Global Competition Policy

EDWARD M. GRAHAM
J. DAVID RICHARDSON
Editors

Global Competition Policy

INSTITUTE FOR INTERNATIONAL ECONOMICS
Washington, DC
December 1997

Edward M. Graham, *Senior Fellow*, was Associate Professor in the Fuqua School of Business at Duke University (1988-90), Associate Professor at the University of North Carolina (1983-88); Principal Administrator of the Planning and Evaluation Unit at the OECD (1981-82); International Economist in the Office of International Investment Affairs at the US Treasury (1979-80) and Assistant Professor at the Massachusetts Institute of Technology (1974-78). He is author or coauthor of a number of studies of international investment and technology transfer, including *Competition Policies in the Global Economy*, with J. David Richardson (1997), *Global Corporations and National Governments*, (1996), *Foreign Direct Investment in the United States* (third edition, 1995).

J. David Richardson, *Visiting Fellow*, is Professor of Economics in the Maxwell School of Citizenship and Public Affairs at Syracuse University and has written extensively on trade and international economic policy issues, including *Competition Policies in the Global Economy*, with Edward M. Graham (1997), *Why Exports Really Matter!* (1995), *Why Exports Really Matter: More!* (1996), *Sizing Up U.S. Export Disincentives* (1993), *International Economic Transactions: Issues in Measurement and Empirical Research* (1991), and *Issues in the Uruguay Round* (1988).

INSTITUTE FOR INTERNATIONAL ECONOMICS
11 Dupont Circle, NW
Washington, DC 20036-1207
(202) 328-9000   FAX: (202) 328-5432
http://www.iie.com

C. Fred Bergsten, *Director*
Christine F. Lowry, *Director of Publications*

Cover Design by Naylor Design, Inc.
Typesetting by Sandra F. Watts
Printing by Automated Graphic Systems

Printed in the United States of America
99 98   5 4 3 2

Library of Congress Cataloging-in-Publication Data

Global competition policy / Edward M. Graham, J. David Richardson, editors.
    p. cm.
    Includes bibliographical references and index.

    1. Competition, International. 2. Commercial policy. 3. International economic relations. I. Graham, Edward M. (Edward Montgomary), 1944- .
II. Richardson, J. David.
HF1414.G558   1997
337—dc21   96-40438
                                                  CIP

ISBN 0-88132-166-4

Contents

III Issue Studies

IV Conclusions

Boxes

Tables

Figures

Preface

In recent years, a number of high-profile international trade disputes have involved private business practices that allegedly act as barriers to market access. In particular, controversy over these practices has been at the heart of United States-Japan conflicts, including those over semiconductors, auto parts, and photographic film. In addition, the United States and the European Union narrowly averted a major clash over their sharply differing reactions to the merger of Boeing and McDonnell Douglas. More such disputes, involving many more nations and occurring especially in sectors that have traditionally been state-controlled but are now privatized, are quite likely.

Government regulation of private business practices falls within the realm of competition (or antitrust) policy. World trade law, as administered through the World Trade Organization (WTO), is not yet well equipped to handle such practices. Nonetheless, trade disputes centered on such issues are being taken to the WTO and more such cases are coming.

New international agreements are therefore needed in this area. The WTO established a working group in 1996 to examine the topic. Establishing new rules will not be easy, however, nor are all key WTO members even prepared to try. There are major substantive and procedural differences on the issue among the key nations and no clear consensus on what constitutes best practice. Indeed, economic analysis of many common private business practices that might impede market entry often shows they have hidden efficiencies so there is no clear intellectual consensus on how to proceed. This is also an area where nations have been especially reluctant to cede authority to an international body.

This book attempts to address these conceptual and policy problems. In the opening and closing chapters, the editors assess the intellectual basis for regulation of competition, concluding that the main goals of competition policy are to achieve fairness and efficiency. The best means of doing so are for governments to ensure that markets are as contestable as possible—that new entry by both domestic and foreign firms be made as easy as possible. At the international level, governments might agree on certain initial steps to accomplish greater contestability: national treatment for foreign-controlled firms, abolition of most international cartels (including those that are now sanctioned), and establishment of mandatory consultation procedures when one government believes that private business practices in another nation foreclose exports or direct investment. There should also be premerger notification requirements for transborder or other mergers having cross-border effects. Further steps might be implemented at a future time.

These conclusions are distilled from chapters profiling the most important competition-policy practices around the world and debating the distinctive cross-border issues they raise. Authors of the individual chapters include the head of the WTO working group on these issues and the chairman of the US Federal Trade Commission, as well as prominent lawyers and economists from all of the regions profiled. These chapters outline the distinctive approaches to competition policies, trade, and investment in Britain, France, Germany, Japan, and the United States, as well as the international agreements governing them within the European Union and between Australia and New Zealand.

In addition to profiling different national approaches, individual chapters analyze contentious functional questions. When do vertical contractual arrangements between manufacturers, suppliers, and distributors make entry by new rivals impossible, whether the rivals come from abroad or from home? Under what conditions are trade practices such as antidumping, voluntary import expansions, and export cartels procompetitive and when are they anti-competitive? Should one size of competition policy fit all sectors, or should there be exemptions of various kinds? Can the exemptions inhibit international market access, and if so, should minimal rules for exemption be negotiated? What about declining sectors?

The views of the expert authors on these issues lead to the editors' policy recommendations: maximum preservation of sovereign initiative; mandatory consultations for vertical practices; a Trade-Related Antitrust Measures (TRAMs) agreement governing international cartels, horizontal restraints, mergers, and national treatment along with corresponding dispute settlement procedures; and, in the longer run, a competition-policy-oriented safeguard arrangement for declining sectors.

The Institute for International Economics is a private nonprofit institution for the study and discussion of international economic policy. Its purpose is to analyze important issues in that area and to develop and communicate practical new approaches for dealing with them. The Institute is completely nonpartisan.

The Institute is funded largely by philanthropic foundations. Major institutional grants are now being received from The German Marshall Fund of the United States, which created the Institute with a generous commitment of funds in 1981, and from The Ford Foundation, The Andrew W. Mellon Foundation, and The Starr Foundation. A number of other foundations and private corporations also contribute to the highly diversified financial resources of the Institute. Partial funding for this project was provided by the American Express Company, the Center for Global Partnership, the Japan-United States Friendship Commission, and the Keidanren. About 12 percent of the Institute's resources in our latest fiscal year were provided by contributors outside the United States, including about 6 percent from Japan.

The Board of Directors bears overall responsibility for the Institute and gives general guidance and approval to its research program—including identification of topics that are likely to become important to international economic policymakers over the medium run (generally, one to three years), and which thus should be addressed by the Institute. The Director, working closely with the staff and outside Advisory Committee, is responsible for the development of particular projects and makes the final decision to publish an individual study.

The Institute hopes that its studies and other activities will contribute to building a stronger foundation for international economic policy around the world. We invite readers of these publications to let us know how they think we can best accomplish this objective.

C. FRED BERGSTEN
Director
November 1997

Acknowledgments

We are indebted to C. Fred Bergsten, Richard N. Cooper, Geza Feketekuty, J. Michael Finger, Robert E. Litan, Patrick A. Messerlin, Douglas E. Rosenthal, Alan Wm. Wolff, and especially to F. M. Scherer for extremely constructive comments on earlier drafts of this book. Helpful input was received from Robert Lawrence and Pierre Souvé.

INTRODUCTION

1

Issue Overview

EDWARD M. GRAHAM AND J. DAVID RICHARDSON

Today's generation, far more than its predecessors, recognizes and pursues the rewards of highly competitive, global markets. Worldwide support for more open-market economic activity is still strong. However, there is resistance. Some is ideological, but much is structural. Structural resistance includes remaining border barriers to fully global market integration, such as tariffs, and entry (or behind-the-border) barriers to fully competitive markets, such as restrictions on the number of suppliers of banking, insurance, transportation, and telecommunications services.

What are the most important remaining barriers to open markets? No one has a persuasive answer. But most agree that border barriers are waning in importance relative to entry barriers. More precisely, tariffs, quotas, and border discrimination are being negotiated away, while regulatory and other barriers that protect incumbent firms by keeping out new suppliers are declining more slowly, especially in large service sectors. Sometimes even privatization replaces a public monopoly with a private monopoly. Consequently, many would agree that, over the past several decades, international trade has liberalized faster than domestic markets have.

This book tries to answer the questions that follow from these observations: If more open global markets are still desired, what is the most promising route? Is that route freer trade, freer entry, or some artful combination of the two? What provides the greatest resistance to open global markets? Is it public border barriers, private anticompetitive practices, proincumbent regulation, or some mix of these? What are the most feasible and attractive ways to enhance market access worldwide (what we will call contestability). Is it access for exporters, foreign investors,

3

and new domestic suppliers alike, or is there already too much contestability? If there is too much, in what sense and under what circumstances does this occur? Finally, what policies support contestability, both within and among countries?

The answers lie in judicious experimentation with a blend of principles, policies, and institutions. The ingredients come from the worlds of competition policy and international trade policy.

This study flows from fundamentals. However, to avoid boring the specialist, our account puts the fundamentals in new light and new context. In this introduction, we describe the raison d'être of competition policy: how it interacts with trade policy, and why that interaction has become an international concern. Efficiency, fairness, and conflict are the key features.

In the concluding chapter of this volume, we outline policy initiatives that are both desirable and feasible in light of the fundamentals. First, we propose sensible first steps toward international cooperation that include fact-finding, consultation, dispute settlement, and maintenance of sovereign initiative. Then we propose a tougher but more rewarding second step: an agreement on Trade-Related Antitrust Measures (TRAMs) patterned on the Uruguay Round's Trade-Related Intellectual Property (TRIPS) agreement. The agreement would cover cartels, market-access-foreclosing practices, and mergers and acquisitions that are international in scope. Finally, we explore the long-run potential for replacing anticompetitive aspects of current trade remedies (antidumping and countervailing duties) with more efficient and more equitable competition-policy safeguards.

Competition policy and international trade policy are already being blended in the World Trade Organization (WTO) via two routes. First, a formal working group on trade and competition policy has been established to examine many of the same issues this book raises (see box 1). Second, certain recent international trade disputes before the WTO spring from issues of competition policy (see box 2).

The Philosophy and Economics of Competition Policies in Open Economies

Concern with competition policy in global trade negotiations has mushroomed.[1] It is at the root of negotiations in airlines, basic telecommuni-

---

1. Scherer (1994) and Green and Rosenthal (1996) compare competition-policy regimes over time and in multiple countries and make policy recommendations. This volume covers these topics but emphasizes the fundamental economics and institutions as well as the integration of existing competition-policy and trade-policy structures at the global level. Scherer (1994) and Levinsohn (1996) are excellent introductions to the economics of competition policies in a global economy. Kühn, Seabright, and Smith (1992) and Ordover

> **Box 1 The WTO Working Group on Trade and Competition Policy**
>
> At the first-ever ministerial-level meeting of the member nations, the WTO authorized the creation of a Working Group on Trade and Competition Policy. Leadership on this matter was exercised largely by the European Union. The formal charge of the working group is as follows (as excerpted from the declaration of the meeting):
>
> > to study issues raised by Members relating to the interaction between trade and competition policy, including anti-competitive practices, in order to identify any areas that may merit further consideration in the WTO framework.
>
> In a press release issued by the WTO, it was emphasized that "[t]he issue is not whether the WTO should negotiate rules in this area but whether it should initiate an exploratory and analytical work programme to identify areas requiring further attention in the WTO framework."
>
> In May 1997, it was announced that the chairman of the working group is Frédéric Jenny of France.

cations, financial services, insurance, and intellectual property. In these areas, international differences in regulatory regimes and rules have created highly varied competitive structures. As noted earlier, differences in generic competition policies have been central to recent trade disputes over market access for autos and auto parts and, more recently, for film and photographic products (see box 2). Such differences have also led to conflict over the announced merger of the US aerospace firms Boeing and McDonnell Douglas, which we address later.

Most of what has been written on competition policy is by and for specialists. By contrast, we make the case for a worldwide approach to competition policy based on economic principles. We then outline a judicious agenda for action, ideally to inform the progress of the WTO's new working party.

Market Competition and Competition Policy: An Introduction

In the broadest sense, competition policy determines the institutional mix of competition and cooperation that gives rise to the market system.

(1990) are equally good introductions to the economics of competition policy, but they pay less attention to the global economy. First, Fox, and Pitofsky (1991); Gifford and Matsushita (1996); and Mathewson, Trebilcock, and Walker (1990) are excellent introductions to legal aspects. Hindley (1996), Hoekman (1997a), Hoekman and Mavroidis (1994), and Lloyd and Sampson (1995) are good political and diplomatic introductions. See Graham (1994, 1995, 1996a, 1996b), Graham and Lawrence (1996), and Richardson (1995, 1997) for our contributions to this literature.

Box 2 Behind-the-border practices and international trade disputes

A number of recent international trade disputes have centered on barriers to market access that are behind-the-border in nature and fall into the domain of competition policy. One such case was the 1995 dispute between the governments of the United States and Japan over auto parts.

The issues raised in this dispute had little or nothing to do with border measures. Rather, the main issue was the level at which Japanese automakers (and firms engaging in servicing automobiles in Japan) purchased parts used as inputs to the production process from nontraditional suppliers. The United States Trade Representative (USTR) alleged that for most purchases of parts the Japanese automakers relied on traditional Japanese suppliers with whom they have long-standing business relations. Foreclosure allegedly resulted, causing US auto parts manufacturers to lose potential sales even though (it was argued that) the US-made product was either better or lower in cost (or both) when compared to the Japanese-made product. It was further alleged that the same exclusive dealing was practiced by the US subsidiaries of Japanese automakers—that is, the Japanese firms Toyota, Nissan, and Honda also sourced most of their parts from only their traditional suppliers (including US subsidiaries of these suppliers).

It is not our intent here to evaluate the allegations or the remedial actions that were announced in June 1995 as part of a negotiated bilateral settlement of the dispute. We simply note that this was not a traditional trade policy dispute. Instead, it centers around basic issues of competition policy: the alleged exclusive dealing by the Japanese firms—a restrictive business practice that is considered a vertical restraint.

This is not the only such case in recent times that has raised issues of market foreclosure by virtue of vertical restraints. Earlier trade disputes between the United States and Japan over semiconductors raised many of the same issues as in the auto parts case, with the key difference that the vertical relationships in this instance were often intrafirm, that is, Japanese users of semiconductors often sourced these items from different divisions of the same company.

A recent US complaint against Japan involves control of distribution channels by Japan's major producer of photo-graphic film and paper products, with the effect of allegedly foreclosing US exports. This case is currently before the WTO disputes settlement body.

While competition is familiar to most, few reflect deeply on cooperation. Almost all market competitors are firms—business organizations (social groupings) that are, for the most part, internally cooperative, not competitive. Firms are the principal suppliers and buyers of most products and services, while consumers (households) generally buy only final goods, which are assembled from materials and components bought and sold many times by firms, through a long series of exchanges in input markets and intrafirm transactions. The economic man or woman so common in elementary economics textbooks is a stylized fiction, and so is the individual entrepreneur. Typical market transactions involve competition among firms. Many of these firms, including subtypes such as labor unions, can legally own and exchange property and differentiate and isolate their legal liability as a group from the liability of their members.

Thus, the market system is socially populated, socially rooted, socially conditioned, and socially constructed. It is far from the chaotically competitive law of the jungle that it is sometimes confused with. A global market system will be socially constructed and conditioned, too, by both policy design and cultural inertia.

This competitive-cooperative market system is governed by formal social regulations called competition policy. Competition policy aims to make the market work better. If designed properly, it is a market-perfecting part of the social infrastructure. It regulates the intensity of competition and the scope of cooperation and defines the legal boundaries for both. Examples of impermissible competition and impermissible cooperation, respectively, are predation (equivalent to the premeditated murder of a market competitor) and coercive collusion (one firm being forced to join a group of others).

Like all social regulations, competition policy reflects history and culture. Therefore, it is constantly changing, and it always differs among countries. Not all countries have a formal, codified competition policy,[2] but all have informal competition conventions. As markets become global, however, differing competition policies and conventions have come into contact. Some of this contact has led to conflict, for example, over market access in China; some has led to constructive com-parison, with an eye to identifying the fittest policies for growing global markets, as in deciding the type and duration of protection that an innovator needs from rivals who would copy his or her intellectual property.

To meet the two broad objectives of competition policies, efficiency and fairness, every country has developed conventions or rules of conduct for firms acting alone and together, over short intervals of time, and over their entire corporate lifetime. Below, we group these conventions into four concerns of competition policy. It turns out, unsurprisingly, that what is welcome competition policy from the perspective of one firm, one industry, or one country is not always welcome in other firms, industries, or countries. In many places, but especially in the last section of this introduction, we describe the ways that competition-policy objectives and concerns differ for an economy as a whole and for multiple economies in global interaction.

---

2. The number of countries implementing formal competition policies in recent years has risen sharply (Green and Rosenthal 1996; Tineo 1997). Most Eastern European and Latin American countries and South Korea, Mexico, and Taiwan have recently promulgated or revised their legislation. A number of other countries have policies in planning or drafting stages.

Objectives of Competition Policy: Efficiency and Fairness

Surprisingly, competition is not the objective of competition policy. Efficiency and fairness are the objectives, and when these conflict, the objective is to evaluate the trade-off between them.

Goals and Instruments

Competition policies around the world seek a blend of efficiency and fairness[3] in their markets. Efficiency has a fairly clear economic meaning. It is a conservational objective; it aims to minimize waste. Efficiency is the ideal of getting the most out of the resources at hand. Examples are an efficient market that generates goods that buyers really want at least cost and an efficient charity that moves resources from one project to another so that the value of the good generated by those resources is at its highest. Likewise, an efficient society seeks the highest standard of living (material and nonmaterial) consistent with its available resources.

If society includes only those people currently living, and the relevant time frame is short (days, months, or even a few years), then that society pursues static efficiency. But if it includes future generations, and the relevant time frame is longer (five years, a decade, a new generation), it pursues dynamic efficiency. Practices that are statically efficient may not be dynamically efficient; the converse is also true. Thus, the simultaneous pursuit of dynamic and static efficiency involves trade-offs.

The meaning of fairness, by contrast, is internationally nuanced and culturally distinctive. In the United States, it often means equality of opportunity or (in our context) free entry into a business endeavor. In other countries, it sometimes means that favored activity or loyalty should be rewarded, or that equity of process or outcome (market division according to historic shares) is valued. Years of acrimonious bilateral negotiations have revealed that Japanese auto and consumer electronics firms characterize loyalty toward and from their traditional suppliers as "only fair," while potential US rivals find it to be an unfair foreclosing of their market access.

Indeed, emphasizing fairness almost invites contention, acrimony, and even international conflict when the protagonists are of different nationalities. But there is no denying the importance of fairness as a motive

---

3. Some countries de-emphasize fairness as an explicit goal of competition policy (e.g., the United States today). Others give it more prominence (e.g., the United Kingdom and France), as seen in chapters in this volume by Hay and Jenny. Virtually all countries, however, include fairness considerations implicitly in implementing their competition policies. Neven, Nuttall, and Seabright (1993, 11) remark that an effective competition authority "must assist in the enfranchisement in the economic process of many of the interests that are naturally underrepresented in the alliance of managers and politicians that makes up the modern corporatist state. Shareholders, consumers, and potential employees. . . . an effective competition authority is the ally of all these excluded groups. . . ."

for competition policy; hence, there is a clear need for definition of what is and what is not fair in a market system and for mutual recognition of threshold standards of fairness in international competition. This need is great because the concepts of fairness and, especially, fair trade have been much abused by special interest groups.

Competition can be a means to attaining efficiency and fairness. For example, a perfectly competitive market—in which there are many small firms that freely enter and exit an industry that produces a standardized product—often achieves efficiency and equality of opportunity (fairness). But this is not always the case. In the market for innovation, perfect competition is generally believed to deliver (inefficiently) too little (see below).[4] For a natural monopoly, a single supplier for the entire market is efficient —competition is not. Where buyers of a product have varied needs and specifications, such that efficiency requires a multitude of varieties rather than one standardized product, monopolistic competition—where numerous producers of those varieties have limited monopoly power and can enter and exit freely—is efficient. And perfect competition makes no promise about fairness of process or outcome, only fairness of opportunity.

Efficiency and fairness are the prizes for competition policy; competition is a secondary objective or, more accurately, an instrument.[5] It will, however, be convenient to use the term anticompetitive (somewhat like the term antisocial) to describe practices and structures that interfere with the objectives of efficiency or fairness. Rule of reason is a corollary legal concept that is relevant to many cases where considerations of fairness or efficiency (and trade-offs between these) require subtle judgments and balancing of arguments. Under rule of reason, these judgments are made on the basis of circumstances and probable outcome rather than fixed per se rules.

Efficiency-Fairness Trade-offs and Cross-Country Conflicts

Efficiency and fairness, like oil and water, do not mix easily. Under most circumstances, neither objective can be met without some sacrifice on the other. Conflict between these objectives occurs within countries and among them.

Within countries, conflict occurs when business practices that enhance the efficiency of some firms appear unfair to others, or when policies that treat all situations fairly have a high efficiency cost. Mergers between firms (e.g., between two large telecommunications companies)

---

4. See also Scherer (1992, 22-40) and Scherer and Ross (1990, chapter 17).

5. Countries differ to the extent that this is true. The United States has sometimes made having many small competitors the chief goal of competition policies, as in the days of trust-busting. Japan, by contrast, explicitly worries about excessive competition (see Suzumura's chapter in this volume).

often involve efficiency for insiders at the apparent cost of fairness to outsiders. Grants of exclusive property rights to patented innovations and unique industrial processes involve the same trade-off.

Nonetheless, apparently even-handed bans on all forms of collusion can force fairness at the cost of efficiency. For some purposes, such as product standard setting, cooperation among firms (collusion to a cynic) can reduce resources expended on the promotion of competing standards (the early competition between VHS and Beta formats for videotapes may be an example of such inefficient expenditures). Global cooperation among firms and governments, as occurs in Mutual Recognition Agreements (MRAs) over the standards each country sets for various products, can also reduce waste.

Cross-country conflicts in competition policies are increasing because concepts of fairness often differ. Some of these differences are endemic (cultural); some are generic. Examples of endemic differences are US insistence on due legal process and continental European and Asian preferences for administrative process (see chapters in this volume by Fox, Jenny, Kühn, Matsushita, and Nicolaïdis and Vernon). Examples of generic differences are the way fairness is seen by would-be entrants and by incumbents; by firms that are small and large; by single-product and diversified firms; and by privately owned, publicly owned, and state-owned firms. Differences in perceived fairness also arise because firm ownership differs from country to country. France and China, for example, have far more state-owned firms than do the United Kingdom, Germany, or the United States. French and Chinese entry barriers in sectors dominated by such firms are contentious to would-be rivals. The United States requires scrupulous financial reporting because most large firms' equities are widely held in public stock markets, but such reporting seems burdensome and unfair to firms that are partly family owned (as in Taiwan) or corporately owned through a tight network of cross-firm shareholdings (as in Japan).

Sometimes, efficiency issues also cause international conflict over competition policies. For example, some countries seek static efficiency and others seek dynamic efficiency. Countries that pursue the former may more strictly regulate cooperative high-technology activities than do those that pursue the latter.[6] Countries that pursue dynamic efficiency may subsidize innovation but force innovating companies to license imitators

---

6. See, for example, Katz and Ordover (1990). Many chapters in Jorde and Teece (1992) argue that US competition policies are insufficiently future oriented for either long-run US welfare (i.e., future gains are inefficiently foregone) or for the ideal US position in the global economy. But competition among firms to arrive at the ideal type and timing of innovations is, on balance, favorable, and strong competition policies that insure entry by energetic new firms often best deliver dynamic efficiency. For a detailed review of the evidence on how market structure affects dynamic efficiency, see Scherer and Ross (1990, chapter 17).

at a regulated price ceiling. These differences cause conflict between firms that compete with each other on seemingly uneven playing fields; such conflict occurred between US and Japanese firms in the early 1980s prior to changes in US competition policy that loosened restrictions on research and development consortiums.

An even more important example is that what's efficient for one country isn't always efficient for the world. Export cartels and monopoly marketing boards are prime examples. Every country can by itself achieve national efficiency—the most output from its national resources—by ensuring perfect competition in the domestic market while charging foreign buyers a monopolistic price in export sales. The country's residents then earn monopoly rents from foreign buyers but do not pay any efficiency cost.[7] However, if every country followed this practice, collective inefficiencies in world export sales world loom large. Such differing effects on national efficiency were well illustrated in the treatment of the proposed merger of Boeing and McDonnell Douglas. European competition-policy authorities initially concluded that the merger might be anticompetitive for Europe, whereas US competition-policy authorities found that it was efficient for the United States. The conflict was resolved with a compromise that somewhat reduced potential efficiency in the United States (e.g., by undoing exclusive-selling agreements between Boeing and certain US airlines that might have led to cost reductions in aircraft maintenance) while reducing what was perceived in Europe as anticompetitive behavior (e.g., undoing the exclusive-selling agreements increased market access for Boeing's European rival, Airbus Industrie).

Finally, and fundamentally, conflict among nations exists for one simple, yet easy-to-forget reason: No firm prefers competition in its output market. However successfully competition may deliver efficiency and fairness to a market system as a whole (sellers, buyers, and final consumers), each firm would rather have less competition as a seller:[8] a monopoly would be most preferred. This is true of market-leading firms and for those hanging on for survival. It is also true for global competition. So skepticism is appropriate when one firm complains about the anticompetitive behavior of a rival (each would do the same if it could get away with it), and also when one country's firms complain collectively about the unfair, anticompetitive behavior of foreign rivals. But skeptics should not be surprised at the complaint nor, for that matter,

---

7. Or, to be maximally efficient, a country by itself could offer foreign sellers a monopsonistic price on imports it buys. That is essentially what the economists' famous optimal tariff does. It beats down world supply prices of imports to the level that a sole national buyer would offer and collects rent (monopsonistic surplus) from the world's sellers of those imports. Alternatively, in a few cases, a government essentially makes itself the sole buyer of imports on behalf of its own constituents, as in certain import-licensing schemes.

8. As buyers of inputs, of course, firms prefer input-market competition, including that created by free opportunities to import and outsource inputs.

be unsympathetic. Global competition policy is an issue precisely because some of these complaints are well taken.

The Efficiency Objective

In almost every country, competition policy aims to reduce inefficiencies. One of the most familiar inefficiencies is the wasteful underproduction and overpricing of a monopolist with market power. Almost as familiar are distortions in relative prices and costs that mislead investors and buyers. Less-familiar inefficiencies are excessive product standardization or its opposite: wasteful product differentiation, unduly sluggish innovation or unnecessary duplication of research effort, inadequate realization of scale economies, and underprovisioning of future generations.

The Fairness Objective

There is also a distributional economics of competition policy, concerned with process and fairness in markets. Its most obvious expression is in policies that oppose coercion and various abuses of market power that imply involuntary action. When economists defend the market system, they require volunteerism. That is, they rule out coercion (no reputable economist recommends markets for slavery, contract murder, or mercenaries to fight wars of territorial aggression). Many competition policies are the legislative expression of the anticoercion principle.[9] Other policies prohibit abuses of market power, such as a horizontal cartel's boycott of distributors that deal with outsiders or new suppliers. Several years ago, Japanese producers of flat glass were found to practice such abuses, and similar issues are at the heart of the ongoing Japan-US dispute in the WTO over alleged abuses in the markets for film and other photographic supplies (see box 2).

Other process-oriented competition policies include those that outlaw fraud, criminalize the theft of intellectual property and industrial secrets, discipline predation, regulate price discrimination (charging different prices to different buyers), and ban foreclosure (contracts and other arrangements with suppliers or distributors that completely exclude new firms). For example, the European Union (EU) recently accused Boeing of negotiating 20-year exclusive-supplier contracts with American Airlines, Continental Airlines, and Delta Air Lines, though some reports suggest that Europe's Airbus had equal chances to compete for and win those and any other contracts.[10]

---

9. From this point of view, for example, laws against employment of underage (child) workers is a species of competition policy.

10. See, for example, Laura D'Andrea Tyson, "'McBoeing' Should Be Cleared for Takeoff," *Wall Street Journal*, 22 July 1997, A14.

The efficiency and fairness objectives of competition policy are discussed at several levels. The most familiar is in the context of a single market for one product. We start there in the next section, and then move to the less-familiar competition-policy concerns of an economy in which many products and services are sold. We conclude this discussion with a treatment of multiple economies in international contact.

Sectoral Concerns of Competition Policy

Competition policy at the sectoral level aims for an efficient and fair market to ensure that short-term decisions, such as pricing, and long-term decisions, such as investments for innovation, are made efficiently and fairly by firms, whether acting alone or with other firms. It also weighs a sector's efficiency and fairness rules against other social objectives, such as the defense industry's role in national security. In subsections below, we describe the four concerns of competition policy as firm behavior, relational behavior, lifetime behavior, and social behavior.

However, competition policy cannot be so easily apportioned. Each subsection describes policy concerns that are linked organically to the other subsections. For example, predation is the premeditated goal of a single firm, but the concept obviously involves a victim firm and is perversely relational.[11]

Firm Behavior

Competition policy is first of all concerned with a firm's behavior and market power. At any moment,[12] this concern involves inefficiencies in prices or marketing, inequities in the treatment of customers or potential rivals, and other abuses of market power. These concerns, sometimes called restrictive business practices, implicitly involve assessments of how close a firm's prices come to its costs; how closely a firm meets buyer demand for products of varying size, durability, reliability, and other characteristics; and how freely a firm will allow rival firms and products to emerge. Competition-policy authorities never try to comprehensively or continuously monitor corporate decision making on these details, much less direct it. But when anticompetitive behavior is

---

11. The technical distinction between the sections called "Firm Behavior" and "Relational Behavior" is that the first involves a firm's noncooperative (i.e., independent) behavior, while the second involves its cooperative (i.e., joint) behavior with some other firm(s).

12. We consider the lifetime behavior of a firm below.

suspected, most authorities have the legal right to summon detailed information from firms in their jurisdiction.[13]

In brief, the first concern of competition policy is to discipline the market power of firms. But what exactly is market power? And what are its inefficiencies and abuses?

Price Setting

Market power is first defined with reference to price and then with respect to attributes. Firms that have the capacity to choose their own price from a menu of options, ranging from high prices with low sales to low prices with high sales, are said to have price-setting power. Firms that can produce any mix of product varieties (e.g., high or low quality, durability, and flexibility) are said to have attribute-selection power.[14] In reality, most firms have some degree of price-setting and attribute-selection power. But both kinds of power are limited by the prices and attributes that rival firms choose. In the perfectly competitive extreme, power is perfectly limited to a single price ceiling and a single attribute floor (e.g., a wheat farmer sells nothing if the price he asks exceeds any rival's price that day or if the cleanliness and purity of the wheat falls short of the minimal acceptable standard of the least-discriminating buyer). In a market structure called monopolistic competition, a firm has price-setting power over the precise blend of attributes that makes its product unique. But other firms produce so many close substitutes to that attribute package that the firm's price choices range over a narrow band, and its power can be severely constrained.[15] At the other extreme, monopoly, both price-setting power and attribute-selection power are maximal, because such a firm is the sole producer of a product with no close

---

13. The problem of gathering such detailed information is reduced in countries such as the United States, which allows firms, presumably well informed, to initiate competition-policy legal action against rivals that they accuse of anticompetitive behavior. The US rewards for successful legal action can be three times as large as the damages (treble damages).

14. Other descriptions refer to a firm's power to select optimal characteristics, differentiation, niche, quality, position, location, performance, and model. Competition over product attributes is sometimes called (blandly) nonprice competition. Besanko, Dranove, and Shanley (1996, part III) describe it as competition for "strategic positioning." Katz and Ordover (1990) and Jorde and Teece (1992) make much of the need for competition policy to ensure the efficiency of competition in innovation, in addition to the more familiar (static) price competition.

15. The technical condition is that every firm's cross-price elasticity of demand with respect to substitute products is very high and increases with the number of substitutes. In that event, its own price elasticity will necessarily be very high as well. When attributes involve many dimensions, however (e.g., quality, location, and durability), an increased number of rivals along any given dimension can sometimes work in the opposite direction, enhancing price-setting and other market power.

substitutes. The term oligopoly describes a market structure in which a small number of firms produce a product with no close substitutes; as the number of rivals and substitutes increases, oligopoly bleeds into monopolistic competition.

Price-setting market power usually leads a firm to boost profits by supplying less to buyers than would be socially ideal but also charging a higher price than is ideal (there is, however, one important exception—see "Price Discrimination" below).[16] That is, of course, fine with the firm's shareholders, but the social ideal is for a firm to keep on selling as long as buyers are willing to pay enough for each successive unit to cover the extra cost of producing that unit.[17] If the firm stops short of this ideal, there is inefficiency (waste) and unwelcome frustration—some buyers are rationed (unfairly, they would claim) and fail to receive units of a product that cost less to produce than their own valuation of those units. That firms will behave this way is at the core of both microeconomic theory and the efficiency objective of competition policy.

Price Discrimination

There is one important exception to these generalizations about price setting. When a firm's price-setting power is enhanced by price-discriminating power, wasteful inefficiency (rationing) can be reduced, although fairness concerns become sharper. Price discrimination is the power of a firm to charge different prices to different groups of customers (who find it impossible or uneconomical to resell the firm's goods among themselves).[18] Examples of price discrimination are time-of-day pricing for telephone calls and power use, loyalty discounts to recurrent customers, and differing fares for the same airline flight for leisure travelers and business travelers. In the extreme, a perfect price discriminator has the power to charge each customer a unique price, as much as each customer can bear to pay to own the product rather than to do without it. Thus, whatever its effect on efficiency, price discrimination accentuates overpricing and makes it discriminatory as well. Both effects raise fairness concerns.

---

16. Microeconomic reasoning shows that, for modest sales reductions, starting at the ideal price and quantity, a firm's overall revenues decline more slowly than its overall costs, generating extra profit, which can often be identified with excess (or supernormal or economic) profit.

17. The technical name for this is the socially optimal price and quantity.

18. Customers who would be charged high prices would otherwise stop buying directly from the firm and start buying indirectly from customers who could get the product at lower prices; these less-desperate customers would begin to buy not only for themselves, but also to resell (arbitrage) merchandise to the first group.

Price-setting power enhanced by this extreme form of price discrimination can restore the ideal volume of sales (and eliminate inefficiency). The firm keeps selling until it reaches the least-willing customer, who values the product so little that he or she bids barely enough to cover the extra cost of the last few units that the firm produces. That is, by definition, the social ideal. But with price-discriminating power, the firm is able to overprice by more, and its profits are higher, because it is able to extract every last dollar of customer benefit[19] above the minimum necessary[20] to keep its customers buying at all!

More common (and less extreme) price-discriminating power may create new inefficiency, rather than relieving it. Currency fluctuations within the European Union, for example, contribute to European firms' power to isolate national markets from each other and charge different prices to different national buyers despite the absence of trade barriers. One of the motives for European Monetary Union is to reduce this type of price discrimination, which inefficiently deters trade between arbitraging buyers in low-price/low-value countries—buyers who become secondary-market sellers to buyers in high-price/high-value countries.[21] Even under a currency union, however, national regulations on which and how many firms can be authorized sellers may continue to support this type of price discrimination. But such regulations are scrutinized strictly by the EU competition-policy authorities. Not only do such regulations support price discrimination, but they also may condemn the overall volume of European sales to be inefficiently lower than even a single-price monopoly would allow.

In any case, price-discriminating power almost always involves a significant and discriminatory transfer of purchasing power from buyers to extra profit for sellers,[22] and this may be considered unfair.[23] So price discrimination changes the nature of the competition-policy problem but not necessarily its intensity, probably putting more weight on unfairness than on inefficiency.[24]

---

19. Technically, the customer's consumer surplus.

20. Technically, the customer's reservation price; such discrimination is called first degree.

21. See, for a discussion, "When the Walls Come Down," *The Economist*, 5 July 1997, 61-63.

22. The extra profit may attract new entrants to the industry, thus shifting the market outcome toward efficient (ideal) outcomes (see Varian 1989, 619-22). Our focus on single-firm behavior allows us to ignore that issue here.

23. It is controversial whether there is a fairness problem at all. Price discrimination in innovation, for example, is considered by many analysts to be part of the reward to those who have pioneered. See, for example, Katz and Ordover (1990, 139).

24. It also changes the confidence economists have giving expert advice. They usually feel more secure discussing efficiency than the fairness of distributional outcomes between buyers and sellers.

The power to price discriminate is increasingly important. The technologies for identifying and isolating customer groups continue to advance (e.g., cash registers and web sites that keep track of what, when, and how much a credit-card customer buys and match such information to socioeconomic characteristics from the customer's credit records). And the cost of frequently varying prices has been greatly reduced by computerized real-time price lists (e.g., airfares in reservations systems) and discounts keyed to coupons and bar codes. For competition policy, the interesting implication of rising price discrimination is a justifiable shift in attention toward ensuring fairness and a competitive process and away from efficiency concerns (which often take care of themselves, especially when entry to price-discriminating activities is unencumbered). Partly for these reasons, we organize our policy recommendations with a priority on competitive process. Our recommendations are aimed at making markets more internationally contestable—that is, making them open to entry by as many new competitors, foreign or domestic, as choose to compete.

Price discrimination has increasing prominence in international conflict as well. Past international trade conventions allowed countries to protect against injurious imports priced lower in their country than in the source country. This form of price discrimination is labeled dumping, and the protective tariffs to combat it are called antidumping duties. To the extent that these duties reduce cross-border price discrimination, they may enhance fairness (indeed, dumping is one example of so-called unfair trade), but they almost surely inhibit efficiency. While all tariffs are price-distorting wedges between foreign and domestic suppliers, antidumping duties are aimed only at dumping suppliers and not all suppliers, making the distortion discriminatory (for a discussion of the trade-offs involved, see the chapter in this volume by Lipstein).

Attribute Competition

Attribute-selection power can sometimes, but not always, have unwelcome effects similar to those of price-setting power, involving both inefficiency and inequity. Powerful incumbent firms may offer too few models or models that are too old—and it may overprice them.[25] For example, airline competition often underprovides desirable attributes.

---

25. Again, the statement implies a social ideal. When buyers differ from each other, their varying tastes for proximity, quality, durability, convenience, and so on will usually make it ideal for a sector to produce many models. But how many models? How many models for each firm? These questions are similar to "How much should a firm produce?" The answers, though, are unfamiliar and not clear-cut. See Besanko, Dranove, and Shanley (1996, part III) for the firm's answers, but see the discussion of lifetime behavior (below) for the conclusion that markets may not always generate the socially ideal attribute selection.

Every airline route serves both business and leisure passengers, whose ideal service requirements differ. Sometimes incumbent airlines will strategically choose (and price) flight times, aircraft, and service to make it unprofitable for a rival firm to generate attribute diversity—that is, to produce substitute models around the ones already in existence.[26] For example, an established business-oriented airline may offer frequent flights to nearby cities and modest (but not rock-bottom) prices to deter a leisure-oriented rival airline from competing. The number and type of service attributes offered by the established incumbent may still be less than ideal;[27] that is, some (leisure) buyers are rationed and, thus, are unable to buy a type of service (e.g., flights on weekends) that would actually cost less to produce than the buyer's valuation of that service. That is wasteful. It may also be an abuse of market power by the incumbent. Exclusionary behavior can undermine both efficiency (measured by the rationing cost) and fairness (because potential rivals are closed out).

This kind of strategic attribute selection may not always be anticompetitive: strategic entry deterrence is not always bad and not always unfair. The incumbent airline in the example does, after all, increase density and frequency and reduce price.[28] In doing so, it no doubt satisfies some leisure travelers. Thus, as is often the case, whether there is an abuse or inefficiency here is a judgment call.[29] That is one reason why competition policies worldwide appeal to a rule of reason in deciding whether practices such as entry deterrence involve exclusion or other distortions or inequities.

Best-Practice Competition

Market power can allow a firm to be nonchalant about maintaining the most efficient production techniques and, thereby, raise its costs. One way this happens is through sluggish innovation, discussed below. However, a firm with market power might also allow costs to rise wastefully unchecked by the discipline of having to keep them in line with costs of rival firms. Inadequate cost control often results in overstaffing and excessive salaries. Also, prices paid for buildings, machines, and intermediate products might be excessive (e.g., a headquarters building that is

---

26. An analogous strategy in innovation is for the innovating firm to design a patent so that it blocks rivals from designing substitute patents around the innovator's patent. For obvious reasons, this is called a blocking patent.

27. But not enough to grant an entrant any profit after it pays the fixed costs of set-up.

28. This is compared to what they would do if entry were not a concern (e.g., if the government had granted them a legal monopoly on the routes).

29. Price discrimination also illustrates the need for judgment calls.

more a monument than an efficient office). Such bloat in organizations is often termed x-inefficiency.

Yet another source of inefficient inputs is costly efforts to deter rivals and maintain market power. These efforts can include lobbying of government agencies that brings benefits to the firm but is wasteful from society's perspective. To deter rivals, the firm might overbuild capacity or commit to making products with attributes that the firm cannot produce as efficiently as can potential rival firms.

Enhanced contestability in a market often leads firms to improve cost control and performance (see Scherer and Ross 1990, 667-78, for evidence on these effects). Likewise, enhanced contestability can lead to favorable restructuring of industries, allowing those firms that are adaptable and effective to absorb the business of those that are not and, thus, improving performance of the industry (see Tybout and Westbrook 1995 for evidence that these effects were important for Mexican industry following liberalization in the late 1980s).

Predation

In an extreme application of market power that is least favorable to efficiency and fairness, an established airline not only deters would-be rivals, but successfully preys upon new entrants. Such predation is the strategic, temporary deployment by the predator firm of attributes that are so attractive (and prices that are so low) that existing rivals leave a market, allowing the predator firm subsequently to enhance market power by reducing quality, raising price, and deterring reentry. Though such predation clearly would be anticompetitive, its real-life occurrence seems rare.[30] Ordinarily, it seems, a firm is only displaced by another firm that offers indefinitely lower prices, better quality, and higher performance. As a temporary tactic to gain market power and then abuse it, predation has proved unsuccessful.[31]

Contestability

However, there is an extreme case of only apparent market power that is favorable to efficiency and equity. An airline resolved to deter rivals

---

30. There are some cases of true price predation in the airline industry. For example, incumbent carriers on North Atlantic routes dropped their prices in response to new entry during the 1980s to drive the new entrants out of the market. However, such predation seems rare. In 95 percent of the US and EU antidumping cases they examined where predatory behavior could, in principle, have motivated the dumping, Shin (1992) and Bourgeois and Messerlin (1993) reject even the possibility of predation. The Organization for Economic Cooperation and Development (OECD) (1989) has a comprehensive treatment of general predatory pricing, whether linked to dumping or not; it covers economic reasoning and historical precedents in all OECD countries.

31. Over the lifetime of firms, discussed below, this more common and procompetitive type of displacement is called creative destruction; Schumpeter (1950) gives its classic description.

or displace an incumbent might be forced (by the ease with which rivals can come and go) to offer so many flights at such low prices for so long a time that the outcome comes close to what would have occurred with realized entry by those rivals. This type of market is called perfectly contestable. In such a market, the varieties offered and their prices come close to the social ideal even when there are only a few firms selling.[32] In general, markets can be made more contestable (hence more efficient) if potential entrants can enter and exit freely and if set-up and withdrawal (exit) costs are low.[33]

From this perspective, global liberalization can be an important force for contestability by multiplying the number of potential entrants and reducing set-up and withdrawal costs. There are usually more potential entrants after trade and investment liberalization. When entering a market, established firms from abroad may have lower set-up costs than would completely new domestic entrants. Thus, liberalization that makes the potential entry of those established firms more likely enhances contestability. Liberalization affects set-up costs in several ways:

- Foreign firms may no longer need to pay for licenses to ship their goods as imports (of the domestic country).

- Foreign firms may no longer need to pay (or bribe) various middlemen (e.g., mandated joint-venture partners) to establish their investors on a par with local firms. Liberalization may alter withdrawal costs as well.

- Suppliers of exports to the domestic market will obviously not have to meet the same withdrawal requirements as a domestic firm that employs local labor and pays local taxes.[34]

In these and many other ways, globalization makes markets more contestable.[35]

---

32. Bresnahan and Reiss (1991) find, for example, in a study of regional markets for professional services, that markets come very close to the social ideal after the third, fourth, or fifth firm enters.

33. Technically, the set-up costs that matter are irrecoverably sunk. That means that they cannot be reclaimed in the event of withdrawal or transferred to some other use. Licensing and license fees are examples of set-up costs that policy has some influence over. Long-term contracts with municipal authorities (e.g., over taxes) and regulations covering the need to notify workers before layoffs are examples of withdrawal costs that policy has influence on.

34. For example, notification and severance requirements, fulfillment of long-term leases, etc.

35. See Graham and Lawrence (1996), Feketekuty and Rogowsky (1996), and Hoekman (1997a) for further development of the presumption that global liberalization makes markets more contestable.

Natural Monopoly

So-called natural monopoly represents still another extreme in which technology dictates either scale economies or high natural set-up costs, with no natural limit on capacity resulting in the relevant market. In this extreme, the average cost per unit for a firm is far lower at high-volume production than at low-volume, because the fixed set-up costs can be spread over many units of production, and capacity constraints never appear.[36] Therefore, it becomes efficient (cost saving) for a firm to operate at high volume. A natural monopoly exists when there are still cost savings from higher-volume production even at the point where a single firm serves an entire market. In this case, price-setting and attribute-selection market power may be the inevitable companions of technological efficiency. Competition policy then traditionally aims to minimize the inefficiencies and inequities that could result under natural monopoly. It may set a ceiling on the price charged by the natural monopolist;[37] it may force firms to rebid periodically on the license to be the natural monopolist; or it may deny the natural monopolist's preference to exclude specialized rivals from using its infrastructure or networks[38] or regulate the price it charges rivals to use them.

Globalization of markets and technological change have clearly reduced the importance of some natural monopolies. Satellites and other forms of wireless communication, for example, have removed the necessity to pay up-front for wire-dependent telecommunications networks.[39] The need for competition policy to deal with natural monopolies has been correspondingly reduced, as has the need for international competition-policy conventions in these cases.

However, globalization and technological change have created a new class of natural monopoly—the global natural monopoly, which has falling average costs for its products and services even if it serves the whole world. Putative examples are hypersonic and large commercial aircraft; high-technology weapons; and some banking, insurance, and satellite

---

36. To be a valid natural monopoly, the set-up costs must also be sunk (see note 36). This makes natural monopoly rare, because many machines or factories can be sold to another sector or to users abroad—as is true of many machine tools and even whole refineries, breweries, and factories (see Andrew Taylor, "Third World Goes Bargain Hunting," *Financial Times*, reprinted in *National Times*, June 1996, 20). Set-up costs in these cases may be large, but they are not sunk.

37. For example, the US Federal Communications Commission sets a maximum price that local owners of wire-based telephone networks can charge long-distance companies for access to those networks.

38. Telecommunications rivals that provide value-added services beyond normal telephone service, such as access to data, are an example. See Graham and Lawrence (1996).

39. The difference between the cost of wire-dependent infrastructure and launch costs has allowed remote, previously unserved areas to have basic telecommunications.

transmission services.[40] For these products, the case for competition policy may have been accentuated, and because the efficient monopoly exists at the global level, the corresponding competition-policy regime is international.[41] The recent merger of Boeing and McDonnell Douglas illustrates the potential for severe competition-policy inconsistency and conflict among subglobal policy authorities.

Size Is Not Power

Natural monopoly and perfect contestability have one trait in common, though they are different types of extreme market structure. They both show that big firms are not automatically bad for efficiency or fairness. "Small may be beautiful," as some say, but it may also be inefficient; to have multiple suppliers may seem fairer than to have only one, but it is not necessarily fairer if one firm has an edge over the others and can serve the entire market best.

By implication, antitrust-mandated breakups of large firms may sometimes be neither efficient nor fair, and, as much as these firms plague populists, visceral concerns over the awesome power of megamultinational firms may be sadly misplaced.[42]

It is not that the market automatically makes all well or that anticompetitive abuses are minimal. On the contrary—that is why competition policy is an issue within and between countries. The point is that the size of a firm is rarely a good indicator of its power. Even small firms can have market power in specialty segments of markets, and even they can abuse that power. And large firms often find their power surprisingly constrained by competition from others.

Furthermore, when big firms and sole suppliers have little market power, they also have close-to-average (normal) profits. They are not making extraordinary amounts of money for their owners, management, or host countries. Competition and trade policies that aim to preserve extraordinary profit pools for one's own domestic firms or to shift them away from foreign firms are less relevant to the extent that even big firms have small and fleeting market power. Many analysts feel that the growth of trade and the investment-based cross-penetration of national markets has produced the situation described above: global markets in

---

40. For the banking and insurance sectors, the potential for global natural monopoly arises from the creation of electronic-payment clearing systems.

41. Yet the strength of the new case is controversial; each example faces close substitutes (e.g., subsonic aircraft, conventional weapons) that may so diminish the efficiency and fairness costs of the global natural monopoly that the problem is not worth worrying about.

42. Scherer (1994, 87-88) concludes that there is little theoretical or empirical support for the proposition that multinational firms (size notwithstanding) are different from "companies that have equivalent market positions but operate from only a single nation."

which the typical structure is monopolistic competition, not oligopolistic. The competition policies that correspond to such a world have many fewer sectoral exemptions, and the trade policies that correspond make less sense from a strategic standpoint.

Relational Behavior

Bad and Good

Competition policy is concerned with interfirm behavior as well as the behavior of each firm alone. This explicitly involves scrutinizing mergers and cooperative joint ventures and challenging those that are anticompetitive.[43] Formal cartels that bind firms together in what is essentially a monopoly are usually banned (with some exceptions), and the authorities watch carefully for less-formal collusion that has the same effect.

Relational concerns aim to make sure that firms do compete with each other, rather than merely fake it. No firm welcomes competition as a seller, as discussed above, so there is always a danger of implicit live-and-let-live collusion. Thus, firms can appear to compete while colluding to avoid aggressive actions such as price competition or while secretly dividing up attribute niches among themselves so that each is a mini-monopolist in reserved models or submarkets or while ostracizing or punishing uncooperative rivals that refuse to join in the collusion such as by denying them access to some vital input (e.g., a pipeline or communications network).

Anticompetitive mergers and collusive practices, such as price-fixing and market-swapping quotas, involve the familiar inefficiencies and inequities. They waste resources, exclude a margin of buyers who would have been willing to pay the costs of more production or more variety, and suck purchasing power away from those buyers that remain.

But not all interfirm cooperation is anticompetitive collusion. A merger in which a strong firm takes over a weak one and restructures the weak one to preserve at least some of its business and employment may enhance overall market efficiency and be fairer than allowing the weak firm to fail and close down. That was an essential part of Boeing's defense of its takeover of McDonnell Douglas's commercial aircraft business. A research joint venture in which each firm takes responsibility for developing and patenting different aspects of a new process or parts of a new product, but then makes licenses available to all members, may efficiently value the spillovers from one firm's innovation to other firms—

---

43. A merger legally blends the ownership and management of two companies. A joint venture (or strategic alliance) is a less-formal form of cooperation, occasionally involving the creation of equity in an entirely new, joint, and dedicated unit but more typically involving no equity exchange or issue. Neven, Nuttall, and Seabright (1993) provide a detailed reference on supranational issues in merger policies for open economies, focusing on the European Union.

spillovers that markets find notoriously hard to value.[44] A system in which a firm bans its retailers and distributors from selling any products except its own (e.g., if Fuji or Kodak insisted that developers and processors of film use only theirs) may enhance informational advertising and efficient quality maintenance—they give each distributor incentives and objectives similar to those of the manufacturer—though such practices may indeed appear otherwise to be anticompetitive barriers to entry. Finally, the incentive for and returns from innovation have been shown (e.g., Geroski 1992) to generally rise when firms are permitted to cooperate with suppliers of complementary inputs (e.g., Microsoft cooperating with both software developers and computer makers or Toyota cooperating with Nippondensu).

Horizontal and Vertical

There are two broad types of interfirm cooperation, horizontal and vertical. Horizontal cooperation involves similar firms at similar stages in the production process (e.g., raw processor, assembler, or distributor); vertical cooperation involves complementary firms at different stages. Competition policy is more suspicious of horizontal cooperation than of vertical. Horizontal cooperation smells more like collusion, like cartels, and the burden of proof to the contrary is usually on the firms. Vertical cooperation, however, has a whiff of integration, the kind of cooperative, nonmarket activity firms do on their own, and the proof that it is anticompetitive usually falls to the authorities.

Horizontal cooperation is generally viewed with suspicion because it seems to reduce competition and, hence, block efficiency and other objectives that competition facilitates. In mergers, after all, the total number of rival firms in the market drops, shifting the market structure toward oligopoly. In joint ventures, the effect can be qualitatively the same, though it is limited to only some activities and is always a less-rigid arrangement than a full merger. However, empirical research shows that the efficiency losses from horizontal cooperation may be quite small as long as three to five rivals remain in a market.[46] And horizontal cooperation can be defended for the efficiencies it may deliver (e.g., a so-called efficiency defense may be based on cost reduction through

---

44. Such spillovers, called externalities, are a classic case of problems that markets do not solve well.

45. See Bresnahan and Reiss (1991). The question regarding merger approval that occupies governments' procedural guidelines is how to define a market for purposes of counting rival firms and evaluating the competitive intensity of the rivalry. If markets are broadly defined (say, chemical products), there are many rivals. If more narrowly defined (say, pharmaceuticals), there are fewer; if still narrower (say, aspirin), even fewer. The narrower the definition, the more likely that governments will find market power and its various abuses.

information sharing and productivity improvement, avoidance of wasteful duplication of fixed costs of research and development, reduction of coordination problems in industrywide rationalization, and facilitation of exit of inefficient firms).[46]

Vertical cooperation is often considered acceptable if rival firms have equivalent opportunities to cooperate and integrate. In this view, equal opportunity vertical cooperation is just another example of free entry—in this case, entry to an organizational structure that spans several production stages. There are, nevertheless, grounds for concern if completely new firms face higher vertical-integration costs than do established incumbents, because the new firms' entry is then limited. This condition is fairly common and may occur, for example, when a new entrant needs to build an integrated distribution network from scratch, or when long-term, almost indefinite contracts and buyer loyalty leave a new entrant with no uncommitted suppliers or distributors. These concerns, of course, have animated Japan-US relations, especially in autos, auto parts, and semiconductors. In the anticompetitive extreme, vertical arrangements among firms may completely choke off comparable entry by rivals. This so-called vertical foreclosure is agreed to be anticompetitive and should be subject to intense competition-policy scrutiny. The classic example of such entry foreclosure is an exclusive contract between incumbent firms and suppliers of some vital input for which there is no substitute—for example, a deposit of ore or diamonds of the purest quality. A more recent, yet controversial, example may be the exclusive, 20-year contracts that Boeing negotiated with American Airlines, Continental Airlines, and Delta Air Lines to be their sole supplier. At least the competition-policy authorities of the European Union thought it was an example; Boeing responded that there was nothing that kept Airbus from competing for these or similar contracts (reports were that they did), and, hence, there was no foreclosure. As noted earlier in this introduction, to gain approval for its merger with McDonnell Douglas, Boeing agreed not to enforce the exclusivity of the contracts but at the same time changed none of their other terms.

Still more controversial gray-area practices include vertical arrangements that enhance price-setting and price-discrimination power, such as those of a manufacturer that prevents its distributors from either independently discounting its products (resale price maintenance) or from remarketing them outside the distributor's designated territory.[47] While

---

46. Sometimes called the failing-firm defense. Dick (1997) finds evidence of efficiency gains even among US export cartels.

47. See Scherer (1994, 74-75) for a discussion of the EU competition authorities' case against Grundig. The authorities at one time prevented Grundig's distributors in one EU member country from shipping its electronics products into another (shipments called parallel imports). Less extremely, Canadian and US auto dealers face different tariffs than do the resident producers of the cars.

such restrictions are anticompetitive because they ban entry by distributors into the business of arbitrage, they also procompetitively support a manufacturer's ability to: ensure local maintenance and repair services, charge an appropriate price for services offered to distributors (avoiding free riding by unauthorized distributors), and charge different prices in different regions, at different times, or to different customers. These types of price discrimination can sometimes promote efficiency when they expand markets or open new ones (while admittedly sacrificing some fairness).

Open-Economy Considerations

Horizontal and vertical cooperation both work differently in an open economy than in a closed one. One reason is that governments represent only their domestic constituents, whereas markets pull firms and customers together across national borders. Collusion may actually be attractive to a government if foreign customers or foreign rivals bear most of the efficiency and equity burdens. That is why many governments allow export cartels that fix prices, restrain attribute competition, divide up markets, and engage in other activities that are usually prohibited domestically. That is also why governments sensibly restrict the rights of foreign firms to join standard-setting or research consortiums (such as the US joint venture Sematech). And that is why many governments favor mergers of domestic firms that enhance their firms' global market power, even though the governments' constituents bear some of the costs. For example, that is one possible reason why US authorities might look more favorably on the merger of Boeing and McDonnell Douglas than do European authorities (though US authorities deny it). Or, for example, a vertical merger between two home firms that impedes the entry of foreign rivals can enhance not just a firm's market power, but also national market power and the national standard of living. (Entry to the US market by oligopolistic and integrated European suppliers was an understandable concern of the United States in recent WTO negotiations over basic telecommunications services.) Of course, in all these cases much of what one country gains is lost by others, engendering conflict and the opportunity for international conflict resolution to discipline these beggar-thy-neighbor competition policies. More ambitiously, international cooperation over trade and competition policies could provide the opportunity to come closer to global efficiency.

Avoiding opportunistic policies is not the only reason for government-to-government agreements concerning relational practices in an open economy. Mergers in one country can often cause inefficiencies or inequities in another, even through exports rather than on-site operations. Thus, a given merger must often clear several different competition-policy reviews, as illustrated by the European Union review of the proposed merger between Boeing and McDonnell Douglas. Some governments have negotiated information-sharing agreements in their merger review procedures, yet one of the contentious issues raised by the Boeing-McDonnell Douglas case is whether an offshore review should defer to a primary review (in this case, by the United States) when the assessments differ. In this case, the European Union pressed on anyway, even in the face of US approval, and Boeing eventually made concessions. Within the European Union, large mergers, meeting other criteria, are evaluated at the community level, not by national authorities.

Although open economies may lead to some inefficiencies, they may also magnify the size of efficiency gains from interfirm cooperation when such gains are there and distribute those gains to all countries. Opportunism is then only an issue in the fair division of the gains. Examples are the on-again, off-again consideration of a joint venture by Boeing and Airbus to build a superjumbo aircraft and joint space research between Russian and US firms.

Some features of an open economy stand in the way of efficient and fair cooperation among firms. Antidumping conventions, implemented at the beginning of the twentieth century to discipline price discrimination in international trade, have metastasized into the weapon of choice against foreign rivals. They are as useful for harassment as for protection and are a facilitator of implicit collusion (see Lipstein's chapter in this volume). Successful antidumping cases are resolved either by erecting inefficient antidumping duties or by allowing firms to negotiate—that is, jointly fix—higher prices (this solution is called a price undertaking). Such sanctioned horizontal collusion raises costs to all users, rations some users, and can slow down innovation. Market-opening tools such as voluntary import expansions (VIEs) and US market-access (Section 301) cases are export analogs to antidumping measures. Whatever procompetitive merit these substitute weapons may have in forcing entry is usually more than offset by their implicit facilitation of cartelization in the target country and collusion at home (Greaney 1996).

Anticompetitive corporate and intercorporate behavior are the immediate concerns of competition policy. But both recur in a longer time frame and in a wider context. We describe the longer time frame as lifetime behavior and the broader context as social behavior.

Lifetime Behavior

Competition policy is also concerned with a firm's long-term market behavior, both individually and in relation to rivals. The key lifetime objectives are efficiency and fairness but with a wider scope than described so far. Efficiency must now include ideal rates of investment, innovation, and attribute introduction that reflect the valuations and varied needs of future buyers—some of whom are not yet discernible or even born. Fairness must now outline the circumstances under which an established firm should be allowed to die, either by absorption into another firm or by liquidation. Efficiency may sometimes dictate the extinction of an entire sector (e.g., television sets), raising especially troublesome fairness questions, especially if the same sector survives in other countries.[48]

So in addition to the classic competition-policy issues enumerated above, this lifetime concern involves extinction, succession, innovation, and change of ownership. These are influenced by policies toward exit and downsizing: bankruptcy and public bailout commitments, education and taxation of research and development, industrial secrets and intellectual property, and takeovers and corporate control. Long-term competition policy involves implicit assessments of questions such as the following:

- What (if any) recourse should shrinking firms in shrinking industries have for temporary relief from global market pressures, from normal competition policy, and from creditors' repayment schedules?

- How easily can the firm abandon weak product lines or sell them to others? How easily can it abandon inefficient production processes or look to outside suppliers for components?

- How actively does a firm work its intellectual property? Can its favorable market position in current technologies or product varieties allow it to slow down its own innovation or that of rivals? What is the optimal amount of protection to be given to intellectual property to encourage the right amount of innovation?

- How easily can outsiders purchase enough equities to gain control of the firm and alter its basic decisions (free entry in the market for corporate control)?

Schumpeterian Competition

Neither research nor competition-policy precedents are well developed with respect to these questions. Nearly all specialists pay lip service to the conviction of the economist Joseph Schumpeter that innovation and corporate displacement and succession cycles (creative destruction) are the keys to dynamic efficiency. But no one has yet worked out the

---

48. But is it really sensible to limit a sector to only television sets, rather than consumer electronics or electronics in general? The broader the characterization, the less compelling is the allegation of unfairness, especially when firms are diversified. The United States led the recent push for an Information Technology Agreement (ITA) despite near absence of US domestic production of consumer electronics.

formal properties of Schumpeterian dynamic efficiency as carefully or persuasively as they have been worked out for point-in-time efficiency (but see Dinopoulos 1994). Hence, competition-policy analysts have relatively little in the way of normative guidelines to design regimes for intellectual property, corporate takeovers, overseas investment, and similar issues.

Other important issues in the social ideal for lifetime behavior are still unresolved. One concerns attribute competition. There is no guarantee, even in theory, that the number of varieties generated by free-market entry of firms into attribute competition (say, the number of fast-food restaurants at a busy intersection) is socially ideal. Markets can in some circumstances create too many varieties (inefficient excessive competition—see Suzumura's chapter in this volume) or, in other circumstances, too few (also inefficient). Thus, highly contestable markets in attribute competition are not necessarily to be pursued as strongly as highly contestable markets in price and quantity competition.[49]

Market Structure and Technological Innovation

What is the effect of market structure on the rate of technological innovation? And what is the appropriate mix of competition policy and intellectual property protection to move that rate toward socially optimal values? The issue is of importance because technological advance is, in the long run, the most important determinant of productivity advances—that is, the rate at which society can increase output without necessarily increasing its tangible inputs.

Most research finds innovation lower at the extremes of perfect competition and perfect monopoly. More precisely, those sectors that are neither highly competitive nor monopolistic tend to create and utilize new technology at faster rates than do other sectors (see Scherer and Ross 1990).

The usual story is that firms in highly competitive industries are not good at creating new technologies because technology is a public good and, in particular, because of what is called nonrivalry. The basic idea is that technology at its fundamental level, is human knowledge; the quantity of one person's knowledge is not depleted if that person passes on the knowledge to someone else. Hence, knowledge is said to be nonrivalrous.

However, the value of specific knowledge to a person might be reduced by passing it on. If only one person knows how to achieve cold fusion, for example, that person might be able to make a fortune from commercializing this knowledge; if everyone else knows what that person

---

49. We are not persuaded of the practical importance of this, however, leaving us still willing to use contestability as a summary guide to our policy recommendations in the concluding chapter of this volume.

knows, any fortune to be made will be spread among millions of people. In the latter case, everyone benefits from this knowledge—we will have a new source of low-cost energy—but no one will become richer than anyone else.

The argument goes like this: If there is considerable competition in a market, no single seller is likely to benefit from developing a new product or new process if the knowledge associated with that development will quickly become known to all other sellers. Indeed, because technological innovation typically is the fruit of costly research and development, the innovating firm might actually be punished, because this firm alone bears the costs, whereas everyone shares the rewards.[50] This situation is generally known as the appropriability dilemma: the innovator cannot appropriate the full value of the knowledge he or she develops, and, indeed, the amount that is appropriated by the innovator might not warrant the irrecoverable (sunk) costs incurred to create the knowledge. The appropriability dilemma has a social dimension: the value of the new knowledge to society (including both sellers and buyers in the relevant market) might be much higher than the costs of developing the knowledge; however, if no one can appropriate enough of this total value to cover research and development costs, the knowledge will never be generated.

The appropriability dilemma is the major economic justification for intellectual property protection; that protection is a deviation from normal competition policy. It gives the innovator a limited monopoly right to work a new technology and, hence, to increase the total appropriable value of this technology.

Advocates of strong intellectual property protection argue that the stronger this protection is, the more that can be appropriated and the stronger the incentive to innovate. This argument cannot be easily dismissed. However, the stronger this protection is, the slower will be the diffusion of new technology from the innovator to other firms (which may then improve upon it). Thus, many economists argue that too much intellectual property protection can be a bad thing by lowering the overall rate of adoption of new technologies, which depends on both innovation and diffusion (and on the improvements that often accompany diffusion). Theory and empirical evidence support this position (Scherer and Ross 1990). Therefore, the socially correct amount of intellectual property protection is, at best, an uncertain matter.

---

50. This assumes that the knowledge diffuses from the innovator to the other firms without cost, an assumption that will not generally hold. Indeed, some highly innovative firms proceed on the assumption that rivals will not be able to easily replicate knowledge generated within the innovative firm or that the time between innovation and imitation will be sufficiently large so that, by the time rivals have mastered the knowledge, the innovator will have moved on to still newer innovations.

The appropriability dilemma also is invoked to justify cooperation in research and development among sellers who otherwise must compete. If the costs of creating new technology are pooled among sellers, then the disincentive to the innovator from having to bear the full costs while sharing the rewards is reduced. This might result in higher rates of innovation. However, as with intellectual property protection, this conclusion is conditional, as shown below.

Both intellectual property protection and cooperative research and development can be seen as restricting competition. But, as we have stressed, competition policy has, as one of its ultimate objectives, long-term efficiency. Thus, even if competition is reduced, if efficiency-enhancing technological innovation is increased, then intellectual property protection and cooperative research and development would be consistent with the objectives of competition policy. However, the "ifs" must be carefully examined: Will higher rates of technological advance result? Again, there is no strong, normative guideline to help with this examination.

If the appropriability dilemma explains why highly competitive industries do not innovate as rapidly as less competitive ones do, then why do monopolies also tend to be noninnovative? After all, a monopolist does not have to worry about other sellers capturing the rewards of technological innovation. Rather, the monopolist gets all of the reward (or, to be more accurate, gets all of the reward that accrues to sellers, because in the absence of perfect price discrimination, some of the reward will be passed to users in the form of additional consumer surplus).[51] From the perspective of the monopolist, the problem is that sinking costs into research and development is to subject oneself to uncertainty: the expenditures might or might not achieve a satisfactory return. And why should the monopolist do this when it already earns monopoly profits? To be sure, if the research and development is successful, profits will increase. But if shareholders are content with current profits, why take the chance that profits will be reduced by unsuccessful efforts at innovation, when to do nothing would be perfectly satisfactory?

Thus, monopolies tend not to be innovative, because there is some risk to spending on research and development but no apparent risk to not spending. Indeed, this reason applies to intellectual property protection and joint research and development ventures: They reduce the appropriability problem but also can reduce the risk of not innovating. In the

---

51. There is a third reward that might be generated by technological innovation, via the creation of so-called positive externalities. Suppose, for example, that the innovation is a better and cheaper device to clean automotive exhaust, which ultimately improves air quality significantly. Then anyone who can stop taking drugs to combat respiratory problems created by the now eliminated smog is a beneficiary of this innovation via this externality: they benefit, but they do not pay.

case of intellectual property, if the protection granted to existing technology is too great, there will be little or no risk that a rival firm will usurp market share by bringing to the market a still better version of this technology. In the case of joint ventures, the temptation might be for all firms to act more like monopolists than innovative risk takers.

It is often argued that in all of these cases the antidote is to make it risky not to perform research and development. This is best accomplished by introducing competition or, at least, contestability in the market. If there is significant risk that, in the event that an incumbent monopolist does not innovate, an innovative entrant will take away market share, then the incumbent will have to balance the risks of doing research and development against the risks of not doing it. And, if there is potential for product or process improvement (and in what sector is there not?), the likely decision will be to undertake the costs and risks of innovation.

The upshot is that an innovative industry is likely to be quite contestable, but innovative firms can still expect to capture significant rewards. This suggests a market structure that is monopolistically competitive, with only fleeting advantages held by the successful innovator. However, the structural determinants of whether an industry is innovative are not wholly understood.[52]

One result is that competition policy does not deal wholly with issues of innovation nor, indeed, with the panoply of lifetime issues facing a firm. Indeed, competition policy does no more than sanction three rather ad hoc institutions: exceptions (or, at minimum, looser regulation) for joint ventures for research and development; monopolistic intellectual property protection regimes; and forbearance for recession and rationalization cartels. The idea in the first two is to reduce the cost of entry for new products and processes and to improve conditions for appropriability; the idea in the third is to reduce the cost of exit for the old, thus encouraging Schumpeterian dynamic efficiency.

With respect to the third, there are few studies to indicate whether these cartels really do reduce the cost of exit. Nonetheless, we suggest experimentation with these and other competition-policy safeguards, because they are more efficient (and often more equitable) than trade remedies (antidumping and countervailing duties) in downsizing activities in which a country's producers have lost comparative advantage.

With respect to innovation, it is clear that markets alone tend to undersupply new technology, but it is not yet clear how competition policy

---

52. For example, traditional 20-year protection of patentable inventions might seem long rather than fleeting. More generally, the issue of the ideal length of patent protection and of patent scope (does the patent cover major variations of a new technology or only minor ones?) is not well addressed by economic reasoning. One consequence is that patent life and scope has been determined by historic precedent rather than by reason and evidence.

can help the market overcome its shortcomings. The recent commitment by all WTO members to historically established systems of intellectual-property protection is an intriguing real-life institutional experiment in policies to encourage dynamic efficiency.[53] Whatever its outcome, in 20 or more years many questions will remain about the optimal design of such institutions, such as how long-lived such protection should be and how broad its coverage should be across varieties of similar innovations.

Globalization, Governance, and Cross-Border Investment

Though competition policy is rarely defined so broadly as to include issues of corporate governance, cross-border investment and trade increasingly force the two together in evaluating the lifetime behavior of firms. Thus, cross-border investment can be a vehicle for both new entry of products and for innovation.[54] Japanese investment in North American steel, rubber, and auto assembly facilities, for example, reestablished US compact-car production and revolutionized US factory organization.[55] Thus, policies that encourage cross-border investment may facilitate the goal of contestability (Graham 1996a, chapter 4). Among other such policies are commitments to rights of establishment and national treatment for foreign firms and discipline of discriminatory performance requirements not covered by the Uruguay Round Trade-Related Investment Measures (TRIMs). But brokerage, forecasting, risk assessment, and risk management are among the important supports and complements to these investment policies. All of these support policies are informational infrastructures that make global investment markets work efficiently and fairly, just as competition policy is a national infrastructure with the same objectives.

Social Behavior

Competition policies are almost always modulated and influenced by broader social objectives.

---

53. This commitment is embodied in the TRIPs agreement. Proponents of this agreement believe that its implementation will encourage the diffusion of technology to nations that, in the past, international investors have been reluctant to transfer technology to because of weak intellectual property protection. Critics, however, worry that full implementation of TRIPs could lead to overzealous protection of intellectual property with the deleterious effects (already noted above).

54. See Noland (1997) for a negative assessment of the hypothesis that cross-border investment is restrained by anticompetitive entry-deterrence practices.

55. Most Japanese investments in steel and rubber involved taking over failing firms; most auto investments involved greenfield investment (building plants from the ground up). Entry was obviously higher than otherwise in the latter case but also higher in the former because exit of US firms, which would have happened without the investment, was allayed.

Sectoral and Corporate Differences

Because it often clashes with other objectives, competition policy varies across sectors. Competition policy is usually tailored to sectoral public-interest regulation—especially in transportation, telecommunications, and utilities—and often tailored to industrial policies that favor agriculture or high-technology sectors over others. Competition policy is almost always made subservient to national-security considerations in defense contracting and defense-sector downsizing.[56] Competition policy has never been applied indiscriminately to financial markets nor to labor markets where labor unions compete with each other and with company representation to represent workers collectively (cooperatively and collusively). Occasionally, competition policy even differentiates among competing firms, with state-owned or state-chartered firms treated with more leniency (but this differential treatment is not sanctioned in either Europe or North America).

Functional Differences

Competition policy is also altered to serve social goals without regard to sector. Examples are the promotion of small or minority-owned businesses, maintenance of indigenous culture, assurance of service to peripheral or declining subregions, and buttressing of government revenue. For example, small businesses in some countries (e.g., France and Japan) are protected by distribution laws that allow mom-and-pop retailers to block the arrival of a new (and often larger) entrant (see chapters in this volume by Jenny and Matsushita). Examples of the policies that maintain indigenous culture are special barriers to ownership of publishing enterprises and mass media by foreigners and, hence, barriers to mergers that involve them (see the chapter by Goldman, Bodrug, and Warner), and antitrust exemptions for local sports (e.g., North American baseball). Until recently, telecommunications and other utilities illustrated policies that support universal service. Firms in these sectors have been allowed to maintain privileged positions of market power in exchange for their pledge to serve the hinterlands, financing an otherwise unprofitable service with excess profits earned from their entry-protected positions.[57] An example of the policies that buttress government revenue is the willingness of governments to compromise competition-policy objectives when privatizing a state-owned monopolist—government revenues from the

---

56. See, for example, "Linking Arms: A Survey of the Global Defense Industry," *The Economist*, 14 June 1997, 7-8.

57. The sanctioned financing is called cross-subsidization. But in the United States and elsewhere, deregulation and international market opening are allowing entry to undercut these cross-subsidies and forcing regulators to find less anticompetitive means to subsidize service in remote regions.

sale are kept higher when the government guarantees the same privileged market position to the private buyer.

When competition policy differs for these reasons across sectors, firms, regions, or activities, efficiency and fairness of the normal sort suffer, as described in the next section. That is the trade-off for or price of meeting other social objectives. However, some commentators argue that this price is rising all too rapidly because of the weakness of existing competition policies (see the chapters in this volume by Rosenthal and Nicolaïdis). And when countries differ in the sectors, firms, regions, or activities that they exempt for social reasons, efficiency and fairness suffer at the global level as well. Conflict over the fairness of differing exceptions becomes inevitable.[58]

Economywide and Worldwide Concerns of Competition Policy

The efficiency and fairness concerns of competition policy are different when viewed from a distance rather than from a sector's vantage point. There are unique insights about the forest that do not characterize the trees.

Economywide and Worldwide Efficiency

Efficiency is achieved by a somewhat different set of guidelines for the economy as a whole than for a single sector or firm. One of the things that matters most for single industries or firms is the relationship of output prices to input costs for given product attributes. But what matters for economywide efficiency are relative prices and costs from sector to sector. At any point, an economy is reasonably efficient if:

- the prices of goods and services from sector to sector have the same relative values as under perfect competition, whether or not this extreme form of competition really exists and whether or not the prices are close to costs, and

- input costs are the same from sector to sector and firm to firm, rather than, for example, being cheaper to incumbents or to favored firms or sectors.[59]

---

58. Suzumura's chapter in this volume outlines the types of considerations that might go into deciding permissible exemptions policies.

59. Favored firms might include those with public ownership or ownership by ethnic minorities, firms with a license to unique resources, or firms with political connections. Favored sectors often include those with prominent places in a development plan, or those meeting social objectives. Price discrimination by input suppliers creates differences across buyer firms, which is presumptively inefficient (Varian 1989, 623-24), unlike price discrimination by final-goods suppliers.

That relative prices and costs are what really matter for economywide efficiency has some surprising implications. The fundamental implication is that, with one important exception, a single economy can still be reasonably efficient when each of its sectors faces comparable competitive imperfections (e.g., if each sector is populated by the same set of rival incumbent firms that block out newcomers and charge prices that are marked up comparably over costs, say, by 30 percent).[60] The economy is still reasonably efficient because excess profits and barriers to entry are roughly the same throughout the economy; there is no economywide incentive to underproduce in one sector relative to another, and the sector-by-sector mix of goods available to buyers is close to that which perfect competition would generate (because the product prices of each sector relative to others are also the same as under perfect competition).[61]

The important exception to this economywide efficiency would occur when relative prices of new products, processes, or technologies that would have often been produced by the blocked, nascent newcomers as their ticket to successful entry are wrong. Product innovation will, as a result, usually be too low, as will the number of product varieties. Process innovation may also be too low, because the costs of new processes are distorted, and entrants with new ideas for how to produce products are also blocked.[62]

This insight on economywide efficiency is less abstract than it may appear. Economies such as South Korea's, in which the same corporate conglomerates (called *chaebol*) compete across virtually all industries, may not have egregious inefficiencies and distortions in any particular sector (except innovation)—as long as South Korea remains reasonably insulated from the world economy. And economies such as Germany's, in which powerful labor unions bargain nationally and represent workers across many sectors, may not have egregious sectoral inefficiencies and distortions—except in innovation and except as the sharp market competition from the rest of the world impinges indirectly on German labor market power.[63] By contrast, economies with sectorally uneven market

---

60. This outcome is sometimes described as the "equal degree of monopoly" environment. See Scherer and Ross (1980, appendix to chapter 2).

61. British competition law actually seeks a "balanced distribution of industry" (see the chapter by Hay in this volume).

62. A less-important exception is that the price of leisure may be distorted, because it cannot meaningfully be produced by the same monopolistic markup process. See Scherer and Ross (1980, appendix to chapter 2). Leisure may be slightly underproduced (excessive labor supply) or slightly overproduced (insufficient labor supply), with the latter slightly more likely, according to empirical estimates of the wage elasticity of the labor supply.

63. The same might be said to be the result of inefficient distribution systems across all sectors in Japan.

power (e.g., government-sanctioned monopolies in transport or telecommunications) often have more inefficiency—visibly bad quality, slow service, and high prices—in those sectors (but they are not so inefficient in other sectors).

Even in an economy with sectorally even market power, however, a lack of innovation might cause static inefficiency to grow over time. This is because innovation itself is uneven across sectors and, hence, causes relative prices to change. An economy that is insulated from such changes will become increasingly inefficient even in the static sense. Additionally, because new technologies will be adopted elsewhere and not at home, producers in the insulated economy will become increasingly technologically inefficient. Put in plain English, they will become backward by failing to adopt technological improvements. The economies of Eastern Europe and the Soviet Union during the 1970s and 1980s are examples. Dominance of these economies by state-owned monopolies led both to increasing static (allocational) inefficiency due to relative price distortions as well as to technological backwardness. One consequence was a high level of so-called x-inefficiency or, in other words, overstaffing (and featherbedding) in the state-owned enterprises.

However, technological backwardness and increasingly inefficient allocation of resources do not necessarily follow if the economy is at least open to imports of technology. South Korea again serves as an example. Although during the 1970s and 1980s it was relatively closed to imports of goods and (nonfactor) services, South Korea was not closed to imports of technology. In fact, Korean firms—including the *chaebol*—paid large fees to gain access to new technologies. One result was that relative prices in South Korea changed in response to technological improvement, and another was that South Korean firms technologically caught up with their rivals in the rest of the world. Also, these firms diversified into new activities, often those where technological advances were occurring most rapidly. Overall, South Korea's economic position in the world (as measured by per capita GDP) rose, at exactly the same time that the position of most of Eastern Europe fell.

For similar reasons, inefficiency is also high in economies in which the cost of the same resource differs dramatically from firm to firm or from sector to sector, say, because of government favoritism or ethnic or family connections. But inefficiency is not necessarily high in insulated economies where everyone faces the same input prices, even if input prices are altered by heavy regulation or taxation (e.g., payroll taxes).

This insight on economywide efficiency means, more precisely, that

■ point-in-time (static) efficiency for an economy in isolation does not require perfect competition; it can be approached when there are competitive distortions that are pervasive yet comparable across activities.

Six more insights follow directly:

- The same economy is likely to be dynamically inefficient: it may not grow quickly if its structure discourages product and process innovation by new firms.

- Efficiency may be ensured, but fairness of opportunity may not; new entrants are uniformly shut out.

- The economy's apparent efficiency may fade as it opens to world markets; every sector in the economy and every input market will be pressured by global counterparts whose corresponding sectors are organized more competitively.

- The greatest pressure will come in the most dynamic sectors—that is, the sectors or input markets that are most innovation-intensive.

- Pressures from global rivals may appear unfair because their economies do not tolerate any modulation or cushioning of ruthless efficiency-enhancing competitive forces.

- Increasingly integrated global financial markets are catalysts for these competitive pressures, creating both opportunity and risk. Efficient corporate cooperation, labor relations, and regulation (e.g., prudential regulation of the financial markets) will actually be rewarded; it is not inevitable that conglomerates and social market economies are eclipsed.

These insights need further discussion by, for example, the working party of the WTO that is now studying them.

One important implication of these insights is that setting an efficient regulatory baseline is a crucial precondition for defining anticompetitive practices. In the long run, there will be no avoiding the need for governments to sit down to negotiate and then recognize efficient competition-policy rules for permissible interfirm cooperation and even for permissible organization of labor markets.[64] Such internationally recognized rules will define (and deliver) baseline efficiency for all countries that agree to them and for all sectors that are covered. The baseline

---

64. These will inevitably involve worker rights to cooperate—that is, organize and collectively transact (bargain), which are rights that mirror the rights of firms to do the same. However, efficient foundational rules would almost surely make union representation more contestable than it is in most countries, reducing the market power of incumbent unions and easing the potential of new-entrant unions to displace inefficient incumbents. Cross-border trade in union organization and representation is a still more distant instrument for achieving efficient foundational labor-relations rules, but it has the same economic rationale as all cross-border competition. Free trade in union representation enhances the contestability of labor markets and has rewards in both efficiency and (arguably) fairness!

may look inefficient relative to some other norm or relative to some definition of efficiency that puts more weight on its dynamic character than its static character (efficiency for growth or for current generations), but arguing over such differences and experimenting with and monitoring alternative baselines will be a crucial part of the process.

Economywide and Worldwide Fairness

Fairness, likewise, is also achieved somewhat differently for the economy as a whole than for each sector. One important reason is that many firms, large and small, are diversified across sectors (large firms that produce in many sectors are called conglomerates). Thus, sectoral differences in competition policy may not be unfair to any particular (diversified) firm. For example, a division of a conglomerate such as General Electric may decide to enter a new line of production such as broadcasting (General Electric owns the National Broadcasting Company [NBC]). Thus, General Electric is less vulnerable from an economywide perspective than from the perspective of the electrical-equipment industry alone—it is a diversified incumbent. And, correspondingly, if it were forced to leave one of its many lines of business, perhaps even by predation from another diversified conglomerate, the inequity seems less compelling if some of its workers, efforts, and rewards are simply reoriented to its other product lines.

This insight also has valuable implications for international conflict. Fairness-motivated competition-policy conventions may be less needful when the underlying constituents are sectorally diversified multinational companies like Daewoo, Mitsubishi, Phillip Morris, and Siemens. Reciprocated entry (cross-penetration) by such firms into each others' diverse domestic markets may make the prototypical global market monopolistically competitive rather than oligopolistic. There would be less need for competition policy of any kind to the extent that market power and its abuse are more tightly constrained by the former market structure than by the latter. Diversified multinational firms can take care of themselves. But market competition among them can take care of disciplining any abuses of market power they may contemplate. The apparent power of each is illusory, undermined by the strong competition of the others.[65]

Smaller firms, however, or those that produce only a single product or handful of products, may be less insulated. So competition policy is more needful to them, especially if small firms can be disproportionately large agents of entry and innovation. However, the large multinationals

---

65. Global cartelization or implicit collusion among these multinationals, such as the cartelization that took place in the 1930s, is clearly to be avoided. This is another natural task of an international competition-policy regime.

often relate vertically to hundreds of small, specialized, domestic suppliers whose need for fair and efficient treatment in global markets is taken care of by the implicit representation of their large corporate customers, not by policy. The place for policy, however, may naturally remain to discipline abuses of market power among large and small firms, whatever their nationality.

Finally, fairness can often be achieved among a few large firms by negotiation alone. The transaction costs of negotiating are generally lower if fewer agents are represented. Thus, there is no need for an elaborate fairness policy if firms can work out their perceived inequities (and potential inefficiencies) through legal joint ventures and other cooperation.[66] This simply illustrates the kind of good interfirm relation described above.

The remainder of this volume is divided into three sections. The first is a series of studies indicating how several nations (and the European Union) have implemented competition policies. What emerges from these chapters is that there are substantial differences among nations in their specific approaches and that these differences can be difficult to reconcile at the international level. Two important sets of differences—those between the United States and the European Union and those between the United States and Japan—are explored in some detail. The following section consists of several studies of specific issues germane to competition policy. The final section contains our recommendations on action that should be taken at the international level.

References

Besanko, David, David Dranove, and Mark Shanley. 1996. *The Economics of Strategy*. New York: John Wiley.

Bhagwati, Jagdish N., and Robert E. Hudec, eds. 1996. *Fair Trade and Harmonization: Prerequisites for Free Trade?* Cambridge: MIT Press.

Bond, Eric. 1996. "A 'Natural Experiment' Using State Level Antitrust Policies." Photocopy. University Park, PA: Pennsylvania State University.

Bourgeois, Jacques H. J., and Patrick A. Messerlin. 1993. "Competition and the EC Antidumping Regulation." Manuscript. Paris: Institut d'Études Politique de Paris.

Bresnahan, Timothy F. 1989. "Empirical Studies of Industries with Market Power." In *The Handbook of Industrial Organization*, ed. by Richard Schmalensee and Robert Willig. Amsterdam: New Holland.

Bresnahan, Timothy F., and Peter C. Reiss. 1991. "Entry and Competition in Concentrated Markets." *Journal of Political Economy* 99, no. 5 (October): 977-1009.

Cho, Soon. 1994. *The Dynamics of Korean Economic Development*. Washington: Institute for International Economics.

Commission of the European Communities. 1997. Green Paper on "Vertical Restraints in

---

66. But there is still a need for competition policy to define the boundaries of cooperation legally and to enforce those boundaries clearly.

EC Competition Policy." Brussels: Commission of the European Communities (22 January).

Dick, Andrew. 1997. "When Are Cartels Stable Contracts?" *Journal of Law and Economics* 39 (April 1996): 241-83.

Dinopoulos, Elias. 1994. "Schumpeterian Growth Theory: An Overview." *Osaka City University Economic Review* 29: 1-21.

EPG (Eminent Persons Group). 1995. *Implementing the APEC Vision*: Third Report of the Eminent Persons Group. Singapore: APEC Secretariat (August).

Feketekuty, Geza, and Robert A. Rogowsky. 1996. "The Scope, Implication and Economic Rationale of a Competition-Oriented Approach to Future Multilateral Trade Negotiations." Manuscript. Monterey, CA: Monterey Institute of International Studies (May).

Finger, J. Michael. 1995. "Can Dispute Settlement Contribute to an International Agreement (Institutional Order) on Locational Competition?" In *Locational Competition in the World Economy: Symposium 1994*, ed. by Horst Siebert. Tubingen, Germany: J. C. B. Mohr (Paul Siebeck).

First, Harry, Eleanor M. Fox, and Robert Pitofsky, eds. 1991. *Revitalizing Antitrust in Its Second Century: Essays on Legal, Economic, and Political Policy*. New York: Quorum.

Fox, Eleanor M. 1997a. "US and EU Competition Law: A Comparison." In *Global Competition Policy*, ed. by Edward M. Graham and J. David Richardson. Washington: Institute for International Economics.

Fox, Eleanor M. 1997b. "Toward World Antitrust and Market Access." *The American Journal of International Law* 91, no. 1 (January).

Fox, Eleanor M. and Janusz A. Ordover. 1995. "The Harmonization of Competition and Trade Law The Case for Modest Linkages of Law and Limits to Parochial State Action." *World Competition* 19 (December): 5-34.

Geroski, P. A. 1992. "Vertical Relations between Firms and Industrial Policy." *The Economic Journal* 102, no. 410 (January): 138-47.

Gifford, Daniel J. 1997. "The Draft International Antitrust Code Proposed at Munich: Good Intentions Gone Awry." *Minnesota Journal of Global Trade* 6, no. 1: 1-66.

Gifford, Daniel J., and Mitsuo Matsushita. 1996. "Antitrust or Competition Laws Viewed in a Trading Context: Harmony or Dissonance?" In *Fair Trade and Harmonization: Prerequisites for Free Trade?* ed. by Jagdish N. Bhagwati and Robert E. Hudec. Cambridge: MIT Press.

Goldman, Calvin S., John D. Bodrug, and Mark A. Warner. 1997. "Canada." In *Global Competition Policy*, ed. by Edward M. Graham and J. David Richardson. Washington: Institute for International Economics.

Graham, Edward M. 1994. "US Antitrust Laws and Market Access to Japan." In *Unilateral Application of Antitrust and Trade Laws*, ed. by Henry B. Cortesi. New York: The Pacific Institute/The Asia Institute.

Graham, Edward M. 1995. "Competition Policy and the New Trade Agenda." In *New Dimensions of Market Access in a Globalizing World Economy*. OECD Documents. Paris: Organization for Economic Cooperation and Development.

Graham, Edward M. 1996a. *Global Corporations and National Governments*. Washington: Institute for International Economics.

Graham, Edward M. 1996b. "Competition Policy in the United States." In *Competition Regulation in the Pacific Rim*, ed. by Carl J. Green and Douglas E. Rosenthal. New York: Oceana Press.

Graham, Edward M., and Robert Z. Lawrence. 1996. "Measuring the International Contestability of Markets: A Conceptual Approach." *Journal of World Trade* 30, no. 5, (October): 5-20.

Graham, Edward M., and J. David Richardson, eds. 1997. *Global Competition Policy*. Washington: Institute for International Economics.

Graham, Edward M., and Christopher Wilkie. 1994. "Multinationals and the Investment Provisions of the NAFTA." *The International Trade Journal* 8, no. 3 (Spring).

Greaney, Theresa M. 1996. "Import Now! An Analysis of Market-Share Voluntary Import Expansions (VIEs)." *Journal of International Economics* 40, no. 1/2 (February): 149-63.

Green, Carl J., and Douglas E. Rosenthal, eds. 1996. *Competition Regulation Within the APEC Region: Commonality and Divergence.* New York: Oceana Press.

Greenhut, Melvin L., George Norman, and Chao-shun Hung. 1987. *The Economics of Imperfect Competition: A Spatial Approach.* Cambridge: Cambridge University Press.

Gual, Jordi. 1995. *The Coherence of EC Policies on Trade, Competition and Industry.* Discussion Paper No. 1105. London: Centre for Economic Policy Research (January).

Hay, Donald. 1997. "United Kingdom." In *Global Competition Policy,* ed. by Edward M. Graham and J. David Richardson. Washington: Institute for International Economics.

Hindley, Brian. 1996. "Competition Law and the WTO: Alternative Structures for Agreement." In *Fair Trade and Harmonization: Prerequisites for Free Trade?* ed. by Jagdish N. Bhagwati and Robert E. Hudec. Cambridge: MIT Press.

Hoekman, Bernard. 1996. *Trade and Competition Policy in the WTO System.* CEPR Discussion Paper No. 1501. London: Centre for Economic Policy and Research.

Hoekman, Bernard. 1997a. "Focal Points and Multilateral Negotiations on the Contestability of Markets." In *Quiet Pioneering: Robert M. Stern and His International Economic Legacy,* ed. by Keith E. Maskus, et al. Ann Arbor: University of Michigan Press. Forthcoming.

Hoekman, Bernard. 1997b. "Competition Policy and the Global Trading System." *The World Economy* 20 (July): 383-406.

Hoekman, Bernard M., and Petros C. Mavroidis. 1994. "Competition, Competition Policy, and the GATT." *The World Economy* 17, no. 2 (March): 121-50.

Horn, Henrik, and James Levinsohn. 1997. *Merger Policies and Trade Liberalization.* National Bureau of Economic Research Working Paper No. 6077. Cambridge, MA: National Bureau of Economic Research (June).

Hufbauer, Gary. 1996. "Surveying the Costs of Protection: A Partial Equilibrium Approach." In *The World Trading System: Challenges Ahead,* ed. by Jeffrey J. Schott. Washington: Institute for International Economics.

Irmen, Andreas, and Jacques-Francois Thisse. 1996. *Competition in Multi-Characteristics Spaces: Hotelling Was Almost Right.* Centre for Economic Policy and Research Discussion Paper No. 1446. London: Centre for Economic Policy and Research (October).

Itoh, Motoshige, and Sadao Nagaoka. 1997. "VERs, VIEs, and Global Competition." In *Global Competition Policy,* ed. by Edward M. Graham and J. David Richardson. Washington: Institute for International Economics.

Jackson, John H. 1990. *Restructuring the GATT System.* New York: Council on Foreign Relations Press for the Royal Institute of International Affairs.

Jenny, Frédéric. 1997. "France." In *Global Competition Policy,* ed. by Edward M. Graham and J. David Richardson. Washington: Institute for International Economics.

Joelson, Mark R. 1993. "Antitrust Aspects of NAFTA." *Federal Bar News & Journal* 40, no. 9 (October): 573-78.

Jorde, Thomas M., and David J. Teece, eds. 1992. *Antitrust, Innovation, and Competitiveness.* New York: Oxford University Press.

Katz, Michael L., and Janusz A. Ordover. 1990. "R&D Cooperation and Competition." *Brookings Papers on Economic Activity: Microeconomics, 1990*: 137-91.

Kühn, Kai-Uwe. 1997. "Germany." In *Global Competition Policy,* ed. by Edward M. Graham and J. David Richardson. Washington: Institute for International Economics.

Kühn, Kai-Uwe, Paul Seabright, and Alasdair Smith. 1992. *Competition Policy Research: Where Do We Stand?* CEPR Occasional Paper No. 8. London: Centre for Economic Policy and Research (July).

Lawrence, Robert Z., Albert Bressand, and Takatoshi Ito. 1996. *A Vision for the World Economy: Openness, Diversity, and Cohesion.* Washington: Brookings Institution.

Levinsohn, James. 1996. "Competition Policy and International Trade." In *Fair Trade and Harmonization: Prerequisites for Free Trade?* ed. by Jagdish N. Bhagwati and Robert E. Hudec. Cambridge: MIT Press.

Lipstein, Robert A. 1997. "Using Antitrust Principles to Reform Antidumping Law." In *Global Competition Policy,* ed. by Edward M. Graham and J. David Richardson. Washington: Institute for International Economics.

Lloyd, Peter, and Gary Sampson. 1995. "Competition and Trade Policy: Identifying the Issues after the Uruguay Round." *World Economy* 18, no. 5 (September): 681-705.

Malueg, David A. 1993. "Bounding the Welfare Effects of Third Degree Price Discrimination." *American Economic Review* 83 (September): 1011-21.

Malueg, David A., and Marius Schwartz. 1994. "Parallel Imports, Demand Dispersion, and International Price Discrimination." *Journal of International Economics* 37: 167-95.

Mathewson, Frank, Michael Trebilcock, and Michael Walker, eds. 1990. *The Law and Economics of Competition Policy.* Vancouver: Fraser Institute.

Matsushita, Mitsuo. 1997. "Japan." In *Global Competition Policy,* ed. by Edward M. Graham and J. David Richardson. Washington: Institute for International Economics.

Messerlin, Patrick A. 1996. "Competition Policy and Antidumping Reform: An Exercise in Transition." In *The World Trading System: Challenges Ahead,* ed. by Jeffrey J. Schott. Washington: Institute for International Economics.

Neven, Damien, Robin Nuttall, and Paul Seabright. 1993. *Merger in Daylight: The Economics and Politics of European Merger Control.* London: Centre for Economic Policy and Research.

Nicolaïdis, Kalypso, and Raymond Vernon. 1997. "European Union." In *Global Competition Policy,* ed. by Edward M. Graham and J. David Richardson. Washington: Institute for International Economics.

Noland, Marcus. 1997. "Host-Country Market Structure and Inward FDI." Photocopy. Washington: Institute for International Economics.

Ordover, Janusz A. 1990. Economic Foundations of Competition Policy. In *Competition Policy in Europe and North America: Economic Issues and Institutions,* ed. by W. S. Comanor et al. Chur, Switerland: Harwood.

Organization for Economic Cooperation and Development (OECD). 1989. *Predatory Pricing.* Paris: Organization for Economic Cooperation and Development.

Peck, Merton J., Richard C. Levin, and Akira Goto. 1988. "Picking Losers: Public Policy Toward Declining Industries in Japan." In *Government Policy Toward Industry in the United States and Japan,* ed. by John B. Shoven. Cambridge: Cambridge University Press.

Richardson, J. David. 1997. "Competition Policies as Irritants to Asia-Pacific Trade." In *East Asian Trade After the Uruguay Round,* ed. by David Robertson. New York: Cambridge University Press.

Richardson, J. David. 1995. Comment on "Can Dispute Settlement Contribute to an International Agreement (Institutional Order) on Locational Competition?" In *Locational Competition in the World Economy: Symposium 1994,* ed. by Horst Siebert. Tubingen, Germany: J. C. B. Mohr (Paul Siebeck).

Rosenthal, Douglas E., and Mitsuo Matsushita. 1997. "Competition in Japan and the West: Can the Approaches Be Reconciled?" In *Global Competition Policy,* ed. by Edward M. Graham and J. David Richardson. Washington: Institute for International Economics.

Rosenthal, Douglas E., and Phedon Nicholaides. 1997. "Harmonizing Antitrust: The Less Effective Way to Promote International Competition." In *Global Competition Policy,* ed. by Edward M. Graham and J. David Richardson. Washington: Institute for International Economics.

Scherer, F. M. 1994. *Competition Policies for an Integrated World Economy.* Washington: Brookings Institution.

Scherer, F. M. 1992. *International High-Technology Competition.* Cambridge: Harvard University Press.

Scherer, F. M., and David Ross. 1990. *Industrial Market Structure and Economic Performance.* Boston: Houghton Mifflin.

Schott, Jeffrey J., ed. 1996. *The World Trading System: Challenges Ahead*. Washington: Institute for International Economics.

Schumpeter, Joseph. 1950. *Capitalism, Socialism, and Democracy*. New York: Harper Collins.

Shaw, R. W. and S. A. Shaw. 1983. "Excess Capacity and Rationalization in the Western European Synthetic Fibres Industry." *The Journal of Industrial Economics* 32 (December): 149-66.

Sheard, Paul. 1997. "*Keiretsu*, Competition, and Market Access." In *Global Competition Policy*, ed. by Edward M. Graham and J. David Richardson. Washington: Institute for International Economics.

Shin, Hyun Ja. 1992. "Census and Analysis of Antidumping Cases in the United States." Monograph. Princeton, NJ: Princeton University.

Smith, P. J. 1997. "Are Weak Patent Rights a Barrier to U.S. Exports?" Photocopy (31 May).

Suzumura, Kotaro. 1997. "Formal and Informal Measures for Controlling Competition in Japan: Institutional Overview and Theoretical Evaluation." In *Global Competition Policy*, ed. by Edward M. Graham and J. David Richardson. Washington: Institute for International Economics.

Thomson, Graeme. 1997. "Australia and New Zealand." In *Global Competition Policy*, ed. by Edward M. Graham and J. David Richardson. Washington: Institute for International Economics.

Tineo, Luis. 1997. *Competition Policy and Law in Latin America: From Distributive Regulations to Market Efficiency*. Center for Trade and Commercial Diplomacy Working Paper No. 4. Monterey, CA: Monterey Institute of International Studies.

Tybout, James R., and M. Daniel Westbrook. 1995. "Trade Liberalization and the Dimensions of Efficiency Change in Mexican Manufacturing Industries." *Journal of International Economics* 39: 53-78.

UNCTAD (United Nations Conference on Trade and Development). 1997. *World Investment Report 1997: Transnational Corporations, Market Structure, and Competition Policy*. New York and Geneva.

Varian, Hal R. 1989. "Price Discrimination." In *Handbook of Industrial Organization*, vol. 1, ed. by Richard Schmalansee and Robert Willig. Amsterdam: North Holland.

II

COUNTRY STUDIES

2

Canada

CALVIN S. GOLDMAN, JOHN D. BODRUG,
AND MARK A. A. WARNER

This chapter has two principal objectives. First, it overviews Canadian competition and foreign investment review legislation and administrative practice, focusing on those aspects that are distinctive or touch on extraterritorial issues in enforcement. In so doing, this chapter also discusses the prevailing economic theory underlying competition policy in Canada, as well as some of the principal characteristics of the Canadian economy and the political institutions that influence that philosophy. Second, this chapter discusses implications of Canadian competition law and policy for Canada's competitiveness and its economic relations with its trading partners. Then, we turn to a broader definition of competition policy to examine how the application of Canadian laws pertaining to foreign investment, trade, and intellectual property rights affects competitive conditions within Canada and between Canada and its major trading partners.

Two broad conclusions emerge. First, the Canadian experience shows that a modern competition policy may be implemented effectively in a relatively small and open economy. Second, the relationship between Canada and the United States illustrates both the difficulties and the advantages of harmonization and convergence of competition policies.

Calvin S. Goldman and John D. Bodrug are partners at Davies, Ward & Beck, Toronto. From May 1986 until October 1989, Mr. Goldman was the director of investigation and research, Bureau of Competition Policy, Ottawa. Mark A. A. Warner is a legal counselor at the OECD Trade Directorate, Paris, and chair of the American Bar Association Section of Antitrust Law International Committee. Mr. Warner's views are his own and do not necessarily represent the views of the OECD or its member states.

The Economic Framework

Canada's economic environment is perhaps best understood in the context of a few basic statistics. In 1995, Canadian GDP was 8.1 percent of US GDP.[1] Canada's exports accounted for 36.4 percent of its GDP, and its exports to the United States amounted to 28.9 percent of its GDP. Canada exported to the United States 79.6 percent of all its exports, while imports from the United States accounted for 66.5 percent of total Canadian imports. By contrast, exports represented 9.0 percent of the US GDP, and US exports to Canada accounted for only 1.9 percent of total US GDP. However, exports to Canada represented 21.6 percent of all US exports, and imports from Canada accounted for 19.2 percent of all US imports.

These data demonstrate three simple themes that are central to understanding the Canadian approach to competition policy, particularly in explaining certain differences from US antitrust policy. First, there is an asymmetric relationship between the importance of the United States to the Canadian economy and the importance of Canada to the US economy. Second, Canada is dependent on international trade for its economic well-being. Third, even though foreign trade is relatively less important to the US economy generally, Canada is nonetheless a significant factor in the US economy.

At various times in Canadian history, Canadians have viewed these factors more as a threat than an opportunity. Up until the mid-1980s, Canada protected its domestic industries with significant tariffs. These tariffs induced foreign firms to establish branch-plant subsidiaries to produce and distribute in Canada rather than to export into Canada. Notwithstanding this policy, Canada periodically displayed skepticism toward the level of foreign ownership in the Canadian economy (Warner 1990, 16). For instance, in the 1970s this concern culminated in the creation of the Foreign Investment Review Agency to screen new foreign investments, and a National Energy Program, which severely restricted foreign ownership of the Canadian oil and gas industry. By the mid-1980s, however, there was widespread understanding in Canada that both of these policies prolonged recessions in Canada by discouraging much-needed foreign investment.[2]

In addition to their macroeconomic effect, these Canadian economic policies increased entry barriers (such as tariffs) and induced firms to establish comparatively small branch plants that produced below an

---

1. The data in this section of the paper are based on calculations made from data contained in *International Financial Statistics* (International Monetary Fund, June 1994) and *Direction of Trade Statistics Yearbook* (International Monetary Fund, 1993).

2. See Rugman and Warner (1988). The authors calculated that between 1980 and 1985 net outflows from the oil and gas sector totaled slightly more than C$15 billion.

efficient scale.[3] The effect of these policies, combined with the relatively small Canadian population spread over a large land mass, was to create small, segmented, and relatively inefficient markets within Canada.[4] Although these policies often led to concentrated markets with few firms, the firms themselves were still not large enough to produce efficiently. Furthermore, excess capacity in these industries, government subsidies and tariffs, and other barriers to entry prevented new competition from emerging and encouraged rivalistic firm behavior within many Canadian markets. Arguably, the horizontal effects of oligopolistic behavior in Canada further reduced the efficiency of the Canadian economy and, in the absence of effective competition in Canada, any efficiency gains from vertical integration did not necessarily accrue to the Canadian economy.

By the mid-1980s, however, the Canadian economy had matured considerably as a result of other developing economic trends. Canada, a traditional host country for foreign direct investment (FDI), also became an important home (or source) country for FDI as Canadians invested in other countries (Rugman 1987, 1990). In 1991, Canada was the fourth largest source of the stock of FDI in the United States, behind the United Kingdom, Japan, and the Netherlands (Borghese 1993, 18 and 24). In fact, between 1981 and 1990 Canadian FDI in the United States grew at an average rate of 12.1 percent, nearly three times faster than the rate of growth of US FDI in Canada over the same period (Rugman and Verbeke 1994, table 2). Furthermore, successive rounds of multilateral tariff reductions under the General Agreement on Tariffs and Trade (GATT) had already forced many multinational corporations to rethink their branch-plant strategies. What emerged was a new generation of multinational enterprises marked by greater bilateral integration, as is evidenced by the importance of intrafirm trade to their profitability. Intrafirm trade dominates the overall bilateral Canada-US trading relationship.[5]

The maturation of the Canadian economy and the adverse effects of the old protectionist policies led the Canadian government to pursue free trade with the United States, which culminated in the signing of the Canada-US Free Trade Agreement in 1988 and the North American Free Trade Agreement (NAFTA) in 1993, and to reform Canadian competition, foreign investment, and intellectual property legislation. As discussed below, these new policies recognize the role of foreign competition in achieving competitive and efficient markets in Canada. The remainder of this chapter discusses the significant aspects of this new

---

3. For a review of the economic literature on this point, see Khemani (1991, 205).

4. See, generally, Eastman and Stykolt (1967).

5. Rugman (1990, 3) estimated that the 50 largest multinationals (whether foreign or Canadian-controlled) operating in Canada account for 70 percent of Canada-US trade. See also Encarnation (1994, 309).

economic policy environment, with particular emphasis on the existing competition and trade law regimes.

Competition Legislation

History and Enforcement

In 1889, Canada became the first western industrialized nation to enact legislation to prevent firms from forming agreements in restraint of trade. (Canada also has the dubious distinction of being the first country to pass antidumping legislation, in 1904.) Legislation with respect to mergers and monopolization (1910), misleading advertising (1914), price discrimination and predatory pricing (1935), price maintenance (1951), and other specific practices followed later. For the most part, this legislation was included in the Criminal Code or the Combines Investigation Act. However, until the enactment of the Competition Act in 1986, successful enforcement of competition legislation was relatively infrequent and rarely accompanied by significant penalties. Between 1910 and 1986, only nine criminal merger charges were laid, and not one contested merger case resulted in a conviction. While the government did successfully prosecute a number of price-fixing cases during that period, penalties were relatively low (at least by US standards), and no one was sentenced to imprisonment. Prior to 1990, the highest fine in a conspiracy case was C$447,000.[6]

This historical, low level of enforcement is partly explained by the fact that, before 1986, Canadian competition law was exclusively criminal legislation. It was very difficult to prove elements such as an "undue" lessening of competition beyond a reasonable doubt—the standard that criminal proceedings require.

Since 1986, mergers, abuses of dominance, refusals to deal, exclusive dealing, tied selling, and several other practices no longer constitute criminal offenses. They are now characterized as "reviewable practices," which may be subjected to an order of the Competition Tribunal, a quasi-judicial body of both judicial and lay members. The tribunal has the power to order that such conduct cease, and in some cases the tribunal also may order divestitures of assets or shares, or other actions to overcome the anticompetitive effects of the particular practice. Failure to comply with an order of the tribunal is a criminal offense punishable by fine or imprisonment and may constitute contempt of court. Conspiracy, bid rigging, price discrimination, predatory pricing, price maintenance, misleading advertising, and several other practices remain criminal offenses under the Competition Act. These offenses are tried by criminal courts and not the tribunal.

---

6. *R. v. Armco Canada Ltd.* (1976), 24 C.P.R (2d) 145 (Ont. C.A.).

Canadian law does not allow individuals to sue for damages suffered as a result of the breach of any of the reviewable practices in the Competition Act, including mergers and abuse of dominance. Only since 1976 has the act provided a right to recover (single) damages and certain costs in respect to a breach of its criminal provisions or of an order of the tribunal. While there have been relatively few such private actions to date, they may become more commonplace in light of the Supreme Court's decision in 1989 confirming the constitutional validity of the act's private-action provisions. However, significant restrictions on contingency fees and class-action suits in Canada, as well as the Canadian rule that the loser generally pays for a significant portion of the winner's costs in a legal action, will likely ensure that private actions in Canada will continue to be much less significant as an enforcement mechanism than they are in the United States.

Similarly, unlike state governments in the United States, provincial governments in Canada have had a very limited role in competition law enforcement to date. While many provinces have passed business practices legislation, such legislation is, for the most part, focused on consumer protection. Some of these provincial laws create private rights of action to recover damages; however, these have also seen limited use to date.

Scope of the Competition Act

The Competition Act applies to all sectors of the Canadian economy, including service, resource, and manufacturing industries. It does not regulate subsidies or state aids to industry at either the provincial or federal level. The act is also binding on Crown corporations in respect to their commercial activities. Certain activities authorized by government legislation may be within the scope of a "regulated conduct" defense; that is, conduct that follows a statutory direction or authorization is exercised in the public interest and, therefore, is generally held to be outside the scope of the act (Goldman 1986, 1989). This defense covers a significant degree of economic activity in Canada, such as price setting and quota allocation by agricultural marketing boards.

In addition, the act exempts collective bargaining, certain activities by associations of fishermen, securities underwriting, and amateur sports leagues.

Underlying Philosophy

Arguably, there is no one philosophy that applies consistently throughout the Competition Act. While the act generally seeks to address market failures and focuses on the acquisition and exploitation of market power, market power is not a necessary element of the provisions governing price discrimination, price maintenance, and several other areas.

The Competition Act itself contains a "purpose clause," which sets out a number of related but sometimes conflicting goals. On the one hand, the Act is intended to promote the efficiency and adaptability of the Canadian economy and expand opportunities for Canadian participation in world markets. On the other, it is intended to ensure that small and medium-sized enterprises have an equitable opportunity to participate in the Canadian economy and to provide consumers with competitive prices and product choices. As will be seen below, decisions of both the tribunal and Canadian courts have displayed a tension in balancing these goals.

Canadian competition law operates on the principle of national treatment, regardless of the nationality of the owners of a firm. While, for example, the possibility of job losses or the acquisition of a Canadian-controlled business by a foreign entity pursuant to a merger of two competitors may be relevant for the purposes of a review under the Investment Canada Act, discussed below, it is not normally relevant in a Competition Act merger analysis.

Administration

The director of investigation and research, who is appointed by the federal cabinet to head the Competition Bureau, administers the Competition Act. The director is an independent law enforcement officer, so ministers in the federal cabinet cannot direct him to make any particular decision or recommendation, although the minister of industry can require the director to inquire into a particular matter.

The director and the bureau investigate and enforce both criminal offenses and reviewable conduct under the Competition Act. But with a staff of only about 240, the bureau has limited resources at its disposal. The director has attempted to use these resources most efficiently by focusing the bureau's resources on conspiracy, bid rigging, mergers, and abuses of dominance (Wetston 1992a, 9); seeking significantly higher fines (most recently a court imposed a C$2.5 million fine for a market allocation conspiracy [Director of Investigation and Research, news release, 27 September 1995]); recommending to the attorney general that more charges be brought against individual directors and officers where appropriate (*Financial Post*, 21 October 1991, and Chandler 1994a); and, in conjunction with the attorney general, instituting a "whistle blowing" policy.[7]

---

7. See Consumer and Corporate Affairs Canada, news release, "Abbott Laboratories Granted Immunity under the Competition Act and Provides $2.122 million restitution," NR-1-898-32. See also Goldman and Crampton (1993), Wetston (1991), and Chandler (1994).

Program of Compliance

Particularly outside the context of conspiracy or bid rigging, directors since 1986 have adopted a proactive approach to Competition Act compliance, generally favoring consultation and cooperation in investigating and resolving issues.[8] For instance, the director will provide advisory opinions on whether proposed conduct would provide grounds for an inquiry.[9] Unlike those under the US business review program, such opinions are not made public.

With respect to mergers, the director may be receptive to reasonable proposals to negotiate a solution (such as a partial divestiture) to concerns about possible anticompetitive effects. Alternatively, the parties and the director can apply to the tribunal for a consent order. The director increasingly prefers this approach, particularly when the merger has significant national implications or when the terms of resolution require a higher degree of enforceability than a negotiated settlement—known in legal parlance as an "undertaking"—or if the resolution involves undertakings once the merger is completed (Goldman and Bodrug, 1997a).

The tribunal was intended to provide both expertise and an expeditious means of addressing mergers that the director had concluded were likely to lessen or prevent competition substantially. However, experience to date has demonstrated that parties appearing before the tribunal in a contested merger proceeding may face a lengthy hearing, in addition to extensive prehearing discovery proceedings comparable to those in any other contested commercial litigation. Delay and cost are at issue, as well as the public disclosure of information relating to the businesses involved. In the *Southam* case, a contested matter, two years passed between the filing of the director's notice of application and the tribunal's final order. The hearings themselves took 40 days, during which 50 witnesses were called. It was not until six years later that a final decision was handed down by the Supreme Court of Canada (*Director of Investigation and Research v. Southam Inc. et. al.* [1997], 71 C.P.R. [3d] 417). Some consent-order proceedings have similarly been significantly delayed, in large measure because the tribunal has let intervenors participate in consent-order proceedings to a much greater extent than US courts have under the Tunney Act in the United States. As a result, only 13 merger cases have gone to the tribunal on either a consent or contested basis since

---

8. Goldman's successor as director, Howard I. Wetston (who is now a federal court judge), served in that post until June 1993. Weston's successor, George Addy, was the senior deputy director of investigation and research during Wetston's tenure and counsel to the director for the latter part of Goldman's tenure.

9. Supply and Services Canada, Director of Investigation and Research, Program of Compliance, Information Bulletin No. 3, 1993.

1986.[10] Many private parties have sought resolutions based on undertakings, and others have apparently abandoned mergers rather than have them come before the tribunal.

In 1995, the director stated that he preferred the use of consent orders because they allowed for greater openness to the public (Addy 1995). However, the director has, for a number of years, been prepared to accept undertakings from parties as an efficient and pragmatic means of resolving certain types of concerns under the Act. Recent decisions of the Tribunal and the Federal Court have confirmed the appropriateness of the director's use of undertakings to resolve issues arising under the Act (Goldman and Bodrug 1997c).

Consent prohibition orders, which do not necessarily involve a guilty plea, may be issued by a court with regard to conduct directed toward criminal offenses. However, the director is more likely to resort to criminal charges with regard to price-fixing or bid-rigging allegations.

The compliance approach gives businesses more assurance that proposed transactions or practices will not run afoul of the law. Nonetheless, some have criticized the lack of transparency of the bureau's review process. They argue that the public and interested parties often do not understand how a particular case will be approached and believe they do not have sufficient input into the director's decisions (see, e.g., Davidson 1991).

Partly in response to these criticisms and based on the limited case law to date, the director has issued enforcement guidelines with regard to strategic alliances, mergers, price discrimination, predatory pricing, and misleading advertising. In May 1995, the director also issued a statement on confidentiality of information under the Competition Act. This statement addresses issues of interpretation of the provisions, the evidence the bureau reviews, and, timing. However, some commentators still question whether the guidelines accurately reflect the bureau's practice in, for example, defining markets and assessing qualitative factors.

Agreements in Restraint of Trade

Section 45 of the Competition Act prohibits conspiracies or agreements to restrain or injure competition unduly. The Supreme Court of Canada has recently defined "unduly" in terms of the ability to exercise market power. In contrast to the approach in the United States, the Supreme Court adopted neither a per se nor a full rule-of-reason standard and characterized the Canadian conspiracy provision as mandating a "partial rule of reason inquiry into the seriousness of the competitive effects of

---

10. For a detailed discussion of the Canadian experience with consent-order proceedings under the act, see Goldman (1990).

the agreement" in the sense that they require a review of the likely prevention or lessening of competition resulting from the agreement, but "considerations such as private gains by the parties to the agreement or counterbalancing efficiency gains by the public lie . . . outside of the inquiry under [section 45]" (*R. v. Nova Scotia Pharmaceutical Society* [1992], 43 C.P.R. [3d]). As such, the act may be less flexible than the US law in accommodating information exchanges, such as benchmarking, which may have significant procompetitive effects that arguably outweigh any lessening of competition. On the other hand, section 45 does not create a per se rule with respect to any particular type of agreement. Even a blatant price-fixing agreement could be permissible if the parties have little or no market power.

Under section 45, the forming of an agreement, understanding, or mutual consent between two or more parties is a prerequisite for proving an offense has been committed.[11] However, an agreement can be proved through a course of conduct or circumstantial evidence, and it is not necessary for the agreement to have been carried into effect.

The "foreign-directed conspiracy" provision of the act (section 46) prohibits a corporation that carries on business in Canada from implementing a foreign agreement or arrangement that, if entered into in Canada, would violate section 45. Whether the officers of the Canadian subsidiary knew of the agreement or arrangement is irrelevant, and two convictions have been registered under this provision to date. Finally, it may be noted that separate provisions make bid rigging, certain forms of price maintenance, and certain agreements or arrangements among federal financial institutions per se offenses (sections 47, 49, and 61).

As noted above, fines or price-fixing offenses in Canada were relatively low until the maximum penalty for a section 45 offense was increased to $10 million in 1986. In this respect, a $2.5 million fine has recently been assessed for market allocation conspiracy.

The director has, in two cases, recommended that the attorney general seek imprisonment for serious antitrust offenses. In 1996, a Quebec judge imposed the first prison term in Canada for a price-fixing offense under the Act. The defendant was sentenced to imprisonment for a period of one year (*R. v. Perrault*, Quebec Superior Court, File #450-27-005489-983, 15 June 1996, unreported). The director has also asked the attorney general to explore possible legal mechanisms to prevent corporations from paying fines on behalf of individuals convicted of an offense under the act (Chandler 1994b). On the director's recommendation, the attorney

---

11. While the Competition Act does not have an equivalent to the prohibition of "unfair methods of competition" similar to that under section 5 of the US Federal Trade Commission Act, it is possible that an attempt to reach an agreement in contravention of section 45 could be an offense under section 24 of the Criminal Code and, in this sense, may capture some conduct that constitutes an incipient violation of section 45.

general applied to US authorities for extradition of an individual in relation to a misleading advertising offense (the individual subsequently submitted to Canadian jurisdiction voluntarily), and the director will likely continue to recommend such proceedings when necessary (Larabie-LeSieur 1994).

Exemptions to the Conspiracy Provisions

Conspiracies or agreements relating only to exported products are exempt from section 45 as long as such agreements are not likely to reduce or limit the real value of the exports, restrict any person from exporting, or unduly lessen competition in export-related services. No registration as an exporter is required to qualify for this exemption.

The act also exempts agreements solely related to cooperation in research and development, exchange of statistics, definition of product standards, advertising restrictions, and measures to protect the environment. However, to qualify for the exemption, any such agreement must not be likely to lessen competition unduly in respect to prices, production, markets, customers, or channels of distribution and must not be likely to restrict anyone from entering into or expanding a business. In light of these limitations, it is unclear whether and to what extent this exemption either permits agreements that would otherwise be prohibited or provides any practical degree of comfort to businesses seeking such agreements.

Abuse of Dominant Position

Abuse of dominance is a noncriminal practice subject to the tribunal's review. The tribunal may issue an order under section 79 of the Competition Act if it finds that one or more persons substantially or completely control a type of business in any part of Canada and engage in anticompetitive acts that prevent or lessen competition substantially. Then the tribunal may prohibit anticompetitive acts or order other actions that it considers necessary and reasonable to overcome the effects of the practice. For example, it might require that assets or shares be divested or that terms of a contract not be enforced.

The act contains a nonexhaustive definition of "anticompetitive acts" that includes a number of vertical restraints designed to prevent entry or eliminate a competitor from a market (section 78).

A supplier may be considered to "control a business" if it has the market power to set prices above competitive levels for a considerable period. In determining whether a supplier has market power, the tribunal will look to indicators such as market share and entry barriers. The tribunal also has indicated that if a firm has a very large market share, it will very likely have market power, but considerations such as the number of competitors and their respective market shares, excess capacity in the market, and ease of entry will also be taken into account.[12] In the six tribunal decisions to date under section 79, market shares exceeded 85 percent, and the tribunal did not adopt any minimum market-share threshold below which a firm would not be considered to possess market power.[13] However, a firm enjoying a large share of a market in Canada relative to its competitors may be subjected to greater restrictions in its pricing and marketing practices than its smaller competitors.

In addition, since section 79 applies where one or more people substantially or completely control a type of business, the abuse of dominance provisions could be applied in the context of a business that is subject to "joint dominance." In 1996, the tribunal issued a consent order under the abuse of dominance provisions in section 79 of the Act in respect to the Interac shared electronic banking network. That proceeding involved allegations by the director that, through the Interac association, the six largest Canadian chartered banks and a number of other deposit-taking financial institutions jointly dominated the shared electrical financial services business in Canada and had engaged in a series of anticompetitive acts, including implementing exclusionary rules and fees that prevented other competitors from participating directly in the network (Goldman and Bodrug 1997c). Section 79 does not appear to require proof of any agreement between the dominating firms, only that they are each engaging in a practice having anticompetitive effects. In the Tele-direct case, the tribunal appeared to give business justifications greater weight than it had in previous abuse of dominance cases. In addition to considering business justifications in the context of assessing whether certain conduct constituted an anticompetitive act, the tribunal also suggested that, in assessing whether the conduct gives rise to a substantial lessening of competition, the anticompetitive effects should be weighed against the business justification or efficiency-enhancing effects of the conduct (*Director of Investigation and Research v. Tele-Direct [Publications] Inc. et. al.* (26 February 1997) [Comp. Trib.] [No. CT 94/03, unreported].

---

12. *Director of Investigation and Research v. Laidlaw Waste Systems Ltd.* (1992), 40 C.P.R. (3d) 289 (Comp. Trib.), 325.

13. *Director of Investigation and Research v. Laidlaw Waste Systems Ltd.* (1992), 40 C.P.R. (3d) 289 (Comp. Trib.), 325; *Director of Investigation and Research v. NutraSweet Co.* (1990), 32 C.P.R. (3d) 1 (Comp. Trib.); *Director of Investigation and Research v. AGT Directory Limited et. al.* (18 November 1994) (Comp. Trib.) (no CT 9402/19 unreported); *Director of Investigation and Research v. Bank of Montreal et. al.* (1996), 68 C.P.R. (3d) 527 (Comp. Trib.); *Director of Investigation and Research v. D&B Companies of Canada Ltd.* (1995), 64 C.P.R. (3d) 216 (Comp. Trib.); and *Director of Investigation and Research v. Tele-Direct (Publications) Inc., et. al.* (26 February 1997) (Comp. Trib.) (No. CT 94/03 unreported).

Deregulation of industries such as telecommunications will likely raise issues under the civil provisions of the Competition Act, such as abuse of dominance (Addy 1994b). The conduct of these industries may also raise criminal law issues. With regard to such industries, the director has commented:

> [i]n rapidly changing industries such as telecommunications, it may be less important to focus on the potential effects of a particular transaction on existing levels of competition. Instead, it could perhaps be more helpful to look forward, and consider if the transaction would likely "prevent" future competition that might otherwise come about as the result of technological expansion. (Addy 1994b)

Similarly, the director, in commenting on his enforcement objectives with respect to the "electronic marketplace," has described a need to deal with "essential facilities" and stated:

> Where any firm—telephone, cable or whatever—controls network facilities essential to competitive entry, obligations must be created for these firms to provide open access to these facilities on a non-discriminatory basis. These obligations should involve the development of common standards, open network architecture, co-location and unbundling or required services. Control of network facilities and proprietary standards should not be used to disadvantage rivals to the detriment of competition. (Addy 1994c)

The director has argued that telecommunications regulators should forbear from regulation where a service is subject to sufficient competition and has promised to intervene in such matters where appropriate (Addy 1994c).

Mergers

The Competition Act defines a merger broadly to include acquisitions of control over, or a "significant interest" in, all or part of a business. The act's merger provisions may apply not only to share and asset acquisitions but also to contracts that give a person the ability to materially influence another business. Asset transactions within the scope of the act include purchases or leases of a brand name or intellectual property rights (Director of Investigation and Research 1991). If a merger is likely to prevent or lessen competition substantially, the director may apply to the tribunal for an order to dissolve or enjoin a merger at any time within three years of the substantial completion of the merger.

Certain large mergers may be subject to prenotification and waiting-period requirements under part IX of the act. Part IX is similar to the US Hart-Scott-Rodino Antitrust Improvements Act. Regardless of size, all mergers are subject to the act's substantive provisions.[14]

---

14. For a discussion of premerger notification, see Goldman and Bodrug (1993, § 10.09).

In defining relevant product and geographic markets, the merger guidelines adopt a "hypothetical monopolist" approach broadly similar to that described in the 1992 US horizontal merger guidelines. The Canadian guidelines do not use the Herfindahl-Hirschman index, a measure of industry concentration, and the Competition Act specifically provides that the tribunal may not rely solely on market shares (section 92). However, the guidelines state that challenges related to a merger's effect on unilateral market power are unlikely if the postmerger market share will be less than 35 percent. Similarly, challenges with respect to interdependent market power are unlikely where the four largest firms would have less than 65 percent of the market or where the merged entity would have less than a 10 percent share (see section 4.2.1. of the guidelines).

These are not fixed rules. A merger below these thresholds could be challenged, and many mergers with market shares above these thresholds are not challenged. In its first contested merger case, the tribunal declined to dissolve a merger that resulted in a 60 percent market share in the rendering business in Southern Ontario.[15] Both the director and the tribunal will tolerate market share thresholds that are clearly much higher than levels that would likely be challenged in the United States.

Another distinguishing feature of Canadian merger enforcement compared with that in the United States is a focus on the ability to exercise unilateral market power rather than an assessment of the likelihood of interdependent conduct.[16] The Canadian deemphasis of market share and the risk of interdependent conduct reflects a recognition that the relatively concentrated markets in Canada may coincide with the need for Canadian firms to achieve internationally competitive economies of scale.

The Competition Act lists factors the tribunal may take into account in assessing a merger: the impact of foreign competitors, the level of barriers to entry (including tariffs and regulatory control over entry), the degree of effective competition remaining, the likelihood of the merger resulting in the removal of a vigorous and effective competitor, and the nature and extent of change and innovation in a relevant market. Of these factors, foreign competition and the level of barriers to entry appear to have the greatest influence on the director's decision on whether to challenge a merger (Khemani and Shapiro 1993).

In general, the director has not applied an incipiency standard to seek

---

15. *Director of Investigation and Research v. Hillsdown Holdings* (Can.) Ltd. (1992), 41 C.P.R. (3d) 289.

16. See merger guidelines, section 2.2. However, the tribunal has identified "enhanced ability for tacit collusion" as one of the issues that should be the focus of attention in any merger case (*Director of Investigation and Research v. Imperial Oil Ltd.*, 26 January 1990, CT./ 89-3, #390, Comp. Trib. at 54 reported in Goldman and Bodrug 1997c at appendix E3.

any remedies where the bureau has identified only speculative concerns about the possible exercise of market power by the merged entity. In some cases, however, the director has advised parties to a merger that the bureau intends to monitor the merged entity and the relevant industry under both the merger and abuse of dominance provisions of the Competition Act. The director has also indicated that he will consider whether mergers in the telecommunications and other technology-intensive industries are likely to prevent competition by making the development of new products or innovations less likely (Addy 1994c).

The act expressly recognizes the "failing firm" factor, and the merger guidelines suggest that if one of the parties to a merger is likely to either fail or exit the market if the proposed merger does not proceed, then a lessening of competition would occur in any event and cannot be attributed to the merger (sections 4.1 and 4.4.1. of the guidelines). By extending the failing-firm defense to exiting firms, the Canadian guidelines may provide a somewhat broader failing-firm defense than the US guidelines. However, it may be difficult for a firm that is not failing to show that there are no competitively preferable purchasers willing to pay more than the net liquidation value of the firm (which is one of the conditions in the guidelines). It may also be difficult to show that the firm will likely leave the market if the merger is stopped.

The Efficiency Exception

In the context of mergers, the Competition Act appears to give greater weight to efficiencies than in the United States, although the tribunal has cast doubts on whether this will be the case in practice. Under section 96, the tribunal may not make an order under the merger provisions if it finds that (1) the gains in efficiency likely to be brought about by the merger will be greater than, and will offset, the effects of any prevention or lessening of competition that is likely to result from the merger, (2) the claimed efficiency gains would not likely be attained if the order were made, and (3) the alleged efficiency gains would not be brought about by reason only of a redistribution of income. In addition, the act directs the tribunal to consider whether such efficiency gains will significantly increase the real value of exports or cause domestic products to be substituted for imported products. But there is no consensus on how these two factors are to be taken into account (Goldman and Bodrug 1993, § 10.05). A full panel of the tribunal has yet to rule on this issue.

In *Hillsdown*, both the director and the acquiror took the position that section 96 directs the tribunal to balance the likely gains in efficiency against the misallocation of resources or loss to society as a whole resulting from the increased prices—that is, the "deadweight" loss—that the merged firm is able to impose as a result of the merger. In the director's view, there is no need to establish that the efficiency gains will be passed on to the consumer. The tribunal suggested, however, that section 96 could be read to permit it to take into account a much broader range of effects, including wealth transfers (*Director of Investigation and Research v. Hillsdown Holdings*, 343).

The tribunal also reviewed "the various purposes served by competition law in relation to efficiency gains" and commented:

> . . . one traditional purpose has been to protect the consumer from being charged supra-competitive prices. While one can argue that this is insignificant from the point of view of loss to the economy as a whole, . . . there is a powerful political argument for preventing such accretions of wealth at the consumer's expense. Another purpose which has traditionally been seen as served by competition law is to encourage the dispersal of power and the distribution of wealth. . . . A third objective of competition law is seen as that of protecting the small firm against more powerful rivals. . . . These objectives can run counter to the fourth objective which is that of furthering the efficiency of the economy as a whole. (*Director of Investigation and Research v. Hillsdown Holdings*, 338–39)

Against this background, the tribunal questioned whether it was appropriate to give precedence to the efficiency objective in the purpose clause over the provision of "competitive prices" and "equitable opportunities for small and medium sized enterprises" (*Director of Investigation and Research v. Hillsdown Holdings*, 343).

Finally, the tribunal questioned whether wealth transfers are always neutral and posed the following two examples: a merger of two drug companies where the relevant product is a life-saving drug, and a merger resulting in a dominant firm that charges supracompetitive prices resulting in wealth transfer out of Canada. These examples suggest that the tribunal may be willing to consider a very broad range of possible negative effects of a merger that must be demonstrated to be offset by efficiency gains in order for section 96 to apply.

Furthermore, Fisher and Lande (1983) have suggested that the combined effect of the deadweight loss and the neutral wealth transfer resulting from a price increase typically far exceeds any efficiencies that may be brought about by a merger. Thus, the approach of the tribunal in the *Hillsdown* case could leave the efficiency exception as a largely academic possibility.[17] Nevertheless, the director continues to apply the approach set forth in the merger guidelines (Wetston 1992a; Sanderson 1997; Ross 1997) and has identified the efficiency exception in the Canadian legislation as one of the factors that led to different decisions by the Canadian Bureau and the European Commission in the *de Havilland* case. The director decided not to challenge the proposed acquisition of de Havilland by Aérospatiale/Alenia on the basis that it was not likely to

---

17. For an alternate perspective on the analysis of efficiencies of merger cases in Canada, see Warner (1994).

lessen competition substantially in Canada, while the European Commission blocked the transaction on the basis that it would create a dominant position in the world market for commuter aircraft (Addy 1991). It should be noted, however, that the efficiency exception has rarely been applied by the director (Warner 1994a and 1997).

Vertical Restraints

Vertical restraints are generally covered under Competition Act provisions dealing with abuse of dominance, exclusive dealing, tied selling, and market restriction. Usually, the tribunal must show that the practice substantially lessens competition in Canada. An exception is the refusal-to-deal provisions that may be invoked when the refusal substantially affects a person in his or her business (in addition to meeting a number of other criteria).

In addition, the price maintenance provisions—one of the more frequently enforced criminal offenses under the act—prohibit refusals to supply or other forms of discrimination against individuals because of their low pricing policies. Certain attempts to influence prices upward (or discourage their reduction) are also illegal. A separate provision also bans certain attempts to induce a supplier, whether within or outside Canada, to refuse to supply individuals with a product because of their low pricing (Goldman and Bodrug 1997b).

International or Extraterritorial Aspects

Some sections of the Competition Act apply only to conduct in Canada; others are not expressly qualified in that regard. The market-power tests are inherently concerned with effects on a national or subnational market and not on the physical location of the businesses. Effective enforcement may, for example, require national officials to assert jurisdiction in a merger review, even when the merger takes place outside its borders, if they believe the country will suffer anticompetitive effects. As many Canadian and US markets continue to integrate, the bureau will be dealing with an increasing number of investigations that raise issues on both sides of the border.

Under the Canada-US treaty on mutual legal assistance in criminal matters (MLAT), in effect since 1990,[18] either the Canadian or US government can request certain assistance of the other. This assistance can include exchanging information, locating or identifying persons, serving documents and taking evidence, or executing searches and seizures.

---

18. Mutual Legal Assistance in Criminal Matters Act, R.S. 1985, c. 30 (4th supp.) and SOR/90-704.

Furthermore, it must be given even if the conduct under investigation in the requesting state does not constitute an offense in the other (Article II, section 3). MLAT provisions have been used in price-fixing conspiracies in the plastic cutlery and thermal fax paper industries.[19] The MLAT does not apply to mergers, abuses of dominance, and other noncriminal matters under the Competition Act.

In addition, on 3 August 1995 the governments of Canada and the United States entered into an agreement regarding the application of their competition and deceptive marketing practices laws (the "1995 Agreement"). This agreement superseded the 1984 memorandum of understanding as to notification, consultation, and cooperation with respect to the application of national antitrust laws between Canada and the United States (the "MOU"). The 1995 Agreement operates in addition to, and not in lieu of, the MLAT. While the 1995 Agreement does not have the force of law, it does provide a framework for intergovernmental notification of antitrust investigations (including noncriminal matters) involving the national interest of the other party or requiring searches for information located in the territory of the other. The MOU is intended to avoid or moderate conflicts of different interests and policies between the two countries. However, it also serves as a useful source of information for the bureau about potentially anticompetitive conduct that may affect Canada. From 1986 through 31 March 1994, the bureau delivered 68 notifications to US antitrust authorities and received 165.[20]

Such information exchanges raise significant confidentiality issues. In Canada, section 29 of the Competition Act prohibits the director and the bureau from divulging, except to Canadian law-enforcement agencies, the identities of those who provide them information. There are exceptions: the director may communicate information to further the administration and enforcement of the act (Goldman and Kissack 1997).

In addition, section 29 may not extend to information voluntarily supplied to the bureau, although the director has indicated it will usually be treated as if it were covered. The director has also indicated that he may disclose confidential information if he is satisfied with the assurances the foreign antitrust agency provides regarding use of the information, and if doing so would advance a matter under investigation in Canada.[21] It is not clear, however, whether a court would agree with this policy. In addition, the director has not guaranteed he will notify

---

19. See 66 Antitrust & Trade Reg. Report 661 (1994); 67 Antitrust & Trade Reg. Report 108 (1994); Goldman and Kissack (1997).

20. See the annual reports of the director of investigation and research, *Competition Act*, for the years ended 31 March 1987-31 March 1993, inclusive (Supply and Services Canada).

21. See the statement on "Communication of Confidential Information under the Competition Act," Bureau of Competition Policy, Industry Canada, May 1995.

those who have supplied confidential information of his intention to share their information.

The MLAT permits but does not require confidentiality restrictions. Thus, individuals who have provided information cannot be certain who has it or what use is made of it. The information the director gets from a foreign antitrust authority is not subject to section 29. However, as noted above, the director has indicated that such information will be protected. Neither current US law or practice nor the International Antitrust Enforcement Act of 1994 appears to require US authorities to provide notice to those who have supplied information before that information is passed on to Canadian authorities.

Canadian Experience with Extraterritoriality

Historically, the Canadian government has asserted that claims of jurisdiction based solely on effects in the country making the claim run counter to international law. This position is understandable, given Canada's past experience with the extraterritorial reach of US antitrust authorities. In the *Alcoa* case, the US Supreme Court held a Canadian company to be in violation of the Sherman Act for agreeing with European producers to allocate world markets and not to supply the American market (*US v. Aluminum Company of America*, 334 US 100, 1947). In another case, the US Supreme Court rejected an act-of-state defense by a purchasing agent of the Canadian government that had prevented the plaintiff from shipping vanadium to Canada (*Continental Ore Co. v. Union Carbide*, 370 US 690, 1962).

In the *Radio Patents* case, three US corporations doing business in Canada through subsidiaries combined to incorporate a Canadian corporation and transferred all their Canadian patents to that company, which in turn required sublicensees to manufacture products in Canada and to refrain from importing products manufactured in the United States (*United States v. General Electric Company, et al.*, 82 F. Supp. 753, D.C.N.J. 1949). It was alleged that these agreements restrained US commerce contrary to the Sherman Act. In the final consent decree, each of the US parent companies agreed that neither they nor their Canadian subsidiaries would exercise their patents or patent licenses to restrict any manufacturer in the United States from exporting products to Canada (1962 Trade Cases §§ 70,342; 70,428; 70,546).

Before 1970, there had been at least 30 US antitrust cases with some effect on Canadian structure and behavior (Henry 1970). One commentator (Kilgour 1963, 101-02) wrote that "a good case can be made for saying that the Sherman Act has had more effect on the Canadian economy than [Canadian competition legislation] has had." At the same time, Henry (1970, 279-81) has suggested that in many of these cases

Canada may have benefited from the extraterritorial application of the US antitrust laws because such action may have blocked an acquisition and ensured the continued independence of a Canadian company, lowered prices in Canada, increased export opportunities, or removed barriers to entry for new firms. One commentator has noted that Canadians "don't so much complain about the injury as the insult" and "there is understandable resentment that Canadians may wake up some day and find that a court somewhere in [the United States] has made a decision which has a large effect on the industrial structure of Canada" (Blair 1979).

Canadian sensitivity has been greatest when attempts to enforce US antitrust law have directly affected Canadian policy. The *Radio Patents* case is arguably an example of a conflict between US antitrust laws and the policy of the Canadian Patent Act to encourage the manufacture of patented articles in Canada (Henry 1970, 280). In commenting on that case, the Canadian minister of justice said that a US decree requiring directors of Canadian companies "to take certain actions with respect to the operations of those companies in Canada, which actions would not be dictated by the requirements of Canadian law, or be in accord with Canadian business or commercial policy, but would be dictated by requirements of United States law and be in accord with United States policy . . . could only be regarded as an infringement of Canadian sovereignty."[22]

In antitrust litigation concerning an alleged international uranium cartel involving uranium producers, a US District Court sought documents from Canadian private corporations through an order known as "letters rogatory." Subsequently, the Canadian government enacted regulations[23] prohibiting release of documentation related to any aspect of uranium production, and the Supreme Court of Canada refused to enforce the letters rogatory on several grounds, including public policy (*Gulf Oil Corporation v. Gulf Canada Limited et al.*, 1980, 2 S.C.R. 39). As a result, some defendants in US civil actions could not obtain evidence to support their defense without violating Canadian law and thus subjecting their officers and directors to fines and prison terms.

Similarly, provincial governments in Ontario and Quebec, during proceedings against Canadian International Paper Company in 1947, passed sweeping legislation that generally prohibited anyone from complying with an order or subpoena of a legislative or judicial authority in any jurisdiction outside the province for removal of business records from

---

22. See the House of Commons debates ([Hansard] 1959, vol. 1, 618). This case led to discussions between the minister of justice and the US attorney general and resulted in an understanding known as the antitrust notification and consultation procedure, a predecessor to the MOU and the 1995 Agreement.

23. SOR/76-644 (P.C. 1976-2368, 21 September 1976).

within either province. In that case, the subpoenas were ultimately withdrawn after negotiations between the Canadian Department of External Affairs and the US State Department. The provincial blocking legislation remains in force and has occasionally been applied (Warner 1994b).

More recently, the *Institut Mérieux* case rekindled concerns about the extraterritorial application of US antitrust laws. That case involved a proposed merger of two pharmaceutical companies completed outside the United States. Neither party to the merger had significant relevant assets in the United States. The US Federal Trade Commission (FTC) issued an order requiring Institut Mérieux to lease part of the acquired business in Toronto, Ontario, to an FTC-approved buyer for a period of 25 years.[24] The FTC exercise of jurisdiction was apparently in conflict with the US Department of Justice's 1988 international guidelines (Owen and Parisi 1991) and was done apparently without at least initial compliance with the notification requirements of the MOU (Rosenthal 1991).

Extraterritorial Assertions of Jurisdiction by Canada

The relatively few policy statements in recent years on extraterritorial application of Canadian antitrust laws reflect the increasing tension between the official position of the Canadian government and antitrust authorities' growing recognition that effective enforcement of competition laws may require at least some extraterritorial reach.[25] However, the bureau has been willing to proceed against conduct that takes place outside Canada. For example, it has reviewed proposed mergers to be effected through share acquisitions where shares are held and traded outside Canada and in which Canadian markets are affected only through a Canadian subsidiary.[26] In one case, the tribunal found that conduct relating to the use of a US patent amounted to an abuse of dominance (*Director of Investigation and Research v. NutraSweet Co.* 1990, 32 C.P.R. 1 [Comp. Trib.]). In addition, Mitsubishi Corporation, a Japanese company, pleaded guilty to and was fined C$500,000 for a price-fixing charge while its Canadian subsidiary pleaded guilty under section 46 and was fined C$250,000 for its role in implementing the conspiracy in Canada. Both companies also entered guilty pleas and were assessed fines totaling C$200,000 for refusing to supply a company because of its low pricing policy in Canada (Bureau of Competition Policy, news re-

---

24. *Institut Mérieux*, 1990 Trade Cases (CCH) ¶22,779 and 66 Antitrust & Trade Reg. Report 509 (1994).

25. For example, compare Hunter (1983) to Addy (1991). See also Goldman (1988).

26. See, for example, the discussion of the Schneider/Square D merger in Goldman, Cornish, and Corley (1992).

lease, 5 August 1994). A US subsidiary of another Japanese company was also fined $950,000 for the same alleged activity (Director of Investigation and Research, news release, 12 July 1994). Finally, Mitsubishi Paper Mills, Ltd. pleaded guilty to and was fined C$850,000 for one count of fixing prices and one count of refusing to supply under the conspiracy and price maintenance provisions of the Act (Competition Bureau, news release, 17 February 1997).

The application of the criminal provisions of the Competition Act in an extraterritorial context is, however, complicated by the Criminal Code, which says that no one shall be convicted of an offense committed outside Canada.[27] Canadian courts have recently expanded their view of what constitutes an offense considered to have been committed in Canada. For example, acts involved in carrying out a conspiracy may be sufficient to invoke criminal conspiracy laws, even if the acts committed in Canada do not constitute a necessary element of the offense.[28] Nevertheless, it remains to be seen how Canadian courts will apply this territorial limitation in the Criminal Code in proceedings based only on anticompetitive effects in Canada resulting from conduct taking place entirely outside its borders.

Effect of Investment and Trade Policies on Competition

Regulation of Foreign Investment

The principal legislation restricting the ability of a non-Canadian to acquire a Canadian business is the Investment Canada Act (ICA). This is currently the only such legislation of general application. Foreign ownership in specific industries, such as airlines, banks, and other financial institutions and broadcasting systems, is regulated by other legislation in a manner similar to foreign ownership restrictions in many other countries, including the United States.

The Investment Canada Act

In general, "non-Canadian" investors who want to establish or acquire control of a business carried on in Canada may only have to notify

---

27. Criminal Code, R.S.C. 1985, c. C-46, s. 6(2), but see also section 465(4), which provides that anyone who, while in a place outside Canada, conspires with anyone to commit certain indictable offenses in Canada shall be deemed to have conspired in Canada to commit the offense.

28. *R. v. Libman* (1985), 2 S.C.R. 178 and *R. v. Rowbotham and Roblin* (1992), 60 O.A.C. 75, affirmed (1993) 4 S.C.R. 834.

authorities under the ICA; in some circumstances—such as a high value of the assets involved—investments are subject to review. Establishments of new Canadian businesses normally require only notification—that is, the filing of very basic corporate information. The ICA applies whether or not the acquired business is currently controlled by Canadians and also applies where a Canadian business is acquired indirectly by a foreign corporation with a Canadian subsidiary. Whether a company is "Canadian" depends on the citizenship or residency of its ultimate controlling shareholders or, in some cases, the members of its board of directors. If the minister of industry considers an acquisition subject to review under the ICA not likely to be of "net benefit to Canada," the acquiror may be required to divest, or be prohibited from acquiring, the business.

The general rule is that acquisitions of Canadian businesses having assets of C$5 million or more, or certain "indirect" acquisitions of Canadian businesses having assets of C$50 million are subject to review. However, acquisitions of some types of "cultural businesses" may be subject to review regardless of the value of the assets involved. Even the establishment of a new "cultural business" can be subjected to a review and, potentially, an order to divest.

For these purposes, a "cultural business" includes the production, sale, or exhibition of books, compact discs, videos, movies, and similar products. The actual scope of this definition is much wider than might first appear because there is no *de minimis* exception to the determination of whether a business carries on any cultural activity. Thus, a convenience store that sells newspapers is likely to be considered a cultural business.

Special Rules for "WTO Investors"

As a result of amendments enacted following agreement on WTO, the ICA contains two sets of review thresholds: the general thresholds (described above), and the higher WTO thresholds, applicable only to acquisitions by or from a "WTO investor."[29] Direct acquisitions of most Canadian businesses by or from a WTO investor implemented in 1997 are subject to review if the assets of the business exceed C$172 million. Indirect acquisitions of most Canadian businesses by or from a WTO investor are not subject to review but must still be notified.

However, acquisitions of Canadian businesses engaged in uranium mining, certain cultural activities, certain financial services, and transportation services are excluded from the WTO review thresholds and continue to be subject to the lower general review thresholds. Again,

---

29. The definition of a "WTO investor" under the ICA is complex but is generally similar to the definition of a "Canadian," discussed above, insofar as it relates to citizenship in a country (other than Canada) that is a member of the WTO.

there is no *de minimis* exception to the determination of whether a business carries on any such activities. Accordingly, a corporation primarily engaged in some other type of business that also, for example, provides some trucking services is excluded from the higher WTO thres-holds even if such services represent a very small part of the corporation's activities.

The Review Criterion: "Net Benefit to Canada"

As noted above, the minister must be satisfied that a proposed acquisition under review is likely to be of "net benefit to Canada." The minister must take into account certain factors: (1) the effect of the acquisition on the level and nature of economic activity in Canada (including employment); (2) the degree and significance of participation by Canadians in the business; (3) the effect of the investment on productivity, industrial efficiency, technological development, product innovation, and product variety in Canada; (4) the effect of the acquisition on competition in Canada; (5) the compatibility of the acquisition with national industrial, economic, and cultural policies; and (6) the contribution of the acquisition to Canada's ability to compete in world markets. However, the ICA does not suggest any weighting or hierarchy for these potentially conflicting factors, and it would appear that the minister's decisions are not subject to judicial review on the merits (*Baril v. Minister of Regional Industrial Expansion*, 1986, 1 F.C. 328).

In order to satisfy the "net benefit" criterion, the minister sometimes requires undertakings from the acquiror, typically related to (1) maintaining existing employees; (2) guaranteeing participation of Canadians as directors or in management; (3) processing resource products in Canada; (4) making capital expenditures or investing in research and development in Canada; (5) transferring technology to Canada; (6) protecting the environment; and (7) supporting local communities.[30] For example, in order to obtain approval of its acquisition of Woolco's retail stores in Canada, Wal-Mart Inc. provided the minister with an undertaking to identify the origin of goods on display in its stores and to "make commercially reasonable efforts to provide Canadian-based suppliers with a full and fair opportunity to supply Wal-Mart Canada" (*Toronto Star*, 3 August 1994; see also undertakings of Viacom Inc., 12 December 1994, in connection with its acquisition of Paramount).

As a practical matter, it may be noted that Investment Canada has not to date instituted any formal process to block any acquisition or

---

30. See, for example, "Investment Canada approves Li Ka-shing's acquisition of Husky Oil Limited," news release, Investment Canada, 20 December 1991; and "Investment Canada Approves Bayer's acquisition of Nova/Polysar's Rubber Division," news release, Investment Canada, 21 September 1993.

require divestiture. All issues arising to date, except with respect to cultural industries or, until 1992, oil and gas industries, appear to have been resolved by undertakings. However, it is impossible to know how many investments were halted because Investment Canada indicated that it would not approve the transaction. Investment Canada does not release information concerning its decision making to nearly the same extent as the director under the Competition Act.

Investment Canada has been more aggressive in enforcing the ICA with respect to both establishments and acquisitions of cultural businesses. In some instances, Investment Canada has requested undertakings from companies that have limited "cultural" activities relative to their business, who may, for example, sell or advertise cultural products of Canadian authors or artists. The federal government also announced in July 1993 a policy to significantly restrict the ability of a foreign-owned magazine publisher to establish new magazines in Canada.[31] Related cultural policies have been successfully challenged before the WTO.[32] "Anti-avoidance" amendments to the ICA enacted in 1993 may also signal more vigorous enforcement of the ICA with respect to cultural businesses. However, the sale of a publishing business by a Crown corporation, apparently in contravention of Investment Canada's guidelines for the publishing industry, was approved by Investment Canada (*Globe & Mail*, 19 February 1994). In 1996, a proposed joint venture between a Canadian firm and Borders Group Inc., a large US book chain, was refused permission to establish a retail book-selling business in Canada under the ICA cultural policy. The minister apparently believed the venture's proposed use of Borders' information and ordering software and the substantial management influence would give the US-based company effective control (*The Financial Post*, 9 February 1996).

The ICA has also imposed significant impediments to investment in the uranium industry and, until recently, the oil and gas industry. However, the federal government in March 1992 abandoned its oil and gas acquisitions policy (which had prohibited the sale of Canadian-controlled oil and gas assets valued in excess of $5 million unless the companies were in financial difficulty). The minister of Energy, Mines, and Resources Canada (news release, 25 March 1992) commented that "the policy imposed increased costs, uncertainty, and delays on the industry" and noted that the change was intended to "allow Canadian and foreign oil and gas companies to rationalize their operations and improve their competitiveness in global markets."

---

31. See related business guidelines, July 1993, issued by the minister of industry, science, and technology under the authority of section 38 of the ICA; see also "Magazines Offered Canadian Shield," *Globe & Mail*, 20 July 1993.

32. See also "WTO Body Orders Canada to Change Magazine Rule," *The Wall Street Journal*, 1 July 1997.

The Relationship between Competition and Trade Laws

Special Import Measures Act

In 1988 the Canadian Parliament enacted the Special Import Measures Act (SIMA) to conform the existing Canadian trade laws to the 1979 Tokyo Round GATT revised antidumping code and the subsidies and countervailing measures code. SIMA governs the imposition of both countervailing and antidumping duties. In both areas, the administrative process begins with a determination of dumping or subsidization by the deputy minister of national revenue for customs and excise (the MNR). Subsequently, a quasi-judicial, government-appointed body, the Canadian International Trade Tribunal (CITT), determines whether there has been material injury or retardation to a domestic industry.

SIMA shares many of the problems found in the trade laws in other jurisdictions, including the United States. Procedures and practices that may favor an ultimate imposition of duties include (1) detailed requests for information and short time frames for response; (2) comparison of individual export prices with a weighted average of home-country prices to determine margins of dumping or subsidization (a procedure that tends to exaggerate the magnitudes of these margins); (3) a low threshold for a causal nexus between the alleged dumping or subsidy and the material injury to the relevant domestic industry;[33] (4) a lack of consistent economic rigor in the determination of the relevant "like good" being produced in Canada; and (5) frequent determination of constructive costs on the basis of average total costs rather than, as many economists suggest should be used, some measure of incremental costs, for the purposes of measuring the margin of dumping or subsidization.

In the past, there were differences between SIMA and US trade law where SIMA appears deficient. For instance, while US law provides that margins of dumping or subsidization less than 0.5 percent are *de minimis* and are, therefore, insufficient to justify the imposition of duties, Canadian law has no similar provision. However, pursuant to the WTO Antidumping Code, Canada amended SIMA to provide for a 2 percent *de minimis* standard for the margin of dumping.[34] Furthermore, following the WTO Antidumping Code, SIMA now provides that if the volume of dumped imports from any one country is less than 3 percent of all imports, it shall normally be regarded as negligible.[35]

---

33. See *American Farm Bureau Federation v. Canadian Import Tribunal* (1990), 74 D.L.R. (4th) 449 (S.C.C.), 488-89.

34. Section 5.8, Agreement on Implementation of Article VI, 15 December 1993, GATT MTN/FA II-A1 A-8.

35. Section 5.8, Agreement on Implementation of Article VI, 15 December 1993, GATT MTN/FA II-A1 A-8.

Both Canada and the United States permit negotiated settlements, or undertakings, in order to avoid facing administrative proceedings. In the past in Canada, however, these negotiated settlements had to be reached before the MNR made a preliminary determination of dumping and had to be entered into by the importers of all or substantially all of the relevant producers. Pursuant to the WTO Antidumping Code, Canada no longer seeks or accepts price undertakings from exporters until after a preliminary determination of dumping and material injury.[36] As a practical matter, these negotiated settlements have not been used as frequently in either Canada or the United States as in other jurisdictions such as the European Union.[37]

Other aspects of SIMA, notably its "sunset" provision, recognize the adverse competitive effects of unfair trade laws. CITT findings, such as the imposition of dumping duties, expire at the end of five years unless they have either been previously removed or interested parties can show why they should not lapse.[38] In the United States and elsewhere, it has been much more difficult to remove such orders once they are granted. However, under the Uruguay Round, US has been brought into conformity with the Canadian practice.[39]

Another Canadian innovation is the inclusion of competition or consumer-welfare concerns in decisions on trade-law administration. There are three ways this can be done. First, section 31 of the Competition Act provides that, following an inquiry by the director or a decision of the tribunal or a court, the federal cabinet may order the reduction or removal of any custom duty it believes to be preventing or lessening competition.

Second, section 125 of the Competition Act provides that the director, on his own initiative or at the request of any federal regulatory agency, may advise the agency on relevant competition issues.[40] Accordingly, the director can make submissions to the MNR about the calculation of the margin of dumping or subsidization or to the CITT about material injury determinations under SIMA. Since 1984, the director has done so on four occasions (Ireland 1991, 23).[41]

In one case, domestic car producers sought to have the CITT impose

---

36. Agreement on Implementation of Article VI, 15 December 1993; GATT MTN/FA II-A1 A-8, section 8.2.

37. See *Stegemann* (1991, 219) and *Rugman and Porteous* (1989, 13-15).

38. SIMA, section 76(5).

39. Agreement on Implementation of Article VI, 15 December 1993, GATT MTN/FA II-A1 A-8, section 11.2.

40. Section 126 of the Competition Act extends this authority to provincial regulatory bodies where they consent to the director's intervention.

41. See also *In the Matter of Preformed Fibreglass Pipe Insulation with a Vapour Barrier, Originating in or Exported from the United States of America*, Inquiry No. NQ-93-002 (CITT 6 December 1993, 9).

antidumping duties on imports from South Korea.[42] The director submitted that there ought not to be a finding of material injury for several reasons: factors other than the imported cars were causing injury to the domestic industry; the imported cars helped maintain competition in the Canadian automobile market; and the relevant product market under consideration was too broad. Ultimately, the CITT found that the imports did not materially injure domestic production for domestic consumption (Ireland 1991, 23-24).

In the director's more recent intervention into the CITT's fiberglass pipe insulation inquiry, the Federal Court of Appeal upheld a CITT ruling that the director's right to intervene "does not include an automatic right of access to all confidential information in the [CITT's] possession" (*Director of Investigation and Research v. Canadian International Trade Tribunal et al.*, 17 November 1993, 3 [Fed. C.A.]). As a result, the effectiveness of such interventions in the future may be limited.

A third mechanism by which competition concerns enter into the trade policy process is through public-interest inquiries under section 45 of SIMA. Generally, SIMA provides that countervailing or antidumping duties must equal the full amount of the margin determined by the CITT (section 3). If the CITT believes that the imposition of such a duty would not or might not be in the public interest, it must formally report its reasoning to the minister of finance. The CITT's statement must be made public, and anyone (including producers and consumers) can weigh in on whether the CITT should issue a report to the minister (section 45[2]). Once the CITT issues such a report, the minister of finance decides whether to lower or to eliminate the duty. As a practical matter, this provision is rarely used.[43] At this writing there have been 13 antidumping investigations and only 3 formal inquiries under section 45, and in only 2 cases has the CITT recommended that the duty be reduced, which the minister of finance did in only one case (although not by the full amount recommended; see Porteous and Rugman 1990, esp. 263-64).

A dispute brought by the CITT over alleged dumping by three US beer producers in British Columbia raises issues on the director's role in such cases. In 1989, the director had decided not to challenge a merger between Canada's second and third largest brewers, partly because of the presence of low-priced US imports in a number of markets, including British Columbia.[44] The merged entity, however, was one of the applicants

---

42. *Statement of Reasons re Inquiry Under Section 42 of The Special Import Measures Act Respecting: Cars Produced by or on Behalf of Hyundai Motor Company* (23 March 1988), CIT-13-87 (CITT).

43. "[S]ection 45 . . . is to be applied on an exceptional basis, as for instance, when the relief provided producers causes a substantial and possibly unnecessary burden to users (downstream producers) and consumers of the product."

44. Consumer and Corporate Affairs, Canada, *Backgrounder: Proposed Merger of Molson/ Carling O'Keefe*, CCAC No. 189 10254 E 89-07, 6-7.

in the antidumping proceedings before the CITT. Significant antidumping duties against the US imports clearly would increase the market power of the merged entity.

The director made submissions in 1991 to the MNR on calculating the dumping margin, and later to the CITT on the material injury question.[45] The director cautioned that considerations such as marketing differences and market segmentation, and not mere physical similarity, should be used in determining the appropriate Canadian beer product to compare with a given US beer import. Furthermore, he said that, wherever possible, the MNR should not resort to constructed cost measures in determining the margin of dumping. However, because the Canadian beer industry is, more or less, a regulated oligopoly, the director argued that the "normal values" should be adjusted to reflect the discriminatory "markups" and "cost of service" fees imposed on importers.

In the subsequent public-interest inquiry, the CITT rejected the director's view that the dumping in the context of this regulated oligopoly would move the market toward an efficient competitive outcome.[46] However, the CITT did agree that it was unnecessary to impose duties equal to the full margin of dumping to remove the injury. Accordingly, in 1991 the CITT recommended that the minister of finance reduce the antidumping duty by any amount that is "superfluous from the standpoint of removing [the] injury."[47]

The beer case shows the CITT's reluctance to use section 45 of SIMA as a "back door" through which competition law may replace trade law. Most recently, in the context of a public interest inquiry into certain antidumping duties imposed on fiberglass pipe insulation from the United States, the CITT again agreed with the director's submission that such duties in the full amount "would likely reduce economic welfare in Canada."[48] However, the CITT also commented:

---

45. Submission of the Director of Investigation and Research Concerning Public Interest Pursuant to Section 45 of the Special Import Measures Act in the matter of certain beer originating in or exported from the United States of America for use or consumption in the Province of British Columbia, NQ-91-002-H3 (19 September 1991); and Submission of the Director of Investigation and Research to the Deputy-Minister of National Revenue for Customs & Excise Concerning an Antidumping Investigation with respect to beer imported from the United States to British Columbia, NQ-91-002 B-26, 22-29.

46. Submission of the Director of Investigation and Research concerning public interest pursuant to Section 45 of the Special Import Measures Act resulting from the section 42 Inquiry No. NQ 91-002, 19 September 1991.

47. In the Matter of the Canadian International Trade Tribunal under Section 45 of the Special Import Measures Act, resulting from the section 42 inquiry No. NQ-91-002, CITT, 25 November 1991, 3-5.

48. Tribunal's consideration of the public interest question in the matter of preformed fiberglass pipe insulation with a vapor barrier, originating in or exported from the United States of America, Inquiry No. NQ-93-002, CITT, 27 January 1994, 4.

> The economic welfare argument would lead to the conclusion that it is in the public interest not to apply antidumping duties in the full amount in virtually every case that comes before the [CITT]. This conclusion would conflict with the public-policy purpose that Parliament recognized in providing protection against injury caused by dumping to Canadian Industry.

In December 1996, a Parliamentary Committee recommended that a nonexclusive list of factors be included in section 45 to guide the CITT respecting whether or how to conduct a public interest inquiry. Among the factors suggested for inclusion are (1) significant damage to downstream users; (2) problems of access to inputs due to imposition of the full duty; (3) restriction of competition in the Canadian market; (4) significant impact on choice or availability of products to consumers; and (5) elimination of competition in the marketplace. The government has agreed that these factors should be considered, however, at the time of writing no amend-ments to section 45 have been made.[49]

The beer case raises the broader question of whether the director should obtain from parties to a proposed merger undertakings not to initiate antidumping actions when foreign competition is a significant factor in the director's decision not to challenge the merger. The director did, in fact, obtain such an undertaking (with a five-year term) in the merger of the large power transformer businesses of ABB and Westinghouse (Ireland 1992, 92).

In conclusion, although the Canadian trade laws are designed primarily to protect domestic producers, Canada has evolved procedural and substantive innovations that may allow for competition policy concerns to enter into the analysis to some extent. However, the CITT has recognized that there is a fundamental policy conflict between the two statutory regimes and has generally been reluctant to embrace competition policy concepts. Nevertheless, there is room for further consideration of how competition policy can promote greater concern for competition and efficiency in the administration of the trade laws.

Dispute Settlement in FTA and NAFTA

The Canada-US FTA made only limited reference to competition policy. Under Article 2010, Canada and the United States could maintain or designate monopolies, which are defined to include any consortium that is designated as the sole provider or purchaser of goods and services.[50]

---

49. Canada, Minister of Finance (1997), "Government Responses to the Report on the *Special Import Measures Act* by a Joint Subcommittee of the Standing Committees on Finance and Foreign Affairs and International Trade."

50. Monopolies arising from intellectual property rights are specifically excluded from the definition and thus are not subject to the limited further obligations set out in the FTA and NAFTA. NAFTA also specifically includes government agencies within the definition of monopoly.

Both countries further agreed that, before designating a monopoly, each would notify the other and would use its best efforts to minimize the impact of such a monopoly on other FTA obligations. Furthermore, both countries agreed that such monopolies would not be allowed to engage in discriminatory sales or other anticompetitive practices that would harm the other country.

Further, the countries were to establish a working group on replacement of certain trade remedy laws with domestic competition laws. As a practical matter, however, the efforts of the "replacement option" working group were effectively overtaken by NAFTA negotiations and the developments in the Uruguay Round. The NAFTA Trade Remedies Working Group concluded its work in spring 1997 without making any recommendations for fundamental reform of each country's substantive trade remedy. However, the NAFTA parties did agree to adopt a number of procedural measures to improve the transparency and predictability in the administration of the trade remedy laws and to simplify each country's trade remedy laws.[51]

The NAFTA also does not address competition policy in detail. Chapter 15 of NAFTA requires each country to maintain a competition law to proscribe anticompetitive business practices and cooperate in its enforcement. Most of the balance of chapter 15 affirms the right of each country to maintain or designate monopolies or to create or maintain state-owned enterprises. Chapter 15 also calls for a Working Group on Trade and Competition to be created and to report with recommendations by 1 January 1999, but it has not been directed to consider replacing trade remedy laws with competition laws. To date, the NAFTA Trade and Competition Working Group has undertaken its mandate via the generation of papers that address trade and competition issues in terms of: (i) setting out the contextual framework of the discussion, (ii) comparing competition laws, and (iii) studying specific issues relevant to trade and competition. The studies undertaken to date identify similarities and differences between the competition laws and policies of the three NAFTA parties, and consider which, if any, of these differences may have implications for trade among the three contracting parties. The working group meets approximately every six months to discuss current and future work.[52]

Interestingly, Article 1501 expressly stipulates that no country may have recourse to any NAFTA dispute settlement mechanism for disputes over competition law or policy. However, as these dispute settlement mechanisms are otherwise relevant for trade and investment disputes,

---

51. NAFTA Trade Remedies Working Group (1997), "Statement by the Governments of Canada, Mexico, and the United States."

52. NAFTA Trade and Competition Working Group (1997), "Interim Report of the NAFTA 1504 Working Group to the NAFTA Commission."

they are briefly reviewed below. The so-called chapter 19 dispute settlement mechanisms of the FTA and NAFTA call for expert panels to review administrative decisions in antidumping and countervailing duty cases. These panels become effective only when the relevant administrative agency has reached a final decision. A panel then determines whether the agency correctly applied the domestic legislation using each country's own standard for judicial review. Under the FTA, panels were chosen from a roster of Canadian and US trade lawyers or economists. However, in response to the US perception that panelists (who were often trade specialists) were applying their own normative perspectives rather than applying the law, NAFTA now provides that the panels should include judges or former judges "to the fullest extent practicable." The panels may uphold a final determination or remand it for further action by the domestic administrative agency. However, the panels cannot substitute a different finding or determination. Both the FTA and NAFTA provide for "extraordinary" challenges on the grounds of bias, breach of a fundamental procedural rule, and an excess of jurisdiction by a panel.

The chapter 19 panel mechanism was created to stem administered protection by agencies that were believed to be improperly interpreting domestic law. However, it did not reduce the number of investigations (Boddez and Trebilcock 1993). In the competition law area, particularly in the United States over the last decade, enforcement policy has been considerably more liberal than the existing judicial precedent (Pitofsky 1991, 530). Hence, recourse to an FTA- or NAFTA-type dispute settlement would not likely be sufficient to deal with competition policy disputes such as those that arose in the *Alcoa* and *Radio Patents* cases, or more recently in *Institut Mérieux*.

Both the FTA (chapter 18) and the NAFTA (chapter 20) also provide for recourse to dispute settlement panels when a party believes that an actual or proposed action of another party would be inconsistent with or would nullify and impair obligations under either agreement. In this case, the panel reports to a commission of the trade ministers of each country.

Even these dispute settlement mechanisms would not likely be effective with respect to competition policy without the parties reaching much greater consensus on the laws and policies to be enforced. The initial competition concern would likely not be remedied, while the withdrawal of trade concessions or other trade disciplines may create new competition concerns over cartel behavior in either market. One alternative with respect to antitrust cases may be to require monetary compensation by the losing party. Here, the experience of courts in assessing damages caused by anticompetitive conduct may provide a useful starting point. The NAFTA-side agreements on environment and labor may provide a partial solution to this problem. Both authorize only the suspension of benefits when a party fails to pay compensation or is not fully implementing a previously agreed-upon action plan (ABA 1994).

In conclusion, the dispute settlement mechanisms of the FTA and NAFTA represent an important step forward in the adjudication of trade and investment disputes in North America. Even so, they have not curbed the use of administered protection. In any case, these mechanisms have only limited applicability for contentious competition disputes. Thus, in the next section we discuss some proposals for the replacement of dumping law with domestic competition law.

Replacing Dumping with Predation Law

In this chapter, we have discussed several problems in the administration of dumping laws in Canada and the United States. In this section, we briefly review the predatory pricing and price-discrimination laws in both Canada and the United States to assess the prospects for the convergence/harmonization of these laws more generally if the abolition of dumping rules can be achieved through NAFTA (ABA 1994, chapter 6; Graham and Warner 1994; Warner 1992; and Feltham et al. 1991).

As tariff and nontariff barriers are reduced and eliminated between and among nations, the incentives for successful dumping should diminish, as any non-cost-justified price differential between the home market and export market should be eliminated by reexporting and other arbitrage activities (Goldman 1987). Accordingly, a separate antidumping regime may be unnecessary within the FTA or NAFTA. To the extent that other incentives for anticompetitive predation remain within the free trade area, these should not be any different from the generic predation issues normally addressed by national predatory pricing and price discrimination laws.

In Canada, predatory pricing is dealt with primarily under the abuse of dominance provisions and the predatory pricing offense in the Competition Act. Paragraph 50(1)(c) makes it a criminal offense to sell at "unreasonably" low prices, which either substantially lessen or tend to lessen competition or eliminate a competitor, or are designed to have that effect. Paragraph 50(1)(c) is not expressly limited to conduct occurring within Canada, but rather refers only to the effects on competition within Canada. It could conceivably be used in cases of alleged dumping into Canada by a foreign producer.

As noted above, one of the principal problems with national dumping laws is the frequent use of constructed measures of costs (in the absence of arm's-length prices) to determine whether dumping has occurred. When constructed costs are used, the MNR compares the export price of the foreign firm against a measure of costs that is at least equal to average total costs. However, Canadian courts have held that if an article is sold for more than the total cost to the vendor, the price is not unreasonably low for the purposes of the predatory pricing offense in the Competition Act, while prices between average variable cost and average total cost may or may not be predatory. Furthermore, courts have held that one may not simply infer that a price is unreasonably low because it is below cost. Courts have held that other competitive factors, such as chronic excess capacity, could justify such prices.[53]

In 1992, the director issued predatory pricing enforcement guidelines. In determining whether to challenge a pricing practice, the director employs an analysis of market power consistent with that used in mergers and discussed above.

"Predatory" pricing that does not constitute an offense under the Competition Act could also constitute an "anticompetitive act" under the abuse of dominance provisions. However, the tribunal is empowered to make a remedial order only if the conduct in question is part of a practice and has a predatory, exclusionary, or disciplinary effect that has resulted, or is likely to result, in a substantial prevention or lessening of competition.

Any replacement option may also have to address price discrimination under Canadian and US law because antidumping laws are often concerned with international price discrimination. National price discrimination laws are arguably a lingering element of the populist roots of competition law. However, except for all but the most restrictive economic assumptions, the efficiency and aggregate welfare effects from price discrimination are, at best, indeterminate (Graham and Warner 1994, 505). Therefore, some have suggested, the replacement option should focus exclusively on harmonizing predatory pricing laws (Ireland 1991, 6). However, it may be that governments will not agree to abolish all laws pertaining to international price discrimination while continuing to apply them domestically. Consequently, it may also be necessary to consider the harmonization of price discrimination laws. We believe this approach, as suggested in the ABA Task Force Report, to be more realistic (ABA 1994, 269-71).

In Canada, price discrimination is dealt with primarily in paragraph 50(1)(a) of the Competition Act. Again, while the provision does not expressly contemplate conduct occurring outside Canada, it may be violated by making a practice of selling the same product to two or more competitors who purchase similar quantities. Unlike the US Robinson-Patman Act, a defendant cannot successfully argue that the price differentials were "cost justified" or necessary to "meet the competition," although such conduct may be permitted if it does not amount to a "practice." Also, a seller can give a preferential discount to a purchaser of a significantly higher quantity even if the discount is not cost justified. The director issued price discrimination enforcement guidelines (1992) that significantly liberalized Canadian enforcement policy in this regard

---

53. *R. v. Hoffman-La-Roche* (1980), 28 O.R. (2d) 164, 200; affirmed (1981), 33 O.R. (2d) 694 (Ont. C.A.).

to generally permit a broader range of functional and other discounts (Goldman and Bodrug 1994). The Canadian law can be applied extraterritorially while the Robinson-Patman Act is unusual among US antitrust laws because its extraterritorial application is somewhat limited (Goldman and Bodrug 1994, 664-67). Each of these issues would have to be considered in detail if harmonization of price discrimination laws were considered an important part of a replacement option.

Other Harmonization Issues

As noted above, the Competition Act exempts conspiracies relating solely to exports from its general prohibition on agreements that unduly lessen competition. Similarly, in the United States, the Webb-Pomerene Export Trade Act (*US Code* 15, sections 61-65 [1988]) exempts from antitrust liability notified conspiracies and combinations that do not affect domestic US commerce. As a practical matter, however, Canadian companies generally do not rely on the export exemption in conspiracies or combinations formed to export to the United States or any other jurisdiction with similar conspiracy legislation. In effect, the exemption facilitates export cartels that sell to less-developed countries that either do not have or do not enforce such competition laws.

Joint Ventures

Intellectual property rights (IPR) encompass patents, trademarks, copyrights, and industrial designs. It is beyond the scope of this chapter to discuss the effects of all the relevant IPR laws and policies on Canadian trade and competition policies. Instead, this section focuses on the competition law treatment of joint ventures and strategic alliances, particularly research joint ventures in Canada.

Under section 95 of the Competition Act, the tribunal cannot use the merger provisions to act against a joint venture that does not involve the formation of a separate corporation. In order to qualify for this exception, the joint venture must satisfy the following criteria: (1) the project would not take place without the venture; (2) the venture results in no change in control of any of the parent corporations; (3) the parties agree in writing to the terms of their relationship, including the contribution of assets; (4) the agreement restricts the range of activities to be carried on by the venture and provides for its termination; and (5) the venture does not prevent or lessen competition except to the extent reasonably required to complete the venture. The director has indicated that covenants barring the parent firms from engaging in independent research could deprive the venture of the benefit of this exception (Wetston 1988, 4). In such instances, or others where the joint venture exception does not apply, the merger review provisions of the Competition Act are fully applicable.

The merger guidelines do not specifically discuss joint ventures. However, the director has elsewhere indicated that a pure joint R&D venture with no restraints on independent research, production, marketing of products, or licensing of technology developed by the parents would not generally be considered anticompetitive. On the other hand, a joint venture that encompasses production and marketing of a new product in an industry characterized by high concentration, barriers to entry, and no foreign competition would probably be considered anticompetitive. This position could still be tempered by the availability of effective substitutes and the expected market share of the parent firms. However, any covenants barring independent competition by the parents would likely make the venture unacceptable absent proof of very substantial efficiency gains (Wetston 1988, 8-9).

There are no publicly reported cases involving this joint venture exception. Section 95 does not require registration, and a similar provision exempts certain joint ventures from the premerger notification requirements. Thus, private parties may have used this exemption without making it public or notifying the bureau. However, section 95 does not exempt a joint venture from a challenge under the criminal conspiracy provisions in section 45 of the Competition Act.

Section 86 of the Competition Act provides for the registration of specialization agreements among competing firms under which each firm agrees to discontinue production of a particular article or service. An agreement registered under this provision is exempt from challenge under either the criminal conspiracy provisions or certain reviewable-matters provisions of the Competition Act. Section 86 was intended to facilitate the rationalization of production within certain industries. The tribunal may register such agreements where it finds that the agreement has been made free of coercion and the efficiency gains are greater than the effects of any lessening of competition. It is possible that even though the efficiency gains will outweigh the likely lessening of competition, there will not be substantial competition remaining in a relevant market. In such instances, the tribunal can make the registration conditional, for example, on the divestiture of assets or the broader licensing of patents. The Supreme Court has been reluctant to consider the positive impact of efficiency gains under a "partial rule of reason" analysis in conspiracy cases. However, section 86 clearly could exempt some types of specialization agreements that would otherwise offend the conspiracy provisions in section 45.

When the specialization agreements and joint venture provisions were created in 1986, officials hoped they would facilitate the restructuring of Canadian businesses, but section 86 has never been used, nor has the joint venture defense (Anderson and Khoshla 1993, 72).

A former director (H. I. Wetston 1991b) has raised questions about the appropriateness of this treatment of R&D joint ventures, export consortia, production sharing, or specialization agreements in the context of emerging global firms. Specifically, will the Canadian economy reap the benefits of the productive efficiencies for which the loss of competition in the national market may be tolerated? These issues have assumed added importance in light of recent legislative developments in the United States (Warner and Rugman 1994), and the succeeding director's announced intention to allocate significant resources into enforcement of policy regarding joint ventures and strategic alliances.

Conclusions

In conclusion, the Canadian experience illustrates how a modern competition policy in a relatively small and open economy can seek to recognize efficiency and innovation. It also provides examples of the tensions that may develop as a result of the extraterritorial application of the antitrust and trade laws of a much larger trading partner, as well as the possible responses. Finally, the attempts by the Canadian antitrust authorities to intervene in antidumping proceedings may instruct future attempts to incorporate competition policy concepts into antidumping laws.

References

Addy, G. N. 1991. "International Coordination of Competition Policies." Speech, 9-11 October.

Addy, G. N. 1993. Remarks, Industry Canada. Speech #S-11274/93-07 (1 October).

Addy, G. N. 1994. "Bureau of Competition Policy Achievements of 1993; Outlook for 1994." *Canadian Competition Record* (5 March): 7.

Addy, G. N. 1994b. "The Competition Act and the Canadian Telecommunications Industry." Speech. Bureau of Competition Policy, S-11410/94-01 (29 March).

Addy, G. N. 1994c. Notes for "Remarks to the Advisory Council on the Information Highway." Ottawa (15 June): 8.

Addy, G. N. 1995. "Competition Policy and Intellectual Property Rights: Complementary Framework Policies for a Dynamic Market Economy." Notes for an address to the Canadian Bar Association, Competition Law Section, 3d Annual Competition Law Conference, Aylmer (29 September).

American Bar Association (ABA). 1994. Report of the Task Force of the Antitrust Section of the American Bar Association on the Competition Dimension of the North American Free Trade Agreement 298 (10 July).

Anderson, R. D., and S. D. Khoshla. 1993. "Competition Policy as a Dimension of Industrial Policy: a Comparative Perspective." Manuscript. Bureau of Competition Policy (June).

Blair, D. G. 1979. "The Canadian Experience." In J. P. Griffin, *Perspectives on the Extraterritorial Application of US Antitrust and Other Laws.* Section of International Law, American Bar Association.

Boddez, T. M., and M. J. Trebilcock. 1993. *Unfinished Business: Reforming Trade Remedy Laws in North America.* Toronto: C. D. Howe Institute.

Borghese, K. J. 1993. "Developments and Trends in Foreign Direct Investment in the United States." In *Foreign Direct Investment in the United States: An Update.* Washington: US Department of Commerce (June).

Canadian International Trade Tribunal (CITT). 1987. Report on Public Interest: Grain Corn.

Castel, J. G., W. C. Graham, A. L. C. DeMestral, S. Hainsworth, and M. A. A. Warner. 1991. *The Canadian Law and Practice of International Trade,* 2d ed. Toronto: Edmond Montgomery.

Chandler, H. 1994a. "Emerging Issues in Competition Law." Speech #S-11414/94-02 to Industry Canada, Ottawa (10 March).

Chandler, H. 1994b. "Getting Down to Business: The Strategic Direction of Criminal Competition Law Enforcement in Canada." Speech #S-11414/94-02 (10 March): 14.

Davidson, R. M. 1991. "Independence without Accountability Won't Last." In R. S. Khemani and W. T. Stanbury, *Canadian Competition Law and Policy at the Centenary.* Halifax, Nova Scotia: Institute for Research on Public Policy.

Director of Investigation and Research. 1991. *Merger Enforcement Guidelines, Information Bulletin 5.* Hull, Quebec: Supply and Services, Canada.

Director of Investigation and Research. 1992a. *Predatory Pricing Enforcement Guidelines.* Consumer and Corporate Affairs, Canada.

Director of Investigation and Research. 1992b, *Price Discrimination Enforcement Guidelines.* Hull, Quebec: Supply and Services, Canada.

Director of Investigation and Research. 1995. Draft Information Bulletin on "Strategic Alliances under the Competition Act" (23 November).

Eastman, H., and S. Stykolt. 1967. *The Tariff and Competition in Canada.* Toronto: MacMillan.

Eden, Lorraine. 1994. *The North American Multinationals.* Calgary: University of Calgary Press.

Encarnation, Dennis J. 1994. "Intrafirm Trade in North America and the European Community." In Lorraine Eden, *The North American Multinationals.* Calgary: University of Calgary Press.

Feltham, I. R., et al. 1991. *Competition (Antitrust) and Antidumping Laws in the Context of the Canada-US Free Trade Agreement. A Study for the Committee on Canada-United States Relations of the Canadian Chamber of Commerce and the Chamber of Commerce of the United States.* Washington: US Chamber of Commerce.

Fisher, A. A., and R. H. Lande. 1983. "Efficiency Considerations in Merger Enforcement." *California Law Review* 1580: 1644-45.

Goldman, C. S. 1986. "The Competition Act as it Relates to the Regulated Sector." Address S-86-45, Consumer and Corporate Affairs, Canada (10 September).

Goldman, C. S. 1987. "Competition, Antidumping and the Canada-US Trade Negotiations" *Canada-US Law Journal* 12, no. 95.

Goldman, C. S. 1988. "Bilateral Aspects of Canadian Competition Policy." *Antitrust Law Journal* 57, no. 401.

Goldman, C. S. 1989. "The Competition Act and the Professions," Speech S-102222. Consumer and Corporate Affairs, Canada (25 April).

Goldman, C. S. 1990. "The Merger Resolution Process under the Competition Act: A Critical Time in Its Development." *Ottawa Law Review* 22, no. 1.

Goldman, C. S., and John D. Bodrug. 1994. "The Canadian Price Discrimination Enforcement Guidelines and Their Application to Cross-Border Transactions." *Antitrust Law Journal* 62, no. 635.

Goldman, C. S., and J. D. Bodrug 1997a. "The Merger Review Process: The Canadian Experience." *Antitrust Law Journal* 65, no. 2.

Goldman, C. S., and J. D. Bodrug. 1997b. "Multinational Distribution—Issues Under Canadian Competition Law and Compliance Strategies." Paper prepared for the

Conference on Managing the Antitrust Risks of Multinational Distribution, New York (10 June).

Goldman, C. S., and J. D. Bodrug. 1997c. *Competition Law of Canada*. New York: Juris Publishing.

Goldman, C. S., and P. S. Crampton. 1993. "The Director's Immunity Program: Some Policy and Practical Considerations." Paper delivered at Insight Conference on Competition Law, Toronto (11 May).

Goldman, C. S., G. P. Cornish, and R. F. D. C. Corley. 1992. "International Mergers and the Canadian Competition Act." *Fordham Corp. Law Institute.*

Goldman, C. S., and J. T. Kissack. 1997. "Cross-Border Issues in Competition Policy: Lessons From the Canadian Experience." Paper prepared for the Pacific Economic Cooperation Council Conference on Trade and Competition Policy, Montreal (13 May).

Graham, E. M., and M. A. A. Warner. 1994. "Multinationals and Competition Policy in North America." In Lorraine Eden, *The North American Multinationals*. Calgary: University of Calgary Press.

Hart, M. 1989. "Dumping and Free Trade Areas." In J. H. Jackson and E. A. Vermulst, *Antidumping Law and Practice: A Comparative Study*. Ann Arbor: University of Michigan Press.

Henry, D. H. W. 1970. "The United States Antitrust Laws: A Canadian View Point." *The Canadian Year Book of International Law* 8, no. 249: 280.

Hunter, L. A. W. 1983. "Extraterritoriality and Antitrust Considerations: The Canadian Perspective." In E. H. Fry and L. H. Radebaugh, *Regulation of Foreign Direct Investment in Canada and the United States*. Provo, UT: Brigham Young University.

Ireland, D. J. 1991. "Enforcement of the Canadian Competition Act under the Free Trade Agreement between Canada and the United States." Speech.

Ireland, D. 1992. *Discussion Paper: Interactions Between Competition and Trade Policies: Challenges and Opportunities*. Consumer and Corporate Affairs, Canada.

Khemani, R. S. 1991. "Merger Policy in Small vs. Large Economies." In R. S. Khemani and W. T. Stanbury, *Canadian Competition Policy at the Centenary*. Halifax: Institute for Research on Public Policy.

Khemani, R. S., and D. M. Shapiro. 1993. "An Empirical Analysis of Canadian Merger Policy." *Journal of Industrial Economics* 41 (June): 161.

Kilgour, D. G. 1963. *The Antitrust Bulletin* 8, no. 1 (January-February): 101-02.

Larabie-LeSieur, R. 1994. "Misleading Advertising and the Competition Act: Compliance and Enforcement in the Nineties." Speech #S-11422/94-04 (9 May).

McKeown, W. P. 1993. Remarks to the Canadian Bar Association, Quebec City (25 August).

Newborn, S. A., and V. L. Snider. 1992. "The Growing Judicial Acceptance of the Merger Guidelines." *Antitrust Law Journal* 60, no. 849: 851.

Owen, D. K., and J. J. Parisi. 1990. "International Mergers and Joint Ventures: A Federal Trade Commission Perspective." *Fordham Corp. Law Institute* 1: 13.

Pitofsky, R. 1991. "Does Antitrust Have a Future?" In H. First et al., *Revitalizing Antitrust in Its Second Century*. New York: Quorum Books.

Porteous, S. D., and A. M. Rugman. 1990. "Canadian Unfair Trade Laws and Corporate Strategy." *Review of International Business Law* 3: 237.

Rosenthal, D. 1990. "The Potential for Jurisdictional Conflicts in Multistate International Merger Transactions." *Fordham Corp. Law Institute* 87, no. 90.

Ross, S. F. 1997. "Afterword—Did the Canadian Parliament Really Permit Mergers that Exploit Canadian Consumers So the World Can Be More Efficient?" *Antitrust Law Journal* 65, no. 2.

Rugman, Alan M. 1987. *Outward Bound: Canadian Direct Investment in the United States*. Toronto: C. D. Howe Institute.

Rugman A. M. 1990. *Multinationals and Canada-United States Free Trade*. Columbia: University of South Carolina Press.

Rugman, A. M., and S. D. Porteous. 1989. "Canadian and US Unfair Trade Laws: A Comparison of Their Legal and Administrative Structures." *Canadian Business Law Journal* 16: 1.

Rugman, A. M., and A. Verbeke. 1994. "Foreign Direct Investment and NAFTA: A Canadian Perspective." In A. M. Rugman, *Foreign Investment and North American Free Trade*. Columbia: University of South Carolina Press.

Rugman, A. M., and M. A. A. Warner. 1988. "Foreign Ownership, Free Trade, and the Canadian Energy Sector." *Journal of Energy and Development* 14, no. 1: 13.

Sanderson, M. 1997. "Efficiency Analysis in Canadian Merger Cases." *Antitrust Law Journal* 65, no. 2.

Stegemann, K. 1991. "Settlement of Antidumping Cases by Price Undertaking: Is the E. C. More Liberal than Canada?" In P. K. M. Tharakan, *Policy Implications of Antidumping Measures*. Amsterdam: North-Holland.

US International Trade Commission (ITC). 1992. *The Year in Trade: Operation of the Trade Agreements Program, 1991*. Washington: US International Trade Commission.

Warner, M. A. A. 1990. "A History of United States-Canada Trade and Investment Relations." In A. M. Rugman, *Multinationals and Canada-United States Free Trade*. Columbia: University of South Carolina Press.

Warner, M. A. A. 1994a. "Efficiencies and Merger Review in Canada, the European Community and the United States: Implications for Harmonization/Convergence." *Vanderbilt Journal of Transnational Law* 27.

Warner, M. A. A. 1994b. "Note on '*Hunt v. Lac D'Amiante du Québec'*." *American Journal of International Law* 88, no. 532.

Warner, M. A. A. 1997. "The Efficiencies Exception to the Canadian Competition Act: Analytical Exception or Unexceptional Analysis." *Antitrust Magazine*.

Warner, M. A. A., and Alan M. Rugman. 1994. "Competitiveness: An Emerging Strategy of Discrimination in U. S. Antitrust and R&D Policy?" *Law and Policy in International Business* 25, no. 945.

Warner, P. L. 1992. "Canada-United States Free Trade: The Case for Replacing Antidumping with Antitrust." *Law and Policy in International Business* 23, no. 791 (Summer).

Wetston, H. I. 1988. "The Treatment of Cooperative R&D Activities under the Competition Act." #S-10064. Consumer and Corporate Affairs, Canada (4 March).

Wetston, H. I. 1991a. Speech #S-10492/91/15. Consumer and Corporate Affairs, Canada (19 August).

Wetston, H. I. 1991b. Speech #S-10612/92-01. Consumer and Corporate Affairs, Canada (1 October).

Wetston, H. I. 1992a. "Competition Law and Policy." Remarks delivered to the Canadian Institute, Toronto (8 June).

Wetston, H. I. 1992b. "Developments and Emerging Challenges in Canadian Competition Law." *Fordham Corp. Law Institute* 195.

France: 1987–94

FRÉDÉRIC JENNY

In 1986 a newly elected conservative administration under French Premier Jacques Chirac set out to abolish a 1945 ordinance that allowed the government to control prices and to rewrite the competition law. It did so partly for a technical reason: various provisions of the competition law had been integrated into the 1945 ordinance. There was also an economic reason: fearing that lifting price controls would fuel inflation, the new administration wanted to strengthen French competition law. Thus the 1945 ordinance on prices and the 1977 competition law were replaced by a 1986 ordinance on the freedom of prices and competition.

The 1986 Ordinance

The leading role in enforcing the antitrust provisions of the new ordinance was entrusted to a new independent administrative authority: le Conseil de la Concurrence, or Competition Council. This council comprises 16 members, made up mostly of civil as well as administrative law judges, though some members have a particular expertise in consumer affairs or competition policy, and some members come from the business community.

Contrary to its predecessor, la Commission de la concurrence, the council is not merely an advisory body. It is first and foremost a quasi-judicial

---

Frédéric Jenny is professor of economics at ESSEC and vice chairman of Conseil de la Concurrence, Paris.

decision-making body, which can on its own decide to open investigations to enforce Articles 7 and 8 of the ordinance of 1986, which prohibit anticompetitive, concerted actions and abuses of dominant position. The council can impose fines of up to 5 percent of total sales on firms found guilty of anticompetitive practices and give them injunctions. Its decisions can be appealed to the Paris Court of Appeals. Thus, a significant aspect of the 1986 reform lies in the fact that the minister for economic affairs has relinquished his powers to decide how to enforce the prohibition of anticompetitive practices.

The civil courts are also competent to enforce Articles 7 and 8 of the ordinance and can award damages to injured parties or nullify agreements that violate the law, which the Competition Council cannot do. Plaintiffs in civil courts bear the burden of proof and must demonstrate the existence of the violation they allege. They can collect only single damages and cannot introduce class-action suits. As a result, relatively few cases of alleged violations of Articles 7 and 8 are adjudicated through the civil courts, and the council plays a major role in enforcing these provisions.

Article 7 of the 1986 ordinance prohibits "concerted actions, conventions, explicit or tacit understandings or coalitions which are designed for or may have the effect of curbing, restraining or distorting competition in a given market." Article 8 prohibits abuse by a firm (or a group of firms) or abuses of the dependency in which a firm holds another firm (supplier or customer) when these abuses have the object or may have the effect of restraining competition.

Although such practices in principle are prohibited unless the firm in question qualifies for a legal or an economic exemption, the scope of the exemptions was significantly reduced in 1986. The legal exemption applies henceforth only if a law imposes the anticompetitive practice. For example, in the agricultural sector some interprofessional agreements imposing quotas or restricting price freedom for certain crops are allowed if the French minister of agriculture approved them or the EU commission imposed them.

In addition, the right to refer cases to the council—previously open only to the minister of economic affairs, trade organizations, certain consumer organizations, and local governments—was extended to firms.

The law with respect to anticompetitive concerted actions, coalitions, and abuses of dominant position was not substantially modified in 1986. A few new provisions regarding the substantive law on anticompetitive practices are, however, worth mentioning.

In 1983 and 1984 several large supermarket chains and common buying agencies of smaller distributors triggered a debate on how to curb "abuses of buying power" when they demanded additional discounts from their suppliers, either because they believed they deserved better terms or because they thought the suppliers were granting better terms to their competitors. They threatened to not carry products of manufacturers failing to meet their conditions. In each case, the name-brand products involved accounted for a minute proportion of the total sales of the distributors but for a significant part (between 10 and 20 percent) of the total sales of the supplying manufacturers. The manufacturers claimed they had no choice but to grant the discounts requested by these distributors (or by the common buying agencies) and then face additional demands by other distributors.

With this recent controversy in mind, and because it wanted to alleviate what it considered to be a growing imbalance in the economic relationship between manufacturers and large distributors, the new administration introduced a provision in the 1986 ordinance making it illegal for firms (even those without a dominant position in the market) to abuse their economic bargaining power vis-à-vis other firms (suppliers or customers) when those firms depend on them and when the abuse constitutes a restraint of competition. The ordinance states, among other things, that the discontinuation by a firm of an established commercial relationship with a dependent firm because the latter refuses unjustified commercial demands could be considered such an abuse.

A 1977 competition law already applied to both public or private firms (and several state-owned firms had been sanctioned between 1977 and 1986 for engaging in prohibited practices). Yet until 1986 it had remained a hotly debated question whether competition law should also apply to divisions of government ministries engaged in commercial ventures—such as the General Directorate for Telecommunications or the Ministry of Post and Telecommunications, which was running the French telephone system without having the status of a public firm.

A comment is in order regarding the council's enforcement of Articles 85-1 and 86 of the EU treaty. Until 1992, French law did not allow plaintiffs to bring a case to the Competition Council solely on the basis of European law, and the council neither had powers to investigate alleged infringement of the European law nor did it have powers to sanction such infringements when they were established. Thus the council could handle Article 85-1 and 86 cases only if the allegedly anticompetitive practices were simultaneously denounced as illegal under domestic law. In 1992 an amendment to the 1986 ordinance made it possible for the council to use its powers of investigation and sanction for the enforcement of European law.

Besides its role as a decision-making body for anticompetitive practices, the council also has specific advisory roles. First, Article 1 of the 1986 ordinance enables the administration to reinstate price controls in a few sectors in which competition is limited either because there is a monopoly or because specific laws prevent it. However, before the administration can impose price controls in these sectors, it must first ask the council whether price competition is indeed limited. Although the council's opinion is not binding on the minister of economic affairs, it must be published with the decree establishing the price control. Sectors in which the administration has reestablished price controls since 1986 include taxis, public transportation, distribution of gas or electricity (through a publicly owned monopoly), and some medical services. Second, whenever the administration considers issuing an administrative order (décret) limiting competition in a sector by establishing quantitative barriers to entry, by giving exclusive rights to some operators in certain areas, or by imposing uniform prices or sales conditions, it must first seek the council's opinion. Third, local governments, trade organizations, trade unions, consumer organizations, and chambers of commerce or of agriculture, as well as permanent parliamentary commissions and the administration, can seek the council's opinion on general questions concerning competition.

The minister of economic affairs must also seek the council's opinion whenever he considers blocking a merger or imposing conditions on the parties to such a merger. The council's opinion, which must include assessments of the merger's potential harm to competition and of its potential contribution to economic progress, is not binding, but the minister must publish it with his decision. The minister of economic affairs controls mergers in two cases: when the combined market share of the parties exceeds 25 percent of a domestic market or when their combined sales total more than 7 billion francs and two (or more) of the parties have sales of more than 2 billion francs each. Notification of a merger to the minister is voluntary, but if notified the merger is implicitly approved if there is no ministerial decision within six months of notification. Merger control thus in practice remains almost solely in the hands of the minister for economic affairs because he alone can decide or refuse to open an investigation and is free to allow or prohibit the merger.

The impetus for enlarging the scope of merger control to include mergers involving firms that did not meet the market-share threshold but were large in absolute terms came, once again, as a result of the hot debate over merger control of the retail sector.

Despite the fact that the merger control law of 1977 was not vigorously enforced before 1985, manufacturers had consistently denounced it as unfair, arguing that different market-share criteria should be used to determine which mergers could be controlled in the distribution and manufacturing sectors. They pointed out that manufacturers typically compete at the national level while competition among retailers is mostly local and that a merger between two chains of supermarkets could well limit competition in many local areas even if the firms or groups of firms involved did not have a significant national market share. They further argued that although a large manufacturer might easily have a market share greater than 25 percent of the national market, not even the largest distributors, who enjoyed considerable buying power, accounted for 25 percent of the retail sales of any given category of goods at the national level and that therefore mergers in the retail sector were "unfairly" immune from controls.

The clamor of manufacturers was thus based on their fear of the growing concentration in the distribution system or, in other words, on the fact that while the merger legislation could prevent manufacturers from gaining "too much selling power," it could not in fact be used to prevent large distributors from gaining "too much buying power."

It is worth noting that the law was significantly changed in the area of individual restraints of trade (i.e., restraints of trade that a firm can impose when it does not have a dominant position or when it does not collude with other firms).

The 1945 ordinance on prices prohibited per se four types of individual restraints of trade: refusal to deal, price discrimination, resale price maintenance, and reselling at a loss. Two of these prohibitions—refusal to deal and price discrimination—were abolished by the 1986 ordinance. It was finally recognized that price discrimination can have procompetitive effects. Regarding refusal to deal, the government came to feel that this per se prohibition—established in the 1960s and deemed necessary at that time to prevent manufacturers, under the pressure of their traditional retailers, from refusing to sell to the emerging large-scale, low-margin retailers—was no longer necessary. While price discrimination and refusal to sell ceased to be per se criminal offenses, they remained civil offenses administered through a rule-of-reason approach.

The 1986 ordinance did maintain as criminal offenses two other individual restraints of trade: resale price maintenance and reselling at a loss. At a time when it was relinquishing its ability to control prices, the administration did not want resale price maintenance to slow the development of discounters. As far as reselling at a loss was concerned, the administration did not want to displease the large constituency of small retailers and name-brand products manufacturers, who had been complaining loudly for years about the "unfair" practices of large-scale retailers and discount stores, which used the most well-known name-brand products as loss leaders to attract customers.

Enforcement

To assess the intensity of enforcement since 1986, it is worth looking at the number of cases the Competition Council has examined since its creation. Between February 1987 and December 1994, 175 out of a total of 551 council decisions were appealed to the Paris Court of Appeals. During the same period, the court examined 166 appeals, reforming 15 decisions and nullifying 13. In the case of the nullifications, the court

Table 1 France: Cases referred to Competition Council, 1987-94

Year	Article 7 and 8 cases	Decisions	Preliminary investigation suggested a violation	Sanctions imposed	Merger cases
1987	86	53	14	5	2
1988	81	50	22	18	1
1989	82	44	17	14	2
1990	84	52	19	19	8
1991	101	60	32	21	1
1992	98	69	38	27	7
1993	91	72	29	22	12
1994	79	75	35	24	10

considered that the council had not followed proper procedures. The court reformed decisions when it found the evidence the council had used to establish violations unpersuasive. In the remaining 138 decisions, the court confirmed the council's reasoning, although in some instances it decreased or increased the fines the council had set.

As far as Article 7 and 8 cases are concerned—that is, cases about cartels or abuses of dominant positions—the minister of economic affairs initiated about half. The remaining half were initiated mostly by firms alleging that they were victims of anticompetitive practices. Trade organizations, chambers of commerce, consumer organizations, or local governments initiated few cases, and most of these concerned horizontal or vertical agreements. Although a large proportion of total cases involved price-fixing or market-sharing agreements between potential competitors, a significant number related to allegedly anticompetitive selective or exclusive distribution arrangements. In contrast, cases involving abuses of market power by firms holding a dominant position (thereby falling under Article 8 of the 1986 ordinance) or abuses of dependency have more rarely been referred to the council. Explicit price-fixing and market-sharing agreements represent roughly 30 percent of all the established violations of French antitrust provisions under the ordinance. Collusions-in-tender offers represent roughly 20 percent of all cases submitted to the council.

Table 1 clearly reflects the council's increased enforcement activity regarding concerted actions (Article 7) and abuse of dominant positions and dependency (Article 8). The pivotal year for this increase appears to be 1990. The fact that the Paris Appeals Court supported the council's analysis in 83 percent of the cases brought to appeal from 1987 through 1994 has contributed to the credibility of the enforcement system and to the establishment of the council's authority.

As far as merger control is concerned, the 1986 ordinance states that the council's opinions should balance the potential adverse consequences on competition of the mergers it examines and their potential contribution to economic progress. The council's analysis therefore differs from that of the EU Merger Task Force on two grounds. The council can recommend that corrective action be taken or that a merger be blocked because it creates a serious threat to competition even if the merger does not lead to the creation or strengthening of a dominant position for the merging firms, and the council can take an efficiency defense into consideration.

Until 1990 the merger control provision of the 1986 ordinance was rarely used, but merger control activity increased when the EU merger regulation went into effect in 1990 (table 1). However, the number of cases referred to the council for formal review may underestimate the importance of merger control in France. Indeed, as was mentioned previously, the minister of economic affairs does not refer all the mergers the ministry examines, but only those he considers to be problematic from the point of view of competition. What is more, some mergers that may hinder competition do not undergo formal review because the parties to the merger agree to meet the minister of economic affairs's demands for corrections during the informal review stage.

Substantive Issues

Scope of the 1986 Ordinance

Because the actions of public authorities were believed to be, directly or indirectly, a major obstacle to competition in many sectors, the scope of applicability of the French antitrust provisions was enlarged in 1986. Article 53 of the 1986 ordinance states that the prohibition of anticompetitive cartels and of abuse of dominant positions applies "to all activities of production, distribution, or service, including those undertaken by public authorities." The courts have held that this provision means that competition law applies to ministries and to local authorities whenever they act as commercial suppliers of goods or services.

Thus, for example, in 1993 the Paris Court of Appeals decided that the National Weather Bureau, which is part of the ministry of equipment and housing and which operates a commercial phone-in service available to the general public, abused its dominant position by refusing to provide a potential competitor with some of the meteorological data that the bureau was required by law to gather and make available for aircraft navigation.[1]

---

1. Decision of the Paris Court of Appeals, 18 March 1993, regarding a 13 May 1992 Competition Council decision (no. 92-D-35). The council had previously considered that the ordinance of 1986 applied to the National Weather Bureau but that its refusal to supply

Similarly, the Post Office, which is a division of the Ministry of Post and Telecommunications and which operates a commercial express mail service as well as banking services that are not part of the ministry's public universal service obligations, is under attack from some of its competitors for abusing its dominant position by using its public service facilities (such as post offices) or public service workers to provide its commercial services without taking into account their full cost. Article 53 of the ordinance also means that municipal governments, which often provide public local services such as water distribution and undertakers could also be found guilty of engaging in anticompetitive practices.

Although the scope of French antitrust law was expanded in 1986, there is still a fair amount of controversy about the extent to which it applies to the public sector. This comes as no surprise in a country in which the public sector remains quite extensive (although shrinking), universal public service obligations are defined broadly, and public services are increasingly supplied by private concerns operating under a concession from public authorities.

One of the problems raised by the interpretation of Article 53, as given by the Conflicts Tribunal (Tribunal des conflits),[2] is that it holds that the ordinance of 1986 applies to administrative bodies only to the extent to which they act as commercial suppliers on the market in which an anticompetitive practice is alleged. The same does not hold true for private firms or organizations. Indeed, a firm holding a dominant position in one market can abuse its dominant position by engaging in an anticompetitive practice in a related market even if it is not present in this related market (for example, by refusing to deal with certain downstream operators). Similarly, a trade organization, which does not usually operate in a market directly, can be found to have violated competition law by organizing price-fixing among its members to restrain competition in the market in which they operate. Thus, although the wording of Article 53 does not distinguish between private and public bodies, case law has restrictively interpreted this provision when public bodies were involved.

However, administrative bodies can help shape competition in commercial markets in which they are not commercial operators via the adjudication of contracts or concessions. French competition law does

---

the specific information requested was not an abuse of its dominant position both because the competitor could have obtained the same information through other means and because it was not established that the weather bureau used this information for its own phone-in service. The case was pending before the French Supreme Court (Cour de cassation) when this was written.

2. This tribunal adjudicates potential conflicts between administrative and civil law. It comprises magistrates belonging to the administrative supreme court (Conseil d'etat) and the civil supreme court (Cour de cassation).

not apply to public authorities in these cases. Although the public procurement code (Code des Marchés Publics) may require public authorities to consult with several potential suppliers when awarding contracts, they are not usually required to consult all potential suppliers or operators or to choose the lowest bidder for the contract or the highest bidder for the concession. Thus administrative bodies enjoy considerable discretion when it comes to deciding which potential suppliers or operators of a public service will compete and which will be chosen. Consequently, personal relationships between suppliers and administrative body officials may determine who gets contracts and concessions rather than the suppliers' or operators' economic performance.

A second problem stems from the fact that public service obligations that are delegated to private bodies are often not precisely defined, making it unclear whether the ordinance of 1986 applies to particular practices. For example, the Ministry for Sports has entrusted sports promotion (which in France is a public service) and the organization of national competitions to sporting federations, which are private bodies. These federations often seek additional revenues either through forcing commercial services on their members or through the selling of exclusive rights to suppliers. The federations then argue that some of the practices, because they are a means to acquire the revenue needed to fulfill their public service obligations, are outside the law's scope—for example, forcing practitioners of a sport who want to join a club to subscribe to federation-selected personal liability insurance or choosing suppliers to equip club players. Competitors of the selected insurance companies or equipment suppliers counter that these commercial activities are distinct from the promotion of the sport and that they are concerted actions (among federation members and the selected insurance companies or equipment suppliers) that restrict competition.

A 1994 amendment to Article 53 has extended the scope of the ordinance to include the concession of public services by public authorities. No cases have yet been referred to the Competition Council under this provision.

Per Se versus Rule of Reason

Articles 7 and 8 of the ordinance of 1986 state that agreements, whether explicit or tacit, and abuses of dominant position are prohibited if their objective is to impair or restrain competition or if they had or could have such an effect. In the antitrust area, the ordinance does not explicitly define practices that should be considered per se violations.

In applying this provision, the council follows a rule-of-reason approach. However, in cases in which the authors of the practice declare that they intended to restrict competition, the council uses a per se approach—that is, it forgoes detailed analysis of how the practice restrained competition, merely stating that the practice had the objective of restraining competition and is therefore illegal.

Although most price-fixing or market-sharing schemes are considered to be illegal anticompetitive practices (and some, such as price-fixing in procurement markets, are per se prohibited), case law provides examples in which such agreements were examined under a rule of reason and were not considered to violate the ordinance.

For example, in its decision on herbicidal products and pesticides (no. 92-D-29), the council decided that minimum price-fixing clauses in co-distribution agreements between chemical manufacturers did not restrain competition (*Rapport du Conseil de la Concurrence pour l'année 1992*, Annexe 36, 260). Herbicidal products and pesticides are typically obtained through the blending of chemical elements. A large number of manufacturers each produce a wide range of products, but practically none of them offers products for all possible uses. Some manufacturers have entered into co-distribution agreements with a competitor, allowing this competitor to add one or several of their products to its product line. In such instances, the manufacturer and its co-distributor market the same product (although under different brand names).

The council found no evidence that the co-distribution agreements it examined in this sector contained ancillary clauses limiting the ability of the co-distributors to engage in research to independently develop products similar to those that were the object of the agreements. However, such agreements typically had a clause whereby both parties agreed to sell the product above a minimum price.

In its decision on herbicidal products and pesticides, the council first determined that the manufacturer in question would enter a co-distribution agreement only to develop its own sales through the marketing efforts of its co-distributor and that it could thereby offer a wider range of products to its traditional clientele. Second, since each product covered by a co-distribution agreement faced competition from products offered by many other manufacturers, the parties' attempt to develop their sales intensified rather than decreased product competition.

Having found that the co-distribution agreements had a pro-competitive effect, the council also considered that without the minimum price clause, both parties to such an agreement could face a free-rider problem. Such a problem would arise for the manufacturer if the co-distributor did not expand the customer base for the product but simply drew customers away from the manufacturer by offering the product more cheaply, or, vice versa, the co-distributor might fear the manufacturer's undercutting *its* price and customer base. Thus, the council held that, given the structure of the industry and the multiplicity of competing products, the price agreements between co-distributors were not illegal because they were necessary to avoid the free-rider problem inherent in co-distribution agreements and because such agreements increased competition.

Defining Competition

From the substantive standpoint, the creation of an independent quasi-judicial body whose decisions could be appealed to the Paris Court of Appeals had important consequences. As with the comparable US and EU laws, the wording of the 1986 provisions prohibiting anticompetitive concerted actions or abuses of dominant positions represents a synthesis of ideas rather than a clear definition of competition and how it is to be achieved. Because of this lack of definition in the ordinance, the enforcement of competition statutes crucially depends on the Competition Council's interpretation.

The council's approach to competition in its area of jurisdiction—which is limited to a narrow definition of antitrust covering cartels, abuses of dominant positions, and mergers—is markedly different from that which permeated some of the debates in French government circles in the 1950s and the 1960s and is much closer to an economic concept of competition.

For example, the council has stated in various annual reports that the following questions should guide its determination of whether a concerted action was anticompetitive:

- Does the concerted practice interfere with the independent decision making of firms in the market?

- Does the concerted practice lessen the uncertainty that each firm should face regarding the strategy other firms will likely follow?

- Does the practice in any way impede the ability of other firms to enter the market or to expand in the market?

These are pragmatic translations of the theoretical conditions for perfect competition suggested by economic theory (atomicity and independence of decision making, lack of barriers to entry). By defining competition in this manner, the council emphasizes the process through which prices and quantities are determined rather than the result of the adjustment process or the fairness of the mechanism. In other words, the council does not think that antitrust law can or should be used to regulate prices or to protect one competitor from another.

For example, in a 1987 decision concerning bakers (no. 87-D-33, *Rapport du Conseil de la Concurrence pour l'année 1987*, annexe 42, 6), the council found that in one geographical area the professional organization of bakers had urged its members to increase the price of bread by a certain amount in January and July 1986 and that most bakers had indeed followed the organization's recommendation. In finding that the organization had initiated an anticompetitive agreement among its member firms, the council refused to consider the organization's claim that in other geographical areas (in which there was no evidence of an agreement among bakers) the price of bread was higher (or increased faster). The council reasoned that the level or rate of increase of bread prices elsewhere was irrelevant because the price in the area in question was not arrived at through independent decision making.

Exemptions to Promote Efficiency

Article 10 of the 1986 ordinance allows exemption of anticompetitive practices when they contribute to economic progress. However, the admissibility of an efficiency defense is restricted to cases in which the authors of the practice "reserved an equitable share of the resulting profits to the buyers" and did not "enable the businesses concerned to eliminate competition on a substantial portion of the markets involved." Additionally, the burden of proof that the exemption conditions are met lies with the authors of the anticompetitive practice.

The wording of Article 10 is thus similar to the wording of Article 85-3 of the EU treaty, but contrary to EU law, economic exemptions can also apply in cases of abuse of dominant position.

Regarding merger control, the 1986 ordinance states that, in its opinions to the minister of economic affairs, the council must weigh both the potential weakening of competition due to the merger and the potential benefits. Thus an efficiency defense of otherwise anticompetitive mergers is allowed in French law, whereas Article 2 of the EU merger regulation does not allow such a defense.

The possibility of an exemption of anticompetitive practices or mergers that contribute to economic progress suggests prima facie that the underlying goal of French competition law is to maximize net welfare rather than consumer welfare. However, this appraisal must be qualified by two considerations. First, because the efficiency defense is admissible only if a substantial part of the efficiency gains have been passed on to consumers, a practice that would entail relatively modest consumer surplus losses and large producer surplus gains cannot be automatically exempted. Second, as was indicated earlier, the council's opinion in merger cases does not bind the minister of economic affairs nor the minister in charge of the sector in which the merger takes place, who together have the ultimate decision-making power.

In interpreting Article 10-2 (or the merger provision of the 1986 ordinance), the council has stuck to a narrow definition of the concept of economic progress by restricting it to cost reductions for the economy as a whole (due, for example, to a reduction in transaction costs) or to innovations that could not be obtained without the otherwise anticompetitive practice or merger. Thus, positive effects on employment, exports, or regional development that could be considered in the public interest are not included in the council's definition of "economic progress."

One case in which the efficiency defense succeeded concerned Interflora, an association of French florists (*Rapport de la Commission de la Concurrence pour l'année 1985*, annexe 18, 123). The council's predecessor, Commission de la concurrence, initially determined that Interflora restricted competition among its affiliates in the same locales when it made an agreement with its independent affiliates on charges for standardized flower arrangements. The commission reasoned that a customer from one city who used the Interflora system to order flowers for delivery in another town was quoted a price that was higher than it would have been had the several local affiliates available to fill the order been free to compete. Subsequently, the commission considered that striking down the price agreement would significantly raise transaction costs for consumers, who without Interflora would have to contact each florist in the town of delivery to find the best price and arrange a transaction. This increased transaction cost would in turn decrease demand for the service. So in the end the commission ruled that Interflora's restriction to competition was in fact a necessary condition for providing this service.

Article 10 also allows the minister of economic affairs to seek a class exemption for certain agreements among small or medium-size firms. Such exemptions can be granted only after the minister has sought the opinion of the Conseil de la concurrence and this opinion is binding on the minister. However, so far, the minister has never proposed granting a class exemption to agreements among small firms. Barring such formal exemptions, the question of whether some anticompetitive agreements could be exempted from competition law depends on whether the Conseil or the Paris Court of Appeals accepts the argument that anticom-petitive agreements violate the prohibition of article 7 only if they have an appreciable impact on competition.

Exemptions Based on Magnitude of Market Effect

A second type of potential exemption, besides that for efficiency's sake, has raised a legal controversy: whether concerted practices or abuses of dominant position with only a minor effect on the market should be exempted.

Because Articles 85 and 86 of the EU Treaty inspired the 1986 ordinance (which is similar but not identical to them), the council simultaneously enforces the European and French law. Hence, differences of approach between the council and the European Commission on agreements with minor effect may cause some difficulty. In its notice on minor agreements,[3] the Commission indicated that it would not investi-

---

3. First published in 1970 and revised in 1977, 1984, 1986, and 1994.

gate concerted practices of firms with less than 5 percent of the EU market or very small firms (less than 300 million ECUs). This does not mean that Article 85 could not apply to anticompetitive agreements of such firms , but only that the Commission, which shares the task of enforcing Articles 85-1 and 86 with the national competition authorities, decided to focus on cases with a larger impact on the European market. The Commission's statement also did not mean that minor anticompetitive agreements are exempt, as has been frequently misinterpreted. In addition, the European Commission and the EU Court of Justice have determined that anticompetitive agreements that do not qualify as minor agreements or abuses of dominant position violate the EU law only if they have an appreciable effect on intra-Community trade and on competition in the European market (or a substantial part of this market).

With these considerations in mind, some legal commentators have argued that anticompetitive agreements among firms with a share of the French domestic market below the Commission's threshold for agreements of minor importance should be exempted because they cannot have an appreciable impact on the domestic market. Furthermore, they argue that other agreements can be found to be Article 7 violations only if the council or the courts establish that they significantly restrain or distort competition.

While the Paris Court of Appeals and the French Supreme Court have occasionally thrown out decisions sanctioning anticompetitive agreements because these agreements had not been shown to appreciably reduce competition, the Competition Council has rarely exempted agreements on such a basis.

The council's position reflects a semantic difference with the courts. When impairing competition has not been established as the agreement's objective, the council examines whether the agreement had an actual or potential effect on competition and thus whether it violated Article 7. But the council holds that an effect, actual or potential, can be established only if the agreement had or could have had an appreciable consequence on the market. In other words, it applies a test of magnitude of market effect in order to determine the actual or potential consequences of an agreement but not as a separate test.

Case Law

Horizontal Agreements

A wide array of practices fall into this category: for example, the exchange of information among competitors, price recommendations by trade organizations, price-fixing and market sharing, collusion in procurement markets, and coordinated attempts to exclude competitors or importers.

Explicit Agreements

Explicit horizontal market-sharing and price-fixing agreements are in most cases considered violations of Article 7 of the 1986 ordinance.

The council has examined several types of explicit price agreements: agreements among competitors to fix prices actually charged or price increases or profit margins, agreements among competitors to determine tariffs (when substantial rebates from the tariff price are common); publication of recommended or suggested tariffs by trade or professional organizations, and the exchange among competitors of information on future prices.

Regarding explicit agreements to fix prices actually charged, price increases, or profit margins, the council in its 1987 annual report stressed its "strong attachment to independent decision making in the price area. Indeed, this independence is a necessary condition for the existence of price competition, which—although it is but one form of competition—is nevertheless a determining factor in forcing firms to be as efficient as possible."

As far as concerted actions among potential competitors to determine tariffs are concerned, the council finds such actions violate the competition law irrespective of whether the prices actually charged consumers were equal to those mentioned on the tariff. Thus, in a decision on thread manufacturers (no. 88-D-50, *Rapport du Conseil de la Concurrence pour l'année 1988*, annexe 54, 111), the council reviewed a concerted tariff that was applied to small customers (representing only 2 percent of total demand), whereas the suppliers granted large rebates to other buyers. There was no evidence that the amount of the rebates had been jointly determined. The council found the tariff agreement to be a violation, noting that it had had an effect on some customers. But it also went on to say that if, as the parties claim, there were differences between the tariffs and the actual prices charged by each firm to other customers, it remains that the concerted tariffs could be used as a common basis for negotiations between suppliers and customers (and therefore could have had an anticompetitive effect).

The council's reasoning regarding trade organizations' publication of recommended prices is quite clear in a 1987 decision concerning architects (no. 87-D-53, *Rapport du Conseil de la Concurrence pour l'année 1987*, annexe 62, 80). In it, the council explained that "besides their purpose, such tariffs may have an anticompetitive effect, . . . in that they may decrease the incentive [of architects] to compute their costs individually [and to determine their prices]. This potentiality is independent of the number of [firms] that actually apply the tariffs."

On a more general level, the council wrote in its 1987 report:

> [T]he publication by trade organizations of price lists, price recommendations or indications on prices to be charged, is prohibited, even in the absence of pressure on the professionals involved to follow the recommendations, because by giving an indication to all firms about the level of what is considered by the profession as a "normal" price or price increase, the trade organizations may give an incentive to some or all of those firms to actually adopt those prices or price increases.

Tacit Agreements and Parallel Behavior

Both the council and its predecessor, the Commission de la concurrence, have repeatedly stated that evidence of parallel behavior among competitors (e.g., simultaneous increases in prices, simultaneous refusal to sell to a discounter, or absolute stability of market shares) is not sufficient to demonstrate the existence of a tacit agreement. A "meeting of the minds" that lies behind and explains the parallel behavior must also be observed (*Rapport annuel du Conseil de la Concurrence pour l'année 1987, XIV*). Thus the ordinance does not prohibit parallel behavior resulting from oligopolistic interdependence. The standard applied in France to cases of parallel behavior is thus similar to the standard applied at the EU level for Article 85.

For example, in its 1992 decision on the distribution of automobile gasoline (no. 92-D-56, *Rapport du Conseil de la Concurrence pour l'année 1992*, annexe 63, 401), the council refused to consider the parallel behavior of major oil companies when unleaded gas was introduced in France as an anticompetitive tacit agreement to reduce price competition in the French market.

When in 1989 the French government decided to grant a special tax exemption for unleaded gas to facilitate its introduction to the French market, each of the major oil companies started selling not only unleaded gas that met the European Commission's minimum standard specifications (called SP 95) but also an unleaded gas with superior specifications (SP 98), which was deemed better adapted to the French market because a much larger proportion of French cars could use it (only 5 percent of French cars could then use SP 95).

Up to that point, the major oil companies had distributed the unleaded gas they produced either through their own gas stations or through supermarket chains, which bought gas from the oil companies on favorable terms because of the huge quantities they distributed (their total share of the retail gas market was about 50 percent). By reselling the gas as a generic product practically at cost, the supermarkets could undersell the gas stations, which was an irritating problem for the oil companies.

When SP 98 was launched, each oil company argued that its product differed from that of its competitors by virtue of its unique mix of additives and therefore could only be sold as a name-brand product.

Between 1990 and 1992, the supermarket chains' access to SP 98 (the sales of which grew very rapidly) was restricted. Some oil companies argued that they did not have enough product for their own gas station networks. Others claimed they had name-brand products they intended to sell only in their own gas stations. The others conditioned delivery of SP 98 to supermarket chains, for instance, building a special tank for stocking their product so that it would not be mixed with other oil companies' SP 98 or affixing company name and brand names to the gas pumps.

In referring the case to the council, the minister of economic affairs and some distributors argued that the de facto refusal to deal was the result of a tacit collusion, the object of which was to prevent large distributors from selling an important gas product and which had the effect of restraining competition.

Doubtless each oil company wanted to decrease the competitive pressure that large distributors represented at the retail level. However, because none of them had a dominant position on the market, the council addressed only the question of whether their parallel behavior could qualify as an illegal tacit agreement.

In its decision, the council first stated that an oil company's wanting to differentiate one (or several) of its products from the products of its competitors (by including additives in its gas and by selling it under a brand name) could not be considered per se anticompetitive. It then said that there was insufficient evidence of a tacit agreement to refuse to deal. Their behaviors had not been sufficiently identical (and simultaneous) to consider them parallel, and, more importantly, each oil company could reserve the sale of its new unleaded gas to its own network, irrespective of what its competitors did, because it was in its interest to do so. Even if other oil companies had decided to market a generic SP 98 both through their gas stations and through large distributors, another oil company could have reasonably sought a more profitable niche market for a higher priced, differentiated, name-brand fuel.

Vertical Agreements

Because Article 7 does not distinguish between horizontal and other types of contracts, this provision may also be applied to restrictive distribution agreements between manufacturers and their retailers, whether explicit or tacit, if they have the object or the effect of restraining competition.

The council examines both exclusive and selective distribution agreements under the same rule-of-reason standard because it recognizes that such agreements may simultaneously restrict competition at the retail level and increase competition among manufacturers. The council further recognizes that the efficiency effect of exclusive or selective distribution contracts (or other vertical restrictions of trade) depends on how much marginal and inframarginal value consumers place on the services distributors provide.

The council's approach to restrictive exclusive distribution contracts is thus more permissive than that of the European Union. Indeed, under European law, exclusive distribution agreements automatically fall under the prohibition of Article 85-1 but can be exempted under Article 85-3 if they meet certain criteria laid down by the Commission in 1967 and regularly revised since then.

The European authorities' reasoning is based on administrative considerations rather than economic analysis. Article 4 of European Commission ruling no. 17 states that the parties to an agreement found to be prohibited by Article 85-1 cannot claim an exemption under Article 85-3 unless they had notified their agreement. Because firms could not foresee what stance the Commission would take on their particular exclusive distribution agreements, thousands of such agreements were notified, and the Commission found it impossible to examine each one. To bring its work load back to manageable proportions, the Commission found it expedient to issue a general ruling on the conditions under which such agreements would be exempted. But since an Article 85-3 exemption can only apply to agreements that fall under the prohibitions of Article 85-1, the effect of the class exemption was to make all exclusive distribution agreements *a priori* illegal.

Under the French ordinance, there is no notification procedure, and the Competition Council investigates only exclusive (or selective) distribution agreements in which either the minister of economic affairs or a private party (for example, an excluded retailer) has lodged a complaint. As a result, the council's work load in this area is lighter than that of the Commission, and cases are adjudicated individually.

The council does not necessarily consider that an exclusive (or selective) distribution arrangement is *a priori* anticompetitive. But when it is convinced that a particular agreement had an anticompetitive object or effect, it will refuse to grant it an exemption on the basis of Article 10 of the 1986 ordinance if the agreement does not meet the standards set for the European Article 85-3 class exemption for exclusive distribution contracts.

As the council has examined many more cases of selective distribution agreements than of exclusive distribution, the following discussion will center on the former.

In its appraisal of the applicability of Article 7 of the 1986 ordinance to vertical restrictive distribution agreements, the council has focused on the market structure for the relevant products, on whether such agreements limit distributors' ability to independently determine pricing, as well as on whether such agreements had the object or the direct or indirect effect of allowing discrimination among retailers or of unjustified exclusion of certain types of retailers.

In line with the per se ban on resale price maintenance (which applies to all manufacturers irrespective of whether they sell through selected distributors and which is enforced through the courts), and in line with European case law, selective distribution agreements imposing resale prices are considered per se anticompetitive and therefore are prohibited. Manufacturers remain free to suggest resale prices to their retailers as long as these retailers do not risk being excluded from the distribution network if they do not follow these suggestions.

Except in the case of resale price maintenance, a selective distribution system is considered potentially anticompetitive if the manufacturer has a dominant position or if a large number of competing manufacturers must distribute their products through a similar distribution arrangement. Thus, for example, the council's predecessor, the Competition Commission, which applied the same principles as the council, ruled that selective distribution had not impaired competition in the tennis racket (*Rapport de la Commission de la Concurrence pour l'année 1984*, annexe 13, 112) or in the wind-sail sectors (*Rapport de la Commission de la Concurrence pour l'année 1984*, annexe 14, 114) because only a few manufacturers representing a small market share distributed their products through selective distribution systems.

However, when the manufacturer has market power (or when restrictive distribution agreements are widespread among competing manufacturers) a selective distribution agreement that does not impose resale prices will be considered a violation of Article 7 if the requirements the manufacturer sets for accepting a distributor are not explicit, objective, and verifiable, or if the manufacturer excludes *a priori* some type of retailers (such as large retailers or mail-order houses) irrespective of whether they meet its requirements, or if the manufacturer discriminates among retailers of the same category (for example, by refusing to deal with some and accepting others in its network regardless of whether they meet its requirements).

The council first examined selective distribution agreements in a case on the distribution of cosmetics by pharmacists (no. 87-D-15, *Rapport du Conseil de la Concurrence pour l'année 1987*, annexe 24, 43). A number of French pharmaceutical firms sell their most successful and well-known brands of cosmetics only in pharmacies. Pharmacies are highly regulated in France (e.g., on the price of prescription drugs and the creation of new pharmacies), and pharmacists are subject to a rigidly enforced code of ethics, which bans behavior that could be considered as discrediting the profession or a fellow pharmacist. Consequently, price competition among pharmacists is nonexistent.

For a number of years large retail chains have tried to gain access to cosmetics sold through pharmacies and have denounced the selective distribution systems as anticompetitive on the grounds that they unnecessarily suppressed intrabrand competition at the retail level.

Although it is likely that the manufacturers refused to sell their well-known name-brand cosmetics to large distributors because they knew that pharmacists would then refuse to carry them, there was no evidence the pharmacists ever threatened a concerted boycott.

The manufacturers defended the distribution arrangement before the council by arguing that cosmetics were dangerous products requiring counseling that only licensed pharmacists could provide. The manufacturers claimed that interbrand competition was strong and that their distribution arrangements did not significantly restrain competition. Finally, the manufacturers pointed out that the cosmetics they sold through pharmacists were competing with cosmetics from other manufacturers who had chosen not to sell through pharmacists but through large retail stores.

The distributors claimed that they were willing to abide by any condition the manufacturers imposed (such as hiring competent salesmen with a degree in pharmacy).

The council concluded that the cosmetics sold only through pharmacists were not close substitutes for other cosmetics distributed through large-scale retailers, as evidenced by the persistent, wide price differentials. The council then ruled that the distribution contracts violated Article 7 because they completely eliminated intrabrand competition since pharmacists did not compete on prices and they prevented distributors who were not pharmacists from carrying such goods even if they were technically able to provide the services (such as counseling) that the manufacturers desired.

The council ordered the manufacturers to spell out the technical, objective, and verifiable requirements necessary to be accepted into their distribution networks and also ordered them to sell to any distributor (whether or not a pharmacist) that met these requirements.

General Sales Conditions and Price Differentiation

Beyond selective or exclusive distribution agreements, general sales conditions of firms that do not have a restrictive retail network have also come under the council's scrutiny, even for firms without a dominant position. Such general sales conditions (which each firm must provide to retailers on request) are considered to be tacit agreements between the firm and the distributors carrying its goods and therefore may be examined under Article 7. The government and distributors have tried repeatedly to bring price discrimination cases under council review. They have argued that differences in buying conditions granted to different retailers—either because the manufacturers' general sales conditions were discriminatory or there were special discounts, not mentioned in their general sales conditions, to selected distributors—prevented retailers that were buying on less favorable terms from competing.

The council has tended to reject these claims, arguing, first, that price differentiation is not necessarily indicative of price discrimination and, second, that price discrimination, when it is established, is not necessarily anticompetitive. The council believes that the government (wrongly) tends to equate competition at the retail level with absolute transparency of general sales conditions and with strict equality of treatment of all competing retailers. Thus the government considers a special discount to a distributor as in itself constituting an agreement restrictive of competition.

The council, on the other hand, expects that some distributors will be able to negotiate more favorable terms and that this is an intrinsic part of the competitive process among retailers. Further, the situation of a particular distributor relative to that of its competitors is in not in itself relevant in assessing the intensity of competition in the market when many retailers are competing. Thus, for the council, the government's position on this issue confuses the distinction between protection of individual competitors and the protection of the competitive process.

Abuse of Dominant Position

Article 10 of the 1986 ordinance prohibits "the abusive exploitation by a firm or a group of firms of its dominant position in the domestic market or a substantial part of the domestic market when it is designed for or may have the effect of curbing, restraining, or distorting competition." As was mentioned earlier, the council has looked at comparatively few cases of potential infringements of Article 10.

The boundaries of the relevant market or markets being considered must be established to determine whether a firm actually holds a dominant position, but they are rarely defined solely on statistical evidence (even if data on cross-price elasticities between various goods or services are available). This reflects the council's and the Court of Appeals's difficulties in assessing the validity of econometrics studies. The council often takes a more qualitative approach to the market definition problem, examining factors such as the extent to which a specific need can technically be met by various products or services, comparison of the prices of these products or services, determinants of their demand over time, product differentiation, brand differentiation, or comparisons of distribution channels.

The overall goal of the council's approach is to establish the extent of demand substitutability. Supply substitutability is generally not used to establish market boundaries but is considered at a later stage of the analysis to establish whether the firm has a dominant market position.

The council has tended to define markets narrowly. For example, in a case involving the possible abuse of dominance of a book club (no. 89-D-41, *Rapport du Conseil de la Concurrence pour l'année 1989*, annexe 48, 139), the council said book clubs and bookstores were different markets because they provided different services. That is, book clubs do not sell to nonmembers: They impose minimum yearly purchases of books on their members, they sell only through mail order, they sell only the books that they have selected (and which have been available in bookstores for a certain time), they provide information on their selections to subscribers, and they can discount books nine months after the books' first editions have been released (which bookstores cannot do, due to a 1981 law allowing resale price maintenance by book publishers).

The courts have sometimes resisted the council's narrow definition. In the book club case, although the Paris Court of Appeals sustained the council's market definition, the French Supreme Court overturned the appellate court, finding the above-mentioned factors insufficient to establish that there was a separate market for book clubs. The case returned to the Paris Court of Appeals, which reiterated its analysis, adding further considerations to buttress its first opinion.

The wording of Article 10, in particular its reference to "a domestic market" or a substantial part of such a market, has led some to question whether the prohibition on abuse of dominant position could be applied to local monopolies such as cable TV, water distribution, undertakers, waste disposal, public lighting, and other sectors where local authorities grant private firms an exclusive license to operate. The council holds that each such local market should be considered to be a specific domestic market (because consumers cannot substitute between the services offered locally and similar services offered elsewhere when an operator has an exclusive concession). In contrast, the courts have wavered in their interpretation of the law and have occasionally used a rather confusing approach, in which they first establish the existence of separate "local" markets in which a firm enjoys a dominant position and then aggregating its dominance in local markets into an assessment of "domestic" market dominance.

In line with the European Court of Justice's interpretation of Article 86 of the EU treaty, in order to establish whether a firm has a dominant position the council assesses whether the firm can to an appreciable degree act independently of its competitors. It takes into account a variety of factors: the firm's market share, distribution of market shares of its competitors, its degree of vertical integration compared with its competitors, the level of differentiation of its product, the ease or difficulty of entry into the industry as well as the history of entry.

Firms belonging to prosperous financial groups will ceteris paribus more likely be considered dominant if their competitors do not belong to similar groups because capital markets are assumed to discriminate in favor of large financial groups, which can offer their affiliates easier and less-costly access to funds than independent firms enjoy.

Article 8 of the 1986 ordinance prohibits anticompetitive abuses by firms "or group of firms" holding a dominant position in a market; this wording raises the question of whether a tight oligopoly could be considered a group of firms collectively holding a dominant position. In such instances, the anticompetitive abuse of each member could be considered as an Article 8 violation and sanctioned even if none of the firms involved had an individual dominant position and even if no tacit agreement existed among them.

The minister of economic affairs has urged the council to adopt this wide interpretation of the scope of Article 10. However, the council and the Paris Court of Appeals have both resisted such attempts, limiting the interpretation of "group of firms" to cases in which the firm under scrutiny had a financial link with some of its competitors (and in which they together had a dominant position on the relevant market).

When it deals with potential abuses of dominant position, the council refrains from taking a normative approach to prices or profit margins. Thus, low output, high absolute price levels, price increases, and large profit margins are not regarded as evidence of an abusive practice by a dominant firm. Practices that may qualify as abuses of dominant position are for the most part limited to attempts to prevent market entry (e.g., no. 92-D-26, *Rapport du Conseil de la Concurrence pour l'année 1992*, annexe 33, 248) or to drive a small competitor out of the market—for example, through predatory pricing (defined as prices below the variable costs of production) or tie-in sales, in which the dominant firm tries to use its monopoly power in one market to acquire a dominant position in a related competitive market.

The only case in which the council made an exception to this rule concerned the French musical authors' guild (SACEM), which has a de facto monopoly on the collection of royalties due to composers and lyricists. In this case the Paris Court of Appeals asked the council not only to deliver a nonbinding opinion on whether SACEM, by overcharging French discothèques, had violated Article 86 of the EU treaty but also to do so following the methodology laid down in a previous opinion of the European Court of Justice. In it, the EU Court of Justice had held that a royalty-collecting agency could be found to have abused its dominant position in a substantial part of the common market (for example, in one member state) if its gross collection per discothèque (including part of its administrative costs and the royalties due to the composers) was significantly higher than the gross collection per discothèque of similar organizations in other European member states. Having found that SACEM charged significantly higher gross royalties to French discos than similar monopolistic collecting agencies did in other member states, the council ruled that it had indeed violated Article 86.

As with its position on general sales conditions cited earlier, the council does not hold that price differentiation is necessarily price discrimination nor that price discrimination by a dominant firm is necessarily an anticompetitive abuse of that position, even if the victims of the discrimination see it as unfair (e.g., no. 91-D-50, *Rapport du Conseil de la Concurrence pour l'année 1991*, annexe 57). Along the same line, the council has stated that manufacturers, even if they have dominant positions, have the right to organize their distribution networks as they see fit (and in particular to dispense with intermediaries or retailers if they decide to sell directly to final consumers). Thus, it has rejected complaints by discontinued distributors or retailers that their elimination from the market violated Article 8 in cases involving the distribution of petroleum products (no. 89-D-44, *Rapport du Conseil de la Concurrence pour l'année 1989*, annexe 51, 164) and games (no. 89-D-39, *Rapport du Conseil de la Concurrence pour l'année 1989*, annexe 46, 136).

However, the council has cited as violations of Article 10 a variety of strategies to prevent entry of competitors or to limit their development (either in the market in which the firm is dominant or in a downstream market if the dominant firm is vertically integrated)—these include predatory pricing or tie-in sales and refusals to deal.

For example, in a case concerning calcium used in foundries, the council established that the dominant supplier had attempted to stifle the development of another firm, which had invented a process for transforming calcium that improved its quality and permitted new uses, by refusing to supply this firm with the raw material it needed until it could come up with a competing process (no. 92-D-26, *Rapport du Conseil de la Concurrence pour l'année 1992*, annexe 33, 248).

In another case, concerning the market for pig-iron water mains, the council held that Pont-à-Mousson, a very well-established and influential firm in France, had a dominant position; its only competitor, a newly established subsidiary of a British firm, had less than 2 percent of the French market. Pont-à-Mousson violated Article 10 by circulating unfounded rumors among local authorities about the quality of its competitor's mains and by systematically lowering its original bids when contracts were awarded to its competitor in order to get the competitor's contract canceled (no. 92-D-62, *Rapport du Conseil de la Concurrence pour l'année 1992*, annexe 69, 429).

Also, when dominant firms practice price discrimination (in some instances) and resale price maintenance (in all instances), these are also considered to be Article 10 violations.

Abuse of Dependency

Article 10-2 also prohibits anticompetitive abuses by firms that do not have a dominant position but hold another firm (whether a supplier or a customer) in their dependency. As was mentioned earlier, this provision was mainly designed to protect manufacturers from the (supposedly abusive) demands of large retail chains, although several cases referred to the council were introduced by small retailers that complained of having lost their contracts as selected distributors of well-known products or of having lost their franchises.

The enforcement of Article 10-2 of this ordinance raises difficult questions. The concept of dependency has no basis in economic analysis and is therefore hard to define. In its most important decision to date on the issue (no. 93-D-21, *Rapport du Conseil de la Concurrence pour l'année 1993*, annexe 28, 206), the council indicated that it considers a number of factors to determine a manufacturer's dependency on a retailer: the retailer's share of total sales of the manufacturer, the importance of the distributor in the sales of the relevant category of products, the notoriety of the manufacturer's brand name or of the retailer, whether the retailer is distributor of the product because of the manufacturer's strategic choice or of technical necessity, and whether the manufacturer has equivalent alternatives. This list suggests that the council will limit its qualification of a manufacturer's dependency vis-à-vis a retailer to cases in which the dependency is the result of objective (structural or technical) reasons but will refuse to find dependency when the manufacturer has deliberately chosen to concentrate its sales with one retailer.

The question remains as to what constitutes an "equivalent alternative." If, for example, a large retailer refuses to carry the products of a manufacturer whose products are sold through all other large retailers, can the manufacturer be considered to have distribution alternatives or should one distributor's refusal to carry the product be characterized as leaving the manufacturer no alternative for selling in all retail shops? (See, e.g., no. 94-D-60, *Rapport du Conseil de la Concurrence pour l'année 1994*, annexe 67, 495).

"Abuse of dependency" is equally difficult to define. Presumably, it refers to large distributors' unjustified (or unfair) demands for discounts on a manufacturer's goods as a condition of carrying them. But economic analysis cannot determine what is a justified (or fair) demand in a vertical negotiation between a manufacturer and a distributor, both of which are interested in dealing with each other and each trying to secure the largest part of the common advantage).

Article 10-2 limits the prohibition of abuses of dependency to cases in which these abuses had the object or may have had the effect of restraining competition. However, unfair dealings between a manufacturer and a distributor do not necessarily restrain competition among the manufacturers or among the distributors. Even in the major cases in which it determined that some manufacturers were dependent on a retailer and that the retailers had made abusive demands, the council remained unconvinced that competition had been restrained (See, e.g., no. 93-D-21, *Rapport du Conseil de la Concurrence pour l'année 1993*, annexe 28, 204).

Merger Control

As was mentioned earlier, the council's task when a merger is referred to it is to assess whether the merger's potential to further economic progress outweighs the potential anticompetitive effect.

Merger control in France can be applied to all mergers that do not have an EU dimension, that meet the thresholds set in the 1986 ordinance, and that may restrain competition even if such mergers will not create a dominant position. Thus the scope of the council's control is in principle larger than the scope for EU merger control, because at the Community level only mergers that create or reinforce a dominant position can be declared incompatible with the Common Market. However, this difference of scope is not as important as it would seem, for two reasons. First, case law at the European level (in particular, the Nestlé/Perrier case) reveals that the Commission broadened the scope of Article 2 of the EU merger regulation by considering that mergers that reinforce an oligopoly can be prohibited on the basis of the fact that they reinforce a collective dominant position for the members of the oligopoly even if they do not confer a dominant position to the merging parties. Second, most of the cases that the French minister of economic affairs has referred to the council have involved firms with substantial market shares. In these mergers, the central question is whether the change in industry concentration is likely to confer or reinforce a dominant position for the merging firms (that is, the ability for these firms to behave independently of their competitors).

In its appraisal of the potential effect of the merger on competition, the council not only takes into account the structural changes to the industry at the time of the merger on French territory but it also considers the international environment of the industry concerned and examines the dynamics of the market.

For example, when it examined a proposed joint venture between Metaleurop and Heubach & Lindgens (no. 94-A-18, 17 May 1994, *Rapport du Conseil de la Concurrence pour l'année 1994*, annexe 95, 671), which both produce lead oxide (used in batteries, glass, and paint), the council did not object, even though in France the combined market share of the parties was close to 90 percent. The council first remarked that it could be economically profitable for major industrial users to produce lead oxide themselves if their level of consumption exceeded a few thousand tons per year. Equipment and know-how were readily available from a number of sources in the world, and the major European industrial users were in fact vertically integrated and ready to sell their excess production, since transportation costs were reasonably low and rarely exceeded 10 percent of production costs for shipment in the European Union. (At the time of the merger, integrated manufacturers accounted for about 20 percent of the commercial supply of lead oxide in the Union.)

The council also noted a high degree of concentration on the demand side; in France the 15 largest customers of the parties to the merger accounted for 95 percent of their total sales, and their 15 largest EU customers accounted for 55 percent of total sales. The council also took into account the fact that concern about the environmental hazards associated with the use of lead or of lead-based products had contributed to the development of substitute products, which were expected to replace lead oxide in the medium term. For all these reasons, the council decided that the joint venture posed limited risks to competition.

When an examined merger is unlikely to lead to the creation of a unified dominant position for the parties but could conceivably lead to the reinforcement of an oligopoly, the council, following the lead of the Merger Task Force of the European Commission, usually focuses on a structural analysis of the industry in which the merger is taking place—including supply-side substitutability, the height of entry barriers, actual or potential vertical integration, concentration on the demand side and the distribution of market shares among the suppliers—to assess whether the mergers are likely to weaken competition. Theories of oligopolistic rivalries (focusing on market transparency, distribution of excess capacity, and game-theoretic considerations) have not so far significantly influenced the council's approach to mergers in oligopolistic markets.

Thus, for example, when it examined a proposed merger between two manufacturers of PET (polyethylène teraphtalate) plastic bottles for soft drinks and sparkling mineral waters, the council first established that nonplastic containers (metal or cardboard) or other plastic containers (such as PVC bottles) were not substitutes for PET bottles, at least for some producers of carbonated drinks (no. 93-A-17, 16 November 1993, *Rapport du Conseil de la Concurrence pour l'année 1993*, annexe 82, 535). Indeed, PET can retain gas better than other materials, and firms such as Perrier and Coca-Cola cannot easily replace PET bottles with PVC bottles. The council then observed that after the merger there would be two major suppliers of PET bottles in the French market: the parties to the merger, with a market share of 35 percent, and Millet PET Packaging, a subsidiary of the American firm Johnson Controls, with an equivalent market share. It also noted that if the price of PET bottles were to increase significantly as a result of the merger, nothing would prevent either carbonated drink producers from making their own PET bottles or new PET manufacturers from entering the market. Entry barriers seemed low, as evidenced by the fact that during the five years preceding the proposed merger three manufacturers had entered the French market, and two of these increased their production capacity during that period. The council also observed that buyer concentration was high; for example, Coca-Cola accounted for more than 82 percent of the total sales of the acquiring firm. Thus the council held that the merger did not threaten competition.

A second difference between EU and French merger control lies in the fact that the possibility of an efficiency defense for anticompetitive mergers is written into the French ordinance, whereas the EU merger control does not formally allow for such a defense. Again, this difference in approach may seem more important than it really is when one considers case law. The Commission has in fact occasionally considered efficiency in assessing whether a particular merger created or strengthened a dominant position. On the other hand, from 1990 on, France's Competition Council has insisted that an efficiency defense for an otherwise anticompetitive merger is admissible only if the parties to it demonstrate that alleged efficiency gains could not be obtained without the merger. The council has thereby aligned its analysis in the merger area with its analysis in the area of anticompetitive practices.

Thus, for example, in its 1990 opinion on the proposed merger between advertising firms Eurocom and Carat Espace (no. 90-A-10, *Rapport du Conseil de la Concurrence pour l'année 1990*, annexe 80, 180), the council indicated that the parties had argued that their merger would allow them to develop synergies—Eurocom being primarily an advertising agency, Carat a media planning specialist, and both of them being major wholesale traders of advertising space. But the council said the firms had failed to establish that, in the French market, Eurocom could not independently develop a media planning capability equal (or superior) to that of Carat or that Carat (which was already the largest wholesale trader of advertising space in France and considered to be the best media planner) could not further develop its business without the support of Eurocom. The council thus argued that the firms involved should be allowed to merge their international networks but not their operations on French territory. Ultimately, the merger was abandoned.

Thus, overall, the council's conditions for admissibility of the efficiency defense mean that such a defense will rarely be successful.

4

Germany

KAI-UWE KÜHN

This chapter presents an overview of the most important areas of German competition policy, with special emphasis on its international aspects. From the German point of view, the most important international aspect concerns the development of competition policy in the European Union (EU). German policy goals for the institutional framework of EU competition policy and Germany's attempts to influence that policy are based on a strong conviction that German competition policy has a successful history. To understand the potential conflicts arising from a globalization of competition policy, it is therefore most important to clearly understand the philosophy of German competition policy and how it is translated into practice. As a result, this chapter is in large measure an exposition of German competition policy. Policy decisions are explained on the basis of the underlying philosophy and evaluated from a welfare economics perspective. Differences between German and other competition policies are pointed out where appropriate.

I begin by giving a brief background on the history of German competition policy, the philosophy underlying the policy's past 30 years, and an exposition of the main aims of competition policy today. I also discuss the important subject of the governance of competition policy. The next section discusses the main pillars of the original 1958 Law

Kai-Uwe Kühn is associate professor at Institut d'Analisi Economica in Barcelona and research fellow of the Center for Economic Policy Research, London. The author is grateful for helpful comments from Edward M. Graham, Luigi Franzoni, Michael Katz, Carmen Matutes, Pierre Regibeau, J. David Richardson, and Amrit Singh. All errors and opinions expressed are those of the author.

against Restraints of Competition: cartel prohibition, industry exemptions, and the control of abuses of "dominant position." The chapter then turns to merger policy—the currently most important policy area—to the policies toward vertical restraints of competition, and to a review of the policies toward research and development cooperation. Finally, I place German competition policies in the international context, in particular discussing issues that arise from European integration and EU competition policy. Furthermore, the relationship between German competition policy, industrial policy, and Germany's attitude to strategic trade policy are discussed.

Development and Philosophy of German Competition Policy

Cartelization and Competition Policy before World War II

Before the nineteenth century, there was no modern market economy in Germany. Most professions, including trading and retail, were closely regulated by the guild system, which also controlled entry. This changed in 1810-11, when Prussia became the first German state to introduce legislation that based the economic system on the freedom to do business and the freedom to contract. This legislation was extended to the rest of Germany in 1869, shortly before the German unification in 1871. Liberalization of the economy coincided with rapid industrialization.

Already in the 1870s, cartel agreements were recognized as a policy problem. However, since the freedom of contracting was a basic feature of the laws governing competition (*Gewerbeordnung*), preventing such contracting practices seemed difficult. In 1897 the Reichsgericht (highest court of the empire) ruled that cartels did not violate the right of other parties to do business. It interpreted the freedom to do business as the right of business to be free from interference by the state in a classical, liberal sense.

This judgment opened the way for rapid cartelization of German industry. By 1905 an official inquiry conducted by the Department for the Interior (Reichsamt des Innern) found 385 cartels with about 12,000 members. Later estimates put the number of cartels in Germany in 1911 at between 550 and 600 and at 1,500 in 1923. The large number of cartels in 1923 also reflects the fact that the state used cartels to run the war economy of World War I.

In 1923 the government tried to combat the growing economic power of cartels with a regulation barring the "abuse of economic power." This earliest attempt to limit the general freedom of contracting in order to achieve competition policy goals has been widely considered ineffective. In particular, scholars point to the further growth in the number of cartels to 3,000 or 4,000 by the end of the Weimar Republic in 1933. It should be noted, however, that the measure was never intended to stop the formation of cartels but only to limit their power vis-à-vis business partners or consumers. The move also has to be seen in the context of the 1923 inflation. The government intended to have powers of price control over cartels so that the monetary reform of 1923 would not lose credibility as a result of drastic price rises by cartels. With the takeover of the Nazis in 1933, the government promoted cartelization as a means of control over national industry, presaging the planned economy of the later war years.

Overall, the pre-World War II experience of Germany was characterized by a rapid process of concentration, which accelerated during the war years. Essentially, the philosophy until 1933 was to give priority to the freedom of contracting unless market power tended to excessively restrict the interest of other market participants. Thus, a strong priority was given to keeping the government from intervening in the structure of the economy except to correct abuses of private power.

Philosophy Underlying German Antitrust Law

Two major influences have shaped current German competition policy. First, after World War II, the Allies imposed a decartelization policy, which substantially reduced the concentration of German industry. This intervention was inspired by US antitrust law but also had a political dimension. The Allies wanted to curtail the political power of German industry, which was seen as detrimental to the development of a democratic political system.

Second, German economic policy in general became strongly influenced by the German neoliberal school of economics and its idea of *Ordnungspolitik*. This school supported a free-market economy but recognized the role of the state in guaranteeing the institutional framework (or *Ordnung*) necessary for market exchange. The exclusive purpose of economic policy, according to this view, is to guarantee such a framework. The whole approach can be seen as one of setting a constitutional structure for economic exchange with the aim of guaranteeing "liberty" not only in the political but also in the economic sphere.[1]

In contrast to the nineteenth century view of economic "liberty," these policies do not aim merely at keeping the state from interfering with the market; they aim more generally at preventing anyone with economic power from limiting the freedom of others to act. While economists of

---

1. Economic policies aimed at guaranteeing economic structures that are conducive to competition and voluntary exchange are usually referred to as *Ordnungspolitik* in the German economic policy debate.

the neoliberal school were quite certain that such a constitutional framework would be economically beneficial, the primary motivation underlying German competition policy rules was a constitutionalist one, not one driven by economic concerns about an optimal allocation of resources (Herdzina 1987, 123).

The two roots of German competition policy manifest themselves quite clearly in the 1958 Law Against Restraints of Competition (*Gesetz gegen Wettbewerbsbeschränkungen*, or GWB). The two main principles were that (with some exceptions) cartels were prohibited and that firms with market power were subject to control for potential "abuse of dominant position." Since then, reforms of cartel legislation have successively tightened the means of control for the antitrust authorities. In particular, the 1973 reform of antitrust law prohibited implicit collusion and introduced merger control into German law for the first time. It also prohibited retail price maintenance.[2] Later changes in the law were mainly concerned with closing loopholes in merger control and controlling of dominant position. In particular, the concept of "financial strength"[3] is now clearly established as an important factor for determining a dominant position. Other changes have mainly concerned strengthening the powers of the German cartel office in response to restrictive interpretations of the law by the courts and adapting German legislation to EU law.

Current German Competition Policy

The central concept in German competition policy today is "dominant position." Dominance is established not just by the possession of a large market share but also by a high degree of forward and backward integration. Another important factor is the financial strength of a firm. The state is supposed to prevent the establishment of dominant positions and control firms holding such positions because they reduce the freedom of other actors in the economy. In this sense, competition policy intervenes in the economy to check the growth of firms.

Competition policy essentially has two parts. Merger policy is aimed at limiting the external growth of firms. Firms that achieve dominant positions through internal growth are subject to control for abuse of dominant position. Most German competition policy falls in one of these categories. Because the courts have made it difficult to prove abuse of dominant position, actual practice seems to be rapidly converging on an

---

2. It should be noted that all of these regulations had been demanded when the GWB was first put through Parliament in 1957, but successful lobbying by industry somewhat undermined the initial goal of a tight competition policy. This explains many of the exceptions, based on efficiency defenses, to the prohibition of cartels.

3. The term "financial strength" is used very loosely and often simply refers to "bigness."

almost exclusive focus on checking the external growth of firms—that is, on merger policy.

The Governance of German Competition Policy

One of the main distinguishing features of German competition policy is the institutional framework within which it is conducted. It is characterized by a very clear allocation of decision rights to specific institutions and a large degree of transparency in decision making. The main executive body of competition policy is the Bundeskartellamt, or Federal Cartel Office, which is responsible for both merger control and control of abuses of dominant position.

While institutionally subordinate to the Ministry of Economics, the Cartel Office independently decides how to treat individual cases. Further, it is restricted to competition policy and cannot consider industrial policy, public interest, or other economic policy concerns the Ministry of Economics might have. The Cartel Office is organized similarly to a court of justice, and its decisions can be appealed through general judicial procedures. In some cases, the minister of economics can overrule the decisions of the Cartel Office or courts on public interest grounds, a feature that will be discussed in the section on merger policy below. Suffice it to say here that this provision adds to the transparency of the process, because the minister of economics has to overrule competition policy concerns publicly and specify the overriding policy interests.

The Monopolkommission, or Monopolies Commission, is another important institution for German competition policy. It is a body of experts, including academic economists and lawyers, who are not directly involved in the policy process. The commission reports every two years on the state of concentration in the economy and critically reviews the Cartel Office's decisions. It can also initiate reports on areas of competition policy it deems particularly important and is usually asked to review firms' applications for ministerial exemptions. The commission's expert opinion is thus particularly important for initiating changes in competition policy practices. Finally, there is a strong federalist element in competition policy, in the sense that cartel offices of the *Länder* (i.e., the states) deal with cases of only regional importance.

Core Elements

In this section, we consider the main ingredients of the original 1958 Law Against Restraints of Competition, the GWB. The more recent rules concerning mergers are relegated to a separate section, as are the rules governing contractual vertical restraints. In this section, we discuss the three remaining elements of German competition policy rules: the prohibition of cartels, the system of exemptions from the cartel prohibition for some sectors in the economy, and the framework for controlling abuse of dominant position.

Prohibition of Cartels

The GWB prohibits cartel agreements between firms that reduce competition, particularly agreements on prices and production quotas. The general cartel prohibition is, however, significantly weakened by a series of exemptions. Efficiency defenses for cooperation and strategic trade policy concerns explicitly encroach on German competition policy via these exemptions.

Cartels on Contractual Conditions and Discounting Cartels

Exemptions for cartels on contractual conditions (*Konditionenkartelle*) and discounting cartels (*Rabattkartelle*) have probably been included in the GWB because they promise to increase market transparency for customers. This seems most credible in the case of cartels on contractual conditions, which cover the standardization in sales contracts of general business conditions, delivery conditions, and payment conditions. Agreements on prices (including discounts) may not be part of such cartels. Numbering about 50 as of 1986 (Audretsch 1989), conditions cartels are relatively important. Unfortunately, little is known about how these cartels operate and what distinguishes their practices from those of other industries in which industry organizations provide sample contracts that are nonbinding for firms (as is the case in the rental housing market). It appears, however, that this form of cartel should raise relatively little competition policy concern.

More dubious is the role of discounting cartels (or rebating cartels), which determine the discounts from a given base price cooperatively, though the base price itself cannot be subject to cooperative agreement. Such discounts would include quantity discounts or discounts for cash payments. While it is again intuitive that such agreements might facilitate the comparison of two offers for a customer, such market transparency always has a downside as well. In particular, the fixing of discounts makes it harder to grant secret price cuts to customers, which would facilitate implicit collusion. More importantly, it appears possible that, by setting discounting schemes in a coordinated manner, firms may be able to also reduce the incentives for competition on the base price.[4]

---

4. I have some doubts that this argument would actually be valid for the discounting strategies observed in practice. It seems that, in order to commit to high prices, firms would want to establish very drastic quantity discounts. This would reduce the incen-

Discounting cartels were initially quite important but have dwindled to an insignificant number. Part of the reason for this has been the hostile position of the Bundeskartellamt toward such agreements.

As with all legal cartels (except for export cartels), the participants in the contract have to notify the Cartel Office that they are forming a cartel. Conditions cartels and discounting cartels are legal as long as the Cartel Office does not object to them within three months after notification.

The cartel authorities have been increasingly restrictive about discounting cartels. In particular, cartels that agreed on rebates based on total turnover were initially allowed but are now prohibited. Such discounts are today interpreted as loyalty rebates, which are seen as detrimental to competition. With this change, the German cartel authorities have adapted their practice to that of the European Union.[5]

Cost-Reducing Cartels

As discussed above, allocative efficiency is not the driving principle behind German competition policy. For example, potential efficiency gains and synergies play an almost negligible role in the Cartel Office's decisions on mergers. Curiously enough, efficiency gains are the most important reason for permitting cartelization in German law. The arguments for allowing some cartels are very similar to those economists would be willing to accept as efficiency defenses for mergers (Kühn, Seabright, and Smith 1992, section 5): synergy effects and capacity reduction in declining industries. Regarding such cartels, competition policy has to consider the potential trade-off between allocative losses and gains in productive efficiency.

A classic efficiency defense is captured in the concept of a "rationalization cartel." To gain the Cartel Office's permission to form such a cartel, firms have to show they will achieve significant cost reductions through the cooperative agreement. Furthermore, these reductions have to outweigh the resulting decrease in competition between the firms. The courts have interpreted the requirement that the member firms of the cartel "improve the satisfaction of demand" by achieving efficiency gains in production to imply that such cartels cannot be formed to coordinate price rises.[6] Nonetheless, Audretsch (1989) finds some evidence

---

tives to lower the base price. In general, firms are much more concerned about limiting the amount of discounts.

5. Note, however, that EU law does not explicitly permit any cartels. Nevertheless, discounts based on total turnover are seen as anticompetitive in and of themselves in EU competition policy.

6. There is a consistent practice in German competition policy where cost reductions are only considered to be beneficial if they are passed on to the consumer in form of price reductions. In this sense, German competition policy is concerned only with consumer surplus.

that such cartels tend to raise prices faster than other firms in the industry. The Cartel Office can also permit the coordination of prices or the formation of joint purchasing or sales organizations "if rationalization cannot be achieved without them."

There seems to be little doubt that rationalization cartels allow firms to raise prices significantly. In this sense, we have a pure efficiency defense for cartel formation. However, it is handled quite restrictively. The main difference between the rationalization cartel and an efficiency defense for mergers is that cartels may not persist. Indeed, because profits are not consolidated within the organization,[7] competitive pressures may (and do) lead to a cartel's eventual dissolution. German cartel law thus raises the question of whether an efficiency defense for cartel formation is preferable to an efficiency defense for mergers.[8]

The grounds for allowing "specialization cartels," which typically limit participants' production to specified product lines, is harder to see. Yet in such cases, no efficiency defense is needed for the cartel to become legalized; the cartel becomes legal unless the Cartel Office objects within three months. Given that specialization cartels are numerically almost as important (20 to 30 at any given time) and given the potential constraints on competition in quality and variety, it seems rather puzzling that this form of cartel is permitted. It is somewhat comforting that the permissive way in which these collusive agreements are handled is fairly unusual in the otherwise tight framework of the law.

The most important type of cartel permitted in Germany in terms of numbers (152 in 1992) is the cooperative agreement between small and medium-size companies aimed at rationalization "as long as competition on the market is not considerably affected" (GWB). The government has in fact promoted cooperation between small companies and even issued a booklet advising small and medium-size companies how to structure such cooperation so that the Cartel Office will not object. While one might see the advantage of strengthening smaller companies in their competition with firms that hold a larger market share, this is almost certainly not the motivation behind allowing and even promoting such cartels. Making cooperation easy for small firms is rather an expression of a conscious policy of favoring small firms, derived from the idea that small and medium-size companies are of themselves desirable for society. It also reflects the considerable lobby-

---

7. This is also one reason efficiency gains from cartelization will tend to be smaller than those from mergers.

8. I do not want to imply that any conscious decision on the part of German policymakers has led to the differences in treatment of cartels and mergers. However, the actual practice seems to make some sense economically. The issue of whether efficiency defenses are more appropriate for cartels or mergers apparently has not been discussed in the economics literature to any extent.

ing power of the organizations representing small and medium-size industries.[9]

In the group of potentially cost-reducing cartel agreements, "crisis cartels" are also permitted. These are meant to lead to an efficient reduction in capacities by participating firms in declining industries. Although there is not much theoretical research on this subject, there may be inefficiencies in the exit pattern in declining industries (Ghemawhat and Nalebuff 1984) that could be avoided by allowing cooperation. Only one such cartel has ever been permitted in Germany.

A similarly negligible role has been played by "emergency cartels," which are cartels authorized by the minister of economics for political reasons. These cartels have been created to give the government the means to let public-interest concerns overrule competition policy considerations in particular cases. As with ministerial intervention in merger policy, this instrument has been used very cautiously. Another fairly innocuous and unimportant form of cartel is the "standardization cartel," which consists simply of contracts between firms that aim at using the same technical standards and norms.

Cartels Affecting Foreign Trade

The principal way in which trade policy has been allowed to affect German competition policy has been through rules permitting the establishment of export and import cartels. The arguments in support of them are classical trade policy arguments: such cartels could not be abolished as long as other countries allowed them and as long as German firms faced trade barriers abroad. Indeed, the United States and the United Kingdom, along with most other countries, permit export cartels. Probably because of the strong concerns of the cartel authorities about competition within Germany, import cartels have never played any role in trade policy and have not existed for 20 years. However, next to cartels established by small and medium-size firms, export cartels are the most important form of legal cartels. They are a classic, pure restraint of competition. While export cartels are illegal under EU law, there were still 53 export cartels in Germany in 1986, down from 66 in 1974.[10]

---

9. This can be seen, for example, in the federal government's comments on the latest report of the Cartel Office. Repeatedly, it is emphasized that the competition policies of the government will be beneficial for small and medium-size businesses, or *Mittelstand* (Deutscher Bundestag, Drucksache 12/5200).

10. Later figures apparently are not available because export cartels only concern extraterritorial markets and, as a result, do not have to be notified to the Cartel Office. German courts have also severely restricted the ability of the Cartel Office to control these cartels, as their effect is purely extraterritorial.

Implicit Collusion

The primary goal of forbidding cartels is to make the cartel contract legally unenforceable. However, cartel agreements may alternatively be enforced through punishments for deviation from cartel behavior such as price wars (as, for example, in the case of the American railroad cartel; see Porter 1985). For this reason, the GWB cartel prohibition extends beyond making cartel contracts unenforceable and threatens to fine firms that practice cartel behavior. This implies that cartel authorities are required to detect and punish implicit collusion.

The ability to act against implicit collusion had been severely curbed before 1973 by the federal courts' insistence that there had to be proof of a cartel contract between the colluding parties, in the sense of German contract law, in order for implicit collusion to be illegal. This led to an explicit prohibition of implicit collusion (*Abgestimmtes Verhalten*) in the cartel law reform of 1973. The new rule (section 25, GWB) now relates to the behavior of firms, not to their contracts.

The fact that most competition policy actions against price collusion are still conducted under the rules of formal cartel contracts and not under rules forbidding implicit collusion is probably due to the general difficulties encountered with proving collusive behavior. The legal doctrine that has developed in this context has further weakened the position of the cartel authorities in tackling implicitly collusive behavior by requiring cartel authorities to prove intent. This seems practically impossible in the absence of a written agreement. Consequently, the main role of a policy prohibiting cartels has to be seen as rendering cartel contracts unenforceable.

An Evaluation of German Cartel Policy

The large number of exemptions gives German competition authorities much scope for permitting cartels. There are more than 300 legal cartels in Germany, most of which were formed on the basis of an efficiency defense. Much of the current practice could probably be defended on economic grounds, in particular when viewed in conjunction with a merger policy that almost completely disregards efficiency defenses. For example, it would seem somewhat contradictory not to intervene in mergers between small firms but to disallow cooperation that allows residual competition to remain. In this sense, the relatively large number of cartels in Germany (compared with those in the United States) may not reflect the whole picture because there is not enough information about the relative frequency of mergers among small and medium-size firms.

The main problem in this area of cartel policy is that the policy goals are unclear. The exceptions to the cartel prohibition as they stand are problematic mainly because they represent a collection of rules adopted to serve special interests. Relating the permission of legalized cartels more closely to merger policy might help focus policymaking in this area and clear up the role of efficiency defenses in German competition policy.

Cartels that affect international trade should definitely be taken out of the catalog of cartel exemptions. Given the typical arguments against their abolishment, it would probably be best to prohibit trade cartels at an international level, preferably in the context of the General Agreement on Tariffs and Trade (GATT).

Industry Exemptions

The law against restraints of competition explicitly exempts several industries from specific competition policy rules, including the cartel prohibition. However, the law explicitly covers government-owned businesses; unless they operate in an exempted industry, the same rules for cartel behavior, merger policy, and other restraints of competition apply. For example, the Cartel Office prohibited the Federal Republic of Germany from acquiring majority ownership in an oil company because it would have strengthened a dominant position in the market for gasoline (*Wirtschaft und Wettbewerb/E* Bundeskartellamt 1457, *VEBA/Gevelsberg*). This provision significantly constrains government intervention in industries with public ownership. But this constraint is not all that critical because government ownership outside the sector of exempted industries takes the legal form of standard private companies in which the state has the role of the owner of shares, which already provides a certain arm's-length relationship from the business's daily operations. Because government-owned companies are subject to the same competition policy rules and therefore to the same competitive pressures as private companies, from a competition policy point of view privatization should not be a major issue in these industries.[11]

More important both for competition policy within the European Union and for Germany's internal privatization debate should be the sectors of the German economy that have been exempted. These include postal services and telecommunications, the transport sector, the

---

11. Official government opinion in Germany certainly contradicts this view. However, from an economic point of view, privatization in most countries, especially the United Kingdom, was important mainly to establish an arm's-length relationship between the government bureaucracy and management, as well as to introduce competition in those sectors. In industries in which such problems do not exist (as, for example, in the German automobile industry, in which the public sector owns a majority of the shares in Volkswagen), one should not expect large gains in competitiveness from privatization.

banking and insurance industries, and public utilities. In addition to these industries, exemptions are granted to agriculture, the Bundesbank, and the government-owned credit institute, Kreditanstalt für Wiederaufbau.

All the exempted industries are subject to extensive regulation. While the general cartel prohibition and restrictions such as retail price maintenance do not apply, the Cartel Office is responsible in varying degrees for control of potential abuses. Independent regulatory bodies govern such sectors as insurance and banking, but in matters regarding competition policy, the Cartel Office shares control. The Cartel Office alone, however, is responsible for mergers affecting these industries. Pressure to change the system of exemptions from cartel law has come mainly from the European Union, which has attempted to bring these sectors under the general control of European competition policy rules.

Abuse of Dominant Position

Definition

The central concept in German competition policy is dominant position (*marktbeherrschend*). A firm is deemed to have a dominant position if it possesses (or nearly possesses) a monopoly, or if it enjoys a much better competitive position than other firms (*überragend*) in a particular product market. To judge the latter, not only market share but also financial strength, access to input and output markets, interlocking shareholdings with other firms, and barriers to entry are considered (GWB, section 22).

The central variables of interest are market share and financial strength. As I will argue later in the analysis of merger policy, financial strength is of much greater importance in German policy than in that of other countries. The law further sets benchmarks for establishing dominant position, including specific levels of both market share and turnover (as a measure of financial strength). A firm is considered to have a dominant position if it has more than one-third of the market share and has turnover of at least DM250 million. This is not a binding benchmark, however. Other factors, such as significant threats of entry, may prevent firms from being judged dominant.

The definition of dominant position extends also to joint dominance by several firms. In particular, three or fewer firms with a market share of more than 50 percent and five or fewer firms with a market share of more than two-thirds are considered to have a dominant position if their turnover does not fall below DM100 million a year. These rules are complemented in practice by an interpretation of the law that considers firms more likely to be dominant if their market share is much larger than that of the next largest competitor. German competition law has therefore established quite exact criteria for what kind of market structures it considers worrisome. Contrary to US practice, the Herfindahl-Hirschman index is not used to measure industry concentration. German authorities do not consider just absolute market shares but the complete distribution of market shares across the relevant industry. In principle, this is preferable to an aggregate measure such as Herfindahl-Hirschman. Yet in so far as both a large concentration and a large dispersion of market shares are considered problematic in German competition policy, the two approaches are in practice very similar.[12]

Following the Monopolies Commission's suggestions, the market dominance criteria established in the law have been applied somewhat more flexibly since the mid-1980s (Monopolkommission 1990). The Cartel Office has made more of an effort to evaluate the threat of entry, in particular from producers outside Germany. This is of particular importance because of the high integration of the German economy into the world economy and the relative ease of entry for foreign competitors. At the same time, the critical market-share criteria have to be seen as the main guideposts for policy. And so they will remain, given the widespread belief in Germany that in tight oligopolies, firms will inevitably achieve implicitly collusive agreements (Höfer 1978). Given the lack of success in controlling implicit collusion, there seems to be some tendency to err on the restrictive side rather than to allow market conditions conducive to collusion.

Since merger control is framed in terms of preventing the establishment of new or strengthening the existing dominant positions in the market, it is in principle based on the definitions of dominant position just discussed. However, for the purposes of merger policy, the criteria for dominant position have been recently extended to allow the cartel authorities to put greater weight on the financial strength of firms.[13] This additional criterion underlines two important aspects of competition policy in Germany. First, the establishment of large firms—and with it, economic power—is seen as a threat to the economic order per se. Second, the financial strength criterion reflects the high credibility that German competition policy implicitly gives to the possibility of predatory pricing, in particular the "deep pocket" variety.

Controlling Abuses of Dominant Position

German cartel law is aimed mainly at controlling dominant positions. The only way to control dominant positions that have not been estab-

---

12. This type of evaluation is not carried through consistently. Sometimes the Cartel Office or the courts argue that very evenly distributed market shares facilitate implicit collusion between firms.

13. These criteria are discussed in section 4 below.

lished by external growth is through controls of the "abuse of dominant position." Although the possibility of giving the cartel authority the right to break up dominant firms has been repeatedly suggested, it has generally been rejected as too interventionist (Höfer 1978; Möschel 1980; Schlecht 1992). What remains are interventions against practices by dominant firms that are considered abusive. "Abuses" are generally placed into two categories: "abuse by exploitation" and "abuse by hindering competitors." The latter generally concerns vertical restraints but would also be applicable to predatory pricing. The former essentially concerns high prices charged by dominant firms. While I will relegate the vertical issues to a later section, I will briefly describe the practices concerning "excessively high" and "excessively low" prices in this section.

Controlling Excessively High Prices

Rules allowing the cartel authority to intervene against excessively high prices[14] are effectively a form of price cap regulation. However, the cartel authority cannot simply set a price cap if it considers a price excessively high. It must prove in court that the price was excessive according to some benchmark. Evidence of exceptional profitability has not been enough to convince the courts. The acceptable method of proof has been to compare the price that is considered excessive to the price in a "comparable market" with significant competition.[15] This rule has made it practically impossible to prove that a price is excessive because the courts generally find the market comparison invalid. This has been shown most dramatically in cases against the oil industry in 1974 and against the pharmaceutical industry in 1980 (Valium).

The case concerning oil prices is closely linked to the first oil price shock in 1973. The six leading oil producers in Germany—Texaco, BP, Shell, Esso, Gevelsberg, and VEBA (ARAL)—had drastically increased their prices between the fall of 1973 and spring of 1974, arguing that increased costs in the international markets had made price increases necessary. After profit increases of 300 percent became public knowledge and published figures showed that oil prices had risen by about 30 percent more than input prices, the Cartel Office intervened, claiming that the five largest firms in the industry were abusing a joint dominant position. After a hearing, which is required in such cases, the Cartel Office ordered firms to take back the price increases as far as they had been instituted. Despite the enormous increases in profitability, the courts lifted the order because they did not see sufficient proof of excessively

---

14. The rules apply equally against oligopsonists that use their market power to gain excessively low prices from suppliers.

15. This rule has been explicitly stated in the GWB since 1980.

high prices. This case demonstrated clearly that profitability criteria could not be used in such cases as evidence.

In the Valium case, the cartel authority attempted to control prices by resorting to competition policy measures. This case was first taken up in 1974, when the Cartel Office ordered Hoffmann-La Roche to reduce its price for Valium by 40 percent and its price for Librium by 35 percent. In the market for tranquilizers, which was considered to be the relevant market, Hoffmann-La Roche had market shares of more than 50 percent in sales through pharmacies and about 85 percent in sales to hospitals. Dominant-firm criteria clearly were satisfied, and the Cartel Office supported the claim of an abuse of dominant position by supplying evidence that German Valium prices were 50 percent higher than in the Netherlands and 300 percent higher than in the United Kingdom.[16]

The case finally failed in 1980 because all possible comparable markets abroad were themselves subject to regulation, and it became impossible for the Cartel Office to convince the court that foreign markets were comparable. Three years before, the court had rejected the claim that prices on foreign markets could be taken directly as a benchmark and had developed a complicated scheme for calculating how a price on a foreign (comparable) market could be translated into a "quasi-competitive price" for the domestic market. Consequently, the Cartel Office has virtually given up its attempt to control excessive pricing. The only recent cases of importance have come with the unification of Germany and the scrutiny of pricing practices by companies in the former East Germany.

Predatory Pricing

Action against the "abuse" of setting too low a price—that is, predatory pricing—has not played a prominent role in German competition policy, but the Cartel Office did attempt to intervene against predatory behavior in 1981 (*Wirtschaft und Wettbewerb/E* Bundeskartellamt 2029, *Coop Bremen*). The case was brought against the retail chain Coop, which was considered a large, integrated retailing company facing mostly small retailers in the region of Bremen. Coop offered about 50 branded products of everyday use at a retail price below the average price it paid for these products, and it did so over a prolonged period. These retail prices were heavily advertised in the local media.

The Cartel Office argued that this strategy threatened the viability of smaller retail outlets. Smaller retailers had smaller product lines and a lower ability to finance advertising. Matching Coop's prices would have implied significant losses that could not be matched by profits in other

---

16. This refers to UK prices before UK government intervention forced the price for Valium down.

areas, as was possible for Coop. Essentially, the situation was seen as a classic, deep-pocket predatory strategy, with the additional advantages to Coop of a product-line effect and advertising advantages. The Cartel Office prohibited the use of prices below average purchase prices (*Einstands-preis*). Coop appealed in the courts, where the case has been stuck since.

This case was probably as strong a case as the Cartel Office could make to show predatory pricing. There was both pricing below average cost and a high potential of exit by competitors. The failure to win this case in court makes it unlikely that further cases will be brought forth. As a response to this situation, there was an attempt to forbid systematic pricing below cost during the last reform of the GWB in 1989. However, the government succeeded in keeping such a rule out of the law (Schlecht 1992). It seems fairly clear that attempts to prove predatory pricing in German courts would essentially be impossible. However, this does not mean that the competition authorities consider predatory practices unimportant. On the contrary, as I argue below, the possibility that such practices are prevalent affects the competition authority's evaluation of mergers that generate cost advantages.

Merger Policy

Horizontal Mergers

The cornerstone of German competition policy since 1973 has been merger control, partly because experience has shown that the behavior of dominant firms cannot effectively be controlled when abuse of dominance has to be proved in court. Price controls through competition policy instruments appear likely to fail in the absence of an explicit regulatory regime. While this leaves no effective means to control firms that become large through internal growth, it apparently underscores the importance of controlling external growth of firms in the eyes of policymakers (Schmidt 1990; Monopolkommission 1980).

When Are Mergers Subject to Control?

The majority of mergers in Germany have to be reported to the Cartel Office as soon as the merger has taken place. The merging firms must have a combined market share of at least 20 percent in some German market. The market can also be a substantial submarket.[17] Second, there

---

17. An exact translation of the wording of the law is: "In the area of applicability of this law or in a substantial part thereof, the merger creates or increases a market share of at least 20 percent, or one of the participating companies has on a different market a market share of at least 20 percent."

is a criterion for firm size, which requires the merging firms to notify the cartel authority if the participating companies jointly exceed an employment level of 10,000 employees or jointly exceed a turnover of DM500 million in the business year prior to the merger. The law is quite meticulous in identifying the merging companies for these purposes with the actual companies controlling ownership.

The number of merger notifications increased from 773 in 1973-75 to 3,750 in 1991-92. The Cartel Office had received a total of 16,147 merger notifications by the end of 1992. The number of mergers significantly increased in the 1980s, with a particularly sharp boost in 1990-91 as a result of German unification, and has stabilized at about 1,500 a year since then.

It has also become more evident over time that consulting the Cartel Office prior to a merger eased procedures considerably. As a result, the facilities for "preventive merger control" have recently been augmented. In particular, mergers that involve one firm with a turnover exceeding DM2 billion or two firms with a turnover of at least DM1 billion each will have to be announced to the Cartel Office in advance so the Cartel Office can delay the merger to investigate its impact on competition and possibly prohibit it. By 1989 two-thirds of all mergers subject to the general notification requirement already fell into this category. Thus, German mergers have become largely subject to prior approval from the Cartel Office.

What Constitutes a Merger?

German law attempts to include in its definition of a merger every agreement that gives one firm a significant influence on a company's policy, not just the complete takeover of a company. This is closely related to the laws on publicly held firms (in particular, the *Aktiengesetz*), in which special rights are given to minority shareholders of substantial size. Under the law, a share acquisition is considered a merger if, as a result of the share acquisition, shareholdings reach 25 percent, 50 percent, or a majority of the shares with voting rights. For example, an increase of shareholdings from 20 to 25 percent would be considered a merger. If the same shareholder were to subsequently increase the shareholding from 25 percent to 50 percent, this would be considered a second merger. Even if smaller minority shareholdings are involved, a share acquisition may be considered a merger under the law if, either directly or indirectly, the minority shareholder gains a significant degree of control in the firm. One case of this, which the law mentions explicitly, would occur if more than half the members of the supervisory committees of two firms involved in the transaction were identical.

German law correctly aims at the control rights that are gained through a formal connection between two firms. It recognizes that, for competition policy purposes, a merger should be defined only on the basis of whether control rights are distributed in such a way that the merging firms will be able to act in concert. This makes the law very satisfactory from an economic point of view.[18]

When Are Mergers Prohibited?

Mergers are prohibited if they are expected to create or expand a dominant position in some market unless the participating companies can prove that the merger will also generate "improvements in competitive conditions and that these improvements outweigh the disadvantages of a dominant position" (GWB, section 24[1]). The formulation "improvements in competitive conditions" does not allow for an efficiency defense for mergers. The clause only applies to market structure criteria.

Essentially, under the practice established by the Cartel Office, an improvement in competitive conditions comes about if the merger allows firms that do not have the largest market share to catch up to the one that does (see *Gemeinschaftskommentar* for examples). The idea is that such a merger reduces the dominant position of the largest firm in the market.

Considerations of public interest, international trade, industrial policy, and, in particular, efficiency gains cannot be used as merger defenses. In fact, claimed efficiency gains often seem to harm the prospects for the merger. A recent case involving the proposed merger between two meat processing cooperatives in Northern Germany is a relatively typical example (*Wirtschaft und Wettbewerb/E* Bundeskartellamt 2428). The two firms had, among other things, claimed that the merger would allow them to realize substantial efficiency gains by rationalizing capacity utilization in an environment of significant excess capacities.

The Cartel Office explicitly agreed that there would be efficiency gains for the participating firms in the merger. However, it argued that these gains would put other firms in the industry at a competitive disadvantage. In particular, the merging firms might push competitors out of the market because the combined firm was financially strong enough to sustain such a strategy.

German merger policy does not take synergy effects into account; instead it sometimes bases its decisions against mergers on the fact that the merged firm would achieve cost advantages. Implicit in this position is the importance attributed to predatory pricing arguments, especially if they are based on deep-pocket arguments.

As we have seen, there is a merger defense for dominant firms if market structure improvements in some markets may outweigh the rein-

---

18. It should be noted, however, that through these procedures the possibilities for a market in corporate control are limited. It is implicit in much of what has been written in Germany about competition policy that the authors consider product market competition, not the financial markets, as the main source of discipline for managers.

forcement of dominant positions in another. Given this policy, it would be logical for cartel authorities to make their agreements to mergers conditional on specific requirements—for example, divestiture in markets for which increases in market dominance are a particular concern. However, they are not allowed to do so. The Cartel Office tries to circumvent these constraints by eliciting "assurances" from firms to divest certain divisions before agreeing to the merger.

Overall the number of mergers prohibited appears remarkably small. From 1988 to 1989 the Cartel Office was notified of 2,574 concluded mergers, only 16 of which were prohibited. These numbers do, however, strongly underestimate the role of the Cartel Office in screening mergers. During the whole period of merger control, 101 mergers were prohibited, but 224 merger proposals were dropped or much altered after consultation with the Cartel Office before formal proceedings were initiated. Clearly, merger control in the preapplication phase was of primary importance. Furthermore, there is a high degree of predictability of Cartel Office decisions because of the clarity of the rules. This predictability can be expected to keep the proportion of mergers proposed and rejected relatively small.

Ministerial Exemptions and Industrial Policy Concerns

If the Cartel Office prohibits a merger, there are two courses of action open to the firms concerned. First, they can appeal to the courts to get the decision overturned. To do so, they must show either that the Cartel Office's assertion of a dominant position was false or that the office had not properly weighed the competitive advantages and disadvantages of the merger. Second, the firms can request special permission from the minister of economics. Unlike the Cartel Office, the minister may let public-interest arguments outweigh competition policy considerations.[19] Through this instrument, synergy advantages of mergers, industrial policy concerns, and strategic trade considerations may enter merger control decisions.

The system is therefore highly formalized and transparent. In order to grant an exemption, the minister has to publicly overrule the Cartel Office. Consequently, the minister of economics has been very reluctant to use the instrument actively. Substantial efficiencies must redound to the whole economy in order to make the minister accept an efficiency defense. Thus synergies that are claimed must be at a very high level. In practice, such synergies have only been recognized in R&D (*Wirtschaft*

19. However, the minister of economics' decisions have often stated that ministers cannot question the Cartel Office's assessments on dominant position and the effects on the competitiveness of markets. They may only allow the merger if they decide that public-interest concerns outweigh the negative effects underlying the decision of the Cartel Office.

und Wettbewerb/E Bundeswirtschaftminister 159, *Thyssen-Huller*) or in otherwise technologically important areas (*Wirtschaft und Wettbewerb/E* Bundeswirtschaftminister 213, *BayWA AG/WLZ Raiffaisen*). Otherwise, like the Cartel Office, the minister is likely to conclude, from the cost advantages of a merger, that firms will be able to push competitors out of the market.

The office of the minister of economics has also repeatedly rejected demands to let industrial policy concerns influence merger decisions. German policymakers largely agree that industrial policy, if conducted at all, should not seek specific market configurations.

Regarding the international aspects of German competition policy, it is remarkable that the minister of economics has been able to insulate himself from industry's demands to allow mergers that strengthen German companies' ability to compete in foreign markets. Ministerial decisions have repeatedly stressed that such mergers could be allowed if they were necessary for market access abroad. However, strengthening of German firms' competitiveness abroad is not seen as sufficient justification for a merger. Furthermore, the minister has emphasized that "considering improvements in international competitiveness at the same time requires an evaluation of the economic disadvantages from restrictions of international competition" (*Wirtschaft und Wettbewerb/E* Bundeswirtschaftminister 177, *IBH/Wibau*). This narrow interpretation of German public interest has led to a situation in which only four mergers have ever been permitted through a ministerial decision, despite the fact that the minister, unlike the Cartel Office, may tie its permissions to merge to conditions.[20] Most of these cases have involved securing energy supplies (*VEBA/BP*, 1979).

Nevertheless, the 1989 case of Daimler/MBB[21] sticks out as a policy inconsistency. The federal government had initially suggested the merger, and thus it appears to be a classic example of industrial policy. The government was interested in transferring German Airbus participation (in particular the financial risk) to the private sector.[22] The German partner of the European Airbus consortium, Deutsche Airbus AG, was nominally owned by MBB, but the government had significant control rights because of the subsidies involved. In Daimler, MBB was to gain a financially strong partner to shoulder the significant risks of the Airbus project in the long run. The competition policy problems arose because in many

---

20. These may not, however, imply a permanent supervision of the firms' policies after the merger.

21. The company MBB (Messerschmidt-Bölkow-Blohm) is one of the largest firms in the German armaments industry.

22. The case has another specific feature: the states of Bayern, Bremen, and Hamburg—major production sites for MBB—jointly had a majority share in MBB. The three have been investing in the company to secure jobs. (Indeed, MBB and Daimler together account for a large share of employment in the state of Bremen).

areas of the defense, space, and aircraft industries the merged firm was to become by far the dominant supplier.

The government essentially supported the claims of the companies that the merger had significant positive effects for the national economy because it improved the abilities for the two companies to win "project leadership" in international high-technology cooperation. Given the relatively small number of such projects and the rather questionable significance of actual technological spinoffs, this move can better be seen as an attempt to increase German bargaining power in partly government-sponsored, international high-technology projects. Despite the Cartel Office's refusal to permit it, the minister of economics finally approved the merger, along with some restrictions that enforced the sale of some divisions of the merged company.

The case also showed the great importance the Monopolies Commission has as an advisory body. The commission supported the merger, conditional on some restrictions. Its report was, however, highly critical. The commission was split in its recommendations, adding to a general uneasiness about the whole case. One reason for finally approving the merger was that the government would otherwise have lost face after having initiated the process in the first place. This atypical case has therefore served to caution the government against using merger policy for industrial policy reasons. The case has also, through the initiative of the Monopolies Commission, once more raised the issue of bank involvement in German industry. Because Deutsche Bank is the largest shareholder in Daimler Benz and because it was influential in initial negotiations with the government, many policymakers felt that the leading banks were getting an excessive amount of bargaining power vis-à-vis the government.

Vertical and Conglomerate Mergers

The treatment of vertical and conglomerate mergers in Germany is very different from the US practice after 1980. While vertical mergers are not considered as dangerous as horizontal mergers, such mergers can be forbidden. For example, if a firm has a dominant position in a market and vertically integrates into the downstream market, it would be considered as having increased its dominant position—partly based on conjectured foreclosure effects, but also on the argument that if a firm can complete more stages of production internally than others can, it is likely to have a wider range of options. This is interpreted as an increase in "market power."[23]

23. Recent research on the welfare effects of vertical mergers in concentrated markets seem to make such restrictive policies toward vertical mergers rather questionable (Mathewson and Winter 1984; Kühn and Vives 1994).

With the fourth reform of the GWB in 1980, legislators particularly wanted to strengthen the instruments of the Cartel Office against conglomerate mergers. This reform led to additional turnover-based indicators for market dominance for the purposes of merger control.

There are essentially three cases that are regarded as market dominance. The first is the case in which the market is fragmented (i.e., it consists of mainly small and medium-size firms, or *mittelständischer Markt*) and a large firm of more than DM2 billion in turnover merges with a firm in that market, yielding a market share of at least 5 percent. Here it is assumed that, with its financial power, the large company will quickly dominate the market. The second case is a merger of a financially powerful company with a company that has a dominant position in a market (and the market turnover is at least DM150 million). Finally, pure financial size is also a criterion. If two firms with at least DM1 billion in turnover each and a combined turnover of at least DM12 billion merge, this is also regarded as increasing a dominant position.[24] These rules cover at least the 100 largest companies in Germany in terms of turnover. As such, the introduction of rules against conglomerate mergers can also be seen as an attempt to stop the overall trend toward concentration in the German economy.

Unfortunately, the role of financial strength, and in particular the role of conglomerate mergers, has not been analyzed to a great extent in the economic literature. It seems sensible to have some means of assessing relative financial power to determine the long-term prospect for concentration in an industry where a merger is proposed. It is somewhat worrisome, however, that financial strength is invariably measured by turnover. Use of this indicator has produced a number of cases in which loss-making firms that were proposing a merger were considered to have a dominant position partly because of their "financial strength." This is not necessarily incorrect because medium- and long-run profitability—and not the immediate financial situation—of the firms should determine a firm's financial strength. Nonetheless, the sole focus on turnover as a predictor of future profits appears rather dubious. Combined with the absence of both an efficiency and a failing-firm defense for mergers, this may very well lead to undesirable outcomes.

Vertical Restraints of Competition

Vertical restraints of competition are regulated in detail in the GWB. Except for the illegality of retail price maintenance (GWB, section 15),

---

24. Again, these rules are complemented by rules for dominant positions of oligopolies. They can be circumvented if the oligopolists can prove that there is significant competition among them.

vertical restraints fall under the prohibition of abuse of dominant position through hindrance of competitors, and therefore are regulated following a rule-of-reason approach. In practice, this rule overlaps the prohibition of discriminatory practices by dominant firms (GWB, section 26). The discussion below is organized according to economic practices.

Prohibition of Resale Price Maintenance

Until 1973 retail price maintenance was permitted under German law for all branded products. With the reform of the GWB in 1973, resale price maintenance (i.e., any contract that limits a contracting party's ability to set prices or conditions in contracts with third parties) was made per se illegal.[25] It was viewed as keeping retailer margins artificially high to the detriment of consumers.

Case studies concerning retail price maintenance show that this rule essentially ensures intrabrand competition while systematically ignoring its presence. An example of this arose from a case concerning a Japanese electronics firm (*Wirtschaft und Wettbewerb/E* Oberlandesgericht 5053), that had trouble persuading retailers to stock its brand because competitive price cuts by other retailers that were carrying the product reduced retail margins too much.

While it was a large firm on world markets, the company held only 0.8 percent market share in the German market, its turnover was falling, and it was starting to incur losses in its German operations. The firm concluded it could secure its presence in the market only by guaranteeing a retail margin, so it imposed retail price maintenance through indirect means. This was deemed illegal. At no point in the procedure did authorities consider the degree of competition with other manufacturers or market-entry conditions.

Given cases of this type and empirical research on retail price maintenance in the United States (Ippolito 1991), it is time to reconsider the strict abolition of retail price maintenance in German law. Fortunately, the per se illegality of retail price maintenance is the only per se rule on vertical restraints that is not tied to the existence of a dominant position.

One of the reasons a change in this rule will probably not come about lies in the basic philosophy of German competition policy. Retail price maintenance is considered as infringing on the freedom of contracting of other parties. This can be seen nicely from a case against a German ski maker (*Wirtschaft und Wettbewerb/E* Bundeskartellamt 2479, *Völkl*), that though it did not produce bindings, imposed a clause on its retailers stating that they could not bundle their skis with another producer's

---

25. The only exception is the publishing industry.

bindings and sell the package at a single price. This stipulation violated the rule against measures that affect retailers' pricing decisions and is a particularly blatant example of the rule to guarantee "freedom of contracting" leading to results that cannot be economically justified.

Refusal to Supply and Exclusive Dealing

"Refusal to supply" can usefully be divided into three categories. First, there is the classic exclusive dealing aimed at restricting distribution channels. Second, refusal to supply may be used to force potential contractual partners to comply with business conditions that cannot be made part of an enforceable contract. Finally, there is the possibility of inducing others to boycott a particular firm. The law prohibits the latter practice by outlawing any attempts at influencing others to terminate or refuse business relationships with third parties. Similarly, the threat of refusal to sell to enforce the pricing policies of another firm is forbidden. This follows from the fact that section 25 of the GWB prohibits the use of threats to induce a particular behavior, and also from the fact that the prohibition of retail price maintenance extends to implicit agreements[26] (*Wirtschaft und Wettbewerb/E* Oberlandesgericht 2822, *Uhren-Kramer/ Seiko*; *Wirtschaft und Wettbewerb/E* Oberlandesgericht 5053).

The problematic case from a policy perspective is that of refusal to supply to ensure exclusive dealing arrangements. This is a common practice, especially in the sale of consumer durables. This is dealt with under the "abuse of dominant position" category. Firms with a dominant position in the market are not allowed to discriminate against firms if this unreasonably hinders the other firm and the discrimination cannot be justified.

The same rule applies if suppliers or downstream firms are "dependent" on a business partner in the sense that they cannot easily shift their business relationships to others. In fact, much of the discussion of competition policy in this area has focused on the question of when firms are considered "dependent." The courts have interpreted dependence quite broadly and have in some areas established a requirement to supply. Surprisingly, this includes forcing firms to supply (*Wirtschaft und Wettbewerb/E* Oberlandesgericht 2390, *Allkauf Nordmende*; *Wirtschaft und Wettbewerb/E* Bundesgericht 1885, *Adidas*). In the Adidas case (similar to the Raleigh bicycle case in Britain), the court put such weight on this principle that it forbade Adidas from continuing to distribute only through specialized sporting goods stores. Although there are many cases in which the right of firms to choose their distribution channels has

---

26. This is the same rule as that covering implicit collusion.

been upheld, the legal practice in the past seems to have excessively restricted firms in their distribution channel management.

Interestingly enough, the Cartel Office has dealt with exclusive dealing mostly under the rules against discrimination, despite the fact that section 18 of the GWB explicitly permits the Cartel Office to prohibit exclusive dealing arrangements. However, the preconditions are somewhat different from those under the discrimination rule. Under section 18, exclusive dealing (including restrictions on trading with third parties) can only be prohibited if many firms are treated in this way, other firms are prevented from entry, and competition is significantly reduced through the exclusive dealing contract. Thus, the rule focuses on foreclosure effects. It is revealing that this economically sensible rule is almost never the basis on which the Cartel Office intervenes.

Price Discrimination and Discounting Practices

Price discrimination and discounting practices essentially fall under the same rules as exclusive dealing. Again, the law addresses only dominant firms, cartels, and dependency relationships. The main issue in discounting practices has been the treatment of total turnover rebates. Similarly to EU policy, the German Cartel Office today considers these practices detrimental to competition and an unwarranted hindrance to competitors (*Wirtschaft und Wettbewerb/E* Oberlandesgericht 1983, Rama-Mädchen; *Wirtschaft und Wettbewerb/E* Bundeskartellamt 1817, *Effem-Tierfertignahrung*). Their arguments are not based on the idea that such schemes relax price competition[27] or prevent entry. Instead, the Cartel Office argues that discounts on total turnover "limit competitors and entrants in their economic freedom and in particular in their freedom of setting prices since they have to grant their customers larger rebates in order to compensate them for not concentrating their purchases on the supplier that provides the turnover discount" (Schmidt 1990, 237).

Price discrimination has mostly been handled under the guise of protecting "dependent" firms. Price discrimination by sellers between buyers has traditionally been treated quite leniently. Usually, the Cartel Office accepted producers' claims that price discrimination was based on economic grounds and therefore justifiable. A case originating in 1976 is a rather worrisome indication that this might have changed. A well-known German producer of brandy, Asbach Uralt, was granting additional discounts to wholesalers specialized in dealing with restaurants and bars if they agreed to a dealership contract with Asbach.

The Cartel Office considered the additional discounts as unreasonable

---

27. See the literature on switching costs, in particular Klemperer (1992), for an overview of the effects of loyalty bonuses.

discrimination between the Asbach dealers and other wholesalers, while the court argued that Asbach dealers were providing special services that justified the discrimination—the traditional argument used to permit discriminatory practices. However, the federal court complained that the lower-court decision had not sufficiently considered the goal of the law—protecting the freedom of competition. As in the earlier refusal-to-supply cases, the court argued that, to be competitive, the wholesalers had to have Asbach Uralt in their product line. Therefore, the restriction of the additional rebate to only Asbach dealers hindered other wholesalers.

Based on this argument, the Cartel Office's position was confirmed. The decision did not take into account whether the rebate had foreclosure effects but was aimed only at protecting the profits of the independent wholesalers—a highly questionable practice that cannot be justified on economic grounds.[28]

The treatment of price discrimination by firms with market power on the demand side has been more controversial. It has been argued in these cases that discounts were simply an expression of effective competition. The Cartel Office nonetheless pursued a case in this area despite rather weak economic grounds for doing so. Metro, a large firm in the food sector, is a large customer of many companies in food supplies. Metro asked supplying companies to pay a fee if they wanted an additional product to be included in Metro's product line.

The Cartel Office interpreted this practice as discrimination between customers who already supplied the product and those who did not. The office argued that this practice made entry more difficult for new suppliers and prohibited the further use of such fees. The case was abandoned when, in a merger case involving Metro, a court decided that Metro did not have a dominant position. Nevertheless, the case raises the issue of whether two-part pricing by an oligopsonist should be prohibited by cartel authorities as anticompetitive. Both cases demonstrate that competition policy authorities seem to have too little economic guidance on how to evaluate vertical contractual relationships.

Tie-In Sales

While tying (or bundling) products was once always considered an abuse of dominant position, the legal assessment became somewhat more lenient in the 1980s. Early cases did, however, smack strongly of attempts to exclude competitors from the market. For example, in the case of *meto-Handauszeichner* (*Wirtschaft und Wettbewerb/E* Oberlandesgericht 995), a firm forced customers to use only their stickers with their sticker-marking device, thereby tying the sale of a durable good in which it

---

28. The extensive reliance on product-line effects to show "dependence" is worrying in itself. It can only be justified economically if foreclosure effects can be demonstrated.

had a monopoly to the sale of stickers in which it would have had to contend with competitors. This practice was rightly prohibited.

Recently, courts have been willing to accept efficiency defenses for tying. In a case involving two newspapers in Stuttgart that were forcing customers to advertise in both newspapers at the same time, the court found that rationalization justified the practice (*Wirtschaft und Wettbewerb/ E Oberlandesgericht 2126*). The Monopolies Commission in its most recent report has advocated following a cautious route in dealing with tying arrangements: "The tying arrangements of a supplier with a powerful market position are only then inadmissible if they threaten to cause substantial deterioration of the market structure on the market for the tied commodity" (Monopolkommission 1992, 525). The commission essentially suggests treating tie-in sales like mergers. If their recommendations are followed, the market structure for the tied commodity would have to be analyzed. If the tying arrangement leads to substantial increases in market share in the market for the tied product (beyond the intervention levels of merger control), tying would be considered illegal. This suggestion is very sensible because it focuses on the horizontal effects of tying and emphasizes the close relationship to merger control.

Research and Development

In all policy concerning research and development, the basic idea that R&D is good for economic development dominates general thinking. Anything that helps intensify R&D efforts is therefore welcomed. This is particularly true of interfirm cooperative R&D and strongly influences competition policy in this area.[29] Firms can choose to do cooperative R&D simply by contractual agreements, or they can form joint ventures. Contractual cooperation could potentially violate the prohibition of cartels. R&D joint ventures will be subject to merger control. If they contain agreements about downstream production, R&D joint ventures may also fall under the cartel prohibition. In this section, I discuss both forms of cooperation.

Contractual Cooperation

For a long time, German competition policy has treated R&D as a precompetitive activity that was an internal organizational matter of the individual firm. Agreements between firms to mount exclusively R&D efforts were thus of no concern to competition policy. This approach is

---

29. EU competition policy related to R&D cooperation is particularly important in practice. For the purpose of exposition, I will concentrate purely on the German side of policy for the moment.

in strange contrast to the often-repeated statement that competition policy is guided by a view of "competition as a dynamic process." It has, however, strongly shaped policy toward R&D cooperation. The Cartel Office regards any cooperation that only involves R&D as unproblematic, but it is concerned with cooperation that extends to production and marketing using R&D results.

As a consequence of this general approach, pure cooperation on R&D is considered as falling outside the GWB's cartel prohibition because it does not "restrict competition." Neither is the Cartel Office troubled by some further degree of cooperation on the use of R&D results nor on licensing (Monopolkommission 1990). The only objections the Cartel Office is likely to raise is that a cooperative effort eliminates competition in "research and development markets." This is generally seen to be the case only if firms cede their right to do independent research.

In contrast, agreements on R&D that also lead to a coordination of production activities should be considered as violations of the cartel prohibition. But in practice, R&D cooperation is almost always regarded as contributing substantially to "rationalization" effects and thus would be permitted as a rationalization cartel. Yet few R&D cooperative agreements have been turned into rationalization cartels, because firms believe R&D cooperation is generally exempt. They thus notify the Cartel Office of few R&D cooperative agreements. Nonetheless, empirical research has found these agreements quite important (Monopolkommission 1990).

R&D Joint Ventures

The formation of R&D joint ventures falls under the usual regulation of merger control. The majority pass by the Cartel Office without objection. When the Cartel Office did prohibit R&D joint ventures or made firms change the scope of the venture, the venture usually concerned cooperation at the production and marketing stage.

Markets in which the Cartel Office prevented R&D-related mergers have characteristically been emerging markets with significant growth prospects, because these mergers were viewed as establishing or strengthening dominant positions. This raises the issue of the extent to which mergers in emerging markets actually prevent the early entry of competitors. Unfortunately for the cartel authority, little is known about the evolution of markets.

One instrument to control R&D cooperation is the imposition of a 10-year limit on the joint venture (Deutscher Bundestag: Drucksuche 8/1925, *Bosch/Deutsche Vergaser Gesellschaft*). This is a sensible way of dealing with the problem and is analogous to the limited duration of a patent grant. Unfortunately, the Monopolies Commission has criticized this practice on legal grounds, so it likely will be discontinued.

One of the big problems in merger control involving R&D ventures is determining the relevant market. In some cases, the Cartel Office considers market share in the "market for R&D" a concept difficult to assess.

Even more problematic is the evaluation of the effects of R&D cooperation on future market conditions. R&D efforts create new markets, and technological developments integrate formerly separate markets. The application of market-dominance concepts would require some information about the market's future, which is not available. The best that authorities can do is to evaluate the likelihood of later potential competition based on other producers' current ability to perform the R&D necessary to compete in new markets.

Reasoning about the role of R&D competition is less developed than in other areas of competition policy. For example, large-firm R&D cooperation is often justified with the argument that today's R&D projects are so big that even large companies cannot undertake them alone. This raises several questions: Are financial constraints the chief impediment to large-scale R&D, and, if so, why is it so difficult for large companies to obtain support in the financial markets? Why do firms need to cooperate on some projects while they are able to continue substantial R&D efforts on other projects on their own? Is human capital a limiting factor for R&D activities?

There are no clear answers to such questions. Essentially, cartel authorities are at a loss when it comes to evaluating the main motivations for R&D joint ventures. There seems to be a growing suspicion, however, that R&D joint ventures are often motivated mainly by the prospect of gaining market power (Monopolkommission 1990, 365).

International Aspects

So far, I have discussed German competition policy in isolation. Although useful for expositional purposes, it does not, of course, capture the international reality. While the GWB is only concerned with the Federal Republic of Germany or parts of it as relevant markets, German competition law is still extensively applied to restraints of competition agreed to outside Germany that affect the German market.

This is clearest in merger policy. Even in 1992, when many mergers involved the Treuhand's sales of companies in East Germany, more than 40 percent of all mergers had some degree of foreign participation (Bundeskartellamt 1993), reflecting the high degree of German integration into the international economy. As a consequence, questions of extraterritoriality frequently arise in merger control. For example, a merger with a firm abroad can be stopped even if the foreign firm neither produces nor sells its product in Germany.

In the case Daimler Benz/MAN-ENASA (*Wirtschaft und Wettbewerb/E Bundeskartellamt* 2445), a merger was prohibited in which Daimler Benz and MAN were to jointly take over the truck production of ENASA, a Spanish company, splitting ENASA facilities between them. Daimler and MAN are virtually the only competitors in the German market for trucks. The Cartel Office ruled the merger would not only allow the two firms to coordinate indirectly through their control in a foreign firm but would also eliminate potential competition. The GWB generally governs foreign mergers that, like this one, affect home markets (see Königs in Gemeinschaftskommentar).

Naturally, the extraterritorial application of German law leads to some competition between legal spheres. The introduction of EU merger control has created a single institution responsible for merger proceedings for large mergers in Europe. Still, there are a significant number of cases in which several authorities deal with control of European mergers. In the recent case of Gillette/Wilkinson, both the German and the British cartel authority prohibited the merger. The Cartel Office tries on a limited scale to coordinate policies through consultations with foreign cartel authorities. There is, for example, a formal information exchange agreement with the United States.

Potential Conflicts between German and EU Competition Policy

In principle, there should not be much conflict between EU and German competition law because EU law, wherever it applies, traditionally has superseded national law. In this sense, national laws would have to converge on EU norms. The federal government expects efforts to harmonize German law with EU rules to dominate the next reform of the law against restraints of competition.

Some rules have already been established. For example, a merger or anticompetitive practice that the European Union has prohibited cannot be permitted at the national level. Similarly, it has been agreed that national law cannot overturn block exemptions the European Union has granted. What this rule means in practice is slightly less clear. For example, if the block exemption is granted for reasons unrelated to trade between member nations, national legal rules should apply. In practice, unresolved questions of this nature will remain a source of conflict for some time.

From the German point of view, conflicts arise mainly over the governance of European competition policy. The German government in particular worries that the European Commission cannot handle the rising case load. Germany has thus been demanding the establishment of an independent European Cartel Office and some more extensive delegation of cases falling under EU law to national cartel authorities. The

German Cartel Office is already conducting some inquiries into cases concerning Article 85 of the Treaty of Rome. So far, the German cartel authorities can only prohibit practices; declaring exemptions remains firmly in the hands of the European Commission. The institutional structure Germany prefers apparently closely resembles Germany's own: a strong, independent cartel authority, which is nonetheless confined to interpreting the rules exclusively on the basis of competition policy aims. On the other hand, a federalist structure in which national cartel offices handle cases with relevance mainly in national markets while the European Cartel Office restricts itself to mergers where international aspects dominate. This would closely resemble the division of authority between the federal and state cartel offices in the Federal Republic.

There is also a reluctance on the part of both the German government and the Cartel Office to reduce the threshold levels on size that determine whether a merger falls under EU jurisdiction. This partly reflects the institutional concerns and partly a concern about implicitly loosening the vigilance of German competition policy.

According to the German Cartel Office, industry largely perceives that EU merger policy is more permissive. The Cartel Office points to the fact that it has observed large companies choosing to arrange mergers in such a way that they fall under the EU merger directive although the purposes of the merger could have been achieved otherwise.

A further area of concern is the transparency of European-level decisions. The Cartel Office in its latest report criticized the Commission for failing to make public its reasoning in the decision against the Aérospatiale/Alenia/de Havilland merger.

Institutional structure explains much of the problem: EU competition policy decisions fall directly under the political influence of the EU Commission. Competition policy and industrial policy concerns are not clearly separated. Indeed, the merger directive does address industrial policy concerns. The German competition policy community, in contrast, presses for a separation of the two policy areas, secured by the institutional structure of an independent cartel authority that must report decisions it takes. Germany will likely link any extension of competition policy powers for the Union to concessions in the institutional sphere and to its general philosophy of competition policy. From a political economy point of view, the German focus on governance may be rather fortunate because it can help the Union avoid regulatory capture problems.

Areas of Exemption

The EU Commission has actively sought to bring the areas exempted from competition policy under regular competition rules. This has put pressure for reform on the German government. Some reforms have already begun in the transport sector through the application of European competition policy rules. In all sectors exempted from competition policy in Germany, regulatory regimes date back to the 1930s. The rationale for some of the rules is hard to understand today, although reasons for ongoing regulatory intervention clearly exist.

The German government has committed itself to "deregulation" in these areas. The German Cartel Office recently tried to force the pace of deregulation in the public utilities sector by challenging exclusive-supply arrangements between an electricity company and a municipality under Article 85(1) of the Treaty of Rome. The Cartel Office is trying to clarify to what extent the rules apply in the electricity industry in an attempt to gain an instrument against exclusive-supply contracts and contracts between suppliers granting each other exclusive rights in certain territories. The government also seems determined to press local governments to withdraw from their ownership of local utilities as part of a general privatization drive.

The main problem in these areas is that elements of natural monopoly remain in these industries, and the introduction of competition can only be seen, as in the United Kingdom, as part of an overall change in the regulatory regime. Unfortunately, the discussion is being conducted as if natural-monopoly problems would never exist. Consequently, policy completely ignores the remaining regulatory problems and the question of what level these should be addressed.

Germany's Specific Entry Barriers

Besides the areas traditionally exempted from competition policy, there are several features of the German economy that may lead to conflicts between EU member countries in evaluations of competition policy. While entry into retailing is free in Germany, there are many professions for which entry into the market requires evidence of relevant qualifications. As with other areas of regulation, this is bound to become a source of conflict should European competition policy concentrate more on government-induced barriers to entry. The difficult decision that has to be made is to what extent member states have autonomy in regulatory decisions and when regulatory regimes become unacceptable barriers to entry.

A particularly important recent example is the introduction of comprehensive regulations on recycling that have been introduced in Germany. French companies complained that the recycling policy puts them at a disadvantage vis-à-vis German companies because very often their products will not qualify for the "green dot," a label that signifies high recycling standards. Given the strong preference of German consumers for "green" products, the green dot gives firms a pricing advantage.

The conflict arises because different governments prefer different solutions to mounting waste problems, and firms want to design their technology according to the requirements in those areas where their sales are highest. The best solution to such conflicts probably lies in requiring that regulations apply equally to all competitors. Anything else would imply a great deal of centralization in political decision making in Europe and a severe reduction in the ability to develop competing ideas for the solution of political problems. Furthermore, if a country decides to incur higher costs for the goods it consumes, supranational competition policy should not prevent it from doing so. A line demarcating where legitimate competition policy intervention ends will have to be drawn.

Industrial Policy and Strategic Trade Policy

In the classic sense of government supporting specific industries, possibly through approving mergers and intervening in industry structure, industrial policy is highly unpopular among German policymakers. "Picking winners" is something everyone rejects. This explains the vigorous opposition of the government, the Cartel Office, and in particular the Monopolies Commission to the intrusion of industrial policy on European merger rules. This does not mean that there is no industrial policy in Germany. There is indeed both on the federal and the state level a very active research and technology policy (Forschungsbericht der Bundesregierung 1993) that consists of a whole range of incentives and subsidies to R&D activities, both for basic and applied research. Based on very activist policies in the 1980s, "technology parks" near universities and state government funding have proliferated. As mentioned earlier, the government in many cases encourages firms to cooperate on their R&D activities (or even requires it as a precondition for funding). There is therefore a strong industrial policy in Germany that basically reflects the conviction that anything that furthers technological progress is good. However, industrial policy geared at sector-specific or project-related promotion of research is seen as inferior to "a technology policy which employs indirect means of promotion and decentralist decision-making structures" (Monopolkommission 1992).

Strategic trade policy raises even greater skepticism. EU member states have delegated trade policy to the Community level. However, unlike some other members, Germany wants to limit trade policy instruments. German policymakers generally agree that "aggressive" strategic trade policy—that is, trade policy aimed at shifting economic rents between countries—should not be used. They even doubt the usefulness of "defensive" strategic trade policy. The Monopolies Commission in its last report severely criticized the use of unilateral countermeasures used by the EU in its trade policy: ". . . the antidumping and antisubsidization regulations and the so-called New Commercial Policy Instrument are in urgent need of reform. They do not move in the right direction and in practice have a protectionist and anticompetitive effect." In particular, the commission would like to see a competition policy regime substitute for defensive trade measures wherever possible but sees difficulties achieving this in the GATT. The commission suggests a larger free trade area, including the European Union, North America, and Japan, within which trade could be regulated by competition policy instead of trade policy.[30] In particular, it envisages substituting antidumping rules with established competition policy on predatory practices and discriminatory behavior.

Naturally, the Monopolies Commission, as a statutory, institutional watchdog over competition policy, will fight for much purer competition-enhancing policies than other institutions. It is therefore remarkable how much official government statements support this thinking. In its comments on the last Cartel Office report, the government suggested increasing the control over export cartels in the international competitive order (Deutscher Bundestag, Drucksache 12/5200).

As demonstrated in the practice of ministerial exemptions to merger control, strategic trade concerns have been expressly limited. One of the largest strategic trade projects, the Airbus consortium, shows, however, that the German government does support some degree of strategic trade policy. It has often stressed that the aircraft industry has very high entry barriers, mostly due to the long lags in development and testing. German authorities see Airbus mostly as a means of opening up a market, making a competitor viable, and thus reducing the complete dependence of the European airline industries on American production. It should thus be seen as the exception that proves the rule in German attitudes toward competition policy. This is, indeed, acknowledged by the Monopolies Commission, despite its opinion that Airbus cannot be termed a success (Monopolkommission 1992). Overall, German policymakers seem to support relatively strongly the notion that trade policy should be treated as international competition policy.

References

Audretsch, D. B. 1989. "Legalized Cartels in West Germany." *The Antitrust Bulletin*: 579-600.

Bundeskartellamt. 1993. *Bericht des Bundeskartellamtes über seine Tätigkeit in den Jahren 1991-92 sowie über Lage und Entwicklung auf seinem Aufgabengebiet* (Report of the Cartel Office, 1991–92). Bonn: Deutscher Bundestag, Drucksache 12/5200.

Busch, A., A. Gross, C.-F. Laaser, and R. Soltwedel. 1987. *Zur staatlichen Marktregulierung*

---

30. This corresponds to the position of Canada that within NAFTA, trade disputes should be resolved through standard competition policy measures and not by the rights of any parties to use trade sanctions.

in der Bundesrepublik (On Market Regulation by the State in the Federal Republic of Germany). Kiel: Institut für Weltwirtschaft der Universität Kiel.

Ghemawhat, P., and B. Nalebuf. 1985. "Exit." *The Rand Journal of Economics* 16: 184-94.

Görgens, E. 1984. "Nachfragemacht im Lebensmittelhandel als Instrument der Strukturanpassung" (Monopsony Power in Grocery Trade as an Instrument for Structural Adjustment). *ORDO* 35: 231-45.

Gröner, H., and H. Köhler. 1980. "Wettbewerbsprobleme der Sanierungsfusion." *ORDO* 31: 87-125.

Herdzina, K. 1987. *Wettbewerbspolitik* (Competition Policy), 2d ed. Stuttgart and New York: Gustav Fischer Verlag.

Höfer, H. 1978. "Abgestimmtes Verhalten—Wettbewerbspolitik am Ende oder am Ende Wettbewerbspolitik?" (Tacit Collusion: The End of Competition Policy or in the End Competition Policy?) *ORDO* 25: 201-43.

Ippolito, P. 1991. "Resale Price Maintenance: Empirical Evidence from Litigation." *Journal of Law and Economics* 34: 767-92.

Klemperer, P. 1992. *Competition in the Presence of Switching Costs: An Overview.* CEPR Discussion Paper No. 704. London: Center for Economic Policy Research.

Kühn, K.-U., P. Seabright, and A. Smith. 1992. *Competition Policy Research: Where Do We Stand?* CEPR Occasional Paper No. 8. London: Center for Economic Policy Research.

Kühn, K.-U., and X. Vives. 1994. "Excess Entry, Vertical Integration, and Welfare." Working Paper. Barcelona: Institute of Economic Analysis.

Mathewson, G. F., and R. A. Winter. 1984. "An Economic Theory of Vertical Restraints." *The Rand Journal of Economics* 15: 27-38.

Monopolkommission. 1990. "Wettbewerbspolitik vor neuen Herausforderungen, 8. Hauptgutachten der Monopolkommission" (Competition Policy in the Face of New Challenges). Baden-Baden: Nomos Verlagsgesellschaft.

Monopolkommission. 1992. "Wettbewerbspolitik oder Industriepolitik, 9. Hauptgutachten der Monopolkommission" (Competition Policy and Industrial Policy). Baden-Baden: Nomos Verlagsgesellschaft.

Möschel, W. 1980. "Wettbewerbsgesetz und Unternehmensentflechtung" (Competition Law and Breaking Up Firms). *ORDO* 31: 69-85.

Schlecht, O. 1992. "Entscheidunglinien der deutschen Wettbewerbspolitik" (Decision Making in German Competition Policy). *ORDO* 43: 319-35.

Schmidt, I. 1990. *Wettbewerbspolitik und Kartellrecht: Eine Einführung* (Competition Policy and Antitrust Law), 3d ed. Stuttgart and New York: Gustav Fischer Verlag.

5

The Antimonopoly Law of Japan

MITSUO MATSUSHITA

A Brief Historical Review

The Original Antimonopoly Law

Enacted in 1947, the Japanese Antitrust Law (known formally as the Antimonopoly Law and referred to as the AML[1]) has often been the focus of political controversy. At present, the AML is an important tool in the effort by Japan's government to open up the Japanese market and restructure the Japanese economy to make it more compatible with the economies of other major nations.

Before the end of World War II, there was limited understanding of the concepts of free enterprise and competition in Japan. With the end of the war came the Allied Occupation Forces, which introduced the Economic Democratization Policy of which the dissolution of *zaibatsu* combinations and the enactment of the AML were both part.

The original AML was quite stringent. Article 4 (which is now defunct) stipulated that cartels were illegal per se unless their effects were *de minimis*. Resale price maintenance was prohibited. Article 3 stipulated that any enterprise possessing disproportionately great economic power in relation to its competitors would be subject to remedial action, including dissolution.[2]

Mitsuo Matsushita is professor of law, Seikei University, Tokyo.

1. For general information on the Japanese Antimonopoly Law, see Iyori and Uesugi (1994); Matsushita (1990); and Matsushita (1993).

2. On the dissolution of *zaibatsu* (large industrial combines), see Bisson (1954).

The Fair Trade Commission of Japan (FTCJ) was created as the enforcement agency of the AML after the model of the United States Federal Trade Commission.

The 1953 Amendment and Subsequent Antitrust Relaxation

Starting around 1950, enforcement of the AML became somewhat more relaxed, for several reasons. For one, in June 1950 the Korean War broke out, causing US policy toward Japan to change quickly from encouragement of a strong antitrust policy to promotion of heavy industry as a means of erecting bulwarks against communist infiltration. Also, it had become evident by about 1950 that the AML in its original form was too ambitious for the Japanese economy, which had been shattered by World War II. Finally, it had also become apparent that there was no popular support for "free competition" and the AML as originally implemented.

In 1953, Japan enacted an amendment deleting Article 4, which had stipulated the per se illegality of cartels. Henceforth, cartels would be controlled under Article 2-6 and Article 3, which stipulated that cartels were unlawful if they restrained competition substantially and if their existence was contrary to the public interest. New provisions (Article 24-3 and Article 24-4) were introduced which authorized, respectively, depression cartels and rationalization cartels. Also, the 1953 amendment introduced an AML exemption covering the resale price maintenance of books and other items subject to copyright; commodities designated by the FTCJ also received an exemption. Another change under the 1953 amendment was the deletion of Article 8, which had provided that a large enterprise could be ordered to partition a portion of its facility, give away technology, or take such measures as appropriate to reduce its economic power if a large gap existed between this enterprise and its competitors in the market. This article was based on the premise that a large enterprise could be subject to an order of dissolution or divestiture without any wrongful conduct on its part as long as there was a large gap in economic power between it and its competitors. This provision was never used during its six-year existence.

The 1953 amendment strengthened one aspect of the AML: the control of unfair business practices. In its original form, the AML had prohibited "unfair methods of competition." The 1953 amendment replaced this phrase with "unfair business practices." It was an objective of the amendment to widen the scope of the law to address practices that were not "methods of competition" but rather were unfairly suppressive of the activities of other enterprises. Examples might include a powerful manufacturer imposing a harsh deal on a subcontractor in a relatively weak bargaining position, or a large retailer such as a department store exacting similarly one-sided terms from its suppliers.

Supplemental legislation enacted in 1956, the Law to Prevent Unreasonable Delay in Payment to Subcontractors and Related Matters (hereafter referred to as the Subcontractors Law), defined prohibited conducts and remedies more specifically. This law remains an important piece of legislation today (*Shitauke Daikin Shiharai Chien Boshi Ho* [Law to Prevent Unreasonable Delay in Payment to Subcontractors and Related Matters], Law 120, 1956, as amended).

A number of exempting laws were enacted granting certain activities immunity from the AML. This legislation included the Export and Import Transactions Law, which permitted the formation of export and import associations; the Marine Transportation Law, which permitted the creation of shipping conferences; and the Medium and Small Business Organizations Law, which allowed trade associations composed of small enterprises to engage in restrictive activities.

Enforcement activity occurred under the AML from about 1950 to the mid-1960s. Only a handful of cases were decided by the FTCJ annually, even though several large mergers took place during those years. These included the merger of three heavy industrial companies to form Mitsubishi Heavy Industries (1963), the integration of Prince Motor Company into Nissan (1965), and the merger of the Yawata Steel Company and the Fuji Steel Company to form the Japan Steel Company (1969).[3]

Revitalization of the AML in the 1960s

A sharp increase in consumer prices in the early 1960s caused the AML to be regarded in a new light: as a weapon to combat high prices, which arguably were attributable to price cartels, resale price maintenance, and price rigidity caused by oligopolistic structures in the economy. More energetic enforcement of the AML in the 1960s was made evident by the increase in the number of cases in which the FTCJ proceeded against price-fixing cartels among enterprises and trade associations and found them to be unlawful (Matsushita 1990, 1-5).

Another important event in the 1960s was the liberalization of foreign trade and capital transactions. Until the middle of the 1960s, external trade and investment were strictly regulated through import quotas and restrictions on the introduction of foreign capital into Japan. Consequently, there was relatively little room for free competition. As liberalization progressed, the role of the AML increased in areas such as international patent licensing, and the need grew for enforcement of the AML. In response to this new situation, the FTCJ, for one, announced a new set of guidelines in 1968 governing how the trade commission would oversee restrictive provisions in international contracts between Japanese and foreign enterprises.

---

3. The best source on these developments is Koseitorihiki Iinkai (1967).

The AML was further revitalized by the emphasis placed on consumer protection by Japan's increasingly affluent society in the 1960s. A supplement to the AML enacted in 1961 (the Law to Prohibit Unreasonable Premium and Representation and Related Matters, hereafter referred to as the Premium and Representation Law) prohibited excessive premium offerings and false and misleading representations; enforcement was entrusted to the FTCJ (*Futokeihinrui Oyobi Futohyoji Boshi Ho* [Law to Prohibit Unreasonable Premium and Representation and Related Matters], Law 134, 1962, as amended). This law continues to be an important piece of legislation.

The 1977 Amendment

The Oil Crisis of 1973 pushed prices sharply upward in Japan. Some oil companies took advantage of the inflation-induced panic by participating in price-fixing agreements. Public criticism was voiced against oil companies, as well as against enterprises whose hoarding practices contributed to higher commodities prices. The FTCJ seized this opportunity by organizing a task force to study the possibility of amending the AML. In a 1974 interim report, the task force recommended an amendment that would make the AML more effective at dealing with cartels and monopolies. The National Diet passed an amendment in 1977 incorporating many new provisions, the three most important of which were the administrative surcharge, structure control, and the price-reporting system.

Until introduction of the administrative surcharge, it had been impossible to forfeit from enterprises extra profits they had gained by means of unlawful price cartels or other cartels affecting price. The FTCJ could only issue orders prohibiting enterprises from continuing the cartels. This weak enforcement mechanism created a situation in which cartels were profitable. The administrative surcharge was implemented as a means of confiscating cartel participants' illegal extra profits and thereby discouraging cartel activity.

Article 2-7 of the AML as amended—the structure control provision— stated that when an enterprise occupied 50 percent or more of a particular market, or two enterprises occupied 75 percent or more, new entry into the market was difficult and undesirable economic outcomes resulted, such as excessively high price and profits or excessive expenditures on general expenses. Under the structure control provision, such enterprises were deemed to be in a monopolistic situation and the FTCJ could order them to be dissolved into smaller entities if other means of remedying the situation failed.

The price-reporting system was designed to deal with simultaneous price increases in oligopolistic markets, a common occurrence. Previously, if there had been collusion among a small number of enterprises to raise their prices, this activity could have been prohibited on the grounds that it constituted the activity of a cartel. However, there would often be no evidence of collusion. Under the provision for a price-reporting system, the FTCJ could now order enterprises that had raised their prices simultaneously in an oligopolistic market to report the reasons for such a price increase and provide supporting data. A summary of the data and their analysis by the FTCJ must be reported to the National Diet. Giving teeth to this provision was the prospect that the FTCJ, when invoking this provision, could require a great quantity of data to be submitted by the enterprises in question, including production costs and customers lists.

The Structural Impediments Initiative (SII)

One of the recent developments promoting revitalization of the AML has been the Structural Impediments Initiative (SII), a trade negotiation between the United States and Japanese governments. The SII was begun in 1989 and concluded in 1990; implementation occurred over the period 1990-93. The task force organized by both governments reported that "structural impediments" existed in the Japanese market preventing penetration by foreign enterprises and foreign goods. Structural impediments in the Japanese market consisted of, among others, *keiretsu* relationships among enterprises (closely interrelated business relationships among enterprises), mutual stockholdings of enterprises belonging to an individual group (such as the Mitsubishi and Mitsui groups), and interlocking directorates among enterprises. The task force recommended that the enforcement of the AML be expanded to cope with these impediments.

In response to the SII report, the Japanese government undertook to increase the enforcement of the AML in several respects. First, the rate of administrative surcharge was raised from 2 percent to 6 percent of the total sales of each participant in a cartel of the product in question (in sectors other than retail and wholesale business). Second, the FTCJ announced a set of guidelines entitled "The AML Guidelines on Distribution and Trade Practices." Third, the maximum criminal fine with regard to corporations was raised to ¥100 million. (Before the amendment, it had been ¥5 million.) Fourth, the FTCJ announced a program whereby it would assist private plaintiffs who brought civil suits for recovery of damages against defendants who violated the AML by providing data and documents so as to enable them to prove the amount of damages and the causal link between the unlawful conduct and the damage.

The number of FTCJ investigators was increased, and the commission established a special office designed to receive complaints from foreign parties claiming their efforts to penetrate the Japanese market had failed because of violations by Japanese enterprises of the AML.

Summary

The AML's enforcement has alternately weakened and strengthened as the result of economic and political pressures both domestic and foreign. On the whole, however, it seems fair to state that enforcement has been strengthened over the years.

A Summary of the Japanese Antimonopoly Law

An Overview

Although the Antimonopoly Law was originally modeled after United States antitrust laws, it has become clear over time that some of the enforcement methods inherited from these laws (such as damage suits and criminal penalties) are not effective in Japan. Therefore, other methods of enforcement, such as the administrative surcharge, have been introduced.

Generally, activities that come under the regulation of the AML are private monopolization (Article 2-5, Article 3), cartels (Article 2-6, Article 3), and unfair business practices (Article 2-9, Article 19).

Private monopolization is defined in Article 2-5 and is prohibited by Article 3 of the AML. Under those provisions, a private monopolization is an "exclusion" or "control" by a powerful enterprise of the business activities of other enterprise(s), thereby causing a substantial restraint of competition in a particular field of trade.

Articles 9 through 13 of the AML (see chapter 4) have been designed to control mergers and acquisitions. They are preventive measures in the sense that, since a private monopoly can be exercised only by an enterprise with a powerful position in a market, the control of mergers and acquisitions so that there will be no excessive concentration of corporate power in a market serves to head off private monopolization in its incipiency.

In Article 2-7, which was incorporated into the AML by its 1977 amendment, a "monopolistic situation" is defined. This provision is designed to deal with an oligopolistic market structure rather than a specific action by an enterprise. In a situation where an enterprise enjoys a large market share—enabling it to charge high prices and to earn high rates of profit—the prohibition of private monopolization is meaningless unless such a monopolistic position has been acquired by means of an exclusion or control by the enterprise of the business activities of other enterprises. As long as such a monopolistic position is the result of natural growth or superior technological or managerial skills, it does not amount to private monopolization even though competition in a market declines. Whether to extend antitrust control to "structure" is a policy matter. In the 1977 amendment, the National Diet decided to incorporate a provision into the AML designed to exert such a control. If a monopolistic situation exists, in order to restore competition the FTCJ can apply a dissolution measure to an enterprise.

Cartels, or Unreasonable Restraint of Trade

Cartels, described as "unreasonable restraint of trade," are defined in Article 2-6 of the AML. Under this definition, a cartel is an agreement (whether overt or tacit) or understanding between enterprises whereby they restrain competition mutually and cause substantial restraint of competition in a particular field of trade. Article 3 prohibits unreasonable restraint of trade. This article corresponds roughly to Section 1 of the Sherman Antitrust Act and Article 85-1 of the Treaty of Rome. Article 2-6 of the AML states that a cartel is unlawful when it is contrary to "the public interest." As will be discussed later, there are differing views on what constitutes the public interest.

Clauses (i) through (iii) of Article 8-1 of the AML prohibit trade associations from engaging in conduct that restrains competition or otherwise limits members' activities. Because trade associations play an important role in the Japanese economy and often engage in restrictive activities, Article 8 is an important provision in the prohibition of cartels. Exemptions for cartels are discussed in chapter 4.

Unfair Business Practices

Unfair business practices are defined in Article 2-9 and prohibited by Article 19. Article 2-9 states that unfair business practices are activities that impede fair competition; that come under any of the six following categories: unreasonable discrimination, transactions with unreasonable price, unreasonable inducement or coercion of customers of competitors, unreasonable control of business activities of other enterprises, abuse of dominant bargaining positions, and unreasonable interference in the matters of competitors; and that are designated by the FTCJ as falling within the framework of these six categories. The FTCJ has announced a set of designations enumerating the activities that fall under the rubric of unfair business practices.

Unfair business practices as defined above include a multitude of practices such as refusals to deal, boycotts, sales below costs, false advertisements, excessive premium offerings, exclusive dealings, and tie-in arrangements. As mentioned earlier, the Subcontractors Law and the Premium and Representation Law provide support to the provisions of the AML governing unfair business practices.

The Enforcement Agency and Its Procedures

The Fair Trade Commission of Japan

The FTCJ is the enforcement agency of the AML. The FTCJ is composed of a commission chairperson, four commissioners, and a secretariat. Altogether, the FTCJ employs more than 500 staff attorneys and other personnel. The chairperson is nominated by the prime minister with the consent of both houses of the National Diet; the fitness of the nominee must also be verified by the emperor. Commissioners are appointed by the prime minister with the consent of the National Diet.

The FTCJ wields administrative, quasi-legislative, and quasi-judicial powers. Its administrative purview includes licensing powers (for example, the power to approve depression cartels and fair-competition codes), the requirement that it receive and examine notifications (such as notifications of the establishment of trade associations and the signing of international contracts), the prerogative to consult with other ministries and give advice to industries, the authority to conduct economic research, and other powers.

The quasi-legislative powers are, in short, the rule-making powers, among which are the powers to designate and elucidate unfair business practices and to name the commodities for which resale price maintenance are allowed.

The quasi-judicial powers include the powers to initiate an investigation, to hold administrative hearings, and to make decisions concerning the legality of conduct. This last power includes the authority to levy an "elimination measure" (the equivalent of a cease-and-desist order of the US Federal Trade Commission). An administrative hearing is an adversarial process with the administrative hearing examiner or the commission presiding.

When the FTCJ deems that a violation exists, it can choose to issue a statement to the offending party that the conduct in question is a violation and recommending that the party discontinue it. If the party accepts the recommendation, the FTCJ does not proceed with a formal hearing process. The FTCJ's decision in such a case is called a *recommendation decision*. If an administrative hearing is initiated, the respondent can propose to the FTCJ that it will accept the allegations of facts and law as stated in the complaint by the FTCJ and that it will take necessary measures to stop the conduct complained of and restore competition. If the FTCJ deems this proposal to be appropriate, it issues a *consent decision*.

A decision of the FTCJ adverse to the respondent may be appealed to the Tokyo High Court and to the Supreme Court. However, the party who receives a recommendation decision or a consent decision cannot bring a suit against it in the Tokyo High Court since such decisions are based on the agreement between the respondent and the FTCJ. When reviewing a case in which a decision of the FTCJ is at issue, the Tokyo High Court is bound by the substantial-evidence rule.[4]

Elimination Measures and Administrative Surcharge

As explained above, the FTCJ issues a decision together with an elimination measure when it has found that an action is in violation of the AML. An elimination measure is a remedy to restore competition and may take various forms according to the nature of the violation in question. It can serve as a means of implementing any order necessary to restore competition. In price cartel cases, for example, the FTCJ usually issues an elimination measure commanding the parties in violation to cancel the cartel agreement and to make public that the cartel has ceased to exist.

As already discussed, the 1977 amendment introduced the administrative surcharge. The details of administrative surcharge are discussed in chapter 3.

Criminal Penalty

Article 89-1 of the AML provides that a person who has created a private monopolization or an unreasonable restraint of trade (cartel) is punishable by a fine not to exceed ¥5 million or by a prison term of not more than three years. The 1992 amendment created a criminal fine on corporations (Law No. 107, 1992 amending Article 95 (l)(i) of the Antimonopoly Law). Under this amendment, which took effect on 1 January 1993, the maximum fine on corporations is ¥100 million. Article 89-2 provides that when a trade association restrains competition substantially in a particular field of trade contrary to Article 8-1 of the AML, the same penalty as that for individuals applies.

---

4. Substantial-evidence rule is provided in Article 80 of AML. It states that the facts in a case determined by the FTCJ is binding on the court that exercises judicial review on the decision only if the facts are supported by substantial evidence. However, this article also states that the court is empowered to decide whether or not there is substantial evidence with regard to the facts found by the FTCJ.

One feature of the system of criminal penalties under the AML is that an accusation by the FTCJ is the prerequisite for public prosecutors to bring an indictment (per Article 96).

Private Damage Action

Articles 25 and 26 of the AML permit a private plaintiff who suffers property damage resulting from a private monopolization, unreasonable restraint of trade, or unfair business practice to bring a suit in the Tokyo High Court for recovery of the damage. The prerequisite of an action under Articles 25 and 26 is that the FTCJ has acted against the conduct in question and a decision (of any kind) has been rendered and become finalized. If an FTCJ decision has been finalized with regard to a conduct and if a private plaintiff brings up a damage action on account of such an act, the defendant cannot claim that there has been no intention or negligence on his or her part. Therefore, the defendant's liability is a no-fault liability.

Article 709 of the Civil Code provides for tort claims generally. Under precedents, whenever there is a violation of the AML, a private plaintiff can bring a tort claim against the malefactor and seek the recovery of damages under Article 709 of the Civil Code; the plaintiff can do this regardless of whether or not there is an FTCJ decision on the action in question (Decision of the Supreme Court, 8 December 1989, *Minshu* [Supreme Court Civil Cases Reporter], 43[11], 1259 et seq. [1989]). Under the general rule of the Civil Code, however, the plaintiff must prove a tortious intent or negligence on the part of the defendant.

Whether a suit occurs under Articles 25 and 26 of the AML or under Article 709 of the Civil Code, the plaintiff in a suit must prove the amount of damage and the causal link between the damage sustained and the unlawful conduct in question. As is touched upon later, the rule regarding this proof is quite stringent, and it is quite difficult for a plaintiff to meet this requirement.

Salient Features of the Enforcement Process

Overview

In this chapter, I take up some aspects of the enforcement of the Antimonopoly Law (AML). The Japanese enforcement system is a mixture of diverse elements. As originally enacted in 1947, the enforcement methods of the AML were modeled after those in United States antitrust laws. There were three primary methods of enforcement. One was the elimination measure (cease-and-desist order) issued by the Fair Trade Commission of Japan. The second was criminal fines and imprisonment. The third was the private suit initiated by the private plaintiff to recover damages sustained by an unlawful conduct.

However, the criminal fines and imprisonment and the private damage suit have proved to be ineffective. In the early 1970s, the Oil Crisis occurred and prices soared. Oil cartels were discovered and a public outcry was raised against them. It was considered necessary to introduce a measure to forfeit profits gained by the participants of a cartel. Consequently, the administrative surcharge was introduced by the amendment of 1977. In the late 1980s, as a result of the Structural Impediments Initiative (SII), the Japanese government promised to strengthen the powers of the AML. As noted in the preceding chapter, the rate of administrative surcharge was raised, as was the maximum fine vis-à-vis corporations; guidelines on distribution and trade practices were formulated; and the FTCJ announced that it would launch a program whereby it would provide assistance to private plaintiffs who brought suits to recover damages by providing documents and data it had acquired in the process of investigation. Consequently, although the process of enforcement in Japan is primarily based on that in the United States, it has become somewhat different from that in the United States and also from that in the European Union (EU).

Administrative Surcharge

The administrative surcharge in Japan resembles the administrative fine in the European Union in that it is imposed by an administrative agency as an administrative measure rather than a criminal penalty. Yet it is different from the administrative fine in the European Union in that whereas the administrative surcharge is regarded as an administrative measure to collect the extra profits gained by the participants in a cartel during the period in which the cartel was effectively implemented, the administrative fine in the European Union is regarded as a "penalty," and the penalty may exceed the actual extra profits gained by participants in a cartel.

The administrative surcharge under the AML is imposed not on actual extra profits gained by an enterprise from participating in a cartel but on an estimated extra profit. This is because it is practically impossible for the FTCJ to calculate the actual amount of extra profit gained by cartel participants in each case.

Article 7-2 of the AML stipulates that a participant in a price cartel or a cartel that affects price (such as that for production quotas) shall pay 6 percent of the total value of sales of the product in question during the period in which the cartel was effectively implemented in the manufacturing industries. In wholesale industries, the rate is 1 percent; in retail industries, it is 2 percent. Before enactment of this amendment, the rate was one-half of 3 percent (=1.5 percent) of the total value (in manufacturing 4 percent, in retailing 2 percent, and in wholesale 1 percent) of sales of the product in question during the period when the cartel was in existence. When a cartel has lasted for more than three years, the administrative surcharge must be applied retroactively to the period beginning three years before the surcharge was imposed.

As part of the SII, the United States government insisted that the administrative surcharge be raised to 10 percent of total sales. In response, the FTCJ organized a task force to examine the issue. The task force concluded that to raise the administrative surcharge to 10 percent would be impossible because the administrative surcharge would then amount to not only a collection of extra profits but also a penalty. Because criminal penalties are also provided for in the AML, the imposition of an administrative penalty in excess of extra profits would be a de facto penalty and violate Article 39 of the Constitution, which prohibits double jeopardy.

Because, as stated earlier, the administrative surcharge is not a penalty but merely a collection of extra profits, the figure cited earlier— 6 percent of total sales of the product of an enterprise that had participated in a manufacturing cartel—is not the maximum leviable administrative surcharge. The FTCJ must impose the administrative surcharge on cartel participants uniformly, calculated on the basis of the formulas provided above, although there are exceptions for small enterprises.

In the European Union, the maximum administrative fine is the greater of 1 million European Currency Units (ECUs) or 10 percent of the total value of worldwide sales in the preceding year of a party in violation. In the European Union, the administrative fine is based on the sales of a violating party in their entirety in the preceding year. In Japan, the administrative surcharge is a fixed rate whose amount is based on the sale of the product in question of a violating party for a period of three years or less, depending on the individual case.

See table 1 for the annual amount of administrative surcharges levied in Japan, in yen, for the years 1985-94.

The total levy for 1990 was unusually high because the Cement Cartel Case (In re Nihon Cement K. K. et al., Decision of the Fair Trade Commission, 25 January 1991, Shinketsushu, vol. 37 [1990-91] p. 59 et seq; In re Onoda Cement K. K. et al., Decision of the Fair Trade Commission, 25 January 1991, Shinketsushu, supra., p. 70 et seq.),[5] in which an unprecedentedly large administrative surcharge was imposed, was decided that year. Even if this year is excepted, however, the record shows a remarkable increase in the amount of surcharges imposed over the 10-year period.

However, it should be noted that the rate of surcharge is fixed by

5. Although these cases were formally decided by the FTCJ in early January 1991, the respondents had accepted the FTCJ measures at the end of 1990.

Table 1   Sum levied as administrative surcharges under Japan's Antimonopoly Law, 1985-94 (in yen)

Year	Cases	Surcharge
1985	4	407,470,000
1986	4	275,540,000
1987	6	147,580,000
1988	3	418,990,000
1989	6	803,490,000
1990	11	12,562,140,000
1991	10	1,971,690,000
1992	17	2,681,570,000
1993	22	4,087,400,000
1994	26	5,668,290,000

Source: Annual report of the FTCJ.

law, which makes it easy for enterprises to calculate how much financial risk is involved in participating in a cartel. Enterprises may take this into consideration as a form of cost, and if projected profits exceed the estimated cost, there will be an incentive to enter into a cartel agreement.

Criminal Penalties

Clauses (i) and (ii) of Article 89-1 of the AML provide that violations of Article 3 (private monopolization or unreasonable restraint of trade) and of Article 8-1 (substantial restraint of competition by a trade association) are punishable by a term of imprisonment not to exceed three years or a fine not to exceed ¥5 million, or both. Article 95 provides that when the natural persons who constitute the representative and employees of a corporation commit punishable offenses covered in Article 89-1, clauses (i) and (ii), the corporation is subject to punishment as well as the natural persons.

The FTCJ has the exclusive power to bring a criminal accusation against individuals and corporations to the prosecutor general; unless the FTCJ has brought an accusation, the prosecutor general cannot bring an indictment.

Through the mid-1990s, the record of criminal prosecutions has been scanty. Typical has been the Oil Cartel (Production Adjustment) Case, decided by the Tokyo High Court in 1980 (Decision of the Tokyo High Court, 26 September 1980, *Hanrei Jiho* [Current Court Cases Reporter], 983, 22 et seq. [1980]). At issue was a program of the Petroleum Association of Japan that was encouraged by the Ministry of International Trade and Industry (MITI) to cut back the amount of oil refining it was doing. The Tokyo High Court held that, although the conduct of the defendants was unlawful, they were not guilty due to the lack of criminal intent. By contrast, in the Oil Cartel (Price-Fixing) Case, decided by the Supreme Court in 1984, a number of oil companies engaged in an agreement to raise prices of petroleum products. The Supreme Court held that most of the defendants were guilty (Decision of the Supreme Court, 24 February 1984, *Keishu* [Supreme Court Criminal Cases Reporter], 38[4], 1287 et seq. [1984]).

Recently, however, criminal enforcement has been stepped up in accordance with the promise made by the Japanese government under the SII. In 1991, the FTCJ brought an accusation against producers of wrap materials who had engaged in price-fixing activities. Indictments were issued, a criminal trial was held, and, in 1993, all the defendants were found guilty (Decision of the Tokyo High Court, 21 May 1993, *Hanrei Jiho* [Current Court Cases Reporter], 1474, 31 et seq. [1993]).

In 1992, the Public Prosecutor's Office indicted a number of individuals alleged to have engaged in bid rigging in the sale of peel-off seals to the Social Welfare Agency, an action in violation of a provision in the Criminal Code prohibiting rigging in public bids. In 1994, the Tokyo District Court handed down a decision in which the defendants were found guilty. Upon notice from the Public Prosecutor's Office, the FTCJ investigated the issue under the AML and issued a decision ordering the enterprises to discontinue the bid rigging. The FTCJ filed an accusation against the corporations with the Public Prosecutor's Office for a violation of criminal provisions of the AML. The Public Prosecutor's Office brought up an indictment and, in 1993, the Tokyo District Court held that the defendants were guilty (Decision of the Tokyo High Court, 14 December 1993, *Hanrei Taimuzu* [Court Decisions Times], 840, 81 et seq. [1994]; Antimonopoly law case, Decision of the Tokyo District Court, 7 March 1994, unreported [criminal law case]).

Although evaluation at this point would be premature, the criminal provisions of the AML may prove to be effective if the current enforcement policy continues. As noted above, in 1992 the AML was revised to increase the criminal penalty to be imposed on corporations. In Japanese criminal law doctrine, a corporation in and of itself is not subject to punishment apart from the criminal responsibility of the individuals belonging to it. Therefore, under Article 89 of the AML, a corporation could be punished only if individuals who were representatives or employees of the corporation had committed a violation of Article 89. Hence, under this doctrine, the maximum penalty a corporation could be assessed could not exceed the maximum for individuals (i.e., ¥5 million).

The maximum fine of ¥5 million was thought to be too small to deter corporate violations, although the social stigma attached to criminal prosecutions was considered to have a deterrent effect.

As part of the effort to step up antitrust enforcement, the FTCJ considered increasing criminal penalties. To this end, it organized a task force, which recommended in a 1991 report that the traditional equivalence between a corporation's degree of criminal liability and that of the individuals associated with it should be ended. Specifically, the task force also recommended that the maximum criminal fine leviable on corporations should be raised to several hundred million yen. The Japanese cabinet decided to introduce an amendment to the AML that would raise the maximum criminal fine for corporations to ¥100 million. As mentioned, the bill was passed by the National Diet in 1992 and took effect in 1993.

In the United States, antitrust laws are enforced by means of criminal penalties as well as treble-damage lawsuits. In the European Union there is administrative penalty, but no criminal enforcement of the kind found in the United States. In Japan, there exist both criminal penalties and administrative surcharges.

When first implemented in the 1940s, the AML introduced criminal enforcement modeled after US antitrust laws. Over the years, however, this form of enforcement proved ineffective. As noted above, after the Oil Crisis of the 1970s, an attempt was made to introduce an administrative surcharge. One means of doing this would have been to introduce an "administrative fine" after the model of the European Union. However, an administrative fine assessed on the extra profit gained by the participants in unlawful activity would amount to a "fine," if not a criminal fine. This would be a violation of the principle of double jeopardy as incorporated in the Constitution.

Therefore, as introduced into the AML in the 1977 amendment, the administrative surcharge was characterized as merely a collection of extra profit. Although the amount collected may not exactly equal the extra profit gained by the parties to an unlawful activity and, therefore, may in fact have the same effect as a fine, in theory it is not regarded as a fine. For the above-stated constitutional reason, an administrative surcharge cannot be raised to a level greater than the amount of extra profit accrued as a result of illegal activity.

It seems that the dualism of the administrative surcharge and the criminal penalties is anomalous in the context of antitrust laws elsewhere in the world. This anomaly creates an obstacle to any attempt to raise the administrative surcharge above a certain level. However, the existence of the administrative surcharge makes it difficult to raise criminal penalties to corporations beyond the maximum fine of ¥100 million, although this amount probably is insufficient in view of the size and power of large corporations in contemporary Japan. In this sense, the counterposing of administrative fines and criminal penalties creates a sort of system of checks and balances that prevents the strengthening of one or the other.

A remodeling of the penalty system under the AML seems necessary. One way of doing so would be to change the AML so that the FTCJ could either impose an administrative surcharge or bring up an accusation if there were a case in which a serious offense apparently was involved. Doing so would avert a double imposition of a criminal penalty and an administrative surcharge. Under such a new regime, the amount (or rate) of administrative surcharge could be raised to a level at which it would be an "administrative fine" in the sense understood in the European Union.

Private Damage Actions

Overview

Articles 25-1 and 25-2 of the AML provide that an enterprise guilty of private monopolization, unreasonable restraint of trade, or an unfair business practice shall be liable to make compensation for the damage sustained by a person and that the enterprise cannot escape from the liability by maintaining that there was no tortious intention or negligence on the part of the enterprise. Article 26-1 provides that a claim based on Article 25 cannot be entertained until and unless an FTCJ decision has been made final with regard to the violation in question. In short, these articles provide for a no-fault liability on the part of an enterprise that has committed a private monopolization, an unreasonable restraint of trade, or an unfair business practice, on the condition that an FTCJ decision has been rendered on the violation in question and has become finalized. Also, as noted above, Article 709 of the Civil Code, which provides for tort liability in general, is applicable when a person has sustained a damage as a result of conduct in violation of the AML.

In the past, private damage actions have been unusual. There may be a multitude of sociological explanations for this. However, as is noted later in this discussion, there is a trend toward more private enforcement today.

Indirect Purchaser and Proof of Linkage
between Illegal Conduct and Damage

As the result of a 1987 Supreme Court decision, it is difficult for private plaintiffs who are indirect purchasers and who seek recovery of damages (e.g., consumers) to prove the linkage between illegal conduct on the part of the defendant and the damage sustained by the plaintiff.

In the relevant case, the Oil Cartel (Price-Fixing) Case, the defendants, oil refineries, fixed the price of petroleum products at the refinery level (Decision of the Supreme Court, 2 July 1987, *Minshu* [Supreme Court Civil Cases Reporter], 41[5], 785 et seq. [1987]). The refineries sold the product to wholesalers, who in turn sold it to retailers, who then sold it to consumers. Consumers brought claims against the refineries, stating that they had sustained damage as a result of price-fixing by the defendants at the refinery level that eventually translated into higher prices at the retail level.

The plaintiffs had to prove that (1) there was a price-fixing, (2) the retail price rose after the refineries' price had risen, and (3) events that occurred between the time of the price-fixing and the time when consumers purchased the product did not affect the price structure of the product. This last requirement would make it very difficult for the defendants to prove the linkage, and indeed, the Supreme Court decided that the plaintiffs had not proved the linkage between the unlawful price-fixing and the damage they as consumers had sustained.

Following the Oil Cartel Case, the FTCJ announced a program to assist private plaintiffs who bring claims against defendants for the recovery of damages. In short, the FTCJ proposed that it provide helpful economic and business data to plaintiffs and to civil courts handling cases that might help prove the existence of links between illegal conduct and damage and help courts determine the amount of such damages.

Recent Private Enforcement Cases

In 1993 and 1994, civil courts in Japan rendered important decisions in which the issue was a restriction imposed by manufacturers or their subsidiaries on dealers and customers. In those decisions, courts struck down restrictions imposed on dealers and customers by manufacturers on the grounds that they were contrary to provisions of the AML. In 1996, more such decisions were pending, and it was expected that even more would be handed down in the near future. Such decisions in private civil cases may lead to more private cases being filed in the future.

The Toshiba Elevator Case The Toshiba Elevator Company (The Toshiba Elevator Case; Decision of Osaka High Court, 30 July 1993), a wholly owned subsidiary of Toshiba engaged in the servicing of Toshiba-made elevators, refused to supply parts and components to independent companies that were also engaged in servicing elevators. There were problems with an elevator made by Toshiba and installed in a building whose owner had entered into a service contract with an independent contractor. The building owner asked Toshiba Elevator to supply parts and components so that the independent contractor could repair the elevator. Toshiba Elevator refused on the grounds of its policy of denying parts and components to anyone not in the business of servicing elevators. However, when an independent servicing company made a similar request, Toshiba Elevator refused to supply parts and components for the same reason.

The owner of the building brought a suit against Toshiba Elevator, as did the servicing company, on the grounds that the refusal to supply parts and components constituted an illegal tie-in arrangement between elevator servicing (the "tying product") and parts and components (the "tied product") in a tortious violation of the AML. The two cases were consolidated into one, and the trial was held in the Osaka District Court. The court handed down a decision in 1990 holding that Toshiba Elevator was liable to indemnify the damage sustained by the plaintiffs.

The defendants appealed, arguing that the tie-in arrangement was necessary to maintain the safety of elevator operations. The Osaka High Court held that, although product safety was an important issue courts should take into account when considering the illegality of a tie-in contract, there was no need to take this into consideration in this case because the plaintiffs were sufficiently equipped to handle Toshiba-made elevators. The court granted the award of damage to the plaintiffs. There were no further appeals. The Toshiba Elevator case was the first in which the plaintiffs were successful in winning a damage award.

The Shiseido Case Shiseido (Fuijiki v. Shiseido, Decision of the Tokyo District Court, 5 September 1993, *Hanrei Jiho* [Current Cases Reporter], No. 1474, p. 26 et seq.), Japan's largest cosmetics company, required retailers to engage in "person-to-person sales." This meant that they had to give personal explanations of Shiseido products to customers who came to their shops. Retailers also could not engage in other forms of selling, such as catalogue sales, and the recommended retail price was set by Shiseido. The possible purpose of these restrictions was to ensure that the retail price of Shiseido products would be maintained at a certain level.

After a retailer violated the contract by offering Shiseido products by catalogue, the cosmetics manufacturer disputed the retailer's action and then terminated the contract. The retailer then brought an action against Shiseido alleging that, since this was a long-term contract, Shiseido had no right to terminate it unilaterally. The Tokyo District Court decided that the termination of contract was wrong and ordered Shiseido to resume the supply of its products to the retailer under the terms of the contract. The court based its decision on the finding that Shiseido's retail-price policy had an effect contrary to "the spirit of the Antimonopoly Law." Shiseido appealed to the Tokyo High Court. On 14 September 1994, the Tokyo High Court reversed the decision of the district court, holding that there was no evidence to show that the requirement imposed by Shiseido that retailers had to engage in face-to-face sales activities was intended to maintain the retail price of Shiseido products at the retail level (see Shiseido v. Fujiki, Decision of Tokyo High Court, 14 September 1994. For details, see Matsushita, "Shiseido Jiken Kossoshin Hanketsu" [The Appeals Court Decision in the Shiseido

Case], Kokusai Shogyo [The Magazine for Cosmetic, Toiletry, & Drug Industries], December 1994, p. 40 et seq.).

Although it is not clear if the court held that the conduct of Shiseido was contrary to the AML, antitrust issues undoubtedly provided a backdrop for the decision.

The Kao Cosmetics Sales Company Case   Kao Cosmetics (Decision of the Tokyo District Court, 18 July 1994. This case was not reported by court case reporters.), a sales subsidiary of the Kao Soap Company, one of Japan's large manufacturers of soap, cosmetics, toiletries, and related items, entered into an agreement with a retailer. The retailer engaged in catalogue sales in which it solicited orders by sending advertisements to business offices by fax and sold the products to customers at a price 10 percent to 20 percent lower than the retail price suggested by the manufacturer. The retailer also sold Kao products to discount shops, which were considered unauthorized retailers.

Kao terminated the agreement on the grounds that the retailer did not observe provisions in the agreement requiring the retailer to sell products by means of "counseling sales." The issue in this case was similar to the "face-to-face sales" matter raised in the Shiseido Case.

The retailer brought a claim against Kao alleging that the termination amounted to an abuse of rights. The Tokyo District Court held that the termination of the agreement was intended to exclude low-price sales by the plaintiff. The court pointed out, among other things, that the plaintiff was singled out for termination by reason of low-price sales and sales to discount shops. The court noted that, although there were some other retailers that engaged in catalogue sales, these retailers did not lower prices and were not subjected to termination of the agreement.

The court held that Kao's termination violated Item 13 of the General Designation of Unfair Business Practices announced by the FTCJ, which prohibits resale price maintenance. For this reason, Kao's action amounted to an abuse of rights. Therefore, Kao was ordered to deliver products to the plaintiff as ordered.

Kao appealed to the Tokyo High Court. Although in the Shiseido case the court used somewhat ambiguous expressions referring to conduct contrary to the "spirit" of the AML, in the Kao Case the court clearly stated that the AML had been violated, although the facts of both cases seemed essentially the same.

Informal Regulation

Although informal regulation of antitrust laws is not unique to Japan, it is probably much more common there than in the United States, the EU states, and other countries. The FTCJ has established several prior-consultation systems in which enterprises receive advice from FTCJ officials prior to the initiation of business plans. For example, under the AML Guidelines on Activities of Trade Associations, a trade association that obtains a go-ahead in prior consultation with the FTCJ when it intends to initiate a business program is protected from legal action by the trade commission as long as the program operates as described to the commission. If a contemplated plan seems likely to involve a violation of the AML, the FTCJ points this out to the party and suggests that it restructure the plan to conform to the law.

Besides the prior-consultation system, there are informal consultation procedures that enable enterprises and trade associations to obtain the views of the FTCJ on proposed business programs. The 1991 FTCJ Guidelines on Distribution and Trade Practices established procedures for these informal consultations. Informal consultation is also used in the enforcement of Article 6 (control of international contracts) and Article 15 (control of mergers and acquisitions) of the AML, and in the enforcement of the Subcontractors Law. Such informal enforcement is considered as important in Japan as formal actions such as elimination measures, administrative surcharges, criminal indictments, and private damage actions.

Between 1987 and 1993, the number of instances in which trade associations consulted with the FTCJ about the lawfulness of proposed activities ranged from 440 to 960. The total was 540 in 1987, 440 in 1988, 600 in 1989, 845 in 1990, 960 in 1991, 808 in 1992, and 725 in 1993.

In 1991, the FTCJ found 36 percent of the proposed programs in clear violation of trade practices law; 17 percent in possible violation, with further analysis needed; and 47 percent in full conformance with the law. In 1992, 34 percent of programs as proposed were in violation of the law, 25 percent were in possible violation, and 41 percent were in conformance. The proportions for 1993 were 26 percent, 25 percent, and 49 percent respectively.

Cartels and Trade Associations

Overview

In the Antimonopoly Law, a cartel is referred to as "unreasonable restraint of trade." Article 2-6 of the AML defines an unreasonable restraint of trade as an agreement, understanding, or communication of wills among enterprises to restrain competition that indeed substantially restrains competition in a market and that is contrary to the public interest. Unreasonable restraints of trade are prohibited under Article 3 of the AML.

Trade associations often engage in restrictive activities such as establishing a standard price to be charged by the member enterprises or the maximum quantity of a product to be produced by the member enterprises. Clauses (i), (ii), and (iii) of Article 8-1 are the special provisions controlling activities of trade associations, among which clause (i) is the most important. This passage prohibits a trade association from engaging in an activity that restrains competition substantially in a market.

There are a number of laws exempting cartels from the application of the AML. To understand the legal aspects of cartels in Japan, it is essential to examine those exempting laws as well as the provisions of the AML that prohibit cartels.

Legal issues with regard to the prohibition of cartels in the AML are not fundamentally different from those that arise in the antitrust laws of other countries. They include, among others, proof of cartel, the roles of circumstantial evidence and conscious parallelism, and permissible scope of remedy. Because the rules that have emerged in the AML with regard to such issues are not so different from those developed in other countries, such as the United States and the member states of the European Union, I refrain here from analyzing those legal principles in details and concentrate, rather, on issues that seem uniquely Japanese.

Cartels and the Public Interest

Like most antitrust laws elsewhere in the world, the AML in principle prohibits cartels. FTCJ has taken the position that business arrangements that can be identified as cartels under the requirements of Article 2-6 are unlawful unless put outside the purview of the AML by an exempting law. Some controversy exists with regard to the meaning of the term "public interest" incorporated in Article 2-6.

Article 2-6 requires that a cartel be "contrary to the public interest" in order to be held unlawful. There are three major schools of thought on the interpretation of the term *public interest*.[6]

The prevailing doctrine of interpretation—that is, the view held by the FTCJ and the majority of commentators—is that the "public interest" as described in Article 2-6 means nothing more than "free competition." Consequently, per this view, "contrary to the public interest" is synonymous with substantial restraint of competition. This view holds that consistency with the public interest is not a separate and independent requirement in the AML.

---

6. See, for details, Matsushita (1993).

Under the prevailing doctrine, the FTCJ or a plaintiff who challenges a cartel need not prove that the cartel in question is "contrary to the public interest" as long as the cartel substantially restrains competition. This interpretation reflects the view that competition is fundamentally important to the economy and may be regarded as an orthodox position on this subject. However, in practice it is difficult to maintain this position in every case. There may be, for example, a situation in which an agreement among enterprises that are selling a product is necessary to create a countervailing power when they are selling the product to a legally sanctioned monopoly enterprise. There might also be a situation in which an agreement among enterprises engaged in production of, say, chemical compounds, is necessary to guarantee that no chemical substance that would damage the environment is produced.

A countervailing perspective on the concept of the public interest is represented within the business community by the Keidanren (Federation of Economic Organizations), that is, that upholding the public interest is not necessarily the same as upholding free competition, and that consequently the term *contrary to the public interest* is not necessarily synonymous with substantial restraint of competition. Under this interpretation, the public interest means a variety of factors such as the interests of consumers and the growth and stability of the national economy. If one accepts this interpretation, a cartel is not necessarily unlawful even if it restrains competition as long as it is useful in meeting other meaningful economic objectives.

A problem with the Keidanren's interpretation of the content of public interest is that this theory is so vague and general that it can hardly provide criteria for judging whether an agreement among enterprises is contrary to the public interest. Such an interpretation creates the prospect of blanket immunity for all agreements among enterprises that restrain competition because some excuse could always be easily found.

The third theory of the public interest was enunciated by the Supreme Court when it decided the Oil Cartel (Price-Fixing) Case in 1984 (Decision of the Supreme Court, 24 February 1984, *Keishu* [Supreme Court Criminal Cases Reporter], 38[4], 1287 et seq. [1984]). Under this interpretation, the term "public interest" in Article 2-6 of the AML means free competition in principle, but there are exceptional situations in which an agreement that substantially restrains competition is necessary to meet a valid objective. In such situations, courts should weigh the benefit of maintaining competition and the benefit of permitting such an agreement; when the benefit of allowing such an agreement outweighs that of maintaining competition, such an agreement is not contrary to the public interest and consequently not unlawful.

The interpretation adopted by the Supreme Court constitutes a middle-of-the-road approach and, if interpreted and implemented properly, seems to be the most balanced interpretation. However, the Supreme Court did not elaborate the details of the meaning of *public interest*. Therefore, it is left to courts, the FTCJ, and commentators to determine the exact meaning of such exceptional circumstances. Generally, however, examples include an agreement among enterprises to avoid hazards to the public, such as an agreement to stop producing an industrial substance that is known to pollute the environment; an agreement to maintain public order and good morale, such as an agreement to restrain publication of obscene literature; and other agreements designed to accomplish additional objectives considered socially valid.

One might argue that such social objectives should be achieved through legislation and should not be left to the concerted efforts of private enterprises. Indeed, legislation is often introduced to provide for such situations. However, there may be a situation in which there is no such legislation or in which such legislation is being considered but has not yet passed despite the immediate need to address the problem. Under such a circumstance, an agreement among enterprises that are designed to achieve a socially acceptable objective may be held as not contrary to the public interest.

Cartels and Administrative Guidance

One of the issues with regard to the prohibition of cartels is the question of whether a cartel initiated under the administrative guidance of a government agency should be immune from the application of the AML. This issue has arisen in the past as a result of the discrepancy between the competition policy enforced by the FTCJ and the industrial policy exercised by the Ministry of International Trade and Industry (MITI). Although the AML prohibits agreements among enterprises or activities by trade associations that restrict competition, the MITI has used agreements and activities of trade associations as a means of implementing industrial policy.

In concrete terms, the MITI has issued "administrative guidance" to enterprises to form trade associations and engage in restrictive activities or to enter into an agreement to restrict competition among themselves. As a result, there have been instances in which activities of enterprises initiated by the MITI have been challenged by the FTCJ as unlawful cartels (examples are given in the following pages).

Recently, the industrial policy of the MITI has changed so that the ministry no longer emphasizes restrictive activities by trade associations or agreements among enterprises that restrict competition as instruments of policy implementation. However, a potential problem lies in the area of control of financial markets by the Ministry of Finance. For example, a uniformity of interest rates exists among banks. If the Ministry of Finance gives guidance to banks to ensure uniformity of interest rates, there results a conflict between the policies of the finance ministry and the AML.

It is worth examining some of the cases in which restrictive activities of enterprises initiated under the administrative guidance of the MITI were at issue and seeing what legal rules have emerged from them, given that some of the rules formulated in this process have a universal applicability. One such case is the Chemical Fiber Production Cutback Case (FTCJ Decision, 16 August 1953, *Shinketsushu* [FTCJ Decisions Reporter], 5, 17 et seq. [1954]), decided by the FTCJ in 1953, in which a production cutback program was implemented by a trade association in the chemical fiber industry based on MITI administrative guidance. In the period following the outbreak in 1950 of the Korean War, the Japanese economy was in recession and the chemical fiber industry in particular was suffering from slackening demand.

The MITI issued a directive to the Chemical Fiber Association that its members should come up with a program to cut back production. In response, the association formulated a plan in which it determined the total amount of chemical fiber to be produced each year and allocated production quotas to its members. The FTCJ regarded this scheme as an unlawful restraint of competition, and an administrative proceeding was initiated to determine whether the production cutback scheme was contrary to the AML.

The Chemical Fiber Association brought a defense that the scheme was based on the administrative guidance of the government and should be immune from the application of the AML for that reason. The FTCJ rejected this defense, holding that the association's scheme was unlawful even though it was based on administrative guidance. The rationale given by the FTCJ was that government agencies other than the FTCJ had no power to interpret and apply the AML and to allow exemption from the application of the AML. Attempting to justify conduct on the sole basis that the conduct was based on administrative guidance was tantamount to granting administrative guidance the same weight as legislation, the trade commission said. The FTCJ further asserted that the unreasonableness of the Chemical Fiber Association's justification of its actions was obvious.

In the late 1990s, the FTCJ's decision in the Chemical Fiber Association Case continues to represent the position of the FTCJ with regard to the relationship between the AML and administrative guidance.

Issues related to those raised in the Chemical Fiber Association Case were addressed in the Oil Cartel (Production Cutback Case Decision of the Tokyo High Court, 26 September 1980, *Hanrei Jiho* [Current Court Cases Reporter], 983, 22 et seq. [1980]) and decided by the Tokyo High Court in 1980. Involved in this case was a program of the Petroleum Association, whose members included every oil refinery in Japan, to restrain production of petroleum products. The association established a plan to limit the maximum amount of production and allocated production quotas to its members. (Legislation already existed—the Petroleum Business Law—that authorized the MITI to announce and carry out the restraint of production of petroleum products as the ministry deemed necessary.) Because the objective of the law coincided with the Petroleum Association's plan to reduce production, the MITI granted tacit consent to the plan and allowed it to be put in place as part of the implementation of the Petroleum Business Law. However, there was no provision in the Petroleum Business Law exempting such a plan from the AML. Consequently, the FTCJ challenged the Petroleum Association program and recommended to the prosecutor general that the association and the individuals involved in the formulation of the scheme be indicted.

The defendants asserted that this program was based on administrative guidance from the MITI and thus should be immune from the application of the AML. The Tokyo High Court held that, in this particular instance, the defendants could not rely on administrative guidance for justification because the conduct in question was not initiated by administrative guidance but rather by private motivation, and that the MITI only stepped in later to utilize an already existing program.

The court responded in the form of a dictum that an activity initiated by an administrative guidance that would be held unlawful were it not for the administrative guidance could be held as *lawful* if the conduct had been commissioned by a government agency or represented an implementation of the policy of the government. Although the scope of exemption based on administrative guidance may be very narrow, the decision of the Tokyo High Court nonetheless allowed an interpretation that administrative guidance could be grounds for exonerating a conduct that would otherwise be considered unlawful.

On 30 June 1994, the FTCJ announced a set of guidelines on administrative guidance. These replaced a memorandum published by the FTCJ on the same subject on 16 March 1981, shortly after the decision of the Tokyo High Court in the Oil Cartel (Production Cutback) Case.

Today, deregulation of economy is a major policy of the Japanese government. Deregulation involves reducing the powers of ministries, including the power of certain ministries to exempt cartels from the AML. Ministries have traditionally used administrative guidance to retain control of industries under their supervision even after the laws that authorized them to exempt some activities of industries from the AML have expired. Cartels have been exempted as a result of such administrative guidance. The FTCJ announced the new set of guidelines to counteract similar possible moves by ministries in the future.

Basically, the FTCJ guidelines promulgated in June 1994 dictate that activities of enterprises and trade associations initiated on the basis of administrative guidance are considered illegal as long as they meet the requirement for illegality found in the AML. The guidelines enumerate, as examples of administrative guidance that tends to generate unlawful activities on the part of enterprises and trade associations, that which relates to: (1) enterprises' movement into and out of particular markets, (2) product price levels, (3) quantity of product produced and utilization of production facilities, and (4) sales methods, quality standards, advertising, representation, and related matters.

It is worth noting that the guidelines mention as a problem area "administrative guidance in which a guidance is given [to enterprises or trade associations] by indicating concrete figures of production, sales, import, the rate of production, the amount of purchase of raw materials, and related matters." It is further stated that "such an administrative guidance tends to cause enterprises and trade associations jointly to decide quantity of production and other terms." In light of the above, if a ministry endeavors to achieve a certain level of imports of a foreign product by issuing administrative guidance indicating the target amount or market share of the product, and enterprises and trade associations subsequently take joint action to achieve this goal, then there is a risk of violating the AML.

Exempted Cartels

Although covered elsewhere, exempted cartels are sufficiently important to warrant a few comments here.[7] Cartels authorized under law include, among other things, depression cartels, rationalization cartels, export/ import cartels, medium- and small-enterprise cartels, shipping conferences, international aviation cartels, and insurance industry cartels.

Although the number of authorized cartels has been reduced dramatically over the past quarter century, there are still many such cartels. Widespread cartelization consequently creates opportunities for enterprises to discuss issues among themselves and generate a sense of exclusivity among participants. These consequences are further evidence of the need to reduce the number of authorized cartels.

It is reported that efficiency is lacking in the areas where cartelization is permitted under law and consumer prices are generally high. The Temporary Administrative Reform Promotion Council announced in 1988 that "the AML is the most universal rule of competition in market and exemptions from it should be limited to its minimum necessity. The number of exemption laws are more than 40 at present. It is necessary to review the need for maintaining the existing exemptions from the competition policy viewpoint" (Matsushita 1996).

The Temporary Administrative Reform Promotion Council released

---

7. Exempted cartels are discussed in greater detail by Suzumura in chapter 14.

its third report in 1992, in which it proposed that, in light of the fact that the Japanese economy enjoyed a high level of international competitiveness, it was necessary to introduce openness to the Japanese market and reform Japan's economic structure so that it would be more compatible with the economies of other major trading nations. To promote this compatibility, the council proposed that the Japanese government reconsider the total legal system with regard to exemptions of cartels, with a view to abolishing some of them. The council concluded its report by recommending that the Japanese government initiate an extensive program to reduce the number of exemption laws and cartels. It urged that, with regard to the review of exempting laws, the FTCJ and the ministries in charge engage in consultation, and that the Japanese government reach a conclusion by the end of 1995.

Reducing the number of authorized cartels or, if possible, effecting these cartels' abolition, is an important objective in light of the trend in this direction among the major trading nations. It is clear that the existence of a large number of exempting laws and cartels impedes a successful harmonization project.

Summary and Conclusion

Although there are some differences between the antitrust laws of major jurisdictions such as the United States, the European Union, Canada, Germany, the United Kingdom, France, Japan, South Korea, Australia, and New Zealand, one element is common to those countries regarding the prohibition of cartels: In every country in which antitrust legislation exists, the cartel is regarded basically as a form of business activity that should be prohibited or at least limited as much as possible. There are some differences among nations with regard to exceptions and justifications for exonerating cartels of one kind or another. However, in every country, including Japan, the number of such exceptions is being reduced. The differences in this area of antitrust law are not nearly as great as those in other areas, such as the regulation of mergers and acquisitions and nonprice vertical restraints. Therefore, one can anticipate that on the subject of cartel prohibition, nations can agree on basic principles with a view to achieving a greater harmonization or approximation of laws.

An important obstacle to harmonization is the existence of exempted cartels. I attempt no detailed discussion of this issue here because it is discussed in another paper. I will only note that there are still many laws in Japan authorizing cartels for various reasons. It is also worth noting that export cartels are permitted not only in Japan but in almost every country in the world. For the sake of harmonization, this situation must also be addressed.

Monopolies and Mergers

An Overview

Article 2-5 of the Antimonopoly Law defines private monopolization, and Article 3 prohibits enterprises from engaging in private monopolization. Under Article 2-5, a private monopolization is an "exclusion" or "control" by a powerful enterprise exerted over the business activities of other enterprises whose effect is to restrain competition in a particular market. These AML provisions are designed to address situations in which a powerful enterprise excludes competitors and dominates a market.

Article 2-7 defines "monopolistic situations." Per Article 2-7, the enterprise or enterprises are regarded as being in a monopolistic situation if (1) an enterprise occupies 50 percent or more of a market, or two enterprises occupy 75 percent or more of a market, (2) new entry into the market is difficult, and (3) the price and profit rates of these enterprises are excessively high. The FTCJ can order an enterprise in a monopolistic situation to accept measures to restore competition, including a deconcentration order, which would split up the enterprise. Article 2-7 was incorporated into the AML by the 1977 amendment and is designed to deal with a situation in which an enterprise has acquired a monopolistic situation through natural growth or any other means that is not unlawful as such under the AML.

Articles 9 through 18 (Chapter 4 of the AML) deal with mergers and acquisitions. Among others, they address matters such as the prohibition of holding companies (Article 9), companies' acquisition of each other's stocks (Article 10), and the control of mergers (Article 15). Provisions in Chapter 4 are regarded as "preventive measures" in relation to the prohibition of private monopolization. Whereas a monopolization is only possible when an enterprise has a substantial market power, such a market power is often acquired through mergers and acquisitions. For the purpose of preventing a monopolization, it is useful to provide for the control of mergers and acquisitions.

Private Monopolization

Although few cases are decided under Article 2-5 and Article 3 of the AML, one worth noting is the Noda Soy Sauce Case, which involved decisions by the FTCJ, the Tokyo High Court, and the Supreme Court (Decision of the Tokyo High Court, 15 December 1957, *Kosai Mishu* [High Court Civil Cases Reporter], 10[10], 743 et seq. [1957]). Noda Soy Sauce Company (Kikkoman) had about 34 percent of soy sauce sales in the Tokyo area. The company's "KIKKOMAN" trademark was the most prestigious trademark for soy sauce; indeed, it was almost synonymous with soy sauce. In the soy sauce industry, there were three grades in terms of quality. They were, from highest to lowest, "Supreme," "Superior," and "Best."

Kikkoman undoubtedly belonged in the Supreme class. Products of three other companies, Yamasa, Higeta, and Marukin, were also regarded as belonging in this class. However, these three brands enjoyed less stable market positions than Kikkoman. Grades generally paralleled prices, with the higher-priced products regarded as being of a higher grade. Because of this price-quality relationship, the other three companies had to price their products at the same level as the Kikkoman product to keep them from being perceived as inferior and consequently being consigned to a lower grade.

Kikkoman pressured its distributors and retailers to raise the prices they charged for Kikkoman products (i.e., to engage in resale price maintenance). In a few days, the other three companies followed suit, raising their prices to match that of the Kikkoman product.

The FTCJ proceeded against Kikkoman, holding that Kikkoman monopolized the soy sauce market by controlling the activities of the other three companies. The gist of this decision was that Kikkoman indirectly controlled the other three companies' price decisions by raising its own price by way of resale price maintenance.

The trade commission's decision was upheld by the Tokyo High Court. The court reasoned in much the same way as the FTCJ, holding that the term "control" in Article 2-5 encompassed indirect control. This means that a control could include a situation in which a powerful enterprise engaged in a unilateral conduct such as requiring its distributors and retailers to raise prices, as long as this conduct had the effect of causing other enterprises to take similar actions. Some commentators argue that this is too wide an interpretation because the term *control* should be interpreted to mean a direct action or pressure by one party on the other parties that causes the latter to engage in an action parallel to that of the former. However, others argue that to deal with the oligopolistic structure of industries, it is necessary to adopt a wide interpretation of the term *control* and support the interpretation of the FTCJ and the Tokyo High Court.[8] This case comes close to being an instance of a "structure control" as contrasted with a "conduct control."

Structure Control

The 1977 amendment introduced the concept of the structure control. Article 2-7 stipulates that if (1) an enterprise occupies 50 percent or more of the market or two companies occupy 75 percent or above, (2) new entry into the market is difficult, (3) the price of the enterprise(s) in

---

8. On this issue, see Matsushita (1986, 78-87).

question is excessively high, and (4) the profit rate of the enterprise is also excessively high, then the enterprise is regarded as in a monopolistic situation and is subject to dissolution if other means to restore competition fail.

As examined above, the prohibition of private monopolization is designed to control a "wrongful conduct" by a powerful enterprise. However, there may be a situation in which an enterprise acquires a predominant position through lawful practices. For example, an enterprise may achieve a market share of 90 percent through a process of "natural growth," in which competing enterprises have lost their ground because of a comparative lack of managerial skills and resources over a long period. Also, an enterprise may dominate the market thanks to a technological invention. In the above situations, there is no "wrongful conduct" on the part of the party that has come to dominate a market; therefore, the actions of such enterprises do not constitute monopolization under Article 2-5. Yet competition in a market may be eliminated by the dominance of such an enterprise.

Article 2-7 was enacted to fill the gap. It is a structure control as opposed to a control over conducts. Although enacted in 1977, it had not been invoked by the end of 1995. If it ever is invoked, it will be as the ultimate measure for dealing with oligopolies. However, invocation of Article 2-7 seems unlikely. This is because, among other reasons, the procedures to invoke this provision are quite stringent, exceptions exist that exempt enterprises in a monopolistic situation from dissolution orders, and the government ministries overseeing enterprises that might face dissolution would be likely to oppose such an action.

However, the existence of Article 2-7 works to deter abusive conduct on the part of enterprises in monopolistic situations. As explained earlier, an enterprise is subject to dissolution if it has a market share of 50 percent or more, new entry is difficult, and the price and the profit are excessively high. Therefore, if an enterprise with a large market share acts as the price leader in the industry, raises price first, and gains a high rate of profit, then that enterprise may be held as being in a monopolistic situation, a finding that could lead to dissolution of the enterprise.

The FTCJ names industries in which market shares of leading enterprises have reached the market share requirement warned of in Article 2-7; such a designation is regarded by named industries as a sign that they are stepping onto a slippery slope. Enterprises with large market shares take into consideration the existence of Article 2-7 of the AML and refrain from acting as the price leader in the industry in question. Such behavior does not necessarily promote competition. If an enterprise with a large market share refrains from raising its price, its lesser competitors may have difficulty raising their prices when they wish. If they are not as efficient as the enterprise in a monopolistic situation, they may be eliminated from the market. This may lead to an even more concentrated market. In this way, the structure control provided for in Article 2-7 may produce a paradoxical result. However, this provision operates as a de facto means of price regulation by the government.

Mergers and Acquisitions

As stated earlier in this chapter, Chapter 4 of the AML (Articles 9 through 18) is devoted to the control of mergers and acquisitions.

Article 9 prohibits the establishment of holding companies. A "holding company" is defined as a company whose main business is to hold stocks of other companies and control them. Article 9 prohibits holding companies regardless of whether they have any anticompetitive effects such as "substantial restraint of competition."

The reason for the prohibition of holding companies can be found in the history of the AML. In 1947, when the AML was enacted, there was a program for the dissolution of *zaibatsu* (large industrial combines that dominated the Japanese economy before and during the World War II), and many *zaibatsu* were controlled by holding companies.[9] When the AML was enacted in 1947, its framers felt that a holding company could easily be used as a tool for the domination of an industry, and thus that it would be necessary to prohibit such arrangements outright.

The absolute ban on holding companies has been criticized by the business community on the grounds that a holding company is a useful tool for business purposes such as reorganization and consolidation of enterprises, that this absolute prohibition is incompatible with other provisions in the AML that control business activities when they do have an anticompetitive effect, and that a holding company is not necessarily anticompetitive in nature.

It is my view that the absolute prohibition of holding companies under Article 9 should be reconsidered with a view to amending it to require proof of anticompetitive effect. The same applies to Article 9-2, which sets the limit on ownership of stocks by large business companies, and Article 11, which prohibits the holding of stocks by financial companies (banks and securities companies) in excess of 5 percent of the outstanding stocks of the acquired company. (For insurance companies, this limit is 10 percent).

Article 10 prohibits the acquisition and holding of one company's stocks by another company when competition in a particular market is likely to be substantially restrained as the result of that acquisition or holding. Article 15 prohibits a merger between companies when the merger is likely to restrain competition substantially in a particular market.

Article 15-2 provides for prior notification of mergers. Under this

---

9. For more information, see Bisson (1954).

article, in effecting a merger the participating companies must notify the FTCJ of the proposed merger plan at least 30 days before its execution. The FTCJ must conduct an examination of this proposed merger within the 30-day period. If it finds that there is sufficient evidence for a possible violation of Article 15-1, it takes an appropriate legal action to cause the companies to revoke the merger plan. Once the 30 days have passed, the FTCJ cannot initiate a legal action. If the companies effect the merger either without notifying the trade commission or before the end of the 30-day waiting period, the FTCJ can bring an action asking the court to declare the merger null and void.

Article 15-1 stipulates that companies shall not effect a merger if, as the result of the merger, competition in a particular market is likely to be restrained substantially. The term *merger* is not defined in the AML. However, it is interpreted in the sense defined in the Commercial Code. This interpretation excludes a de facto consolidation of enterprises by a means other than two companies establishing a third company, transferring its businesses to the third company, and subsequently dissolving themselves.

In view of the fact that a wider economic concept of "enterprise" is applied to merger control by the antitrust laws of major countries (see the use of terms such as "concentration" in the European Union and "mergers and acquisitions" in the United States), it is worth reviewing this narrow concept of mergers in the AML in order to widen the scope of it.

The FTCJ announced a set of merger guidelines in 1980. In order to respond to criticisms that they were too general, the FTCJ announced new guidelines on 18 August 1994 (referred to as the FTCJ Merger Guidelines). Under this set of guidelines, mergers are classified into (1) horizontal mergers, (2) vertical mergers, and (3) conglomerate mergers, and FTCJ's enforcement policies are laid out with regard to each of these categories. I will touch on only the most salient features of the guidelines.

If the value of assets of merging companies is ¥10 billion or less, the FTCJ conducts only a cursory review of whether the filing of the proposed merger satisfies the formal requirements, such as provision of the necessary information. This practice provides a "safe harbor" for mergers of small enterprises because it means that there will be no substantive investigation into the lawfulness of a merger if it is below this threshold.

Under the FTCJ Merger Guidelines, the trade commission conducts a close scrutiny of a proposed merger under the following conditions:

1. If one or both of the parties to a merger (1) occupy 25 percent or more of a market, (2) rank at the top in terms of market share, holding 15 percent or more of market share, or (3) rank at the top in terms of market share, with the market share of one or both parties

at least one-quarter more than that of the second-ranking or third-ranking company

2. If, in the market in which one of the parties to a merger operates, one or both of the parties rank within the top three in terms of market share, and the total market share of the three top-ranking companies is 50 percent or more

3. If the number of competitors in the market in which one of the parties to a merger operates is seven or fewer

4. If the total value of the assets of one of the parties is ¥100 billion or more, and the total value of assets of the other is ¥10 billion or more

If a merger between companies falls into any of the above categories, it is closely examined by the FTCJ. However, this does not mean that the merger is held unlawful or is presumed to be unlawful. Rather, a number of factors are taken into consideration in the FTCJ's examination.

In horizontal mergers, factors such as the conditions of competition in the relevant market, the conditions in the related markets, the total business ability and resources of the merging companies, the nature of the relevant market, and the environment in which the new entity will operate are considered.

As to efficiency, the FTCJ Merger Guidelines state that increased efficiency is considered a factor only if the merger in question is expected to promote increased competition.

The FTCJ Merger Guidelines state that, with regard to a vertical merger, factors such as degree of market foreclosure and increase of entry barrier will be considered. With regard to a conglomerate merger, factors such as the existence of potential competition among the parties to a merger, the degree to which the position of the parties to a merger will be improved by the merger, and the increase of entry barrier are considered.

The FTCJ Guidelines show some improvements over the previous guidelines in terms of predictability. It is clearly stated, for example, that the market share figure of 25 percent is not a rigid requirement and that other factors are weighed. Likewise, the requirement that market competitors must number at least seven if scrutiny is to be averted is also not rigidly observed by the FTCJ.

The US Department of Justice announced merger guidelines in 1992. These establish three categories in terms of market concentration measured by the HHI (Herfindahl-Hirschmann Index), in which likelihood of action by the Department of Justice is indicated according to the principle that as one moves up to a category of higher concentration ratio, there is more likelihood of action. Relative to the US guidelines, the FTCJ guidelines lack predictability and allow the FTCJ a wider discretion in deciding which factor will be given weight in a given case.

Vertical Restraints

Overview

The Japanese distribution system has long been a focal point of trade issues between Japan and its major trade partners. The United States and the European Union have claimed that the distribution system in Japan is "too long," "too complex," and "exclusive," and that it has prevented foreign enterprises from penetrating the Japanese market.[10] In fact, exclusivity in the distribution system was one of the major issues negotiated under the Structural Impediments Initiative (SII). In response to the request of the United States, the Federal Trade Commission of Japan announced "Guidelines on Distribution and Trade Practices" in 1991 (hereafter referred to as the FTCJ Distribution Guidelines),[11] in which the FTCJ articulated its enforcement policies toward restrictive business practices in distribution. An account of the FTCJ Distribution Guidelines is provided later in this chapter.

Antitrust issues in distribution in large part concern vertical restraints. Generally they involve restraints exercised by a powerful manufacturer over its distributors and dealers such as a resale price maintenance, a vertical territorial allocation of business, an exclusive-dealing arrangement, a tie-in clause, and related matters. Also, sometimes a powerful distributor (for example, a large trading company or a large-scale retail store) will exercise control over manufacturers by means such as requiring manufacturers to give them a sole distributorship.

Some of the practices mentioned above have the effect of excluding outsider parties. For example, an exclusive-dealing arrangement and a tie-in clause exclude outside parties from supplying goods, and a sole distributorship excludes competing goods from the distribution channel. Although a resale price maintenance and a vertical territorial allocation do not exclude outside parties as such, the close relationships they create may have the de facto effect of hindering penetration by outside parties.

Although the term *keiretsu* is both general and vague, it is often used to mean a vertical arrangement between a manufacturer and its distributors (i.e., a distribution *keiretsu*), or such an arrangement between a manufacturer and the producers of parts and components (production *keiretsu*), or between a bank and borrowers (financial *keiretsu*). Although

---

10. For similar claims, see Goldfarb (1995).

11. For a summary of these guidelines, see "The Antimonopoly Act Guidelines Concerning Distribution Systems and Business Practices," *FTC/Japan View*, September 1991, 11 et seq. A full translation of these guidelines is published by the Executive Office of the FTCJ (1991).

a *keiretsu* is not necessarily a vertical relationship (it can be a horizontal or conglomerate *keiretsu* or a mixture of the two types), a vertical relationship is undoubtedly an important feature of it.

Because antitrust issues in distribution are enormously complex, I deal here only with selected issues that seem important in light of trade issues. In the following pages, I examine case law development in areas such as resale price maintenance, territorial and customer restrictions, exclusive-dealing arrangements, and tie-in clauses. I then analyze the contents of the FTCJ Distribution Guidelines. The chapter concludes with some remarks on the effectiveness of the Antimonopoly Law in relation to vertical *keiretsu* issues.

Resale Price Maintenance

A resale price maintenance arrangement whereby a manufacturer causes wholesalers and/or retailers to maintain wholesale or retail prices at a certain level is generally regarded as unlawful unless exempted from the application of the AML under that law's Article 24-2. Resale price maintenance comes under Article 2-9 of the AML and Article 12 of the FTCJ Designation of Unfair Business Practices. Under Article 12 of the FTCJ designation, if a seller of a commodity imposes a condition on a purchaser that the purchaser must maintain a price level as dictated by the seller when the commodity is resold by the purchaser, this imposition constitutes resale price maintenance and is thus unlawful unless there is a good reason for the action. Good reasons are considered by the FTCJ to exist only under very limited circumstances, such as when a manufacturer mandates the price that its subsidiary or distributor will charge to customers.

In practically all cases in which the FTCJ and the courts, including the Supreme Court, have dealt with resale price maintenance, such an arrangement has been found unlawful. One example, which was heard by the Supreme Court, is the Wakodo Case (Decision of the Supreme Court, 11 July 1975, *Minshu* [Supreme Court Civil Cases Reporter], 26[6], 888 et seq. [1975]), in which the sole distributor of powdered milk imposed an elaborate scheme under which retailers had to register themselves with the sole distributor and to pledge that they would abide by the retail price level as directed by the sole distributor. This scheme was held unlawful by the FTCJ and upon appeal came up to the Supreme Court. The Supreme Court supported the FTCJ decision, stating that a resale price maintenance was unlawful as long as it stifled competition among distributors and retailers with regard to the terms of resale of the product supplied by the manufacturer. This has meant that a resale price maintenance is unlawful as long as it stifles "intrabrand price competition" among distributors and retailers of the commodity in question. This doctrine has the broad effect of making resale price maintenance generally unlawful because the very nature of a resale price maintenance is to eliminate intrabrand competition among distributors and retailers.

In the Wakodo Case, the respondent argued that a resale price maintenance was useful for rationalization of the distribution system. The Supreme Court rejected this argument, stating that the lawfulness of a resale price maintenance must be reviewed only from the viewpoint of maintenance of fair competition, and that the mere fact that a resale price maintenance served the purpose of rationalizing the distribution system did not justify it.

In March 1993, the FTCJ challenged a disguised resale price maintenance scheme exercised by sales subsidiaries of Toshiba, Hitachi, Sanyo, and Matsushita. These television manufacturers announced their "suggested retail price" as well as a "reference price." The reference price was lower than the suggested retail price and closer to the market price. The sales subsidiaries instructed the large-scale retail discounters not to advertise the TV sets below the reference price. The FTCJ held that this amounted to an "attachment of unreasonable condition on other party to a transaction" and was thus unlawful (FTCJ Decision, 8 March 1993, *Shinketsushu* [FTCJ Decisions Reporter], 39, 236 et seq. [1994]). In this case, the four television manufacturers took parallel actions in imposing conditions on discounters with regard to advertised price. If there were communications of intentions among the sales subsidiaries, this would be a case of horizontal cartel rather than of vertical restraint.

Viewed narrowly, the case of the four television manufacturers was not one of resale price maintenance because the sales subsidiaries imposed restrictions on "advertisement" rather than on pricing itself. However, the intention of the sales subsidiaries was to keep the retail price from falling below the reference price; therefore, this case can be classified as one of de facto resale price maintenance.

Article 24-2 exempts books and other articles that are subject to copyright (such as music recordings) from the AML. Also exempted are certain commodities expressly designated by the FTCJ. Many commodities have been exempted from the AML. Recently, however, the number of commodities so exempted has been greatly reduced. At present, pharmaceuticals and cosmetics are the sole commodities designated by the FTCJ for exemption from the AML.

Vertical Territorial Restraint

Article 13 of the FTCJ Designation of Unfair Business Practices states that to attach an unreasonably restrictive condition to a transaction is unlawful. "Unreasonable attachment of restrictive condition" is a broad concept and applies to various types of products. Vertical territorial restraint belongs in this category. In this area, precedents have not fully developed yet. The only well-known case is that of Fuji X-Ray (FTCJ Decision, 11 May 1981, *Shinketsushu* [FTCJ Decisions Reporter], 28, 10 et seq. [1982]). A subsidiary of the Fuji Film Company, the Fuji X-Ray Company held about 70 percent of the market for X-ray equipment in Japan and allocated exclusive territories to its distributors. The FTCJ proceeded against this arrangement and held it to be unlawful.

Some rules are included in the FTCJ Distribution Guidelines; they are analyzed later in this chapter.

Exclusive-Dealing Arrangements

Article 11 of the FTCJ Designation of Unfair Business Practices stipulates that to attach a condition to a transaction that the other party to the transaction cannot deal with the producers of competing products is unlawful if such a condition is considered unreasonable. Exclusive-dealing arrangements are included in this category. An exclusive-dealing arrangement whereby, for example, a manufacturer requires that distributors and dealers not handle competing products is held unlawful if it is exercised by a powerful enterprise. There are several cases in which it was found that an exclusive-dealing arrangement was unlawful. A representative case is that of Muto Kogyo (FTCJ Decision, 22 November 1974, *Shinketsushu* [FTCJ Decisions Reporter], 21, 148 et seq. [1975]), in which a manufacturer of drafting instruments holding a 70 percent market share required distributors not to sell competing products. The FTCJ proceeded against this arrangement and held it to be unlawful. The FTCJ Distribution Guidelines set out rules on this subject, which I discuss later in this chapter.

Tie-In Clause

Article 10 of the FTCJ Designation of Unfair Business Practices provides that a tie-in arrangement is unlawful if the freedom of choice of the party on whom a tie-in clause is imposed is unreasonably restricted. Comparatively few cases have involved tie-ins. These include the Textbook Case (1964) and the Farmers' Cooperative Case (1976) (FTCJ Decision, 22 November 1974, *Shinketsushu* [FTCJ Decisions Reporter], 21, 148 et seq. [1975]). The most recent case is the Draque Case (1991) (FTCJ Decision, 28 February 1992, *Shinketsushu* [FTCJ Decisions Reporter], 38, 41 et seq. [1992]), in which a distributor of game software programs tied the sale of such products that it had difficulty selling (i.e., the tied product) with the sale of a very popular game software program called "Dragon Quest" or "Draque" (i.e., the tying product). The FTCJ initiated an administrative hearing procedure, and this tie-in arrangement was held to be unlawful.

As noted earlier, the Osaka High Court handed down a decision in the Toshiba Elevator Case in which the court granted a damage award to plaintiffs seeking the recovery of damage sustained by a refusal to sell by a service company (a company wholly owned by Toshiba).

The FTCJ Distribution Guidelines

As mentioned earlier, the FTCJ announced its Guidelines on Distribution and Trade Practices in 1991 ("The Antimonopoly Act Guidelines Concerning Distribution Systems and Business Practices," *FTC/Japan View*, September 1991, 11 et seq.).[12] This action was an outcome of the Structural Impediments Initiative. Under the SII, the United States government demanded that the Japanese government increase enforcement of the AML in relation to restrictive trade practices and *keiretsu* relationships to improve market access.

The guidelines are divided into three parts. Part 1 contains provisions dealing with restrictive practices in relation to the distribution of capital goods, raw materials, parts, and components. Part 2 deals with restrictive practices in the distribution of consumer goods. Part 3 deals with restrictive business practices in import trade and related matters such as the exclusionary activities of sole import distributors.

Part 1 is entitled the "Guidelines on Continuous and Exclusive Transactions among Enterprises." It includes provisions prohibiting collusive activities of enterprises that restrict purchases from and sales to outside parties of a commodity—in other words, a cartel. There are also provisions on boycotts. In those provisions, a boycott is described as an unreasonable restraint of trade if it curbs competition substantially. Even if it is not an unreasonable restraint of trade, it is held as an unfair business practice. In both cases, a boycott is considered unlawful in principle. However, a refusal to deal exercised by a single enterprise is held as an unfair business practice when it is used as a means of enforcing a term that is unlawful. For example, a refusal to deal is unlawful if it is used to enforce a resale price maintenance.

There are several rules on exclusive-dealing arrangements in Part 1. Under those rules, an exclusive-dealing arrangement constitutes an unfair business practice if it is exercised by a "powerful enterprise" and business opportunities of competing enterprises are unduly reduced. If the market share of an enterprise is 10 percent or more, or if the enterprise ranks in terms of market share within the top three in its field, then that enterprise is subject to scrutiny as a "powerful enterprise."

---

12. See also Federal Trade Commission of Japan (1991).

However, this market share does not automatically establish an entity as a powerful enterprise. The FTCJ also takes into consideration such factors as the conditions of the market in general, the position of the enterprise in the market, the number of competitors and their positions, and the possible impacts of the arrangement on these competitors.

Part 1 also deals with reciprocal dealings in which one party (for example, a buyer) deals with the other (for example, a seller) on the condition that the latter purchase a commodity from the former. If, for example, a powerful department store conditions its purchase of a commodity from a subcontractor on the purchase by the subcontractor of a commodity that the department store sells, this arrangement may constitute an unlawful reciprocal-dealing arrangement. Of course, a reciprocal-dealing arrangement is not held as unlawful per se. However, if there is coercion, intimidation, or undue pressure to buy or sell, as the case may be, the reciprocal dealing is held to be an unreasonable arrangement.

Also dealt with in Part 1 are such actions as offering a customer a price below that offered to competitors for the purpose of excluding competitors from a particular transaction, and an acquisition of stocks of a party to a transaction for the purpose of excluding competitors from transactions with that party.

Part 2 of the Distribution Guidelines, entitled "Antimonopoly Guidelines on Transactions in Distribution Sectors," deals with restrictive practices in the distribution of commodities. It includes provisions on vertical price restrictions (resale price maintenance) and vertical nonprice restrictions.

With regard to resale price maintenance, Part 2 enunciates the general principle that this practice is unlawful. Although an indication of suggested price or a recommended price is lawful as such, if a manufacturer takes steps to make it a de facto binding obligation, it is held as unlawful. Various examples of unlawful resale price maintenance are provided in the Guidelines on Distribution and Trade Practices.

Part 2 addresses exclusive-dealing arrangements and vertical territorial arrangements. Under the provisions of Part 2, an exclusive-dealing arrangement is not unlawful as such. However, if it is undertaken by a "powerful enterprise" (as referred to earlier), and a new entrant and the existing competitors experience difficulty finding alternative distribution channels, then the exclusive-dealing arrangement is unlawful.

Four categories are mentioned in Part 2 with regard to vertical territorial arrangements. One is the setting up of an "area of primary responsibility" in which sales territories are allocated by a manufacturer to distributors and dealers as their primary areas of responsibility without the imposition of a strict restraint on activities outside the allocated territory. The second category concerns restrictions on the siting of sales establishments. In such instances, a manufacturer designates a location for a sales establishment to distributors and dealers and obligates them to refrain from establishing their shops and stores at sites other than the designated location. The third category concerns the practice of strict territorial allocation, in which a manufacturer allocates sales territories to dealers and distributors and obligates them not to sell in territories other than those allocated by the manufacturer. The fourth category involves restrictions on sales to customers outside the allocated territory, in which a manufacturer prohibits distributors and dealers from selling the commodity of the manufacturer to customers who order that commodity from outside the territories allocated by the manufacturer.

Among the four categories of vertical territorial arrangements, the setting up of an area of primary responsibility and the placement of restrictions on the location of sales establishments are both lawful in principle. However, a strict territorial restriction is unlawful if it is used by a powerful enterprise and the price of the commodity involved tends to be artificially maintained. Likewise, a restriction imposed by a manufacturer on distributors and dealers requiring that they not sell the manufacturer's commodity to customers who order it from outside the territories allocated by the manufacturer is held unlawful if the price of the commodity tends to be artificially maintained.

Another category mentioned in Part 2 is customer restriction. Generally this involves a restriction imposed by a manufacturer on distributors requiring that they sell the commodity of the manufacturer only to designated customers. Although a customer restriction is not unlawful as such, it is held unlawful if it has the effect of artificially maintaining the price of the commodity.

Rebates given by a manufacturer to distributors and dealers are also discussed in Part 2. A rebate is not unlawful in itself. However, it is unlawful if it is used to achieve restrictions that are unlawful, such as a resale price maintenance, an unreasonable exclusive-dealing arrangement, a strict territorial arrangement, or an unreasonable customer restriction.

Part 2 also enunciates some rules on unreasonable interference by manufacturers in the managerial matters of distributors and dealers and abuse of dominant position by large retailers.

Part 3 of the Guidelines on Distribution and Trade Practices is entitled the "Guidelines of the Antimonopoly Law with regard to Sole Sales Agencies." Part 3 includes rules on the activities of a sole sales agency of a commodity, including rules on parallel importation of genuine goods. Because the rules articulated in Part 3 are essentially not different from those announced in Parts 1 and 2, detailed discussion is omitted here.

Effectiveness of the Antimonopoly Law Relative to Vertical *Keiretsu* Issues

One of the focal points of trade disputes between Japan and its major trade partners, especially the United States, is the issue of production and distribution *keiretsu*. Trade negotiators in the United States and the European Union have argued that *keiretsu* systems in production and distribution make up an important part of the trade barriers preventing the entry of foreign enterprises and commodities into the Japanese market. Of primary concern are vertical *keiretsu* systems. There are various arguments over the vices and virtues of such *keiretsu* systems. A comprehensive analysis of *keiretsu* issues is made by Sheard in chapter 16. A few comments are provided here with regard to the effectiveness of the application of the AML vis-à-vis vertical *keiretsu*.

Increased enforcement of the AML will have a substantial impact on corporate behavior. In fact, there is evidence indicating that some manufacturers have changed their distribution agreements with their distributors and dealers and eliminated restrictive provisions from these agreement so as to make them conform to the norms of the AML. This trend undoubtedly will enhance the openness of the Japanese market in general. Although the ways in which manufacturers changed their distribution systems in response to an increased enforcement of the Antimonopoly Law belong to trade secrets and are not disclosed, it is evident that such changes have occurred. Some companies have announced antimonopoly compliance programs in which they stated their basic objective was observance of Antimonopoly Law rules. For an example, see the recently announced Antimonopoly compliance manual by Shiseido Company (1996).

It should be noted that there is a limit to the effectiveness of the application of the AML to *keiretsu* systems. First, there is often intensive interbrand competition between *keiretsu* systems (for example, competition between Toyota *keiretsu* and Nissan *keiretsu*), including price competition. As long as there is strong interbrand competition, including price competition, between *keiretsu* systems, such systems generally are considered lawful under the AML. This is true if one accepts rules announced in the Guidelines on Distribution and Trade Practices as stated above and rules enunciated in US Supreme Court cases such as the Sylvania Case and the Business Electronics Case (*Continental TV, Inc. v. GTE Sylvania, Inc.*, 433 US 36 [1977]; *Business Electronics Corp. v. Sharp Electronics Corp.*, 485 US 719 [1988]). Yet each system may be a closed system. If such a system is to be challenged, it should not be by a means based on a traditional antitrust concept.

Second, *keiretsu* systems are not necessarily arrangements in which contractual agreements are involved. Sometimes a *keiretsu* system is a de facto relationship among enterprises. For example, in automobile distribution, dealers that sell automobiles of a manufacturer may remain loyal to the manufacturer and refrain from selling competing products simply because they expect, among other things, that it is the policy of the manufacturer to protect dealers, that the manufacturer would guarantee that the businesses of dealers continue, and that financial assistance would be forthcoming from the manufacturer if they faced business difficulties.

There is a widespread view among manufacturers that if a dealer under their particular *keiretsu* goes bankrupt, the reputation of the manufacturer will be hurt. Also, if bankruptcy hits a dealer under the sponsorship of a manufacturer, it may affect the morale of all the dealers under this sponsorship. This may, in turn, drive the manufacturer to adopt the policy of providing some kind of measure to ensure that dealers will be protected if they get into serious financial trouble.

In the above-mentioned situations, the relationship between enterprises is more sociological than contractual. Challenges to such sociological entities under the AML would be difficult. Despite this limitation, an increase in the purview of the AML over distribution would be worthwhile because it would contribute to more openness in the market structure.

Abuse of Dominant Position

Overview

Control of abuse of dominant position, which is provided for under the Antimonopoly Law, is given an interpretation that is perhaps unique to Japan. In the European Union, Article 86 of the Treaty of Rome provides for the prohibition of abuse of dominant position. This prohibition is aimed at controlling abusive conduct by an enterprise that is dominant in a market and therefore has the power to control the market. However, the AML concerns itself with dominant position at the *transaction level*. Therefore, a small enterprise with little influence in a market may be in a dominant position in relation to the other party to a transaction if the other party is smaller still (Decision of the Supreme Court, 20 June 1977, *Minshu*, [Supreme Court Civil Cases Reporter], 31[4], 449 et seq. [1978]).

The AML's approach to dominant position is aimed at protecting small enterprises such as subcontractors that supply parts and components to manufacturers, as well as suppliers of commodities to supermarkets and department stores, from abusive conduct on the part of manufacturers and large-scale stores. It is in this sense that it can be said that this control is designed to protect small enterprises. Therefore, the control of abuse of dominant position in the AML is structured differently and for a different purpose than in the European Union.

In Japanese business society, there are many vertical, horizontal, or conglomerate systems in which participants are "captive members." Mobility between different systems is not high. For example, it is not easy for a dealer of one automobile manufacturer to shift to another manufacturer. Although this situation appears to be changing, this lack of mobility between different business systems is expected to persist for some time.

Defining Dominant Position

Article 14 of the Federal Trade Commission of Japan Designation of Unfair Business Practices prohibits an abuse of a dominant position by an enterprise. Article 14 states that if an enterprise engages in a transaction with another party and uses its dominant position to impose unreasonable conditions that appear contrary to commercial customs, then an abuse of dominant position has occurred.

A dominant position is not the same as market domination. It suffices to say that dominant position exists if an enterprise is dominant in a particular transaction and is able to impose conditions on the other party that would be impossible if there were equality of bargaining power. In the Miyagawa Case (Decision of the Supreme Court, 20 June 1977, *Minshu*, [Supreme Court Civil Cases Reporter], 31[4], 449 et seq. [1978]), a financial institution (a cooperative established under the Medium and Small Enterprises Cooperatives Law) loaned money to an enterprise on the condition that the borrower deposit a certain amount of money in the institution. The enterprise that had borrowed money could not pay it back, and the financial institution seized a property that had been offered by the borrower as security. The borrowing enterprise argued that it was an abuse of dominant position under the AML on the part of the financial institution to condition the loan on the deposit by the borrower. The enterprise further argued that the loan agreement was null and void because it had had to borrow the amount required for the deposit and consequently had to pay interest on two loans.

The Supreme Court handed down a decision in which it stated that the financial institution's requirement that the borrower deposit money constituted an abuse of dominant position. It added, however, that the loan agreement could not be declared null and void just because the agreement was contrary to the AML. The Supreme Court also stated that the interest charged by the institution was excessive in light of the Antiusury Law (Risoku Seigen Ho [Antiusury Law], Law 107, 1954), and that the amount of interest in excess of the limit established under this law would be regarded as payment of the principal.

The financial institution in this case was a relatively small one without a dominant position in any market. However, in the particular transaction involved in the case, the borrower was even smaller and, in relation to the borrower, the financial institution had a stronger bargaining power. Therefore, the decision established a rule that a dominant position under Article 14 need not be in a market but was sufficient as long as a party was dominant in a particular transaction.

Defining Abuse

Article 14 of the FTCJ Designation of Unfair Business Practices enumerates five categories of conducts as abuses on the part of a dominant enterprise: (1) requiring the other party to a continuous transaction to purchase a commodity or a service from the dominant enterprise that is different from that involved in the transaction; (2) requiring the other party to a continuous transaction to offer to the dominant enterprise money, services, or any other economic benefit; (3) setting terms of a transaction or changing them to the disadvantage of the other party; (4) causing disadvantage to the other party with respect to the terms of a transaction or the implementation of it in a manner other than those above mentioned; and (5) requiring the other party to a transaction (when it is a company) to observe a prior direction by the dominant enterprise or to obtain the approval of the dominant party when the other party appoints members to its board of directors. This definition is illustrative rather than exhaustive; other activities may come under Article 14. Also, this definition is necessarily general. It is not clear, for example, whether an abuse requires any "coercion" or "oppression." In the Mitsukoshi Case (FTCJ Decision, 17 June 1982, *Shinketsushu* [FTCJ Decisions Reporter], 29, 31 et seq. [1982]), a large department store, Mitsukoshi, sold luxury items to suppliers and asked them to contribute money to Mitsukoshi for the purposes of remodeling sales space and financing festivals sponsored by Mitsukoshi. The FTCJ proceeded against these practices on the grounds that they constituted an abuse of dominant position on the part of Mitsukoshi in regard to its suppliers of goods.

Mitsukoshi argued that it had only asked suppliers to purchase items and contribute money on a voluntary basis, with no coercion or oppression. The FTCJ argued that suppliers of goods had no choice but to comply with such requests owing to the bargaining power held by Mitsukoshi, because the arrangements between them and Mitsukoshi could be ended if they did not comply. The case was terminated at the request of Mitsukoshi for a consent decision.

The Mitsukoshi Case had the potential to establish the meaning of abuse by a dominant enterprise. However, because Mitsukoshi requested a consent decision and the FTCJ disposed of the case without certifying any facts, no legal interpretation on this issue is shown in the decision. It seems, however, that some elements of coercion or oppression are necessary to constitute an abuse; otherwise, the coverage of Article 14 would be too wide and too intrusive upon freedom of business action.

Abuse of Dominant Position and Its Impact on Foreign Trade

Although an abuse of dominant position as exercised by Japanese enterprises and controlled by Article 14 is not aimed at preventing imports generally, it may have some impact on imports. For example, there is a widely practiced business custom, which might be described as "return of goods," in which large-scale Japanese retailers such as supermarkets and department stores return unsold goods to suppliers. If this is done excessively, it may constitute an abuse of dominant position under Article 14 on the part of the party returning the goods, such as a supermarket or department store. It has been pointed out that this business custom tends to discourage imports because retailers have difficulty returning goods to foreign exporters when they cannot sell them out and therefore are less willing to handle imported goods.[13]

Supermarkets in Japan often require suppliers to supply goods in small quantity and with great frequency. They require this in order to meet the purchasing demands of customers quickly without holding a large stock of goods. Although there is no evident business reason for this practice, it is said to affect imported products adversely because foreign exporters generally cannot meet such requirements as quickly as Japanese suppliers can. Also, this practice may be an abuse of dominant position under some circumstances.[14]

Abuse of Dominant Position and Competition Policy

Some observers hold that the control of abusive conduct on the part of a dominant enterprise in a particular transaction does not belong to the realm of competition policy but to other areas of law such as the law of torts, and that it makes more sense to require that the wrongdoer be at least a "powerful enterprise" as defined in the FTCJ Distribution Guidelines. There are several interpretations given to this part of the AML that attempt to place this type of regulation in the proper place in the context of the AML. However, none of these interpretations appear satisfactory.

In the context of harmonizing competition laws internationally, the segments of the AML concerned with abuse of dominant position may present a difference between the AML and the competition laws of other countries and thus become the focus of review.

Conclusion

The Antimonopoly Law was originally modeled after United States antitrust laws. It retains some features characteristic of US antitrust law such as criminal enforcement. However, over a period of close to 50

---

13. For a discussion of the issue, see Sanekata (1994).

14. See Sanekata (1994).

years, other features have evolved. The 1953 amendment introduced control of an abuse of dominant position, interpreting this concept in a way probably unique to Japan. The 1977 amendment introduced the administrative surcharge system, which is akin to the European system of administrative fine, yet with significant differences. Further distinguishing Japanese antitrust has been the emergence of an informal enforcement system.

Although the AML is different from US antitrust laws and from competition rules in the European Union, it shares principles with competition laws of other countries in areas such as the prohibition of cartels. Also, to some extent the AML resembles US antitrust laws, as well as competition rules of the European Union, in that it controls excessive concentration of corporate powers created through mergers and acquisitions.

The many causes of trade imbalances between Japan and other countries include saving rates, investment trends, budget deficits, and Japan's embattled but still-present lifetime employment system, as well as microeconomic factors such as the restrictive practices of Japanese enterprises. Indeed, it may be that the restrictive business practices of Japanese enterprises constitute a comparatively small part of the large problem of trade imbalance, and that an increase in enforcement of the AML will have, at least in the short run, little effect on the trade imbalance between Japan and its major trading partners.

Nevertheless, the AML can play an important role in creating a market in Japan that is more conducive to open competition by eliminating restrictive business practices and creating more favorable conditions for business enterprises to compete with each other. This will contribute to the establishment of an international trading system in which differences in competitive conditions for enterprises among the major trading nations can be reduced to a tolerable level.

References

Bisson, Thomas Arthur. 1954. Zaibatsu *Dissolution in Japan*. Berkeley: University of California Press.

Federal Trade Commission of Japan. 1991. *The Antimonopoly Act Guidelines Concerning Distribution Systems and Business Practices*. Tokyo: Federal Trade Commission (11 July).

Goldfarb, Lewis H. 1995. "Trade and Competition Policies in the Global Market Place." In OECD Documents, New Dimensions of Market Access in a Globalizing World Economy, p. 125 et seq.

Koseitorihiki Iinkai [Japan Fair Trade Commission]. 1967. *Dokusenkinshi Seisaku Nijunenshi* [A 20-year history of Japanese antimonopoly policy]. Tokyo: Fair Trade Association.

Iyori, Hiroshi, and Akinori Uesugi. 1994. *The Antimonopoly Laws and Policies of Japan*. New York: Federal Legal Publication.

Matsushita, Mitsuo. 1986. *Keizaiho Gaisetsu* [Economic law]. Tokyo: Tokyo Daigaku Shuppankai.

Matsushita, Mitsuo, with John D. Davis. 1990. *Introduction to Japanese Antimonopoly Law*. Tokyo: Yuhikaku.

Matsushita, Mitsuo. 1993. *International Trade and Competition Law in Japan*. New York: Oxford University Press.

Matsushita, Mitsuo. 1996. "The Japanese Antimonopoly Law." In Jagdish Bhagwati and Robert Hudec, *Fair Trade and Harmonization*, vol. 2: Legal Analysis. Cambridge, MA: MIT Press.

Sanekata, Kenji. 1994. "*Ryutsu Torihiki Kanko Shishin no Jikkosei*" (The Effectiveness of Distribution on Trade Guidelines). *Keizeihogakkai Nenpo* (The Annual of Economic Jurisprudence) 34, no. 15: 7-11.

Shiseido. 1996. *Fair Trade Business Observance Guide. Manual Q & A*. Japan: Shiseido.

6

United Kingdom

DONALD HAY

There is a growing recognition by international institutions of the importance of the interface between trade policy and competition policies, broadly defined (OECD 1984 and 1995; IMF 1992; Lloyd and Sampson 1995; Hoekman and Mavroidis 1994; Commission of the European Communities 1995). The context is one in which a growing proportion of international trade occurs in markets that, because of economies of scale and scope in production or because of product differentiation, are imperfectly competitive, with firms exercising some degree of market power. Many of the industries involved in international trade are R&D-intensive, so that process and product innovation play a major role in firms' competitive strategies. These firms are often multinational, and their production and distribution decisions have a marked effect on trade flows. Imperfectly competitive markets, and the behavior of firms within them, have long attracted the attention of competition policy authorities. The actions (or inaction) of those authorities will clearly have implications not only for domestic markets but also for international trade. This chapter focuses on these issues as they affect the UK economy, including the additional dimensions that arise from UK membership in the European Union. The interface between trade policy and competition policy is of

Donald Hay is research associate at the Institute of Economics and Statistics at Oxford University. This chapter has benefited greatly from the helpful comments of John Vickers, Derek Morris, Hans Liesner, Edward M. Graham, J. David Richardson, Mark Williams, and participants at a meeting in Paris in January 1993. The valuable research assistance of Michael Buchanan and Robin Nuttall is gratefully acknowledged.

considerable interest.[1] Various aspects can be explored. The first is the general point that removing protectionist impediments to trade (such as tariffs, quotas, and subsidies) does not necessarily ensure access to domestic markets. There are several ways in which firms may be able to keep imports out of the domestic market, even in the absence of protection. One is predatory behavior, practiced either by a dominant firm in a market or by a colluding group (Tirole 1988, chapter 8.4). The entrant faces price cutting or aggressive marketing responses in the markets it is seeking to enter. The incumbents may, for example, sink costs in capacity to create a credible threat of severe competition. A second barrier to access is a vertical constraint to entry, such as that an importer faces when it cannot gain access to existing distribution networks and must incur expenditure in setting up its own network of dealers and outlets. These examples immediately raise questions about the effectiveness of domestic competition policy. Is the legal framework of policy framed in such a way as to inhibit predatory or exclusionary behavior and are competition policy authorities willing and able to act, not least when it is a domestic firm that is seeking to keep out a foreign supplier? In addition, it is possible that trade policy (as opposed to competition policy) may connive in anticompetitive responses to foreign suppliers by requiring those suppliers to accept voluntary export restraints (VERs) or by identifying competitive entry as dumping and invoking antidumping measures (Scherer 1994, 78-87; Hoekman 1994).

If the overseas entrant wishes to set up manufacturing facilities in the domestic market rather than just supply the market via exporting, then there are additional hurdles that may be put in its way. The constraints on access to the distribution network described above may be matched by refusal to supply productive inputs, where all the existing suppliers are exclusively linked to existing manufacturers.

But the most crucial issue of all is whether the entrant can expect parity of treatment with national firms in all respects. Does it, for example, have the same rights to establish a business, to take over a domestic firm as a base for entry to the market, to bid for government contracts, and to obtain patent and copyright protection for its products and processes?

Even if the overseas entrant can expect equal treatment, there is still the issue of how effective domestic competition policy is. Indeed, it is evident that a weak competition policy may be a substitute for protection, enabling established domestic firms to resist the entry of more efficient overseas suppliers, whether they are trying to export to the domestic market or set up production facilities. There will, of course, be social costs incurred by a weak policy. Unless the domestic firms are

---

1. Dixit (1984) made this point in his seminal article on international trade policy for oligopolistic industries. Cowan (1989) has explored the interaction of trade policy and competition policy in a theoretical treatment.

consistently singled out for different treatment (which could be difficult to implement), the lack of an effective policy will hinder competition among them. Furthermore, the empirical studies surveyed by Richardson (1989) suggest that protection of any kind, in the presence of imperfect competition, is likely to generate welfare losses (or, to make the same point, there are gains from liberalization of trade).

One possible exception to this conclusion is the Krugman (1984) model of import protection as export promotion, where the aim of protection is to enable domestic producers to realize scale economies, to progress along the learning curve, and to recoup R&D costs before being exposed to international competition. The idea of creating "national champions" has also arisen in discussions of competition policy. One strand of these discussions is that competition policy should not be overly concerned with the emergence of dominant firms or with mergers that will create firms with large shares of the domestic market if large scale is essential to success in world markets. The issue might be seen as one of appropriate market definition: if the market is truly global, then a high share of domestic *production* is of no concern to the competition policy authorities. (This begs the important question of how national competition policy authorities should deal with firms, especially multinational ones, that are dominant in world markets.) However, as our previous discussion has shown, firms that are dominant in domestic markets may be able to reserve those markets for themselves despite having many effective competitors in international markets. This would then be the equivalent of the "protected" domestic market of the Krugman model—that is, as a base for success in export markets.

The same desire to give domestic firms an edge in export markets may be reflected in less-stringent policies on agreements that affect their performance in export markets. Examples are export cartels and joint ventures in the supply of overseas markets. The problem here for the competition authorities is to know how to prevent cooperation in overseas markets from being translated into collusion in supplying the domestic market. The gain from cooperation in overseas markets is that the firms do not compete against each other and dissipate the monopoly rents available. Joint ventures—for example, in marketing overseas—may enable medium-size domestic firms to penetrate markets that they might not have been able to tackle on their own, given the high costs of establishing a distribution network. Joint ventures and other forms of cooperation involving domestic firms may also be permitted by the competition authorities in R&D-intensive sectors. The arguments for such agreements are that they prevent wasteful duplication of research efforts by domestic firms, that a larger R&D unit may be able to defeat foreign rivals in the race to innovate, and that they can solve some of the incentive problems arising from inappropriability and spillover (Geroski 1993).

These general aspects of the interface between trade policy and competition policy form the framework for the discussion that follows. The next section reviews the overall structure and objectives of competition policy in the United Kingdom, including the role of EU policy, which is likely to become even more significant with the completion of the single European market. Subsequent sections consider the role of competition policy in the protection or liberalization of the domestic economy and in the promotion of internationally competitive sectors, especially with respect to exports.

The discussion touches on a number of issues outside the scope of competition policy, which here is narrowly defined as policy toward abuse of market power, collusive behavior, and mergers. One such issue is the question of national treatment for foreign firms in such areas as rights of establishment, public procurement, and protection of intellectual property rights. A second issue is the existence of public monopolies or regulated industries, where competition is excluded as a matter of policy. A third issue is industrial policies to assist the restructuring of industries in decline or to promote the development of industries or products: state aids, subsidies, and the organization of R&D joint ventures are among the policy instruments that have been employed to these ends.

Competition Policy in the United Kingdom and the European Union

The competition policy of the European Union (EU) is now an integral part of the UK competition policy regime, so that in practice the two are no longer separable. After describing legislation and institutions relating to competition policy in both the United Kingdom and the European Union, this section goes on to look at the issue of conflicts between and priority in the application of the two regimes. The section concludes by discussing the issue of extraterritoriality, that is, the degree to which authorities charged with enforcing competition policy seek to apply remedies to firm behavior outside their jurisdiction. In practice, conflicts of policy and the issue of extraterritoriality often arise because the relevant market is international and because the enterprises that serve it are multinational.

Competition Policy in the United Kingdom

There are four main elements of competition law in the United Kingdom: the Fair Trading Act (FTA) of 1973, the Competition Act of 1980, the Restrictive Trade Practices Act (RTPA) of 1976, and the Resale Prices Act (RPA) of 1976. The FTA consolidated previous legislation and established the Office of Fair Trading (OFT). It gives the Secretary of State and the Director General of Fair Trading (DGFT) powers to refer to the Monopolies and Mergers Commission (MMC) cases in which it appears that a "monopoly situation" exists with respect to the supply or acquisition of goods or services in the United Kingdom. Commissioners are appointed to the MMC by the Secretary of State for fixed terms of four years. They include lawyers, economists, and businesspeople, as well as people distinguished in public service. Appointments can therefore reflect the stance of the Secretary of State toward competition policy, although once appointed the commissioners are completely independent. The act's definition of "monopoly" is legal rather than economic. Monopoly is deemed to exist where a single company accounts for at least 25 percent of a relevant market. In addition, a "complex monopoly" exists where two or more companies that together account for at least 25 percent of the relevant market act so as to restrict competition (however, if such action resulted from, or implied, agreements as defined in the RTPA, the matter would be considered under that legislation and not under the FTA). The secretary of state or the DGFT, in making the referral, determines which products constitute the relevant market. The MMC then investigates and reports on whether a monopoly situation exists and on whether it operates against the public interest. When the MMC reports that a monopoly situation does have effects contrary to the public interest, the secretary of state can either seek undertakings by the companies to refrain from the practices found to be detrimental or can remedy or prevent them by issuing an order (i.e., a decree that can be enforced in the courts), or, exceptionally, can ignore the findings of the MMC and clear the companies involved.

Section 84 of the FTA gives the MMC very wide discretion as to what it may take into account in determining the public interest, but it lists the following five criteria to be taken particularly into account:

- maintaining and promoting effective competition between persons supplying goods and services in the United Kingdom

- promoting the interests of consumers, purchasers, and other users of goods and services in the United Kingdom in respect of the quality and variety of goods and services supplied

- promoting, through competition, the reduction of costs and the development and use of new techniques and new products, and facilitating the entry of new competitors into existing markets

- maintaining and promoting the balanced distribution of industry and employment in the United Kingdom

- maintaining and promoting competitive activity in markets outside the United Kingdom on the part of producers of goods, and on the part of suppliers of goods and services in the United Kingdom

This broad notion of the public interest, which extends considerably beyond the promotion of effective competition, is also used in merger references and in references under the Competition Act.

The FTA also empowers the Secretary of State, on advice from the DGFT, to refer to the MMC mergers that create or enhance market shares of at least 25 percent, or that involve assets of more than £30 million. The MMC has a limited time (normally no more than three months) in which to report on whether the merger may be expected to operate against the public interest. The presumption is therefore that the merger will be permitted unless the MMC reports adversely.

Merger policy was the subject of a review by the UK Department of Trade and Industry in 1988. Despite considerable criticism of the policy —that it was too soft on mergers, that case-by-case application of the public-interest criterion gave rise to uncertainties for business, and that the policy failed to account adequately for the international dimension of many mergers—the review concluded that the basis of the policy was broadly correct. In particular, there was an unwillingness to interfere in the market for corporate control, despite evidence (summarized in an annex to the report) suggesting that the gains from mergers were quite modest, and despite the kinds of theoretical difficulties with the take-over process identified by Grossman and Hart (1980). The outcome of the review was a number of procedural changes, notably an arrangement for optional prenotification of mergers to the OFT, which then has four weeks to clear the merger or to raise objections. There was also a sensible provision to permit the OFT to seek solutions where mergers raise competition issues, and for the parties involved to enter into enforceable undertakings (e.g., to sell off part of the merged firm, or, in the case of a vertical merger, not to cut off supplies to a competitor). There was also a new requirement on the MMC to report on cases referred to it within three months of referral.

Section 2(i) of the Competition Act introduced the concept of "anti-competitive practice," defined as those business practices where "in the course of trade or business a person pursues a course of conduct which of itself, or when taken together with a course of conduct pursued by persons associated with him, has or is intended to have or is likely to have the effect of restricting, distorting or preventing competition in connection with the production, supply or acquisition of goods . . . or the supply of services in the United Kingdom or any part of it." The purpose of the legislation was to enable practices such as tie-ins, full-line forcing, and other actions to prevent or deter entry to be dealt with without a full-scale MMC inquiry and report. (A tie-in is a requirement that buyers wishing to purchase one of a firm's products also buy a related good or service from the same firm; full-line forcing is the requirement that distributors carrying any of a firm's products must carry the firm's entire product line.) Under the act, the DGFT has the right to investigate an allegedly anticompetitive practice and to seek undertakings from the company that it will refrain. Only if the company refuses to give an undertaking is the matter referred to the MMC.

The RTPA requires agreements between two or more companies that involve certain types of restrictions to be registered with the DGFT. Registrable restrictions include those that affect supply, pricing, and distribution. The act provides for certain exceptions as well. Once an agreement is registered, the DGFT must refer it to the Restrictive Practices Court (unless relieved of this duty by the secretary of state, in the case of innocuous restrictions). The presumption is that such agreements are contrary to the public interest, and the burden of proof is on the parties to demonstrate the contrary. The act lays down certain criteria, known as "gateways," by which agreements may be justified. But even if an agreement succeeds in passing through one or more of these gateways, it may still be struck down if the court decides that the detriments to the public interest are greater than the benefits demonstrated in terms of the gateways.

The effect of the RPA has been to make resale price maintenance more or less illegal per se. Although suppliers can seek exemption from the ban on public-interest grounds, only suppliers in the book publishing and pharmaceutical industries have succeeded so far, and it is doubtful whether any other product would be similarly successful. (Moreover, the agreement between publishers, the NET Book Agreement, was abandoned by them in 1995.)

This mixture of legislation and institutions has attracted a good deal of criticism. One criticism is that the definition of the public interest in much of the legislation is so wide that policy lacks focus and certainty, which is thus making it difficult. Much, of course, depends on how the competition authorities decide to interpret their brief. For example, the "gateways" incorporated in the RTPA might in principle be interpreted in a way that would allow many restrictive agreements to pass. In practice, since the *Yarn Spinners* case in 1959, most parties to such agreements concluded that they had little hope of getting them past the court, and they simply abandoned their agreements. The fate of referrals to the MMC has been much more varied, with public-interest arguments being accepted in a number of cases. However, since the advent of the "Tebbit doctrine" (discussed below) in 1984, there is little doubt that competition issues have been more prominent in referrals to the MMC, and this has had an effect on the weight given to competition issues relative to other public-interest concerns in the commission's reports. It is perhaps unsatisfactory that competition policy should be so susceptible to shifts in emphasis, depending on who holds the office of Secretary of State at the time a given case arises.

UK competition policy has also been criticized for its emphasis on legal definitions rather than economic effects. For example, the RTPA concentrates on the form of agreements between firms, with the result that careful drafting can take an agreement outside the provisions of the act even though its economic effects may be identical to another agreement that the act would prohibit. The definition of "monopoly" in the FTA is also formal rather than based on the existence of real market power with economic effects. "Anticompetitive practices" may be identified, under the terms of the legislation, in situations where the firms involved have no discernible market power.

The legislation is not consistent on the issue of burden of proof. Whereas under the RPA and the RTPA the onus is on the firms to demonstrate that their behavior is in the public interest, under the FTA and the Competition Act the onus falls on the DGFT or the MMC to identify where the public interest is harmed. Critics have repeatedly suggested that it would be helpful to make the procedures consistent, preferably by adopting the RTPA procedure in merger cases.

The Competition Law of the European Union

The purpose of European competition policy is to ensure that firms do not frustrate the overall objective of a unified common market by means of anticompetitive practices that hinder trade in goods and services between member states. Article 3(f) of the Treaty of Rome calls for the "institution of a system ensuring that competition is not distorted." In contrast with the wide formal definition of the public interest in UK competition policy, EU policy is specifically intended to promote and maintain effective competition.

The main provisions of EU competition law are Articles 85 and 86 of the Treaty of Rome. Article 85 prohibits and declares void agreements between firms and concerted practices that have the object or the effect of "preventing, restricting, or distorting trade" within the European Union and that affect trade between member states. Price and nonprice, horizontal and vertical restrictions all fall within the compass of Article 85. All restrictive agreements must be notified to the European Commission, but exemption may be sought under Article 85(3) on the grounds that the agreement contributes "to improving the production or distribution of goods or to promoting technical or economic progress." Exemption may not be granted if the restrictions are not necessary to obtain the benefits claimed, or if there is a risk that competition will be eliminated.

Article 86, which is concerned with abuse of market dominance, condemns

> . . . any abuse by one or more undertakings of a dominant position within the Common Market or a substantial part of it . . . in so far as it may affect trade between Member States. Such abuse may, in particular, consist in:

(a) directly or indirectly imposing unfair purchasing or selling prices or other unfair trading conditions;

(b) limiting production, markets or technical development to the prejudice of consumers;

(c) applying dissimilar conditions to equivalent transactions with other trading parties, thereby placing them at a competitive disadvantage;

(d) making the conclusion of contracts subject to acceptance by the other parties of supplementary obligations which, by their nature or according to commercial usage, have no connection with the subject of such contracts.

Within the European Commission, competition policy is the responsibility of Directorate-General IV (DGIV). That office is empowered to investigate breaches of Articles 85 and 86, to require firms to desist from practices or agreements that constitute breaches, and to impose fines of up to 10 percent of annual worldwide turnover. DGIV may act on its own initiative or in response to complaints received from affected parties. Firms may appeal to the Court of First Instance and then to the European Court for review of Commission decisions. Over the years, there have been a large number of such appeals, so that in its judgments the Court has had a significant role in shaping EU competition policy. For example, in a 1978 case involving the pharmaceutical company Hoffmann-La Roche, the Court addressed the issue of market dominance in Article 86, defining it as ". . . a position of economic strength enjoyed by an undertaking which enables it to prevent effective competition being maintained on the relevant market by affording it the power to behave to an appreciable extent independently of its competitors, its customers and ultimately of the consumers." This definition requires a prior inquiry to determine the relevant market and the presence or absence of dominance within that market before the question of the abuse can be tackled. The Commission and the Court have not always followed this logic in practice: there has been a tendency to identify an abuse first, and then to infer that the firm must be dominant (Fairburn et al. 1984). The judgment in the *Michelin* case (1981) in particular has been criticized on this basis (Hay 1985).

Two other features of the European Commission's application of competition policy are worthy of note. The first, which is particularly relevant in the context of this paper, is that the policy is applied very much with the goal of a single market in mind: hence any agreements or behavior that might have the effect of dividing or segmenting the markets of member states are attacked with particular vigor. As will be seen below, the practice of charging different prices in different member states, where such pricing is unrelated to the costs of supplying the different markets, is particularly condemned. So are any practices that might have the effect of closing the market of a member state to interstate trade. The second feature is that the European Commission is keen to assist small and medium-size enterprises (SMEs, which has become a term of art in EU competition law), which can benefit from block exemptions from Article 85 for R&D or specialization agreements, and for joint ventures. The particularly tough line taken by DGIV on price discrimination is at least partly due to a desire to protect SMEs.

A long-term weakness of EU policy was the lack of any reference to mergers in Article 86. Article 86 attacks only the abuse of a dominant position: it is apparently silent on the process by which a dominant position may be achieved. This lacuna, with respect to mergers at least, was in part patched up by the judgment in the Continental Can case (1972), which argued that the act of taking over a competitor to reduce competition in a market would itself constitute an abuse. In principle, however, that could only apply where a merger is instigated by a firm that is already dominant. A merger that built a dominant position where none existed before would escape, as would a merger in which a non-dominant firm takes over a dominant firm. A further difficulty with Article 86 was that it has no equivalent of Article 85(3), allowing for offsetting public benefits to be considered. In principle, these problems with merger policy were finally overcome by the adoption of Regulation 4064/89 (the Merger Regulation), which came into force in 1990 and was drafted specifically to control mergers. This regulation took merger policy outside Articles 85 and 86 and established both criteria and procedures for dealing with them. The operation of the policy in its first few years has been comprehensively reviewed by Neven et al. (1993).

A key passage of the regulation (in Article 2) defines its objective: "A concentration which creates or strengthens a dominant position as a result of which effective competition would be significantly impeded in the common market or a substantial part of it shall be declared incompatible with the common market." This appears to secure competition as the criterion by which mergers are to be judged; however, as Holzler (1990) observes, the fine print of the regulation is less explicit and leaves open the possibility of admitting some public-interest criteria. But DGIV has made it clear that it intends to focus on competition issues. A further concern is whether DGIV is adequately staffed to take on the task of reviewing major European mergers: even without responsibility for merger control, DGIV had a large backlog of cases. Even the most complex merger cases are supposed to be resolved within five months: other cases must be dealt with, in the first instance, within one month. The danger is that DGIV will not be able to complete an adequate analysis of a complex merger within that time, let alone the procedures for review within the Commission before a decision must be arrived at.

To conclude, EU competition policy has a number of positive features that UK policy lacks. The focus on competition rather than on a broad concept of the public interest makes the objectives and rationale of the policy clear, not least to firms and their advisers. The attention to economic effects rather than concern with the legal forms of agreements or market practices ensures that policy is not diverted from appropriate economic analysis. The procedures for dealing with cases, which include a wide-ranging investigation and decision by experts within DGIV but with appeal to the European Court on both substance and legal matters, could in principle combine the best aspects of administrative and legal approaches to competition policy. In practice, the procedures have been widely criticized. The main criticisms are of the backlog of cases under Articles 85 and 86, the insufficient expertise of the Commission staff, and the long delays in getting appeals to the Court heard. There is also a concern that deals are often struck between DGIV and the parties under investigation, to which third parties are not privy and are therefore unable to raise objections.

Conflicts Between UK and EU Competition Law

Conflict between UK and EU competition law could arise either from questions of jurisdiction or from fundamental differences in the content of policy. Before considering how these work out in current practice, it is worth noting some theoretical points, which have been explored by Gatsios and Seabright (1989), on the appropriate division of labor in regulatory matters between the European Commission and governments in member states.

The key problem is that the regulatory actions (or lack of action) of a member state will often have impacts in other member states. Examples are state aids or lax application of competition rules, which may be used strategically by a member state to protect domestic markets or to promote domestic producers in export markets. Similarly, a member state may be less than rigorous about enforcing environmental standards if pollution has its major effects elsewhere. The question is whether this international prisoners' dilemma is best solved by centralizing policy—for example, by making it the responsibility of the European Commission— or whether agreements between member states on the rules to be enforced will be sufficient.

There are major difficulties in relying on agreements between states. The first is asymmetric information: each state is better informed about its own industries and firms than about others. A second is that there is likely to be a range of possible solutions, with different distributions of benefits between states. Third, even if agreements can be reached, there is the further problem of credibility, given that there will always be incentives for member states to cheat, and such lapses may be quite difficult for others to detect given asymmetric information. In these circumstances, there may be considerable advantages in ceding both formulation and implementation of policy to a supranational authority such as the European Commission. At the level of policy formulation this does not necessarily solve the problems already noted of asymmetric information and the distribution of benefits between member states, but the Commission is perhaps in a better position to broker an agreement. At the level of implementation, ceding authority to the Commission almost certainly helps with the problem of credibility, and it may be that the Commission is less prone to regulatory capture than are regulatory authorities within member states. An intermediate situation arises where the Commission issues policy directives to member states, which the member states are required to implement, with sanctions for noncompliance. The difficulties here are detection (for example, many state aids to public corporations are concealed within public-sector accounts) and possibly the willingness of member state governments to accept the risk of being sanctioned for noncompliance (which might even be politically popular at home).

The varied application of this theoretical analysis to competition and industrial policies within the European Union is instructive. For example, on product standards the Commission has adopted the policy of mutual recognition of the standards of each member state. This probably gives recognition to too many products, which confuses consumers and forfeits potential economies of standardization. It also creates undesirable incentives for standards authorities in each member state to give their producers an advantage by lowering standards (not least because of the greater possibilities of capture).

In the area of competition policy, EU policy has developed as an upper tier of policy, superimposed on member state policies and concerning itself with abuse of market power, anticompetitive agreements, and mergers with a "European dimension," that is, those that affect competition, and hence trade, in more than one member state. In principle, this policy should be able to deal with the danger that member state policies are less than fully rigorous in seeking to promote competition at least in traded goods and services. In practice it has not been so easy. Disagreements about appropriate scope and content held up the formulation of European merger policy for many years before 1989. Furthermore, if some member state policies are "weak," then the EU authorities cannot depend on national policy institutions to be effective, and therefore a greater burden falls on DGIV. The ideal would be convergence between member state policies and EU policies so that the load can be shared. This would also make jurisdiction less of an issue. By the criterion of subsidiarity, it would be appropriate to devolve competition policy responsibilities to member states, which have better information about their own industries and firms and are therefore more able to identify anticompetitive market structure and behavior. But that solution will not work if EU and member state policies are divergent. Even if they are not ostensibly divergent, the EU authorities will probably have to continue to monitor member state policies to ensure that they are not being used to protect or promote the interests of their industries.

The basic position is that Community law takes precedence over domestic UK competition law, so that in an apparent conflict between the two, the former must be applied. Thus, for example, if an agreement between firms is granted an exemption under Article 85(3) or falls within a block exemption (under Regulation 418/85), the view of the Commission is that exemption is a positive action (and not just a permissive one) and therefore has to be respected nationally. This doctrine has not, however, been tested in the European Court. A different example is one where Articles 85 and 86 do not apply because, for instance, interstate trade is not affected in any way. Then domestic UK competition policy applies, and a UK firm cannot appeal to the Commission authorities against any decision of the UK authorities.

Prior to 1989, merger control was the area in which there was the most uncertainty about jurisdiction. A number of UK mergers, including those between British Airways and British Caledonian (1987) and between GEC and Siemens/Plessey (1989), were considered by both the MMC and the European Commission. In the former case, the Commission significantly strengthened the conditions for allowing the merger after what many judged had been a weak response by the UK authorities. In principle, of course, the Commission should only be involved where a merger is likely to affect competition in the European Union as a whole, including competition in interstate trade. That requires some assessment of what is the relevant market effected by the merger: is it domestic, or does it extend into other member states? The regulation adopted by the European Union in 1989 applies to any merger where the aggregate world turnover of the firms involved is at least 5 billion ECUs and Community-wide turnover at least 250 million ECUs, unless each of the firms achieves more than two-thirds of its EU turnover within the same member state. This last proviso is intended to exclude mergers that only affect a single member state's domestic market, which would remain the province of the domestic competition authorities. There are also provisions for member states to claw back powers from the Commission on such grounds as ensuring plurality of ownership in the media, fulfillment of prudential regulations in the financial sector, and national security. It remains to be seen how effective this regulation will be in distinguishing EU and UK jurisdictions (it is to be reviewed in 1994). However, the basic reasoning seems to be sound.

More fundamentally, it is apparent that there are real differences in the content of UK and EU competition law. It is therefore significant that reviews of policy in the United Kingdom in the last five years have given serious consideration to moving UK policy in the direction of EU law (for a fuller account than can be attempted here, see Williams 1993).

The first review, of policy on restrictive trade practices or "anticompetitive agreements," resulted in a White Paper (Department of Trade and Industry 1989) that promised legislation. The key proposal was that the United Kingdom should adopt legislation similar to Article 85, prohibiting all agreements and concerted practices that have as their object or effect the distortion of competition. The key features of the policy are that it is to be based on effects and not on legal form, that the OFT is to be given much more extensive powers to investigate suspected breaches, and that a newly instituted Restrictive Trade Practices Tribunal (consisting of members of the MMC specially selected for the task) should have power to impose fines of up to 10 percent of UK turnover on firms found in violation and to fine company directors and managers. To assist firms in compliance with the law, the EU precedent of an illustrative list of banned practices is envisaged, including resale price maintenance, price-fixing, collusive tendering, market sharing, and collective boycotts. The legislation will also provide for both block and individual exemptions along the lines of Article 85(3), with the block exemptions following the EU list (but with scope for more to be added later). Interestingly, the proposed test for individual exemptions will not include a public-interest criterion, despite pressure on this point from the professions: an exemption will be permitted only if it "improves the supply of goods or services, or produces economic or technological improvements."

These proposals, if implemented, would represent a desirable toughening of UK policy on collusive behavior. Although a promise to implement these proposals was included in the Conservative party manifesto for the 1992 election, there is no immediate prospect of legislation. However, it is clear that the intention is that UK policy should be brought into line with that of the European Union.

A second review, this time of policy toward the abuse of market power, was initiated by a consultative document in the autumn of 1992 (Department of Trade and Industry 1992). It outlined three options for change. The first option was merely to strengthen, in helpful ways, existing legislation and policy institutions. The advantages of the present policy were identified as its flexibility and the range of remedies available (which include termination of an anticompetitive practice, required divestment, and price controls). The main disadvantage was seen to be weak deterrence. The second option was to introduce Article 86-type legislation parallel to EU policy. The legislation would include a general prohibition of abuse of monopoly power plus an illustrative list of banned practices, provide additional powers of investigation for the OFT, give the MMC the power to impose fines, and permit third-party actions. Apart from the obvious advantages (for firms as well as policy) of alignment with EU policy, the main advantage of this option would be the increased deterrence. The shortcomings would be the difficulty of defining and identifying abuses satisfactorily and the loss of some of the flexibility of existing policy (e.g., the possibility of investigating complex monopolies and the availability of structural and regulatory remedies). The third option would meet some of those objections: Article 86-type legislation would be introduced for anticompetitive practices, but the antimonopoly provisions of the previous legislation would be retained to permit wide-ranging investigations and a range of remedies in monopoly situations.

The consultative process arising from this document was completed early in 1993, and the government announced that it had ruled out major reform and would content itself with the first option described above. The reasons given were that representatives of business had indicated that an Article 86-type policy would introduce too many uncertainties as to what was and was not permissible market behavior, and that compliance costs were likely to be high. The concern is that this decision reflects a turning back from the procompetition stance on industrial policy that has been an important feature of the UK government since 1979.

Extraterritoriality

The growth of international trade in the postwar era has created new problems for competition law. One is that the relevant market for a good may be international, but the suppliers may be multinational enterprises with production facilities in several countries. Any one country's competition policy may therefore be totally inadequate to deal with any competition issues that may arise. A related problem is that the behavior and actions that are perceived to be affecting domestic competition adversely may originate in another country, which raises both theoretical and practical problems of jurisdiction for the competition authorities.

UK competition law ducks these issues by restricting its focus to goods supplied within the United Kingdom. Thus the RTPA does not apply to agreements between firms that concern goods exported from the United Kingdom or services supplied outside the United Kingdom. Furthermore, it applies only to firms that are carrying on business in the United Kingdom: a cartel in another country that is exporting to the United Kingdom would not be subject to the provisions of the legislation, unless both the action and the effects were within the UK market. The UK approach in these matters is also manifest in a strong resistance to any attempt by foreign authorities to enforce their foreign competition law within the United Kingdom. Thus the Protection of Trading Interests Act of 1980 enables the Secretary of State to issue an order expressly forbidding a UK firm from complying with a ruling of an overseas competition authority if the trading interests of the United Kingdom might be harmed thereby. Other sections of the act inhibit the supply of information to an overseas competition authority and provide that multiple damages assessed in foreign antitrust actions should not be enforceable in the United Kingdom.

EU competition law is apparently less formalistic on the issue of extraterritoriality. Articles 85 and 86 apply where there is judged to be an effect on interstate trade within the European Union. It is perfectly possible that conduct by a set of Japanese firms—for example, an agreement to share markets within Europe—might pass this test, but this "effects doctrine" has never been tested in the European Court. In all cases to date involving non-EU firms, there has been evidence that the firms have entered into an agreement with an EU firm or have taken some action within the European Union.

The 1985 *Wood Pulp* case is a good example. The Commission found that there was a concerted practice by a group of non-EU firms, and it sought to condemn the practice on the basis of the effects within the European Union. The European Court avoided confirmation of the effects doctrine by arguing that the concerted practice had been implemented within the European Union, and therefore Article 85 could be directly applied. This argument relied on the "economic entity" doctrine of the Court, which identifies the behavior of a subsidiary or agent within the Union with that of its controlling non-EU firm on the grounds that they are a single economic entity. Thus any EU order can be served on the EU subsidiary rather than the non-EU parent. The Court has also held that it is perfectly valid for an order to be served directly on the non-EU parent (and for requests for information to be directed to it). But it is recognized that it would be difficult to enforce orders outside EU boundaries, and for this reason they are usually served on the EU subsidiary or agent.

Foreign Access to the Domestic Market

This section reviews a number of aspects of UK and EU policy that might affect a foreign supplier seeking to enter the UK domestic market either through exports or through direct investment. The review goes somewhat beyond competition policy proper to include the issue of national treatment for foreign firms and the use of trade policy instruments such as voluntary export restraints (VERs) and antidumping regulations.

National Treatment for Foreign Firms

In its treatment of foreign firms, UK legislation is remarkably lacking in xenophobia. In principle, any foreign firm wishing to set up operations in the United Kingdom through direct investment is subject to exactly the same procedures as any UK firm. The same applies to the registration of patents and copyrights. Competition policy is applied to the actions of suppliers within the United Kingdom, regardless of their nationality. Thus a foreign supplier's behavior will not be judged on any basis different from that on which a domestic firm is judged, and anticompetitive behavior by a domestic firm will not be condoned on the grounds that it is designed to exclude a foreign supplier from the market. Nor is there any evidence of substantial barriers to entry by foreign suppliers arising from a preference of UK consumers for British goods (the situation is indeed, if anything, the contrary) or of UK manufacturers for British sources of materials, semimanufactures, or machine tools. In other words, there is no equivalent of the vertical *keiretsu,* which some believe creates an informal barrier to access to the Japanese market for foreign suppliers (Lawrence 1991; Weinstein and Yafeh 1995).

Public procurement was, for a long time, an area where preference was accorded to UK suppliers. The European Commission has been active in breaking down barriers in this area, although undoubtedly some remain, for example, in the awarding of defense contracts (European Commission 1988, section 3.4). At the EU level, access by non-EU firms to EU contracts has been made contingent on reciprocal access to non-EU markets, especially the United States and Japan. Rules for procurement by public utilities and transport permit European preference, where bid prices differ by 3 percent or less, and permit exclusion of bids where the European content is less than 50 percent. These provisions raise issues of compliance, given that origin and content rules are difficult to apply objectively.

Requirements of reciprocity have also been applied in the services sector, especially financial services, where a regulatory regime seeking to promote prudential or safety objectives may also restrict access to markets and reduce competition (European Commission 1988, section 5). Initial deregulatory moves were taken by the United Kingdom in the 1986 Financial Services Act. Reciprocity of treatment for UK financial services firms in overseas markets was made a condition of licensing for foreign operators in the UK market. Within the European Union, DGIV has been much more active since 1985 in the pursuit of anticompetitive practices, including the use of Article 90 of the Treaty of Rome to open up services markets assigned to public enterprises or state monopolies by member states (Sapir et al. 1993).

Standards are another area where access of foreign firms to domestic markets can be impeded (European Commission 1988, section 3.3). As noted above, current EU policy (see Pelkmans 1987) is to allow national authorities to continue to set their own technical regulations, subject to scrutiny by the Commission for their trade-impeding effects, which may lead the Commission to insist on changes. In principle, goods made according to national regulations in any one member state must be permitted entry into any other member state, even if they do not meet the standards applied locally. Meanwhile, the Commission is pressing ahead with the promotion of European standards. The United Kingdom historically has had a well-developed set of national standards, which may have had the effect of excluding goods of lower quality. European policy has therefore almost certainly precipitated liberalization of the UK market, although the United Kingdom has also argued for more stringent EU standards.

The UK program of privatization has been linked to some liberalization of markets (Armstrong, Cowan, and Vickers 1994). Thus the statutory telecommunications monopoly of British Telecom (BT) was broken by the licensing of Mercury Communications to operate an alternative long-distance network, with access to BT's local networks assured by regulatory action. Further liberalization is planned in the latter half of the 1990s, including the granting of licenses to non-UK telecommunications companies to operate in the United Kingdom. Similarly, the privatization of the electricity industry, by splitting the industry into generators, the national grid, and local distribution companies, in principle facilitated new entry into generation. The least satisfactory privatization was that of the natural gas industry, where British Gas was allowed to retain its vertically integrated structure, which made it difficult for effective competition to develop. Despite some weaknesses in implementation, there can be no doubt that the UK privatization program of the 1980s opened up the prospect of more competition in public services, although it will be important that the regulatory authorities maintain a procompetition stance in encouraging entry. There is no reason why at least some of that entry should not come from efficient non-UK suppliers.

One area where the issue of access to the UK market is perhaps slightly less clear-cut is that of a takeover of a domestic firm by a foreign firm, where the size of the takeover brings it within the criterion for review by the OFT. In a number of cases the MMC has made reference to the effect of the proposed merger on UK imports and exports in a particular sector. Thus its 1981 report on the proposed takeover of Davy International, a UK company, by Enserch, a US company, expressed the fear that the result might be a restriction on UK exports, and the MMC recommended that the merger be blocked, even though it would have enhanced competition. In its 1984 report on the proposed merger of Hepworth Ceramic Holdings and Streetley, the MMC made reference to a likely decline in UK exports.

Two other cases appeared to establish a bias against foreign control per se in some circumstances. In a 1982 report on the proposed merger of Shanghai Banking Corporation with Royal Bank of Scotland, the case against the merger was based on the argument that part of the UK bank clearing system should not be allowed to pass out of national control, given the significance of clearing banks for monetary policy. It is noteworthy that similar fears were not expressed in regard to the 1992 takeover of the Midland Bank by the Hongkong & Shanghai Banking Corp. Similarly, in the 1988 case involving the Government of Kuwait and British Petroleum, it was argued to be against the public interest for a major UK oil firm to be controlled by an overseas producer. But in not referring Nestlé's 1988 bid for Rowntree Mackintosh, the secretary of state advanced the general proposition that there was no inherent objection to inward investment in the United Kingdom, so the nationality of the bidder (in this case Swiss) was of no significance.[2] Only competition mattered. A similar line was taken in the 1989 case involving Minorco and Consolidated Gold, where the MMC declared that the (South African) nationality of the bidder was of no significance to its deliberations.

The report on the proposed merger between Elders IXL and Allied Lyons (1986, paras. 8.15 to 8.18) raised the issue of lack of reciprocity in different competition policy jurisdictions. The bidder, Elders IXL, was an Australian concern; the issue was that a foreign bidder for an Australian firm would not enjoy the same freedom to make a bid as Elders IXL did in bidding for Allied Lyons. The report also noted that, under sections 11 to 13 of the Industry Act of 1975, the Secretary of State does have general powers to prohibit the acquisition of a UK manufacturing company by a foreign firm—powers that could, for example, be used where there is a lack of reciprocity of this kind. In practice, the Secretary of State has never exercised this power under the Industry Act. The (informal) view of civil servants within the Department of Industry is that there would be great difficulties should the Secretary ever do so: in particular, it might raise questions about the need to compensate shareholders, who would be effectively deprived of the right to dispose of their holdings to a particular bidder.

Finally, note should be taken of what has come to be known as the "Lilley doctrine." A previous secretary of state, in referring a number of proposed mergers to the MMC, noted that the prospective purchaser of a UK company was an overseas company that was publicly owned. The expressed fear was that this could result in back-door nationalization, especially of utilities. The more substantive point was that foreign state ownership often gave the purchaser privileged access to funds to make bids while remaining immune from bids itself. Insofar as this is a serious problem, it would be more appropriate to deal with it through EU state aids policy than by extending the scope of public-interest considerations in UK policy. In practice, the Lilley doctrine was never a substantive issue for the MMC, which continued to base its judgments on the effects on competition.

---

2. The main argument for a referral was lack of reciprocity, in that the distinction between registered and bearer shares allowed in Swiss company law effectively inhibited any bid for a Swiss company by a UK company.

Predation and Other Horizontal Exclusionary Behavior

The concept of predation is not difficult to grasp, but predatory behavior may be hard to identify in practice. Single dominant firms, or groups of firms acting in concert, may take actions designed to inhibit the entry of competition in their markets or to drive out an existing rival. This is, of course, an issue that has exercised competition policy for a long time, and the debate is helpfully summarized by Ordover and Saloner (1989). The definition of predation focuses on the strategic implications for future profits of the predator's current actions. One implication is that a current action (e.g., cost-reducing investment or R&D, or product innovation) may credibly commit the predator to a more aggressive strategy in future periods. A second is that the action may affect the behavior of rivals (or potential rivals) in a way that benefits the predator.

There are three possible circumstances in which a predatory course of action may be profitable. The first is the "deep pockets" story. Here the predator has sufficient reserves that it can sustain a price war longer than its rivals. In principle, a price war need not even occur: knowing that it will not be able to compete, the rival will retire gracefully (or may never enter). In practice, however, the rival may not be well informed about the depth of its rival's pockets, and some limited predatory offensive may be needed for the dominant firm to make the point. The puzzle in such cases is why the rival firm is under greater financial constraint than the predator—if its prospects of survival beyond the price war are good, it should be able to gain access to financial resources equal to those of the predator. Fudenberg and Tirole (1986) and Bolton and Scharfstein (1990) have endeavored to address this question in terms of asymmetric information in financial markets.

The second type of predatory behavior occurs when a firm behaves aggressively in order to establish a reputation for being tough. In ordinary circumstances an entrant might expect accommodating behavior from an independent monopolist, if there is no means to create a credible barrier to entry by sinking costs. If, however, the entrant has some uncertainty about the motives of the dominant firm, then by acting tough when its position is challenged, the dominant firm can establish a reputation that will permit it to retain its monopoly (Milgrom and Roberts 1982).

A third type of predatory behavior has characteristics similar to those of the second type. Here the question is whether the incumbent firm is a low-cost or a high-cost producer. The entrant's problem is that entry will only be profitable if the incumbent is a high-cost producer, but the entrant does not know if this is the case: the only evidence available is the price the incumbent charges. In some circumstances, the entrant will pay a high-cost incumbent to masquerade as a low-cost producer in order to keep out competitors.

The difficulty in all this for competition policy is to distinguish behavior that is predatory from normal commercial practice. Thus a price cut (or an increase in marketing expenditures) in response to another firm's entry may reflect no more than a normal competitive response to the new market situation. Even more difficult to evaluate are loyalty bonuses, rebates, and discounts available to repeat purchasers, which clearly may deter them from considering the product of a new entrant, and other forms of price discrimination.

Given the difficulty in distinguishing predatory practices from acceptable commercial practices, the UK competition authorities take a pragmatic approach. The MMC Report on Discounts to Retailers (1980-81) argued against a general prohibition of price discrimination, holding that each case needed to be weighed individually for its pro- and anticompetitive effects. Loyalty rebate schemes have been generally condemned where the producer has a large share of the market. Predatory price cutting was identified and condemned in a number of sectoral reports, including Industrial and Medical Gases (involving British Oxygen, 1956-57) and Concrete Roofing Tiles (1981-82). Pricing practices may also be challenged by the OFT under the Competition Act of 1980, and in a number of cases firms have given undertakings to refrain from practices that might be exclusionary.

The European Commission's rules on price discrimination have to be more precisely defined, given that a dominant firm that is condemned under Article 86 can be fined and required to pay damages to injured parties. A number of rulings have affected UK firms. For example, in a 1989 case, BPB Industries was fined for offering discounts to retailers that stocked its plasterboard only, thus excluding competition from other EU producers. This judgment followed precedents set by a number of previous cases, where loyalty rebates and similar discounting practices by dominant firms were ruled against because the rebates or discounts could not be clearly linked to objective cost advantages and were therefore interpreted as exclusionary. EU competition authorities are, in general, very suspicious of price discrimination of any kind practiced by a dominant firm, particularly where it leads to price differentials between markets in different member states. A firm serving markets in different states is likely to attract attention if it cuts price in one market where it is facing new entry competition. The line between "meeting competition" and predation is not well defined, and a firm that wishes to steer clear of the competition authorities is likely to avoid any behavior that might be identified as predatory.

Exclusionary agreements among a group of firms may take a number of forms. A group of suppliers and a group of distributors may agree only to deal with each other. There may be arrangements for aggregated rebates: a purchaser's rebate will be calculated on the basis of purchases from all members of the supplying group. The group may impose a collective boycott on any distributor who deals with an "outsider." Members may also agree to practice predatory pricing. All such anticompetitive horizontal restraints are unreservedly condemned under both UK and EU competition law. The relevant UK law is the RTPA: even in those exceptional cases where the Restrictive Practices Court has upheld price-fixing arrangements, it has normally taken steps to remove any horizontal exclusionary restraints from those arrangements. The European Commission has consistently condemned exclusionary behavior by groups of firms, particularly where it is designed to keep inputs out of the domestic market, as an infringement of Article 85(1).

The conclusion is that this area of competition policy in the United Kingdom (including EU policy, where it applies) is procompetitive. An overseas supplier seeking to enter the UK market is unlikely to face predatory or exclusionary tactics by established firms, given that the competition authorities (UK, and especially EU) are alert to the possibility of such tactics and have acted vigorously against them in the past.

Vertical Relationships Between Firms and Barriers to Entry

Full vertical integration (e.g., where a producer also sets up its own distribution system) is to be distinguished from vertical agreements. The former has not attracted as much attention from competition authorities as the latter. However, both UK and EU authorities have become more concerned in recent years about vertical integration involving dominant firms because of the danger that markets will be foreclosed. Some recent theoretical analyses of vertical integration and market foreclosure give these concerns added weight. Earlier work by Salop and Scheffman (1983, 1987) explored the possibility that dominant firms might be able to put their rivals at a disadvantage by raising their costs. Hart and Tirole (1990) have identified situations in which vertical integration has the effect of foreclosing the market and is the optimal strategy for the firms involved.

In a controversial 1989 report on the UK beer industry, the MMC recommended that leading brewers be required to divest themselves of a large number of their outlets, on the argument that control of outlets represented a barrier to entry to brewing and to the retail market for other suppliers. Other reports have looked critically at mergers involving a dominant firm taking over a supplier or a customer. Thus in a 1986 report on the proposed merger of BT and Mitel, the MMC identified a danger that BT was taking over a competitor in the market for automated branch telephone exchanges just as that competitor was beginning to make inroads in the BT-supplied market. The recommendation was not that the merger be disallowed, but that Mitel be required to operate at arm's length from BT at least for a number of years and to limit its share of the UK market. The EU competition authorities have no basis for intervention where vertical integration results from internal growth of the firm, unless the firm involved is a dominant firm (Article 86): where vertical integration arises by merger, the recent EU guidelines might apply, depending on the size of the firms involved.

Vertical restraints have attracted greater attention from the competition authorities (Waterson 1993). One concern is with those restraints that might constitute a barrier to the entry of new suppliers (including overseas suppliers) and that may operate either in intermediate goods markets or in the distribution system. The main concerns are with exclusive dealing and purchasing agreements and with refusal to supply. Exclusive dealing and purchasing often, though not invariably, go together: the downstream firm or distributor agrees to accept supplies from only one source in return for an agreement that the supplier will not supply potential competitors (e.g., in a particular regional market). The downstream firm will sometimes be given inducements, such as loyalty rebates or discounts, to practice exclusive dealing in the absence of a formal agreement. The concern about these agreements is that they cut out new suppliers from the market unless those suppliers are able to enter both upstream and downstream (e.g., by setting up their own distribution network). Franchising arrangements, which involve licensing a package of rights, including intellectual property rights and brand names, are one form of exclusive dealing agreement.

UK and EU competition policy lacks consistency in dealing with vertical restraints. There is an influential view in the United States that restraints should not, of themselves, be of interest to the authorities. It is up to each firm to decide on its marketing strategy, and if that involves vertical restraints, then let the market decide between suppliers. In other words, the issue is not whether vertical restraints are good or bad, but whether there is adequate competition in the market. The existence of restraints, in this view, should never be used to infer market power.

In the United Kingdom, an investigation of exclusive agreements can be undertaken in the context of a monopoly referral to the MMC under the FTA, where there is a case for investigating whether a firm has a dominant position, or under the Competition Act, where the firm in question does not fulfill the monopoly criterion. One example of the former was the MMC's 1981-82 *Car Parts* report, where the requirement by certain automobile manufacturers that distributors only stock replacement parts supplied by them, thus excluding other suppliers, was condemned, and the manufacturers were ordered to remove the requirement for their contracts with distributors. A subsequent MMC inquiry, *Motor Car Parts* (1992) investigated other aspects of manufacturer-distributor relationships, such as manufacturers' payment of bonuses to franchised dealers, giving the dealers an incentive to supply only that manufacturer's parts, and the refusal to supply name-brand parts except to franchised dealers. The report concluded that these practices did not contravene the public interest. Cases investigated under the Competition Act have mainly concerned minor markets in services. The EU competition authorities are concerned mainly with the economic effects of exclusive agreements: where the firm or firms involved are dominant, and the effect of the agreement is judged to be anticompetitive, the agreement will be regarded as an abuse of a dominant position under Article 86.

Refusal to supply raises issues that go beyond competition issues alone. The legal systems of most market economies, including those of Europe, adopt the view that firms and individuals may choose to contract with whomever they wish, without giving justification. For example, a firm may believe that a customer is unlikely to pay, or it may genuinely be unable to supply the customer because of limited output capacity. However, it is also evident that a firm might refuse to supply a rival so as to deter its entry in a downstream market. The rival would then have to set up (or find) alternative upstream sources, thus increasing the risk of entry and the capital required. The issue was examined in the MMC's *Refusal to Supply* report (1970), which concluded that there was cause for concern where refusal to supply was practiced by firms in a dominant position. In fact, the MMC has considered very few such cases, and none in a significant market. Under EU law, refusal to supply can be condemned under Article 86 as an abuse of a dominant position. The judgment in *Commercial Solvents v. Commission* (1973–74) established the presumption that withdrawing supplies from an established customer is an abuse when the supplier is in a dominant position. In this case, it was evident that the firm in question was seeking to ease the entry of its own subsidiary into a downstream market by cutting off supplies of an important input to the established firm in that market. Perhaps more significant for the current discussion, in a 1989 case involving London European and the Belgian airline Sabena, the Commission held that Sabena had to give London European access to its computer reservation system for flights between the United Kingdom and Belgium. Sabena had withheld access to bring pressure on London European to raise fares. By contrast, the EU authorities have adopted a permissive stance toward vertical restraints (exclusive dealing, refusal to supply nonfranchised dealers) in the distribution of new motor vehicles, with a block exemption under Article 85(3) granted in 1985 and renewed in 1995 for a further seven years.

The conclusion is, however, that UK-EU competition policy is generally procompetitive in respect to vertical restraints in those circumstances where dominant firms might seek to use exclusive agreements and/or refusal to supply to prevent the entry of a competitor.

Recession Cartels, VERs, and Antidumping

This subsection looks mainly at a set of instruments that are usually classified as trade policy but that equally affect competition from overseas firms in domestic markets. All of these are instruments that can be brought to bear in situations where domestic producers are facing import competition, and where the rapid consequent adjustment of domestic industry could generate economic distress. As with all forms of protection, where the aim is to ease adjustment in the domestic economy, there is a danger that uncompetitive sectors and firms will be encouraged to remain, given that any protection generates a lobby to preserve it (Neven and Vickers 1992).

One possibility is that the firms in an industry under pressure will enter into a restructuring agreement to ensure that the adjustment process is orderly and that those firms and production facilities that are viable in the long run are preserved. In principle, such agreements must be registered under the RTPA and hence would need to be defended before the court on one of the grounds identified in the gateways. In the 1959 *Yarn Spinners* case, the court accepted an argument that the agreement was designed to alleviate the prospect of localized unemployment, but it concluded that the agreement overall failed to meet the criterion that its benefits should outweigh its costs. The European Commission has been willing to accept restructuring agreements for social reasons—although these are not strictly relevant to the provisions of Article 85(3) under which exemption may be given—and to ensure that as many competitors as possible survive in the market in the long run. Thus in the 1984-85 *Synthetic Fibers* case, the Commission approved an agreement involving an 18 percent reduction of capacity over three years, with the expectation that a more efficient industry would emerge with no diminution of competition. A number of similar arrangements have been permitted subsequently, notably in petrochemicals. From this description of the responses of the competition authorities, it is clear that these exemptions from the provisions of RTPA and Article 85 are unlikely to present a barrier to entry to international competition in the UK market, since no predatory response to new entry would be permitted.

Voluntary export restraints (VERs) are a tool of trade policy rather than competition policy. Their impact on competition has been reviewed by the Organization for Economic Cooperation and Development (OECD; 1984, paras. 96-125). There are three kinds of VERs. The first consists of those arranged by the government of the importing country, which sets up agreements either with the government of the exporting country or directly with the exporters—these "orderly marketing arrangements" are designed particularly to deal with adjustment, where a domestic sector is under threat of rapid decline due to imports. VERs of the second type are organized by the government of the exporting country, perhaps under pressure from the importing country's government. Those of the third type are organized by groups of exporting firms themselves who fear protectionist measures being imposed by the importing country if their exports grow too quickly. In the European context, the main VERs have been those instituted by Japan in 1985 on a range of exports, including videocassette recorders, color television tubes, light commercial vehicles, small motorcycles, quartz watches, stereo equipment, and machine tools.

The legality of VERs under the General Agreement on Tariffs and Trade (GATT) is not an issue as long as the exporting country agrees to accept the restraint voluntarily, since it is only the exporting country that would have the standing to register a complaint. Because VERs are undertaken by third-country exporters, they do not fall within the scope of Article 85 relating to competition and trade within the European Union. Private VERs might, however, be caught. Thus the decision in the 1985 *Wood Pulp* case went against a group of US exporters who had formed an export cartel to fix prices in the European market, having been exempted from US antitrust legislation under the Webb-Pomerene Act. The reason given was that although the agreement was between firms outside the European Union, it was implemented within the European Union and could therefore be challenged. (The agreement would not have been challenged under the RTPA because of the doctrine of extraterritoriality applied by the UK competition authorities.) Obviously, VERs are implicitly collusive because of the market-sharing element. It has been noted that the response of Japanese exporters has generally been either to raise the quality of their exports (and hence achieve higher margins) or to locate at least some final product assembly in the European Union so as to bypass the restraints.

Antidumping measures are a second type of trade policy instrument with effects on competition. These measures are permitted under Article VI of the GATT, and a code of practice was agreed to in the Kennedy Round of GATT negotiations in the 1960s. The code provides that, to establish dumping, the price in the importing country's market must be shown to be lower than that in the producer's domestic market, the impact on the importer's market must be material, and causality must be established (i.e., it must be shown that the low-priced imports are causing the difficulties of domestic producers in the market). These rules have been adopted by the European Union: private parties have the right to file complaints with the European Commission, which was quite active on this front in the 1980s. Most cases have been resolved by voluntary price undertakings by the exporting firms. The issue does not arise for the United Kingdom alone, as all antidumping cases are now referred to the European Commission.

There is always a danger that firms in the domestic market will abuse antidumping legislation by lobbying for actions designed to keep out foreign competitors. There is an obvious parallel with the treatment of predatory pricing by competition policy. Antidumping measures are (possibly) called for if and only if the imports are priced predatorily, and not if the price simply reflects the producer's low costs (Hindley

1991). The difficulty is to establish the reasons for the low price. For example, a firm may have a monopoly in its domestic market and therefore be willing to set a higher price there than in the export market. A low price in the export market may be a procompetitive weapon for a firm seeking to enter new markets. The information required to establish predatory behavior (or dumping) may simply not be available to the authorities, given that the pricing decisions have probably been made in the exporting country, at the headquarters of the firm or firms involved (Messerlin 1991). In practice, under EU (and US) policy, predation does not have to be established before antidumping measures are implemented. There is also some evidence that antidumping measures are linked to collusive behavior on the part of the domestic producers. In a review of Article 85 cases (suspected cartels) in the chemical industry over the period 1980-89, Messerlin (1990) found that in half the cases there were parallel antidumping cases, the implication being that antidumping measures provided the context for collusion (and vice versa).

Promotion of Domestic Producers

This section explores the possibility that competition policy (or the lack of it) may be used to promote the interests of domestic firms, both in the domestic market and in exports. Policies toward dominant firms, export cartels, and joint ventures (especially, but not exclusively, in R&D) are discussed.

Dominant Firms, Mergers, and National Champions

In certain circumstances it may be in the interest of national authorities to support domestic producers, enabling them to realize scale or learning economies that will allow them to compete more effectively in international markets in the long run (Brander and Spencer 1983; Krugman 1984; Grossman 1986; Itoh et al. 1991). This raises the possibility that a relaxed attitude toward the emergence of dominant firms, whether dominance is achieved through internal growth or through merger, could achieve the same objective. The popular concept is that of creating "national champions," particularly in high-growth or high-technology sectors.

This is an area of policy where, in principle, the UK approach looks rather different from that of the EU authorities. The relevant legislation in the United Kingdom is the FTA. This act enables the Secretary of State or the DGFT to refer monopoly situations to the MMC for investigation (in practice it is virtually always the DGFT who makes the referral). The definition of "monopoly" is structural: any situation where at least 25 percent of supply of a good in the United Kingdom is supplied by (or to) one firm (or a group of connected firms). The emphasis is on supply rather than production: thus an overseas firm with no production facilities in the United Kingdom could still be referred under the legislation if it supplied at least a quarter of the market. The 25 percent threshold is merely a trigger that may precipitate a referral—whether the situation in the market is contrary to the public interest is for the MMC to deliberate upon. Thus in its 1967-68 report on *Flat Glass*, the MMC noted that Pilkington had 89 percent of the relevant market, but the commission could find nothing untoward in the firm's behavior.

It was noted above that the FTA's definition of the public interest is widely framed: although three of the criteria laid down in the act relate to competition in supplying the domestic market, another refers explicitly to employment, and a third to competitive activity in markets outside the United Kingdom (presumably in export markets). In principle, therefore, given the wide definition of the public interest and the generally discretionary nature of the whole procedure, the competition authorities could use their powers to promote the interests of a domestic firm against foreign competition by taking a relatively relaxed view of market dominance. But it is difficult to identify any report on a "monopoly" where such considerations have affected the thinking of the commissioners.

The situation with regard to mergers under the FTA is basically similar. The MMC is asked to consider the public interest, using the same criteria as for monopoly cases. Since 1979 the UK government has stressed that the primary consideration in deciding whether to refer a merger will be that of competition. In July 1984, then Secretary of State Norman Tebbit made a policy statement to this effect (since then known as the "Tebbit doctrine"), and there is no evidence that the government has weakened in its resolve on this matter since. It is, however, possible to identify two cases where enabling domestic firms to compete internationally may have had some effect on the commission's thinking.

The first is the 1987 report on the merger between British Airways and British Caledonian. The MMC recognized that the merger would create a national champion better able to compete internationally, but it also noted the adverse effects on competition with smaller UK airlines. The merger was allowed after British Airways entered into undertakings (subsequently strengthened after intervention by the European Commission) to cede some of its landing slots at London's Gatwick Airport to competitors (see Hay and Vickers 1988 for a further account).

The second example is that of the 1989 consortium bid of GEC and Siemens for Plessey. The MMC's 1986 report on the proposed merger between GEC alone and Plessey had identified an adverse effect on competition in the domestic defense and telecommunications markets, and that merger was blocked. The 1989 report, however, placed conditions on a merger involving the same two companies but did not seek to block it. The MMC noted that the market in question had become more international, and that GEC and Plessey were already involved in a joint venture in the telecommunications sector. The view was taken (and not subsequently contradicted by the European Commission) that competitive pressures from Japanese and US companies in the telecommunications market required larger UK (and European) units to compete. The conditions required by the MMC related mainly to defense contracts, seeking to alleviate the fears of the Ministry of Defence that a merger with a large foreign company might jeopardize national security.

Formally, the approach of the European Commission to dominant firms under Article 86 is quite different from that of the United Kingdom. Article 86 attacks the abuse of a dominant position within the European Union or part of it. An economic concept of dominance is introduced, making it essential to define the relevant product market(s) within which the firm is potentially dominant. If products can be regarded as interchangeable, they are deemed to fall within a given market. The relevant market having been defined, it remains to identify the level at which a firm becomes dominant. A large market share is not enough; there also has to be evidence that conditions of entry are such that the firm could effectively exercise market power. In practice, a market share of 40 to 45 percent has been taken to indicate dominance (in a 1978 case involving United Brands and in a 1976 case involving Hoffmann-La Roche). Once a firm has been judged to have a dominant position, it remains to be considered whether it has abused that position. Article 86 gives examples of such abuses—unfair prices, limiting production, price discrimination—but the scope of the article is not limited to these examples, and in principle the European Commission may consider a wide range of behavior.

One difficulty with (or, some would argue, a strength of) Article 86 is that it gives no room for a firm to argue for countervailing benefits from its dominant position. It is unlikely therefore that a lax application of Article 86 could be used "strategically" to permit EU champions to emerge. Perhaps this is right—the scale of the EU internal market is such that it should be possible both to preserve competition between producers and to realize the scale economies needed for international competitiveness. Similar issues are raised by the EU Merger Regulation, in force since 1990. As previously noted, the imprecise drafting of some points of the regulation leave the door open to a defense of a merger as creating a European champion. It is therefore reassuring that in the one case where the commission has ruled against a merger (the proposed merger of Aérospatiale-Alenia and de Havilland, decided in 1991), the decision emphasized the need to maintain competition in EC and world markets.

Export Cartels

Agreements between exporters are sometimes defended on the grounds that they enable a group of firms to share expertise and services in supplying foreign markets. In practice, for such agreements to be effective, they need to cover relatively homogeneous products and involve few participants. In the United Kingdom in the late 1970s, export cartels covered less than 5 percent of exports and were most common in the engineering industry (OECD 1984, paragraphs 14-23). Competition authorities do not generally concern themselves with export cartels, and the authorities in the importing country have not been able, as a rule, to act against them. The main fear of domestic competition authorities is that agreements over exports may be conducive to collusive behavior in the domestic market. In the United Kingdom, an export cartel is required under the RTPA to register but is treated as exempt from that law's provisions. The EU position is that an export cartel in one member state that affected trade with another member state would be dealt with under Article 85(1); however, an export cartel that affected only trade with a non-EU country would not be challenged.

R&D Agreements, Specialization Agreements, and Joint Ventures

Domestic firms may enter into R&D agreements in order to reduce the costs of undertaking the R&D they need to compete successfully internationally. For the competition authorities the familiar trade-off reappears: the gains in terms of international competitiveness may be offset by extension of the cooperation to supplying the domestic market. Under UK legislation (the RTPA), any agreement in which the parties accept restrictions on production and commercial exploitation of an innovation must be registered. Agreements that solely involve sharing of R&D and exchange of technical information need not be registered. If the agreement is registrable, the firms may seek to persuade the DGFT to get a direction from the Secretary of State not to take action against the agreement, or they may go to the court and seek to have the agreement upheld under one of the gateways, or they may appeal to the European Commission for exemption under Article 85(3).

In fact, the EU competition laws are generally sympathetic to R&D agreements and joint ventures in the high-technology and energy sectors and between small and medium-size firms, and to any cross-frontier cooperation. Regulation 418/85 gives block exemptions to pure R&D agreements, R&D agreements extending to joint exploitation, and joint exploitation flowing from an earlier R&D agreement. Joint exploitation can include joint manufacturing and licensing but does not extend to joint marketing and selling. Agreements that do not gain exemption under this regulation can then seek individual exemptions under Article 85(3)—in practice these are often granted, although the procedure involves detailed investigation by DGIV, and there may be protracted negotiations over the precise form of the agreement. R&D agreements and joint ventures in high technology have been particularly favored, perhaps reflecting concerns about Europe's ability to compete with Japan and the United States. Indeed, in some high-technology sectors the European Commission has taken active steps to promote European cooperation in R&D (Geroski 1989).

Specialization agreements—whereby one firm agrees to specialize in one product and another to specialize in a second, and both agree to supply each other (and each other's customers)—can generate obvious economies of scale and enable the firms to compete more effectively internationally. Treatment of such agreements under UK and EU competition law parallels that of R&D agreements, with one exception: the regulation granting block exemption is restricted to smaller undertakings (with specified threshold firm sizes). In general, the European Union prefers specialization agreements to agreements that involve joint production.

Joint ventures in production and/or marketing that affect the supply of goods in the United Kingdom may be investigated under either the RTPA or the FTA. In the case of production joint ventures, the RTPA rules apply if the venture takes the form of a collusive agreement between the firms. The FTA applies in cases where the joint venture will have more than 25 percent of the relevant market. The key distinction between the two pieces of legislation is that the RTPA has a presumption against agreements, whereas under the FTA each joint venture agreement is to be considered on its merits. Under EU competition law, joint ventures are mainly considered under Article 85. Exemptions can be obtained under Article 85(3), but the tests are quite stringent. The advantages from the joint venture must be objective and significant, and close cooperation must be indispensable. The joint venture must not be used to eliminate competition within the European Union or any geographical market within it. Exemptions are limited in time, and arguments for continuing the exemption must be presented for renewal.

In February 1993 the commission issued a "Notice on Cooperative Joint Ventures." This notice distinguished cooperative joint ventures, which continue to be dealt with under Article 85, from concentrative joint ventures. The latter perform "on a lasting basis all the functions of an autonomous economic entity" and do not "give rise to coordination of the competitive behavior of the parties." These ventures are dealt with under the Merger Regulation. (For further discussion of joint ventures, see OECD 1986, Geroski 1993, Jacquemin 1988, and Jorde and Teece 1990.)

State Aids

The European Union has recognized, from its inception, that the strategic use of subsidies by member state governments could undermine the gains from reductions in tariffs and other barriers to trade within the Union (European Commission 1991). Policy has developed within the framework of Articles 92 and 93 of the Treaty of Rome. Article 92 contains a general prohibition of state aids, unless the commission specifically grants a derogation. Since the mid-1980s the commission has taken a tougher line on state aids (Gilchrist and Deacon 1990), and there has been an overall decline in support for manufacturing, especially sector-specific aid schemes (e.g., in steel and shipbuilding). This decline has been particularly marked in the United Kingdom, which now has the lowest level of subsidies among the major EU economies. But the UK record is far from blameless: in 1992 the UK government was required to claw back from British Aerospace some of the substantial "sweeteners" that had been granted to induce the company to take over the unprofitable (nationalized) car manufacturer Rover in 1988. In contrast, the European Commission has been willing to countenance the development of European consortia backed by member states. The most notable example is Airbus Industrie (Baldwin and Krugman 1988; Neven and Seabright 1995), set up in 1970 by the governments of France, Germany, the United Kingdom, and Spain. The "aid" to Airbus is in the form of nominal debt, which has to be repaid only if Airbus is profitable (i.e., the arrangement is closer to a venture capital arrangement). The objective was to create a European competitor to the developing monopoly of Boeing in world markets for wide-bodied commercial jet aircraft. There is some debate as to whether this objective has been achieved and, if so, whether there has been a net gain in European welfare.

Conclusions

This paper has explored the interface between trade policy and competition policy in the United Kingdom, exploiting the natural links between the theory of trade in imperfectly competitive markets and the concern of competition policy for such markets. Two broad themes have been identified: access to the domestic market for foreign suppliers, and actions to promote the interests of domestic producers, especially in export markets. In exploring these themes, the contributions of the UK and the EU authorities in shaping policy in the United Kingdom have been noted.

Regarding access to the domestic market for foreign suppliers, four areas were considered. The first is whether a foreign supplier will be accorded national treatment, either to supply or to produce in the United Kingdom. Our conclusion is that the policies put in place in the 1980s—especially the deregulatory and privatization policies of the UK government, but also those of the European Union—have made the United Kingdom relatively open to foreign suppliers and producers. There has in the past been a slight question mark over the acquisition of UK firms by foreign bidders, but currently that is not an issue. The second and third areas are those of predatory response by UK firms to entry by a foreign supplier, and vertical restraints practiced by UK firms that might make entry difficult. Our conclusion is that in both these areas UK and EU policy is procompetitive in its stance. The fourth area is that of policy responses where domestic producers are under pressure from imports. On the competition policy side, recession cartels established to allow orderly adjustment in the industry have been permitted (and even promoted) by the European Commission in some instances. Regarding trade policy, which is the responsibility of the Commission alone, there has been a willingness to protect domestic suppliers through voluntary export restraints negotiated with foreign suppliers and through antidumping measures. There is some evidence that these measures have had adverse effects on competition between European suppliers.

Regarding promotion of domestic producers, especially in export markets, there are three areas of interest. The first is policy toward dominant firms and toward mergers that seek to create dominant firms. The popular conception is that such firms are national champions, which can realize scale or learning economies to enable them to compete more effectively in world markets. In principle, UK competition policy is more open to such arguments than EU policy, and there is evidence in a few UK cases that they have been significant in reaching decisions. The second area is agreements between firms: export cartels, R&D agreements, and joint ventures. Both UK and EU policies have been generally permissive of such agreements, especially where the main objective is competition in export markets. The third area is that of state aids, which have been a particular concern of the European Union in the 1980s. Britain now has the lowest level of subsidies among the major EU economies. However, the Commission has been willing to permit aid to European consortia in high-technology sectors to preserve a European competitor in world markets. Our conclusion is that UK and EU policy is not unsympathetic to the notion that national champions are needed to compete effectively in world markets. Policy is in part simply permissive (e.g., UK merger policy), and in part openly promotional (e.g., toward R&D joint ventures): the main concern of EU policy is that no member state policy should benefit producers in that state against producers in other member states.

A final question is whether there are significant conflicts in the competition policies being pursued by the United Kingdom and the European Union. The impression given by a review of the legislative and institutional frameworks is that there are significant divergences of thought; in particular, the UK public-interest criterion differs from the EU emphasis on promoting and maintaining effective competition. In practice, this difference of view has not been a serious issue in recent years, with the emphasis of the UK government on deregulation and competition generally. However, it is unfortunate that the UK government has not up to now been willing to take steps to bring the UK policy framework more into line with that of the European Union. If nothing else, problems will arise for major UK producers from their being subject to different competition policy regimes in the United Kingdom and the European Union. The differences may also exacerbate any conflicts over jurisdiction in particular cases, which may not be entirely avoided by rules for assigning jurisdiction (as in the EU Merger Regulation).

References

Armstrong, M., Cowan S., and J. Vickers. 1994. *Regulatory Reform: Economic Analysis and British Experience.* Cambridge, MA: MIT Press.

Baldwin, R., and P. Krugman. 1988a. "Industrial Policy and International Competition in Wide-Bodied Jet Aircraft." In R. E. Baldwin, *Trade Policy Issues and Empirical Analysis.* Chicago: University of Chicago Press for the National Bureau of Economic Research.

Baldwin, R. E., and P. R. Krugman. 1988b. "Market Access in International Competition: A Simulation Study of 16K Random Access Memories." In R. Feenstra, *Empirical Studies of International Trade.* Cambridge, MA: MIT Press.

Bolton, P., and D. Scharfstein. 1990. "A Theory of Predation Based on Agency Problems in Financial Contracting." *American Economic Review* 80: 93-106.

Brander, J. A., and B. J. Spencer. 1983. "International R and D Strategy and Industrial Rivalry." *Review of Economic Studies* 50: 707-22.

Brander, J. A., and B. J. Spencer. 1985. "Export Subsidies and International Market Share Rivalry." *Journal of International Economics* 18: 83-100.

Commission of the European Communities. 1995. *Competition Policy in the New Trade Order: Strengthening International Cooperation and Rules.* Luxembourg: Office for Official Publication of the European Communities.

Cowan, S. G. B. 1989. "Trade and Competition Policies for Oligopolistic Industries." *Weltwirtschaftliches Archiv* 125: 464-83.

Department of Trade and Industry. 1988. *Mergers Policy.* London: Her Majesty's Stationer's Office.

Department of Trade and Industry. 1989. *Opening Markets: New Policy on Restrictive Trade Practices* (cm 727). London: Her Majesty's Stationer's Office.

Department of Trade and Industry. 1992. *Abuse of Market Power: A Consultative Document on Possible Legislative Options* (cm 2100). London: Her Majesty's Stationer's Office.

Dixit, A. K. 1984. "International Trade Policy for Oligopolistic Industries." *Economic Journal Conference Papers* 94: 1-16.

Dixit, A. K., and G. M. Grossman. 1986. "Targeted Export Promotion with Several Oligopolistic Industries." *Journal of International Economics* 21: 233-49.

European Commission. 1988. "The Economics of 1992." *European Economy* 35 (March).

European Commission. 1991. "Fair Competition in the Internal Market: Community State Aid Policy." *European Economy* 4 (September).

Fairburn, J., J. Kay, and T. Sharpe. 1984. "The Economics of Article 86." IFS Working Paper. London: Institute for Fiscal Studies.

Fudenberg, T., and J. Tirole. 1986. "A 'Signal Jamming' Theory of Predation." *Rand Journal of Economics* 17: 366-76.

Gatsios, K., and P. Seabright. 1989. "Regulation in the European Community." *Oxford Review of Economic Policy* 5, no. 2: 37-60.

Geroski, P. 1989. "European Industrial Policy and Industrial Policy in Europe." *Oxford Review of Economic Policy* 5: 20-36.

Geroski, P. 1993. "Antitrust Policy Towards Cooperative R and D Ventures." *Oxford Review of Economic Policy* 9, no. 2: 58-71.

Gilchrist, J., and D. Deacon. 1990. "Curbing Subsidies." In P. Montagnon, *European Competition Policy*. London: Pinter for Royal Institute for International Affairs.

Grossman, G. M. 1986. "Strategic Export Promotion: A Critique." In P. R. Krugman, *Strategic Trade Policy and the New International Economics*. Cambridge, MA: MIT Press.

Grossman, S., and O. D. Hart. 1980. "Takeover Bids, the Free-Rider Problem, and the Theory of the Corporation." *Bell Journal of Economics* 11: 42-64.

Hart, O., and J. Tirole. 1990. "Vertical Integration and Market Foreclosure." *Brookings Papers on Economic Activity: Microeconomics* 205-76.

Hay, D. A., and J. S. Vickers. 1987. *The Economics of Market Dominance*. Oxford, UK: Blackwell.

Hay, D. A., and J. S. Vickers. 1988. "The Reform of UK Competition Policy." *National Institute Economic Review* 125: 56-68.

Hay, G. A. 1985. "Competition Policy." *Oxford Review of Economic Policy* 1: 63-79.

Hindley, B. 1991. "The Economics of Dumping and Anti-dumping Action." In P. K. M. Tharakan, *Policy Implications of Antidumping Measures*. Amsterdam: Elsevier/North Holland.

Hoekman, B. M. 1994. *Antitrust-Based Remedies and Dumping in International Trade*. CEPR Discussion Paper No. 1010. London: Centre for Economic Policy Research.

Hoekman, B. M., and P. C. Marvroidis. 1994. "Competition, Competition Policy and the GATT." *World Economy* 17: 121-50.

Holzler, H. H. 1990. "Merger Control." In P. Montagnon, *European Competition Policy*. London: Pinter for Royal Institute of International Affairs.

International Monetary Fund (IMF). 1992. "The Interface Between Trade and Competition Policies," appendix II. In *Issues of Developments and International Trade Policy*. Washington.

Itoh, M., K. Kiyono, M. Okuno-Fugiwara, and K. Suzumura. 1991. *Economic Analysis of Industrial Policy*. San Diego: Academic Press.

Jacquemin, A. 1988. "Cooperative Agreements in R and D and European Antitrust Policy." *European Economic Review* 32: 557-60.

Jorde, T., and D. Teece. 1990. "Innovation and Cooperation: Implications for Competition and Antitrust." *Journal of Economic Perspectives* 4: 75-96.

Krishna, K. 1989. "Trade Restrictions as Facilitating Practices." *Journal of International Economics* 26: 251-70.

Krugman, P. R. 1984. "Import Protection as Export Promotion: International Competition in the Presence of Oligopoly and Scale Economies." In H. Kierzkowski, *Monopolistic Competition and International Trade*. Oxford, UK: Blackwell.

Lawrence, R. Z. 1991. "Efficient or Exclusivist? The Import Behavior of Japanese Corporate Groups." *Brookings Papers on Economic Activity* 1: 311-41.

Lloyd, P., and G. Sampson. 1995. "Competition and Trade Policy: Identifying the Issues after the Uruguay Round." *World Economy* 18: 681-705.

Messerlin, P. A. 1990. "Anti-Dumping Cases or Pro-Cartel Law? The EC Chemical Industry Cases." *World Economy* 13: 465-92.

Messerlin, P. A. 1991. "The Uruguay Negotiations on Antidumping Enforcement: Some Basic Issues." In P. K. M. Tharakan, *Policy Implications of Antidumping Measures*. Amsterdam: Elsevier/North Holland.

Milgrom, P., and J. Roberts. 1982. "Limit Pricing and Entry Under Incomplete Information: An Equilibrium Analysis." *Econometrica* 50: 443-59.

Neven, D., R. Nuttall, and P. Seabright. 1993. *Merger in Daylight.* London: Centre for Economic Policy Research.

Neven, D., and P. Seabright. 1995. "European Industrial Policy: The Airbus Case." *Economic Policy* 21: 313-58.

Neven, D. J., and J. S. Vickers. 1992. "Public Policy Towards Restructuring: Some Issues Raised by the Internal Market Programme." In K. Cool, D. Neven, and I. Walter, *European Industrial Restructuring in the 1990s.* London and Basingstoke, UK: Macmillan.

Ordover, J., and G. Saloner. 1989. "Predation, Monopolization and Antitrust." In R. Schmalensee and R. Willig, *Handbook of Industrial Organization.* Amsterdam: North Holland.

Organization for Economic Cooperation and Development (OECD). 1984. *Competition and Trade Policies: Their Interaction.* Paris.

Organization for Economic Cooperation and Development (OECD). 1986. *Competition Policy and Joint Ventures.* Paris.

Organization for Economic Cooperation and Development (OECD). 1988. *International Mergers and Competition Policy.* Paris.

Organization for Economic Cooperation and Development (OECD). 1989. *Competition Policy and Intellectual Property Rights.* Paris.

Organization for Economic Cooperation and Development (OECD). 1991. "Industrial Policy." In *OECD Countries: Annual Review 1991,* 145–54. Paris.

Organization for Economic Cooperation and Development (OECD). 1995. *Guidance for Cooperation between Authorities in Controlling Competition as it Affects International Trade.* Council text C(95)130, 29 September.

Pelkmans, J. 1987. "The New Approach to Technical Harmonization and Standardization." *Journal of Common Market Studies* 25: 249-69.

Richardson, J. David. 1989. *Empirical Research on Trade Liberalisation with Imperfect Competition: A Survey.* OECD Economic Studies 12. Paris: OECD.

Salop, S., and D. T. Scheffman. 1983. "Raising Rivals' Costs." *American Economic Review* 73: 267-71.

Salop, S., and D. T. Scheffman. 1987. "Cost Raising Strategies." *Journal of Industrial Economics* 36: 19-34.

Sapir, A., P. Buigues, and A. Jacquemin. 1993. "European Competition-Policy in Manufacturing and Services: A Two Speed Approach?" *Oxford Review of Economic Policy* 9, no. 2: 113-32.

Scherer, F. M. 1994. *Competition Policies for an Integrated World Economy.* Washington: Brookings Institution.

Smith, A., and A. J. Venables. 1988. "Completing the Internal Market in the European Community: Some Industry Simulations." *European Economic Review* 32: 1501-25.

Tirole, J. 1988. *The Theory of Industrial Organization.* Cambridge, MA: MIT Press.

Waterson, M. 1993. "Vertical Integration and Vertical Restraints." *Oxford Review of Economic Policy* 9, no. 2: 41-57.

Weinstein, D. E., and Y. Yafeh. 1995. "Japan's Corporate Groups: Collusive or Competitive? An Empirical Investigation of *Keiretsu* Behavior." *Journal of Industrial Economics* 43: 359-76.

Whish, R. 1989. *Competition Law.* London: Butterworth.

Williams, M. E. 1993. "The Effectiveness of Competition Policy in the United Kingdom." *Oxford Review of Economic Policy* 9, no. 2: 94-112.

7

United States

ELEANOR M. FOX AND ROBERT PITOFSKY

This chapter provides an overview of US antitrust law, with emphasis on those portions that affect international trade and global competition. In a few instances, aspects of US law that do not directly affect international trade are summarized because the US approach is significantly different from the approach of other countries to comparable problems.

Goals of US Competition Policy

Economic and Noneconomic Goals

The goals of US antitrust law are multiple and vary somewhat from statute to statute. The Sherman Antitrust Act of 1890, the oldest US federal antitrust law, was a child of the industrial revolution. The giant industrial trusts of that era, in addition to their many productive contributions, engaged in a course of conduct to stamp out and swallow up their competitors and exploit their suppliers and customers. The Sherman Act was passed to regulate these trusts. Its legislative history is replete with concerns about the unfair use of power and disparities in wealth and power. Farmers, small proprietors, consumers, and those who sim-

Eleanor M. Fox is Walter Derenberg Professor of Trade Regulation at the New York University School of Law. At the time this paper was prepared, Robert Pitofsky was professor of law, Georgetown University Law Center, Washington. Subsequently, he was appointed chairman of the Federal Trade Commission.

ply suffered "inequality of condition, of wealth and opportunity" were all identified as victims. Economists generally opposed the bill.

In 1914 Congress passed the Clayton Act. Born of the Progressive Era, this legislation was enacted during the term of President Woodrow Wilson as a part of his "new freedom" initiative, which promised "the little man" a better opportunity to succeed. One of the law's best-known proponents was Louis Brandeis, later an associate justice of the Supreme Court, who fought to protect opportunities for small business. The Clayton Act introduced a merger law in section 7, and in section 3 a law against tie-in sales (where one product is used to force the sale of another) and exclusive dealing and requirements contracts between buyers and sellers that may lessen competition. "Lessen competition" did not then have particular reference to consumer harm. The law was designed to unclog the channels of competition so that small firms would not be fenced out of business opportunities by larger and powerful competitors.

In 1936, in the wake of the Great Depression and especially in view of the hardship small businesses were suffering in the shadow of large and powerful firms, Congress passed the Robinson-Patman Anti-Price Discrimination Act. This act was an extensive amendment of section 2 of the Clayton Act.

The events of World War II gave rise to the next important amendment to the antitrust laws. Americans observed how the concentration of industries in Germany had played into the hands of fascism. In the 1940s, responding to a call from President Franklin D. Roosevelt to protect "the liberty of democracy," Congress established the Temporary National Economic Committee to study the causes and effects of economic concentration and to offer solutions to the widely accepted "problem" of economic concentration. The TNEC hearings and monographs, as well as parallel discussions and debate, led to the Celler-Kefauver Merger Act, an amendment to section 7 of the Clayton Act, in 1950, which strengthened the merger law. The purpose of the amendment was to check the increasing concentration of assets into fewer and fewer hands. The law aimed to preserve a society of small, independent, decentralized businesses in order to keep economic power dispersed and thereby keep political power diffused.

For scores of years, through the 1960s, neither Congress nor Supreme Court majorities acknowledged the tension between protecting small firms' freedom to participate in open markets, on the one hand, and protecting the interest of consumers in low prices, on the other. But in the mid-1970s the Supreme Court began to speak more frequently of the economic grounding of antitrust and began to apply a limiting principle to antitrust precedents so that conduct that served consumers was not unlawful. When the tension between the interests of small firms and those of consumers finally did surface, the courts and government agencies framed it as one between protecting inefficient small competitors and protecting consumer welfare. In the 1980s, under the Reagan administration, federal enforcement agencies resolved this dilemma in favor of protecting consumer welfare, by which phrase some enforcers meant promoting allocative efficiency—that is, efficiency of the total economy—while others meant, more literally, consumer interests. Enforcement officials in the Reagan administration resolved to use the antitrust laws only to challenge inefficient transactions. Beyond outright cartels, however, it was hard to find such transactions, and enforcement activity dwindled.

The Reagan administration's enforcement officials, whose ideology is popularly referred to as that of the Chicago School, were strong advocates of their new paradigm for antitrust, and many judges, especially newly appointed ones, were sympathetic to the relatively noninterventionist antitrust law that the paradigm implied. Other judges were also concerned with the rather bloated body of antitrust law that was the legacy of the 1960s, and all were aware of the Supreme Court's signals in the late 1970s heralding economic "soundness" as a basis for resolving antitrust issues. These influences converged to give great prominence to economic efficiency as a goal of antitrust law in contemporary antitrust jurisprudence.

By the end of the 1980s, some antitrust watchers believed that the Chicago School had won, not only in its quest to make allocative efficiency the sole goal of US antitrust law but also in its effort to confine the category for permissible intervention to output-limiting transactions, and to begin analysis of a problem by assuming that markets work well, that business acts efficiently, and that government intervention is clumsy. It is now clear, however, that the Chicago School, although very influential, has not prevailed.

First, as to goals, certain surviving antitrust rules are clearly not based on allocative efficiency. These include the per se rule against resale price maintenance agreements (discussed below), the modified per se rule against tie-ins by firms with market power, and the rule against naked competitor boycotts. These rules imply the right to be free from coercion and bullying and the right to participate in unclogged markets. Even the per se rule against cartels was driven not so much by allocative concerns as by a concern for fairness in distribution and by the political-economy interest in assuring that markets, not people, control the terms of trade. Even the law against market power-increasing mergers was driven by a desire to maintain the diversity thought necessary to preserve the interplay that underlies competition, and the pluralism that anchors democracy. That many of these rules, as refined, are consistent with allocative efficiency goals does not imply that allocative efficiency explains their adoption.

Second, US antitrust jurisprudence of the 1990s shows no signs of adopting into law an assumption that markets work well and virtually always pressure firms to operate efficiently—or the motto that one should "trust markets, not government." The Supreme Court rejected just this approach in the case of *Kodak v. Image Technical Services, Inc.* (504 U.S. 451, 1992).

Third, the question of how to use (or withhold) antitrust enforcement to achieve efficiency remains open. Targeting inefficient transactions may be one way to gain efficiency, but it is no longer accepted that all other enforcement conduces to inefficiency. Another way to keep markets efficient and firms robust may be to keep markets free of artificial blockages (see the *Aspen* and *AT&T* cases discussed below and complainants' allegations in the cases against Kodak and Microsoft). These issues are still being explored by enforcement agencies and the courts.

Influence of Industrial Policy

We confine industrial policy in this discussion to government policy that promotes national champions or otherwise facilitates the successful participation of US firms in international or world markets. Competition is one industrial policy. Indeed, US efforts to maintain competition through antitrust enforcement have no doubt greatly facilitated the growth of robust US firms and their successful participation in world markets, whereas lax antitrust enforcement seems to have had the converse effect.

Has industrial policy been an influence on the development of antitrust law? It may be an influence in two senses: industrial policy interests might be taken into account in considering what is anticompetitive, and "competitiveness" might be asserted as a trump over antitrust. Industrial policy interests have influenced antitrust in both ways, but most significantly the former. In the 1970s the United States reexamined its antitrust analysis against the background of an overgrown body of antitrust law, a declining economic growth of the nation, a recession, and the rise of efficient foreign competitors. Antitrust policy was revamped in the late 1970s and the 1980s, with new sympathy for freedom of action of even large firms, removing what some called the handicap of US antitrust.

As for industrial policy as a trump, policymakers may decide that it is worth bearing some anticompetitive loss in order to gain international or transnational competitiveness. Some legislative initiatives along these lines have failed (e.g., a merger proposal by Secretary of Commerce Malcolm Baldrige during the Bush administration), but others have passed. Sematech, the research and development consortium of US semiconductor chip makers, received both government funding and an antitrust exemption. Other legislation has been more modest. Two statutes simply lessen the available remedies against certain transactions, namely, research and development joint ventures and production joint ventures that are notified to the government, described below. Finally, a 1982 statute removes from the scope of the law US activity that harms only markets abroad.

Influence of Trade Policy

Trade policy has been linked with antitrust policy since the birth of US antitrust law. In 1890 many Republicans who supported the McKinley Tariff Act to protect US business from low-priced imports also supported the Sherman Act as the price of protection. If foreign goods were to be kept out of the United States, the nation had to be assured of a competitive national market.

In a very different sense, trade policy had a dramatic influence on antitrust in the 1970s. Because tariffs in the United States had by then been reduced to relatively low levels and there were few other trade restraints, foreign firms had easy access to US markets. Newly efficient firms from countries such as Germany and Japan, having finally recovered from the devastation of World War II, offered intense competition to US firms, some of which had grown lax with success. Antitrust became a scapegoat. Firms that were less than efficient tended to blame their failures on constraints imposed by US antitrust laws, and they often suggested that foreign firms were free of similar constraints.

In the early 1990s antitrust was again linked with trade policy. The US trade deficit with Japan had soared, and US businesses decried what they saw as the closure of Japanese markets by private as well as government restraints. The United States and Japan were then engaged in the Structural Impediments Initiative (SII). Then-US Assistant Attorney General James Rill joined then-US Trade Representative Carla Hills in suggesting antitrust policy as well as trade policy as a tool to pry open cartelized foreign markets (an initiative discussed in the section on extraterritoriality below).[1] Although this initiative has provoked cries of impermissible extraterritoriality, it has also raised to the level of international discussion the problem of private blockage of market access and the extent to which antitrust law can and should be used to police the openness of markets.

Trade policy influences day-to-day antitrust analysis in a more technical way. Tariffs and voluntary import restraints are barriers. If, because of trade restraints, merging domestic producers would be able to raise prices without triggering a flow of foreign imports that would defeat the price rise, the merger would be more likely to be found anticompetitive. But

---

1. A related problem for both antitrust and trade policy is raised in the context of low-priced imports made possible by monopoly profits in the closed foreign markets. A devastated US industry may seek protection against such imports.

if a production joint venture in the United States is the vehicle for a foreign producer to jump over a voluntary export restraint (VER) barrier, the joint venture may be procompetitive. Thus, the presence or absence of trade restraints is a background fact influencing competitive analysis.

Federal and State Antitrust Statutes

Federal Statutes

The substance of US federal antitrust enforcement derives from the four statutes described above: the Sherman Act, the Clayton Act, the Robinson-Patman Act, and the Celler-Kefauver Merger Act. Although they are the primary source of US competition policy, these statutes (with the exception of the Robinson-Patman Act) are relatively concise and lacking in detail. In reality, most antitrust policy in the United States originates in court interpretation of the broad language of the statutes.

The Sherman Act

The Sherman Act consists of two brief operative paragraphs. In section 1, contracts, combinations, and conspiracies "in restraint of trade" are declared illegal. The phrase "restraint of trade" has been interpreted to cover such hard-core violations as price fixing and market division, and also practices that are less harmful from a competitive point of view, such as exclusive-dealing contracts and joint ventures, when they are anticompetitive. The section covers both horizontal arrangements (agreements between competitors) and vertical arrangements (agreements between a producer and its suppliers or distributors). Violation requires more than one participant, for there must be a contract, combination, or conspiracy.

Section 2 of the Sherman Act makes it a violation to monopolize, attempt to monopolize, or combine or conspire with others to monopolize trade. A single firm may violate this provision. It is noteworthy that the section prohibits "monopolizing" and not the status of holding a monopoly position. Thus, some behavioral component is normally regarded as necessary before the provision is violated.

The Clayton Act

Provisions of the Clayton Act prohibit a variety of business practices whose effect may be to substantially lessen competition or tend to create a monopoly. Among the practices covered are price discrimination (section 2 of the act), tie-in sales and exclusive-dealing contracts (section 3), mergers and joint ventures (section 7), and interlocking directorates (section 8).

The Robinson-Patman Act

This statute covers in great detail discrimination in price and the provision of services. It covers not only discriminatory pricing but also the knowing receipt of a discriminatory discount.

The Celler-Kefauver Act

This legislation declares illegal those mergers or joint ventures (horizontal, vertical, and conglomerate) whose effect may be substantially to lessen competition or to tend to create a monopoly.

State Statutes

State antitrust laws, similar in most respects to federal antitrust laws, exist in most of the 50 states. These statutes are normally interpreted in a fashion consistent with federal court interpretation of the Sherman and Clayton Acts.

State statutes are enforced primarily against local restraints of trade, that is, practices that have an effect exclusively or primarily within a single state. There are important exceptions, however. A state may challenge in court any transaction that has a significant effect on commerce within its borders, even if the transaction is of national or even international dimension.

Enforcement

There are four centers of antitrust enforcement: two federal agencies with largely concurrent jurisdiction (the Antitrust Division of the Department of Justice, and the Federal Trade Commission), state enforcement, and private enforcement by companies or individuals injured in their business or property by practices that violate the antitrust laws.

The Antitrust Division of the Department of Justice

The Antitrust Division is responsible for enforcing the Sherman and Clayton Acts. Although authorized to do so, the division has not brought a proceeding under the Robinson-Patman Act for almost half a century.

Violations of sections 1 and 2 of the Sherman Act can be challenged in civil proceedings seeking an order to cease the practice, or in criminal proceedings, where conviction is punishable by imprisonment for up to three years and fines in amounts up to $350,000 for individuals and up to $10 million for corporations for each offense, or, if greater, double the amount gained from the violation or lost by the victim. Beginning in the mid-1970s, the Antitrust Division put new emphasis on criminal prosecutions and routinely seeks imprisonment for serious antitrust offenses such as price-fixing.

The Federal Trade Commission

The Federal Trade Commission (FTC) is an independent regulatory agency, established in 1914 by the Federal Trade Commission Act, which declares unlawful "unfair methods of competition."[2] The provision has been interpreted to give the FTC concurrent jurisdiction with the Department of Justice to enforce the Sherman and Clayton Acts.[3] The FTC has no criminal jurisdiction. The two agencies have certain overlapping jurisdiction and responsibilities, most notably with regard to mergers. They have developed a liaison system to avoid duplication of effort and unnecessary interference with businesses.

Private Enforcement

Individuals and corporations injured by violations of the antitrust laws may sue on their own behalf to enjoin behavior that causes them antitrust harm. If successful, they are entitled to three times the amount of their damages plus court costs and attorneys' fees. In the 1970s and early 1980s, an average of almost 1,500 private actions were brought each year by customers, competitors, or other private parties. Partly because of procedural restrictions on access to the courts, private actions have declined in recent years, but they still totaled more than 500 in 1992. Moreover, groups of complainants similarly situated can join forces in a class-action suit seeking damages on their joint behalf.

Successful antitrust actions can involve huge costs and damages. General Electric and other companies paid more than $350 million in the early 1960s to litigate and settle price-fixing cases. Treble damages of more than $1 billion were more recently awarded to a pipeline company against a group of railroads (*ETSI Pipeline Project v. Burlington Northern, Inc.*, No. B-84-979, E.D. Tex. 1989).

---

2. It has been suggested at times that the act be interpreted to cover transactions that violate the spirit if not the letter of the Sherman and Clayton Acts, making the act an independent source of restrictions. In practice, that notion has not significantly modified antitrust coverage.

3. The statute also empowers the FTC to enforce a variety of other statutes, including those concerned with fair packaging and labeling, consumer credit, and deceptive advertising.

State Enforcement

State enforcement officials may bring antitrust cases for injunctive relief or for damages to the state itself and on behalf of individuals residing in the state. These officials may seek treble damages, costs, and attorneys' fees in addition to injunctive relief.

State antitrust enforcement has increased sharply in recent years, particularly in the 1980s when it was widely thought that federal antitrust enforcement was inadequate.[4]

Selected Competition Issues That Affect Global Markets

Measurement of Market Power

Except in areas of per se prohibition, the consequences of conduct or transactions vary depending on the market power of the firm or firms engaged in the transaction. For example, a merger or joint venture is more likely to lessen competition and therefore be held illegal if the parties to the transaction account for 40 percent of the market than if they account for 10 percent.

The first step in measuring market power in the United States is to define the relevant market. The US approach to market definition, particularly with emphasis on future competitive responses if prevailing prices are raised, is somewhat different from market power measurement in other parts of the world.

General Concepts in Case Law and Guidelines

In defining the relevant market under US law, the central question is whether a firm or group of firms can raise their price by a significant amount without losing so much business to substitutes (which may be other products available in the same geographic area or the same product produced in other geographic areas) that the price rise would be unprofitable. A product market includes all products or services for which there is reasonable interchangeability in consumption or production. A geographic market is defined by identifying the area within which purchasers can practically turn for an alternative source of supply. If

---

4. Under certain circumstances, even foreign governments may sue in US courts to recover damages for injuries to those governments. See *Pfizer, Inc. v. Government of India*, 434 US 308 (1978). The principle entitling foreign government buyers to treble damages was modified by amendment to section 4 of the Clayton Act of 29 December 1982, P.L. 97-393.

a firm or firms that raised their price would lose a significant amount of business to other products or to the same product produced in other geographic areas, those other products are within the product market, and those alternative sources of supply are within the geographic market.

The leading US case on the subject is *United States v. E. I. du Pont de Nemours & Co.* (351 US 377, 1956), in which Du Pont was charged with monopolizing commerce in cellophane. If the court determined that cellophane was a separate relevant product market, Du Pont, with almost 75 percent of sales, might have been found guilty of monopolizing behavior. If, however, all flexible packaging material (including wax paper, aluminum foil, polyethylene, and other materials) were considered part of the market, Du Pont's share was only 20 percent, and Du Pont was not even a candidate for monopolization. The US Supreme Court concluded that there was cross-elasticity of demand between cellophane and other flexible packaging materials, so that if Du Pont raised the price of cellophane significantly, many customers would switch to other flexible packaging materials; therefore the product market was not cellophane but all flexible packaging materials.[5]

A measurement of market power should not end with an examination of presently available substitutes. One should inquire whether the firm or firms in question, if they raised the price, would face competition from producers that could easily shift their facilities to make the relevant product ("supply substitution"), products currently sold outside the geographic market that could be diverted into it ("geographic diversion"), or new entry in the form of expanded capacity or totally new production. Even a firm with 100 percent of an existing market would lack market power if, upon raising its price slightly, it would be swamped by an avalanche of diverted production or prompt new entry.

What standard must be satisfied to establish that potential production constrains market power (and therefore is in the relevant market)? During the 1980s, US enforcement agencies and some courts became very lenient in examining whether future hypothetical shifts in purchasing or supply patterns constituted checks on market power. Often the courts were satisfied with a finding that substitute production *could* appear (i.e., that there were no insurmountable barriers to entry) rather than whether it actually *would* appear in the market.[6] Rejecting this lenient approach, the 1992 Merger Guidelines (US Department of Justice and

---

5. There is a notorious and much-criticized logical flaw in the application of the test used in this case. It is possible that DuPont was already charging a higher than competitive price for cellophane, and for that reason substitute competition was effective in preventing further price increases (Pitofsky 1990 summarizes criticism of the doctrine).

6. See, for example, *United States v. Waste Management, Inc.,* 743 F.2d 976 (2nd Cir., 1984) and *United States v. Syufy Enterprises,* 903 F.2d 659 (9th Cir., 1990).

Federal Trade Commission 1992) provide that substitute competition or new entry will only be taken into account where such entry *would* be "timely, likely and sufficient in its magnitude, character and scope to deter or counteract the competitive effects of concern." It remains to be seen whether US courts will also adjust their approach to the question of substitute competition or new entry constraining the exercise of market power.

Global Competition: Effect on Relevant Market Analysis

A few products (jet engines, some financial services) compete in a market that is essentially global. Alternative sources of supply worldwide may check anticompetitive behavior and ensure that no market power exists. The list of such products is short, but it may grow as competition changes from national to global.

More frequently, global competition considerations relating to measurement of market power revolve around the question of imports. The established view in the United States is that imports are counted in the market and are relevant for purposes of measuring market power. The argument put forward by some—that international trade is fragile, easily disrupted, and unpredictable and therefore should not be counted in measuring domestic market power—has been rejected. As a result, market power in the United States is directly affected by the level of imports.

If imports would promptly increase upon a price rise, this potential pressure on prices may be taken into account as well. The pressure from imports and potential imports may prevent market power from arising, but such a conclusion cannot be assumed; it depends on specific facts, including the reliability of the flow of imports. Since importers may be actual competitors of domestic firms, many transactions (mergers, joint ventures, distribution contracts) entered into between non-US firms that export to the United States and US firms will be regarded as horizontal transactions. In general, arrangements that lessen horizontal competition are treated more stringently under US antitrust law than those that lessen competition between firms that are not presently or only potentially direct rivals.

Cartel Policy

Both in law and in enforcement, the United States has an exceptionally strict anticartel policy. Naked agreements between competitors to fix or affect price or divide markets are illegal.

Scope of Policy

Agreements are regarded as price-fixing if they set or have the effect of setting either maximum or minimum prices (*Arizona v. Maricopa County*

Medical Society, 457 US 332, 1982) or related terms of sale such as discounts, rebates, transportation charges, and credit terms (*Catalano, Inc. v. Target Sales, Inc.*, 446 US 643, 1980). A market division agreement divides markets geographically or by product (*Palmer v. BRG of Georgia, Inc.*, 498 U.S. 46, 1990). Finally, agreements to allocate or rotate bids are a form of price fixing.

Reflecting a general antagonism to cartel behavior, US law provides that price fixing and market allocation between rivals are illegal per se. In these cases, it is no defense that the participants lack market power, are motivated by a benign business purpose, or have good business reasons for their conduct. Experience reveals that such conduct almost always results in adverse competitive effects and is almost never justified by business reasons sufficiently persuasive to counteract those effects.[7]

The Issue of "Agreement"

Since direct price-fixing is almost impossible to justify, the central issue under US law is whether price setting occurred unilaterally (which is legal) or by agreement. The necessary agreement can be express or implied and is often inferred from circumstantial evidence. Parallel pricing is not in itself sufficient to prove the existence of an agreement, but parallel pricing together with other evidence (often referred to as "plus factors") can establish an agreement. Plus factors might include evidence of meetings among competitors (particularly if clandestine), exceptionally high profits, or lock-step pricing over a long period of time and in the face of varying economic conditions. If defendants' conduct or behavior would not have made business sense if done unilaterally, an inference of collaboration might be drawn, and conversely if a hypothesis (e.g., that defendants conspired to fix a low price) does not make business sense, an inference that no agreement existed might be indicated. US law has not yet grappled with the problem that what makes business sense might be a function of culture. For example, it is said that Japanese firms might employ strategies to increase their market shares even at the expense of profit maximization.

Characterization Questions

There occasionally is a preliminary question concerning whether competitively ambiguous behavior constitutes price-fixing. Particularly where the effect on price is indirect, and where the arrangement challenged as price-fixing can be defended on the grounds that it produces efficiencies, the court will take a "quick look" to determine whether the severe per se

---

7. The cases establishing the per se rule are old but still valid: *United States v. Socony-Vacuum Oil Co.*, 310 US 150 (1940); *United States v. Trenton Potteries Co.*, 273 US 372 (1927).

rule should apply. This characterization phase is an abbreviated procedure in which the courts examine market power, purpose, effect, and business justification—the very issues that would be excluded by a per se approach. (The leading case illustrating the characterization approach is *Broadcast Music, Inc. v. Columbia Broadcasting System*, 441 US 1, 1979).

Exceptions

Although antitrust condemnation of cartel behavior is sweeping and covers almost all industries, there are a few exceptions, primarily based on express legislative provisions. These are discussed below.

"Dominant Firm" Policy

Antitrust limits on business behavior designed to achieve monopoly power and on the behavior of companies that possess monopoly power have been a central feature of US antitrust policy from the beginning. In the first half of the 20th century, the courts adopted exceptionally restrictive rules. The history of enforcement and interpretation in recent decades reflects a general easing of those restrictions, to the point where US policy with respect to dominant firms is now more lenient than policy in the European Union and most European countries.

Monopoly Power

There is no precise market-share threshold necessary to support a claim that a firm possesses monopoly power under section 2 of the Sherman Act. A famous dictum from the *Alcoa* case states that 90 percent of a market is enough to constitute a monopoly, 60 or 64 percent is doubtful, and 33 percent is insufficient (see *United States v. Aluminum Co. of America*, 148 F.2d 416, 424, 2d Cir., 1945). In fact, the issue of what level of market share qualifies does not lend itself to easy formulas. A firm with monopoly power may be content to charge extremely high prices and exercise its market power and a distinctive good by reaping high profits on less than a 50 percent market share. However, a firm with 90 percent of the market may not have market power if it is earning only ordinary profits and would lose a substantial portion of its business if it raised its price even a small amount. Despite these complexities, it has been observed that the leading US cases upholding monopolization claims involved defendants that controlled from 70 to 100 percent of the market.[8]

---

8. *Broadway Delivery Corp. v. United Parcel Service of America, Inc.*, 651 F.2d 122 (2d Cir.), *cert. denied*, 454 US 968 (1981); *Hiland Dairy Inc. v. Kroger Co.*, 402 F.2d 968, 974, n.6 (8th Cir., 1968).

Monopolizing Behavior

As noted earlier, in the United States the mere possession of a monopoly does not violate the antitrust laws; unacceptable conduct to achieve or maintain such a monopoly seems to be required for violation. In some early cases the conduct component was much attenuated. For example, in the *Alcoa* case cited above, the defendant, holding a dominant position in the production of aluminum ingot, was found to have violated section 2 because it had doubled and redoubled its capacity in anticipation of demand.[9] The court appeared to hold that "deliberate" conduct that has an exclusionary effect is illegal even if motivated by legitimate business concerns. The court's attitude on the question was complicated by the fact that it carved out as an exception conduct that constituted nothing more than superior skill, foresight, and industry (*United States v. Aluminum Co. of America*, 148 F.2d 430, 2nd Cir., 1945). The *Alcoa* case and others decided during this period thus reduced the conduct element of a section 2 violation to a bare minimum.[10]

The most common example of monopolizing behavior is the acquisition of a direct rival by a dominant firm in a high-barrier market (see, e.g., *United States v. Southern Pacific Co.*, 259 US 214, 1922). Other instances might involve predatory pricing (pricing below cost under certain conditions with expectation of recoupment), long-term lease arrangements with penalty clauses if the customer switches to a challenger of the monopolist, and refusals to deal for no business purpose other than to achieve or maintain a monopoly position.[11]

In the past several decades, US courts have become far more solicitous of protecting a monopolist's ability to compete in order to defend its position or even achieve greater market share, particularly where that monopoly position was legally acquired.[12] As a result, government and private challenges to monopoly behavior have repeatedly been unsuccessful. A single glaring exception, however, is the federal govern-

---

9. The court's decision was no doubt influenced by the fact that, in the early years of its operation, Alcoa had clearly engaged in anticompetitive conduct such as participating in an international cartel and entering into exclusionary contracts that prevented potential competitors from acquiring power sites in areas adjacent to raw material deposits. Because of technicalities, this earlier anticompetitive behavior was not before the court.

10. Although more serious anticompetitive conduct was involved, courts appeared to embrace the test that called only for deliberate exclusion, regardless of business justification, in *United States v. United Shoe Machinery Corp.*, 110 F.Supp. 295 (D. Mass., 1953), *aff'd per curium*, 347 US 521, 1954; and *United States v. Grinnell Corp.*, 384 US 563, 1966.

11. See *Otter Tail Power Co. v. United States*, 410 US 366 (1973) and *Lorain Journal Co. v. United States*, 342 US 143 (1951).

12. *Olympia Equipment Leasing Co. v. Western Union Telegraph*, 797 F.2d 37, 375-76 (7th Cir., 1986), *cert. denied*, 480 US 934 (1987); *Telex Corp. v. IBM*, 510 F.2d 894 (10th Cir., 1975), *cert. dismissed*, 423 US 802 (1975).

ment's challenge to the monopoly position and practices of the American Telephone & Telegraph Company (AT&T), but that is explained on the grounds that the defendant possessed vertically integrated monopolies (in long-distance and local service) and the court found that the Justice Department made a prima facie case that the company protected its monopolies through highly anticompetitive exclusionary conduct (*United States v. AT&T*, 524 F.Supp. 1331, D.D.C., 1981) (later settled by consent decree, which was vacated by the Telecommunications Act).

There remains a basic lack of clarity in US law on how to distinguish between economically exclusionary or predatory conduct, which is illegal, and exercise of superior skill, foresight, and industry, which is legal. Part of the problem rests with the reliance on such words as "exclusionary" because so much desirable competitive conduct exemplifying "superior skill" has an exclusionary effect. One of the Supreme Court's most recent effort at clarification was *Aspen Skiing Co. v. Aspen Highland Skiing Corp.*, 472 US 585 (1985), where the owner of three ski slopes abruptly discontinued the offer to consumers of a joint four-mountain ticket with a fourth, smaller ski slope and made it impossible for the smaller ski slope owner to buy up tickets to offer a package deal. Although the court recognized that a monopolist has no generalized duty to cooperate with competitors, it found Aspen Ski's behavior illegal, apparently on the ground that the discontinuance was injurious to its competitor and was entirely lacking in business justification, depriving consumers of an option they desired and disabling the smaller competitor from serving that demand. That formulation is probably a fair, though ambiguous, statement of current law. See also the *Eastman Kodak Co. v. Image Technical Services, Inc.*, 504 U.S. 451 (1992) holding that Kodak's cut off of independent repair suppliers can be a violation of section 2 where it is an exercise of market power to exploit its machine customers.

Merger Policy

Mergers are reviewed primarily under section 7 of the Clayton Act, which declares illegal those mergers that may substantially lessen competition or tend to create a monopoly. US antitrust policy with respect to mergers has varied widely. In the 1960s the United States had by far the most stringent antitrust merger policy in the world, striking down mergers among small firms in unconcentrated markets. It was not unusual for the government to challenge successfully mergers among direct competitors holding no more than 5 or 6 percent of the market,[13] and in one case a merger between customer and supplier was successfully challenged where

---

13. *United States v. Pabst Brewing Co.*, 384 US 546, 550 (1966); *United States v. Von's Grocery Co.*, 384 US 270, 281 (1966).

the acquired company accounted for between 1 and 2 percent of the market (*Brown Shoe Co. v. United States*, 370 US 294, 347–48, 1962). By the mid-1980s, the United States had moved to an extremely lenient merger policy. No challenges to nonhorizontal mergers occurred, and billion-dollar mergers were regularly allowed to be completed without government challenge, even when they involved direct competitors.[14] Current federal enforcement is more visible. It extends to horizontal, potential horizontal, and vetical mergers.

Philosophy of Merger Enforcement

The twin themes of US merger enforcement involve concerns that the merger will allow the combined firm, acting unilaterally, to raise prices, or that the merger will result in the reduction of the number of firms in a high-barrier, concentrated market, which in turn will facilitate explicit or implicit coordination of action to extract higher prices and earn greater profits at the expense of consumers.[15] Also, merger enforcement may preserve innovation competition in highly concentrated markets. Beyond these specific concerns about the possible anticompetitive effects of mergers, there is a generalized view in the United States that, in noncompetitive markets, incentives to achieve efficiency, innovate, and drive down prices will diminish.

Merger Rules

The initial step in analyzing the legality of a merger is to define the relevant market (see "Measurement of Market Power" above). Within that market, current fashion in the United States is to measure market shares and industry concentration by the Herfindahl-Hirschman index (HHI), calculated by summing the squares of the market shares of each firm in the market. For example, in a market with ten equally sized firms the HHI is 1,000 (10^2, or 100, for each of the ten firms); in a market with five equally sized firms the HHI is 2,000 (400 for each of the five firms).

With modest differences in emphasis, the current guidelines and earlier versions (reflecting judicial decisions as well) are consistent in describing different enforcement attitudes depending upon concentration after the merger. If a postmerger HHI for a horizontal merger were 1,000, the guidelines would treat it as an unconcentrated market, and the government would be extremely unlikely to sue; if the HHI exceeded 1,800, the guidelines would treat that market as concentrated,

---

14. For a summary of data on the question see Fox and Pitofsky (1992, 319, 325-27).

15. The US Department of Justice and the Federal Trade Commission restated these themes of merger policy in the 1992 Horizontal Merger Guidelines (US Department of Justice and Federal Trade Commission 1992, section 0.1 at 4-5).

and the government would be far more likely to challenge it. Markets with HHIs between 1,000 and 1,800 are characterized as moderately concentrated, and the government and the courts will examine a wide variety of factors to determine whether market power has increased, justifying enforcement. Even where collusive or collaborative behavior is not a matter of concern, a single firm might be able unilaterally to achieve anticompetitive effects. The guidelines assume that such a result will occur when the combined market share of the merging firms is at least 35 percent.

When the enforcement agencies and the courts look beyond market share and concentration to "other factors," the most important by far involves conditions of entry. When entry is sufficiently easy, US courts have occasionally held that the merger is not a serious problem regardless of market share (*United States v. Waste Management, Inc.*, 743 F.2d 976, 2d Cir., 1984). Other factors that have been examined include homogeneity of the product (cartels are easier to establish and maintain when homogeneous products are involved), availability of key information concerning transactions and individual competitors that make cartel behavior feasible, and a history of collusion in the market.

The most controversial "other factor" is the presence or absence of efficiencies. Claims of efficiency can be considered as a relevant factor in the enforcement agencies' exercise of prosecutorial discretion (US Department of Justice and Federal Trade Commission 1997 amendment, section 4), but according to Supreme Court precedent in the 1960s, efficiencies are not relevant as an offset or a defense when a transaction is examined in court (see *FTC v. Procter & Gamble Co.*, 386 US 568, 1967). Even in the context of prosecutorial discretion, the government's posture toward efficiency claims has sometimes been skeptical. The burden of persuasion and proof is on the party asserting the efficiency, and it probably is essential to demonstrate that the claimed efficiencies occur in a market setting that ensures that the savings from the efficiencies will be passed along to consumers (Pitofsky 1992 summarizes current law). Many lower courts are beginning to take efficiency claims into account, but the US Supreme Court has not had an opportunity to reconsider its position.

To clarify their own position, the government agencies amended their 1992 merger guidelines in 1997, stating that they will not challenge mergers with substantiated efficiencies unlikely to be produced absent the merger if these efficiencies are sufficiently great to counteract any consumer harm, and that the greater the probable adverse effect of the merger the greater must be the efficiencies to nullify the effect.

Finally, US law takes into account the economic condition of the acquired company. Even where a merger is otherwise illegal, a company (or one of its divisions) that is failing may be sold to any purchaser. A "failing firm" is defined very narrowly. The firm must have "resources so depleted and prospects for rehabilitation" so remote "that it faces the grave probability of a business failure" (*United States v. General Dynamics Corp.*, 415 US 486, 507, 1974, quoting *International Shoe v. FTC*, 280 US 291, 302, 1930), and there must be no other prospective purchaser available that poses a less-severe danger to competition (*Citizen Publishing Co. v. United States*, 394 US 131, 136, 138, 1969). The 1992 Horizontal Merger Guidelines adopt similarly stringent language and in addition provide that the defense is available only if the allegedly failing firm would not be able to reorganize successfully through bankruptcy proceedings, and only if, absent a merger, the assets of the failing firm would exit from the market (US Department of Justice and Federal Trade Commission 1992, section 5.1). In effect, firms must be virtually insolvent before the defense is permitted. If the *industry* is in economic distress (for example, it has chronic overcapacity) but the firm in question is not failing, no defense is available under US law. Of course such factors would be taken into account as a matter of prosecutorial discretion.

Joint Venture Policy

Characterizing and Distinguishing Mergers, Cartels, and Joint Ventures

Joint ventures are a preferred device by which US and non-US firms combine resources to compete in a particular product or geographic market. Joint ventures may include any cooperative arrangement among firms. Normally they are undertaken to share talents and pool risks, in order to undertake a job that neither partner could do as well alone.

Joint ventures may be loose contractual arrangements, or they may be corporate joint ventures. The joint venture partners may form a new corporation in which they hold shares, and they might jointly control the new corporation. Since corporate joint ventures are normally subject to section 7 of the Clayton Act, the principal merger law, as well as to the Sherman Act, characterization questions at the borderline between merger and joint venture are relatively unimportant. In this respect, US law differs from law in the European Union, under which a joint venture must be classified as either concentrative (merger-like) or cooperative, and much turns on the characterization (although an amendment to the European Merger Regulation may alleviate the problem).

When loose forms of cooperative arrangements are involved, characterization questions at the borderline between cartels and joint ventures are, however, very important. Cartels, in US usage, are agreements among competitors designed to fix price or divide markets in order to override the market (see "Cartel Policy" above.) Cartels are illegal per se and a criminal violation. Joint ventures are subject to the rule of reason and, currently, are treated hospitably. Cartelists might seek to conceal a cartel under the rubric of a joint venture, as has been done in such notorious international cartel cases as *Timken Roller Bearing v. United States,* 341 US 593 (1951) and *United States v. Imperial Chem. Indus., Ltd.,* 100 F.Supp. 504 (S.D.N.Y., 1987). Often, whether a collaboration is a joint venture or a cartel presents a difficult question of fact (see *United States v. Columbia Pictures Indus., Inc.,* 507 F.Supp. 412, S.D.N.Y., 1980, *affirmed without opinion,* 2d Cir., 1981).

General Analysis

Joint venture analysis may be divided into three parts: essence, ancillary restraints, and, in rare cases, the duty to admit competitors.

The *essence* question is whether the formation of the joint venture is likely to produce or increase market power. To perform this analysis it is necessary to define the market. Often there is more than one relevant market in the case of a joint venture; for example, the market in which the joint venture operates and the market within which the parents operate or stand in a buyer-supplier relationship. Anticompetitive problems usually arise, if at all, from one of the following two situations.

First, the parents may be competitors outside the joint venture market, and the fear is that the joint venture will bring them closer together and provide a forum for collaboration; thus their collaboration might spill over to lessen competition in an adjacent market. This concern arises in the case of export associations composed of the few firms in a concentrated US market. The spillover concern was also expressed in connection with the General Motors-Toyota joint venture to make and sell a small car, which was permitted to proceed subject to consent decree restrictions (*In General Motors Corp.,* 103 FTC 374, 1984) (decree later vacated). Anticompetitive effects would not be expected to arise unless the market is concentrated and entry not easy, for otherwise the forces of competition would make the spillover collaboration unprofitable.

Second, the parents may be potential competitors: for example, a US parent may be a dominant firm in the US market, and a foreign firm may be in the same line of business in its home market and one of a few potential entrants into the United States. The two might enter into a joint venture, for example in a specialty market in the United States. The joint venture might co-opt the foreign firm, which might then lose its incentive to become a competitor of its partner. This concern, too, was raised in the General Motors-Toyota joint venture: a hypothesis was that Toyota would lose its incentive to establish its own production facilities in the United States. The consent decree addressed this problem by limiting the joint venture's output to approximately 5 percent of the US small car market.

"Strategic alliance" is a label given to certain joint ventures, particularly where the collaboration gives each partner advantages in penetrating the market of the other or gives the partners synergistic advantages in technology. The label itself tells very little. The anticipated strategic benefit may be anticompetitive exclusionary advantages, or it may be procompetitive means of market entry. Each case must be analyzed on its facts.

A joint venture may be likely to create market power but also likely to result in efficiencies or technological progress. We know of no US court that has explicitly confronted this tension, although the General Motors-Toyota joint venture was potentially such a case. From dictum in contemporary cases under section 2 of the Sherman Act, we believe it is likely that courts will treat hospitably joint ventures that promise to create significant efficiencies or technological progress not likely to be achieved otherwise, even if the joint venture might create some market power in the short run.

Ancillary restraints may limit the competition of the joint venturers against one another or between the joint venture and its parents, and they may set the terms by which the fruits of the joint venture are exploited. Where a joint venture is procompetitive and ancillary restraints are important to make it work, covenants are normally upheld. On the other hand, covenants not to compete, entered into in connection with the joint venture, may be a way to protect the partners from one another's competition and may be far broader than necessary to make the joint venture work (*Yamaha Motor Co. v. FTC*, 657 F.2d 971, 8th Cir., 1981).

There is very little contemporary law on the rights of joint venture partners to *share the technological fruits* of their joint venture. They may, for example, wish to divide the fruits so that one partner has the exclusive right to use a product or technology in a given field or in its home country, and the other the exclusive right in a different field or its home country. They also may wish to agree not to sublicense their new technology. A first question is whether any of the above provisions are illegal per se. Under contemporary principles, they are not likely to be so treated where the covenant was an important part of the bargain that produced the joint venture and is reasonably related to achieving its goals. As a result, if the technology produced does not prove to be highly desirable and unique, the parties are not likely to face antitrust concerns. If, however, the joint venture is successful and the technology confers market power, the problems are of a different dimension and the outcome cannot be predicted.

It is less likely that a court would require the joint venture to give competitors access to the technology, in recognition of the fact that the joint venture parents have taken risks and invested efforts to produce the technology. But the collaborative aspect of the joint venture would make its refusal to deal more vulnerable than a refusal to deal by a single actor.

Before the mid-1970s it was generally thought that dominant joint ventures might have *duties of inclusion*; that is, they might be obliged to accept all competitors who wished to take part in the enterprise (or make available the advantages of membership) and who were willing to share its costs (see *Associated Press v. United States*, 326 US 1, 1945). Under contemporary law and thinking, the duty of inclusion is very narrow. It is recognized that, if collaboration is important to competitiveness, several competing groups are far better than one.

There remains a rare instance in which dominant joint ventures would have a duty of inclusion, namely, when the joint venture is or owns an essential facility that cannot feasibly be duplicated, and access to it is necessary in order to compete. Even then, if the "facility" consists of technology created by the foresight of the joint venturers, a court may well deny a right of access. This, too, is a cutting-edge problem on which the law is not clear.

Predation

Definitions

Under US law predation is a strategy to disable competitors by first using low prices, strategic exclusions, or other means designed to impose costs on the competitors, and then raising prices after achieving monopoly or oligopoly. It is a strategy that would not make sense if the market were expected to be as competitive after the period of predation as before it began. Thus we say that a firm "invests" in predation—it takes a loss today in the expectation of a future payback in the form of higher than competitive profits that more than repay the loss.

Most commonly, predation is price predation, but it can also be product-change predation, as when IBM slowed the speed of a unit that it manufactured just so peripheral compatible manufacturers' equipment would fail. In *Transamerica Computer Co. v. IBM*, 481 F. Supp. 965, 1007-08 (N.D. Cal. 1979), *aff'd*, 698 F.2d 1377 (9th Cir.), *cert. denied*, 464 U.S. 955 (1983), the court held that IBM had no monopoly power and dismissed the case.

Price predation is a complex issue because low prices are good for consumers, and the law should not discourage sustained low pricing. Price predation cases normally arise, where they do arise, in the context of section 2 of the Sherman Act, where the defendant (at least allegedly) either has monopoly power or is likely to obtain it as a result of its pricing strategy. A number of courts have required, to reach a finding of predation, that the defendant was charging a price below cost (e.g., below marginal cost, with average variable cost as a proxy).[16] In addition, some courts inquire into the defendant's intent to destroy competitors and

---

16. US precedent is summarized and policy considerations are examined in *Barry Wright Corp. v. ITT Grinnell Corp.*, 724 F.2d 227 (1st Cir., 1983).

whether it had a reasonable chance to do so, and, thereafter, whether it had a reasonable chance to recoup the losses by charging higher than competitive prices. In some courts it is sufficient that the defendant's prices were below average total cost, and some fewer courts accept pricing above average total cost with clear proof of anticompetitive intent. Some courts have not required proof of probable recoupment, but a recent Supreme Court opinion declares probable recoupment a necessary element of the case (*Brooke Group Ltd. v. Brown & Williamson Tobacco Corp.*, 509 U.S. 209, 1993).

Comparison with Trade Policy

Trade law protects US industry against dumping, which is sustained low pricing (pricing at "less than fair value") of imports into the United States that causes material harm to a domestic industry. "Less than fair value" may mean less than the price at which the goods are sold in the home country, less than their price in a third country, or less than some constructed value (i.e., a value computed by estimating costs). Procedures for the finding of "less than fair value" are not rigorous.

Accordingly, it has been argued that trade law may keep out of the United States goods sold at sustainably low prices even in cases in which the importers have no possibility of winning market power in the United States, and thus no possibility of raising prices above competitive levels later. See Lipstein's chapter in this volume for a discussion of the tensions between and proposals for convergence of antitrust and antidumping policy.

Price Discrimination

Definition and Enforcement

The Robinson-Patman Act prohibits price discrimination where its effect may be substantially to lessen competition or to injure, destroy, or prevent competition with a competitor or customer. "Primary line" discrimination harms a competitor of the firm engaging in price discrimination and may threaten to lessen competitiors on this level at which the defendant and its competition compete. Secondary line discrimination may harm competition on the line of the disfavored customer.

For at least the last 20 years, enforcement authorities have been acutely aware of the tension between the Robinson-Patman Act and the policy of the Sherman Act. The Robinson-Patman Act has the potential to chill price cutting. Accordingly, the act has been little enforced at the federal level; its enforcement has largely been by way of private treble-damage actions.

In 1993 the Supreme Court handed down a decision in a Robinson-Patman primary line case (*Brooke Group Ltd. v. Brown & Williamson*

Tobacco Corp., 509 U.S. 209, 1993). The case involved a price war in un-branded cigarettes. Brown & Williamson, the company in the oligopolistic branded-cigarette market with the most to lose from the incursions of generic cigarettes, waged the low-price war with the intent to destroy Liggett, the innovator in generic cigarettes. Brown & Williamson charged prices below its average variable cost. The Supreme Court held that the jury verdict for Liggett could not stand because Liggett had not proved the defendant's probability of recoupment. The Supreme Court seem-ingly brought primary line Robinson-Patman cases into line with price predation cases under section 2 of the Sherman Act, except that under the latter the low pricing must be en route to monopoly, whereas under the Robinson-Patman Act it may be en route to solidifying market power among oligopolists.

Comparison with Trade Law

Trade law against international price discrimination (see above) remains much more far-reaching than the Robinson-Patman Act's restrictions on domestic price discrimination. For example, a recoupment scenario is not a necessary element in finding a trade law violation. Moreover, pric-ing below cost is not a requirement of the trade law violation; typically, a respondent prices below average total cost but not average variable cost.

Vertical Agreements

Contractual arrangements whereby manufacturers influence the market-ing behavior of distributors can affect—indeed, sometimes control—the ability of foreign manufacturers to obtain access to markets in the United States. For that reason, vertical arrangements are examined at some length in this section. In addition, other countries, particularly Japan and Germany, are struggling now with some of the same issues that have attracted the attention of US enforcement authorities and courts in recent years.

Resale Price Maintenance

Agreements to fix maximum or minimum resale prices (resale price main-tenance, or RPM) are illegal per se (*Dr. Miles Medical Co. v. John D. Park & Sons,* 220 US 373, 1911). In the last decade, however, there has been judicial erosion of this rule by narrowing the definition of "agree-ment," narrowing the definition of "price-fixing agreement," and in-creas-ing the plaintiff's burden in proving that an agreement exists. Proof of a manufacturer's cutoff of a discounter in response to a full-price dealer's complaints is not sufficient to take the case to a jury, either with regard to proof of agreement or with regard to proof that an agreement, if one exists, sets a resale price (*Business Electronics Corp. v. Sharp Electronics Corp.*, 485 US 717, 1988). To prove that an agreement exists, the plaintiff's evidence must tend to exclude the possibility that the manufacturer was acting independently from the nonterminated distributors. To prove RPM, the plaintiff must show that the agreement fixed a price or a price level.

The back-door erosion of the per se rule parallels the minimalist position, widely publicized in the 1980s, that almost all vertical restraints are good for competition. According to that position, vertical restraints are likely to prevent free riding on the investments and services of full-price distributors, and interbrand competition will police the market to make sure that producers respond to buyers and do not exploit them.

The erosion noted above has particular regard to minimum vertical price fixing. Maximum vertical price fixing—putting a lid on prices—and minimum price-fixing may be quite different. Maximum vertical price-fixing may be a way to compete. The per se rule against maximum vertical price-fixing rule has been eroded by standing rules (who can sue) and antitrust injury concepts (what kind of harm is compensable). Thus, the Supreme Court has held that a competitor hurt by nonpredatory low pricing brought about by maximum price fixing has not suffered antitrust injury and cannot complain (*Atlantic Richfield Co. v. USA Petroleum Co.*, 495 US 328, 1990). At the time of this writing, a case pending before the Supreme Court challenges the per se rule against maximum vertical price fixing (*Kahn v. State Oil Co.*, 93 F.3d 1358 [7th Cir. 1996], cert. granted).

Division of Customers and Territories

Since the *Sylvania* case (*Continental T.V. v. GTE Sylvania*, 433 US 36, 1977), vertical divisions of customers and territories are judged by a rule of reason. This treatment recognizes that intrabrand customer and territorial divisions can improve a manufacturer's efficiency, either by preventing free riding or simply by clarifying lines of responsibility and thus accountability, and that intrabrand efficiency can improve interbrand competition. Vertical customer and territorial allocations are illegal only if they create or increase market power. This would be possible if, for example, the market is concentrated and not easy to enter and the same vertical restraints are adopted by all of the leading firms, thus easing their coordination. A minority of courts take a different approach and would find such restraints illegal if they seriously lessen intrabrand competition and the intrabrand restraints are not offset by benefits to interbrand competition.

The *Sylvania* rule is very different from the rule in the European Union, which prohibits tight territorial restraints at member state borders, regardless of the intensity of interbrand competition (see Fox, this volume). The European rule is designed both to enhance free movement and market integration and to promote competition. Border restraints are viewed as a distortion of competition, and the requirement that borders be kept open is seen as a dynamic enhancement to competition. (The Europeans are less persuaded than the Americans that free movement, intrabrand, undermines efficiency; they are also less persuaded that there is a serious free rider problem.)

Tie-ins, Exclusive Dealing, and Reciprocity

Congress enacted section 3 of the Clayton Act to protect small and medium-sized businesses from being squeezed out of markets and business opportunities by their powerful and better situated bigger competitors. In the 1950s and 1960s the spirit of this section of the Clayton Act crept into the handling of Sherman Act section 1 cases, and both statutes were interpreted to prohibit what were viewed as unfair foreclosures: blockages of substantial segments of markets for reasons other than competitive merit (see, e.g., *Standard Oil Co. of California v. United States*, 337 US 293, 1949). Although sometimes consumer harm might appear, this was not a necessary element of the case. Unjustified blockage, or "fencing out," was implicitly assumed to harm consumers, because by definition consumers were deprived of an option they would or might otherwise choose (*Northern Pac. R.R. Co. v. United States*, 356 U.S. 1, 1958).

In the early 1980s, foreclosure law was rarely accepted as the basis of a violation. Enforcers urged applicaton of the price theory paradigm: no vertical restraint is illegal unless the plaintiff can prove that it creates or enhances market power, raising price and limiting output. The law against reciprocity—agreements to deal with a customer on condition that the customer deal with the seller—has all but disappeared. Exclusive-dealing, exclusive-purchasing, and requirements contracts are recognized to have strong efficiency properties and have usually been found legal by the courts. They are illegal under a rule of reason if they can be proved to increase the coordinative behavior of competitors in an oligopoly, or if they raise barriers to entry and thus enhance unilateral price-raising power.

The tie-in law, however, was too well developed to yield to the price theory model. Tie-ins are subject to a modified per se rule: a firm with market power in the market for one product cannot legally use that power to force its customer to accept another separate product in cases where a not-insubstantial amount of commerce in the tied product is affected (*Jefferson Parish Hospital No. 2 v. Hyde*, 466 US 2, 1984). Even then, the tie can be defended if there is a plausible business justification; for example, that product A will not perform well if the supplier cannot control the quality of product B (*Mozart Co. v. Mercedes-Benz of North America*, 833 F.2d 1242, 9th Cir., 1987). The law is justified today largely on grounds of coercion of the consumer, but in fact it appears to be one of the last vestige of the once-robust market access rules that arose from the sense that foreclosures were unfair.

Unlike much contemporary US law, law in the European Union does not force the distinction between what is anticompetitive and what is "merely" unfair. Unjustified exclusionary practices may amount to abuse of dominance (and a firm with 40 percent of a market may be deemed dominant). Exclusive dealing and tying by large firms not uncommonly run afoul of this law (see Fox, this volume).

Exceptions to General Antitrust Policy

The United States has a number of derogations from general antitrust policy, although perhaps fewer than most other countries. Most of the derogations are justified on grounds that market failure is so great that competition cannot be counted on to bring about the economic benefits that markets provide, or that noneconomic goals are paramount.

Labor policy is informed by both justifications. The labor exemption, contained in section 6 of the Clayton Act, provides that the labor of a human being is not an article of commerce. It is interpreted to allow workers to combine, for example, for collective bargaining, which could involve employee wage fixing. A nonstatutory exemption provided by case law allows employers to combine to negotiate with labor unions and allows agreement on terms of labor.

A number of industries are regulated by statute and by administrative agencies, and some of these statutes provide limited antitrust exemptions—for example, in the electric power industry and the insurance industry. Through a series of Supreme Court opinions it is now well settled that the exemptions are narrowly construed, and that application of antitrust law is normally consistent with regulatory regimes; competition should prevail wherever it can work. In the absence of express exemption, it is possible to have an implied exemption, but only if and to the extent that the regulatory system so displaces competition that the two cannot operate side by side.

At least two exemptions do not fit either of the above categories of justification: those for professional baseball and for export cartels. The baseball exemption arose by historical accident: an exemption was judicially decreed for the "performance" or "exhibition" of the game when the commerce clause of the US Constitution was narrowly construed and the performance was held not to be in interstate commerce.

A less-important but similar provision exempts from the antitrust laws associations or joint ventures organized for the sole purpose of engaging in export trade (see the Webb-Pomerene Act 1918, *Stat.* 40, 516, as amended, *US Code Appendix* 1987, Vol. 15, sections 61-65). The export cartel exemption was enacted only in 1982 (technically, the Sherman Act was cut back so as not to cover export cartels), as part of an effort to promote exports by removing the so-called antitrust handicap.

Trade and Investment Policy

Trade and investment policy in the United States is developed and implemented in a wide array of governmental units, including cabinet departments (Commerce, State, Defense, Treasury, and Justice, among others), regulatory agencies (the International Trade Commission, the Environmental Protection Agency, and the Federal Trade Commission, among others), the Council of Economic Advisers, the National Security Adviser, and the US Trade Representative. Description of the responsibilities of each of these governmental units in the trade and investment area is beyond the scope of this chapter.

One recent development deserves comment, however. In early 1993 the Clinton administration created the National Economic Council (NEC) to coordinate the administration's international trade and domestic economic policy. Aside from providing the president with economic advice, the NEC was designed as a vehicle to avoid policy conflicts that have burdened previous administrations and to coordinate economic policy much as the National Security Council coordinates foreign policy.

In the past, US competition policy was implemented in a manner largely independent of the goals and programs of other trade and investment policies. For example, monopolies such as the telephone system were dismembered regardless of the impact on trade issues, and mergers were permitted or challenged without reference to noncompetition trade objectives.

National Security Considerations

Until recently, national security considerations were not formally examined in connection with enforcement of competition policy. Occasionally, the Defense Department or the Commerce Department would comment upon the national security implications of proposed enforcement actions or remedies—for example, in connection with investigations of monopoly behavior by AT&T or by US oil companies—but such instances were relatively rare. In 1988 Congress passed the Exon-Florio amendment, which authorized the president to investigate and eventually block or suspend any acquisition or other foreign investment where US national security is threatened (the term "national security" was not defined; *US Code App.* 1988, Vol. 50, section 2170). The president's exercise of discretion in approving or blocking a foreign investment is not re-viewable.[17] In 1992 Congress amended Exon-Florio so as to create a presumption against allowing foreign government-controlled entities to make acquisitions in the US defense industry.[18]

Because the Exon-Florio amendment does not provide a clear defini-tion of national security, the statute has the potential for extremely broad application. To date, however, the Exon-Florio amendment has been an insignificant factor in merger enforcement. Of 805 notifications of pro-posed foreign acquisitions from 1988 to 1995, only 15 have been subject to full investigations, and only 1 has been blocked. That may understate slightly the influence of the statute, since three other transactions sub-jected to full investigation were withdrawn and one was restructured.

The single transaction that was blocked provides little guidance about the future of US merger policy. A company owned by China's Ministry of Aerospace Industry sought to acquire MAMCO, a Seattle-based manu-facturer of metal commercial aircraft components, including tail and wing assemblies and other smaller parts. Boeing was MAMCO's principal cus-tomer, and MAMCO had no contracts involving classified products. Never-theless, then-President George Bush, relying on "credible confidential information," blocked the transaction (Tolchin and Tolchin 1992, 57). Some have speculated that the decision was more a reaction to China's violent crackdown on prodemocracy demonstrators at Tiananmen Square in 1989 than one based on any national security information or technol-ogy possessed by MAMCO. In any event, other transactions that appear to have had a more direct impact on national security were either not investigated or cleared. These included the acquisition by a Japanese firm of up to a 25 percent interest in Titanium Metals Corp. of America, which provided 50 percent of the titanium purchased by the Depart-ment of Defense, and the proposed acquisition by Nikkon Corporation of Japan of Perkins-Elmer Corporation, the last major US manufacturer of silicon chip-etching machines, which involve key defense applications (Tolchin and Tolchin 1992, 64-65).

To date, enforcement of Exon-Florio has been an insignificant factor in the development of competition policy. To the extent that the statute has been enforced (or not enforced), the US government has given very ambiguous signals as to the type of transactions that would be subject to its provisions.

---

17. The legislation directs the president to block or divest a foreign investment if there is credible evidence that leads the president to believe that the foreign interest exercising control might take action that threatens to impair the national security, provided that national security is not adequately protected by other statutory schemes (50 USC App. section 2170[e]).

18. P.L. No. 102-484, *Stat.* 1992, 106:2463. For extensive discussions of Exon-Florio, see Graham and Krugman (1995).

Comparative Treatment of Foreign and Domestic Transactions under US Law

As a general matter, the United States has not taken into account the nationality of parties to a transaction in examining its legality. However, a modest departure from the general proposition that nationality is not a factor may have occurred in the enactment of the National Cooperative Production Act of 1993 (P.L. 103-42, section 3[a], *Stat.* 107:117, *US Code* 15, section 4301, 10 June 1993). The statute provides that lawsuits against joint ventures for research, development, and/or production will be treated under a rule of reason, and in the case of ventures notified to the government, damages will be limited to single rather than treble damages. These benefits are available, however, only if "the principal facilities for such production are located in the United States or its territories," and any foreign person controlling the joint venture is from "a country whose law accords antitrust treatment no less favorable to United States persons than to such countries' domestic persons with respect to participation in joint ventures for production. . . ."

The practical effect of the statute is minor, because there has not been a challenge to a production joint venture (lacking coordinated sales as well) under US antitrust law since the federal law was enacted in 1890— that is, the 1993 statute limits legal challenges in an area where legal challenges are virtually unknown. Moreover, production joint ventures are clearly entitled to rule of reason analysis. Also, the reciprocity provision is framed in such a way that it will be difficult to find a foreign country that does not accord equal treatment.

Extraterritorial Reach of US Antitrust Laws

The Sherman Act prohibits restraints that affect commerce. The word "commerce" expressly includes that between and among the states of the United States and with foreign nations.

The United States has adopted the effects doctrine, derived from the *Alcoa* case, under which the Sherman Act applies even to foreign actors acting abroad when they intend to and do affect US commerce. The doctrine is sometimes restated to hold that the Sherman Act applies when the acts, although performed abroad, have a direct, substantial, and reasonably foreseeable impact on US commerce. The effects doctrine is based on the notion that if a regulating nation or its citizens are hurt directly, the nation has a stake in regulating the conduct and ought to be able to do so.

In view of trading partners' claims of US jurisdictional overreaching, some—but not all—US courts tempered the effects doctrine with balancing tests, the best known of which was declared by the Court of

Appeals for the Ninth Circuit in the case of *Timberlane Lumber Co. v. Bank of America*, 549 F.2d 597 (9th Cir., 1976). Under *Timberlane*, after considering whether the conduct has an effect or intended effect on US commerce and whether the effect is sufficiently large to present a cognizable injury to plaintiffs and therefore an antitrust violation, the court must consider seven factors: purpose, effect, foreseeability, nationality, location, comparative significance of effects in the United States and elsewhere, and degree of conflict with foreign law and policy. The court is enjoined not to exercise jurisdiction if the "interests of, and links to, the United States ... [are not] sufficiently strong, vis-à-vis those of other nations, to justify an assertion of extraterritorial authority" (*Timberlane Lumber Co. v. Bank of America*, 549 F.2d 613–14, 9th Cir., 1976).

In 1982 Congress passed the Foreign Trade Antitrust Improvements Act (FTAIA; 15 USC, sections 6a, 45, 1982). The FTAIA limits the Sherman Act and the Federal Trade Commission Act. By its terms, the limitation does not apply to conduct involving import trade or commerce. As to conduct involving all other (i.e., nonimport) US trade or commerce with foreign nations, the Sherman and FTC Acts are declared inapplicable unless the conduct has a "direct, substantial and reasonably foreseeable effect" on US commerce or on the export trade of a person engaged in such trade or commerce in the United States.

The principal effect of the FTAIA is to remove from the scope of the US antitrust laws US firms' actions in foreign commerce where the only persons hurt are foreign competitors or foreign consumers. Thus, as far as the US antitrust laws are concerned, US firms may form export cartels as long as the cartel activity does not spill over into price rises in the United States and does not otherwise harm US competition.

A companion statute, the Export Trading Company Act of 1982 (15 USC sections 4011-21, 1982), provides a procedure whereby persons wishing to engage in export activity may receive a certificate of review from the secretary of commerce. To qualify, the applicant must satisfy the attorney general and the secretary of commerce that the export activity will neither lessen competition within the United States nor substantially restrain the export trade of a competitor of the applicant. A certificate, when granted, protects the holder against both criminal and civil actions brought by the government and limits an injured private party's recovery to single damages for all conduct described in the certificate.

The Antitrust Division of the Department of Justice issued Enforcement Guidelines for International Operations in 1977 and revised guidelines in 1988; in 1995 the division, jointly with the Federal Trade Commission, promulgated new guidelines that replaced the 1988 document. The 1988 guidelines stated, in footnote 159, that the Justice Department was "concerned only with adverse effects on competition that would harm US consumers by reducing output or raising prices." Moreover, in a case example (case 4), the department gave guidance that it would not challenge a merger despite a substantial anticompetitive effect in the United States where both merging firms are foreign and all of their assets relevant to the antitrust concern are located outside of the United States, on grounds that it would be difficult to obtain effective relief.

The guidance value of the guidelines was eroded in 1990 when the FTC challenged an acquisition by a French producer of rabies vaccine, Institut Merieux, of a Canadian producer of polio vaccine, Connaught BioSciences. The case was settled upon the filing of a consent order that required Merieux to lease the rabies vaccine business of Connaught to an FTC-approved lessee (an order expanded only belatedly, at Canada's insistence, to require also approval by Canadian authorities). So important was the US market to the merging companies that they accepted the order without contesting jurisdiction.

In 1992 the 1988 guidelines were eroded once again. US businesses complained that they were unfairly fenced out of foreign markets, especially the Japanese market. The United States and Japan were then engaged in the Structural Impediments Initiative (SII) to break down artificial barriers to trade. To advance the objectives of the SII and unclog channels for US exporters, US Assistant Attorney General James Rill announced that, in a proper case in which comity concerns were satisfied, the Antitrust Division would consider challenging a foreign import cartel that excluded US exporters; he would consider lawsuits against US subsidiaries of the foreign cartelists, in the United States under US law, if the import cartel was also illegal in the excluding country and the excluding country declined to enforce its own law. On announcing this initiative, Attorney General William Barr and Assistant Attorney General Rill withdrew footnote 159 of the 1988 guidelines. Consistently, the 1995 international guidelines envisage lawsuits in certain cases where foreign firms' private restraints on their own territory directly and foreseeably exclude US exports.

In 1993 the US Supreme Court had its first opportunity in more than a quarter century to clarify the law on extraterritoriality and comity with regard to antitrust. Nineteen states and numerous private plaintiffs had brought Sherman Act section 1 cases against domestic insurers and domestic and foreign reinsurers of general commercial liability. The plaintiffs alleged that the insurance companies had cut back commercial insurance coverage through illegal collaborations and conspiracies that allegedly rendered occurrence ("long-tail") and pollution coverage unavailable or nearly unavailable in the plaintiff states.

The defendant foreign reinsurers, which operated on the London market under the aegis of London market regulation, moved to dismiss the case against them. The district court granted the motion on grounds of comity. It found that a "significant" conflict with English law and policy would result from application of US antitrust law to the UK reinsurers' conduct and operations in the United Kingdom and that the interference and harm caused by the conflict was not outweighed by other factors, such as the effect and foreseeability of effect of the defendants' conduct in the United States. The court stated that the purpose of the foreign defendants' collaboration to deny certain coverages was to reduce exposure to certain risks and thus control losses—"a legitimate business purpose." The Court of Appeals for the Ninth Circuit reweighed the factors that figured in the comity balance and reversed the decision.

The Supreme Court, in a 5-4 decision, held that comity did not justify dismissal (*Hartford Fire Ins. Co. v. California*, 509 U.S. 764, 1993). The Court first found that subject matter jurisdiction existed. Plaintiffs had alleged that the foreign conduct "was meant to produce and did in fact produce some substantial effect in the United States." Writing for the majority, Justice David Souter said, "[I]t is well established by now that the Sherman Act applies to foreign conduct that was meant to produce and did in fact produce some substantial effect in the United States" (*Id.* at 796). The Court then rejected the claim that conflict with foreign law existed and that the conflict counseled dismissal. The Court determined that conflict did not exist because the British defendants *could* have complied with the law of both nations at the same time. The four dissenting justices, in an opinion by Justice Antonin Scalia, would have treated the question as one of intended reach of the US law and would have held that the US law did not apply to what they saw as essentially a London market transaction. This case settles very little regarding the confused law of extraterritoriality and comity. (For a proposed framework for resolution see Fox 1993, 1995, and 1997.)

Bilateral and Multilateral Treaties and the OECD Recommendation

The United States is party to four bilateral agreements on cooperation in antitrust enforcement. Moreover, as a member of the Organization for Economic Cooperation and Development (OECD), the United States works within the framework of that organization.

The first US bilateral cooperation agreement was signed with Germany in 1976. The agreement provides that the antitrust authorities of the two countries will cooperate with and render assistance to one another. The parties agree that each will provide to the other "significant information" that comes to its attention involving restrictive business practices that have a substantial effect on the trade of the other. Upon request, each party agrees to obtain for the other advice, assistance, and information regarding such referred restrictive business practices (subject to a right to decline on grounds such as confidentiality and public policy). The parties agree upon request to consult regarding possible coordination of concurrent antitrust investigations or proceedings. They agree that neither shall interfere with an antitrust investigation or proceeding of the other, to the extent compatible with domestic law and policy. Moreover, where application of the laws of one party "will be likely to affect the important interests of the other party," the former agrees to notify the latter and to consult and coordinate "to the extent appropriate" (4 CCH Trade Reg. Rep. ¶ 13,501). The agreement was designed to reflect and build upon the already close ties between the West German Federal Cartel Office and the US enforcement agencies (see Glynn 1991).

Bilateral cooperation agreements were also signed with Australia in 1982 and with Canada in 1984. A superseding agreement with Canada was signed in 1995. The 1982 and 1984 agreements rose out of several cases involving international transactions and stemmed from a desire to ease the tensions that had developed from extraterritorial application of US law.

The Australian agreement provides that, when a US agency decides to undertake an antitrust investigation that may have implications for Australian interests, it must notify the government of Australia of the investigation; Australia, for its part, "may" notify the United States when it has adopted a policy that may have antitrust implications for the United States. After notification, either party must consult upon request of the other, and both must "seek earnestly to avoid a possible conflict between their respective laws, policies and national interests," giving "due regard to each other's sovereignty and to considerations of comity." The United States agrees to consider Australia's interest in exports before bringing or continuing litigation. When a private suit that has been the subject of notification and consultations is pending in a US court, the government of Australia may request that the government of the United States participate in the litigation, whereupon the latter must report to the court on the substance and outcome of the consultations (4 CCH Trade Reg. Rep. ¶ 13,502).

The 1984 Canadian agreement was similar to the Australian agreement, but it was more detailed and the obligations it imposed were reciprocal (4 CCH Trade Reg. Rep. ¶ 13,503). The 1995 Canadian agreement adds "positive country" obligations such as those undertaken in the US-EC agreement described below (4 CCH Trade Reg. Rep. ¶ 13,503).

The OECD recommendation forms the major framework for notifications and sharing of information between and among most industrialized countries of the world. The last revision was adopted in 1986. Compliance with the recommendation is voluntary. The recommendation recites that when a member country intends to take action that may affect the important interests of another member country, it should notify the latter in sufficient time to hear and take into account the views of the affected country. An appendix contains guiding principles and procedures for notifications, exchanges of information, consultations, and conciliations (OECD document printed in Hawk 1990; Glynn 1991).

A more innovative form of cooperation agreement was crafted in 1991 by the United States and the European Community. This is the Executive Agreement with the European Community of September 1991 (printed at 61 BNA Antitrust & Trade Reg. Rep. 382, 26 September 1991). Although held void on a technical ground by the European Court of Justice, the agreement was officially validated upon approval by the Council of Ministers in 1995. The concept of the agreement can be traced to speeches by Sir Leon Brittan, then EC Commissioner for competition, who expressed concern about the multitude of jurisdictions regulating the same merger and suggested consultations to allocate jurisdiction.

The US-EC agreement covers much more than mergers. Its purpose is "to promote cooperation and coordination and lessen the possibility or impact of differences" in the parties' application of their competition laws. It provides that when antitrust enforcement by one party, including remedies, may affect important interests of the other party, notification shall be given far enough in advance to take the other party's views into account. The agreement also calls for consultations. It requires exchange of information and meetings at least twice a year for this purpose and to discuss policy changes. Most significantly, it provides for "positive comity"—helping one another in enforcement efforts. If anticompetitive activities carried out in the territory of one party adversely affect the other, the latter may request the former to initiate discovery and other enforcement actions, and the former must sympathetically consider the request. The agreement provides a framework for coordinating enforcement activities when both parties have an interest in pursuing the same conduct or transaction.

The agreement also provides for "negative comity" (i.e., restraint) where one party's enforcement may adversely affect the important interests of the other. The parties agree to seek "an appropriate accommodation of the competing interests" and, in doing so, to take into account all relevant factors. The listed factors are similar to those in the *Timberlane* case, discussed above. (The agreement is printed at 61 BNA Antitrust & Trade Reg. Rep. 382, 26 September 1991.)

The Antitrust Division of the Justice Department is devoting continuing efforts to coordinating enforcement activities with the antitrust authorities of other nations. To facilitate this effort, the division sought and obtained enactment of the International Antitrust Enforcement Assistance Act (IAEAA) of 1994 (*US Code App.* 15, sections 6201-12). Pursuant to the IAEAA, the US antitrust authorities are empowered to share evidence (other than pre-merger filings) regarding antitrust violations with the antitrust authorities of foreign nations that enter into antitrust mutual assistance agreements with the United States. Upon request by foreign authorities who have entered such agreements, the US authorities may, if they choose, investigate possible violations of foreign anti-trust laws. Australia has entered into a mutual assistance agreement with the United States (printed at 4 CCH Trade Reg. Rep. 13,502A).

The IAEAA and the US-EC agreement focus on positive comity—helping one another to enforce the law against cross-border transgressions. They reflect the reality that competition and competitive offenses have reached a global dimension, and they reflect the challenge of the law to meet this economic reality.

Conclusion

Thus US antitrust law has moved from a law designed to limit power, preserve diversity, and open markets, to a law guided by the goals of robust business and consumer interests. While antitrust law has become quite separate from trade law and other disciplines, the pulls of the world economy are once again bringing specialists in antitrust, trade, and industrial policy into dialogue.

References

Fox, Eleanor M. 1993. "The Tenth Milton Handler Lecture: Antitrust, Trade and the 21st Century—Rounding the Circle." *Record of the Association of the Bar of the City of New York* 48: 535.

Fox, Eleanor M. 1995. "Competition Law and the Agenda for the WTO: Forging the Links of Competition and Trade." *Pacific Rim Law and Policy Journal* 4: 1.

Fox, Eleanor M. 1997. "Toward World Antiturst and Market Access." *American Journal of International Law* 91: 1.

Fox, Eleanor M., and Robert Pitofsky. 1992. "Antitrust Division and Federal Trade Commission Antitrust Policy." In Mark Green, *Changing America: Blueprints for the New Administration.* New York: Newmarket Press.

Glynn, E. 1991. In B. Hawk, *International Agreements to Allocate Jurisdiction Over Mergers.* New York: 1990 Fordham Corporate Law Institute.

Graham, Edward M., and Michael E. Ebert. 1991. "Foreign Direct Investment and National Security: Fixing the Exon-Florio Process." *The World Economy* 14, no. 3 (September): 245-68.

Graham, Edward M., and Paul R. Krugman. 1995. *Foreign Direct Investment in the United States,* 3d ed. Washington: Institute for International Economics.

Hawk, B. 1990. *United States, Common Market and International Antitrust: A Comparative Guide,* 2d ed. Englewood Cliffs, NJ: Prentice Hall Law & Business (has 1993 supplement).

Pitofsky, Robert. 1990. "New Definitions of Relevant Market and the Assault on Antitrust." *Columbia Law Review* 90: 1805, 1845-46.

Pitofsky, Robert. 1992. "Proposals for Revised United States Merger Enforcement in a Global Economy." *Georgetown Law Journal* 81: 195, 206-08.

US Department of Justice and Federal Trade Commission. 1992. *Horizontal Merger Guidelines.* Washington.

8

Competition Policy and Trade Policy in the European Union[1]

KALYPSO NICOLAÏDIS AND RAYMOND VERNON

Three decades of experience in the European Union (EU) provide materials of incomparable richness for our efforts to define the relative realms of competition policy and trade policy. Faced with the challenge of creating a common internal market, free of barriers to the movement of goods, services, labor, and capital, the Union has fashioned and applied instruments of competition policy and trade policy without precedent. In the process, it has highlighted the institutional requirements to be met and the policy issues to be overcome when a region attempts to enlarge the role of competition policy and to shrink that of trade policy.

The Union as a Laboratory

Before the six charter members of the European Community (EC) (later to be a part of the European Union) agreed to its terms in 1957, nothing quite like it had existed in the annals of international economic relationships.

By the terms of the Treaty of Rome, which created the European Community, the member states agreed to relinquish to it their powers

1. Yun W. Choi made a substantial contribution to this paper with an extensive analysis of major cases arising in the European Community and under the General Agreement on Tariffs and Trade. Minghong Lu and Mingcheng Lian also provided valuable research support.

Raymond Vernon is professor of international affairs emeritus, and Kalypso Nicolaïdis is assistant professor of public policy, both at the John F. Kennedy School of Government, Harvard University.

to regulate the flow of goods, services, money, and workers among them, with a view to creating a common market without frontiers. In that common market, therefore, the member states would relinquish the usual instruments of trade policy, relying upon the institutions of the Community to ensure that the market remained open and competitive. On any definition of trade policy and competition policy, therefore, the so-called *acquis communautaire* covered both.

By observing the Union's behavior in the succeeding decades, the rest of the world may be able to draw some lessons on the relationships between competition policy and trade policy in the handling of problems that arise when goods or services cross national borders. In particular, one can gain impressions of the substitutability of competition policy for trade policy and can identify problems in the maintenance of competitive markets that do not fit comfortably in either the competition policy or trade policy category.

What a study such as this cannot provide, of course, is an evaluation of the relative efficacy of competition policy as a substitute for trade policy. The general case for substituting competition policy for trade policy rests heavily on the assumption that the actions of any trading area based on competition policy are less likely to be vulnerable to special interests and more likely to reflect the area's overall interests. In practice, the execution of trade policy depends heavily on restrictions imposed at the border, such as import and export duties and licenses, whereas competition policy usually relies on measures that proscribe offending practices or reduce the threat of dominance by large firms. As the EU experience confirms, both can be shaped with an eye to the well-being of the producers in the area, but competition policy is less likely to prescribe measures that discriminate against foreign suppliers and that burden consumers.

There is nothing in EU experience to suggest that the assumptions regarding the relative merits of these two lines of policy are invalid. On the other hand, many of the competition policy measures taken by EU institutions—including the Commission, the Council, and the Court—have often evoked sharp criticism, and in some cases it seems, deservedly so. We have not regarded the Union's experience, therefore, as if it were an ideal case of the possibilities of competition policy. Instead, we have sought to use it to identify institutional problems and policy issues that are likely to arise when a government enlarges the role of competition policy at the expense of trade policy.

Analysis of the relative roles of these policies, however, depends to some extent on how one defines the terms. How are we to classify measures taken against predatory dumping by foreign firms that are aimed at destroying domestic firms? Or measures by governments that encourage mergers in order to strengthen exports? As it turns out, one encounters a gray area of policy in which either label will do, according to one's tastes.[2] Our approach is to be clear about the nature of the measures under discussion without identifying them as either competition policy or trade policy when such classification appears arbitrary.

The experiences of the Union in reducing barriers to cross-border movements of services have proved particularly useful in demonstrating the arbitrary character of such definitions. Unlike trade in goods, governments usually apply their restrictions on the sale of services of foreign origin inside their territories rather than at their borders. There are some cases in which border controls will be relevant, as when foreign truckers are required to pay a border tax. But in other cases, as in the practice of medicine or banking, border controls are not involved. Achieving a common market in services, therefore, has presented a more complex challenge than in goods. And there have been enough differences in approach so that, in the pages that follow, we distinguish trade in merchandise from trade in services without always categorizing the relevant policies as competition or trade.

At the Creation

The Background

Both political and economic objectives drove the six EC charter members in 1957 to create a European common market. The paramount political objective was the desire of France and Germany to intertwine their economies so that hostilities between them in the future would be unthinkable. A second political objective, often visible in the motivations of the governments of France, was to pool the economic power of Europe in an effort to increase its political and economic weight in international affairs. But European leaders also had their eye on the added economic advantages that might accrue from increased scale and scope as well as from increased opportunities for their exports.[3]

The provisions of the Rome treaty that emerged out of the negotiations of the 1950s were obviously deeply conditioned by the historical experiences of the signatory countries. One experience that all had shared in the decades preceding was an extensive exposure to cartels and trade restrictions.

Although the period before World War I in Europe is usually described as one of low trade barriers and easy interchanges of goods and services, that sweeping generalization overlooks some salient facts (see,

---

2. For an ambitious effort to create a precise delineation between the two fields, see OECD (1993).

3. France placed particular emphasis on the possibility of expanding its markets for agriculture, an emphasis that continues to the present day (Lynch 1993, 59-87).

e.g., Milward and Saul 1977, 468-69). By 1914, interchanges of manufactured goods among the industrial leaders of Europe, including France, Germany, the Low Countries, and Britain, were subject to pervasive cartel restrictions aimed at restraining the movement of manufactured goods between major national markets.[4] Sometimes, especially in chemical products, these cartel agreements were reinforced by an exchange of patent rights. But at other times, as in the case of the International Steel Cartel, the firms involved simply established their market divisions by private contract, including provisions for quotas and fines.

Between the two great wars, the official restrictions of governments, taking the form of tariffs, quotas, and licenses, supplemented the cartels to create formidable obstacles to trade among the European states. But after World War II, a number of factors served to reduce the levels of both private and official restrictions.

One such factor was the European Recovery Program. Under that program, with the financial support of the United States and the institutional support of the Organization for European Economic Cooperation, the countries of Western Europe sought to close the manifest gap in productivity and technological achievement between European industry and US industry (Maier 1987, 121-52). On the trade policy front, those countries launched a series of programs aimed at reducing trade barriers among them, while discriminating collectively against goods and services from outsiders, including the United States. In the field of competition policy, each of the countries participating in the European Recovery Program undertook in bilateral agreements with the United States to prevent restrictive business practices harmful to the achievement of the program's objectives.

Experience under the program suggested a generalization that would be affirmed and reaffirmed in subsequent decades. Trade agreements designed to dismantle restrictions on goods imposed at national borders require comparatively little international apparatus for their implementation. Agreements to restrain the use of restrictive business practices or the abuse of dominant positions by enterprises, on the other hand, depend heavily on the presence of an effective implementing apparatus. Where restrictive business practices are concerned, the facts tend to be elusive and complex, so that complaints are not as readily forthcoming nor as readily pursued. Without an effective apparatus for enforcement in the European Recovery Program, therefore, the commitments regarding restrictive business practices by enterprises proved to be practically a dead letter.

---

4. Svennilson (1983, 17) remarks on the limited volume of such trade. Hexner (1946, 43-56) documents the principal cartels. Another study reports 114 international cartels before 1914, covering industries in coal, steel, metals, chemicals, textiles, pulp and paper, and various other industries; see Hallinan (1928, 18-19).

Another reason competition policy proved much less important than trade policy in this early period, however, was that the cartels of the prewar period were slow to reestablish themselves in the decade or two after the war. In the first postwar decade, widespread scarcities in Europe reduced the incentives for enterprises to develop private restrictive agreements. Soon after, the presence of US-owned subsidiaries in large numbers in Europe presented an added obstacle.

After the adoption of the European Recovery Program, the next major opportunity for defining the relative roles of trade policy and competition policy arose with the negotiation of the European Coal and Steel Community (ECSC) in the early 1950s (Diebold 1959, 8-20). At the time, coal and steel were perceived as providing the sinews of war, hence as central in intertwining the German and French economies. On the face of it, creating a common market in these industries would be a daunting task, given their history and their structures. Apart from the fact that the International Steel Cartel had been one of the most powerful of prewar Europe, the postwar facilities commonly involved state financing and state ownership (Lister 1960, 84-88, 123-76). Coal pits, too, were in state hands in several countries, and the price of coal was heavily subsidized in Germany. On the other hand, political decisions were still being taken in a spirit of crisis during the early 1950s, and the usual interest groups were exercising less than their accustomed authority. Undaunted, the drafters of the ECSC treaty set out to overcome the national borders among the six member countries for the production and sale of coal and steel.

The motives of the treaty's guiding genius, Jean Monnet, were economic as well as political. Coming away from five difficult years as the head of France's Commissariat du Plan, Monnet was eager to expose the French coal and steel industries to new stimuli that might increase their efficiency. Accordingly, Monnet rejected early drafts of the treaty that seemed to ape the structure of the prewar International Steel Cartel, including geographical divisions of the market along national lines and production and price-fixing by the producing firms. Instead, two seemingly divergent concepts fought their way into the treaty's text, both ostensibly aimed at increasing efficiency: The treaty creates a strong central authority, with powers that could be used for maintaining a highly planned and regulated market among the member countries. But the treaty also contains strong provisions against restrictive business practices and monopolies.[5]

---

5. The intellectual roots of the provisions against restrictive business practices and monopolies go back to provisions adopted as a chapter in the Charter for an International Trade Organization. Compare Article 34 of the proposed ITO Charter with Articles 65 and 66 of the ECSC Treaty, for which see US Department of State (1951). See also Diebold (1952, 26-27).

Within a few years of the adoption of the ECSC, its six member countries were negotiating the terms of the much more ambitious and comprehensive European Economic Community (EEC).[6] In the course of that negotiation, the idea of a strong central authority was diluted a little, the victim of a German distaste for dirigiste governmental powers and a French distaste for overt challenges to its national sovereignty. Although the powers of EC institutions remained formidable, the dominant authority rested in a Council of Ministers, composed of representatives of the member states, rather than in an independent High Authority. But the basic idea of a common market survived, constituting the core of the treaty.

Trade and Competition Provisions

The bedrock agreement embodied in the Treaty of Rome was the abolition of tariffs among the member states pursuant to a timetable and the creation of a common external tariff. The formula by which the rates for the common external tariff were established reflected the spirit of the drafters—a joint desire to suspend the usual industry-by-industry haggling over levels of protection in favor of a sweeping approach to the completion of the common market structure. Except for some 70 especially sensitive items, the six member countries agreed to determine the common external rate for each tariff category simply by taking the arithmetic average of the rates in that category previously applied by France, Germany, Italy, and the Benelux customs union.

Among the factors that distinguished the Community from that of any other customs union in history was its adoption of the proposition that private agreements should not be allowed to impede the easy movement of goods and services across national borders inside the market, an objective embodied in a remarkable set of provisions aimed at controlling cartels and dominant enterprises (see, e.g., Rosenthal 1990, 293-343). The Community was charged also with addressing "all measures having equivalent effect" to tariffs and quotas, an open-ended responsibility that would prove important in its subsequent activities. Moreover, it secured some powers to place a lid on measures by which national governments provided financial aid to enterprises on their territories. But how these powers were actually to be implemented was left for future development.

From the first, the organizers recognized that a common market in agriculture would differ drastically from the regime that would apply in other products. With France in the lead and Germany not far behind,

---

6. Treaty establishing the European Economic Community, 25 March 1957, 298 UNTS 3, often referred to as the Rome treaty.

the treaty reflected the members' view that agriculture should be highly protected from outside competition, even if this required extensive intervention by the Community. Subsequent EC agricultural policies followed lines fully consistent with these early hints.

The treaty's provisions with respect to services, however, were to prove especially revolutionary. The provisions themselves were very general, simply authorizing and directing the Community to see to the free movement of services within the common market (Articles 59 and 60 of the Rome treaty). Effective action under that provision was slow to materialize. But after the enactment of the Single European Act in 1985, it took on major importance.

Institutional Arrangements

Apart from the path-breaking content of the substantive provisions of the Rome treaty, an equally unusual feature was the administrative apparatus adopted for their implementation and enforcement. The Commission of the European Union (the current name of the organization that inherited the responsibility for the execution of the Rome treaty) is the executive arm of the organization, composed today of 20 members nominated by governments for four-year terms, all of them committed to act "with complete independence" and sworn neither to seek nor to accept instructions from any government.

As provided for in the treaty, the Commission is the only institution authorized to initiate proposals for a regulation, a directive, or a recommendation of the Union, but such proposals, as a general rule, cannot enter into force without enactment by the Council of Ministers, composed of ministers of the member governments. However, in the application of the rules relating to the competitive practices of enterprises, addressed under Articles 85 and 86 of the treaty, the Council has delegated its powers to the Commission. And in the handling of individual cases of state aids under Article 92, the treaty itself names the Commission as the executing authority, subject to an override by a unanimous vote of the Council. In all these areas, of course, the Commission's actions are subject to an appeal to the Union's Court of Justice.

Clearly, the Union comprises an unusually powerful set of institutions, with authority and competency not often found above the nation-state level. Functionaries from the constituent member states, it is true, have played a critical role in the Union's decision making. Indeed, the various permanent representatives of the member states residing in Brussels have created an elaborate structure of committees and subcommittees staffed by national civil servants (collectively known as the COREPER) who advise the Commission and the Council of Ministers on a continuous basis.

Yet the outcomes from the Union process have been quite different from those that would have been achieved by a string of international agreements negotiated by the national representatives of those same states. The differences have been due to various factors, including the fact that the Commission has extensive powers of initiation, that EU bodies do not ordinarily require unanimous votes in order to reach decisions, and that the ultimate authority of the European Court of Justice in interpreting its treaties and enactments has so far not been directly challenged. Taken in combination, these features have created an institution that, in addition to enjoying supranational attributes, is heavily insulated from the subnational grass-roots influences to which the constituent national governments of Europe are ordinarily exposed.

There have been times, to be sure, when the Union's supranational attributes seemed under siege. When in the 1960s, the sovereignty implications of the treaty began to be apparent, France's President Charles de Gaulle sought belatedly to curtail the Union's autonomous powers. He demanded and secured a commitment that whenever any member state claimed that its vital national interests were involved in a decision, the provisions for majority voting in the Council of Ministers should be suspended in favor of a requirement for unanimity. And the unanimity rule prevailed until the adoption of the Single European Act in 1985.

Despite that fact, however, EU institutions continued to gain in strength during the decade or two following the 1966 agreement, largely as a result of a series of decisions by its Court of Justice. These decisions embodied a set of principles that clarified and strengthened the Union's jurisdictional reach.[7]

One such proposition formulated by the Court has been the doctrine of direct effect.[8] According to the Court, the unambiguous responsibilities of the Union under the Rome treaty, such as the progressive abolition of customs duties among its members, the creation of a common external tariff, and other measures necessary for the completion of the common market, require no further action by the member states for their validation; they represent legal obligations between member states and their own nationals and even among individuals, obligations that are enforceable in national courts as well as in the judicial system of the Union itself.

A second proposition developed by the Court serves to strengthen the impact of the direct effects doctrine. Any norm that the Union develops within the area of its jurisdiction, whether by EU law or by

---

7. The key role of the Court of Justice, having been belatedly discovered by political scientists in the 1980s, has generated a spate of theorizing on causes and consequences. See, for instance, Burley and Mattli (1993, 41-76).

8. This section draws heavily on Weiler (1991, 2403-83). See also Hartley (1981, 185-223).

regulation, enjoys the attribute of supremacy—that is, it supersedes any conflicting national law. Accordingly, the Union has the extraordinary power through its directives of commanding member states to change their laws or adopt new laws in order to conform with Union law. And, even if a country fails to do so, its nationals are entitled to appeal to EU directives as a basis for determining their rights before their own national governments (*Italy v. EC Commission*, Case 41/83, [1985] ECR 873).

In another line of decisions, the Court has strengthened the Union by recognizing some implied powers—powers not explicitly granted in the treaty but recognized by the Court as essential for the achievement of the treaty's purposes. One of these is the Union's right to enter into international agreements in the areas of its competence, agreements binding not only on the Union but on member governments as well. In some of these areas, the Union's power to enter into international agreements is seen as exclusive, precluding agreements of any kind by the member states. In others, the Union is seen as sharing jurisdiction with the member states. But if the Union legislates in these areas of shared jurisdiction, such action may have a preemptive effect, creating a barrier against independent action by the member states.

When we observe the actions of the Union, then, what we are observing are not the actions of national governments as constrained by international agreement but the measures taken by a supranational institution with some of the attributes of sovereignty in a defined area of competence.[9] True, numerous questions have been raised regarding the Union's legitimacy, given the extraordinary powers it purports to exercise (Weiler 1992, 1-16). Such questions became particularly insistent after 1992, with the adoption of the Treaty of European Union (the Maastricht treaty), which extends the mandate of the Union into areas heretofore largely reserved to the member governments. These include the creation of a common European currency and a European Central Bank, along with some carefully circumscribed measures for the coordination of foreign policy and the support of pan-European communication and transport networks.[10] But no serious sentiment has existed in Europe for the dismantling or even the substantial reversal of the giant strides already taken toward the creation of an economic union.

---

9. Not all observers agree with such a view. See, for instance, Hoffmann (1982).

10. The "democratic deficit" of the Community has been widely discussed in various sources, reflecting the fact that the only body of the Community whose members are directly elected to their Community positions is the European Parliament, a body whose powers are largely consultative in nature (Hartley 1981, 18). The Treaty of European Union, adopted in 1993, and the Treaty of Antwerp, negotiated in 1997, augment those powers, but not to the extent usually associated with a parliament.

Trade Policies

Dominance of the Common Market Goal

From the Union's birth in 1958 to the enactment of the Single European Act in 1986, the objective of creating a common market among its members shaped and dominated EU trade policies, affecting the members' trade relationships with nonmember countries as well as with each other. As we observed earlier, a driving goal of the Community's founders was to so intertwine the economies of France and Germany as to render economic independence an impossibility for either. As long as that goal determined the policymakers' actions, relations with other countries were bound to take second place. That outcome, however, might not have prevailed if the Union's institutions had not been endowed with their extraordinary powers.

On matters of trade with the outside world, the treaty placed the lawmaking function of the Union squarely in the hands of its Commission and its Council of Ministers and, with an assist from the EU Court of Justice, reduced the powers of national governments to "cases of emergency." The covenants that bind member countries in the development of a common market, therefore, are far more powerful than any other agreements they can enter into, whether with each other or with outside countries. In disputes among EU members, for instance, a country cannot invoke the provisions of other international agreements, such as the General Agreement on Tariffs and Trade (GATT), if those provisions are inconsistent with the Rome treaty, nor can it turn to Union institutions in an effort to enforce such provisions; neither can a member state appeal to such outside commitments as grounds for failing to fulfill its obligations under the Rome treaty.[11]

In the exercise of its trade powers, therefore, the Union has developed a structure of trade relations that builds outward from a European core. The core, of course, consists of the trade among the members; as membership grew from the original 6 to 15 countries, intra-Community trade gained in importance. Whereas trade among members amounted to only 44 percent of the total trade in 1960, it represented 68 percent of the members' total trade in 1995. Layers outside the core are made up of a variety of preferential relationships, involving scores of nonmember states. That element of EU foreign trade, representing about 30 percent of the total in 1960, has declined to about 18 percent since then.[12] Fur-

---

11. For an analysis of the relationship between obligations under the Rome treaty and obligations under the GATT, see Tumlir (1986, 1-22), Petersmann, (1981, 23-72), and Maresceau (1981, 107-26).

12. Preferential trade arrangements include agreements with the African, Caribbean, and Pacific (ACP) countries; various Mediterranean countries; countries in Eastern Europe;

ther out from the core lie those members of the GATT not included in the preferential arrangements of the Union—the United States and Japan, among others, as well as a few states in remote outer darkness toward which the Union has no trade commitments. Trade with these groups, which amounted to about 26 percent of total Union trade in 1960, stood at about 13 percent in 1995.[13]

The Common Market Core

By the terms of the Rome treaty, member states were obliged to eliminate customs duties and quantitative restrictions in trade between them through a step-by-step process that was effectively completed by 1968. During the same period, the common external tariff provided for in the treaty was gradually being put in place.

The principle that trade restrictions inside the common market were to be abolished in effect barred member states from using their usual trade policy tools in that domain. After a period of transition, antidumping actions between member countries were abolished, along with national measures that had been applied to offset the state aids of other member countries. And the responsibility for initiating dumping and state-aid measures against nonmember countries was shifted from the individual member states to the Community (Green, Hartley, and Usher 1991, 14-19).

In assuming its responsibilities, the Community inevitably had to deal with a variety of problems, some relating to the special circumstances of an individual industry, some to difficulties facing a single member. In dealing with those problems, the Community began to exhibit a characteristic that would typify its behavior in the decades to follow—a tendency to improvise. EC institutions, particularly the Council of Ministers, exhibited a suppleness in individual cases that seemed more akin to the negotiation and renegotiation of a contract among its member states than the application of a treaty provision.

This flexibility in implementing the common market has in fact been so pronounced at times as to raise doubts in some eyes as to the achievement of the underlying concept. From the beginning, the Rome treaty has included a provision, Article 115, under which the Commission could authorize individual member states to impose "protective measures" against imports from nonmembers, where such action was needed

---

and the approximately 130 countries that fall under the Community's Generalized System of Preferences (GSP).

13. Data are based on various annual issues of GATT, *International Trade*, Geneva and IMF, *Direction of Trade Statistics Yearbook*, Washington.

to avoid "economic difficulties."[14] With the Commission's assent, member states have made extensive use of Article 115, especially in protecting their automobile, textile, and consumer electronic industries, and in favoring selected foreign sources of bananas in their home markets. But to implement such restrictions, member states have been permitted to maintain so-called surveillance arrangements within the common market aimed at preventing the frustration of their restrictions. By 1985, 1,800 surveillance measures were in place inside the common market, and in several scores of cases, actual import restrictions were being imposed (Henrichs-Cohen 1993, 564).

The threat that such measures posed to the common market concept was, of course, widely recognized. And in the years following the adoption of the Single European Act in 1986, the Commission would succeed in reducing considerably the use of these individual-country measures.

Efforts were made to remove the provisions of Article 115 completely in the sweeping treaty revisions adopted in 1993, but these efforts failed. Instead, the Union sought to "communitarize" the remaining restrictions by folding them into Community-wide schemes that took account of the special demands of individual countries; country-specific restrictions on foreign automobiles and bananas, for instance, were incorporated in such schemes.

A Layer of Preferences

In accordance with the treaty's provisions, the Commission conducts trade negotiations, pursuant to Council directives and with the advice of a special committee composed of national representatives, the so-called 113 Committee, which has performed as a Council of Ministers in miniature.

In the decades prior to the adoption of the Single European Act, as we observed earlier, the European Community found itself developing preferential arrangements with third countries. There were free trade agreements with other European countries—members of the European Free Trade Area—covering nonagricultural goods. There were bilateral agreements with countries in the Mediterranean Basin, the Middle East, and eastern Europe, giving them preferential access to EC markets over a specified range of products. There was an oft-renewed agreement with several dozen former colonies in Africa, the Caribbean, and the Pacific, giving them even wider preferential access to EC markets. And there was a system of lesser preferences for several scores of other developing countries.

---

14. For a careful review, see Henrichs-Cohen (1993, 553-587). For an analysis of these measures, see Bronckers (1983, 53) and Henri Froment-Meurice (1988, 65-117).

In formulating these preferential relationships, however, the Community typically retained all the usual tools of trade policy, such as antidumping duties and emergency import restrictions. Cases were common, therefore, in which exporters to the common market encountered such obstacles despite their preferential status.

The World Beyond

Trade relations with the world beyond these preferential areas have been governed largely by the GATT, as well as by agreements covering selected services, such as banking, telecommunications, and air travel. Despite the GATT's lack of standing in matters that involve relations between EU members, the Union readily acknowledges the GATT's imposition of obligations on the Union as a whole. And the Union has played an active role in trade negotiations under the aegis of the GATT.

Yet the Union's status in the GATT has been utterly anomalous. All the member countries of the Union are also GATT signatories, but the Union itself is not. Nevertheless, the non-Union signatories of the GATT look to the Union, as they must, to carry out the obligations of its member countries.

Although the Union generally has provided for nondiscriminatory treatment of goods at its borders, it has exercised its propensity for ad hoc solutions with particular freedom in matters relating to its GATT obligations. True, all GATT members have tended toward ad hoc solutions of their disputes; this is because GATT provisions encourage countries to settle them bilaterally before invoking its dispute settlement machinery. But the Union's preferential agreements have been tailored to each country, without much regard for the standards contained in the GATT.

This ad hoc approach has been especially pronounced in EC application of antidumping duties. From 1970 to 1974, the Commission initiated only two or three cases a year alleging dumping by outside countries into EC markets. Between 1976 and 1980, however, the number had risen to about 25 a year; from 1980 to 1984, it had increased to over 40 (Commission of the European Union 1993). In the years following the adoption of the Single European Act, from 1986 to 1995, the number of new cases per year leveled off; but as of midyear 1995, the number of EU antidumping measures in force stood at 178 (Trade Policy Review Body 1996).

Moreover, with the increase in antidumping cases, the Community's use of the antidumping concept seemed to grow increasingly creative (McDermott 1988, 315-30; Steele 1996). One development of considerable importance was the Community's increasing tendency to accept "price undertakings" from foreign exporters as a basis for settling investigations of alleged dumping. By the 1980s, price commitments were being used twice as frequently as antidumping duties as a basis for closing antidumping cases.[15] Moreover, the Court of Justice was routinely affirming such decisions in cases of appeal, assessing the appeal costs on the appellant defendants in such cases (Van Bael and Bellis 1990, 220).

The Community's expanded use of antidumping provisions produced its inevitable aftermath: a game of cat-and-mouse between multinational enterprises and the regulatory authorities. Some firms set up subsidiaries inside the common market with the ostensible purpose of importing components at prices above those required by existing antidumping measures, assembling them inside the Community, then selling the assembled products at unacceptably low prices. The Community countered with its well-known "screwdriver plant" regulation, subjecting the output of such European plants to the same antidumping treatment as that accorded to imports.[16] Quite clearly, the Community chose to regard the output of such plants as if they posed a trade problem rather than a competition problem, notwithstanding that the plants themselves lay inside the common market.

Another device that multinational enterprises used to deal with EC antidumping efforts was to shift their sourcing of the targeted imports from the foreign facility charged with dumping to another controlled source. That tactic elicited another blocking response, embodying still another use of a trade policy instrument in the form of an "anti-circumvention tax" imposed on the products from the substituted source.[17] Eventually, a GATT complaints panel would find such measures in violation of the agreement, but the problem did not subsequently go away (GATT 1990).

All told, the history of the EC application of trade policy points to two lessons. One is the dominance of the common market objective over the global commitments relating to trade policy, epitomized in the GATT: When conflicts occur, the common market objectives of the Union usually take precedence. At the same time, there are signs that the increasing importance of multinational enterprises in the world economy

---

15. From *Annual Reports of the Commission on the Community's Anti-dumping and Anti-subsidy Activities*, various years. The series begins in 1983 (Commission of the European Communities 1983).

16. Council Regulation (EEC) No. 2423/88, *Official Journal of the European Communities* (hereafter *OJ*) 1988, L209/2. The regulation applies to assembled products made up of components subject to antidumping procedures, provided such components constitute 60 percent or more of the value of the assembled product. The regulation has been applied to plants in the Community assembling typing machines and photocopy machines.

17. For a discussion of the implications and legality of EC regulation No. 2324/88 establishing the anticircumvention tax, see Torremans (1993, 288-30) and GATT (1991, 1075).

offers a growing challenge to the efficacy of Europe's trade policy measures, as such enterprises seek effective entry into the huge European market.

Competition Policy: Restrictive Business Practices

Inside the common market, competition policy has been a powerful weapon. And one obvious application of such policy has been in the field of restrictive business practices.

The Provisions

The Charter for an International Trade Organization, negotiated in 1947, contained an elaborate set of provisions for dealing with such practices. Although the charter failed to materialize, its influence was reflected in the content of the Rome treaty on restrictive business practices. But the more immediate forerunner of the relevant sections in the Rome treaty consisted of similar articles in the treaty creating the ECSC.

The spirit that drove these provisions in both treaties, however, was not a simple commitment to competition. The prewar cartels, it will be remembered, had usually divided up markets along national lines. The provisions in these treaties, therefore, included a political determination that the national barriers lifted by the elimination of governmental trade restrictions would not be thwarted by private restrictions.

Article 85 of the Rome treaty lays down a draconian prohibition against agreements and concerted practices among enterprises that may prevent, restrict, or distort competition in the common market, including the fixing of prices; the control of production, procurement, marketing, investment, and innovation; and the discriminatory treatment of sellers. Agreements or decisions prohibited by the provision are automatically void, so that they cannot be invoked or enforced by any of the parties anywhere in the common market.

Up to that point, one can detect the shades of US antitrust statutes; but then Article 85 takes a distinctly European turn, endowing the Commission with broad powers to exempt any agreement, decision, or practice, singly or by category, that satisfies specified criteria. An exemption may be earned if the agreement satisfies four conditions:

- It must contribute to improving the production or distribution of goods or to promoting technical or economic progress.
- It must allow consumers a fair share of the resulting benefits.
- It must not impose restrictions superfluous to the achievement of these objectives.

- It must not afford the possibility of eliminating competition "in respect of a substantial part of the product in question."

Cynics wondered at the time these Janus-like provisions were adopted if any substance remained, but subsequent events demonstrated that the provisions have considerable substantive importance.

Because Article 85(1) rendered null and void any agreement that fell under its prohibitions and because the treaty's provisions dominated national legislation to the contrary, the Community was under great pressure to settle a number of issues as rapidly as possible: how to define the outer limits of the prohibitions in order to take account of the special positions of various sectors under the treaty, including agriculture, transport, defense, public monopolies, and the like; how to integrate EC action with the action of national governments under their respective antitrust statutes; and how to formulate and issue exemptions from Article 85(1).

By 1962, the Council of Ministers had adopted a key regulation laying out a process by which the Commission could administer these provisions.[18] The regulation provided that any enterprise that concluded agreements containing any of the proscribed provisions of Article 85(1) could report those agreements to the Commission, requesting an exemption from the prohibition, with the understanding that any exemptions granted would ordinarily be retroactive to the date of notification. Failing notification, firms faced the risk of heavy penalties in the event their agreements were later found in violation of Article 85. Another part of the regulation set out a procedure by which an enterprise could obtain a "negative clearance" from the Commission; that is, an acknowledgment that a specified agreement lay outside the scope of the prohibitions in Articles 85(1) and 86.

Agreements among Competitors

Not surprisingly, the reporting requirements turned up very few cases of simple market-sharing arrangements among potential competitors fashioned on the cartels of the prewar period. But eventually a number of such cases did surface, providing a platform on which the Commission and the Court could interpret and apply Article 85.[19] A series of

---

18. Regulation 17 of the Council of 6 February 1962 implementing Articles 85 and 86 of the treaty, *OJ* (1962) 13/204; amended *OJ* 1962, 58/1655, *OJ* 1963, 162/2696, and *OJ* 1971, L285/49.

19. See *Aluminum Imports from Eastern Europe, OJ* 1985, L92/37; *Woodpulp, OJ* 1985, L85/1; *Rio Tinto Zinc Corporation & Others v. EC Commission,* Joined Cases 8, 50, 54-56, 111, 113 & 117/73, [1975] *European Court Reports* (hereinafter ECR), p. 1663; *ICI v. EC Commission,* Cases 48-57/69, [1972] ECR 619; and *International Quinine Agreement, OJ* 1969, L192/5.

such decisions reaffirmed the fact that the Union was prepared to move energetically against arrangements that had the explicit effect of carving up markets among potential competitors within the Union. Nor was the Commission tolerant of blatant efforts among competitors at fixing prices, limiting production, or restricting technological change when these had a distorting or restraining effect on trade within the common market and could not be justified by the standards for granting exceptions under Article 85. Even when such agreements were ostensibly contained within a single member country, the Commission felt free to condemn them if they demonstrably affected the trade of that member country with other countries in the Union.[20] And eventually, following a doctrine adopted much earlier by the United States, the Court also asserted its jurisdiction over agreements entered into outside the Union that had effects on the Union's markets.[21]

The exemption criteria of Article 85, however, proved sufficient in the eyes of the Commission and the Court to allow for some restrictive agreements among competitors. After some soul-searching, the Commission cautiously acknowledged that it might be prepared to allow some agreements designed to reduce excess capacity in a given industry. Eventually, in a number of decisions that were widely interpreted as bending to the pressures of special interests, it granted several such exemptions.[22] The Commission also allowed some "no-future-competition" commitments to stand that the parties had entered into in connection with the takeover of firms, although it insisted that the terms of such restrictive clauses should not be so extensive as to outweigh the gains generated by the takeover.

Vertical Agreements

Although the reporting requirements adopted by the Council of Ministers in 1962 produced few cases of old-fashioned cartels among potential competitors, it provoked a deluge of reports of agreements between producers and their distributors, between licensers and licensees, and between principals and agents of various sorts. Collectively, these reports revealed a network of business arrangements that appeared prima

---

20. See *Vereniging van Cementhandelaren v. EC Commission*, Case 8/72, [1972] ECR 977 and *Groupement des Fabricants de Papiers Peints de Belgique & Ors v. EC Commission*, Case 73/74, [1975] ECR 1491.

21. Re the "Woodpulp Cartel" (1988) 4 *Common Market Law Reporter* (hereinafter C.M.L.R.) 901: *A. Ahlstrom Oy and Others v. EC Commission*, Joined Cases 89/85, 104/85, 114/85, 116-117/85, and 125-129/85.

22. See Commission of the European Communities 1982, 43-45). See also *Synthetic Fibres Agreement, OJ* 1984, L207/17.

facie to be creating numerous barriers between national markets inside the Union. The greatest number of these consisted of bilateral agreements between suppliers and their distributors, designed to grant the distributor a monopoly over the supplier's product inside a given national market and to grant the supplier the assurance that the distributor would not handle rival products in that market.

Thereafter, the administration of competition policy became a major preoccupation of the Commission. Well over 100 professional administrators were involved in the process (apart from the ubiquitous translators required in the operation of the Union's institutions), and a considerable part of the docket of the Court of Justice consisted of cases under review (Van Bael and Bellis 1990).

The problem of maintaining a common market against the challenge of restrictive business practices forced the Union to confront still another major issue that trade policy specialists had commonly overlooked. The agreements that flooded the Union's offices in Brussels typically appeared to consist of nothing more than an arrangement between a principal in one country and an agent in another, without any attributes of independence residing in the agent. The agent, for instance, might even be a wholly owned subsidiary of the principal.

From a trade policy viewpoint, the fact that the agent's transactions might represent no more than a transfer within a single organization constitutes no basis for waiving the usual measures by which dumping is measured. Trades between a parent and a wholly owned subsidiary, therefore, are exposed to all the tests that would apply if they were trades between independent parties. But, as the Union soon learned, any serious application of competition policy requires the administering public agency to recognize when a single party is both buyer and seller in an observed transaction. Eventually, therefore, the Commission and the Court came to recognize the possibility that a "group economic unit" might be responsible for a given pattern of international trade, and with that recognition, these institutions set the stage for some of the critical judgments that were required in the application of competition policy (Goyder 1988, 79-83).

Developing Policy

Predictably, the task of sorting out private agreements under the Rome treaty criteria proved overwhelming. The exemptive standards laid out in Article 85 of the treaty seemed at first to require a study of each individual agreement in order to determine if it met the requirements for exemption. Besides, many of the agreements between suppliers and their distributors that seemed to create divisions between national markets were fortified by licenses to patents, trademarks, or unpatented technology. With Article 36 of the treaty exempting restrictions by member states imposed for the protection of "industrial and commercial property," the risk existed that otherwise unexceptionable private arrangements might be parceling out national markets, thereby imperiling the common market concept. But in the end, a series of decisions by the Commission and the Court substantially reduced that risk.

It is beyond the scope of this report to review all the subtle distinctions and nuances that the Commission developed in the course of its administration of the "negative clearance" procedures and the exemptive provisions of Articles 85 and 86. But as the Commission gained experience, certain propositions began to emerge as characteristic features of its decisions. The Commission, for instance, was prepared to accept the desirability of producers marketing through a network of distributors, if the distributor could be assured of its position as the sole designated agent in a given territory, and the producer could be assured that the distributor would not take on rival products. But such arrangements were more easily tolerated if the products had complex marketing requirements and if other producers were in the market, as in the case of automobiles. Moreover, the Commission was especially allergic to restrictive provisions that could be applied after the appointed distributors had sold their products in the market; even where patents existed covering such products, the Commission limited their use as a means of blocking cross-border transactions inside the common market.[23]

In the course of time, the Commission gained enough confidence in its ability to distinguish desirable from undesirable agreements that it began issuing group exemptions covering specified types of provisions. Between 1967 and 1985, eight such exemptions were issued, covering exclusive purchase and distribution agreements, specialization agreements, research and development agreements, and patent license agreements. The terms of these group exemptions offer a snapshot of EC policy under Article 85.

One of the most elaborate of the group exemptions, covering joint research and development agreements, was issued in 1984 following a long struggle.[24] At issue was the familiar problem of finding the right balance between the conditions for encouraging research and development and the conditions for preventing collusion or monopoly. To limit the possibility of abuse, the exemption was hedged in numerous ways to ensure that such an agreement would not be converted into a market-sharing arrangement. One such provision terminated the exemption itself five years after the first marketing of a product that issued

23. See *Consten & Grundig v. EC Commission*, Joined Cases 56 & 58/64, (1966) ECR 299; *Davidson Rubber Company*, OJ 1972, L143/31; *Burroughs-Delplanque* CMLR D67, (1972). For a discussion, see Goyder (1988, 258-62).

24. Regulation No. 418/85 on the application of EEC Treaty Article 85(3) to research and development agreements, OJ 1985, L53/5.

from the research program, or when the market share of the parties to the agreement reached 20 percent. Within these constraints, various restrictive measures are explicitly permitted, such as an undertaking by the parties not to enter into research and development agreements with third parties in the field covered by the agreement, and even an assignment of exclusive territories among the parties during the five-year marketing period. But there is also an extensive blacklist defining practices that are not permitted by the exemption, such as agreed restrictions on quantity and price, as well as undertakings not to challenge the validity of patents issuing from the research program inside the common market.

Competition Policy: Monopoly and Dominance

From the first, the drafters of the Rome treaty had been aware that overcoming the barriers that separated national markets inside the Community would require much more than the provisions of Article 85 could deliver. One problem they would have to confront, for instance, was the existence of legal monopolies that were created for a variety of social, fiscal, or other purposes and that all member countries maintained—from telephone systems to tobacco monopolies. In this area, it was evident the Community would have to proceed cautiously.

Article 90 of the treaty reflected that caution: such enterprises would be subject to the anticompetitive prohibitions contained in the treaty, but the application of such rules was not to obstruct "the *de jure* or *de facto* fulfillment of the specific tasks entrusted to such enterprises." Predictably, this delphic provision would be the subject of a continuous battle in the decades to follow. It would not be until the enactment of the Single European Act in 1986 that the Commission would attempt to deal effectively with those state monopolies.

In addition to dealing with the problems created by the threatened dominance of legal monopolies, the treaty also addressed the potential dominance of enterprises that were not state supported. Article 86 of the treaty prohibits enterprises from taking improper advantage of a dominant position in the common market to the extent that their actions affect trade between any member states. Such actions include, for instance, imposing "inequitable" purchase and selling prices; placing limits on production, markets, or technical development to the detriment of consumers; discriminating among trading partners to their competitive disadvantage; and attaching supplementary tie-in conditions to contracts.

As in the case of Article 85, Article 86 has given the Union considerable room for interpretation, especially in determining when an enterprise is dominant and when it uses that position abusively. In a series of decisions, the European Court confirmed that various enterprises in fact held dominant positions, including in some instances enterprises that consisted of partnerships among firms in the same line of business.[25] The key characteristic of a dominant enterprise, according to the Court, was the ability to prevent effective competition, a capacity that derived from its power to behave independently of its competitors and customers. The signposts that such a condition existed obviously were not rigid. But where sellers were found to hold a dominant position, they usually were in control of a large share—say, 35 percent—of some defined market.

What the Court determined to be abuses within the meaning of Article 86 covered a wide range. In a few instances, the Court found the existence of abuse under circumstances that would have evoked anti-dumping duties if trade policies were being applied. There was, however, a critical difference between the Court's application of a remedy in such cases and the application of dumping duties as practiced in the wide world beyond—a difference that epitomizes a fundamental distinction between competition policy and trade policy. In the application of trade policy, the central question is whether "dumping," however defined, has occurred, but in competition policy, the central question is whether the conduct of the offending enterprise, viewed broadly, is deemed injurious to the maintenance of a competitive market (ECS/AKZO, OJ 1985, L374/1).

Much more common than dumping cases, however, were cases involving anticompetitive practices of other types. Some of these had been dealt with under national laws, but many had been tolerated in the national jurisdictions of member states. One group of cases addressed by the Commission involved the use of so-called "fidelity rebates." As the name implies, these were special rebates available only to customers who committed themselves to buying from a specified list of sellers.[26] Other anticompetitive practices were dealt with as well: withholding supplies from a customer in order to stifle competition, charging different prices to different customers, and charging "excessive" prices, defined as prices that have no reasonable relation to the economic value of the product supplied.[27] Neither the Commission nor the Court, how-

---

25. *United Brands v. EC Commission*, Case 27/76, (1978) ECR 207, p. 277 (para. 65). The definition of dominance in this case was later applied in *Hoffman-La Roche v. EC Commission* ('Vitatims'), Case 85/76, [1979] ECR 461; *Michelin v. EC Commission*, Case 322/81, [1983] ECR 3461; and *CBEM-Telemarketing S.A. v. Compagnie Luxembourgeoie de Telediffusion (CLT) and Information Publicitie Benelux SA (IFB)*, Case 311/84, [1985] ECR 3261. For a case dealing with a dominant buyer, see "Railway Rolling Stock," in the Commission of the European Communities (1975, 60-61). For a case dealing with a dominant group, see *European Sugar Industry*, OJ 1973, L140/17.

26. See *Suiker Unie & Ors OJCooperatieve Vereniging v. EC Commission* (joined cases 40-48, 114/73) 16 December 1975 (1975) ECR 1663.

27. See *United Brands v. EC Commission*, cited above. The case turned in part on whether United Brands was discriminating in response to its own competitive needs or in response to the interests of its favored distributors, the latter being seen as more objectionable.

ever, saw any of these practices as a violation per se of Article 86, each one being adjudged for its effect in the context in which it was practiced.[28]

EC concern with the abuses that could be practiced by dominant firms eventually led it into an area pioneered by US law, namely, the control of mergers among large enterprises. In 1972, the Commission had brought a case against Continental Can, aimed at preventing it from acquiring a rival firm in the Netherlands through a German subsidiary. The Commission's argument was that the acquisition was illegal under Article 86, creating a dominant position in packaging materials in the common market and threatening its competitors (*Continental Can, OJ* 1972, L7/25). Although the Court overrode the Commission's decision in the individual case, it nevertheless chose to use the case as an opportunity for approving the use of Article 86 to prevent mergers that would have the effect of stifling competition (*Europemballage and Continental Can v. EC Commission*, Case 6/72, [1973] ECR 215).

With the tie between mergers and anticompetitive practices having been recognized, the Commission sought to gain the right to screen mergers routinely before they were consummated, as some EC countries had the power to do under their national laws. Sixteen years would pass, however, before the Council of Ministers could agree on a regulation empowering the Commission to review prospective mergers, launching a program on which we comment below.[29] During that interval, there were continuous discussions of the relative merits of fostering competition in the Community versus building up "champions" to do battle in world markets, a tension that continues to the present day.

Competition Policy: State Aids

To establish a common market, the members of the European Community were obliged to grapple not only with the market-sharing and predatory propensities of individual enterprises, but also with the widespread lending of financial support by European governments to firms operating in their respective jurisdictions. As long as governments were free to impose restrictions at their borders, they retained the option of imposing countervailing duties against foreign goods that had benefited from such official support. But with the initiation of the common

---

28. See, for instance, "Gillette Received Brussels Ultimatum," *Financial Times*, 12 November 1992, 18, a case in which Gillette's acquisition of a 70 percent share of the market was seen by the Commission as an abuse of a dominant position.

29. Council Regulation (EEC) No. 4064/89 on the control of concentrations between undertakings, *OJ* 1990, L257/13.

market, member countries had to look to competition policy in order to deal with state aids.

In Europe, government financial support to industry has a rich and extensive history (Shonfield 1965; Wilson 1985). Accordingly, Articles 92 and 94 of the Rome treaty relating to state aids are much more equivocal in their recognition of the virtues of an open, competitive market than Articles 85 and 86. True, Article 92 begins with a broad condemnation of state aids in any form that distort competition and adversely affect trade within the common market. But the article then explicitly defines some categories of state aid as compatible with the common market: aid of a social character that does not discriminate on the basis of the origin of products (such as a subsidy for the purchase of medicines); aid to deal with natural disasters or other such events; and aid to specified areas of Germany to overcome the problems of German partition.

Having narrowed the scope of its prohibitions a little, Article 92 then goes on to define state aid programs that the Commission may in its discretion find compatible with the common market. These cover a very wide range, including programs to elevate depressed regions, programs to execute important projects (such as the Chunnel, the pan-European high-speed train system, and the Airbus family of aircraft), programs to remedy "serious economic disturbances," and programs that the Council of Ministers approves on recommendation of the Commission. To put teeth in these provisions, the treaty prescribes a screening procedure that subjects existing and future state aid programs to the scrutiny and approval of the Commission. Where new programs are involved, the Commission has two months in which to demur, and, in the absence of such action, the member state is entitled to proceed with its state aid program.

Reflecting the spirit of these treaty provisions, the Commission's administration has exhibited much less doctrinal fervor than in the case of Articles 85 and 86. Indeed, the Commission has gone to some pains to describe its administration as "basically realistic" (Commission of the EC 1972, quoted in Goyder 1988, 375-76). That realism has been manifested in various ways, beginning with the Commission's recognition that state aids can take many forms, from outright grants and preferential loans to more subtle infusions of cash in the form of tax exemptions and stock purchases.

More to the point, however, has been the Commission's pragmatism in distinguishing between acceptable state aid programs and those that did not merit approval. One criterion has been that of *selectivity*; accordingly, schemes that provide support for a well-defined geographical region are more acceptable, as a rule, than schemes that are much less specific regarding the areas and industries to be supported. The *transparency* and specificity of the proposed aid provide a second criterion. *Temporary measures* are more acceptable than those of indefinite duration, especially if the measures are designed to tide over the affected enterprises in the handling of a transitory problem rather than to prop up a chronically sick sector. The *appropriateness* of the proposed aid, given the problem it is designed for, provides yet another criterion. And the measure of *benefit or harm* to the Union as a whole provides still another peg for the Commission's final verdict.

However, one has to recognize that the decisions of the Commission in this area are fundamentally pragmatic, taken with a strong sensitivity to the nature of the political pressures that its member states face. This does not mean that the Commission's reviews are altogether perfunctory. During 1981-85, for instance, the Commission reviewed more than 761 state aid schemes. While 77 percent were allowed to pass without objection, the remainder encountered some obstacle in the review process, commonly leading to revisions.[30] After the adoption of the Single European Act in 1986, the Commission visibly tightened its review standards. But the Commission's disposition to avoid confronting any member state with a politically intolerable decision remains evident.[31]

The Single Act and Its Aftermath

The Background

In 1985, the EC states agreed to launch into a new phase in the process of integration, a decision that introduced a decade of frenetic change.[32] Despite the remarkable developments of prior decades, the common market was still very far from being a single economic unit. On the contrary, national frontiers inside the common market continued to offer substantial impediments to the easy movement of goods and services and of the resources required to produce them.

The remaining impediments, although substantial, on the whole had received little attention from economists and policymakers in the past. They took the form of national monopolies such as those in telecommunications and energy distribution, national regulations such as those in the fields of environmental control and consumer safety, national

---

30. The figures do not include aid to agriculture, fisheries, and transport (Commission of the European Communities 1990, 135, table 2).

31. The Commission's decision to allow Italy to subsidize the closure of 68 steel plants in June 1994 represented an especially striking illustration of the Commission's willingness to bend its own rules. See "Brussels Resurrects Steel Plan," *Financial Times*, 16 June 1994, 1. See also "The Aidbusters' Charter," *Financial Times*, 14 December 1996, 15.

32. There are several other interpretations regarding the factors that produced the Single Act initiative (see, e.g., Sandholtz and Zysman 1989, 92-128; Moravcsik 1991, 651-88; Keohane and Hoffmann 1992, 1-40; Cameron 1992, 23-74).

qualifications for the practice of the professions such as those in engineering and law, and national recognition and enforcement of privately developed product standards such as those in consumer durable goods.

Throughout the 1970s and early 1980s, the Commission had been sponsoring piecemeal efforts to reduce these diverse impediments, largely by attempting to harmonize the relevant national regulations. Now and again, these efforts came to a head in ambitious proposals sponsored by prestigious committees, but until 1985, the results were distressingly meager. As a result, the prices of products and services typically varied substantially from one member country to the next, with differences that could not conceivably be explained by transportation costs (Emerson et al. 1988, 147-50). Thus, in 1985 the dispersion of price for goods and services bought by households, as reflected in national averages, came to about 22 percent of the average prices prevailing in the Community (Emerson et al. 1988, 147, 277). The prices of wine, vegetables, and automobiles displayed much larger differentials, rising to 60 percent in some automobile categories.

What helped bring matters to a head in 1985 were several trends, deeply disturbing to Europe's leaders and that convinced them that the EC economy was headed toward a crisis. One such development was the persistent slippage of Europe in its competitive race against Japan and the United States, a trend already visible in the 1960s (OECD 1970). By the early 1980s, EC sources were observing that of 37 technological sectors "of the future," 31 were dominated by the United States, 9 by Japan, and only 2 by Europe; that 4 out of 5 patent applications for new materials were being filed by US and Japanese companies, and that the leading European company in computers occupied only 10th place in the world computer industry.[33]

To make matters worse, Europe in the 1980s was being challenged from the low end of the technology spectrum as well as from the high end. Countries such as Korea, Taiwan, Brazil, and even India were beginning to compete effectively against Europe in standardized products such as steel, bulk chemicals, small motors, computer software, and the like. From the viewpoint of European industry, Europe's competitive advantages were evaporating. In all, between 1980 and 1986, the EC share of world manufacturing exports fell from 23 percent to 19.5 percent ("A Rude Awakening: A Survey of the European Community," *Economist*, 3 July 1993, 50).

According to conventional wisdom at the time, the remaining impediments in the common market were preventing the firms in any member country from looking on the whole of Europe as a home market. That situation, in turn, was discouraging businesses in Europe from engaging in cross-border mergers, building firm resources to the levels of their

---

33. For an overview, see Sharp (1993, 200-26).

competitors in Asia and North America and using those resources in the global race to develop new products and to invest in new processes. In response to this diagnosis, the leading firms of Europe plunged into a campaign to accelerate the move toward a single market (Sandholtz and Zysman 1989, 116-18; see also Green-Cowles 1994).

The advances of the single-market concept on the political front during the early 1980s offered the bureaucrats in Brussels the opportunity they had persistently sought. The brilliance with which they exploited that opportunity was due in considerable measure to the leadership of Jacques Delors and Lord Cockfield, who developed a program to implement the political decision that was far more extensive than anyone could reasonably have expected.

The strength of the bureaucrats' response was augmented by the fact that the Court had been so quietly persistent in interpreting the Rome treaty in ways that would support a single-market concept. The idea that national regulations and national professional requirements might violate the Rome treaty by creating an impediment to the common market's realization had appeared in its opinions for a decade or more before the political decision to move toward a single market. As early as 1974, the Court observed that "all trading rules by member states which are capable of hindering, directly or indirectly, actually or potentially intra-Union trade are to be considered as measures having an effect equivalent to quantitative restrictions" (Case 8/74 *Procureur du Roi v. B. & G. Dassonville* [1974]). Eventually, that idea would be applied not only to the movement of goods but also (with some caveats) to the sale of services.[34]

The Brussels bureaucrats, however, chose to pin their proposed program for a single market on a more recent and more widely advertised opinion of the Court, the celebrated *Cassis de Dijon* decision, which obliged Germany to suspend its restrictions on the importation of a French cordial (Case 120/78, *Cassis de Dijon*, [1979] ECR 649). In that case, the Court concluded that although French regulations differed from those of Germany, they were equivalent in effect and hence had to be recognized by Germany as satisfying German objectives. Building on that opinion as if it were a clear break with the past, the Commission proposed to generalize the concept of "mutual recognition" as a central element of the new single-market program.[35]

There were other factors that helped to explain the willingness of member states to consider a great leap forward toward a single market,

---

34. For cases concerning services, see *Reyners v. The Belgian State* (Case 2/74, [June 1974] ECR 631) and *Van Binsbergen v. Bestuur van de Bedrijfsvereniging voor de Metaalnijverheid* (Case 33/74, [1974] ECR 1299).

35. For a discussion of the history and implications of this principle, see Nicolaïdis (1993).

factors that showed up in the detailed negotiations that were to follow concerning regulations in the various fields of goods and services. Two seemingly barren decades of negotiation aimed at harmonizing national regulations had not been altogether in vain. In the process, as it turned out, national officials had learned a great deal about the regulations of other member countries, evaluating their strengths and identifying their inadequacies. Moreover, in some cases, from food product specifications to physicians' diplomas, member states had already taken substantial steps toward harmonization. Once the political conditions turned favorable, therefore, bureaucrats were better able to identify areas in which the regulations of exporting member states seemed adequate, as well as the provisions that were indispensable to restrain, condition, and manage a Europe-wide regime.

With the formulation of the Single European Act, the Community vigorously moved toward a single market. Among the telling signs that the movement might be having some success was a rapid increase in the relative importance of intra-Community trade. By 1991, trade within the Community reached 60 percent of the total trade of its members, as compared with 50 percent in 1980 (European Community 1992a, 9). At the same time, transborder mergers and acquisitions among enterprises in the common market were increasing at a more rapid rate than mergers and acquisitions between firms within single member countries, a development quite new in Europe's business history. Between 1984 and 1989, the total value of transborder mergers and acquisitions within the Community jumped from $8 billion to $167 billion (Smith and Walter 1991, 3).

Trade in Goods

Taking off from *Cassis de Dijon*, the Community extended its efforts to overcome differences in the national regulations that were impeding the flow of goods inside the common market.[36] Under this approach, two types of situations were envisaged. One was the situation in which national regulations, though different in detail, would be considered as essentially equivalent in purpose and effect. Such cases, it was estimated, would cover the large majority of cases. In those circumstances, member states importing the goods were to accept the regulations of the exporter country as equivalent to their own.

Under the remaining cases, where substantive differences existed among national regulations, the Community developed a two-stage process to ensure that these differences would not impede trade inside the common

---

36. This new approach was originally stated in "The New Approach Resolution" adopted by the Council in May 1985 (Commission to the European Council 1985, 26).

market. In the first stage, the Council of Ministers would adopt a directive that embodied the "essential requirements" to which any national regulatory system would be expected to adhere, along with guidelines pointing to the means by which such adherence might be achieved. "Essential requirements" would be restricted to basic considerations of safety, health, consumer protection, and environmental protection. Detailed technical standards embodying these essential requirements were left for formulation to private organizations in Europe organized for such purposes, such as the Comité Européen de Normalisation. As far as exporting member countries were concerned, however, products that met the "essential requirements" promulgated by the European Council were entitled to certificates of conformity whether or not they satisfied any technical standards so promulgated. And importing member countries were under an obligation to accept such qualifying certificates.

To implement this approach, the Community needed to ensure that certificates of conformity issued by one member state would be recognized by the others. Thus, in 1990 a "global approach" was initiated by member states' certification bodies. The European Organization for Testing and Certification was created to provide a structure for negotiating mutual recognition agreements and for cooperating in their operation.

Another feature of the new approach was that the Council was prepared to formulate its "essential requirements" by broad product categories rather than by narrowly defined products. By early 1993, 11 such broad directives were adopted, including machine tools, toys, pharmaceuticals, medical devices, and food products (Commission of the European Communities 1993). In earlier discussions aimed at harmonizing national regulations, the products in any one of these broad categories had been the subject of dozens of separate discussions.

Indicative of both the efficacy and the limitations of the new approach was the history of EC efforts to harmonize safety standards in toys. The Toys Safety Directive broke a deadlock of nearly 20 years of stalled harmonization negotiations. It put down stringent criteria regarding flammability and toxicity without spelling out technical specifications for conforming to such criteria (Directive 88/378 EEC, 3 May 1988).

Despite such progress, the new approach has been less effective than many within the Commission envisaged in 1985. The specified requirements still tend to be detailed, lengthy, and difficult to negotiate. On the average, they take about three years to make.

More basic, however, is the question of what the Union has actually achieved under the label of "mutual recognition" when applied to goods. To what extent has the Union simply fobbed off the difficulties of harmonizing national official regulations to private national bodies? To what extent are the solutions of such bodies consistent with the Union's objectives of maintaining open markets inside the Union? Have these bodies managed to avoid the temptation of developing standards that non-

European producers would find especially difficult to meet? Answers to these obvious questions await the careful scrutiny of future researchers.

Trade in Services

Even more difficult and complex has been the range of directives devoted to overcoming the many impediments to the sale of services inside the common market, notably in transport, finance, and information services, and in the practice of medicine, nursing, law, accounting, and teaching. As noted earlier, these restrictions have taken many forms, including those formulated, administered, and enforced by the public bureaucracy, and also those developed by private bodies such as professional associations. The original formulation of the Single European Act envisaged that 54 directives would be required to cover such subjects. But ultimately the total mounted to 84.

In part, the variations in the form and substance of these national measures reflected the different weights that governments placed on various public objectives. In many cases, of course, the object of the restrictions was simply to protect a national market from foreign competition. But in other cases, as in banking and in medicine, a genuine concern for consumer safety provided part of the explanation for some of the government restrictions.

In any event, in relinquishing their controls over the delivery of services by firms from other EC members, host countries have demanded far more extensive limits, conditions, and safeguards than in the sale of goods (Nicolaïdis 1993). Illustrative of the problems involved were two Council directives adopted in 1988 and 1992, covering professional services.[37]

In substance, the first directive deals with the cross-border provision of services in professions whose practice requires a diploma or license, and it establishes a general system for the recognition of diplomas requiring three years or more of study, awarded on completion of professional training. Under the directive, member states cannot refuse to recognize such diplomas awarded by other member countries, thereby opening the door for applicants from other member states.

Following that sweeping grant, however, the directive addresses other problems that so often distinguish the sale of services from that of goods. First, some member countries do not require a diploma for the sale of specified services, as in the United Kingdom and Ireland; instead, private bodies rather than the state recognize the professional accreditation of a barrister or an accountant. For such cases, complex equivalency

---

37. Council Directive 89/48/EEC of 21 December 1988 and 92/51/EEC (*OJ* January 1989 and July 1992).

rules are laid down. More importantly, host countries retain the right to subject applicants to residual entry requirements where "substantial" differences exist in training between the countries concerned. The host country could require, for instance, a specified amount of professional experience in the home state, the completion of an adaptation period under the responsibility of a qualified professional in the host country, or passage of a test on the subject matter. Given the imprecision of the directive's wording and the widespread resistance of national professional associations to it, provisions such as these are readily abused. Finally, the new system is predicated on the development of an extensive system of mutual monitoring of training requirements among member states that is a far cry from the unqualified reliance on the standards of the service provider's home state (Nicolaïdis 1992). Other key directives in the field of services have reflected different applications of the basic idea of mutual recognition. Thus, the Second Banking Directive, passed by the Council in December 1989, introduced the Single Union banking license, otherwise referred to as the European passport.

The directive attributes the primary task of supervising the financial institutions to the competent authorities of their home state.[38] As with the General Service Directive, however, the banking directive falls short of requiring member states to rely totally on the regulatory controls of home states. Instead, the scope of mutual recognition is restricted to two fields: the initial authorization granted to financial institutions to engage in business and the responsibility to supervise solvency requirements.

Even in the case of initial authorization, however, mutual recognition in banking does not mean that the right of access acquired by financial institutions in the markets of other member states can thus be exercised without any formalities; foreign branches still need to provide host governments with detailed information regarding their financial standing. Moreover, the Second Banking Directive is accompanied by an array of harmonization directives dealing with solvency ratios, accounting rules, supervisory control over major shareholders, deposit guarantee schemes, the monitoring of large exposures of credit institutions, and the transparency of banking operations. Accordingly, the system that has been put in place is closer to a state of "co-regulation" involving the Union and national regulatory authorities than to a simple system of mutual recognition, a feature that reduces the risk of a competitive degradation of national standards.

All told, the Union has sought to carry out the mutual recognition principle as "managed mutual recognition," an approach replete with

---

38. Council Directive 89/646/EEC of 15 December 1989 on the Coordination of Laws, Regulations and Administrative Provisions relating to the Taking up and Pursuit of the Business of Credit Institutions (*OJ* L386, 1989).

provisions for national authorities to learn about each other and for safeguards that limit the automaticity of the rights of the nationals of other EU countries. Less has been achieved under the new approach than its strongest supporters had hoped. (Only a few dozen lawyers, for instance, have managed to acquire cross-border rights under the new regime.) But the system qualifies, nonetheless, as a remarkable experiment in liberalization (Nicolaïdis 1995, 269-304).

Building Technological Strength

Convinced that the technological gap between Europe and its industrial rivals was growing, Europe's leaders also have sought to narrow the gap by increasing the flow of public financial support, whose source until the early 1980s had mainly been national governments. In 1984, the member states agreed to develop a multiyear framework program to stimulate and support the establishment of what the Commission referred to as an authentic "European Research and Technology Union" (European Community 1988a, 1993). With the negotiation of the Single European Act in 1985, such programs were institutionalized and expanded.[39]

Of the various activities supported under this general heading, the most relevant for competition and trade policy has been a program to provide initial stimuli for technological cooperation among industrial firms in Europe. Of particular importance, in the eyes of Union officials, has been the need to help European industry increase its competitiveness in information technology and telecommunications.

Programs devoted to this goal constituted 45 percent of the total value of the 1987-91 framework program. Foremost among them was ESPRIT, the European Strategic Program for Research and Development in Information Technology, launched in 1984 and designed for a 10-year period. Projects carried out under ESPRIT involve at least two independent industrial partners from different member states and are linked together by an electronic information network, Eurokom.

The first phase of ESPRIT had a budget of 1.5 billion ECUs and financed 219 projects involving 450 partners. In light of the apparent success of the first phase, the budget for the second phase of ESPRIT was doubled. In addition, in 1987, the Community launched the RACE telecommunications program with a 1.5 billion ECU endowment; its principal objective was to develop the technology required for broadband fiber-optic networks. The program, completed in 1995, included about 350 organizations and 2,000 individuals in the course of its existence.

---

39. The Single European Act added a new article 130f to the treaty that called for supporting the efforts of European undertakings to cooperate with each other, to "become more competitive at the international level."

Strengthening Competition

The efforts of the European Union to support European business, while apparently successful in various respects, at the same time have heightened the tension that has always existed between two lines of EU policy: between ensuring, on the one hand, that European business is amply endowed with the necessary financial, managerial, and technological strength to do battle in world markets, and, on the other hand, maintaining enough internal competition to keep European industry on its toes.

Inevitably, some measures intended to increase the resources of European industry also risked reducing competition in the common market. For instance, encouraging research consortia among European enterprises, coupled with an increase in transborder mergers, may have strengthened the hands of dominant firms.

A new merger regulation responsive to this concern was adopted in 1989. Under it, EC reviews of proposed mergers were to preempt any national reviews, but EC reviews were to be limited to very large firms with substantial business within the common market.[40] The standards for such reviews were quite general, acknowledging both the desirability of strengthening competition and the desirability of promoting technical progress. But one decisive test, according to the regulation, was whether the merger would create or strengthen a dominant position in the common market.

In the five years following the institution of the Commission's new merger powers in September 1990, its staff had received about 400 cases for review. In the exercise of its powers, however, the Commission exhibited an exceedingly cautious approach as it sought to develop appropriate standards (Sandrock and Van Arnheim 1991, 859-74). Some observers complained that the Commission was giving too much weight to the efficiency gains sought by such mergers and not enough weight to consumer welfare effects (Neven, Nuttall, and Seabright 1993). Indeed, by 1996, the Commission had blocked only one merger project, which involved the proposed acquisition of a Canadian commuter aircraft producer by a joint venture of French and Italian firms engaged in the same line of production (*Aerospatiale-Alenia/de Havilland*, OJ 1991, L334/42). Despite the infrequency of such formal actions, however, the parties did alter the conditions of the various proposed mergers during the Commission's investigations.

The merger regulation, it should be noted, applies not only to firms

---

40. More precisely, the standards defining the area for review of proposed mergers were those that would create an entity whose worldwide revenues exceeded five billion ECUs, had 250 million ECUs of business in the Community by each of at least two of the "undertakings" (that is, the firms concerned), and had not more than two-thirds of that business in a single member country (Downs and Ellison 1991, 54-56).

headquartered within the Community, but also to firms headquartered elsewhere if they otherwise meet the size criteria and other criteria defining the regulations scope. Some member states have worried that such an approach would increase conflicts over extraterritorial jurisdiction, in particular with the United States. Accordingly, in 1991, the Community signed an unprecedented agreement on competition policy with the United States, including an undertaking by the administrations in both to take into account the important interests of the other party at all stages of their enforcement activities. The agreement obliged the parties to notify each other of relevant investigations and to exchange information in order to better understand "economic conditions and theories" relevant to their actions (Jacquemin 1993, 91-102).

In 1996, Boeing's prospective takeover of its rival McDonnell Douglas presented the first serious test of the effectiveness of the US-EU agreement. It remains to be seen if differences in national interests and antitrust concepts would prevent a common approach to such situations.

In addition to stepping up its surveillance of mergers, the Community also reacted to disturbing signs that enterprises might be increasingly organizing themselves in restrictive agreements inside national markets in order to control the sale of goods and services (Swaddled, *Economist*, 24 July 1993, 67).

The grounds for expecting an increase in restrictive business practices and in the abuse of enterprises' dominance have been particularly strong in the case of services. Until the 1980s, the Commission had largely overlooked restrictive agreements in the sale of services, given the other barriers that stood in the way of transborder transactions. With the new initiatives under the Single European Act, however, there were signs that some services' operators were looking actively for arrangements to protect themselves from increased competition. For instance, proprietary computer networks, such as those already existing for ATMs among an exclusionary group of banks and for air reservations among a group of airline companies, seemed to threaten the objectives of Articles 85 and 86. How such issues would eventually be resolved was not clear.

Finally, in the spirit of the Single European Act, the Commission turned to some of the anomalies in the European market for services, such as state-owned monopolies in telecommunications and electric power, that had been tolerated in earlier years. In the second half of the 1980s, some member states had independently started to implement deregulatory programs in these areas. But, in the view of the Commission, these programs were not sufficient to achieve a market without frontiers by 1993. Accordingly, the scope of competition policy was extended to include not only private-sector services, such as banking, but also those provided by the state, such as telecommunications.

The EC approach to the activities of state-owned enterprises in the service sectors, however, reflected some of the limitations of classifying its actions under the dichotomy of competition policy and trade policy. The provisions of the Rome treaty seemed to offer a number of ways to deal with the issue. Articles 30 and 59, endowing the Union with the power to create a common market in goods and services, seemed to offer one channel; Articles 85 and 86, empowering the Commission to strike down barriers to competition and to restrain the use of dominant positions, seemed to offer another; and Article 90, providing some circumscribed powers to the Commission over state enterprises, suggested another avenue. For EC bodies, the distinction was sometimes critical. The Union's powers vis-à-vis the governments of its member states was different in each approach. And inside the Union itself, the relative powers of the Commission and of the Council of Ministers differed in each approach.

Therefore, when in the late 1980s the Commission sought to restrain state telecommunications monopolies from exercising some of their powers of exclusion, it had to decide whether to proceed under the Union's powers over governmental trade restrictions in the common market or under its less-exclusive powers over competition contained in Articles 86 and 90 of the Rome treaty (European Community 1988b). Its decision to use Articles 86 and 90 was subsequently modified by the European Court of Justice, which placed the justification for the action more squarely on EC plenary powers over trade in the common market.

Considerable liberalization was achieved under the program in the years that followed. But some countries clung to their existing monopolies over voice transmission. Eventually, however, the year 1998 was fixed as the deadline for liberalization.

EC efforts to terminate state monopolies in the generation and transportation of gas and electricity have underlined the complexity of the liberalization of services trade. The reasons some of these state monopolies existed, it became apparent, was to control not only production and trade in the affected areas but transportation and distribution as well. Unwilling to deprive national governments altogether of their rights to maintain some measure of control in these cases, the Community began to look for arrangements that would entail some degree of negotiation among the states, such as was already common in the establishment of mutual recognition regimes in other services.

Other decisions in the services area added to the impression of complexity and sometimes seemed almost ad hoc. On the one hand, the Court ruled that the German public employment agency's monopoly in placements for various job categories and the exclusive right of certain designated companies to load ships in the port of Genoa violated Article 86 of the treaty (*French Republic and Others v. Commission*, 23 April 1991; *Höfner v. Macroton*, 10 December 1991). On the other hand, the Court relied on the trade obligations contained in Article 59 to limit some of the exclusive rights of the Greek state television company over the Greek television market (*Ellinki Radiophonia Tileorassi*, 18 June 1991).

From all appearances, the choice between the use of competition policy or trade policy in the context of services has been guided both by questions of practicality and by politics. Because the Commission shares its powers with the Council of Ministers in the application of trade-liberalization provisions, activists in the Commission sought to control state monopolies through the antitrust provisions, where the Commission exercises almost exclusive jurisdiction. But the ministers representing the member states and the Court have preferred to rely on the trade-liberalization provisions as the platform for EC actions against these state monopolies.

Conclusions

By the terms of the Rome treaty, both the trade policies and the competition policies of the European Union are tilted toward improving market efficiency by reducing or eliminating barriers erected by governments or firms. Although the Community (and its successor, the European Union) has pursued those objectives by fits and starts over the decades of its existence, and although some of its programs can be seen as significant departures from the trend, the basic direction has been maintained, testimony to the power of a continuous learning process. But, of course, the Community's goals, as well as its preferred means of achieving them, have been quite different for trade between its members than for trade with outside countries.

In the internal market, the dominant goal of both competition policy and trade policy is to overcome the restrictions that would separate national markets from one another; exceptions to that general principle must bear a heavy burden of proof of their compelling necessity. In dealing with other countries, however, the Union incorporates the usual caveats that typify the behavior of countries in international trade, including an insistence on maintaining special restrictions for agriculture, a reservation with respect to measures that might impose serious injury on any industry in the Union, and a readiness to impose restrictions in individual cases without prior authorization from any external source.

The differences in the Union's approach to problems in the internal and the external front are especially marked in other respects. Where the internal market may be affected, the Union maintains extensive programs aimed at restraining measures, such as cartel agreements and state subsidies, that imperil market efficiency. But when the effect of such measures would be borne largely by outside countries, as in aircraft manufacture, the restraints on such practices are few. In this respect, of course, EU practices are not unlike those of most other countries.

Inside the common market, the Union has relied on competition policy to deal with some problems that would otherwise be addressed by trade policy, such as dumping. Exceptionally, however, the Union has sometimes been obliged to tolerate restraints inside the common market in response to pressures from member countries, a situation reflected in persistent price dispersion in some products.

One of the Union's major contributions, from which the rest of the world could learn, has been its attempts to overcome the distortions and restraints in the internal market that arise as a result of different regulatory approaches among its member states, notably approaches to consumer protection, health, and the environment, and as a result of state monopolies such as those found in electric power and telecommunications. Such restraints have received far less attention in the past from economists and policymakers than their impact on trade appears to warrant. Restraints such as these affect trade in both goods and services, but they are especially important in the services sector. The measures taken by the Union to deal with such issues cannot be easily classified under either the competition policy or the trade policy rubric, as they are ordinarily defined. Commonly, they entail extensive negotiation among the states involved, and they restrict the movement of goods and services across borders and limit the freedom of firms to develop cross-border alliances.

Finally, if the lessons of the Union can be generalized, they teach that the effective development of competition policy, as well as of the hybrid measures associated with regulatory regimes, demands a much more elaborate apparatus among the countries concerned than now exists in international regimes in the trade policy field. The facts to be established and the judgments made in competition cases are far more nuanced than in trade cases. The bodies rendering judgments in competition cases, therefore, are much more vulnerable to challenges on the merits of their decisions. The effectiveness of EU institutions in competition cases is explained in considerable part by the extraordinary powers with which the founding treaties endowed them. Until that fact is recognized, governments in the rest of the world are unlikely to be able to replace trade policy effectively with competition policy.

References

Bronckers, Marco C. E. J. 1983. "A Legal Analysis of Protectionist Measures Affecting Japanese Imports into the European Community." In J. H. J. Bourgeois et al., *Protectionism and the European Community*. Deventer, Netherlands: Kluwer.

Burley, Anne-Marie, and Walter Mattli. 1993. "Europe Before the Court: A Political Theory of Legal Integration." *International Organization* 47, no. 1 (winter): 41-76.

Cameron, David. 1992. "The 1992 Initiative: Causes and Consequences." In Albert Sbragia, *Euro-politics*. Washington: Brookings Institution.

Commission of the European Communities. 1972. *First Annual Report on Competition Policy*. Luxembourg: Official Publications of the European Communities.

Commission of the European Communities. 1975. Third Report on Competition Policy. Luxembourg: Official Publications of the European Communities.

Commission of the European Communities. 1982. *Twelfth Report on Competition Policy.* Luxembourg: Official Publications of the European Communities.

Commission of the European Communities. 1983. Annual Reports of the Commission on the Community's Anti-dumping and Anti-subsidy Activities. Luxembourg: Official Publications of the European Communities.

Commission of the European Communities. 1985. *Completing the Internal Market.* White Paper from the Commission to the European Council. COM (85) 310 final, Brussels.

Commission of the European Communities. 1990. "Activity in the Control of State Aid." In *Twentieth Report on Competition Policy.* Luxembourg: Official Publications of the European Communities.

Commission of the European Communities. 1993. *A New Community Standards Policy* 4. Luxembourg: Official Publications of the European Communities.

Commission of the European Union. 1993. *Eleventh Annual Report of the Commission on the Community Anti-Dumping and Anti-Subsidy Activities,* Com (93).

Diebold, William Jr. 1952. *The End of the ITO.* Princeton: International Finance Section, Department of Economics and Social Institutions, Princeton University.

Diebold, William Jr. 1959. *The Schuman Plan: A Study in Economic Cooperation, 1950-1954.* New York: Council on Foreign Relations.

Downs, T. Anthony, and Julian Ellison. 1991. *The Legal Controls of Mergers in the EC.* London: Blackstone Press.

Emerson, Michael, Michel Aujean, Michel Catinat, Philippe Goybet, and Alexis Jacquemin. 1988. *The Economics of 1992: The EC Commission's Assessment of the Economic Effects of Completing the Internal Market.* Oxford: Oxford University Press.

European Community. 1988a. *Research and Technological Development in the EC.* Luxembourg: Official Publications of the European Communities.

European Community. 1988b. *Towards a Competitive Community-Wide Telecommunications Market in 1992.* Brussels.

European Community. 1991. *Opening the Internal Market.* Luxembourg: Official Publications of the European Communities.

European Community. 1992. *The Single Market in Action.* Luxembourg: Official Publications of the European Communities.

European Community. 1993. *Twenty-sixth General Report on the Activities of the European Community.* Luxembourg: Office for Official Publications of the European Communities.

Froment-Meurice, Henri. 1988. *L'Europe de 1992-Espace et Puissance.* Paris: La Documentation Française.

General Agreement on Tariffs and Trade (GATT). 1990. *Basic Instruments and Selected Documents* (BISD) 132, 37th Supplement.

General Agreement on Tariffs and Trade (GATT). 1991. *Panel Report on EE Regulation on Imports of Parts and Components (Screwdriver Case).* Adopted 16 May 1990. GATT Document L/6657: 132-199.

Goyder, D.G. 1988. *EEC Competition Law.* Oxford: Clarendon Press.

Green-Cowles, Maria. 1994. "Transcending Political Representation: the Mobilization of Big Business in the European Community." Paper presented at the American Political Studies Association Conference, Washington, September.

Green, Nicholas, Trevor C. Hartley, and John A. Usher. 1991. *The Legal Foundations of the Single European Market.* Oxford: Oxford University Press.

Hallinan, Charles T. 1928. "Introduction." In Robert Liefmann, *International Cartels, Combines and Trusts.* London: Europa Publishers.

Hartley, T. C. 1981. *The Foundations of European Community Law.* Oxford: Clarendon Press.

Henrichs-Cohen, Starla. 1993. "EEC Treaty Article 115." *Law and Policy in International Business* 24, no. 2 (Winter): 553-87.

Hexner, Ervin. 1946. *International Cartels*. Chapel Hill: University of North Carolina Press.

Hoffmann, Stanley. 1982. "Reflections on the Nation-State in Western Europe Today." *Journal of Common Market Studies* 21 (September-December).

Jacquemin, Alexis. 1993. "The International Dimension of European Competition Policy." *Journal of Common Market Studies* 31, no. 1 (March): 91-102.

Keohane, Robert, and Stanley Hoffmann. 1992. "Institutional Change in Europe in the 1980s." In Keohane and Hoffmann, *The New European Community*. Boulder, CO: Westview Press.

Lister, Louis. 1960. *Europe's Coal and Steel Community: An Experiment in Economic Union*. New York: Twentieth Century Fund.

Lynch, Frances M. B. 1993. "Restoring France: the Road to Integration." In Alan S. Milward et al., *The Frontier of National Sovereignty*. London: Routledge.

Maier, Charles S. 1987. *In Search of Stability: Exploration in Historical Political Economy*. Cambridge, UK: Cambridge University Press.

Maresceau, Marc. 1986. "The GATT in the Case Law of the European Court of Justice." In Meinhard Hilf et al., *The European Community and GATT*. Deventer, Netherlands: Kluwer.

McDermott, Patrick J. 1988. "Extending the Reach of Their Antidumping Laws: The European Community's 'Screwdriver Assembly' Regulation." *Law and Policy in International Business* 20, no. 2 (Spring): 315-30.

Messerlin, Patrick A. 1990. "Anti-Dumping Regulations or Pro-Cartel Law? The EC Chemical Cases." *The World Economy* 13, no. 4 (December): 465-93.

Milward, Alan S., and S. B. Saul. 1977. *The Development of Continental Europe, 1850-1914*. Cambridge, MA: Harvard University Press.

Moravcsik, Andrew. 1991. "Negotiating the Single European Act: National Interests and Conventional Statecraft in the European Community." *International Organization* 45, no. 1: 651-88.

Neven, Damien, Robin Nuttall, and Paul Seabright. 1993. *Merger in Daylight*. London: Centre for Economic Policy Research (CEPR).

Nicolaïdis, Kalypso. 1992. "Mutual Recognition, Regulatory Competition, and the Globalization of Professional Services." In Yair Aharoni, *Coalition and Competition-The Globalization of Professional Services*. London: Routledge.

Nicolaïdis, Kalypso. 1993. "Mutual Recognition among Nations: Trade in Services in the European Community," Ph.D. dissertation. Cambridge, MA: Harvard University.

Nicolaïdis, Kalypso. 1995. "International Trade in Information-based Services: Beyond the Uruguay Round. In William Drake, *The New Information Economy*. New York: Twentieth Century Fund.

Organization for Economic Cooperation and Development (OECD). 1970. *Gaps in Technology: Analytical Report*. Paris: OECD Publications.

Organization for Economic Cooperation and Development (OECD). 1993. "Trade and Competition Policy: How They Interrelate." Revision 1, SG/IW/TC(92) 5, Labour/Management Program, OECD, Paris, 6 July, restricted.

Osenthal, Douglas E. 1990. "Competition Policy." In G. C. Hufbauer, *Europe 1992: An American Perspective*. Washington: Brookings Institution.

Petersmann, Ulrich. 1986. "The EEC as a GATT Member—Legal Conflicts between GATT Law and European Community Law." In Meinhard Hilf et al., *The European Community and GATT*. Deventer, Netherlands: Kluwer.

Sandholtz, Wayne, and John Zysman. 1989. "1992: Recasting the European Bargain." *World Politics* 42 (October): 92-128.

Sandrock, Otto, and Elke Van Arnheim. 1991. "New Merger Control Rules in the EEC." *The International Lawyer* 25, no. 4 (Winter): 859-74.

Sharp, Margaret. 1993. "The Community and New Technologies." In Juliet Lodge, *The European Community and the Challenge of the Future*, 2d ed. New York: St. Martin's Press.

Shonfield, Andrew. 1965. *Modern Capitalism: The Changing Balance of Public and Private Power*. New York: Oxford University Press.

Smith, Roy, and Ingo Walter. 1991. "The First European Merger Boom Has Begun." Center for the Study of American Business Formal Publication No. 103, Washington.

Steele, Keith, ed. 1996. *Anti-Dumping under the WTO: A Comparative Review*. London: Kluwer Law International.

Svennilson, Ingvar. 1983. *Growth and Stagnation in the European Economy*. New York: Garland Publishing.

Svennilson, Ingvar. 1983. *Growth and Stagnation in the European Economy*. New York: Garland Publishing: 17.

Torremans, Paul. 1993. *Anti-circumvention Duties after the Screwdriver Panel Report*. E.L.R.: 288-30.

Trade Policy Review Body. 1996. *Overview of Developments in International Trade and the Trading System: Annual Report of the Director-General, 1995*. Geneva: WTO Publications.

Tumlir, Jan. 1986. "GATT Rules and Community Law." In Meinhard Hilf et al., *The European Community and GATT*. Deventer, Netherlands: Kluwer.

US Department of State. 1951. *Suggested Charter for an International Trade Organization of the United Nations* and the *Treaty Establishing the European Coal and Steel Community (ECSC)*. Pub. No. 2598, Commercial Policy Series No. 93, 18 April, 261 UNTS 140.

Van Bael, Ivo, and Jean Francois Bellis. 1990. *Anti-Dumping and Other Trade Protection Laws of the EEC*, 2nd ed. Chicago: Commerce Clearing House.

Weiler, Joseph H. H. 1991. "The Transformation of Europe." *Yale Law Journal* 100: 2403-83.

Weiler, Joseph H. H. 1992. "After Maastricht: Community Legitimacy in Post-1992 Europe." In W. J. Adams, *Singular Europe*. Ann Arbor: The University of Michigan Press.

Wilson, Graham K. 1985. *Business and Politics: A Comparative Introduction*. Chatham, NJ: Chatham House.

III

ISSUE STUDIES

9

Competition in Japan and the West: Can the Approaches Be Reconciled?

DOUGLAS E. ROSENTHAL AND MITSUO MATSUSHITA

Some Western policy analysts, prominently including Clyde V. Prestowitz Jr. and Karel van Wolferen, are convinced that Japanese culture is fundamentally incompatible with the Western ideological commitment to economic competition.[1] Some Japanese observers, such as Shintaro Ishihara (1989), who would like to see Japan distance itself from the West, share this view. These are sincerely held views on the part of perceptive and knowledgeable observers and should be taken seriously. Indeed, the idea is not a new one, nor is it contradicted by serious scholarship. In her classic study of Japanese national character, *The Chrysanthemum and the Sword*, written during World War II, Ruth Benedict wrote that:

> it is especially important for Americans to recognize that competition in Japan . . . does not have the same degree of socially desirable effects that it does in our own scheme of life. . . . Psychological tests show that competition stimulates us to do our best work. . . . In Japan, however, tests show just the opposite. It is especially marked after childhood has ended, for Japanese children are more playful about competition and not so worried about it. With young men and adults, however, performance deteriorated with competition. Subjects

---

Douglas E. Rosenthal is a partner in the law firm of Sonnenschein, Nath & Rosenthal in Washington. He served as chief of the Foreign Commerce Section, Antitrust Division, US Department of Justice from 1977 to 1980. Mitsuo Matsushita is a professor of law at Seikei University.

1. A recent study by Prestowitz (1994) concludes that Japan and the United States operate under basically different models of capitalism and that these cultural variations significantly preclude commonalities of economic interest (see also *New York Times*, 10 June 1994, D1, and Karel van Wolferen, *Washington Post*, 26 June 1994, C3).

who had made good progress, reduced their mistakes and gained speed when they were working by themselves, began to make mistakes and were far slower when a competitor was introduced. (Benedict 1946, 153)

In Japan, as in Germany, the idea of competition generally, and of economic competition in particular, has often connoted something dangerous and unstable—in Japan the word is often preceded by the adjective "excessive" (see Niino 1993, 171-89). In his fascinating study of postwar Japan, William Chapman observes that the bureaucrats of the Ministry of International Trade and Industry (MITI) were genuinely perplexed by the US Occupation Force's imposition of an antitrust law:

> It seemed contrary to everything that had been learned about national economic management during the war. Big companies were efficient producers. The law's "antibigness" feature genuinely confused post war planners, who had first assumed it was part of the Occupation's plan to gain revenge on Japan for having waged war. . . . MITI's top planners discussed antitrust policy as if it were a severe penalty. (Chapman 1991, 103)

Vigorous competition has long been missing and is missing still from many aspects of Japanese economic life. Japanese culture has not traditionally embraced the idea of competition as expressed by Adam Smith. But the same was true of Germany and much of the rest of Europe, well beyond the end of World War II. Must one therefore assume that the Japanese cannot or will not, in the near future, accept competition in some approximation as a norm for economic behavior? Must one assume that Japanese social and economic institutions cannot or will not become more compatible with the stated Western goals of open national markets and substantial consumer sovereignty in an open global trading system? If so, persistent trade conflict and instability of relations between Japan and the West are inevitable. But if these assumptions are wrong—if Japan, the United States, and Europe are at least "reading from the same page" in discussing broadly shared national and international microeconomic goals and concepts—the prospects need not be so grim. We believe the more hopeful is also the more realistic perspective.

There are three main reasons why it will increasingly be possible for American policymakers to engage the Japanese in a constructive dialogue about competition both within Japan and globally. First, there is already greater acceptance of free market ideas in Japan today than is generally understood in the West. Japan does have a meaningful antitrust law, which is increasingly being enforced in ways comparable to Western antitrust laws. Although it means different things to different people, the idea of deregulation in Japan is powerful and pervasive. Neither bureaucrats, business leaders, nor politicians dare *openly* oppose a policy of deregulation, even if privately there is foot dragging. The direction of change in Japan is definitely toward stronger consumer sovereignty, less central planning, consensus on the need to reform a distribution system that makes goods too costly, and greater transparency in government decision making.

None of this is to deny that there are in Japan certain entrenched ideas, institutions, and practices resistant to competition. Japan's phenomenal postwar rate of economic growth was driven by forced saving and only gradual satisfaction of domestic consumer demand. Many still believe that a continuation of such input-driven growth is possible and desirable. Deregulation will be a serious threat to many presently protected interests. But the new prominence of an alternative deregulatory and more consumer-focused growth model must also be acknowledged.

In 1993, for example, a potentially important Administrative Procedure Act was enacted, aimed at increasing transparency and fairness in the Japanese governmental process. The law sets out basic principles that government agencies must use in awarding licenses to enterprises, and it further provides that "administrative guidance" should not be given beyond the scope of the agency's legal authority, should be employed only after truly voluntary cooperation has been obtained, and should be stated in writing when so requested. In keeping with Article III of the Japanese Constitution, foreign and domestic firms and individuals are to be treated equally in this regard. The Japanese government has announced a deregulatory initiative consisting of some 300 specific proposals. It is hailed by its proponents as a framework for major structural reform to promote competition (*Wall Street Journal*, 29 June 1994, A13). Whether or when this objective will be substantially met, that this is the stated goal shows a shared viewpoint on the validity of regulatory reform and a promise of institutional change.

Second, although Japan has been dramatically more protectionist than either the United States or Europe, progress has been made over the last 10 years in increasing market access, especially for many foreign consumer goods, although less so for durable goods or services. Substantial further progress can and should be made in all sectors. Particular attention should be paid to financial markets and other basic product and (often) services markets regulated by ministries such as those of health, construction, agriculture, telecommunications and posts, energy, and housing, which even now have little incentive to deregulate. The divisions of MITI dealing with basic and intermediate industries have so far continued long-standing protectionist policies, which cannot be reconciled with the agency's self-professed new market orientation (*New York Times*, 9 November 1994, C1). There are institutional reforms already under way, however, which can be promoted to bring change—if Western leaders take them seriously and make it their policy to encourage them. For example, in 1993, for the first time, Japanese courts awarded antitrust damages in private civil cases alleging injury to competition. This contradicts the idea that existing Japanese institutions cannot adapt to Western ideas of competition law and policy. Promoting the necessary political consensus, removing obstacles to deregulation, strengthening the responsiveness of the political process to consumer interests, and accelerating reform are more problematic. In what follows, we offer several incremental suggestions.

Third, dialogue is possible because Japanese ideas of protection and market regulation are not qualitatively different from corresponding ideas in the West. Protectionism remains attractive to many Westerners today and is the subject of ongoing debate in the United States and Europe. In fact, many so-called traditional Japanese ideas are Western transplants. That the same ideas are constructively debated within all developed countries strongly suggests that they can be constructively debated between Western and Japanese cultures.

"Excessive Competition"

Several general ideas historically embedded in Japanese culture support a wariness about the market mechanism and encourage trust in economic planners to minimize the impact of market disruptions. The market mechanism is the antithesis of central planning. It rewards luck, foresight, and diligence. It identifies winners and losers and often deals harshly with the latter. A Confucian ideal of order and harmony is not easily reconciled with the disorder of an unfettered marketplace (Komiya 1990, 297-301).

Central planning in Japan is perceived to have worked well during the Meiji Restoration of the late 19th century and again during the post-World War II reconstruction. The prestige of being a Japanese civil servant has attracted bureaucrats of a generally high level of ability, who have been educated for careers as administrators and who stay in government for the duration. Given this background, they probably have done better at planning than their US counterparts. Until recently, respect for authority has been a Japanese trait, and Japanese voters and politicians have been willing to cede much authority to senior civil servants.

Such delegation of authority was consistent with US policy toward Japan in the late 1940s and early 1950s. First, fear of the strength of Japanese pro-communist groups and then, after the North Korean invasion of South Korea, the need for a bulwark against the spread of communism in Asia led to US encouragement of Japanese bureaucratic control over a managed Japanese economy with protected home markets (Chapman 1991, chapter 5). The United States did not object when the Ministry of Finance set interest rates on Japanese bank deposits at low levels and limited access to luxury consumer goods, thereby increasing the rate of saving and providing the funds for low-interest loans to Japanese corporations. Many Americans would have the same done in the United States—if they could have been persuaded to make the sacrifice. Cartelization of Japanese financial institutions was an almost inevitable byproduct of Ministry of Finance planning.

Industry trade associations also promoted cartels. By 1965 there were 1,079 established cartels exempt from the Antimonopoly Law. This is what we get for answered prayers, and US policymakers of both parties share responsibility for turning Japan away from deregulation so as to further US Cold War defense policy. By 1991, however, the number of authorized cartels had shrunk to 248. It is now widely recognized that such cartels tended to be inefficient and to raise prices artificially. Their abolition is now a part of the deregulation program. As we know from US experience, this program will undoubtedly meet resistance both from the industries that have been protected and from the government regulators who will lose the power to control them.[2] However, that does not mean deregulation in Japan will not happen.

American and European policymakers frequently pay lip service to the market mechanism, yet sometimes find the temptations of industrial policy interventions irresistible. The Europeans complain that US cold war defense policy played a major role in protecting and indirectly subsidizing key US defense industries. President Bill Clinton, in a reaction to the distaste of the Reagan and Bush administrations for government targeting of investments in innovative technologies, has been tempted to take a leaf from MITI's book. For example, the United States is now encouraging a joint venture among the Big Three US automakers (excluding the Japanese automakers with closely controlled US manufacturing subsidiaries) to pool their research and development efforts to produce a new, fuel-efficient automobile engine (Reed 1993, 25). In contrast, 25 years ago the Justice Department sued under the antitrust laws to stop such a collaboration to jointly develop a standardized pollution control device (*United States v. Automobile Mfctrs. Assn., Inc., et al.*, 1969 Trade Cas., section 72,907, 1969). If the United States is now willing to promote such central planning, does it not show a shared ambivalence among US and Japanese policymakers about deregulation? Perhaps part of the reason such an abrupt US policy change is under consideration is the US recognition that many Japanese companies have learned very well how to compete effectively in foreign markets and to compete with each other in Japan. Toyota, Nissan, and Honda compete aggressively with each other far more than they cooperate. Nonetheless, some cooperation may facilitate market performance and promote consumer welfare.

This is not the place to belabor the point, but economic competition serves not a single goal but several. The first is economic efficiency in

---

2. At this writing, a coalition of regulators and the regulated are fighting to block abolition of the US Interstate Commerce Commission, which regulates trucking, busing, and railroads in North America.

the marketplace. Another is fairness of business practices. A third is equality of market access. A fourth is the absence, by definition, of inefficient government regulation. There is a spirited dispute in the United States about whether deregulation should include reduced antitrust enforcement. As antitrust becomes more powerful in Japan, the same debate can be expected there, too. A fifth goal of competition is to discourage excessive concentration of economic power in the hands of a few market participants. A sixth is to restrict collaboration among competitors that facilitates collusion. A seventh is to promote consumer sovereignty by encouraging manufacturers to give consumers the products and services they want. An eighth is to lower costs of production and pass the savings on to consumers.

These goals often conflict. That is why, given imperfect knowledge, some advocates of competition may favor a particular joint venture between competitors while others, equally sincere, oppose it. Important segments of Japanese industry have, it would seem, done extremely well in promoting the seventh goal listed above, and the eighth, in highly competitive markets.[3] In a deregulated and open environment, the competitiveness of firms and the presence of competition in the overall market are positively related. But the fact that the Japanese automobile industry competes aggressively in the West is not sufficient to prove that Japan is committed to competition at home. That commitment is not yet broad or deep. The United States, too, departs from the single-minded pursuit of competition in many economic sectors, but that does not mean that US policy is not basically committed to competition.

If absence of market regulation other than antitrust, absence of market access restrictions, and consumer sovereignty are the core competition values, the United States is exceeded only by Hong Kong in its commitment to competition. Nonetheless, the differences between the United States, Europe, and Japan begin to look more like differences in degree than in kind (even if they remain far apart on the continuum) when one parses different specific indicators of the commitment to competition. Competition values are regularly compromised in the United States and Europe, as in Japan and elsewhere, when they conflict with other important values such as national security, jobs, protection of influential competitors, social fairness, the environment, property rights, and investment targeting. At least it becomes possible to compare, measure, and discuss relative performance when it is on the same continuum. The basic economic and political geography of the modern

---

3. With respect to goal number eight, however, the large staffs of many Japanese corporations, in which meritorious performance is not specially rewarded, probably reflect a significant excess cost that has yet to be trimmed. The high cost of Japanese labor will probably change that, although some think lifetime employment will be preserved by many corporations, even at great cost.

nation-state, thanks to the end of the Cold War, has never been more congruent.

In the sixth century, Prince Shotoku, a great Buddhist thinker and leader regarded as one of the greatest influences on the Japanese national character, stressed the importance of peace and harmony rather than competition and rivalry. Until recently, many Japanese industrial leaders advocated a philosophy of "live and let live" among competing enterprises, particularly when markets were stagnant or declining. Adopting this business philosophy, protecting jobs, protecting traditional social institutions, and avoiding the determination of clear winners and losers in the marketplace in bad times are seen as more important than economic efficiency and consumer welfare. This explains the Foodstuffs Control Law, which protects Japanese rice farmers; the Large Scale Retail Stores Law, which protects small food shops from the entry of large supermarkets; and the *keiretsu* relationships between Japanese automobile manufacturers and dealers, under which dealers are given de facto guarantees against bankruptcy in times of slack demand, in return for ceding important controls over their operations to the manufacturers.[4]

Yet even with respect to these traditional ideas the situation is changing fundamentally. It may have been appropriate to require sacrifices of consumers, investors, stockholders, and taxpayers when Japan was recovering from the destruction of World War II. But in an affluent society in which Japanese per capita income is now among the world's highest, such policies are widely recognized to be outmoded. There is no longer any reason for the Japanese public to pay the costs of over-regulation and excessive consumer prices. The Japanese recession of the past three years, which is continuing, and the sharp rise in the value of the yen have accelerated the appeal of more open markets, at least for consumer goods, which are more directly visible to the consuming public than infrastructure goods.

Contrary to popular lore, it is doubtful that lifetime employment is deeply rooted in Japanese tradition, although it did emerge for perhaps a third of the work force during the postwar period. Lifetime employment was immediately embraced as a mechanism for achieving economic and social stability (Chapman 1991, 109-11). The perceived benefits of lifetime employment promote the idea that corporations are worth preserving, even when they suffer economic distress. If corporations have a

---

4. Americans, too, remain ambivalent about the benefits provided by the small business and the family farm. This is reflected in some local efforts to blunt the competitive edge of the highly successful Wal-Mart Stores discount chain, and even to try to keep Wal-Mart out of certain rural areas, in the hope of keeping small businesses, which are believed to anchor town communities, viable. Of course, there is a rich religious and philosophical literature in Western culture, reaching back to Saint Thomas Aquinas, debating the Christian morality, social justice, and social costs of broad deregulation and wholesale adoption of the market mechanism (Maritain 1936; Lindblom 1977).

validity independent of their success in the marketplace, there is a justification for limiting opportunities for corporate takeovers by those who would raise stock values at the expense of jobs. Anticompetitive limitations on market exit result. Cross-ownership of Japanese corporations and suspicion of shareholder democracy are thereby justified.

Sometimes, self-imposed limits on market exit can promote innovation and consumer welfare. Kenichi Ohmae tells a revelatory anecdote about the Yamaha Piano Company (Ohmae 1990, 38-41). Pianos were an industry in decline in Japan: there were no prospects for successful competition with low-cost Korean producers. Yamaha was advised, as most American firms would be in Yamaha's situation, to divest. Instead, Yamaha developed a combination of digital and optical technology that could reproduce, on an electronic piano, notes of 92 different degrees of sound volume and duration. This technology permitted the retrofit of a standard piano into an instrument capable of being played by CD-ROM, reproducing in the home the great musical performances of the most celebrated pianists. The company was restored to health. Without management's commitment to the survival of the enterprise, regardless of its near-term market prospects, this innovation might not have happened.

The US corporate shareholders of a Japanese company recently replaced its Japanese chief executive officer. The new boss was willing to pay higher dividends to shareholders rather than accumulate cash for new investments in this mature industry.[5] Such behavior is shortsighted and selfish by traditional Japanese cultural values, although it may be good business for profit-maximizing investors.

Even on this issue, however, there are opportunities for constructive dialogue between Americans and Japanese. Lifetime employment practices in Japan are eroding at the same time that there is an increased American perception that the US merger wave of the 1980s produced an excessively harsh social and economic dislocation. There is renewed thinking about the desirability of giving US business leaders some insulation from Wall Street's focus on short-term profitability. Many Japanese enterprises have satisfied their shareholders for decades with a combination of double-digit sales growth, a steady trend of reduced costs, and annual profits of about 3 percent. As Japanese growth continues to slow, however, profitability should become more important to investors in Japanese enterprises.

A closer look at those Japanese ideas that are supposedly idiosyncratic and incompatible with competition shows that they are also Western ideas, never entirely abandoned in the West. The quotation from Ruth Benedict cited above expresses some of the anxieties of workers in

---

5. See *New York Times* (17 January 1994, D2), the article that describes the effort by Mobil and Exxon, as joint shareholders of the Tonen Corporation, to replace the president and change basic Tonen corporate policy.

American factories that led to the successful rise of the trade union movement at the beginning of this century. Recent polls of white-collar employees, which show significantly high levels of unhappiness in the American workplace, reveal similar anxieties.

W. Edwards Deming was a successful American management expert before he was discovered by the Japanese in the 1950s—and rediscovered by Americans in the 1970s. According to the Deming management model:

> [T]he fundamental problem of American management is that we are systematically destroying the people who work in the system, both hourly workers and managers alike. Our reward system destroys any possibility of teamwork by incorrectly distinguishing the above average from the below average when the difference is due to chance. . . . [N]o rational person will divulge techniques that lead to superior results in an [competitive] environment of fear. If divulging his methods may lead to someone else getting a higher rating at his expense, he would have to be a fool to cooperate. (quoted in Aguayo 1991, 95)

The Deming model is in partial conflict with the free market model of resource maximization. The tension is suggested by the following Deming maxim:

> End the practice of rewarding business on the basis of price tag. Instead, minimize total cost. Move toward a single supplier for any one item, on a long-term relationship of loyalty and trust. (quoted in Aguayo 1991, 124)

American competition theory suggests that quality is important, but price is important too. Generally, staying with a single supplier for a generation or two has been thought less efficient than encouraging competitive bids among several suppliers, at least from time to time. Deming was no apologist for monopolies: he did favor limiting some types of competition to enhance continuous cost cutting and stimulate innovation in the development of products that would be attractive to consumers. In this aspect of competition, the Japanese became early converts.

Under most versions of Western competition theory until relatively recently, a sole supplier is suspect for its potential to exploit its protected relationship, undisciplined by competition from other suppliers seeking to supplant it. Some US companies, however, such as Boeing and General Motors, have followed Deming's advice, often with success. Ironically, some American enterprises are now asking that US antitrust law be enforced to require Japanese firms to give up long-term sole supplier relationships so that potential new American suppliers can gain market access in Japan. Would Boeing be pleased to be told it had to give up its long-standing long-term supplier policy? We can agree on the need to end Japanese buyer monopolies and to end resistance to buying superior imported nonconsumer goods without imposing unwanted suppliers on firms facing competition. Such a requirement would not be imposed under US antitrust law today.

Some of Deming's ideas have been popularized by the Boston Consulting Group (BCG). Going beyond Deming's management theories, the BCG has encouraged enterprises, as a long-term profit-maximizing strategy, to seek to be number one or number two in market share in concentrated industries with relatively high entry barriers. This strategy appears to have paid off handsomely for some multinationals, including General Electric. This "American-sourced" philosophy, attractive to firms of various national origins—including Japanese firms—does not unreservedly embrace unbridled competition in perfectly open markets. Instead, it looks to practical positioning as a means of employing market power in competitive but still oligopolistic markets. Although it departs from the traditional free market model, it is not fundamentally irreconcilable with it. Oligopoly markets are much to be preferred over cartelized ones. How to improve competition within oligopoly markets is a continuing concern of competition policy and enforcement everywhere in the world.

"Western" Ideas of Competition Reflected in Japanese Law and Policy

The Japanese Anti-Monopoly Law is comparable to the antitrust laws of other developed nations. Of course, as other chapters in this book indicate, national antitrust laws vary and evolve over time with different emphases. Accordingly, comparability does not mean harmonization. Japanese antitrust law proscribes anticompetitive agreements and monopolizing conduct in the forms proscribed by US antitrust law. It is thought in the West that Japanese merger law is almost nonexistent, since there has been no report of a blocked merger for more than 40 years.

Mergers have, however, sometimes been blocked or restructured by administrative guidance, MITI officials report. The Japan Fair Trade Commission (JFTC) has had a set of merger regulations in place since 1980. These have been effective in precluding mergers in relatively concentrated industries where the merging firms have a combined market share of 25 percent or more. According to MITI officials familiar with the process, it has been almost impossible to clear such a merger up to now. Recently, however, we have been advised that some exceptions have been made. Approval, the regulations notwithstanding, has been based on such criteria as the imminent failure of the acquired party—criteria that would apply under US merger doctrine as well.

The prevention of mergers constituting 25 percent of a market is a reasonable and reasonably significant, if rather blunt, restriction against excessive industry concentration. Surprisingly, therefore, it may reflect an even more stringent merger enforcement policy than now exists in the European Union, which still primarily blocks mergers causing the formation of monopolies, but not mergers leading to concentration in oligopoly markets. In Canada, which has a relatively small domestic market and relatively open access to US and other imports, mergers leading to a combined market share of 35 percent are generally permitted. Of course, if, as in Japan, foreign market access is often restricted, a general 25 percent rule may not be sufficiently strict. Merger review should also be made more transparent.

The JFTC has announced revised merger guidelines to bring still greater convergence with Western approaches to merger enforcement. Ironically, these "Westernizing" revised guidelines may actually promote concentration by encouraging efficiency-enhancing mergers, where the merging firms have a greater than 25 percent share of relatively concentrated markets—especially if entry barriers are higher to foreign competition. As a matter of explicit policy, the market access of imports should be made highly relevant to whether the JFTC should permit a more relaxed domestic merger policy. US policymakers should watch to see that this happens. By discouraging mergers in sectors where foreign goods and services are excluded, the JFTC may enhance its power to force resisting "patron" ministries to adopt regulatory reforms promoting market access.

Resale price maintenance (RPM) has generally been prohibited under Japanese law, and the JFTC has frequently taken action against RPM arrangements. Of course, even under US law, merger and RPM enforcement can be selective and lax, as was seen during the Reagan years. However, the Supreme Court of Japan has held RPM to be illegal in principle, and the JFTC has announced plans to further strengthen enforcement against such arrangements.

JFTC enforcement of regulations prohibiting bid rigging has only recently become aggressive. New rules announced by the JFTC in July 1994 clarify that bid rigging by construction companies is illegal. For nearly two decades—since the prosecution of the oil distribution cartel after the OPEC oil shock of 1973—there had been no criminal antitrust enforcement. But in 1993, a year of significantly intensified enforcement by the Justice Ministry, assisted by the JFTC, three criminal antimonopoly convictions were obtained.

The first case involved the successful prosecution of both individuals and enterprises for price fixing of "plastic wrap materials." The second involved rigging by several printing companies of bids tendered to the Social Welfare Agency for peel-off seals used on official documents. The Public Prosecutor's Office brought an indictment under the criminal code—which makes bid rigging a crime—against several individuals. At the recommendation of the JFTC, a bid-rigging indictment was also brought under the Antimonopoly Law against the implicated corporations. Guilty verdicts were returned in both cases. Two individuals received (suspended) jail sentences of 18 and 12 months, and each corporation paid a total of about $200,000 in non-tax-deductible criminal fines and administrative surcharges. In addition, the Social Welfare Agency has brought a civil suit against the criminal defendants under the Government Procurement Law, claiming unjust enrichment. The damages sought are the charges in excess of what "would have been the competitive price." If this suit is successful, the defendants will have faced a JFTC administrative surcharge, civil liability and damages, a permanent injunction, and criminal liability and fines. This is a meaningful enforcement breakthrough.

The chapter by Matsushita in this book indicates that there have been literally thousands of enforcement actions by the JFTC against horizontal price-fixing activity. Although often brought primarily against smaller fish, or against big fish only in small, less economically significant, markets, and until recently usually only calling for an end to the illegal conduct, such enforcement has not been insignificant and has been a meaningful part of Japanese law enforcement for almost 35 years.

In practice, the Antimonopoly Law has not been enforced aggressively against collusion in major industries. It has rarely addressed collusion, through important trade associations or otherwise, among heavy industrial firms or other major Japanese enterprises—especially exporters, importers of key materials, or established, prestigious providers of financial services. Exceptions are the oil cartel cases, the sheet glass case, and a few others. (There have been more than 700 enforcement actions against trade associations in smaller industries, such as the barbers' association.) This omission was properly alluded to in a 1994 speech by Anne Bingaman, US Assistant Attorney General for Antitrust (Bingaman 1994a). She noted (as we did above) that at various points in modern history the Japanese government has tended to use trade associations to further official policy. Such a practice invites at least tacit horizontal collusion and can spill over rather easily into significant overtly collusive agreements.

Access to government regulators means access to standards setters and compliance certifiers. Such access is often dependent on membership in trade associations. Foreign firms frequently find it difficult to gain full membership status and therefore equal access. But these problems are not qualitatively different from those found in other countries, even the United States.[6] The problem is one of determination and

---

6. See, for example, *American Society of Mechanical Engineers v. Hydrolevel Corp.* 456 US 556 (1982), in which the court held a trade association liable for the anticompetitive acts of its agents acting within the scope of their apparent authority, where the agents, acting for several firms in the industry making low-water fuel cutoffs for boilers, used the association's safety standards to foreclose one firm from the market by keeping it from qualifying to sell its distinctive products.

authority to enforce laws and regulations effectively against politically powerful sectarian interests, not failure to understand competition.

The Japanese Antimonopoly Law addresses anticompetitive expansions of monopoly rights conferred by intellectual property laws. For four decades the JFTC's enforcement policy as to the licensing of patents and know-how between foreign and Japanese firms was to protect and promote domestic industries rather than competition. American and European licensors were required to reduce royalties and limit grantbacks and other restrictions on Japanese licensees. Finally, in 1989, after many years of US objections, the JFTC issued a set of formal guidelines covering licensing of patents and know-how. Although not free of continuing national bias, these guidelines are an improvement. They apply to both international and domestic licensing agreements. The Antimonopoly Law has not been actively applied to prevent unreasonable intellectual property rights claims by Japanese firms in Japanese markets to restrict the innovations of competitors. This is an area where reform is needed. However, it is an area where more vigorous antitrust enforcement is needed in the United States as well—something that Assistant Attorney General Bingaman has promised and that the US Department of Justice has begun to deliver (Bingaman 1994b; see also the consent decrees in the *Pilkington* and *Microsoft* cases).

On rare occasions, Japanese antitrust enforcement can be even more aggressive than US enforcement. The first successful private antitrust action before the Osaka High Court was brought by a small independent company providing maintenance service for Toshiba elevators. It challenged the efforts of the manufacturer's service subsidiary, Toshiba Elevator, to monopolize the aftermarket for maintenance of its own equipment by preventing independent elevator repair companies from gaining access to Toshiba elevator parts. Toshiba Elevator defended its behavior on several grounds, including safety and the claim that elevator maintenance was not a separate market from the sale of elevators.

The parties, in their briefs and in their oral arguments, cited a then-recent decision of the US Ninth Circuit Court of Appeals (in *Image Technical Services v. Kodak*). This US lower court case influenced the decision of the Osaka court to reject the defendant's motion to dismiss the complaint. This decision was rendered before the US Supreme Court upheld the Ninth Circuit's decision in the *Kodak* case. The Supreme Court established the US federal precedent that single-brand equipment service aftermarkets may be separate markets open to monopolization and tying restrictions by a single equipment manufacturer. The fact that this and other Japanese courts, as well as the JFTC, are influenced by US antitrust case precedents in applying Japanese law indicates that US and Japanese approaches to competition can be compatible when one gets down to cases.

During the summer of 1994, a Japanese retailer of cosmetics won an important victory in Tokyo District Court to enjoin Kao Toiletries Company from successfully terminating its distribution agreement and ceasing to supply it with cosmetics for resale. The plaintiff had violated a policy embodied in the distribution agreement requiring it to sell Kao Cosmetics only to people to whom the cosmetics could be demonstrated and whose questions could be answered on the spot, with the cosmetics only being sold in the shop. Instead, the retailer sold through a catalog at a substantial discount. For the first time, a Japanese court found that evidence of termination upon discovery of mail-order sales was sufficient to prove RPM and to void the distributor cancellation clause in the contract. The court found that the failure to provide service was a mere pretext to punish price cutting and mail-order sales. This case suggests that Japan may be at the point where private antitrust enforcement has become more aggressive than in most of Europe and Canada.

Two institutional reforms could significantly increase the effectiveness of growing antitrust enforcement in Japan. The first is new legislation to make it substantially easier for private parties to obtain preliminary injunctions in private cases brought in Japanese courts. If a plaintiff can show by a preponderance of the evidence that it is being foreclosed from the Japanese market by private collusive or monopolizing conduct, it should get prompt judicial relief—as is sometimes possible in the United States. Preliminary Japanese antimonopoly injunctions should be made at least as easy to obtain as under US law (such suits are successful about 10 to 20 percent of the time). If foreign firms were given the right to seek such injunctive relief, without having to rely on the slower and less certain administrative processes of the JFTC, a tool for importer self-help could be created. Court injunction decisions should be rendered within one year. The potential benefits of such changes, allowing foreign corporations to win access themselves through the courts without being dependent on administrative bureaucrats, could exceed the benefits of 50 bilateral framework negotiations.

We also suggest that the system of appointment of the five commissioners to the JFTC be reformed. From the commission's inception, the chairman of the JFTC has been appointed (by the prime minister, with consent from both houses of the Diet) from the Ministry of Finance. The Ministry of Justice often has a "reserved" seat on the commission, as do MITI and the Ministry of Foreign Affairs. Although we do not object in principle to the appointment of ex-officials of these ministries, the custom of secured seats for retired bureaucrats is not conducive to an independent JFTC engaged in vigorous enforcement. The Antimonopoly Law states that commissioners should have knowledge of law and economics. Strong, well-qualified, and independent candidates should be sought not primarily from among the "old boys" of the ministries, who may sometimes have conflicting interests, but also from the bar, universities, journalism, and commerce.

In recent years, contrary to popular impression, significant elements within MITI, the government agency "responsible" for most of Japanese industry, have become more competition-oriented. Japanese industry needs access to foreign markets. Insufficient responsiveness to foreign pressures promotes protectionism in foreign markets vital to Japanese exporters. Weak demand for foreign goods and services in Japanese markets helps raise the international value of the yen, making Japanese exports less price competitive. High costs of imported raw materials, high domestic labor costs, and inefficient distribution of resources to plants in Japan make Japanese manufactures too expensive abroad. Japanese plants close and Japanese jobs are lost. This is of major concern to MITI.

In 1992 it was MITI that played a leading role in lobbying the Diet to adopt new legislation increasing penalties under the Antimonopoly Law. MITI officials are well schooled in Western economics, many having done graduate work in economics at American universities. Japanese industrial organization economists in MITI, academia, and the private sector see the successes that opening to market forces and deregulation have promoted in South China and in Hong Kong and Singapore. It is increasingly common to encounter Japanese policy analysts who worry that if Japan fails to deregulate promptly and sweepingly it will jeopardize its position of Asian market leadership.

Because the Ministry of Finance does not at present support competition law enforcement or policy, and the Ministry of Justice is less directly concerned, the JFTC needs a freer rein to implement its mandate. We do not propose that MITI take the place of the Ministry of Finance in having the chairmanship of the JFTC reserved for it. We suggest instead independent designation by the prime minister's office of JFTC commissioners who have a market-oriented philosophy and the willingness to exercise authority. We also emphasize the need for less stereotypical thinking on the part of Western authorities and media in dealing with Japanese institutions such as MITI as they evolve.

Ideas Are Changing in Both Societies

Ichiro Ozawa, the perceived power behind the opposition New Frontier Party, has published a bestseller entitled *Blueprint for a New Japan*. His argument that Japan needs to become more like the rational, individualistic West has not come in for much criticism in Japan. Almost every day brings reports of new consumer-oriented initiatives. A new law, for example, will make it easier to sue for product liability (*New York Times*, 8 March 1993, D2). Companies are springing up to sell used computers at substantial discounts, and they are finding customers looking for bargains and willing to forgo the latest models (*Japan Times*, 4 January 1993, 18). There are reports of price wars and increased introduction of cheaper private brands for food, clothing, and electronic appliances (*Financial Times,* 14 July 1994, 1). Meanwhile editorials call for increasing disclosure in the government's decision-making process (*Japan Times,* 15 December 1992, 20).

One of the themes of this volume is that the American approach to competition law and policy tends to be more absolutist and ideological than the European or the Japanese approach (see, e.g., the chapter by Nicolaides and Rosenthal). For the Japanese, this purported purity and consistency of the US commitment to antitrust and free markets is difficult to understand and accept. Two years ago the Keidanren (the Japanese Federation of Economic Organizations, which speaks for Japanese industry and commerce) was stressing the need for *kyosei.* (*Kyosei* means respecting the values and practices of others while continuing to compete with them aggressively.) The idea was that Japan needed to tone down its aggressiveness and its competitiveness to avoid trade warfare.

Akio Morita, before his recent illness, gave several speeches expressing his shock at the hostility others felt toward what they considered high-handed Japanese business practices (Morita 1992). As a member of Keidanren (the Japanese Federation of Economic Organizations), Morita visited Germany, Belgium, the Netherlands, and the United Kingdom in November 1991. What observers in the West see as coordinated foreclosure of Western products from Japanese markets, Morita and others in Japan see as Japanese excellence (resulting primarily from superiority in engineering) and Japanese producers' greater attention to customer preferences (another form of consumer welfare) winning out competitively in the Japanese marketplace.

When they hear Westerners talk about the need for greater commitment to competition in Japanese economic life, Morita and other Keidanren officials have wondered if this isn't really a complaint that the Japanese have been too successful as competitors, flooding the West with Japanese cars not by dumping them at cut-rate prices, but by producing a superior product at a lower price and being satisfied with lower profits. There is room for debate here. Japan is more closed than many Japanese like to admit. But it is also true that many in the United States fear Japanese competition and want the protection of unbalanced trade laws to restrict it.

For example, some Americans are having second thoughts about the appropriate level of openness to innovation in computer technology. In the past, many Silicon Valley entrepreneurs have been confident in Americans' ability to be world leaders in technological innovation, especially in computer software. As a consequence they have not favored reading intellectual property rights in software patents and copyrights so broadly that competitors were unable to get royalty-free access to their computer codes, especially interface codes. With such access, innovators have often been able to invent around or build upon existing technology to further technological progress.

Recent US policy reflects a loss of this self-confidence. For example, a recent effort by the US government was successful in pressuring Japan into retaining certain restrictive provisions in its existing copyright law. Japanese reformers seeking to promote innovation in the design of computer software had sought to permit competitors to engage in reverse engineering to produce separate, new competing products:

> Many leading American computer and software companies—including Apple, IBM and Microsoft—say . . . that such a change would help the Japanese catch up to American software companies. Washington has adopted this position and has said it views the possible change with "gravest concern."
>
> But another group of companies, led by Sun Microsystems, [has] testified . . . that a revision of law would spur innovation and competition and make it easier for different programs and computers to work together. (*New York Times*, 15 December 1993, D12)

US law on this subject is in flux. However, there are indications that the balance between encouragement of innovation and expression and enforcing intellectual property rights broadly is shifting back toward innovation—not least in the field of computer software copyright. We may thus be asking the Japanese to keep in place a more protectionist domestic law than many courts will now be enforcing in the United States.[7]

Such policy disputes, as well as the numerous ways in which the United States protects certain favored domestic interests in the US market, lead many friendly Japanese to wonder whether the United States is really all that serious about making competition paramount. Some seem sincerely to believe that the US policy of pushing Japan to be more open and market-oriented is transitory, and that the US commitment to strong antitrust enforcement will recede, as it did in the Reagan years.

The dramatic political changes in Japan over the last year and a half have reopened to debate within Keidanren issues of competition and competitiveness, industrial policy, and deregulation. Keidanren is now more committed to (and more outspoken in promoting) deregulation as economically beneficial to Japan, not just as politically expedient. However, some members still disbelieve in deregulation as a spur to economic recovery, notwithstanding the supporting empirical evidence in Europe, China, and elsewhere. Resistance to major market penetration from abroad is not surprising in a period of serious recession.

One of the ironies of US policy focusing so doggedly on getting the

---

7. See *Sony Corp. of America v. Universal City Studios, Inc.* 464 US 417 (1984); *Lotus Development Corp. v. Borland Intern. Inc.* 49 F.3d. 807 (1st Cir. 1995), cert. granted, 64 U.S.L.W. 3199 (27 September 1995) (No. 94-2003); *Sega Enterprises Ltd. v. Accolade, Inc.* 977 F2d 1510 (9th Cir., 1992); and *Atari Games Corp. v. Nintendo of America, Inc.*, 975 F2d 832 (Fed Cir., 1992); but see, contra, *Advanced Computer Systems, Inc. v. MAI Systems Corp.* 845 FSupp 356 (E.D. Va. 1994).

Japanese to accept American ideas of competition is that, if it works, others may benefit more than American exporters. Asia now surpasses the United States as Japan's largest export target. In 1993 Japan's trade surplus with Asia exceeded for the first time its trade surplus with the United States. Nonetheless, Japan is a net importer of color televisions, home appliances, and cars, many of them made by Asian transplants of Japanese enterprises. As market access increases in Japan over the next decade, it may well be the Asian exporters who are the primary beneficiaries (*Financial Times*, 15 July 1994, 13). Deregulation may also make Japanese industry even more competitive. If that happens, it will test the Western commitment to competition.

Establishing a successful dialogue between the United States and Japan requires greater constancy and consistency from both sides. To be more effective in persuading Japan that Westerners want more-competitive Japanese markets, the United States and Europe must continue to strengthen their own competition policies and law enforcement. Western neomercantilism understandably undercuts Western credibility in Japan.

Japan has been critical of threatened unilateral extraterritorial US antitrust enforcement, which could be applied against Japanese enterprises in Japan. Since the Sherman Act was passed in 1890 there have been about 40 cases in which US antitrust law has been applied to stop conspiracies or monopolizing conduct foreclosing US exporters from foreign markets. We do not see this enforcement as a serious threat to Japan. US antitrust laws (unlike the restrictive trade laws of the United States and other World Trade Organization member states) seek to promote market access and competition. Antitrust disputes are resolved employing substantially fairer legal safeguards than trade law disputes. For example, Japanese companies have won the two biggest private international antitrust suits so far brought against them in US courts.[8] One was the result of a verdict by a lay jury in Arizona. To the extent Japan develops a strong and responsible domestic antitrust enforcement regime, extraterritorial US enforcement becomes less necessary and less likely. That should be a further incentive to the Japanese government to accelerate the strengthening of Japanese antitrust enforcement. In any event, too much antitrust enforcement by governments is not a problem anywhere in the world today (see chapter by Rosenthal and Nicolaides).

US Policy and Competition in Japan

To promote competition in Japan, the United States must continue to promote competition and open access in the United States. US trade

---

8. See *Matsushita Elec. Indus. Co. Ltd. v. Zenith Radio Corp.* 475 US 574 (1986) and *Go-Video Inc. v. Akai Elec. Co., Ltd.* 885 F2d 1406 (9th Cir., 1989).

policy should not undermine antitrust enforcement in the United States or Japan. Early in 1994 it was reported that a high official of the US Commerce Department had met

> individually with the heads of the major Japanese automobile producers in the U.S.—Honda, Toyota and Nissan. Industry sources said that [the official] was seeking some assurance from the transplant companies that they could meet the targets for increased parts purchases that the U.S. is proposing in the framework negotiations.

> The U.S. is asking for a Japanese commitment that purchases of U.S.-made parts by Japanese companies will continue to grow at the 1990–94 rate, a figure somewhere between 20 and 30 percent. In addition, the Administration is seeking a commitment by the transplants to increase their domestic content level in U.S.-produced vehicles to that of the Big Three automakers. (*Inside U.S. Trade,* 4 February 1994, 12)

If this report is accurate, the US official may have been attempting to organize a hub-and-spoke quantity-allocation antitrust conspiracy, with himself at the hub. An automobile manufacturer cannot agree with a US government official or, indirectly through that official or the press, with its competitors, to buy fewer parts from Japanese national suppliers and more from American national suppliers. This not only could be a criminal violation of US antitrust law, but could also give Japanese auto parts manufacturers transplanted to the United States, as well as their counterparts located exclusively in Japan, a potential private treble-damage antitrust claim. There would also be potential exposure to lawsuits under state antitrust laws, such as California's, if these pressured purchases resulted in higher retail prices of Japanese cars to US car buyers. Under the law in these states, indirect purchasers have standing to sue. Although the US official might not be held personally liable, if these were the facts, the official could not immunize the three Japanese automobile manufacturers.[9]

In mid-1995, it was announced that the United States and Japan had narrowly avoided a trade war over the sale of US automobiles in Japan and US auto parts in both Japan and the United States. Our assessment of early evaluations of the settlement is that it may not hold over time, as it is not clear that the two sides are in accord about the specifics of the Japanese commitment. It remains to be seen whether this agreement will promote competition and deregulated markets in either the United States or Japan.

Many have criticized the numerical quotas demanded by US trade officials to promote and measure market access in Japan. If the goal is to

---

9. See *Consumers Union v. Kissinger,* as discussed in American Bar Association (1992, 911-12).

promote deregulation in Japan, one should not demand that Japanese bureaucrats meet numerical quotas. The virtually inevitable response of any bureaucracy in any culture to such a demand, if acceded to, would be to establish market allocation cartels and disrupt free markets. That lesson should have been learned at the end of the American occupation of Japan. Some officials in prior US administrations may have failed to grasp this as well. In 1986 the United States and Japan struck what became implemented as a de facto cartel agreement in semiconductors. It is widely believed that, during the Bush administration, a secret addendum to the Semiconductor Trade Agreement, still in effect, was reached between US and Japanese officials to raise foreign semiconductor exports to Japan to a goal of 20 percent of the Japanese market (*Washington Post*, 7 March 1989, C1). This was intended to be the measure of competitive success.

Apparent Japanese acceptance of this informal numerical target may well have emboldened trade officials in the Clinton administration to try to expand this arrangement, formally, to several other sectors. Japan should never have been pressured to accept numerical targets as goals for the private sector. Such targets may be appropriate for public sector procurement, or in other cases where the buyer is a monopsonist. They should not, however, be more than one crude indicator of performance in open markets. Only a free market can determine what an appropriate competitive market share should be.

According to a recent anecdote, a senior official of the Office of the US Trade Representative was approached by a senior Japanese official seeking to break the US-Japan trade policy deadlock. The Japanese official reportedly asked, "What five reforms from your list of 100 do you need absolutely? As we have done before, I can give you these to avoid a deadlock." The US official is said to have replied, "I need all 100—anything less will not do." Although this story has been used to illustrate the naïveté and impracticality of the US negotiating position, it may illustrate even better a failure on the part of the unnamed Japanese official. If the story is true, the US official was wrong to focus just on targets for Japanese government intervention, whatever the number was, but the Japanese official should not have been trying to conduct "diplomacy as usual." How much Americans sell in Japan should depend primarily upon the free operation of Japanese markets—not the free operation of bureaucrats. The old way of negotiating will not do. True deregulation and market access must be extensive. The US and Japanese governments should be focusing on what they can do to remove government and private restraints to market access—not on regulating that market to greater American advantage.

It is currently suspected in the West that threats of vertical boycotts by Japanese manufacturers who do not want wholesalers or retail chains to stock more foreign imports are having much greater effect in limiting market access than MITI concedes. So far the JFTC has not been energetic in investigating these charges or in taking effective action where confirming evidence is found. Meaningful improvement in enforcement to address these suspicions is preferable to setting quotas for foreign import purchases by Japanese distributors.

To the extent that a greater push is required to overcome Japanese consumers' suspicion of foreign goods, some import subsidies might be considered. Why not a discount for certain categories of foreign imports, paid for by the Japanese government, for example? Of course this would be a competition "tax" on Japanese domestic firms, but perhaps it is a fair trade-off to promote market access. New entry into Japanese markets is difficult for many reasons. The high cost of land limits the establishment of a network of distribution outlets in Japan. One way of promoting market access would be for the Japanese government, perhaps through the Japan Export-Import Bank or the Japan Development Bank, and the US government, perhaps through the US Export-Import Bank, to lend funds to US automobile manufacturers and others to buy land in Japan for distribution outlets, or to build factories.[10]

Another possibility is to reduce the tying up of blocks of shareholdings in public companies by private agreement so that foreign acquisition of significant stock interests in major Japanese companies becomes easier. This is a problem in the European Union as well, except in England and France.

The encouragement of more dispersed shareholdings, including to foreigners, would be complemented by greater accountability of corporate officials to shareholders generally. Japanese law gives shareholders the right to sue their company's directors for wasting corporate assets through illegal activities. The law provides for both damages and injunctive relief. On 20 July 1994, a group of shareholders of Kajima, a large construction company, filed such a suit, alleging among other things that the firm had paid illegal bribes to government officials and participated in anticompetitive bid-rigging schemes. Effective enforcement of this law would make it more difficult for directors of Japanese companies to engage in illegal activities such as price-fixing.

If the law were strengthened to impose potential liability on the directors of companies victimized by the price-fixing of others, for failing to sue to recover private antitrust damages owed to their companies, private antitrust enforcement would be significantly enhanced. It was

---

10. After the last paragraph was drafted, it was reported that the Japan Export-Import Bank will lend $300 million to the Big Three US automakers, at a rate of interest below prime (4.4 percent), to produce right-hand-drive cars outside of Japan to sell in the Japanese market. (*Wall Street Journal*, 27 July 1994, A13). It was also reported the same day in the *Nihon Keizai Shibun* that the Japan Development Bank had in the past loaned money to these same companies to build facilities in Japan to facilitate auto parts imports.

the threat of exposure to this liability that led the directors of US electrical utilities to sue General Electric and Westinghouse for damages resulting from their purchases from an electrical turbine and generator cartel prosecuted by the Justice Department in the 1950s.

To the extent that market access is viewed as a problem of microeconomic policy—and to some degree it is—the United States should continue to focus attention on specifically identified structural impediments. Past pressure to redress specific market access barriers, private and governmental, and to modify noncollusive traditional social practices, has made and can continue to make a difference. The difference will be greater, however, if the Japanese government speeds up the dispute resolution process.

The US government should also focus particular attention on helping to promote and monitor nascent Japanese deregulation initiatives. The American deregulatory experience is the most extensive in the world. Some Japanese policymakers will welcome constructive US assistance toward reform. But that US policy assistance should promote deregulation, transparency, and the operation of the market mechanism, not protectionist quotas or other neomercantile bargains designed merely to address the current account imbalance. Instead of criticizing the Structural Impediments Initiative of the Bush administration as misguided, the Clinton administration should devote substantially more resources and more continuous effort to push for specific, targeted regulatory reforms.

It will also help to improve trade relations with Japan if Americans can improve resolution of serious disagreements about what exceptions to the market mechanism are necessary in US society and how they should be adopted, monitored, and limited. The debate between free trade and protectionism, and between deregulation and industrial policy, is an important ongoing debate within both nations, as much as it is a bilateral and multilateral debate. Japanese protectionists and free traders need to participate in this debate. This requires a US policy of engagement, not rejection.

Conclusion

The focus of this chapter has been both more fundamental and less ambitious than merely to offer yet another critique of US and Japanese bilateral trade policy. Nonetheless, it is important to identify what practical steps could be taken now to further competition goals in the bilateral relationship.

We have identified several reform proposals for Japanese competition law and policy. Among these are the following: make competition policy a domestic Japanese political issue, promote massive deregulation, promote private antitrust self-help litigation through reform of Japanese laws and elimination of judicial delay, have the prime minister's office appoint an aggressive and independent JFTC, and design government-induced incentives to attract foreign investment and imports.

We have also proposed a greater commitment on the part of US government officials to more open US markets, and less restrictive US intellectual property and industrial policy laws—the United States cannot expect to succeed by asking the Japanese to do as it says, and not as it does. We encourage both governments to assign more personnel to the intergovernmental effort to monitor, publicize, and negotiate for more sweeping and meaningful deregulation of Japanese markets and the removal of nontariff barriers.

As Rosenthal and Nicolaides indicate elsewhere in this volume, we think that antitrust enforcers should play a larger role in forming and implementing US and Japanese international economic policy, at least on issues involving trade-offs between competition and such noncompetition goals as enhancing intellectual property rights, protecting jobs, national security interests, and so-called essential forms of continuing government regulation. Reciprocally, trade and commerce officials' views on necessary policy trade-offs that reduce competition must be discussed more openly both in Japan and the United States. US extraterritorial antitrust enforcement against egregious private exclusionary conduct in Japan is preferable to restrictive trade law enforcement, especially unilateral section 301 actions, which are of doubtful legality under international law. Legal standards that we would not impose in the United States under US law should not be imposed on Japanese society because of "national systemic differences." However, competition and consumer welfare cannot and should not always be the overriding policy goal imposed by law on a democratic polity. Choices between competition and protection should be matters of political choice, within Japan, within the United States, and in the US-Japan relationship.

Japanese nationalists may be unhappy at the idea, but it is nonetheless true that the major changes in Japan toward greater competition have been achieved through foreign pressure (*gaiatsu*). It was true in the case of the Meiji Restoration, which created the modern Japanese state, and of the major reforms that followed World War II, including the enactment of the Antimonopoly Law. The Japanese people should admit that every time the United States "bashes" Japan, the Japanese economic system is improved. This points to some defect in the political process in Japan that renders the Japanese legislature unable to initiate major policy changes when these call for sacrifice. This is regrettable. However, the Japanese should acknowledge that trade pressures from the United States have been instrumental in reforming their society in a way that has lessened incompatibility between the United States and Japan.

For two decades Americans have rightfully chided the Japanese for their persistent feelings of victimization, which are wholly inconsistent with Japan's true role as an international economic power. Within the past few years, however, the Japanese people have shown a readiness, finally, to go beyond this traditional defensive attitude. They are seeking a new level of democratic and consumer-oriented self-confidence. This is not the time for the United States and Europe to overreact by themselves assuming the role of defensive, insecure victim. Japan, Inc., is not systematically victimizing the West, any more than the West has victimized Japan over the past 50 years.

Before the pessimists among us conclude, as have Prestowitz, van Wolferen, and Ishihara, that Western and Japanese ideas of capitalism and competition are incompatible, we need to try more persistently to make a renewed commitment both to competition and to transparency and temporal limits when anticompetitive compromises are negotiated, both in the West and in Japan.

We have tried to show that Japanese and Westerners are indeed "reading from the same page." Although that does not assure that the rate of growth of competition in Japan will be swift, it does mean that the timing, pace, scope, and specifics can be joined constructively as both domestic and international policy issues.

References

Aguayo, Rafael. 1991. *Dr. Deming: The American Who Taught the Japanese About Quality.* New York: Simon & Schuster.

American Bar Association. 1992. *Antitrust Law Developments (Third),* vol. II. Chicago: Section of Antitrust Law, American Bar Association.

Benedict, Ruth. 1946. *The Chrysanthemum and the Sword.* Boston: Houghton Mifflin.

Bingaman, Anne. 1994a. "The Role of Antitrust in International Trade." Speech to the Japan Society, New York, 3 March.

Bingaman, Anne. 1994b. "The Role of Antitrust in Intellectual Property." Speech before the Federal Circuit Judicial Conference, Washington, 16 June.

Chapman, William. 1991. *Inventing Japan: An Unconventional Account of the Postwar Years.* New York: Prentice Hall.

Ishihara, Shintaro. 1989. *The Japan That Can Say "No."* New York: Simon & Schuster.

Komiya, Ryutaro. 1990. *The Japanese Economy: Trade, Industry, and Government.* Tokyo: University of Tokyo Press. Reprinted in F. M. Scherer.

Scherer, Frederic M., ed. 1993. *Monopoly and Competition Policy,* vol. 1. Brookfield, VT: E. Elgar.

Lindblom, Charles E. 1977. *Politics and Markets.* New York: Basic Books.

Maritain, Jacques. 1936. *Integral Humanism.* New York: Scribner.

Morita, Akio. 1992. "A New Management Philosophy." *Bungei Shunju,* 10 January. Translation.

Niino, Kojiro. 1993. "The Logic of Excessive Competition—With Reference to the Japanese Interfirm Competition." Reprinted in F. M. Scherer, *Monopoly and Competition Policy,* vol. 1. Brookfield, VT: E. Elgar.

Ohmae, Kenichi. 1990. *The Borderless World*. New York: Harper Collins.

Ozawa, Ichiro. 1994. *Blueprint for a New Japan: The Rethinking of a Nation*. Tokyo: Kodansha International.

Reed, Donald. 1993. "A New Generation of Vehicles: Government Action." *Automotive Engineering* 101, no. 12 (December): 25.

Prestowitz, Clyde V. Jr. 1988. *Trading Places: How We Allowed Japan to Take the Lead*. New York: Basic Books.

Prestowitz, Clyde V. Jr. 1994. *Shrinking the Atlantic: Europe and the American Economy*. Washington: Economic Strategy Institute.

10

US and EU Competition Law: A Comparison

ELEANOR M. FOX

On the surface, there appears to be much in common between competition law in the United States and competition law in the European Union. Article 85 of the Treaty of Rome,[1] which prohibits agreements that distort competition and, accordingly, agreements that fix prices, is roughly comparable to section 1 of the US Sherman Act (*US Code*, Vol. 15), which prohibits agreements in restraint of trade. Article 86 prohibits abuse of a dominant position and seems roughly comparable to section 2 of the Sherman Act, which prohibits monopolization and attempts or combinations to monopolize.

US and EC competition systems also have common objectives. Both seek to advance the interests of consumers and protect the free flow of goods in a competitive economy. Both seek to protect competitors' access to markets and protect to some extent consumer freedom of choice and seller freedom from coercion.

The respective competitive systems of the two areas have developed, however, out of different histories and different concerns, and upon closer examination, significant variations in law, policy, and enforcement become apparent.

Eleanor M. Fox is Walter Derenberg Professor of Trade Regulation at the New York University School of Law. The author thanks Robert Pitofsky for his helpful comments on an earlier draft of this chapter.

1. This is the treaty establishing the European Economic Community, 25 March 1957, Article 85. The Treaty on European Union (or, the Maastricht Treaty), adopted in 1993, did not alter the competition provisions in the Treaty of Rome.

Goals of Competition Policy

US competition policy derives from statutes enacted at different times in US history, and therefore the goals of these statutes are not identical. Overall, US antitrust policy is primarily designed to protect consumer welfare (i.e., produce a variety of products at reasonable prices), with modest elements of fairness (right of firms to be free of coercion) and of hostility to vast concentrations of economic power. Through much of its history, US enforcement agencies and courts were not very sensitive to claims of efficiency; they assumed that a robust competitive market would automatically be efficient. However, many contemporary commentators believe that efficiency claims are likely to be given more weight in the future.

Sophisticated economic analysis is a centerpiece of American antitrust enforcement. "Industrial policy," defined here as overt efforts to strengthen domestic firms to serve goals other than competition and efficiency, such as successfully competing in global markets, has not had much influence on US antitrust law. Occasionally, industrial policy concerns such as promoting research and development influence competition rules, but those concerns rarely trump antitrust policy entirely. Fundamentally, competition has been the industrial policy of the United States.

In the European Union,[2] economic integration of the various member nations is a dominant objective of competition policy. The common market evolved from the perceived need to break down trade barriers between Western European nations, and Community policy therefore reflects as a cardinal principle the desirability of free movement of goods and people across member state lines. By contrast, the free movement of goods in the United States was achieved through a sympathetic interpretation of the commerce clause provisions of the US Constitution that effectively demolished local or regional preferences and state barriers.

While economics has a role in EU analysis, it is much less center stage than in the United States. The European Union is concerned about competitive opportunities for small and medium-size firms, raising the economic level of worse-off nations, and general notions of "fairness." There is also a sense in the European Union that joint ventures, mergers, and other collaborations may be necessary to enhance technological development and therefore to allow European firms to compete effectively in global markets. Article 85(3) of the EC Rome treaty embodies these notions, providing that otherwise void agreements or combinations may be exempted where they "contribute to improving the production or distribution of goods or to promoting technical or economic

---

2. The Maastricht Treaty created the European Union (EU). The European Economic Community, now called the European Community (EC), is a constituent part of the European Union. The competition law remains in the EC Treaty of Rome.

progress . . ." as long as consumers enjoy a fair share of resulting benefits. While hard to judge, the language of the EC Rome treaty and EU enforcement policy seems to accept a larger element of "industrial policy" and of "fairness" than is accepted in the United States.

Systems of Enforcement

US enforcement of competition policy is both complicated and litigation-oriented. The statutes are in most cases concise, and the law has been made through judicial interpretation during a century of litigation. Opportunities for the federal government to make law or adjust policy by edict or guidelines are limited.

Complications in American competition policy derive from the fact that there are so many sources of enforcement and regulation. At the federal level, two agencies, the Antitrust Division of the Department of Justice and the Federal Trade Commission (FTC), have roughly coextensive jurisdiction, though the FTC has no criminal enforcement authority and the two agencies' policies are not always congruent. States and private parties injured in their business and property also have access to the courts, and they frequently bring cases that go beyond or are flagrantly inconsistent with prevailing federal policy. Finally, competition policy is sometimes influenced by protectionist efforts of the Department of Commerce and the International Trade Commission, and regulations and subsidies emerge from a broad variety of departments and agencies (for example, the Department of Defense with respect to the defense industry and the Federal Communications Commission with respect to telecommunications).

Enforcement in the European Union is far more regulatory and bureaucratic. Much regulation is based on a system of notification and approval by negative clearance, individual exemption, or block exemption. Block exemptions exist for the most common types of contracts—for example, distribution contracts—and companies seek the advantages of the block exemption by molding their transactions to fit its rigid structure, which lists the clauses that are permissible and those that are not.

In many areas of law—merger enforcement is a notable example—the substantive standard contained in the relevant EU regulation may be similar to the standard of US statutes and guidelines, but enforcement in the European Union to date has been more lenient.

Enforcement against Cartel Behavior

US and EU law and enforcement attitudes are probably most similar in their hostility to price-fixing, market division, bid rotation, and other forms of hard-core cartel behavior.

In the United States, price-fixing and related behavior is treated as illegal per se, which means that practices such as price-fixing violate the law regardless of the market power of the participants, their motives, or purported business justifications.[3]

The assertion that price-fixing and related cartel behavior is treated with exceptional severity under American antitrust law is subject to a qualification. When the effect on price is indirect and the practices being challenged can contribute to efficiency (for example, through integration of resources), courts will take a "quick look" to determine whether the strict per se rule, as opposed to a more lenient rule of reason, should apply.[4] The contours of this vague exception remain under consideration by the US Supreme Court, but in any event the US approach is not likely to undermine overall stringent treatment of hard-core cartels. Price-fixing and related practices often result in criminal penalties in the United States, and fines and damages to injured parties can be enormous.

The EU law against cartels is similar to US law. Cartels in the Community are covered by Article 85(1), which deals with market sharing, price-fixing and related practices. There are several EC exemptions that do not apply in US law. For example, there is some limited room for an exemption for crisis cartels (i.e., rationalization cartels in which there is chronic industry overcapacity) if the industry adheres to very strict conditions.[5] Also, small and middle-size firms may enter into specialization agreements, agreeing to specialize in certain product markets and stay out of the markets of one another.[6] Finally, collaboration among European firms is subject to a *de minimis* exception not present in US law.[7]

The major difference between US and EU cartel enforcement is in levels and quality of enforcement. Price-fixing and other cartel behavior usually fall within the province of the US Department of Justice and are commonly treated with criminal sanctions. A substantial staff in the Justice Department's Washington office, as well as in regional offices in several major cities, is primarily devoted to detecting and challenging cartels.

The EC staff for cartel enforcement is very thin. There is no investigative staff and, as a result, cartels are normally uncovered, if at all, by complaint. In many parts of Europe, cartels were a customary way of life before the Treaty of Rome was adopted, and there is a serious ques-

---

3. The leading American case is *United States v. Socony-Vacuum Oil Co.* (310 U.S. 150, 1940).

4. Two cases exemplifying the approach are *Broadcast Music Inc. v. Columbia Broadcasting System* (441 U.S. 1, 1979) and *Northwest Wholesale Stationers, Inc. v. Pacific Stationery & Printing Co.* (472 U.S. 284, 1985).

5. See Synthetic fibers (Commission Decision 84/380, O. J. L. 207/17).

6. See Fine papers (Commission Decision 72/291, O. J. L. 182/24).

7. Regarding the *de minimis* exception, see *Volk v. Vervaecke* (case 5/69, 1969, ECR 295).

tion concerning whether EC law (which has no criminal component) and EC enforcement have reduced the level of secret cartels significantly.

Dominant Firm Behavior

Restrictions on business behavior designed either to achieve or maintain dominant power is an important element of competition policy in both the United States and the European Union. On closer examination, however, the definition of what constitutes a dominant firm and the types of conduct that constitute violations of law differ in the two jurisdictions.

While the controlling US statute is silent on the point and case law somewhat ambiguous, leading US cases appear to treat firms as holding monopoly power only if they control about two-thirds or more of a relevant market.[8] Moreover, market power (even monopoly power) alone is not enough to violate American statutes; there must be an element of unacceptable conduct to achieve or maintain that position.

US law on the question of monopolizing behavior has changed markedly over the years. In early cases such as *United States v. Aluminum Co. of America* (148 F.2d 416, 2d Cir., 1945) and *United States v. Griffith* (334 U.S. 100, 1948), it appeared that virtually any conduct that had an exclusionary effect on actual or potential competitors would violate the statute—unless it could be defended, in the words of the *Alcoa* decision, as an example of "superior skill, foresight, and industry." In recent years, American courts have backed away from such a stringent approach and generally allow firms to achieve or defend their legally acquired monopoly position through aggressive competitive behavior.[9] Examples of conduct that go beyond acceptable behavior include "predatory" pricing (i.e., below-cost pricing en route to greater power), acquisition of direct rivals, long-term lease arrangements with penalty clauses if the customer switches to a challenger of the monopolist, and refusals to deal for no business purpose other than to injure a competitor.

In the European Union, Article 86 declares illegal "any abuse . . . of a dominant position within the Common Market" and goes on to indicate examples of dominant-firm abuse. The founders of the Community did not oppose bigness. Rather, they believed that European firms were often below optimum scale and therefore not large enough to achieve

---

8. Companies with only 30 or 40 percent of a market may "attempt to monopolize," but conduct must be plainly anticompetitive and lacking in business justification to be deemed a violation, and it must predictably produce monopoly if allowed to continue to operate. For example, see *Spectrum Sports, Inc. v. McQuillan* (506 U.S. 447, 1993) and Turner (1975).

9. See, for example, *Telex Corp. v. IBM* (367 F. Supp. 258, N.D. Okla. 1973, *rev. per curiam* 510 F.2d 894, 10th Cir., *cert. dismissed*, 423 U.S. 802, 1975).

maximum efficiency or to compete with foreign-based multinationals, particularly those based in the United States. Therefore, the initial conception was to regulate power rather than to prevent its acquisition (Joliet 1970).

According to *Hoffman-La Roche v. Commission* (case 85/76, 1976, ECR 461, para. 38), a dominant firm under EU law is one that has the power "to behave to an appreciable extent independently of its competitors, its customers, and ultimately of the consumers." A 40 percent market share, in the presence of significant barriers to entry, can constitute dominance, and a firm with 50 percent of a market or more is presumed to have dominance (*AKZO Chemie BV v. Commission*, case C-62/86, 1991 ECR I-3359)—a level substantially below the point that "monopolization" restrictions begin to apply in the United States.

Article 86 itself lists some examples of dominant-firm abuse, including the imposition of unfair purchase or sales prices, limits to production, application of dissimilar conditions to equivalent transactions, and extraction of supplementary obligations from customers that are not connected with the subject of the transaction.

In several respects, the conduct declared illegal under Article 86 would probably be legal if a US firm with monopoly power engaged in it. For example, a firm that legally acquires a monopoly position can sell at any price it chooses under US law and can intentionally limit production in order to drive up the price. That is so because US law is not regulatory (in the sense of direct regulation of price and output) but rather concentrates on preserving conditions, whereby free-market forces can constrain price and can induce optimal production.

EC case law demonstrates that conduct constituting "abuse" ranges beyond the four examples in Article 86. A dominant firm has broad duties to deal and may offend the law by not serving all demand.[10] In other respects, standards of conduct may appear similar to those in the United States—for example, abusing a dominant position through predatory pricing or discrimination in price is illegal, but EC law has far looser standards for proof of either offense.[11]

Dominant firms may escape what otherwise might otherwise be a violation of Article 86 by "objective justification" of their practices—e.g., that the conduct was important to serve the market (Gyselen 1989, 616, n. 49).

---

10. Höfner and Elser/Macrotron (case C-41/90, 1991 ECR I-1979). See also *Radio Telefis Eireann v. Commission* (cases C-241/91 P and C-242/91 P, 1995 ECR I-743) concerning the duty to license intellectual property when necessary to create a new product that consumers demand.

11. Compare *AKZO Chemie BV v. Commission* (case C-62/86, 1991 ECR I-3359) with *Brooke Group v. Brown & Williamson Tobacco* (509 U.S. 209, 1993).

Vertical Contractual Arrangements

US and EU differences of approach to antitrust regulation of contractual arrangements between suppliers, distributors, and customers reflect significant differences in competing policy considerations and in balancing goals of competition policy against goals of enforcement.

In the United States 20 or 30 years ago, regulation of a wide range of distribution arrangements was fairly restrictive of private firms' conduct. Not only were maximum and minimum resale price maintenance agreements declared illegal per se,[12] but stringent rules applied as well to division of customers and territories among distributors,[13] exclusive dealing contracts,[14] and tie-in sales.[15] At least in part, these older rules reflected a concern for the preservation of fair opportunities for distributors to compete and to act independently of their suppliers. Distributors' freedom—viewed as freedom to respond to the market—was assumed to be consistent with consumers' interests.

In the 1980s, a "minimalist" school of US antitrust took the very different position that almost all vertical restraints were procompetitive. The animating notion appeared to be that such restraints were likely to prevent free riding on investments and services of full price distributors and, in any event, interbrand competition among rivals would adequately police any intrabrand restrictions applied. This minimalist approach was controversial, and in its extreme form is unlikely to prevail.

The most stable rule regulating vertical contractual arrangements in the United States declares agreements to set minimum resale prices illegal per se. There has been criticism of the rule in scholarship and some roundabout erosion by increasing the plaintiff's burden of demonstrating an "agreement" between a supplier and its customers and narrowing the cateogry of resale price agreements.[16] Nevertheless, there is strong congressional support for a rule against minimum vertical price-fixing (largely viewed as manufacturers' techniques for limiting the aggressive competitive activities of discounters) and no indication that the US Supreme Court will back away from its position that such activity is illegal per se.

---

12. See *Dr. Miles Medical Co. v. John D. Park & Sons Co.* (220 U.S. 373, 1911) regarding minimum price-fixing and *Albrecht v. Herald Co.* (390 U.S. 145, 1968) regarding maximum price-fixing.

13. *United States v. Arnold, Schwinn & Co.* (388 U.S. 365, 1967, *overruled*) and *Continental T. V. Inc. v. GTE Sylvania, Inc.* (433 U.S. 36, 1977).

14. *Standard Oil Co. of California v. United States* (337 U.S. 293, 1949).

15. *Northern Pacific Railway v. United States* (356 U.S. 1, 1958).

16. A good example is *Business Electronics Group Corp. v. Sharp Electronics Corp.* (485 U.S. 717, 1988).

A comparable rule of *per se* illegality for vertical customer and territorial allocation has been abandoned (*Continental TV, Inc. v. GTE Sylvania, Inc.*, 433 U.S. 36, 1977). Conservative economic analysis has successfully made the case that such restrictions are often designed to protect the investment of distributors against free-riding challengers who make no comparable investment. As a result, US courts will not entertain a challenge to vertical territorial and customer allocation unless the manufacturer accounts for a very large portion of the market—probably at least 30 or 40 percent—and some courts may require a further showing that the other major competitors followed a similar plan and the effect was to facilitate producer cooperation. Therefore, few challenges to such arrangements have been successful in the last decade. Similarly, exclusive dealing contracts (providing that the supplier will not set up a second distribution outlet in a defined area) are treated under a lenient rule of reason and seldom successfully challenged.

Restrictions on tie-in sales in the United States have waxed and waned. In the 1950s and 1960s, the law was interpreted stringently against arrangements to force distributors or customers to take unwanted products, largely on grounds that it prevented competitors of the seller from competing on the merits for business in the tied product (*Northern Pacific Railway v. United States*, 356 U.S. 1, 1958, n. 24; *United States v. Loew's, Inc.*, 371 U.S. 38, 1962). The fenced-out competitors' right of access was equated with the consumers' right to choose. The market power of the firm that was coercing purchase of the unwanted product was often modest. At that time, most illegal tie-ins were invalidated under the modified per se rule. More recently, the law has eased so that, for the modified per se rule to apply, the tying firm must have substantial market power in the market for the tying product (again, probably at least in the 30 percent range; see *Jefferson Parish Hospital District No. 2 v. Hyde*, 466 U.S. 2, 1984). The plaintiff's burden of demonstrating that there are in fact two products and that the defendant used its power over the first to force the second on buyers has become substantial. Still, a tie might be defensible or at least not subject to the modified per se rule if a defendant can show that the conduct is necessary to respond to the market (*Jefferson Parish*, 466 U.S. 2, 1984, 25, notes 41 and 42).

The US Supreme Court in *Eastman Kodak v. Image Technical Services, Inc.* (504 U.S. 451, 1992) reaffirmed its commitment to prohibit tie-in sales where the necessary conditions are met. The *Kodak* case is unique in that it concerned an intrabrand aftermarket (tie-in of services to spare parts), and the Court rejected conservative economic theory that competition in the interbrand original equipment market would guarantee responsive behavior in the aftermarket.

In the European Union, development of the law on vertical restraints was much influenced by the goal of assuring market integration among the nations of Europe. The influence of that objective is most apparent in connection with territorial restraints. In the famous case of *Consten and Grundig v. Commission* (cases 56, 58/64, 1966, ECR 299), the European Court of Justice held that no firm may have airtight territorial restraints at member-state borders because such restraints impair the movement of goods across state lines. The Court of Justice affirmed the exclusion of evidence of interbrand competition and ignored arguments about the necessity of territorial restriction to prevent free riding on the investments of existing distributors (Bermann, Goebel, Davey, and Fox 1993, 634-35). Many other cases have reinforced the conclusion that tight territorial allocation at member-state lines is among the most egregious of restraints in the Union. Intra-Community export restraints, or agreements such as those for dual pricing (a higher price for goods to be exported), are illegal for the same reason—they block or discourage the flow of parallel imports (see *Distillers Co. Ltd. v. Commission*, case 30/78, 1980, ECR 2229). In other areas of the law, there is greater congruence between US and EU law. For example, in both, agreements to maintain resale prices are illegal.

Block exemptions cover exclusive distributorship and exclusive purchasing arrangements.[17] Regulations state what clauses must be included and excluded to get the benefit of the block exemption. Selective distribution is not covered by block exemption but is generally allowed as long as the manufacturer does not restrict the number of distributors to be designated (*Metro SB-Grossmarkte GmbH & Co. KG v. Commission*, case 75/84, 1986, ECR 3021).

In the European Union, tie-ins and fidelity rebates are treated under Article 86—that is, as an aspect of dominate-firm behavior—and are normally illegal if they increase the share of the dominant firm and do not pass a stringent test of objective justification (*Hoffmann-LaRoche v. Commission*, case 85/76, 1976, ECR 461; Tetra Pak *International SA v. Commission*, C-333 94P, [1996] ECR I-__, 16 November 1996).

The European Union is reexamining its law on vertical restraints. The Commission adopted a Green Paper on vertical restraints in January 1997 and has asked for comments on four options: maintaining the current approach, widening the block exemptions, focusing the block exemptions, and reducing the scope of Article 85 (1).

Mergers and Joint Ventures

Prevention of mergers and joint ventures that threaten anticompetitive changes in market structure has been a centerpiece of American competition enforcement. Levels of enforcement have varied widely, from

---

17. Commission Regulation 83/83 O. J. L 173/1 (30 June 1983); Commission Regulation 84/83, O. J. L 173/5 (30 June 1983).

extremely lax in the 1920s and 1980s to exceptionally vigorous in the 1960s. Overall, many believe that the reason most American industries are less concentrated than counterpart industries in Europe and Japan is because of enforcement and the threat of enforcement of antimerger restrictions.

The history of enforcement against mergers in the European Union is entirely different. At the genesis of the European Community, there was no concern about mergers. The founders did not believe that bigness was a problem but rather were concerned about inefficient smallness resulting from the balkanization of markets (Bermann et al. 1993, chapter 24). Even as to bigness, the solution was thought to be regulation rather than deconcentration. Thus, mergers were often welcomed, especially cross-border mergers that could help integrate the Common Market. To the extent that the Community seriously considered merger enforcement, it focused upon a concern that mergers would lead to abuse of dominant power. Eventually, mergers were considered an appropriate concern for EC law. Only after many years were the member states prepared to cede sovereignty, and thus national policy initiatives necessary for a Community-wide merger policy. In 1989 the Council of Ministers agreed on a merger regulation[18] still focused primarily on single-firm dominance. When the law applies, it supersedes member-state merger laws (Bermann et. al. 1993, 859-60), in contrast to the US system of dual federal-state enforcement.

American case law and guidelines with respect to mergers focus primarily on a concern that mergers might lead to undue concentration, which in turn would facilitate the exercise of market power. Market power is the ability-profitably to maintain prices above competitive levels for a substantial period and is thought to occur when barriers are high and either there are so few firms in the market with entry barriers that they can implicitly coordinate their actions or when a single firm unilaterally gains power.

US case law tends to find violations in three types of mergers:

- **Direct horizontal mergers between competitors.** Serious scrutiny begins where the combined market share of the merging parties is roughly 20 percent in a concentrated market with significant barriers to entry (US Department of Justice and Federal Trade Commission 1992).

- **Mergers between customers and suppliers.** Serious scrutiny starts when each firm accounts for 20 percent or more of the market and there are significant barriers to entry (*Fruehauf Corp v. FTC*, 603 F.2d 345, 2d Cir., 1979).

---

18. Council Regulation 4064/89, O. J. L 395/1 (30 December 1989), corrected, O. J. L 257/ 14 (21 September 1990), amended effective 1 March 1988, Council Regulation 1310/97 (30 June 1997).

■ **Conglomerate mergers.** Violations are effectively limited now to situations in which one of the merging parties would have entered the market of the other if the merger did not occur, or one of the parties exerted a procompetitive effect from the edge of the market, thus producing a potential horizontal problem (*United States v. Marine Bancorporation*, 418 U.S. 602, 1974). A substantial majority of merger actions involves horizontal mergers where there is a threat that concentration will lead to coordinated anticompetitive action.

At least in the older cases, there was no opportunity to claim efficiencies as a moderating factor.[19] The American enforcement agencies are willing to take efficiencies into account in the exercise of prosecutorial discretion, but their overall attitude has been skeptical. Efficiency claims must be "merger-specific" (not achievable through some less anticompetitive arrangement) and must be verifiable. The efficiency gains must be sufficient to prevent any consumer harm.

When a company or one of its divisions is "failing," restrictions on mergers and joint ventures are loosened. However, the definition of a failing firm or division under US law is extremely demanding. The firm must show that it is unable to meet its financial obligations in the near future (i.e., it is virtually in bankruptcy), that it could not reorganize successfully, and that there is no other buyer tendering a reasonable offer that would keep the firm in the market and create a less-severe danger to competition (US Department of Justice and FTC 1992; *Citizens Publishing Co. v. United States*, 394 U.S. 131, 1969). In court, it is rare that US firms can successfully assert a failing-company defense. As to situations in which there is chronic overcapacity (so-called "distressed industries"), there is no provision in US law or guidelines for more lenient antitrust treatment.

With respect to joint ventures, US law is generally lenient. When two firms otherwise unable to enter the market on their own join forces to create a new competitor, that transaction is probably legal. Problems arise principally when the two firms are already in the market and combine forces, perhaps claiming achievement of efficiencies, and try to characterize their combination as a joint venture rather than as a merger. It is mainly these joint ventures that have been challenged under American law. For some time, it was thought that a joint venture between a firm in the market or one committed to entry and another firm that appeared unlikely to enter but that remained a potential competitor might

---

19. In recent years, lower courts in the United States have been willing to entertain claims of efficiency, but no merger, otherwise illegal, has been allowed on the basis of an efficiency claim (*FTC v. Universal Health, Inc.*, 938 F.2d 1206, 1222, 11th Cir., 1991, and *United States v. Rockford Memorial Corp.*, 717 F. Supp. 1251, 1289-91, N.D. Ill. 1989, *affirmed* 898 F.2d 1278, 7th Cir., *cert. denied*, 111 S. Ct. 295, 1990).

be actionable (*United States v. Penn-Olin Chemical Co.*, 378 U.S. 158, 1964). More recently, American courts have imposed so many preconditions on a challenge in the "one-in/one-out" situation—for example, the outside firm must be one of only a few entrants and would have a significant effect on competition if it entered independently—that violations of this sort are unlikely to be found (*Tenneco, Inc. v. FTC*, 689 F. 2d 346, 2d Cir., 1982).

The EC merger regulation, cited above, prohibits mergers that create or enhance "dominance" so as to substantially impair effective competition (Bermann et al. 1993, 862). Language regarding oligopolies or cartel-like behavior was consciously omitted from the regulation. Nonetheless, the issue of coverage remains an open one. In *Néstle/Perrier* (case IV/M 190, Commission Decision 92/553), the Commission articulated and accepted a theory of oligopolistic dominance. This issue is now before the EC Court.

Efficiencies and economic progress are relevant in an examination of competitive effects under the merger regulation, but only if they are "to consumers' advantage and [do] not form an obstacle to competition." In the *de Havilland* case (Commission Decision 91/619, O. J. L 334/42, 5 December 1991)—the first merger struck down under the merger regulation—the Commission avoided the question of efficiencies. Without deciding whether efficiencies could be a defense, it examined the record in the case and concluded that the combined firms would produce no substantial efficiencies. The Commission's approach is perplexing in that it referenced economies of scope without identifying them as such and expressed fears that realization of this advantage would disadvantage the single-line competitors.

The EC merger law has not yet squarely addressed a failing-company claim or a "distressed industry" claim. Political considerations seem to penetrate the EU decision-making process more easily and frequently than in the United States, and therefore it is more likely that industrial policy will creep into the decisions and influence outcomes, despite language that may appear, on the surface, faithful to the standards of the merger regulation.

As in the United States, joint ventures of various sorts are treated leniently under EC law. Cooperative joint ventures (those not treated as mergers) are rather liberally exempted under Article 85(3), although the Commission often exacts conditions, such as striking exclusivity clauses, that US law would not be likely to treat as anticompetitive. Exemptions are granted only for a term of years so that surveillance of cooperative joint ventures continues.

Under the stewardship of a talented merger task force (the staff in the Competition Directorate that analyze the mergers and make recommendations), EC merger law shows increasing sophistication. By the nature of the Commission system, however, the law is not insulated from political influence, leading some contingents to advocate for an independent antitrust agency.

Predation

Price predation is a strategy to injure competitors by low prices, strategic exclusion, or other means of forcing rivals to bear costs that the predator does not incur itself, thereby enhancing or entrenching its market power. Almost all predatory pricing behavior involves extremely low pricing.

A definition of unacceptable predatory behavior has been far more controversial in the United States than in the European Union. Moreover, EU treatment of predation, consistent with EC law generally, suggests a concern to protect competitors as well as future consumers from both exclusionary and exploitative abuses.

Elements of predatory pricing ordinarily include pricing below some appropriate measure of costs and some indication of exclusionary or monopolistic intent. There is increased recognition in the United States that cases or rules restricting undesirably low pricing must be carefully considered so as to avoid law enforcement that chills or deters vigorous, aggressive pricing—that is, the essence of behavior that the antitrust laws are designed to protect.

To prove predation in the United States, many courts require evidence that the defendant charged prices below reasonably anticipated marginal cost. Because marginal cost is difficult to measure, many courts use average variable cost as its surrogate.[20] In some parts of the United States, prices above average full cost can still constitute a violation—particularly where there is evidence of intent to destroy competitors and/or high barriers to entry so that a predatory campaign is plausible.[21]

Even when prices are below some acceptable level, some US courts have concluded there can be no predatory pricing if actual or potential rivals are so numerous that a predator would not be able recoup its investment in low prices after some or all existing rivals are eliminated. A Supreme Court case—*Brooke Group v. Brown & Williamson Tobacco* (509 U.S. 209, 1993)—declares the ability to recoup an essential factor.

---

20. Marginal cost is the increment to total cost that results from producing an additional item of output (see *Northeastern Tel. Co. v. AT&T*, 651 F. 2d 76, 87, 2d Cir., 1981, *cert. denied*, 455 U.S. 943, 1982); variable costs are the sum of all costs that vary with output, excluding overhead, depreciation, taxes, and similar items *(Morgan v. Ponder*, 892 F.2d 1355, 1360, n.11, 8th Cir., 1989).

21. For a summary of applicable US rules, see *Barry Wright Corp. v. ITT Grinnell Corp.* (724 F.2d 227, 1st Cir., 1983).

In combination, these two tests—sales below average variable cost (at least in most jurisdictions) and a market structure conducive to recoupment —have made it extremely difficult for a plaintiff, whether government or private party, to win an antitrust challenge based on low pricing. The consensus appears to be that predation is not a promising area for aggressive law enforcement.

The European Union employs a different standard. In *AKZO* (1991 ECR I-3359), AKZO and its competitor, ECS, sold organic peroxide, the former primarily to plastics manufacturers and the latter for flour. When ECS started selling to AKZO's plastics customers, AKZO began to price low—sometimes below average variable cost—to ECS's flour customers in order to discipline ECS.

AKZO was found to have abused its dominant position. The Court's opinion indicated that such abuse can occur with a campaign designed to eliminate a competitor by pricing below average variable costs, or even above average variable costs but below average total costs. It was unlikely that ECS would have been eliminated and, even if it were, there was another important competitor in the market and AKZO probably could not have recouped its profits lost in the siege of predation. The EU court focused on the problem of eliminating or disciplining a competitor in contrast with US jurisprudence, which reflects the worry that legal "protection" against a competitor's low prices is likely to be costly to consumers, who are denied the advantage of low pricing. The reasoning and concerns of the Court of Justice in AKZO are confirmed in Tetra Pak, which held that recoupment is not a necessary element of a price predation case (*Tetra Pak International SA v. Commission*, C-333 94P, [1996] ECR I-__, 14 November 1996).

Enforcement Levels

In many respects, US and EC substantive law is quite harmonious. Cross-fertilization of thinking among scholars and practitioners across the Atlantic is likely to further this convergence. However, substantive law diverges at a number of points as noted; the enforcement system has many differences, and enforcement levels are quite different.

Even in the 1980s, when US enforcement was dominated by a "minimalist" enforcement attitude, there were over 500 lawyers and economists in the Antitrust Division of the Department of Justice and a similar number engaged in competition enforcement at the Federal Trade Commission. Enforcement against cartel behavior and large horizontal mergers has been constant. In the late 1980s during the Bush administration, and the 1990s under the Clinton administration, a broad range of antitrust enforcement activities has been resumed. In addition, state attorneys general and private parties continue actively to challenge anticompetitive behavior. Even with sharp drops in private enforcement that have occurred over the last 20 years, there are still approximately 1,000 private treble-damage and injunction cases filed annually in the United States.

Compared with those in the United States, enforcement levels in the European Union, especially against cartels, are low. Competitors' complaints trigger most proceedings to the EC Commission, other than those involving mergers. All mergers that pass the high threshold of "Community dimension" are reviewed by the Commission, but there have been only about eight cases that have resulted in a flat prohibition order. A number of other cases involved consent arrangements where some portion of the merged assets were spun off or other relief was accepted.

There is no provision under EC law itself for private antitrust action, but Articles 85 and 86 allow suits in member states for damages or injunctive relief in accordance with whatever procedures and remedies the member-state law provides. Some EU officials and others advocate greater use of private actions.

Conclusion

In sum, US and EC competition laws have many similarities, but the substantive center of gravity of each is unique. EC competition law is derived from the impulse for market integration and is closely connected with the EC principle of free movement of goods and services across member-state lines. It seeks to preserve opportunities for small and middle-sized business, though it is also motivated by concerns for efficient businesses and for consumers' interest.

Moreover, analysis of cases in the European Union has been less technical than in the United States. The Commission and the Court readily presume dominance and increases in dominance without the kind of factual record that might be required in the United States.

The intensity of enforcement is much lower in the European Union than in the United States. Competitors' complaints and notifications of agreements are the principal triggers of official activity, and minimal resources are devoted to anticartel activity. Resources are devoted to mergers, but few challenges are made. This contrasts with the United States, where anticartel activity is much greater and many more mergers are challenged or subject to spinoff requirements.

Procedurally, the enforcement regimes are quite different. While both are affected by politics, in the United States enforcement is more likely to be influenced by the political philosophy current in the administration rather than direct interference in particular cases. In the European Union, enforcement activity and disposition of cases is more likely to be swayed by ad hoc political influences brought to bear by one of another member state that perceives an interest in the outcome of the case or the competitive position of EU firms.

There is a perception in both the United States and Europe that EC Article 85 is underenforced with respect to cartels and cartel-like behavior. It is considered underenforced because 1) only the Commission has the right to grant an exemption, and therefore, as a practical matter, all agreement/combination cases must be funneled to it; 2) the Commission has limited resources; and 3) single damages with no significant discovery and the specter of a double bill for lawyers' fees provide no incentive for private parties to become effective private attorneys general. There is also a US perception that, beyond cartels, Articles 85 and 86 are both overenforced, deterring firms from taking aggressive action that could serve buyers. However, Europe perceives US antitrust as the captive of big business and Chicago free-market theory and as defaulting in its role to protect against abuses and to limit or regulate power.

The differences are not likely to be worked out by "pushing" the systems into greater harmony, but there are sufficient, important, substantive commonalities that can be maximized if and as the world demands more harmony in the laws governing global transactions.

References

Bermann, G., R. Goebel, W. Davey, and E. Fox. 1993, Supp. 1995. *Cases and Materials on European Community Law*. Minneapolis: West.

Gyselen, L. 1989. "Abuse of Monopoly Power within the Meaning of Article 86 of the EC Treaty: Recent Developments." In B. Hawk, *Fordham Corporation Law Institute*.

Joliet, R. 1970. *Monopolisation and Abuse of Dominant Position: A Comparative Study of American and European Approaches to the Control of Economic Power*. Netherlands: Nijhoff.

Turner, D. F. 1975. "The Scope of 'Attempt to Monopolize'." *Record Association Bar* (New York City) 30: 487.

US Department of Justice and Federal Trade Commission. 1992. *Revised Merger Guidelines*. Washington.

11

Harmonizing Antitrust: The Less Effective Way to Promote International Competition

DOUGLAS E. ROSENTHAL AND PHEDON NICOLAIDES

Efforts to harmonize national competition laws, whether by multilateral code, bilateral agreement, or unilateral national action in response to an emerging international consensus on appropriate standards, are drawing increased interest. In December 1996 a ministerial meeting of the World Trade Organization (WTO) considered the future establishment of multilateral rules to discipline anticompetitive actions by companies. In the fall of 1994, Congress passed the International Antitrust Enforcement Assistance Act, which authorizes the Justice Department and the Federal Trade Commission (FTC) to cooperate with foreign antitrust authorities in multinational antitrust enforcement. One hope for this legislation is that it will increase the effectiveness of antitrust investigations and enforcement actions involving international activities and reduce enforcement conflicts between jurisdictions. In the summer of 1993, a team of experts with a strong German representation published a draft harmonized international competition code. Under the auspices of the prestigious Max Planck Institute, the draft code was proposed as a treaty amendment supplementing the GATT's traditional trade rules. It met with a storm of criticism for being premature and overambitious. The European Union Commission was recently successfully challenged by France before the European Court of Justice for signing, without prior

Douglas Rosenthal is a partner in the law firm of Sonnenschein, Nath, & Rosenthal, in Washington. He served as chief of the Foreign Commerce Section of the US Department of Justice's Antitrust Division from 1977 to 1980. Phedon Nicolaides, an international economist, is professor and head of the unit on EC policies at the European Institute of Public Administration, Maastricht, the Netherlands.

approval of European Union (EU) member states, a bilateral Antitrust Cooperation Agreement with the United States. As a result, the Commission had to go back to the EU Council for formal approval. Antitrust harmonization is under serious study by the Competition Committee of the Organization for Economic Cooperation and Development (OECD), although progress is slow.

North American antitrust officials and experts are exploring ways to achieve greater harmonization of Canadian and US competition laws—both legislated more than 100 years ago—while helping Mexico implement a competition law after their example. The new Mexican competition law went into effect in June 1993. This harmonization effort was a predicate to Mexico's entry into the North American Free Trade Agreement (NAFTA), which includes a largely hortatory chapter inviting the strengthening and harmonization of the national antitrust laws of the three signatories. A recent American Bar Association Task Force Report optimistically hails the NAFTA as a landmark on the path to North American economic integration. Similar developments, although not as ambitious, are taking place in Latin America as well. The Rio Group, comprising the largest countries in Latin America, is currently considering the adoption of common competition rules.

More advanced efforts at integration are taking place on the European continent. The European Economic Area Agreement (EEAA) between the European Union and all member states of the European Free Trade Association except Switzerland, which took effect in January 1994, and all of the EU's Association Agreements with other European countries contain competition provisions that virtually duplicate Articles 85, 86, and 92 of the Treaty of Rome. The EEAA also provides for a common enforcement authority, while the Association Agreements provide for consultation and conciliation procedures. Numerous additional examples could also be identified.

The significant academic support for antitrust harmonization contrasts with the broad, although not always outspoken, opposition from many government officials and practitioners. We do not oppose the effort, however, and cite with approval the chapter by Fox and Pitofsky in this book, comparing US and EU competition law, as a positive step in this direction. We believe that a different and more important form of harmonization exists that requires more immediate attention: putting the objectives of antitrust in accord with those of other economic laws and policies by making their conflicts more transparent and open to policy debate.

The role of laws and policies governing competition, at least within each of the major states of the world trading system, needs strengthening and increased visibility. By comparison, harmonizing national antitrust laws with each other is a less urgent concern. Competition law and policy in the United States, Europe, Japan, and Canada are relatively weak vis-à-vis five sets of national laws and economic policies that most directly restrict national and global competition: (1) protectionist trade measures, (2) measures intended to attract or exclude categories of foreign investors, (3) nonborder regulations that confer a competitive advantage on local products or firms, (4) industrial policies intended to promote national champions and save jobs, and (5) overly broad protection of intellectual property rights in some nations, which has had the effect of discouraging innovation and competition not involving industrial pirates. Making different antitrust laws more consistent will not address the sometimes profoundly anticompetitive provisions of these five nonantitrust law and policy sectors. Because competition policy is often weak nationally, it is necessarily weak in multilateral forums.

The theme of this chapter is that differences in antitrust enforcement between nations do not significantly impede the functioning of open markets. Rather, low-visibility resistance to competition outside the scope of antitrust law and policy, particularly expressed in the five sectors enumerated above, often is an impediment. If advocates of free trade are serious about promoting open global markets and reducing regulatory inefficiencies, a constituency of efficient producers and consumers who welcome a global marketplace needs to mobilize around antitrust policy. Furthermore, this constituency needs to be encouraged to play a larger and more effective role in making national as well as international economic policy. Leadership should come from the industrialized states if stronger competition policy is to be adopted by the industrializing nations, which likely will be among the major traders of the next century.

Before intersectoral harmonization can advance, and before significant multilateral progress can be made in international deregulatory agreements relating to protected sectors, national commitments to competition must be strengthened. While antitrust enforcement in the United States, Europe, Canada, and Japan may be somewhat stronger and more aggressive than it was 10 years ago (see the relevant chapters in this book), it still plays a very modest part in determining the trade, investment, intellectual property, regulatory, and industrial policies and laws of these respective governments—or of any government today.

There are too many exceptions to, and exemptions from, national competition laws in the service of these other national governmental policies. Even US and European competition laws, which are among the most actively enforced, are riddled with the five sectors of preemption enunciated above. Until these five sets of laws and policies are themselves more transparent and open to debate on the costs and benefits of their anticompetitive purposes and effects, antitrust harmonization will be of marginal significance. Where antitrust is not preempted, political and budgetary pressures limit "politically sensitive" enforcement. This is seen clearly in Japan (see Rosenthal and Matsushita, chapter 9). But it is also a fact in Europe, Canada, and even the United States.

National and International Antitrust
since World War II

At the end of World War II, no nation had a strong antitrust law. The US law was the strongest, with a maximum $50,000 fine for price-fixing among corporate competitors. This law was a criminal statute in name only. No one went to jail. Indeed, there was little punishment and therefore little deterrence. Important economic sectors such as agriculture, transport, utilities, the professions, and sports were largely exempt from rules enforcing open markets. Canada's competition law was even weaker. The fact that the only thing it enjoined was criminal anticompetitive activity virtually ensured that the Canadian law would be rarely enforced. Great Britain's law was weaker still, and quite a few important industrial countries, such as Germany and Italy, had no competition law at all until years later.

The Depression, along with the political polarization and territorial aggression of the 1930s, had led to the abandonment of the goal of open international and national markets. The international trading system through World War II was largely defined by national and international cartels in the major industrial sectors—especially chemicals and mining.

Postwar reconstruction, however, brought an about-face—a surprisingly broad commitment to try again to develop open international markets. Many Western economic policymakers, academics, and business executives believed in the possibility of establishing an international trade organization (ITO), which would provide a political structure and set of principles for reducing tariff barriers between nations. This ITO would also provide a means of ending cartels and private and governmental restraints on national market access. It would channel funds for reconstruction and economic development, enabling nations shattered by the war to reach a level of prosperity that would enable them to remove regulations protecting home industries. An international monetary fund promoting stability in international currency exchanges and fiscal and monetary self-discipline, along with reduced restrictions on investment to promote nondiscriminatory investment opportunities, could make an open trading system work where it had failed before.

It was well understood in the 1940s that open and competitive markets required more than reduced tariffs, more than national competition laws, more even than an international competition code. They also required rules of national nondiscrimination in investment regulations and fair but not overly broad standards for intellectual property protection and deregulation of nontariff governmental trade barriers. The Havana Charter, drafted in 1948, was to set the standard for open national markets, after a short period of reconstruction. It was widely hoped that an institutionalized ITO would lead to an open international system of world trade investment and competition, with the deregulation of markets the primary stimulus to greater economic growth.

By 1950, the ITO initiative was dead. William Diebold's assessment at the time (1952, cited in Gardner 1956) still seems sound. The ITO was killed by a combination of (1) the Cold War; (2) postwar reconstruction taking longer and costing more than had been anticipated; (3) lack of consensus about what the competition, deregulation, and investment norms should be, and how rigorously they should be applied in the face of protectionist resistance; and (4) the same tension between pragmatism and idealism that had undermined the League of Nations. Many free traders in the US business community came to the conclusion that too many of the market-opening deregulatory norms had been qualified to the point that national implementing laws would end up being used more often as nontariff barriers, blocking the access of US enterprises to foreign markets. Protectionists, by contrast, were relieved. Tariff and monetary reform went forward. But a norm of open markets through a multilateral initiative was largely abandoned—except, of course, within Western Europe.

It probably is wrong to assume that, if the Havana Charter had been adopted, an international commitment to the enforcement of competition law would have come sooner than it actually did. Approval of the ITO would not have led to its immediate implementation. The factors that killed it may have slowed the development of antitrust enforcement outside the United States. However, several nations adopted and began to develop competition laws anyway: Germany and Japan were influenced by their American occupiers. Admittedly, the national antitrust laws at that time permitted a number of restrictive practices that would be illegal now. These laws were largely powerless against nationalized enterprises, private national champions protected by regulatory authorities, and broad, continuing industry self-regulation justified by the "imperatives" of reconstruction. Competition agencies received modest funds for law enforcement and continued to exercise weak sanctioning authority. The principal enforcement weapon was the cease-and-desist order. Because there was little deterrence to misconduct, violating the law until discovered could be highly profitable. Even injunctions, without penalties or damages, were rarely applied in significant ways to conduct in heavy industries or important service sectors—except in the United States.

But in Europe, starting in the late 1950s, a number of competition-distorting practices and policies were increasingly brought under supranational control. The six founding member states of the European Community established the first multinational competition law. As Vernon and Nicolaïdes in their chapter on the European Union properly emphasize, for the first time since the Havana Charter the norm of competition, by being included in the Treaty of Rome as a fundamental norm, was given constitutional status—a bedrock status it does not even have under US law. Regulation 17, adopted in 1962, provided an enforcement mechanism with teeth. Within a relatively short time thereafter, Directorate General IV (DG IV), the competition law directorate of the European Commission, began successfully to prosecute horizontal cartel cases, abuses of dominant market positions, and anticompetitive state subsidies. These had never before been the subjects of sustained enforcement in Europe.

In the United States, throughout the 1940s and 1950s, the Justice Department brought important prosecutions attacking cartels and monopolies in major industries and service sectors. Every major unregulated sector was affected: chemicals, steel, automobiles, investment banking, electrical equipment, construction, and oil. In the 1960s, the private antitrust suit, with automatic treble damages plus attorney's fees for prevailing plaintiffs, became an even more important enforcement tool than action by the FTC and the Department of Justice. Many significant economic sectors remained largely immune from open access and vigorous competition, but their number diminished under a surge of deregulation in the 1970s and 1980s in transportation (excepting shipping), energy industries, telecommunications, financial services, and the professions. By the middle of the 1980s, about a dozen US state governments had begun to enforce both state and federal antitrust laws, sometimes in direct conflict with federal enforcement policy.

The European Union has had similar experiences. As a result of its "1992" program, the Union has begun to deregulate and to apply competition law to several previously sheltered sectors, among them telecommunications, air and maritime transport, postal services, and energy utilities. Competition law has been applied even to firms with special or exclusive rights conferred by law. More broadly, in addition to the sectors mentioned above, the "1992" program has opened up public procurement and financial and professional services, and has simplified procedures for product certification and acceptance of partner countries' national standards.

The Relative Weakness of Antitrust Today

US and European antitrust today is stronger than that of other countries, and much stronger since World War II than it was prewar. Despite that, antitrust officials have had disappointingly little impact on their jurisdictions' policies governing industry, investment, intellectual property, trade, and regulatory matters. The following sections provide a cursory look at the limited role of EU competition policy, and of EU competition enforcement officials, in regard to these five sectors.

Industrial Policy

The European Union has long had an industrial policy, even though it was not given the legal competence to formulate such a policy until promulgation of Article 130 of the Maastricht Treaty on European Union.[1] (The Maastricht Treaty took effect on 1 November 1993.) The absence of legal competence did not prevent the European Commission from proposing industrial policy initiatives to member states. The Commission got involved in industrial policy because it feared that, in the absence of any EU initiative, member states would act in support of their own national firms. The Commission's desire to avoid fragmentation of the Common Market along national lines also explains why its early initiatives primarily protected industries of declining competitiveness. It is the propping up of ailing industries that governments find politically irresistible.

The European Union ventured deeply into industrial policy in the 1970s by permitting the establishment of the so-called crisis cartels, which rigged the market (e.g., by means of consensual output cuts and state subsidies) in the false hope that reducing competition would restore longer-term global competitiveness. This medicine did not work, and the declining industries of the 1970s, such as shipbuilding and textiles, are now nearly moribund.

Subsequent EU initiatives have been more subtle. The Single European Act, which revised the Treaty of Rome in 1987, gave the Commission additional responsibility to formulate and implement policies intended to encourage cooperation in basic research and procompetitive technological development. The Commission has always been concerned that the EU research and development effort is suboptimal because it is largely undertaken within the framework of national rather than Union policies. Hence, it traditionally has put a premium on cross-border cooperation and has been willing partly to subsidize it. The Commission has been careful, though, generally to avoid subsidies that would have a direct, adverse effect on competition.

In addition to providing overall horizontal support of European R&D, the European Union still maintains a small number of significant schemes that protect specific key industries such as electronics, automobiles, and textiles from import competition, especially from Asia. The Commission's

---

1. The European Union has had much stronger powers for more than 40 years to regulate the coal and steel industries, exempt from operation of the Treaty of Rome antitrust articles. These powers were conferred by the treaty establishing the European Coal and Steel Community in 1952. The European Union has used these powers primarily to subsidize these costly, inefficient, but labor-intensive sectors, and to protect them from import competition.

position on such sectoral protection has gradually become less accommodating to demands from member states' governments. However, it is not clear in the present political environment if there will be a complete withdrawal of subsidies and other protectionist measures for these sectors.

A shift in the European Commission's view was also evident in its willingness to interpret more strictly the rules of the Treaty of Rome (Articles 92-94) on state aids or subsidies. Several years ago, under the direction of the then-commissioner for competition, Sir Leon Brittan, the Commission enunciated the "private investor" principle: All state aids schemes would be assessed as if the state were a private investor. If there were no indication of commercial return on a government's investments in private or even state-owned industries, that government would be adjudged as offering subsidies that were distorting competition and would therefore have to withdraw them. This policy commitment has not been eroded with the change in portfolios for Brittan. Karel Van Miert, the current commissioner responsible for competition, is no less aggressive in promoting competition over industrial policy. Here, too, important policy conflicts can be expected between calls for competition and calls for protection in the coming years. Antitrust harmonization will have little impact on this conflict.

Investment Policy

The European Union has no active investment policy that applies to all member states. Nonetheless, a de facto investment policy is expressed in certain trade decisions that have specified rules of origin for manufactured products. It is believed that these have been applied in certain cases to induce foreign manufacturers to relocate within the European Union if their products (e.g., photocopiers and semiconductors) were to be considered European.

Compared with the United States, the European Union may be said to have a negative investment policy. It imposes certain limits on the incentives that member states may offer to foreign or domestic companies that establish offices or plants within their borders. Because of the European Union's concern for integration, such state aids generally are prohibited, unless the investment takes place within a designated underdeveloped region and the received subsidy conforms to strict criteria that specify its final use and intensity (ratio of subsidy to output). Replacing member states' protectionist policies with EU-wide ones may promote market integration; however, it does not promote international competition. Rules of origin and other investment restrictions should be subjected to competition analysis and criticism.

Intellectual Property

The Commission has been trying for years to persuade member states to establish a common framework for patents, copyrights, and trademarks. Even though member states are parties to the relevant international conventions (e.g., Bern and Paris), and despite the progress that has been achieved within the context of the 1992 movement to a single market, member states are still far from a common legal framework. There is considerable tension over where to draw the lines, whether primarily to reward those who assert broad property rights or to limit those rights—for example, as to computer software innovations—for the sake of encouraging nonproprietary innovation. DG IV officials do not play a major role in the formation of intellectual property policy. At this writing, the European Court of Justice has ruled that in at least limited circumstances (not clearly identified), copyright rights conferred by national laws may not be enforced to restrict consumer welfare by denying the introduction of new, efficient products or services into the Common Market (*Radio Telefis Eireann et. al. v. Commission* and *Magill TV Guide Ltd.* Cases C-241/91 and C-242/91 P, 6 April 1995). Compulsory licenses for patents and copyrights are rare in competition law. It remains to be seen how the principle applied in this case will be expressed. It is not, we suspect, likely to be extended to even most situations where intellectual property rights confer significant market-realizing powers.

Trade Policy

Trade measures have distorted competition in several ways. The most significant are antidumping actions which, on several occasions, have shielded already cartelized industries from foreign competition (Messerlin 1989, 563-87). The EU antidumping regulation is more extensive than the domestic competition law provisions on predation (Article 86) in the sense that foreign firms are penalized when they choose aggressive low-pricing strategies as means of injuring domestic competitors. They are not rewarded for promoting consumer welfare through greater competition. International competition is also distorted when in antidumping cases the EU seeks or accepts undertakings by third-country exporters to raise their prices in order to avoid punitive antidumping duties.

Before the advent of the single market on 1 January 1993, the existence of controls at the internal borders of the EC allowed member states to make effective use of a provision in the Treaty of Rome (Article 115) that permitted the imposition of restrictions on third-country products whenever domestic industries faced serious economic difficulty. To its credit, since January 1993 the European Commission has not authorized any so-called Article 115 derogations. Still, EU competition officials have little impact on Union trade policy. Although these officials are formally consulted on competitive consequences before trade restrictions are imposed, something that is not done at all under US trade law, they rarely affect significantly the imposition of such restrictions.

Regulated Sectors

With the exception of the products covered by the European Coal and Steel Community, the EU has no power to regulate any industry in the way utilities are "normally" regulated. That is, the Union cannot set prices, determine output, specify detailed conditions of supply, or determine the number of licensed operators. This does not mean that member states do not have their own regulations or that EU rules do not affect a great many industries. In fact, hardly a day passes without a new regulation or directive being issued that imposes new standards on some industry. In their majority, such EU rules impose on private firms certain quality or technical standards and on governments or their agencies certain obligations toward those firms.

Until the advent of the single market, two of the EU's main problems concerning competition in its internal market were that, first, national regulations differed to such an extent that entry into certain sectors was virtually impossible for foreign firms, and, second, to make things worse, some sectors were controlled by legal monopolies. No matter how vigorously EU competition rules were enforced by the European Commission or national authorities, certain firms led sheltered lives. National regulators granted exclusive operating rights, or laid down such idiosyncratic technical standards or stipulated such complex certification procedures that no foreign firm found it financially feasible to develop products according to those standards and take the trouble to have them certified. This happened routinely in, among other fields, telecommunications, air and road transport, electricity and gas distribution, and virtually all those service industries in which service providers had to be licensed.

The European Union is seeking to overcome this regulatory hurdle basically by doing three things. First, it has defined common licensing procedures and is developing more EU-wide technical standards. Second, it is establishing a "one-stop-shop" system of certification or licensing based on the principle of mutual recognition. Third, in certain monopolized sectors such as telecommunications and air transport, it traditionally has succeeded in abolishing legal monopolies and the exclusive rights granted to certain national firms.

The EU's hard work to create a single market in monopolized sectors is an apt example of how powerless competition policy can be when a sector is heavily regulated or when it is dominated by state-owned companies. Competition is hardly possible when disparate national regulations lead to market segmentation. Although the effort to standardize and deregulate is well under way, certain obstacles still remain. Complex standards, enforced arbitrarily, can place a profound drag on competition. These standards will be a source of policy conflict for at least the next decade. Indeed, the Commission has recently declared that one of its main objectives in the next few years is to achieve a uniform application throughout the EU of single market measures.

Because the European Commission is responsible for overseeing the elimination of distortions to intra-Union trade, greater attention is paid to internal competition issues than in the more decentralized US executive policy process. Nonetheless, the competition directorate, DG IV, plays a relatively limited role in this policy process—except in enforcing EU antitrust law and in reviewing state aids.

The relative ineffectiveness of US antitrust law and policy in promoting the procompetitiveness of US trade, industrial, intellectual property, and regulatory policy in international markets is discussed in greater depth later in this chapter (and in the Rosenthal and Matsushita chapter 9). The interplay between US competition and US investment policy does evidence some existing transparency and public debate. An example of the weakness of antitrust in making US investment policy is the National Cooperative Research and Production Act of 1993 (NCRPA; US Code 15 § 4301[7][2]). This legislation requires that joint production, if it is to be entitled to NCRPA's benefits, must take place principally in the United States and be controlled by US citizens or by persons from countries whose antitrust laws are no less favorable to US citizens than to the nationals of that country.[2] NCRPA provides certain clear exemptions from possible application of US antitrust law to qualifying research-and-production joint ventures. Its effect is to discourage the participation of foreign enterprises with foreign production in qualifying joint ventures (Warner and Rugman 1994, 945). An example of the strength of antitrust in US investment policy is the difficulty of blocking a foreign acquisition of US assets on national security grounds under the Exon-Florio provision in the Omnibus Trade and Competitiveness Act of 1988.

There are dozens of legislative, regulatory, and judicial exemptions from and exceptions to US antitrust law. Many affect international trade and investment. To take a few examples, US shipping and ship building are subsidized. Restrictive trade agreements affect many important economic sectors such as agriculture, semiconductors, machine tools, textiles, minerals, and, until recently, steel and autos. There are restric-

---

2. This equivalence standard is vague and would be difficult to enforce.

tive orders in numerous US dumping cases that significantly reduce competition in US markets. Although it cannot be proved, it is likely that officials of the Bush administration negotiated acceptable price and output levels for exported Saudi oil. This action may have produced a net benefit to US consumers and may have furthered perceived US foreign policy interests, but it was in likely violation of US antitrust law. Saudi-US price-output understandings probably were negotiated as well by previous administrations. It is unlikely in any of these cases that the US attorney general was consulted. When major economic policy issues, especially trade issues, are addressed, antitrust concerns may sometimes play a role—but not a major one. This was further evidenced in US domestic health policy, where antitrust policymakers were given a minor role in developing the Clinton administration's ultimately unsuccessful proposal for health care reform. The Department of Justice is not even represented on the president's Economic Policy Council.

Greater Antitrust Harmonization Will Not Significantly Strengthen Antitrust in International Markets

The norms of US and EU competition law are largely, though not completely, congruent (Fox and Pitofsky, chapter 10). So are those of the other developed states. The norms of member state competition laws and EU law are largely congruent; so are the norms of the antitrust laws of the 50 states and those enforced federally in the United States. All oppose monopolies that abuse monopoly power, and all oppose mer-gers that create monopolies. They all oppose cartels that are price-fixing, supply-restricting, and/or market-allocating. They all oppose extending exempted monopolies beyond the boundaries of their legal exemption. They all proscribe group boycotts and attempts to monopolize through predatory practices.

If one focuses closely on the United States, one sees nontrivial differences in antitrust enforcement approaches and even in substantive doctrine—such as the standing of competitors to attack mergers, or what constitutes predation—among the 13 US circuit courts of appeal. All apply the same federal antitrust law, subject to binding decisions of the US Supreme Court. But the result is a surprising degree of uncertainty about when one may be sued, and by whom, and how many times, and with what potential exposure to damages, for alleged anticompetitive conduct. Proper antitrust standards and the best way to enforce them are both topics of controversy. Evolving judgments, lacking many of the verities one might think could be applied with confidence to legal activities such as interpreting contracts and deciding when a person has committed fraud, limit the potential benefits of harmonization. The FTC and the

Justice Department have some differences in approach. Each new administration's antitrust enforcers are different from their predecessors and successors. Some enforcers of antitrust law at the state level have differences in approach, albeit incremental, from federal officials and from each other. So do the 50 substantive antitrust laws in the 50 states.

But this disharmony does *not* work against vigorous antitrust enforcement. If anything, the emergence of the state attorneys general as antitrust enforcers, plus the willingness of the Justice Department to take over the Microsoft investigation, which the FTC had closed after only two years of effort, and fight to enforce a consent decree against district court disapproval, suggest that disharmony can be compatible with active and decentralized antitrust enforcement authority (Katten 1994, 32).

Outside the United States and the European Union, some competition laws give some protection to small businesses. Some permit crisis cartels. Only US law imposes a virtually automatic treble damage remedy, even in a case in which the law was previously unsettled, and the malice or recklessness required before punitive damages can be invoked in most other legal fields is entirely absent. Still, actual damages and levels of fines against enterprises engaged in anticompetitive activities are increasing in most non-US jurisdictions, often dramatically, as in Europe, Japan, and Canada. Only the United States, so far, has put senior corporate officials in jail for price-fixing. Some jurisdictions, such as the European Union, require extensive notification for big mergers. Some, such as the United States, have modest initial notification requirements. Others, such as Italy, require almost no antitrust notification at all. Some jurisdictions, such as Canada, are more tolerant of mergers that promote oligopolies. Most jurisdictions do not encourage private antitrust enforcement. Only US law strongly encourages private antitrust enforcement as an important supplement to government action.

Many of the jurisdictional differences in antitrust enforcement, internationally and within the United States, are less the result of conflicting norms and more a question of either different ideas about what will best work to achieve common norms or bureaucratic turf battles over who will decide. For example, DG IV has set stricter definitions of geographic and product markets than have enforcement officials, scholars, and the courts in the United States. In Europe, where markets have until very recently been segmented along national lines and where consumer preferences vary considerably, it has been difficult to persuade enforcement authorities that products that do not seem plausibly to be close substitutes may in fact be so. It is not so difficult in the more homogeneous United States. Furthermore, in Europe the Commission requires that notifiers seeking authorization for a large merger tell its staff what they think are the relevant product and geographic markets. In the United States, this burden is not imposed on those making premerger notifications.

An international code is not likely to accomplish harmonization of means to shared ends when there are legitimate grounds for disagreeing as to the best means, and no simple empirical test that will show one approach to be correct and another to be wrong. Conflict between the United States and the European Union over merger enforcement is now inevitable. Some conflict of enforcement policy between the European Union and Canada in the *de Havilland* case, and some conflict between the Union and a US district court in the *Minorco-Goldfields* case. There is now the possibility of a trade war over the merger between Boeing and McDonnell Douglas. If such a collision does happen, absent an as-yet unestablished dispute-resolution mechanism, the merger at issue will probably be stopped. It only takes one authority in one important market saying "no" to stop a big merger. But the question now is whether the EU Commission would risk a major confrontation with United States trade and security officials.

Changes in perception of where the proper balance lies between conflicting values that both supposedly promote competition can be found throughout the body of antitrust doctrine. These perceptual changes are reflected in ongoing differences, domestic and international, about: (1) the actual harm predatory pricing can cause in the marketplace; (2) whether and when restrictions on intrabrand competition cause more harm than the benefits of interbrand competition that such restrictions may facilitate; (3) whether monopolists should have a unilateral right to refuse to deal with individuals or classes of customers; (4) whether antitrust law and policy enforcers should be concerned when some competitors are driven from the marketplace by joint anticompetitive practices of others, even though no surviving firm in the industry has market power; and (5) what presumptions, or shifts in the burden of proof, concerning liability and damages, should be made from certain types of direct and indirect evidence. The concept of market power itself, central to antitrust enforcement, is the subject of strongly contrasting views about what it is and when it can be abused. As pointed out in Rosenthal and Matsushita (chapter 9), the goal of competition is multivalued, and these values often conflict, even where available facts are reasonably developed—which is unusual. In sum, greater antitrust harmony than already exists will be hard to achieve.

Through the 1970s, there was no strong impetus for an international antitrust code such as that envisaged in the Havana Charter, nor for international harmonization of national competition laws. In Europe, Germany was developing a strong competition law and a relatively strong competition enforcement agency, the Bundeskartellamt. But national antitrust enforcement remained relatively weak elsewhere. To some extent, this did not matter because DG IV continued to gain strength. However, since the directorate's principal mission was to promote a single European market for goods and services, more energy and attention were directed at attacking vertical territorial restrictions than at going after anticompetitive horizontal agreements. DG IV was preoccupied with these restrictions because competition policy was and still is perceived fundamentally as an instrument for breaking down territorial barriers that isolate national markets. Such policy is not equally concerned with opening domestic markets to nonmember state competition.

Perhaps the most important accomplishment of the European Union was the prohibition of protectionist national trade laws such as anti-dumping regulations, trade-distorting subsidies, quantitative import restrictions, and other measures of equivalent effect applied to trade between member states. This protectionist set of trade regulations was replaced with a single EC competition law enforced by the Commission. Italy, for example, could no longer restrict competition from French products by applying an Italian dumping or subsidies law. The only "legitimate" trade law remedy was to get the Commission to bring an enforcement action against a French manufacturer for abusing its dominant market position in Italy, or to bring a challenge to the anti-competitive nature of subsidization by the French government of exports to Italy. Of course, nontariff barriers such as the establishment of "quality," health, or packaging standards discriminating against foreign imports was one way to evade competition law. However, this kind of evasion has become increasingly difficult as a result of stricter interpretation of the provisions of the Treaty of Rome that prohibit trade restrictions (in particular Articles 30 and 36) and as a result of the "1992" program promoting a system of mutual recognition of national technical, health, safety, and quality standards.

Australia and New Zealand (see Thomson, chapter 12) are the only other nations where competition law has replaced trade law inter se. Both countries offer an open binational market with consumer protection rather than a trade-protection remedy featuring predatory pricing and state subsidization, both of which disadvantage the consumer.[3] The United States rejected an invitation from Canada to dismantle trade barriers between the two countries in the United States-Canada Free Trade Agreement. An opportunity for North American market reform, which would have ended dumping cases in US-Canada trade to the benefit of both nations, was thereby lost. It was never a serious option as part of the NAFTA, once again due primarily to resistance from some US and Canadian businesses and much US labor opposition.

In the late 1970s, the United Nations Committee on Trade and Development (UNCTAD) did adopt a nonbinding international antitrust code. The UN showed sufficient consensus on general competition standards to

---

3. For a discussion of the broader potential applicability of this approach, see Marceau (1994).

obtain endorsement of the code by the UN General Assembly in December 1980. However, the code was much less an exercise in promoting markets free of monopolizing restraint than an initiative to promote a redistribution of income from have to have-not nations. A majority of the signatories had no interest in open and deregulated national markets, let alone international ones. The UNCTAD code's only discernible impact has been to promote the formation of national competition agencies in several developing states. Indeed, the Thatcher Revolution—with its passionate commitment to the market mechanism as maximizer of economic welfare for all states, developed and developing—probably would have had the same modest impact even had this UN code never existed.

The experience with antitrust harmonization since World War II supports four conclusions:

- Expanding antitrust into closely regulated or protected national and international sectors, over time, was recognized 50 years ago as a key element in the structure of international economic reform, something that has been largely forgotten today.

- Merely harmonizing broad, substantive antitrust norms will not have much impact on anticompetitive behavior and practices tolerated or promoted by other national and international economic laws and policies.

- Antitrust enforcement grew stronger in many nations, even against powerful restrictive policies, but not to the point where it could challenge significant anticompetitive provisions in the GATT, such as the dumping laws, and other national and international laws and policies that adversely affect international competition.

- Complete antitrust harmonization would require the establishment of a single global competition authority or dispute-resolution tribunal—something all but the most ardent national proponents of antitrust harmonization find unacceptable.

US Extraterritorial Antitrust Jurisdiction As a Spur to Antitrust Harmonization

There is one continuing source of international tension arising from national antitrust enforcement which can, but usually does not, adversely affect open international markets: extraterritoriality (ET). In antitrust, export controls, securities law, and discovery in US civil litigation, ET became a significant political issue in the decade from the mid-1970s to the mid-1980s (Rosenthal and Knighton 1982). ET is the conflict between the extraterritorial enforcement of US antitrust (and other) laws to command or punish conduct in a foreign state, on the one hand, and the local regulatory laws or policies of that state which ET enforcement nullifies or undermines, on the other hand. Under US law going back to the Supreme Court's 1911 decision in *United States v. American Tobacco Co.*, US courts have broad "effects" jurisdiction to try to break up international cartels formed and operated abroad that have a substantial adverse effect in United States domestic markets. In the past 80 years, this doctrine has been used more aggressively to challenge and frequently to nullify restrictive practices exempt from foreign-competition laws that are not exempt from US competition law.

In the 1960s, the Supreme Court determined that US antitrust law could be applied to attack private restraints foreclosing US firms from access to foreign markets—as long as requisite minimum contacts with the United States could be attributed to those engaging in concerted exclusionary conduct (*Continental Ore v. Union Carbide & Carbon Corp.* 370 U.S. 690, 1962). Several foreign governments have been outraged at the notion that US law could force open access to their domestic markets if they determined as a matter of sovereign national policy that in some particular policy area some largely domestic protectionist conduct was appropriate or even desirable. The ruling seems particularly arbitrary to these governments since there are numerous protectionist exceptions to antitrust law in the United States. For three main reasons, there was and continues to be little sympathy in the United States for this point of view.

First, Americans do not know what it is like to have other nations use their laws to punish conduct in the United States that is legal under US law. Only the member states of the Arab League have adopted an extraterritorial law making conduct in the United States illegal (trading with or investing in Israel) that is legal and, indeed, encouraged under US law. It is unlikely that US public opinion would be very sympathetic if, say, a US supercomputer manufacturer that obtained US government subsidies by congressional lobbying was found thereby to be in violation of the competition law of a US trading partner, such as Germany, which believed that its computer industry thereby had been anticompetitively disadvantaged by private foreign lobbying.[4] Since the United States has not been the target of such extraterritorial enforcement, many Americans fail to appreciate the viewpoint of others that extraterritorial enforcement by the United States that undermines their local law can be humiliating, appear cynically imperialistic, and frustrate the local political process. To compound this insensitivity, there is an inconsistency in US and European antitrust laws in the sense that both governments' sets of laws attack foreign price cartels aimed at their

---

4. The United States took just such a view, affirmed by the US Supreme Court, in applying US antitrust law to hold anticompetitive lobbying to influence the Mexican legislature to be illegal *(United States v. Sisal Sales Corp. 277 U.S. 258, 1927)*.

respective markets but at the same time immunize their respective export cartels aimed at collusively raising prices in third markets.

Second, the US government often compartmentalizes responsibility. The Treasury and State Departments used to be jointly responsible for US trade policy. They still retain some indirect involvement. The Commerce Department and the US Trade Representative, with some emerging independence by the International Trade Commission, now share control with Congress of most US trade law and policy. The Justice Department and the FTC are responsible for federal competition law and policy. The intersection of US trade and antitrust law and policy, both in the executive branch and in Congress, is almost nonexistent.

This lack of interaction between law and policy governing the trade and antitrust spheres can have inconsistent, ill-considered consequences. In the 1940s, as part of its Cold War policies, the United States encouraged Canada, France, Australia, and South Africa to develop domestic uranium industries. By the 1960s, the US uranium industry wanted restrictions placed on these foreign producers' access to US markets so that US uranium producers could monopolize the market among private American electrical utilities for fuel to generate nuclear power. With weak opposition from the executive branch and no participation by the Justice Department, Congress passed legislation imposing a multiyear embargo on imported uranium for private sector power generation. Foreclosed from perhaps two-thirds of their potential customers by this US act of protectionism, foreign uranium producers, with the support of their own governments, formed a defensive cartel to salvage their access to the severely reduced electrical utility market still open to them. A few years later, US policy compartmentalization led the Justice Department to challenge this foreign government-supported international cartel as illegal under US antitrust law. This government enforcement facilitated the bringing of additional successful private US antitrust enforcement actions. These led to the payment of more than $100 million in damages by these producers to US utilities, to the Westinghouse Corporation, and to these plaintiffs' lawyers.

The foreign uranium producers and American electricity consumers were the victims of a misguided policy of US trade protectionism beyond the reach of US antitrust law and policy. The problem here was not lack of harmonization among the antitrust laws of the concerned jurisdictions but rather the lack of harmonization, more precisely the failure to intersect, of US trade and competition law and policy with respect to the sale of uranium fuel for commercial purposes in the United States.

The third and only good reason the United States supports extraterritorial national enforcement is that failure to do so discriminates in favor of persons who form and conduct cartels aimed from abroad at US markets. To fail to enforce US antitrust law extraterritorially is unfair to producers in the United States who have to comply with US antitrust law. Mere territorial enforcement fails to protect US consumers and producers who are the victims of foreign cartels.

Experience with extraterritorial enforcement of US antitrust law within the European Union has led most EU competition officials to see the merits of extending EU antitrust enforcement outside Europe. However, this is still a matter of controversy. The United States remains the only nation with an aggressive extraterritorial antitrust policy, feared abroad but popular at home.

Renewed concern over US extraterritorial antitrust law enforcement has led some nations, Japan in particular, to support in principle the drafting of an international competition code. This would, some hope, submerge extraterritorial national enforcement incompatible with agreed international norms. However, there is no near-term prospect for such multilateral consensus on this still-divisive issue. New conflicts in the next few years would not be surprising. Nonetheless, relatively limited ET antitrust enforcement in the United States has not had a major or sustained impact on either the growth or the restraint of the free international movement of goods, services, and capital.

Unwelcome ET conflict, however, does not justify premature efforts at jurisdictional harmonization. It is not a conflict over the conditions of international competition and access to national markets. Rather, it is a conflict over national sovereign prerogatives. Aggressive US extraterritorial law enforcement is perceived by the United States' allies as coercing them to modify their domestic laws illegitimately, outside the framework of diplomacy, and absent an agreed basis in international law. But competition law is only one field among many in which this conflict arises.

ET conflict is present in trade law, in debate, for example, over the validity and propriety of the United States' employment of unilateral trade retaliation under section 301 and super 301 of US trade law for the failure of foreign states to provide access to US exporters in foreign markets. It is increasingly an issue in intellectual property law, for example, whether there should be ET application of national copyright and trademark protection. ET conflict is raised in employment discrimination law and is a major by-product of US insistence on using export controls to prevent its allies from shipping to Cuba from their own foreign ports, even when the goods never pass through the United States, and even when it is illegal under these countries' laws to acquiesce to US laws applied extraterritorially to circumvent the trade policy of exporting jurisdictions. ET conflict is a big problem in criminal law enforcement, especially the episodic circumvention in the United States of bilateral extradition treaties, and it is a problem in civil litigation, where US jurisdictional claims and broad pretrial discovery rules often conflict with foreign adjudicatory standards. ET conflict is therefore too broad an issue to be resolved by harmonized standards of antitrust alone.

ET eventually will diminish as a problem if the United States becomes more accommodating to the desires of foreign states to control activity that takes place predominantly in their home territories, or, conversely, if powerful jurisdictions such as the European Union, Germany, Japan, or even Canada begin to apply their laws extraterritorially to sanction conduct in the United States supported by US laws or policies that adversely affect competition in their home markets. It would have been poetic justice if Canada and the European Union had prosecuted the US uranium industry for conspiring to have Congress legislate an embargo on foreign exports of uranium to US utilities. Foreign uranium producers probably could have proven billions of dollars in actual damages.

Bilateral antitrust cooperation agreements are not likely to reduce ET frictions in the short run, either. These agreements, one of which has been in effect since the late 1950s, provide primarily for notification and consultation. Neither side in any bilateral understanding negotiated to date has been willing to defer, as a matter of principle, to the primacy of the jurisdiction of the other, if the other has predominant contacts with the conduct or persons under scrutiny or a more compelling claim to assert jurisdiction. To so agree would be to cede control, to surrender turf. Governments are bureaucracies, and bureaucracies rarely do this willingly. Moreover, the US executive branch historically has claimed to be particularly concerned that if it agreed to avoid extraterritorial antitrust conflict by deferring to foreign competition authorities in some international cases, it could face congressional criticism for "selling out US interests," and might even face a legal challenge for failing diligently to enforce US laws.

The one legal area where international harmonization is working to avert ET conflict is the prosecution of international securities fraud. The US Securities and Exchange Commission has successfully assisted several foreign governments in establishing enforcement programs to stop stock fraud, including fraud aimed at investors in the United States. But that is a special case not easily adapted to competition enforcement. As a rule, stock fraud is no longer tolerated in many countries. All nations *do* tolerate numerous restrictions on competition. Anticompetition policies are actively and extensively promoted by every nation, including the United States, in selected areas.

One cannot harmonize international ET enforcement in antitrust or, for that matter, substantive and procedural antitrust norms, until one gets consensus on a methodology or procedure for deciding which anticompetitive restrictions should be exempt from antitrust enforcement and which should not. But that brings us back to the insight that stimulated the ITO exercise. Harmonizing competition standards will not work domestically or internationally unless there is substantial harmonization with other standards promoting open markets: nondiscriminatory investment rules; short-term, transparent trade protection measures; limits on beggar-your-neighbor industrial policy subsidies; and greater deregulation of regulated market sectors.

The Real Need for Harmonization: Competition with Mercantilism in the National Economic Policy Process

We have argued that harmonization of substantive antitrust laws is likely to have little impact on market access. Where then is the need and opportunity for competition harmonization? Where it was 50 years ago. It remains necessary to harmonize or initially to engage with transparency the policy process *within* each of the major trading nations if the international economic policy process among them is to become harmonized.

We are not talking about a harmonization that makes competition law and policy paramount and rejects in all cases the legitimacy of values expressed in restricted competition. That will never happen. As this is written, there is concern that rising job insecurity is increasing the level of fear, violence, and alienation in Western societies. This is a threat, if such a concern is well founded, to democratic stability itself. Democratic governments must pay attention. Competition is not an absolute good. There are legitimate national security goals that require trade restrictions—for example, restrictions on sales of armaments to Iraq or of biological weapons to anybody. Some sectors require some government intervention in an otherwise free marketplace to promote equality, fairness, and personal security—health care, for example. Some targeting via industrial policy of high-technology winners is irresistible to policy planners, and sometimes, if too rarely, governments do stimulate economic growth without enormous economic waste. However, US trade law encourages inefficiency when it takes no account of the impact on downstream producers and ultimate consumers when a dumping case is reviewed. It is wrong that US trade law gives monopolists standing to exclude foreign competitors for dumping when these outside firms are merely competing on price for the purpose of getting a toehold in the US market. Such exclusion is disharmonious.

It is wasteful and inefficient when the governments of US states offer subsidies worth tens of millions of dollars to manufacturers to build factories within their borders rather than within neighboring states. In recent years, some of these subsidies have been sufficiently large to provide nontrivial competitive advantages in the marketplace. US competition authorities have no impact on decisions made about either state or federal subsidies.

The US Supreme Court decided two cases in 1993 that represent lost opportunities to begin to harmonize competition law and policy with legitimate noncompetition concerns under US law. In one, the Court refused to find the possibility of antitrust injury, notwithstanding un-contradicted evidence of one competitor's intent to injure another to a point that would lead it to raise its prices back to "appropriate" levels. The Court found that there was little possibility that the predator could in fact recoup its economic losses expended in the predation (*Brooke Group Ltd. v. Brown and Williamson* 113 S.Ct. 2578, 1993). Because the consumer was the beneficiary of the predatory pricing, and competition would remain in the marketplace, even if not, perhaps, as provided by the target of the predation, the Court saw no need to apply the antitrust laws. In international trade, the dumping law, which started out as a predatory pricing law, is now primarily applied in cases in which there is no evi-dence of below-cost sales, let alone evidence of the possibility of recoup-ment from price discrimination by the exporter. The antitrust law on predatory pricing and the antidumping law are moving in diametrically opposite directions. The disharmony is manifest. It should be addressed.

Although the Uruguay Round has tightened the definitions of *normal price*, *dumping margin*, and *injury*, it still has not introduced criteria to distinguish between predatory and other, possibly harmless, forms of dumping. Even the Uruguay Round's major innovation, a definition of *de minimis* dumping, has not gone far enough.[5] In competition policy, the concept of *de minimis* normally is applied to two or more firms that collaborate. It does not normally apply to single firms. The actions of a single firm are found to infringe upon competition law only when that firm commands a dominant market position (usually with a market share exceeding 35 to 40 percent). Antidumping rules would still apply to single firms with, say, a 3.5 percent market share.

One of the many problems with the dumping laws is that merely threatening to bring an antidumping action is often sufficient to en-courage foreign competitors to raise prices. Following a dumping action through to a determination of material injury is not required. Price sig-naling through the threat of—or mere commencement of—dumping actions can have anticompetitive purposes and anticompetitive effects. The question of whether this form of nonprice predation could be an antitrust violation presented another important opportunity for harmoni-zation to the Supreme Court. Unfortunately, the Court made such con-duct immune from antitrust enforcement when there is any "colorable" (arguable) basis for bringing the dumping action (*Columbia Pictures In-dustries Inc. v. Professional Real Estate Investors Inc.* 113 S.Ct. 1920, 1993). The Court will not even consider having lower courts look into whether

---

5. Dumping is considered to be *de minimis* when the dumping margin is less than 2 percent or when the volume of dumped imports is less than 3 percent (as measured by the share of dumped imports in relation to total imports).

there is an anticompetitive purpose or effect in the way the dumping law is used. As Lipstein has documented (chapter 13), it is now so easy to prove dumping injury under the dumping laws of the United States and other jurisdictions, even in the absence of predatory conduct, that it is almost impossible to conceive of a threatened dumping action that could not, if challenged, have some arguable basis for success. Ironically, based on a naive notion of predation, the courts are reducing the potentially constructive impact of US competition law and policy on US trade law and policy. Fragmentation is so complete, and antitrust is so compartmentalized from other areas of international economic policy such as trade, that the courts and many competition experts are not sensitive to these issues.

How to Begin Promoting Competition in Protected Sectors

What we propose here to promote competition in protected sectors can be done without new international agreements and without new international institutions. The first step is to open up the national policy process in each major trading country—to break down the barriers that separate competition from trade, investment, deregulation, intellectual property, and industrial policy. The different ministries and departments need to consult with and debate each other. The second step is to build a strong competition value component into any national law that restricts investment, imposes trade restrictions, endorses selective industrial subsidies, defines the scope of intellectual property protections, or continues regulation of limited-access markets. Conversely, limited possibilities for nonenforcement of the antitrust laws to further other important values, without the requirement of exempting legislation, should be explored. In the United States, this means that antitrust officials should be participants in executive policy in these other areas, and officials representing State, Treasury, Commerce, the US Trade Representative, and the White House who deal with these issues should play a role in shaping antitrust policy. A parallel task in Europe would be to strengthen the role of DG IV in EU economic policymaking.

Recent years have witnessed the Thatcher Revolution, the political scandals in Italy, the despoliation of resources in the former communist states, and the continuing international noncompetitiveness of many companies protected over the past half century by national industrial policies. These events have created a climate in which market access and opportunities to compete are recognized as economically necessary and desirable. State socialism and heavy-handed government regulation are on the defensive. A world with limited resources and a great hunger for democratic accountability promotes greater use of the market mechanism.

However, competition enforcement must pay its dues. To obtain access to the international economic policy process of major jurisdictions, antitrust enforcers must show a willingness and ability to be effective participants in that process. That means, among other things, the ability to make as well as obtain concessions. In the United States, since the days before World War II when Thurman Arnold headed the Justice Department's Antitrust Division, antitrust enforcers generally have welcomed isolation from the national economic policy process. They have said that antitrust enforcement is nonpolitical, like the enforcement of any other criminal statute such as those concerning theft or fraud. Antitrust law, it is said, must be enforced without political interference. Policy interaction, it is believed, invites interference.

The international economic policy process within developed nations is grounded in a recognition that, from time to time, competition concerns must give way to other legitimate policy concerns. This depoliticization of antitrust has had the ironic effect of isolating it from an economic policy process in which concerns about competition need, but often lack, effective advocates or supporters. This, in turn, weakens the voicing of competition concerns when international economic policy is made. Independence from politics has not assured the predominance of antitrust over other values. Arguably, this independence has marginalized antitrust's impact. Independence in most criminal enforcement of per se rules is necessary and appropriate. It is neither necessary nor appropriate in deciding which civil cases to bring under a rule of reason where difficult economic policy trade-offs exist.

Over the past quarter century, there have been some—though not many—major antitrust victories in the conflict between antitrust law and policy and mercantilist policies. In the European Union, it is only recently that competition policy has been applied in traditionally regulated industries such as telecommunications, air transport, and utilities, and only recently has it challenged the preeminence of state-owned firms with legal monopoly rights. It is also encouraging that the Commission has recently begun a study of how to ensure that antidumping measures are in the "interest of the community." The Commission is required by EUs antidumping regulation to examine before the imposition of any antidumping duties whether such duties would be contrary to community interests. Traditionally, community interests have been equated with producer interests. If they are interpreted more broadly to include both user and consumer interests, then the protectionist element of antidumping action will decline. Not surprisingly, the Commission's study has been severely criticized by some industry lobbies. In the United States, a significant victory for antitrust was achieved by Bill Baxter, President Ronald Reagan's first antitrust chief. Baxter won out over Secretary of Defense Caspar Weinberger in getting White House support for deregulation of the US telephone monopoly. In the late 1970s, antitrust officials did play a part in congressional deregulation victories in trucking, rail transport, aviation, and the sale of securities. The Antitrust Division needs an institutionalized policy presence to encourage and empower more such successes.

One formidable obstacle to the effective joining of competition with laws and policies governing trade and other areas is that antitrust law tends to have absolute standards. Anticompetitive conduct, subject to relatively few and limited defenses, is flatly illegal. Horizontal anticompetitive conduct is a felony in the United States, Canada, and Japan and is prosecuted with increasing energy—if still-insufficient resources—in the European Union. Trade law encourages horizontal industry price undertakings that would be illegal if they were not exempt from the antitrust laws. In the attempt to promote national interests, trade policy often encourages international horizontal price-fixing cartels. Criminal enforcement in the United States triggers special rules and procedures—such as grand jury secrecy and prosecutorial independence. These special requirements limit the possibility that antitrust enforcers will participate effectively in the trade policy process—at least when operating in established ways. How does one protect the integrity of the antitrust enforcement process while encouraging those with the greatest relevant knowledge and the greatest potential to develop a procompetition constituency to participate in the wider international economic policy process? It is not an easy question to answer. Today, it is not even being discussed.

At the urging of the Antitrust Division, in the mid-1970s the Supreme Court ruled that noncompetition values such as the promotion of health or safety could never be evoked to justify anticompetitive practices so as to provide a defense against antitrust prosecution (*National Society of Professional Engineers v. United States* 435 U.S. 679, 1978). Although this decision simplified antitrust enforcement, it has worked against a harmonizing of competition and other legitimate policy concerns, not only in law enforcement but in policymaking. It should be reconsidered. Congress included the Exon-Florio provision in the Omnibus Trade and Competitiveness Act of 1988 as a means of taking national security interests into account in assessing whether to permit mergers affecting United States commerce that would be permissible under the antitrust laws. This legislation was opposed by the Antitrust Division. It was feared as a threat to the purity of competition values as the only legitimate basis for the prevention of mergers. Harmonization of competition with other international policy sectors will sometimes, perhaps often, mean a retreat for competition. This will be especially so in periods of strong protectionist sentiment, particularly during economic recessions.

But there cannot be rewards without risks. If the policy process can be made transparent, if the anticompetitive impact of restrictive policies upon the public can be identified and publicized, if the tensions between competition goals and mercantilist goals can be made accessible to the people in continuing public debate, then Americans will be truer to their democratic beliefs. This is so even if it cannot be assured that competition concerns will prevail. There is too little awareness of these issues today, too little debate.

One step toward national harmonization that promotes international competition policy is, we believe, easier than often assumed. Competition criteria should be used to evaluate trade remedies. This can be achieved to a large extent unilaterally or regionally, rather than within multilateral settings. A case in point is competition-distorting and trade-distorting subsidization by a foreign government. Should the importing country's authorities not take any action against the subsidized imported products? We suggest that the question is not whether countermeasures should be taken. It is, rather, what kind of countermeasures? The following case from the European Union illustrates that it may not always be so difficult to achieve the harmonization for which we have argued.

In December 1993, the EU Council decided to levy customs duties on televisions and gear boxes made in Austria[6] because their manufacturers had received state aid (subsidies). The EU-Austria Free Trade Agreement banned state aid that led to distortions of competition between the EU and Austria. The European Union imposed the tariffs to offset the effect of subsidies.

In the case of televisions, the European Commission learned in January 1993 of the decision taken by the municipality of Vienna to grant Grundig's subsidiary in Austria a subsidy that could exceed $11 million. The Commission deemed this an infringement upon the relevant provisions of the EU-Austria Free Trade Agreement. According to the Agreement, before any duties were imposed (or, as in this case, reimposed), there had been prior consultations between the two parties in the Joint EU-Austria Committee. Although this Committee appointed a group of experts to investigate the case and find a solution acceptable to both parties, none was found.

The European Commission proposed a duty of 14 percent because the Vienna area was not eligible for regional aid. The EU Council authorized that duty. It was to be applicable until the aid would no longer have any distorting effects on trade and competition, or at most for a period equivalent to the average duration of the fiscal depreciation. In January 1994, however, following a decision by Grundig to refund two-thirds of the aid, the EU Council reversed its earlier decision.

In a similar case involving trucks manufactured in Austria by Steyr Nutzfahrzeuge, the European Commission in December 1993 withdrew a proposal for duties ranging between 6 and 22 percent because at the

---

6. Austria acceded to the EU as a full member on 1 January 1995.

consultations in the Joint Committee it accepted Steyr Nutzfahrzeuge's eligibility for regional aid under the European Union's own criteria.

Both cases show how trade measures should be used to offset distortions of international competition. First, the European Commission sought to consult the other party. One might note that the consultation was, after all, required by the EU-Austria Free Trade Agreement. But GATT rules also encouraged such consultations, which members rarely made in a serious way. In this context, it is encouraging that the recent Association Agreements that the EU has signed with 10 central and east European countries contain provision for consultation before antidumping action is taken and for reliance on EU internal rules on state aid in cases of public assistance to industry. Second, the cases were put to a group of experts to find mutually acceptable solutions. Third, the Commission relied on competition policy criteria used to review regional aid within the European Union (i.e., it did not apply one standard to imports and another to products manufactured within the Union). Fourth, the duties were to remain for as long as there was a distortion of competition, not for as long as there was danger of injury from imports. Fifth, the Commission accepted a compromise for repayment of the aid. It recognized that small amounts of aid did not significantly distort trade or competition. In normal countervailing-duty cases, the Commission would not have to accept this argument, and indeed usually did not.

In the United States, a desire for harmonization also needs to be fostered in Congress. The increasing allure of mercantilist solutions in the legislative branch requires more public focus on the interplay among competition and these other policies both nationally and internationally. It would help if international trade, investment, and competition issues were not the responsibilities of different congressional committees. The courts also need educating as to the international context of antitrust, which itself needs to be brought into the mainstream of national and international economic law and policy.

We said at the outset of this chapter that we do not oppose the harmonization of national antitrust laws or the continuing effort to draft an international antitrust code with supernational authority. Those pursuing these projects rightly point out that there is a chicken-and-egg problem involved in finding the precise point of maximum impact. Without a growing international commitment to effective competition laws, competition policy inevitably will be trumped at both the national and international levels by less competitive alternatives. We are just less sanguine, for the reasons set forth here, that these antitrust harmonization efforts have "legs" for the foreseeable future. We are concerned that these efforts could, like the UNCTAD code, result in the capture of competition policy by those hostile to the market mechanism. National deregulation successes, however, have been significant over the past decade on every continent. Catching the momentum of national reform, having national competition agencies more explicitly promote national competition policy in national forums, seems to us a more practical near-term strategy for global-competition reform.

Raymond Vernon, one of the deans of international economy policy analysis, is skeptical about the reality of a remedy, as here proposed, which encourages more extensive and effective interaction between the Antitrust Division and other makers of US international economic policy. He properly points out that effective coordination and consensus building among officials in different US executive branch agencies, and between executive branch and congressional leaders responsible for international economic policy—especially when they are from different political parties—is rare (Vernon, Spar, and Tobin 1991, chapter 1). Our point is that competition officials have hardly tried to be policy participants, to build industry alliances, and to work with the White House to develop and pursue competition policy goals outside a very narrow range of antitrust law enforcement issues. Even if the obstacles are tall, it is unduly negative to conclude that the effort to build a procompetition constituency is not even worth making. It has not been attempted in a concerted manner since Thurman Arnold headed the Antitrust Division more than half a century ago.

Now that the Cold War is over and substantial reconstruction and development have been accomplished in Europe and Asia, perhaps there can be a return to the idea that inspired those who drafted the Havana Charter. The initial focus might be on the desirability of harmonizing antitrust and national economic policy within the United States and Canada and within the European Union. One expects both Europe and the United States to continue to press the Japanese government for more of this harmonization within Japan, in particular for an enhancement of the role of the Japan Fair Trade Commission in Japanese economic life.

This harmonization effort will be difficult and protracted. Support for open markets is broad but shallow. People like competition for their suppliers and customers but do not much like it for themselves. After all, antitrust lawyers are not happy about competition from other antitrust lawyers, and free market academic economists like the tenure system. In the rough-and-tumble of politics, protectionists who can mobilize narrow but deep constituencies often triumph, especially where backed up by ethnocentrism—and today, ethnocentrism is on the rise. It is important that further harmonization efforts go forward internationally on trade, intellectual property, deregulation, open investment, and favoring national champions. But if those efforts are to promote competition and open markets, greater national reconciliation of these policies should be predicate.

Protectionists do not always win, however. Promoting open markets over restricted ones goes to the heart of the key public policy issues of our day. Harmonizing competition with state protectionism is not, like antitrust harmonization, an arcane issue for technical experts.

References

Diebold, William Jr. 1952. *The End of the I.T.O.* Essays in International Finance 16. Princeton: Princeton University Press.

Gardner, Richard N. 1956. *Sterling Dollar Diplomacy.* Oxford: Oxford University Press.

Katten, Joseph. 1994. "The Microsoft Deal and Antitrust Limits." *Legal Times of Washington* (8 August): 32.

Marceau, Gabrielle. 1994. *Anti-Dumping and Anti-Trust Issues in Free Trade Areas.* Oxford: Clarendon Press.

Messerlin, P. 1989. "The EC Antidumping Regulations." *Weltwirtschaftliches Archiv* 125: 563-87.

Rosenthal, D., and W. Knighton. 1982. *National Laws and International Commerce: The Problem of Extraterritoriality.* London: Chatham House.

US Department of State. 1948. "Havana Charter for an International Organization." Reprinted in Pub. No. 3206. *Commercial Policy Studies* 114: 86.

Vernon, Raymond, Debora Spar, and Glenn Tobin. 1991. *Iron Triangles and Revolving Doors: Cases in U.S. Foreign Economic Policymaking.* New York: Praeger.

Warner, Mark, and Alan Rugman. 1994. "Competitiveness: An Emerging Strategy of Discrimination in U.S. Antitrust and R&D Policy?" *Law and Policy in International Business* 25: 945.

12

Australia and New Zealand

GRAEME THOMSON

Australia and New Zealand were relatively late starters in significant enforcement of competition laws. Both countries have had national competition laws since early in this century, but for nearly 60 years the laws were either unenforced or ineffective.

Australia

Australia, which is a federation with a written constitution, enacted a national competition law in 1906. The Australian Industries Preservation Act of 1906 was inspired by the Sherman Antitrust Act of 1890 (Nieuwenhuysen and Norman 1976, 15). It prohibited "monopolization" and "combinations" in restraint of trade or commerce, or that injured or destroyed Australian industries through unfair competition. However, a restrictive interpretation of the federal government's constitutional powers in 1910 substantially limited the scope of the act, so it fell into general disuse until the mid-1960s. The federal government sought unsuccessfully to remedy the limitation on constitutional interpretation by seeking authority in four separate but failed referendums between 1913 and 1944.

A number of the Australian states also had laws promoting competition, but these were not comprehensive in scope and state jurisdiction was limited. In the 1950s, increasing concern was expressed in academic

Graeme Thomson is principal adviser, Department of Foreign Affairs and Trade, Australia. The views expressed in this chapter are those of the author and not necessarily those of the governments of Australia.

and government circles over cartelization and excessive concentration of industry in Australia. In 1962 the government proposed a Federal Restrictive Trade Practices Act, but in the following debate the proposed legislation was seriously weakened through the lobbying of business interests. However, a Trade Practices Act became law in 1965. It required registration of certain restrictive agreements with the possibility of disallowance of such agreements if they were found to be contrary to the public interest. Initially, the act had no provisions for dealing with resale price maintenance. These were inserted in 1971. In 1971, the Trade Practices Act of 1965 was held invalid by the High Court, but in so doing the court handed down a new interpretation of the federal government's constitutional powers that allowed the government wider regulation of business conduct. So the grounds were finally established in 1971 for the enactment and enforcement of a national competition law in Australia that applied uniformly to corporations.

A New, National Approach

In 1972 the Australian Parliament legislated a replacement act, but with a new federal government elected to office in late 1972 a change in policy approach also occurred. No longer was the approach to restrictive business practices to be based on administrative investigation of behavior and authorization of conduct deemed to be in the public interest; the approach was now to be based on prohibition of restrictive activity either on a per se basis or subject to a competition test (Nieuwenhuysen and Norman 1976, 46). A new Trade Practices Act was passed in 1974 to prohibit anticompetitive conduct. Significantly, this act provided for private rights of action in most instances. This act was further amended in 1977 following a review of the 1974 act. The main changes in 1977 were the replacement with respect to mergers of the "substantially lessening competition" test with the weaker test that it "achieve or strengthen market dominance." Additionally, tougher provisions were added to deal with price-fixing agreements, special provisions were introduced dealing with collective boycotts, antimonopolization provisions were tightened, and exclusive dealing provisions were extended to cover restrictions imposed by buyers or sellers.

During the 1980s the importance of competition in building a more flexible, dynamic, and efficiently functioning economy became more embedded in the public mind and official policy in Australia. Prohibition of anticompetitive behavior and judicial enforcement have remained the basic approach to competition policy law in Australia since 1974. Some changes occurred in the 1980s—for example, in 1986 the prohibition on misuse of market power was amended, and the merger provisions were extended to certain overseas mergers. In 1992 the merger test was strengthened back to the pre-1977 criteria of "substantially lessening competition" while penalties for contravention of competition provisions were increased substantially.

In 1983, as part of its commitment to the newly agreed Prices and Incomes Accord—a 1983 agreement on certain labor and economic policies between the federal government and key union and business interests—the federal government enacted the Prices Surveillance Act of 1983. It provided for the establishment of a statutory authority to monitor and examine prices of a nominated range of goods and services. The goods and services monitored and examined would change over time and would "focus on areas where effective competitive disciplines are not present." Also, the activities of the former Petroleum Products Pricing Authority, itself a remnant of the previous Prices Justification Tribunal, were subsumed under the new authority.

The Prices Surveillance Act of 1983 did not apply to state/territory authorities, and there were no penalties for failure to comply with the Prices Surveillance Authority's findings, but the treasurer noted that "the force of public opinion and companies' recognition of their public responsibilities will be powerful factors ensuring compliance with the findings of the Authority" (Paul Keating, second reading of speech, "Prices Surveillance Bill, 1983," House of Representatives, *Hansard*, 30 November 1983). The act requires that "declared persons" supplying "declared" goods or services must give prior notice to the Prices Surveillance Authority of price increases. More generally, the authority is empowered to hold inquiries into the prices charged by any legal entity and to make recommendations to the federal government. In recent years the number of declared persons and the number of notifications of price increases has been declining as a result of the increased competitiveness of the economy.

In 1993 a major review of competition policy conducted in Australia (Hilmer 1993), inter alia, recommended the extension of competition rules to include previously exempt government instrumentalities. The accompanying report addressed both the Trade Practices Act itself and existing government policies and practices.

With regard to the act, the reviewing committee recommended, inter alia:

■ removing unjustified distinctions between goods and services,

■ relaxing the prohibition on third-line forcing,[1] by requiring that it "substantially lessen competition" (this would bring it into line with the rules on exclusive dealing, but this recommendation was not accepted by the government),

---

1. Third-line forcing occurs where a contract between two persons requires one of the parties to purchase products (which are unrelated to the contract) from a third party.

■ allowing resale price maintenance to be authorized where it can be demonstrated to offer net public benefits, and

■ deleting the prohibition on price discrimination and relying on the section in the act dealing with misuse of market power.

The Hilmer Report then went on to recommend application of the act to the Crown in right of the states and territories (i.e., "binding the Crown"). The act already applied to the Crown in right of the federal government to the extent it engages in business activity. The court has held in the absence of an act specifically applying to the Crown in right of a state, the Crown is not bound. In 1997 this issue is on the list before the High Court.

Another policy area giving rise to anticompetitive behavior was in the area of legally mandated business arrangements, as often happened when state parliaments provided for legislated monopolies for state-owned service providers such as power generation and distribution or for exclusive buying arrangements such as agricultural commodities boards. It was also noted that the states often extracted substantial monopoly rents from many government-owned business enterprises.

The report recommended that any new firms attempting to compete with existing GBEs would need to have a guaranteed right of access to essentials such as power and rail services.

The report also pointed out that the act, operating as it did under the existing constitutional powers of the federal government, did not cover noncorporate entities such as proprietorships and partnerships unless they were engaged in interstate or overseas trade. It was suggested that a "referral of powers" be negotiated with the states/territories for this type of business activity to be covered in future.

Finally, the committee recommended establishing a National Competition Council composed of representatives from federal, state, and territory governments, which would oversee policy aspects, and the amalgamation of the existing Trade Practices Commission and the Prices Surveillance Authority.

In February 1994 the federal, state, and territory governments agreed to the principles articulated in the Hilmer Report. Agreeing to implement most of these reforms, however, required complex negotiations between the federal, state, and territory governments. Agreement was finally reached on 11 April 1995, when the state and territory governments accepted phased payment over five years of a share of the tax gains expected as a result of the benefits from the implementation of the Hilmer reforms. The federal bill was passed on 29 June 1995, and state and territory legislation have followed. The reforms will lead to a truly uniform application of competition law and a largely borderless national market.

Two new national competition agencies have been created: the Australian Competition and Consumer Commission, which merges the Trade

Practices Commission and the Prices Surveillance Authority; and the National Competition Council, an advisory and research body. Competition laws have been extended to all businesses, including professionals, partnerships, and other unincorporated enterprises. Legislation governing government business enterprises is being reviewed to ensure that it is competition neutral or that distortions are justified on public interest grounds. As a consequence, government marketing authorities will face more competition. Effective access to essential services has been assured. The reforms, when fully implemented, will see benefits to consumers estimated at up to A$9 billion a year, with an overall gain in Australia's GDP of 5.5 percent (Industry Commission estimates).

New Zealand

First Beginnings of Competition Law

New Zealand, like Australia, has a relatively long history of legislating to enforce competition law but not exercising strong judicial or executive will to rigorously or widely enforce those laws until relatively recently (Ahdar 1991).

Unlike Australia, New Zealand has a unitary system of government, and it first enacted competition law provisions in 1908. This was the Monopolies Prevention Act of 1908, which applied only to designated agricultural implements—flour, wheat, and potatoes—and had very circumscribed but somewhat novel competition provisions, given the current debate about linkages between trade and competition policy. For example, with flour and wheat, the act protected consumers from unduly high prices by exempting these products from customs duties if prices were restrictively raised above competitive levels or were otherwise unduly high. The act became nonoperative long before its repeal in 1975.

The 1908 act was followed by the more comprehensive Commercial Trusts Act of 1910, which sought the "repression of monopolies in trade or commerce." However, the act was still of limited coverage, applying to food, coal, petroleum products, and agricultural implements.

The Board of Trade Act of 1919 also contained powers to make regulations controlling monopolies, unfair competition, and prices. Effectively, this law was repealed in 1956 as part of a move to dismantle controls.

By the 1920s New Zealand had begun to implement protective tariffs and establish government-sponsored marketing boards for agricultural products, actions that tended to cloud judicial interpretation of the public interest. Like Australia, New Zealand began a slide into a range of anticompetitive policies that was to last some 60 years.

In 1927, the *Crown Milling* case severely undermined the Commercial Trusts Act of 1910. This case dealt with an arrangement that controlled the price of flour. The Privy Council, the final court of appeal for New Zealand, determined that such arrangements must be shown to hurt the public interest, and that it was not the role of any tribunal to adjudicate conflicting theories of economics. With anticompetitive policies in ascendancy, the New Zealand government chose not to deal with the problems the Privy Council's decision raised. Although the 1910 act did not cease effect immediately, it fell into disuse and was finally repealed in 1975.

While Australia's attachment to the principles of competition declined with the impact of the Great Depression of the 1930s, New Zealand went even further into price control, stabilization arrangements, and marketing through marketing boards. After World War II, New Zealand persisted with price controls. Even by 1954, when price controls had been substantially dismantled in most industrialized countries, New Zealand still had controls in place for basic foodstuffs and gasoline. Politically, New Zealand had become locked into a false choice between continuing price controls in the public interest or instituting a comprehensive competition policy. Indeed, a draft bill establishing competition laws was prepared but dismissed by the then-prime minister in 1957 as the product of someone "socialistically inclined."

New Beginnings of Competition Law and Enforcement

In 1958, following a change of government, the Restrictive Trade Practices Act was passed into law. The thrust of the 1958 act was to control monopolistic practices through corrective orders, although price controls were also retained, as it was believed these remained necessary to deal with the effects of monopolies whose power could not be removed by orders. The 1958 act did not proscribe anticompetitive behavior as such; rather it required that certain practices be examined to determine if they met a public-interest text. While something of a threshold, the 1958 act was countered by the government's continuing attachment to extensive regulation, which included restrictions on entry to certain industries.

A Prices Commission was able to recommend that goods be put under price control. Eleven categories of agreements (e.g., boycotting, collective price-fixing, resale price maintenance) were covered by the act and had to be registered. Price discrimination was not covered.

In 1961, 1965, and 1971, further legislative changes were effected—the latter two changes amounting to tightening of provisions against anticompetitive behavior.

In 1974 the Trade Practices and Prices Commission was renamed the Commerce Commission. In 1975, the Commerce Act of 1975, which amounted to an amalgam of the Trade Practices Act of 1958 and the

Control of Prices Act of 1947 with some added monopoly and merger control provisions, was passed. As a result of changes to competition law, resale price maintenance and collective pricing arrangements required the prior approval of the commerce commissioner, services were covered in the area of unjustified refusal to supply, exemptions were tightened, and the burden of proof, which had rested upon the government examiner, was loosened slightly. An examinable approach to restrictive trade practices was continued. Prior to 1975 there had been no comprehensive scrutiny of mergers or takeovers. Under the new act, two classes of mergers became subject to prior approval: special product groups, and those with asset levels above a defined threshold. Between 1975 and 1986, a number of amendments were made that effectively widened the scope of coverage and improved enforcement.

In 1984, a new government came to office with a vision of changing the highly regulated, largely closed, and, by then, very uncompetitive New Zealand economy. Competition and consumer policies were seen to play an important role in restructuring the economy to become more open, efficient, and adaptable.

The Commerce Act of 1986 drew heavily on Australian experience and represented a sea change in New Zealand attitudes to competition law.

Finally, a Real Competition Law

The 1986 act reconstituted the Commerce Commission as a true enforcement agency. Private rights of action were established for most contraventions of the act. The act is directed at business practices that substantially reduce competition, to prevent firms in a dominant position from using that position for anticompetitive purposes. The act scrutinizes mergers and takeovers to prevent acquisition or strengthening of market dominance.

Because it represented such a major change in approach, the act was subject to review after two years' operation. This began in 1988 and was implemented largely in the Commerce Amendment Act of 1990. The main change was to drop a proposed premerger notification scheme and simply require that anticompetitive mergers be prohibited per se. This is effected through a voluntary clearance process. The amendments also extended coverage of the act to trade across the Tasman Sea between Australia and New Zealand by outlawing use of a dominant position in that market. In particular, the use of a dominant position in a market in Australia for exclusionary purposes in a New Zealand market was prohibited. Another effect was to move the focus solely away from international price discrimination to price and nonprice discrimination. The move arose from the Australian and New Zealand governments' decision to abandon the antidumping remedy on such trade from

1 July 1990 following the 1988 Review of the Australia/New Zealand Closer Economic Relations Trade Agreement (CER) (Vautier 1990).

In 1991-92 the Commerce Act of 1986 was comprehensively reviewed following expressions of concern that the act was not giving sufficient weight to such factors as economies of scale. The review addressed the following issues:

- the nature of the economic cost-benefit analysis undertaken and the scope of the "public benefit" test applied by the Commerce Commission

- application of the act to markets for primary products and to labor practices that affect markets for goods and services

- the treatment of mergers and takeovers

- arrangements for enforcement, thresholds for determining anticompetitive conduct, resale price maintenance, and harmonization issues

However, the Commerce Act of 1986 was not amended, as had been recommended, to replace "benefit to the public" with "benefit to New Zealand" in sections of the act relating to authorization of anticompetitive mergers and practices and provide that productive, allocative, and dynamic efficiency to be the principal elements of the analysis to assess applications for authorization. No general exemption for primary products was provided, and the government's consideration of the review confirmed the existing law respecting labor practices, and a range of operational amendments were implemented or identified for further consideration (Ministry of Commerce et al. 1992).

Enforcement of competition law on a comprehensive front in both Australia and New Zealand has been a contributing factor to a reversal in the competitive decline in both economies evident until the 1980s.

Trade and Competition Policy

It is ironic that Australia and New Zealand throughout this century have promoted, as a first-order preference, freer and less distorted international agricultural markets and policies while pursuing domestic policies (including often those for agriculture) that were increasingly anticompetitive—that were, in essence, the antithesis of policies to promote efficiently functioning, flexible, and open economies. However, this has not been true of either country since the mid-1980s.

Tolerance of anticompetitive behavior, which reached its pinnacle in New Zealand in the postwar period, found political justification in both New Zealand and Australia as a response to the closure of European and North American markets to efficiently produced and cheap Antipodean agricultural products. It was also a response to tariff escalation and other protectionist policies that kept Australia and New Zealand as residual suppliers of generally low-value-added commodities. In turn, in order to build employment and growth at home and then to sustain competitiveness, successive Australian and New Zealand governments adopted policies that placed a low priority on competition: import protection, import substitution, and regulatory practices including subsidies.

While Australia abandoned import licensing in 1960, New Zealand did not do so until the mid-1980s. However, both economies maintained high tariff protection until the mid-1980s, when both tariff and the relatively few nontariff barriers (NTBs) employed by Australia and New Zealand began to be liberalized or, in the case of NTBs, largely eliminated.

Trade Policy Reform and Trade Liberalization

Since the early 1980s in Australia and the mid-1980s in New Zealand, trade policy reform has been a principal instrument for substantially improving conditions of competition in both economies. In Australia, assistance to manufacturing was reduced between 1981-82 and 1995-96 from 25 percent to 5 percent of the value of manufacturing output. With only two industry sectors as exceptions (motor vehicles and textiles, and footwear and clothing)—where maximum nominal tariffs will be 15 percent and 25 percent, respectively—by 1996 tariffs for all other products imported into Australia have been 5 percent or less. Australia's average tariff in 1996 was less than 4 percent and is expected to fall to 3 percent by 2000. All border, nontariff barriers, such as "voluntary" export restraints, import quotas and the like, of which Australia had few, were eliminated by 1992. In 1997 the Australian government announced that the tariff on motor vehicles would be frozen at 15 percent from 2000 to 2005. For New Zealand, which had significantly higher border protection than Australia, similar dramatic, unilateral reductions have been implemented since the mid-1980s. New Zealand, however, did not adopt the policy-neutral setting that Australia adopted in 1991 of a maximum tariff of 5 percent (with two exceptions) and of 1996 as the date for final implementation (Industry Commission, Australia 1993, 439). However, from July 1997 New Zealand was to broadly parallel Australian tariff policy to the year 2000 and in some sectors reduce tariffs below Australian levels.

Since 1984, the New Zealand government has pursued an extensive program of regulatory reform aimed at generating sustained, noninflationary growth. The reforms included deregulation of key sectors (finance, communications, and transport) a revamp of the tax system, privatization of government business enterprises, elimination of agricultural subsidies and sharp cuts in export assistance—a very liberal approach to rules of origin—and lowering of border protection, most notably through the 1983 CER Trade Agreement with Australia. Tariffs in 1996 were 5.7 percent (simple average applied tariff rate). As with Australia, New Zealand motor vehicle and textile clothing and footwear tariffs remain high: in 1996, motor vehicle tariffs were 25 percent, and clothing and footwear, 30 percent. Post-1996 tariff reductions have been announced with a three-tier structure of 5, 10, and 15 percent to operate by the year 2000. Apparel, footwear, motor vehicles, and components will fall to 15 percent, with textiles and replacement vehicle parts falling to 10 percent. New Zealand's average tariff in 1996 will be under 6 percent, underlining the massive elimination of protection achieved by New Zealand in recent years (New Zealand Ministry of Commerce estimate).

New Zealand, closely followed by Australia, has the lowest levels of assistance (subsidies, transfers, and price-raising import barriers) to agriculture of any of the industrialized nations. In 1995 New Zealand's net percentage producer subsidy was the equivalent of 4 percent (as measured by Organization of Economic Cooperation and Development [OECD]), and Australia's was 9 percent, in comparison with the OECD average of 41 percent (OECD 1996). Overall, when assistance to agriculture, manufactures, and services is considered, Australia and New Zealand each are at the least-protected end of the OECD countries. New Zealand's transformation in moving from the position of perhaps the most closed OECD economy in 1983 is particularly impressive.

Separately taking place, but associated with this trade policy reform in both countries, has been an ongoing deregulation of a range of factor markets and promotion of competition, together with privatization of government business enterprises. Underlying all these changes, including reforms of labor markets to improve productivity and work place flexibility, has been a clear perception in both countries that their economic performance and relative standards of living had slipped significantly and that, without significant change, decline would accelerate and the effects would become more endemic and serious. Prime Minister Paul Keating of Australia summarized this thinking in a speech on 26 February 1992: "The engine which drives efficiency is free and open competition."

The policy debate and action agenda in both countries now comprehend eliminating or reducing exemptions from competition laws, such as those favoring government businesses, the professions, and agricultural marketing. Many of these exemptions have already been discontinued; others may be soon or may be changed so as to create greater competitiveness and efficiency. A key objective has been increasing the efficiency of GBEs through commercialization and introduction of competition (so ending monopoly). While these changes will deal with basic concerns over lack of competition, concerns over "competitive neutrality" remain in some areas (i.e., the advantages that GBEs can enjoy vis-à-vis private enterprises arising from cost advantages and pricing opportunities).

Moreover, because of the policies of its state governments, such as preferential purchasing, Australia until recently had never fully enjoyed the advantages of a truly national market. Throughout the 1980s, consensus grew on the importance of a national market free of market fragmentation, and reforms were made of state/territory and federal legislation to facilitate this goal—including abandonment of state and territorial government purchasing preferences and establishment of national food and other product standards. Substantial progress has been made in creating a trans-Tasman market (referred to variously as "a single market" or the "joint domestic market") either through harmonization of regulations or mutual recognition of standards.

With regard to research and development activities, Australia does not provide for any specific competition policy adjustment for this sector. The federal government currently provides a 125 percent tax deduction for eligible R&D expenditure. New Zealand's practice on R&D is similar to Australia's.

Exceptions to the Competition Policy Rules

Both the Australian Trade Practices Act and the New Zealand Commerce Act have similar exceptions to their general provisions. It is beyond the scope of this account to assess the specific advantages and disadvantages of each exception other than to note that some exceptions have an undoubted justification to secure economic efficiency while other exceptions may have less to do with competition and efficiency and more to do with political economy. By comparison to other economies, however, following on the implementation of the Hilmer reforms, Australia (and New Zealand with its own separate policy reforms) has sound competition policy exemptions. In Australia, the Trade Practices Commission can grant immunity from prosecution for an agreement or conduct that would otherwise be prohibited under the act. The act provides that this "authorization" might be granted for anticompetitive agreements, primary boycotts, secondary boycotts, anticompetitive exclusive dealing arrangements, exclusive dealing involving third-line forcing, and mergers leading to a substantial lessening of competition in a market. Authorization is not available for such activities as misuse of market power, resale price maintenance, price discrimination, or most types of price agreements. Generally, in assessing the merit of an application for authorization, the commissions must weigh the public benefit from the proposed arrangements.

More specifically, the legislation includes additional requirements for the authorization of mergers. A company's gain or strengthening of a dominant position through a proposed merger must be balanced against the broader public benefit that might flow from the merger. The commission is specifically required to take into account in its public benefit analysis a significant increase in the real value of exports and significant import substitution. Issues relating to international competitiveness are also to be considered.

Possibly of more trade-related interest are the statutory exceptions for certain restrictive trade practices under section 51 of the Trade Practices Act:

- export agreements (notification required within 14 days)

- conduct that is specifically authorized by the legislature of a state or territory

- certain arrangements relating to patents, copyrights, trademarks, and designs

- compliance with a Standards Australia standard

- conduct arising from labor agreements

- a contract for the sale of a business where the condition is for the protection of the purchaser in respect of the goodwill component of the business—that is, the seller will not attempt to poach customers from the buyer or undermine the customer base

- partnership agreements between individuals

- consumer boycotts

Both in Australia and New Zealand, the relevant acts generally bind the Crown, although no prosecution can be undertaken for breaches. Additionally, section 51(1) of the Trade Practices Act allows federal, state, and territory governments to explicitly exempt otherwise prohibited conduct.

Exemptions in both acts are also available for international shipping "conferences." In Australia, the agreement is to be registered with the federal Department of Transport and Communications. However, these exemptions only apply to specified practices that might otherwise breach anticompetitive agreements and exclusive dealing other than third-line forcing. No exemptions are available for secondary boycotts, misuse of market power, or mergers and acquisitions.

When the federal government introduced legislation exempting international liner shipping, it also stipulated that a review would be made "not later than seven years after [the exemption] enters into force." That review panel reported to the government on 23 December 1993, recommending that the provisions be retained, with some minor adjustments to strengthen the hand of importers when negotiating freight rates. In October 1994, the federal government accepted the basic thrust of the recommendations and added a few enhancements. Under part 10 of the Trade Practices Act, members of the international liner shipping conferences that operate in Australia's liner trades are allowed limited exemptions from the general competition provisions of the act. Nevertheless, the government will amend certain provisions of part 10, including penalties and civil-remedies provisions, where there are anomalies. The amendments will enable greater scrutiny of the effects of shipping accords and discussion agreements and will clarify several other provisions. The federal government would be able to grant injunctions where negotiated settlements—called undertakings—have been breached. The amendments will also provide for effective low-cost dispute resolution and conciliation (Australia 1993).

Arising essentially out of the Westinghouse and other private, treble-damage antitrust actions in the uranium industry of the 1970s, Australia enacted three pieces of legislation to thwart and contest US assertion of extraterritorial jurisdiction. The first was the Foreign Proceedings (Restriction of Certain Evidence) Act of 1976, which allows the attorney general to prohibit companies or individuals from producing Australian documents for discovery proceedings in foreign courts. The second blocking act was the Foreign Antitrust Judgments (Restriction of Enforcement) Act of 1979, which could by order make a foreign judgment unenforceable in Australia, and the third was the "Recovery Back" amendments to this act introduced in 1981. These amendments permit the attorney general to "attach" assets under Australian jurisdiction that belong to a plaintiff facing a judgment when the Australian government contests the extraterritorial effects of that judgment. Though still in effect, these statutes are dormant following settlement of the cases that gave rise to their enactment.

New Zealand also had blocking legislation—the Evidence Amendment Act (No. 2) of 1980—which provides only for the blocking of the supply of documents and records held in New Zealand.

In mid-1997 Australia had only one bilateral agreement related to competition policy. This is the "Agreement between the Government of Australia and the Government of the United States of America, Relating to the Cooperation on Antitrust Matters," which was signed and came into force on 29 June 1982. The agreement obliges US authorities to notify Australia of any US antitrust investigation that may have implications for Australia's laws, policies, or national interests. The Australian government has an option to notify US antitrust authorities of trade policies that it believes may have antitrust implications for the United States. The agreement contains provisions dealing with consultations, each party's obligations to consider the other's interests, the provision of written opinions, and the participation by the US government in private legal actions to inform the court of the substance and outcome of consultations with the Australian government.

The agreement was a landmark of its type at the time because it not only provided for cooperation in antitrust enforcement but also provided a mechanism to avoid or resolve conflicts between Australian trade policies and US enforcement of antitrust laws. Since coming into force, the agreement has formed the basis of a much-improved relationship between the parties on antitrust enforcement and extraterritoriality issues.

It is now understood that a substantially revised Antitrust Mutual Assistance Agreement is awaiting approval in the United States and Australia. The agreement by both countries to cooperate would assist the relevant authorities to gather antitrust evidence, facilitate administration or enforcement of each country's competition laws, reduce duplicaton of effort and inconsistent treatment, and notify the other authority about anticompetitive activities that may warrant enforcement activity by that authority. Legislaton in Australia (the Mutual Association in Business Regulation Act 1992 and the Mutual Assistance in Criminal Matters Act 1987) and the United States (the International Antitrust Enforcement Act 1994) provides the framework for enhanced cooperation.

There is also a memorandum of understanding between the Australian Trade Practices Commission and the New Zealand Commerce Commission that provides for cooperation in administration and enforcement matters. It was signed on 27 July 1994.

Free Trade: A Powerful Tool for Improved Competition and Change

The centerpiece of the review in 1988 of the Australia/New Zealand CER Trade Agreement was the achievement of free trade between Australia and New Zealand without exception in goods, from 1 July 1990. An agreement of treaty status—governing and substantially establishing, from the same date, free trade in services between Australia and New Zealand—was also an important outcome. New Zealand has been able also to enjoy the benefits of open and free access to the Australian market (with a population of 17.5 million), thus expanding its own domestic market beyond its small population of 3.4 million. But the price of this advantage was accepting Australian competition in the smaller New Zealand market and adjusting without assistance to that added competition. Of course, both economies gained from the removal of the remaining barriers to trade between them, particularly as the barriers then remaining were frequently aimed at preventing or limiting trade from the others.

Further, significant decisions resulting from the 1988 CER review were the elimination of the antidumping remedy for trans-Tasman trade and the decision to rely instead on protection against predatory trading practices through harmonized competition-law provisions. These were implemented beginning in mid-1990 (Thomson and Langman 1991) and have taken on added relevance with the current debate on convergence of trade and competition policy.

In making this decision to abolish antidumping within the free trade area, the Australian and New Zealand governments recognized that use of such measures was anomalous to achieving a single trans-Tasman market and would hamper their efforts to promote competitiveness. Different thresholds for establishing dumping and applying competition-law remedies between the two countries—significantly lower in the case of dumping—would have maintained protection for relatively inefficient sectors in the open trans-Tasman market and therefore hampered the efficient allocation of resources. And it would have required a bigger bureaucracy, which itself would have spawned private-sector operations to service antidumping investigations, which would be costly to both countries.

Both governments believed that the removal of trade barriers would make the resort to antidumping action increasingly redundant, as the scope for price discrimination between the domestic and export market decreased and the threat of cross-Tasman retaliation by competitors increased, with the possible occurrence of arbitrage. Moreover, maintaining antidumping remedies risked continuing prolonged disputes at an official level (as well as at the commercial level), which neither government wanted. Without exception, the whole approach—and this is what makes the CER Trade Agreement unique—has been to promote a competitive, level playing field between the two countries without creating bureaucratic, private enforcement, or adjudication processes, as has been the case in the European Union, the Canada-US Free Trade Agreement, and the North American Free Trade Agreement (NAFTA). That is why the CER also proscribes subsidies for goods and services that affect the other trade partner. These provisions are clearly a step ahead of the relatively weak subsidy provisions of both the Canada-US FTA and NAFTA. This proscription has also served to decrease the payment of more generally available industry subsidy schemes in both countries, with ensuing benefits for all.

Thus, the principle of competition promotion without bureaucratic regulation and enforcement underpinned the novel development of eliminating the antidumping remedy between Australia and New Zealand. Instead, the two countries rely upon the market as the first and main determinant, with backup enforcement action by the commercial parties directly affected to be adjudicated by the courts.

Developing the elements of the agreement was made easier by the fact that there was already a significant level of compatibility between the competition laws of Australia and New Zealand. New Zealand had closely modeled the competition-law provisions of its Commerce Act of 1986 on those of part 4 of the Australian Trade Practices Act of 1974. There were, nevertheless, differences in constitutional frameworks, drafting style, and policy objectives, which contributed to some difference between the two pieces of legislation. Representatives from business and professional countries were extensively consulted about jurisdictional aspects of the package. There was concern, especially from some in the Australian and New Zealand agricultural and manufacturing sectors, but industry and business provided a significant level of support for the governments' goals.

To a considerable extent, Australia once used antidumping actions to protect its domestic industries. This trade remedy was also used against imports from New Zealand before the 1990 package. There were 31 antidumping or countervailing actions brought against New Zealand goods that were accepted in Australia for formal investigation between 1985 and 1988. In three of these cases, antidumping duties were imposed, while eight were resolved by undertakings. New Zealand antidumping cases against imports from Australia, while fewer than Australian cases against New Zealand, increased as New Zealand phased out its extensive administered system of protection based on import licensing and high tariffs and began to liberalize its import regime.

The two governments harmonized their competition laws applicable to trans-Tasman trade in 1990 by agreeing to extend the prohibitions on the anticompetitive use of market power in section 36 of the New Zealand Commerce Act and section 46 of the Australian Trade Practices Act. This was achieved in Australia by inserting a new provision, section 46A, into the Trade Practices Act, which is based on section 46. New Zealand inserted a corresponding provision, section 36A, into its legislation.

The legislation extends the competition-law provisions to trans-Tasman trade in goods and services, but it does not extend to trade exclusively in services. As noted previously, there are slight differences between the two countries' new laws covering trans-Tasman trade. New Zealand's new provision prohibits any persons with a dominant position in a market in either Australia or New Zealand or both from using that position to restrict entry into, or to deter competition in, or to eliminate a person from, a market in New Zealand. Australia's law provides that a corporation with a "substantial degree of market power in a trans-Tasman market" must not seek to eliminate or substantially damage a competitor, or prevent the entry of a person, or deter competition, in a market in Australia.

To enable the new provisions to operate effectively, a number of further changes were made to various laws. In Australia's case, changes were made to the Trade Practices Act of 1974, the Federal Court of Australia Act, and the Evidence Act. These amendments were necessary to ensure that trans-Tasman competition-law proceedings were hampered as little as possible by national boundaries. To enforce the new trans-Tasman prohibitions on the anticompetitive use of market power, both governments agreed to give new investigatory powers to the Australian

Trade Practices Commission and the New Zealand Commerce Commission, enabling them to obtain evidence in the other country.

These changes allow the New Zealand Commerce Commission to issue a notice requiring an Australian company to provide information and any documents needed during its investigation of a complaint. A failure by a company to comply is punishable under the Australian Trade Practices Act. The relevant court in New Zealand is able to sit in Australia or to take evidence and submissions by electronic means for trans-Tasman matters. The relevant Australian court has reciprocal rights. Further, any judgments and orders, including injunctions, made by the relevant courts of each country are enforceable in the corresponding court of the other country.

The Australian and New Zealand commissions at the outset expressed their willingness to consult with business about the legislation, to keep each other informed, and to cooperate in administration and enforcement. This cooperation was extended to investigations; one commission will commence preliminary hearings on behalf of the other. The commissions can also jointly investigate a complaint.

The Australian Trade Practices Commission has adopted a similar approach in dealing with abuses under section 46A as it has under section 46. The Trade Practices Commission's guidelines distinguish between conduct which it believes does not generally restrict competition, that which may, and that which does. It further considers whether the conduct in question hurts consumers in terms of prices, quality, or availability; choice and/or convenience; impedes the competitive process; raises the cost of entry to a market, or prevents or hinders potential competitors from entering; and whether the conduct can be justified in terms of economic efficiency or the desire to engage in genuine competitive rivalry.

The New Zealand Commerce Commission takes a slightly different approach. It gives priority to enforcing the law against conduct seen as having a widely detrimental effect on competition in the market. The Commerce Commission looks first at the concentration of market power. Then it examines the practice in terms of the wording in the legislation. The Commerce Commission seeks to avoid making any a priori judgments about particular practices.

No cases have been initiated under the legislation. Most agree that the removal of antidumping remedies was important in opening the trans-Tasman market to complete free trade in goods. It has also helped secure the maximum economic efficiency and welfare gains possible from the creation of a single market. Future challenges include the complete incorporation of trade in services into the CER agreement, although there already has been further progress toward liberalization in services trade on both sides since the initial but substantial steps were undertaken in 1988 (Thomson 1989). When the CER became effective on 1 January 1989, Australia had 13 service sectors—and New Zealand 8—that were termed exceptions under the negative listing provisions of the CER Trade in Services Agreement. In mid-1997, these had been reduced to 9 for Australia and 3 for New Zealand, and further liberalization may occur soon.

Conclusion

Australia and New Zealand are interesting studies in the linkages between trade and competition policy because of the substantial steps each is taking to bring about economywide, competitive improvements through competition policy, legislation, and enforcement, and to seek greater competition in their economies through trade liberalization and subsidy elimination or reduction (Vautier, Farmer, and Baxt 1990). They have done this by adopting both the traditional approach of prohibiting anticompetitive behavior as well as adopting measures to achieve competition at the microeconomic level.

Each country still has a relatively high dependence, by industrialized-country standards, on basic commodity exports. They also have relatively large and efficient service sectors. However, they both have large degrees of foreign ownership and control of their industries and face very high levels of protection against many of their commodity and potential services exports in global markets, notwithstanding the liberalizing outcomes of the Uruguay Round and subsequent WTO sectoral negotiations. These impediments include effective import barriers, distortions caused by subsidized production and/or exports, tariff escalation in major commodities markets inhibiting value adding, significant volumes of exports subject to single purchaser arrangements in importing countries, widespread controlled or allocated conditions for import access, regulatory regimes that favor domestic producers or service providers, and export franchise restrictions of foreign-owned enterprises that limit capacity to capitalize on enhanced domestic competitiveness by accessing a wider range of markets. In these circumstances, both Australia and New Zealand have a real interest in a new and innovative international effort to inculcate principles of competition more widely into the global economy either in traditional trade policy terms or through wider and more effective application of national competition policy principles or through convergence of both trade and competition policy.

Accordingly, as discussion of trade and competition policy dialogue develops between governments and in international forums such as the OECD, the Asia Pacific Economic Cooperation forum, and the World Trade Organization, Australia and New Zealand have both the experience and commitment to be effective participants. Both countries are likely to promote a strong, all-sectors approach, comprehensively applied and enforced, that encompasses old and new policy techniques and comprehends all measures that hinder or distort competition.

References

Ahdar, R. J., ed. 1991. *Competition Law and Policy in New Zealand*. Sydney: Law Book Company Limited.

Australia. 1993. *Report of the Committee of Inquiry, Liner Shipping: Cargoes and Conferences: The Part X Review in Brief*. Canberra: Australian Government Publishing Service.

Australia. 1995. Science and Technology Budget Statement. Canberra: Australian Government Publishing Service.

Bollard, A., and Kerrin M. Voutier. 1996. "The Convergence of Competition Law within APEC and CER." *PAFTAD*.

Hilmer, F. G. 1993. *National Competition Policy*. Report by the Independent Committee of Inquiry. Canberra: Australian Government Publishing Service.

Industry Commission, Australia. 1993. *Annual Report 1992-93*. Canberra.

Ministry of Commerce, the Treasury, the Department of Justice, the Department of the Prime Minister, and Cabinet of New Zealand. 1992. *Review of the Commerce Act 1986*. Wellington.

Nieuwenhuysen, J. P., and N. R. Norman. 1976. *Australian Competition and Prices Policy*. London: Croom Helm.

Organization for Economic Cooperation and Development (OECD). 1994. *Agricultural Policies, Markets and Trade, Monitoring and Outlook 1994*. Paris.

Thomson, Graeme. 1989. "A Single Market for Goods and Services in the Antipodes." *The World Economy* 12, no. 2: 207-18.

Thomson, Graeme, and Christopher Langman. 1991. "The Removal of Trade Remedy Law in Trans-Tasman Commerce." *Canada-United States Law Journal* 17, no. 1: 203-07.

Vautier, Kerrin M. 1990. "Trans-Tasman Trade and Competition Law." In Kerrin M. Vautier, J. Farmer, and R. Baxt, eds., *CER and Business Competition—Australia and New Zealand in a Global Economy*. Auckland: Commercial Clearing House, New Zealand Limited.

Vautier, Kerrin M., and Alan E. Bollard. 1996. "Competition Policy in New Zealand." In Carl J. Greer and Douglas E. Rosenthal, *Competition Regulation in the Pacific Rim*. New York: Oceana Publications.

Vautier, Kerrin M., and Peter J. Lloyd. 1997. *International Trade and Competition Policy: CER, APEC, and the WTO*. Wellington: Institute of Policy Studies.

Vautier, Kerrin M., J. Farmer, and R. Baxt, eds. 1990. *CER and Business Competition— Australia and New Zealand in a Global Economy*. Auckland: Commercial Clearing House, New Zealand Limited.

13

Using Antitrust Principles to Reform Antidumping Law

ROBERT A. LIPSTEIN

For more than 70 years, the United States has had two standards for dealing with international predatory pricing. The first, the Antidumping Act of 1916, addressed what competition policy normally conceives of as predation. The latter, the Antidumping Act of 1921, came to be the international version of price discrimination policy.[1] These statutes may thus be thought of as the international counterparts to section 2 of the Sherman Act and section 2(a) of the Robinson-Patman Act, which prohibit, respectively, predatory pricing and price discrimination within the domestic market.[2] However, the jurisprudence under these four statutes, particularly since the Antidumping Act of 1921 was superseded by the Trade Agreements Act of 1979, has shown a remarkable and even alarming degree of divergence.

True predatory pricing in its original sense remains difficult to prove in both the domestic and international contexts; domestic price discrimina-

---

Robert A. Lipstein is a partner in the Washington law firm Lipstein, Jaffe & Lawson, L.L.P.

1. Antidumping Act of 1916, *US Code* 15 § 71 et seq. The Antidumping Act of 1921, codified at *US Code* 19 § 161 et seq., was repealed by the Trade Agreements Act of 1979. The current administrative antidumping law is found at 19 U.S.C. § 1673 et seq.

2. Sherman Act, § 2, *US Code* 15 § 2. Robinson-Patman Act, *US Code* 15 § 13. Similar concepts exist in many other countries that have well-developed antidumping and competition regimes. For Canada, see the 1986 Competition Act (competition policy—§ 45 prohibition on restraint of competition, § 50 price discrimination, § 79 predatory pricing), and the 1988 Special Import Measures Act (antidumping). For the European Union, see Articles 85-86 of the Treaty of Rome (EEC Treaty—competition policy) and Regulation 3283/94 (antidumping measures).

tion cases are relatively few, and plaintiffs rarely win them.[3] This is true whether the claim is one of predation by a horizontal competitor for a primary line injury under the Robinson-Patman Act, or whether the claim is for discrimination by a single seller between competing purchasers, which constitutes a claim of secondary line injury under Robinson-Patman.

Antidumping law unquestionably was aimed, at least in part, at price predation undertaken by companies with the intent to harm their competitors. Although there is no direct analogy to secondary line injury cases in the antidumping context, modern antidumping law notions of less-than-fair-value (LTFV) sales are more akin to the lower standards of proof found in secondary line cases. Antidumping law merely requires proof of crossborder discrimination in the form of a seller's lower return on US sales as compared with home-market sales. Antidumping law thus targets not *price discrimination* but *profit discrimination* and seeks to force foreign sellers to earn the same profit, or return, on export sales as on domestic sales. Despite this difference, antidumping law can be analyzed using tools developed in both primary- and secondary-line domestic price discrimination cases.

Contrary to the difficulties of private plaintiffs attempting to prove price discrimination by their domestic competitors, in the international context price discrimination has become relatively easy to establish, using rules that tilt heavily in favor of US Department of Commerce (or counterpart administering authority) findings of less-than-fair-value sales.[4] In this chapter, I will explore some of the "rules of the game," focusing on those applied by the US International Trade Commission (ITC) and the Commerce Department's International Trade Administration (ITA) in antidumping duty investigations and administrative reviews. I then suggest specific proposals to make an antidumping case more like price discrimination litigation under US competition law. While specific regimes from Canada, the European Union (EU), and similar developed-country jurisdictions are not discussed, I submit that a similar degree of divergence between antidumping and antitrust exists in all developed countries, and that similar reforms are also warranted there.

---

3. *Brook Group Ltd. v. Brown & Williamson Tobacco Corp.*, 509 U.S. 209 (1993); *Orscheln Brothers Truck Lines, Inc. v. Zenith Electronics Corporation*, 498 U.S. 933 (1990); ABA Antitrust Section, *Antitrust Law Developments* (3d ed. 1992), 401–51.

4. Throughout this chapter, I use terminology established under the new US antidumping law. The Antidumping Agreement concluded as part of the GATT Uruguay Round was enacted into US domestic law by the Uruguay Round Agreements Act (URAA), P.L. 103-465, *Statutes at Large* 208, 4809 (8 December 1994). The GATT Agreement defines dumping as the sale of a product from one country into another at "less than its normal value." Such a sale occurs if the "export price of the product is less than the comparable price of the like product when sold in the exporting country" (Agreement on Implementation of Article VI of the GATT 1994, Article 2 [hereafter, cited only to the article number of the Agreement]).

I do not here debate the wisdom of defining price discrimination, or even predatory pricing, differently for international and domestic purposes. Rather, I assume that there is a political consensus, and perhaps even an economic justification, favoring some greater protection of domestic producers from international, as opposed to domestic, competition and, therefore, that there is a need for a different framework for addressing discriminatory pricing in the international context.[5] This chapter's more modest goal is to examine whether antidumping laws and their enforcement have so markedly tilted the playing field that dumping is being found, and duties are being imposed, for pricing or other behavior that is not only accepted in the purely domestic context but is even encouraged as being fair, aggressive competition.

The Divergence of Trade and Competition Policies

The degree of divergence between trade and competition approaches to price discrimination can best be demonstrated by the following hypothetical case.

A producer of stainless steel tubing located in the Northwest United States, by virtue of its longevity in the area and its relative geographic isolation from other producers of stainless tubing, has enjoyed substantial economic success and has developed solid and long-standing customer relationships. But because of the shutdown of a major customer, this producer decides that it must sell its product in Southern California, where it has not traditionally done business. To penetrate the Southern California market, the steel producer offers lower prices to new customers in Southern California than it offers to existing customers in the Northwest. Its policy of offering lower prices to California customers earns it a 10 percent share of the California stainless steel tubing market and angers Southern California producers of stainless steel tubing, which traditionally have not faced competition from the Northwest.

Since this hypothetical case involves purely domestic, localized price cutting, the legal remedy available to the Southern California producers is limited to domestic price discrimination laws, principally the Robinson-Patman Act. Under the facts presented, the Southern California producers would be unable to persuade any respectable antitrust lawyer even to bring a Robinson-Patman Act action against the Northwest competitor. A competitor would have to allege primary line injury in such a case, tantamount to an "attempt to monopolize" antitrust case against the Northwest producer for predatory pricing in violation of section 2 of the Sherman Act (*Brook Group Ltd.*, 509 U.S. 209). This would have no

5. An excellent and up-to-date discussion of the subject can be found in Hart (1997). For the view that antidumping law should be scrapped altogether, see Lipstein (1993, 43).

chance of succeeding under US competition law because of the Northwest producer's small market share, inability to recoup lost profits, and the absence of below-cost sales. Moreover, it could not be credibly argued that the Northwest producer would greatly expand its Southern California market share, as it enjoys much more profitable business closer to home.

Rather than resorting to a legal remedy at all, the California producers would most likely retaliate in kind by shipping their newfound excess capacity to the Northwest, thereby lowering prices in the Northwest and undermining the Northwest producer's ability to continue to charge lower prices in Southern California. Such arbitraging of price discrimination is quite common in the purely domestic setting. The Southern California steel producers most likely would elect to compete rather than seek legal protection because the competition law remedies available to them do not offer the option of protectionism.

Now assume the stainless steel tubing mill is located not in the Northwest United States but in Canada. Under the same facts, the Canadian steel producer is now selling at less than fair value in the United States. Whether the Canadian producer is dumping or not depends entirely on whether its less-than-fair-value sales are causing material injury, or threatening to cause material injury, to the domestic stainless steel tubing industry—here conceived as a regional industry comprising the Southern California producers. In arguing their case before the US International Trade Commission, the Southern California steel producers would point to their own lost sales in Southern California, price undercutting by the foreign supplier, and price suppression effects by the foreign supplier, where its lower bids have forced the California producers to lower their own prices to retain business. There will also be arguments about lost employment, reduction of profits, and a continuing threat of injury because, under the hypothetical case, the Canadian supplier's sales to the US market are driven by the permanent loss of a major Canadian customer, thereby creating long-term capacity for the US market.

Under US antidumping law, the Southern California producers would almost certainly obtain legal relief on the very same facts that would not support an antitrust *claim*, let alone antitrust relief. The dumping remedy, in the form of an antidumping duty order, would effectively raise prices to stainless steel tube consumers in the Southern California market. Note, too, that the imposition of antidumping duties would remove the incentive for US producers to arbitrage the higher prices in the Canadian market, thereby allowing higher prices to prevail in both the Southern California and Canadian markets.

At this point, it seems appropriate to ask the competition policy question: Why should there be different schemes for price discrimination *across* national boundaries than for price discrimination *within* national boundaries? Put differently, one could also ask the trade policy question: why should a country be permitted to deviate to such a significant extent from principles of national treatment in the enforcement of its price discrimination laws?[6] The principal answer is largely historic, and in many cases, no longer accurate.

Specifically, it was generally the case when the Antidumping Law of 1921 was enacted that the goods being targeted were fully manufactured, or almost fully manufactured, in the country of export. It was also true that one did not, or could not, arbitrage international price discrimination by exporting back to the dumping firm's home market, thereby bidding away his home-market profits and thus his ability to sustain discriminatory prices. As a result, there was a policy presumption implicit in antidumping law that the imposition of antidumping duties on the merchandise in question would not produce a dynamic response from other domestic industries.

Modern US experiences, however, such as the antidumping case against flat-panel displays, are reason enough to question the continuing validity of these assumptions ("High Information Content Flat Panel Displays and Display Glass," *Federal Register* 56: 32376, 16 July 1991; ITC 1991). As that case and others demonstrate, manufacturing today is a global business, and antidumping measures interfere with efficient structuring of global manufacturing.

Moreover, a US company can, in many instances, effectively arbitrage international price discrimination by taking business away in the dumping firm's home market, or in third-country markets in which both compete. The Canada-US Free Trade Agreement, for example, moved those two countries' markets to this standard of openness, thereby eliminating a fundamental original premise of antidumping law.[7]

---

6. The concept of nondiscrimination in treatment of domestic and foreign companies underlies the General Agreement on Tariffs and Trade (GATT), and exceptions to national treatment, for example, for reasons of national security, are specifically enumerated in the GATT. The Antidumping Agreement, of course, is part of the GATT and therefore a permitted departure from the national-treatment principle. The question here is not why such a departure should be recognized, but rather, why the degree of departure should be tolerated.

7. For a scholarly analysis on the reasonableness of replacing antidumping law with competition law for US-Canada trade, see Feltham et al. (1991). The economic integration of Europe has resulted in the elimination of a cause of action for dumping among member states of the European Union, leaving dumping only as a border measure and competition principles as the measure for addressing intra-Union price discrimination. Australia and New Zealand have also eliminated the use of antidumping measures for trade between them, likewise relying on competition rules instead (see the 1988 Australia/New Zealand Closer Economic Relations Trade Agreement, described by Graeme Thompson in chapter 12). These examples, as well as the hypothetical case in the text, underscore the lack of relevance of antidumping measures for trade between economically integrated and open markets.

Where international arbitrage is not possible—that is, where the foreign market is "closed"—the increasingly frequent remedy has been more widespread use of antidumping or other trade measures. This likely explains why Japan and China have been the primary targets of US antidumping cases in recent years. But this approach has not solved the underlying problem—the closed foreign market remains closed. Indeed, as the hypothetical case suggested, the availability of an easy and effective dumping remedy dulls the incentive for private interests to pry open the closed market, again with the result that higher prices prevail all around.

The adoption of antidumping regimes has increased nontariff trade barriers and genuinely threatens to undo much of the benefit realized by decades of multilateral tariff reduction. When the United States enacted its first modern antidumping law, the Trade Agreements Act of 1979, there were less than 10 countries in the world that had antidumping laws in place. In 1990 there were 24 countries with such laws, and by 1996 nearly 60 countries had enacted antidumping laws.[8] US exporters—indeed, exporters from all countries—should be concerned that the seemingly arbitrary application of their own country's dumping laws will create new and higher barriers to trade, just when tariff barriers are being negotiated down to minimal or zero levels. The better approach is suggested by competition law and the use of public and private antitrust actions to open up markets to international trade.

If governments are to ease the trade-distortive effects of the ever-increasing number of antidumping regimes being created, it will be necessary for antidumping law to be less arbitrary and less tilted in favor of the domestic industry. This will require that the concepts of "unfair" trade practices in domestic and in international trade begin to converge, using competition law principles as the paradigm.

A Comparison of International and Domestic Price Discrimination Requirements

US Antidumping Law

The US antidumping law, Title VII of the Tariff Act of 1930, as amended by the Uruguay Round Agreements Act (URAA), like its domestic counterpart, the Robinson-Patman Act, uses specialized terms of art to define

---

8. *1996 Trade Policy Agenda and 1995 Annual Report of the President of the United States on the Trade Agreements Program* (US Government Printing Office 1996, 39). See also, "Dumping Complaints Rapidly Rising," *Financial Times*, 28 April 1993, 5 (citing GATT figures showing the rapid growth of antidumping investigations worldwide); "Mexican Dumping Cases Unsettling US Businesses," *Journal of Commerce*, 14 May 1993, 1A (describing the surge in Mexican antidumping cases against US exports).

its primary findings: "less-than-fair-value sales" and "material injury." Each aspect of the antidumping law, however, is enforced by separate agencies, each of which employs its own terminology and its own standards to reach what are, in some areas, overlapping decisions.

Before antidumping duties can be imposed, the Commerce Department must determine that a class or kind of foreign merchandise is being or is likely to be sold in the United States at less than fair value, and the ITC must determine that an industry in the United States is materially injured or threatened with material injury by reason of LTFV imports of the foreign merchandise. (The key terms will be defined below.) An antidumping investigation proceeds through four separate stages: preliminary determination of injury, preliminary determination of LTFV sales, final determination of LTFV sales, and final determination of injury (*US Code* 19 §§ 1673 and 1677).

Almost all antidumping investigations are initiated by the private filing of a petition, which is required by law to be on behalf of a domestic industry. While the Department of Commerce is considering the sufficiency of the petition, the ITC proceeds with its preliminary injury determination, which must be in the affirmative if the ITC finds that "there is a reasonable indication" that an industry in the United States is materially injured or threatened with material injury by reason of imports of the merchandise that is the subject of the investigation. An affirmative preliminary injury determination permits the investigation to continue; a negative preliminary determination terminates the proceeding.

The statute contains a number of defined terms:

Industry is defined as the producers as a whole of a "domestic like product," or those producers whose collective output of "a domestic like product" constitutes a major proportion of the total domestic production. If, however, some of the domestic producers are related to the exporters or importers, then the statute permits industry to be defined in certain circumstances to exclude those producers from the scope of the domestic industry.[9]

Material injury is defined simply as "harm which is not inconsequential, immaterial, or unimportant." As a result, virtually any injury will be deemed to be material under this definition.[10]

In determining whether material injury is *by reason of* the imports

---

9. The 1994 GATT Antidumping Agreement, Article 4, defines domestic industry as "the domestic producers of the like products as a whole or those producers whose collective output constitutes a major proportion of the total domestic production of the like products." The Agreement also allows the domestic industry to be defined to exclude producers related to the exporters of the merchandise, or that are themselves importers of the merchandise. (US implementing legislation generally follows the language of the Agreement.)

10. The 1994 GATT Antidumping Agreement modified the injury test in several significant aspects (see, generally, footnotes 11-14 and accompanying text).

under investigation, the statute directs the ITC to consider the volume of imports, the effect of imports on prices in the United States for the domestic like product, and the impact of imports on producers of the domestic like product, with respect to their US operations.[11] The statute further elaborates on each of these factors. Critically, the statute requires the ITC to cumulate the volume and effect of imports from two or more countries subject to investigation if such imports compete with each other and with the domestic like products in the United States.[12]

Domestic like product is defined in circular terms as "a product which is like, or in the absence of like, most similar in characteristics and uses with," the merchandise that is subject to investigation. The 1994 GATT Antidumping Agreement defines *like product* to mean "a product that is identical to the product under investigation, or in the absence of such a product, another product which, although not alike in all respects, has characteristics closely resembling those of the product under investigation" (1994 GATT Antidumping Agreement, Article 2). While this would appear to be an improvement, there is still substantial discretion left to the agencies to define which characteristics "closely resemble" those of the product under investigation, and US implementing law made no substantive change.

The Department of Commerce is obliged to determine whether a class or kind of merchandise is being or is likely to be sold in the United States at *less than fair value*. Merchandise is sold at less than fair value if its export price or constructed export price (CEP) is less than its normal value.[13] Export price or CEP is, effectively, the selling price of the merchandise to the first unrelated party in the United States, less deductions for US Customs duties and brokerage charges, and all movement charges associated with delivering the merchandise from its point of production in the foreign country to the unrelated US customer, less expenses incurred in selling to the customer in the United States.

Normal value is, generally speaking, the price at which the foreign like product is sold in the home country, again adjusted for movement charges and selling expenses. Thus, both export price and normal value

---

11. Article 3.5 of the 1994 GATT Antidumping Agreement requires affirmative proof that the "dumped imports are, through the effect of dumping, causing injury within the meaning of this Agreement." The 1994 GATT Antidumping Agreement further requires that all factors contributing to the injury of the domestic industry, other than the dumped imports, be isolated and not considered in the causation analysis. US implementation of this requirement, however, has treated the 1994 GATT Antidumping Agreement as not requiring a substantive change in US law, a position that, to this author, is untenable.

12. Cumulation is expressly permitted, though not required, by Article 3 of the 1994 GATT Antidumping Agreement.

13. The new GATT terminology, which has been implemented into US law, substituted the concept of normal value for foreign market value, and export price, or constructed export price, for US price.

measure prices adjusted to an ex-factory basis; assuming the actual home-market price is above the cost of production, US sales are made at less than fair value when the manufacturer realizes a lower rate of return on export sales to the United States than on domestic sales. As noted earlier, this concept of profit discrimination, not price discrimination, is unique to trade law.

As in the case of domestic like products, the statute defines *foreign like product*, but it sets forth here a specific hierarchy: (1) subject merchandise that is identical in physical characteristics with and produced in the same country and by the same person as that merchandise; (2) merchandise produced in the same country and by the same person as the subject merchandise which is like the subject merchandise in component materials and in the purposes for which it is used, and is of approximately equal commercial value; (3) merchandise produced in the same country by the same person, of the same general class or kind as the subject merchandise, which is like that merchandise in the purposes for which it is used, and that the Department of Commerce may determine may be reasonably compared (*US Code* 19 § 1677, 16).

Further, normal value is to be based on sales for home consumption "in the usual commercial quantities" and "in the ordinary course of trade."[14] Finally, normal value is to be determined by prices prevailing, at a time reasonably corresponding to the time of the sale used to determine the export price or constructed export price. This introduces into the antidumping margin analysis a requirement that US sales be compared with home-market sales that are made reasonably contemporaneously to the US sale.

Where there are no home-market (or third-country) sales of the foreign like product, or such sales occur below the cost of production, then normal value may be based on "constructed value," which is the cost of all materials and labor used to produce the product exported to the United States, plus actual selling, general and administrative expenses (SG&A), plus profit.[15]

The foregoing is merely a review of the statutory framework. Examples of how the ITC and the Department of Commerce have implemented this framework in specific cases will follow. These will demonstrate the degree

---

14. In implementing legislation, the United States has defined "ordinary course of trade" to be only those home-market sales that survive the "sales below cost" test. Further, since the GATT Agreement provides that the profit for calculating constructed value (normal value based on cost of production, plus expenses and profit) will be profit on sales in the ordinary course of trade, this US definition of ordinary course of trade will actually increase dumping margins based on constructed-value comparisons. This certainly was not the intent of GATT negotiators when they bargained for US elimination of its minimum 8 percent profit and the use instead of "actual profit" information.

15. See discussion in footnote 14 regarding the impact of the 1994 GATT Antidumping Agreement on this statutory provision.

to which the implementation of the antidumping law deviates from either predatory pricing or price discrimination standards under domestic antitrust law. Antitrust standards are discussed in the context of specific proposals for reform of antidumping law later in this chapter.

Requirement of Contemporaneous Sales

For antidumping investigations, the Department of Commerce generally examines a 12-month period of sales in the United States. Section 773(a)(1) of the Tariff Act provides that the Department use as the normal value the price "at a time reasonably corresponding to the time" of the US sale.[16]

As a result of changes made by the WTO Antidumping Agreement and the URAA, Commerce will normally calculate a single weighted average price for each "averaging group" covering the 12-month period of sales in both the United States and in the home market. Averages will be calculated based on groups of identical or virtually identical merchandise in each market and at the same level of trade.[17] Under this average-to-average methodology, US sales that occur toward one end of the period of investigation could, effectively, be compared to home-market sales made several months earlier or later than the "contemporaneous" home-market sale(s).[18]

In administrative reviews, Commerce normally will compare sales of identical merchandise in the home market in the same month as the US sales. If there are no sales of identical merchandise in the home market in the same month as each monthly average of US sales, Commerce will search for monthly weighted average sales values of identical merchandise in the home market up to three months, or 90 days prior to the month of the US sales. If there are no sales of identical merchandise in the home market up to 90 days prior to the month of the US sales, Commerce will search for monthly weighted average sales values of identical merchandise in the home market up to two months, or 60 days subsequent to the month of the US sales. If no home-market sales of identical merchandise are located, the 90-60 search is repeated for home-market sales of "similar" merchandise. If Commerce is *still* unable to find contemporaneous sales in the home market, Commerce will use constructed value as the basis for normal value.[19]

---

16. For a comparison with pre-1995 law, see "Certain Forged Steel Crankshafts from the United Kingdom," *Federal Register* 56 (14 February 1991): 5975 and 5976.

17. 19 CFR § 351.414(d)

18. Note, however, that the use of averages on both sides does not give full credit for US sales made above normal value. See discussion of US sales below.

19. This matching process obviously introduces the possibility that margins will be created, exaggerated, or eliminated solely by virtue of movements in exchange rates. Dur-

In some annual reviews before 1995, Commerce had examined home-market transactions to determine whether prices on a part-by-part basis had been stable throughout the period of review. When prices were stable, Commerce used an average value of sales for the entire period of review, effectively treating all home-market sales as contemporaneous to each and every US sale.[20]

Contemporaneous is not defined by a US statute. However, the ITC follows a general practice of reviewing data for a full three-year period before the investigation as well as data for the current partial year and the corresponding data from the immediately preceding partial year.

Thus, ITC review of relevant economic factors covers the entire industry within a broad period. Findings of injury may, therefore, be based on conduct occurring well before Commerce's 12-month period of investigation. This bifurcated approach is unlike US domestic antitrust law, where the plaintiff is required to demonstrate that the very sales for which discriminatory prices were charged are the source of competitive harm.

Cumulation

In making its determination on material injury, the ITC must evaluate the volume, price effects, and impact on domestic producers of the subject imports, as well as any other economic factors deemed relevant. In conducting its evaluation, the ITC is required to:

> cumulatively assess the volume and effect of imports of the subject merchandise that compete with each other and with domestic like products in the United States market. *US Code* 19 § 1677(7)(G)(i)

Traditionally, the ITC has evaluated four factors in determining if products compete with one another and with domestic like products as

---

ing 1994 and early 1995, for example, the Japanese yen strengthened considerably, and at times rapidly, against the US dollar. Because Commerce converts the price of a home-market sale using the exchange rate in effect on the date of the US sale, a comparison two or three months back would produce significantly higher margins, even if the exporter had raised US prices to offset the currency fluctuation. The 1994 GATT Antidumping Agreement, Article 2.4.1., provides that enforcement authorities must allow exporters 60 days to adjust to sustained currency movements and that temporary movements are to be disregarded in margin calculations. The new US antidumping law provides for a 60-day lag on currency conversions where there has been a sharp and unexpected movement in exchange rates. See section 773A of the Tariff Act of 1930, as amended by section 225(a) of the Uruguay Round Agreements Act. The United States has limited this change, however, to "investigations" and has not applied it to "annual reviews," where the actual margin of dumping for duty assessment purposes is calculated.

20. US implementation of the 1994 GATT Antidumping Agreement prevents such "annual averaging," limiting Commerce to monthly averages (section 777A[d][2] of the Tariff Act of 1930).

required under this cumulation provision: fungibility of imports with both other imports and the domestic product, sales or offers of sales in the same geographic markets, existing common or similar channels of distribution, and the simultaneous presence of imports in the market (ITC 1993c, 66). In evaluating these factors, the ITC only has to find a "reasonable overlap" of competition to mandate cumulation. The ITC asserts that it is its general practice to "cumulate imports even where there were alleged differences in quality between imports and domestic products, although considerations of quality differences are relevant to whether there is 'reasonable overlap' of competition" (ITC 1993b, 12). Imports already subject to trade relief were, under prior US law, eligible to be cumulated with imports under investigation if the antidumping order was "sufficiently recent such that those unfairly traded imports which resulted in the imposition of the order are continuing to have an effect on the domestic industry" (ITC 1993a, 12-13).[21]

As a result, injury can be established through the magic of cumulation even where the volume of imports from one country under investigation is small. In the *Flat-Rolled Carbon Steel Products* case (ITC 1993c), the ITC considered the issue of "reasonable overlap" of competition to mandate cumulation according to the market share of the countries in question.

The ITC rejected challenges that were based on claims that the imported merchandise did not compete with the products of the domestic industry. Thus, the ITC rejected arguments by French producers of hot-rolled sheet that a large percentage of French products did not compete with other subject imports and the domestic like product because they were of higher quality and because domestic manufacturers were unable to manufacture similar products. The ITC said it was sufficient that a significant minority of products did compete more directly. It reached a similar decision with respect to hot-rolled sheet from the Netherlands, stating:

> We also specifically reject the Dutch respondent's arguments that the Commission has the 'inherent authority' to exclude from its cumulation analysis a certain portion of a country's imports that are found to be noncompetitive with the domestic like product and other subject sources. We have consistently declined to exclude a portion of a country's imports which may be less than completely substitutable with domestic products and other imported sources and only analyze competition with respect to the remaining imports. (ITC 1993c, 56, note 202)

As noted, the injury portion of the antidumping statute permits an exception to mandatory cumulation for negligible imports. Import levels

---

21. The 1994 GATT Antidumping Agreement, Article 3.3., limits cumulation authority to imports simultaneously subject to investigation. The United States implemented this requirement under the Uruguay Round Agreements Act.

Table 1   Imports by selected countries of hot-rolled sheet as a percentage of US apparent consumption, 1990-92
(percentages)

Country	1990	1991	1992
Non-negligible import levels subject to cumulation			
Canada	1.2	1.3	1.9
France	0.9	0.6	0.8
The Netherlands	0.4	0.5	0.6
Negligible import levels not subject to cumulation			
Germany	0.6	0.5	0.4
Japan	0.4	0.4	0.3
Brazil	0.3	0.2	0.3
Belgium	0.1	0.2	negl.[a]

a. Import levels of less than 0.1 percent.

were found *not* to be negligible in Canada, France, and the Netherlands. By contrast, imports from Belgium, Brazil, Germany, and Japan were found to be negligible and therefore escaped cumulation (table 1).

In the decision involving Germany, the ITC ruled: "We believe that the volume and market share of the imports alone, together with the fact that there was significant overselling of German products, indicates that German imports are negligible. . . ." (ITC 1993c, 66). Compared with the decision concerning the Netherlands, the crucial factor seems to be one of a very marginal trend line.

The new US antidumping law defines negligible imports as imports that account for less than 3 percent of all such imports by volume in the most recent 12-month period, unless the total of all negligible imports from all countries exceeds 7 percent of import volume (*US Code* 19 § 1677, 24).

Domestic and Foreign Like Products

Again, under the antidumping law, the determination of what merchandise is involved in an investigation is loosely defined by statute and requires separate analyses by both Commerce and the ITC. Commerce determines whether subject merchandise has been sold at less than fair value. In calculating antidumping margins, Commerce must go further than simply identifying the subject merchandise—it must identify merchandise sold in the home market or in third countries that is "such or similar" to the merchandise allegedly being dumped in the United States. For its part, the ITC determines "domestic like product" categories to determine whether injury, or threat of injury, to the domestic industry exists. These analyses are not uniform and allow for varying levels of discretion by each agency. Furthermore, Commerce and ITC may or may not come to similar conclusions, and often include products that do not truly compete with the allegedly injured producers of the domestic like products.

An example of the application of the statutory language governing Commerce's foreign like-product determination is the case of "Certain Cold-Rolled Carbon Steel Flat Products From Argentina, et al." (*Federal Register* 58: 37062, 9 July 1993, Notice of Final Determination). Here, Commerce determined that the products constituted four classes or kinds of merchandise, as well as four categories of "such or similar merchandise." This determination was reached despite claims by both respondents and interested parties that some of the merchandise should not be included because it was neither available domestically (at all or in the required quantities), nor were there any substitutable products (*Federal Register* 58: 37062 and 37075, 9 July 1993). Commerce rejected these arguments, noting that petitioners are not required to produce every product covered by the scope of the investigation, nor is Commerce required by law to consider such arguments as "available substitutes" when considering what products to include under a scope exclusion request.[22]

The antidumping statute requires the ITC to determine what constitutes domestic like-product categories for determining injury. To determine whether the petitioner in an antidumping case has been injured, the ITC examines the industry that produces the domestic product it has determined is "like" the merchandise under investigation. The petitioner, however, has the first opportunity to define this merchandise and therefore to influence the scope of the domestic like-product determination. The statute itself provides little guidance on how the ITC should determine when one product is "like" another.

ITC analysis of injury is producer based, not consumer based, as would occur under competition law principles. In the recent antidumping investigation of *Certain Steel Wire Rod from Brazil, Canada, Japan, and Trinidad and Tobago,* for example, the ITC preliminarily determined that all products under investigation constituted a single like product.[23] In the public hearing, suppliers of steel wire rod testified that only the high-quality, high-carbon content wire rod could be used for certain applications such as tire cord and bead; lower-grade rod could not be substituted. Furthermore, there was testimony that the domestic industry had neither the capacity nor the capability to produce acceptable tire

---

22. "Certain Cold-Rolled Carbon Steel Flat Products From Argentina et al., (Notice of Final LTFV Determination)," *Federal Register* 58: 37,076, 9 July 1993. In contrast, under price discrimination law, a key issue is product substitutability, discussed later in this chapter.

23. *Certain Steel Wire Rod From Brazil, Canada, Japan, and Trinidad and Tobago,* USITC Publication 2647 (June 1993, 9).

wire rod.[24] Thus, the effect of the ITC's one like-product determination was to allow injury to be found by reason of imports of all grades of wire rod, regardless of differences in market circumstances surrounding the different grades of steel wire rod covered under this investigation.[25]

The ITC's producer-oriented focus is further highlighted in the recent steel case decisions in which it determined that the products under investigation constituted four separate like products. Here, the ITC reiterated that its practice is not "to fragment like product definitions where a continuum of products exists" (ITC 1993c, 13). The ITC deviates from this practice only where *more than minor* differences exist to distinguish products. In the steel cases, however, even though the foreign producers alleged, and the ITC found, differences in price and customer and producer perceptions and a lack of interchangeability in end uses, the ITC determined that these differences were not significant enough to warrant additional separate like-product distinctions (ITC 1993c, 17-18).

The Robinson-Patman Act

The Robinson-Patman Act, passed in 1935 as an amendment to the Clayton Act, was expressly intended to protect competitors and is the only antitrust law that has that express purpose. It therefore provides a framework of analysis that should be acceptable to supporters of the antidumping law. To establish a prima facie case of price discrimination under the Robinson-Patman Act, the plaintiff must demonstrate:

- reasonably contemporaneous sales
- of commodities
- of like grade and quality
- at differential prices
- where the effect of such price differentials may be to lessen competition or tend to create a monopoly in any line of commerce.

Each of the above is a statutory element of the violation, and therefore the plaintiff bears the burden of proof as to all of them and must separately establish each element as to each defendant.

The statute provides for certain defenses from liability even where

---

24. USITC hearing, 14 May 1993, Steel Wire Rod case, Inv. no. 731-TA-646-649, pp. 161–69.

25. The ITC, in its final determination, found that there was no injury to the domestic industry, but retained its one like-product conclusion *(Certain Steel Wire Rod from Brazil and Japan*, Inv. Nos. 731-TA-646 and 648 [Final], USITC Pub. 2761, March 1994).

price differentials exist. Most significantly, the statute allows a price differential to be charged in good faith to meet a lower price offered by a competitor. Lower prices are also permitted where a price differential can be cost justified. Finally, the statute recognizes that certain inventory clearances or other unusual sales do not give rise to a lessening of competition.

Initial enforcement of the Robinson-Patman Act, particularly by the Federal Trade Commission (FTC), established some inflexible standards, the effect of which was to reduce merchants' abilities to compete with one another on price. As a result, the Robinson-Patman Act came under significant attack by antitrust commentators, and its enforcement, particularly by the FTC, virtually lapsed. In the last 15 years, however, there has been renewed litigation under Robinson-Patman, both by private parties and the FTC. Recent interpretations of the act have generally attempted—successfully, in my view—to harmonize enforcement of the act with the fundamental principle embodied in other US antitrust laws, namely, the protection of consumers through lower prices for goods. To that end, decisions under Robinson-Patman have eliminated the so-called "automatic damages" rule (*J. Truett Payne Co. v. Chrysler Motor Corp.*, 451 US 557, 1981) and have expanded the "meeting competition" defense. Recent cases have confirmed that this defense is available so long as the seller acted in good faith, it is not lost if the seller ultimately proves to have beaten, rather than merely to have met, the competition (*Great Atlantic & Pacific Tea Co. v. Federal Trade Commission*, 440 US 69, 1979), and they have allowed for areawide use of the defense based upon available information as to the competitor's marketing strategy (*Falls City Industries v. Vanco Beverage, Inc.*, 460 US 428, 1983).

While a showing of predatory pricing now requires an objective likelihood of recoupment, such requirement has not generally been imposed in secondary-line Robinson-Patman cases. Following on the thesis of this chapter that antidumping law is more like secondary-line injury cases than predatory pricing or primary line cases, the following reforms do not include a suggestion that possibility of recoupment be demonstrated before relief under antidumping laws can be obtained.

Specific Reforms of Antidumping Law

Changes in ITC Injury Determinations

Applying Antitrust Principles to Domestic Like Product Definition and Injury Analysis

As we have seen, the ITC conducts its injury analysis on the basis of data about the industries that produce domestic products that are "like" the merchandise under investigation. The domestic like-product concept, however, typically allows the petitioner to establish very broad product categories and to seek relief even for imports of individual products it does not produce. In the *Flat Rolled Steel* cases, for example, several foreign producers demonstrated that the specific products they sold to the United States were high-value, niche, or specialty products that did not compete with US production. In most instances, however, the ITC ignored such arguments, finding that it was sufficient that some portion of the foreign production competed with domestic production. In other words, the ITC would not segment the "domestic like product" into narrower groups of products.

Commerce's "class or kind" analysis is not much better. While Commerce often follows the ITC's preliminary like-product analysis, it is not bound to do so. In *Brass Nozzles* (*Federal Register* 50: 8354, 1 March 1985), for example, Commerce found five classes or kinds of merchandise, while the ITC found seven like products. As a result, Commerce had to recalculate its dumping margins to exclude the sales of the noninjurious products. Such differences are not only wasteful but downright silly. After all, the agencies are ultimately enforcing the same statute.

The contrast between the antitrust and trade law approaches to these issues could not be more stark. In antitrust cases, price discrimination is actionable only when the products involved are of "like grade and quality" (*US Code* 15 § 13[a]). Factors considered in determining whether products are of like grade or quality include cross-elasticity of demand, substitutability, physical appearance, and identity of performance (*Checker Motors Corp. v. Chrysler Corp.* 283 F. Supp. 876, 888-89, S.D.N.Y. 1968). True physical differences that affect either consumer use or the marketability of the product can be sufficient to make two products not of like grade and quality (*Quaker Oats Co.*, 66 F.T.C. 1131, 1964).

Like grade and quality can even be influenced by the relative time at which two sales occur. In *Lombino & Sons v. Standard Fruit & S.S. Co.*, bananas that were shipped in the same shipment but sold at different times were deemed to be *not* of like grade and quality due to their perishable nature (1975-2 Trade Cas. [CCH] ¶60,527, 67,329, S.D.N.Y. 1975). Thus, under the Robinson-Patman Act, the determination of like grade and quality is conducted under strict provisions that attempt to ensure that products are truly alike.

While the Robinson-Patman Act focuses on comparisons between individual products, the US government's Horizontal Merger Guidelines (US Department of Justice and Federal Trade Commission 1992) provide a framework for defining "relevant markets" within which to measure a variety of effects, including whether imported products compete sufficiently with domestic products to be a cause of material injury. Unlike the producer orientation of the ITC's injury analysis, the Merger Guidelines' analysis is based primarily on consumer substitution responses.

The Justice Department and the FTC "define a market in which firms could effectively exercise market power if they were able to coordinate their actions" (US Department of Justice and Federal Trade Commission 1992, 7). The core of this definitional process is the price increase test, which analyzes potential consumer response to a "small but significant and nontransitory" price increase. It is the consumer response that then defines the product market:

> A price increase could be made unprofitable by consumers either switching to other products or switching to the same product produced by firms at other locations. The nature and magnitude of these two types of demand responses respectively determine the scope of the product market and the geographic market. (US Department of Justice and Federal Trade Commission 1992, 8)

Thus, the Merger Guidelines define the product market, as described by a product or group of products, and a geographic market, based solely on demand substitution factors (US Department of Justice and Federal Trade Commission 1992, 8).

Proposal for Reform

The like grade and quality analysis of Robinson-Patman provides a single, workable framework for analyzing both margins and injury. Adopting a specific standard applicable to both determinations ought to be non-controversial. Adopting a tighter standard, while most assuredly controversial, nonetheless makes sense. The current standards allow for import relief against whole groups of products that do not, in an antitrust sense, *compete* with the domestic products.[26] There is no trade policy rationale for such broad relief.

If, as we suspect will be argued, the like grade and quality standard is too narrow, then the product and geographic market analysis of the Merger Guidelines is an appropriate alternative. If the flow of imports of a specific product will not change in response to a higher US price for a second product, the two products are in different markets. The volume and value of imports of the one product cannot, by definition, injure producers of the second, and relief should not be allowed against both products merely because, in some vague sense, they are "like" each other.

By adopting a competition-based analysis of like product and injury, trade relief will be available only against truly competitive products.

---

26. The domestic industry retains a strong incentive to include such noncompeting products within the requested scope of relief because antidumping duties on such products raise rivals' costs and therefore enhance the effectiveness of any remedy obtained on directly competing products.

Emphasizing consumer substitution responses will eliminate from the scope of relief products that are not substitutes and that are not obtainable domestically. Such an analysis would limit remedies to competitive situations and would prevent injury both to downstream producers and consumers, who should not be forced to pay higher prices for imports when competitive domestic products are not available. This reform would return antidumping analysis to its roots and eliminate one of the more pernicious aspects of the current approach.

Requiring Proof of Injury

Nearly 10 years ago, Congress added a provision to Title 19 of the US Code that requires the ITC to cumulate the effects of imports from different countries if those imports compete with each other and with the like product; that provision, § 1677(7)(C)(iv), has a counterpart section in the Uruguay Round implementing legislation, *US Code* 19 § 1677(7)(G). As we have seen in the *Flat Rolled Steel Cases*, cumulation has permitted injury to be found from imports constituting as little as 0.5 percent of apparent consumption. Contrast this with the typical antitrust price discrimination case, where injury must be affirmatively demonstrated as to each defendant. Indeed, in such cases there is typically only one manufacturer as a defendant.

The concept of cumulation is nothing more than a petitioner's invention to broaden the reach of trade laws to remedy even the smallest perceived hurt. One cannot help but wonder how US domestic industries expect to be competitive in the rough-and-tumble of global competition when they enjoy such a protected home life.

Proposal for reform An antidumping petitioner should be required to prove his case element by element, exporter by exporter, or, at a minimum, country by country—bearing the burden of proof just as antitrust plaintiffs do. Of course, if an antidumping petitioner can establish the existence, or likelihood, of a cartel among two or more respondents, cumulation as to those respondents would be appropriate.[27]

One clear benefit of limiting or eliminating cumulation is that it makes the results of an antidumping case potentially destabilizing. While differing margins create winners and losers within a country under investigation, the prospect for a no-injury finding against some exporters but not others from the same country would be far more destabilizing. It may well improve the quality of information generated by the injury

---

27. The 1994 GATT Antidumping Agreement permits but does not require cumulation. Thus, it would be possible, consistent with the Agreement, to implement the proposed reform into domestic law.

investigation, as it could divide the foreign respondents, who now are virtually always united in opposing relief. By giving some respondents an incentive to lay the blame on others, a clearer picture of injury or threat of injury is likely to emerge.

Establishing a "Meeting Competition" Defense

Price discrimination under the Robinson-Patman Act is not actionable if the discriminatory price is offered in good faith to meet the lower price of a competitor. There is, however, no counterpart to the "meeting competition" defense under antidumping law. In part, this relates to the amorphous standard of "material injury" "by reason of" imports under the antidumping statute. The concept of meeting competition as a defense under the Robinson-Patman Act is that one supplier should not be prohibited from offering lower prices if a competitor is offering such prices. Under the antidumping law, however, if a domestic producer is the first to offer lower prices, the foreign producer is not permitted to meet those prices if, in doing so, it would be selling at less than fair value and such sales would be a cause of injury to the domestic industry. As we have seen, whether the domestic industry is presently suffering injury is oftentimes more a factor of general economic conditions, including global downturns in demand and global increases in capacities. Under such circumstances, it is quite easy to find LTFV imports to be a cause of that injury.[28]

Maintaining such disparate standards between domestic and international price discrimination has a wide variety of consequences. First, it most likely encourages a greater level of foreign direct investment than would otherwise be optimum. Domestically produced merchandise, even if produced by a foreign owner, will still enjoy the benefits of the Robinson-Patman Act's meeting-competition defense. Second, the disparities allow domestic petitioners who are suffering as a result of more efficient domestic competitors to obtain relief from import competition even though the import competition is not the most significant, or even a major, cause of the inefficient producers' problems. If imports are not the primary source of the domestic industry's problems, higher import duties will not be of much help to the petitioning domestic producers, as they must continue to face domestic competition that is already more efficient. For relief to be effective under such circumstances, an antidumping case would have to be coupled with a domestic cartel. That alone is reason enough to allow a meeting-competition defense in antidumping actions.

---

28. Although the 1994 GATT Antidumping Agreement was intended to remedy, in part, the lack of clarity in injury standards, US implementing legislation left current US law unchanged.

Proposal for reform The burden should be on the exporter to show that its US prices, to the extent they were lower than its home-market prices, were offered to meet the competitive situation created by a US seller. This will assure that the ITC takes into account the prices of the most efficient US producer when it determines whether price underselling by imports has caused injury to the US industry. This would essentially allow a foreign seller to sell below its home-market price, as low as the price of the most efficient US seller.

Department of Commerce Procedural Changes

In addition to the changes described above to the ITC's standards for determining injury, there are a number of changes to Commerce's practices that would restore some semblance of balance between producers' and consumers' interest in antidumping enforcement. Some of these practices, in particular the procedures for identifying "such or similar" merchandise, have analogs to ITC determinations. Others, however, are issues unique to Commerce's LTFV calculation methodology.

Standing

The Department of Commerce alone determines whether an antidumping petitioner has the requisite standing. As noted above, a petitioner's action must be on behalf of the domestic industry that produces the product under investigation. Commerce has taken an expansive view of standing, so that a petitioner that makes some, but not all, of the products in the class or kind of merchandise under investigation will be presumed to have the requisite standing to maintain the action against the entire class of products. Further, opposing interests must challenge the petitioner's standing before Commerce will even survey the domestic industry to determine whether it supports the petition. Those opposed to a petitioner's claim of standing thus have the affirmative burden of persuading the Department of Commerce that a majority of producers in the industry are against the action.

Is it really necessary to change the standards for establishing standing? After all, one may reason that no antidumping measures will be imposed unless Commerce is satisfied that the imports under investigation are being sold at less than fair value and the ITC concludes that such LTFV imports are injuring the domestic industry.

Such a simplistic view, however, ignores the real-world consequences of an antidumping proceeding. One need look no further than the recent round of steel cases to appreciate the tremendous impact that the pendency of an antidumping case has on supply and pricing. Shortly after the steel cases were initiated, domestic steel producers increased prices on flat rolled products, even though the ITC eventually found imports of such products not to be causing material injury and did not impose duties. With each milestone in the case, the domestic industry hiked price again. After the preliminary LTFV determination, many foreign suppliers virtually abandoned the United States as a market, rather than risk millions of dollars in antidumping duty liability. Talk of shortages arose as the cases drew to a conclusion and, despite the negative injury determinations, price increases were not rolled back.

Merely the credible threat of an antidumping duty action can cause market impacts, even if a petition is not filed. In early 1993, the US auto industry was openly discussing commencing antidumping actions on virtually all automobile imports. Foreign producers scrambled to increase prices for automobiles sold in the United States in response. This allowed US producers to implement unheard-of midseason price increases, all of which occurred without any antidumping cases actually being filed. The results can be readily seen in the profits of Ford, Chrysler, and General Motors for the balance of 1993 and for 1994.

These examples demonstrate the enormous power of antidumping proceedings. Before 1 January 1995, access to such power was essentially not circumscribed. A single private party could bring to bear on its foreign competitors forces that closed the door to the United States as a viable market. The 1994 GATT Antidumping Agreement, Article 5.4, raised the threshold necessary to establish petitioner standing. The Agreement requires that a petition be supported by domestic producers representing a "major proportion" of domestic production, which means 50 percent of the output of those producers expressing views on the petition and at least 25 percent of total domestic production of the domestic like product; see *US Code* 19 § 1673a(c)(4)(A). Both the Agreement and the proposal for reform discussed below have the same objective: eliminating the presumption of standing.

Proposal for reform   Once a petition is lodged, Commerce should be required to establish that the petitioner has the requisite standing *before* it begins an investigation. The burden should be on the petitioner to (1) identify each and every production source within the United States, whether US or foreign owned, that is engaged in the manufacture of the products under investigation, and (2) produce written evidence from those manufacturers supporting commencement of the proceeding.

For those production facilities located in the United States but owned by non-US companies, rules need to be established to determine *ex ante* whether such facilities will be considered part of the US industry. If the facility is owned by a parent company located in a country that is not the target of the petition, that facility should unequivocally be included in the concept of domestic industry. If the facility is owned ultimately by a company headquartered in a targeted country, then inclusion of the US production facility as part of the domestic industry should turn on the degree to which the US facility would be gaining a comparative advantage through the purchase of LTFV imports of components.

Two benchmarks would seem to be appropriate. First, there should be a minimum threshold of component cost as a percentage of total material costs of the US production facility. Second, total material cost should be measured against total US cost of manufacture: if imported components are a significant portion of total material costs but total material costs are only a fraction of the total cost of manufacture, then the "unfair advantage" conferred by the importation of LTFV price components is *de minimis*.[29]

Again, adopting this proposal would mean antidumping petitioners would have to meet standards more like those faced by a plaintiff in an antitrust action, who bears the burden of establishing certain jurisdictional prerequisites, including standing.

Foreign Like Product (Such or Similar Merchandise)

Under the antidumping law, Commerce calculates the US price for the merchandise under investigation and compares it to the normal value of the foreign like product.[30] The flexibility of the concept of foreign like product, or its predecessor, such or similar merchandise, often leads to comparisons that, under the Robinson-Patman Act, would never be allowed beyond a motion to dismiss.

Commerce, for example, has developed an elaborate methodology for

---

29. The standard, as construed in the *Forklift* case, is that total US value added of more than 25 percent precludes circumvention. I therefore propose the obverse: Domestic production that is foreign owned is part of the domestic industry if imported components are less than 25 percent of material costs *or* total material costs are less than 25 percent of total cost of manufacture. For comparison, see "Internal Combustion Engines for Forklift Trucks from Japan, Negative Final Determination of Circumvention of Antidumping Duty Order" *(Federal Register* 55: 6028 and 6031, 21 February 1990):

> Value Calculation. Based upon our analysis of the comments received, we have amended our value calculation and determined that the difference in value between forklift trucks completed and sold in the United States and the value of the Japanese components used in the production of that merchandise ranged from 25 percent to 40 percent.

and

> . . . we determine that no circumvention of the anti-dumping duty order is occurring. This negative determination is in accordance with section 781(a) of the Tariff Act (*US Code* 19, section 1677j(a).

30. In accordance with language provided for in the 1994 GATT Antidumping Agreement, US law was amended to delete the "such or similar merchandise" language and to instead use "foreign like product." That change, however, had no substantive impact on the analysis.

identifying which tapered roller bearings (TRBs) sold in Japan are to be deemed identical or similar to tapered roller bearings sold in the United States. Commerce basically permits comparisons on a price-to-price basis of US TRBs to Japanese TRBs so long as the Japanese TRBs' variable cost of manufacture is no more than 20 percent of the total cost of manufacture of the US product. Within this basic parameter, Commerce will accept comparisons even if the Japanese TRB deviates from the US product in its size (outer diameter, inner diameter, or width), load rating, or precision rating by 100 percent or more. As far as Commerce is concerned, for example, a high-precision TRB sold in Japan is identical to a commodity-grade TRB sold in the United States, as long as it has the same dimensions and load rating. Even though the high-precision product will command a price premium as a result of extra steps in superfinishing that provide for closer tolerances, longer life, and quieter running, no adjustments are made for these differences, and dumping margins result not from price differentials for identical merchandise, but because a higher-value product is being treated as identical to a lower-value product.

Such flexible notions of foreign like product totally undermine the notion that the antidumping law addresses international price or profit discrimination. Domestic price discrimination law requires that the differential pricing involve sales of commodities of like grade and quality. As noted above, the concept of like grade and quality has been construed narrowly to prevent findings of price discrimination when, in the domestic context, the products cannot fairly be said to be comparable. In the international context, however, the United States has vested in an administrative agency virtually unfettered discretion to determine what can be considered comparable merchandise.

Proposal for reform In Robinson-Patman jurisprudence, there is a body of decisional law that fleshes out the concept of "like grade and quality." If Commerce were to apply the antitrust concept in the anti-dumping context, it would be forced to match US sales to a more limited home-market sales base or to compare US sales to a benchmark of cost-constructed value. This would have the salutary effect not only of eliminating margins derived solely from comparing prices of merchandise that shouldn't be compared, but also of substantially reducing the administrative burden imposed upon respondents who must participate in these proceedings.[31]

---

31. See, for example, "Comments of Assistant Secretary Garfinkel before the Practicing Law Institute," *International Trade Reporter* 6 (27 September 1989): 1222 and "Certain Small Business Telephone Systems and Subassemblies Thereof from Japan, Korea, and Taiwan," (Notice of Initiation of Investigation), *Federal Register* 54 (24 January 1989): 3516. The Department of Commerce data requests were so burdensome that the Japanese companies defaulted ("Certain Small Business Telephone Systems and Subassemblies Thereof from Japan" [Final LTFV Determination] *Federal Register* 54 [17 October 1989]: 42541).

Levels of Trade

The 1994 GATT Antidumping Agreement requires that "fair comparisons" of home market and export sales normally be partly based on comparisons made at the same level of trade. For matches made at different levels of trade, the US implementing legislation for the first time introduced into the antidumping statute a preference for matches at the same level of trade and adjustments based on the level of trade.

Commerce collects from respondents information on the selling functions performed in connection with the respondents' sales to home-market customers and sales to the export market. Based on an analysis of these selling functions and where in the chain of distribution each customer is located, Commerce will classify customers into different levels of trade. By law, export sales will be matched first to sales in the home market at the same level of trade, if such sales exist. If sales must be matched to a different level of trade in the home market, Commerce will grant an adjustment for the level of trade—but only if the need for such an adjustment is demonstrated and the amount of the adjustment can be quantified. In the case of CEP sales, if the amount of the adjustment for the level of trade cannot be quantified—as will often be the case—Commerce will grant a CEP offset equal to the lesser of the indirect selling expenses deducted in calculating CEP or the indirect selling expenses incurred on the home-market sales.

The new adjustment methodology based on the level of trade is a substantial improvement over prior law and, where it is used, will tend to eliminate the creation of artificial dumping margins arising from "cross-level of trade" matches. Under prior law, a high-volume, low-priced OEM sale in the United States often was compared to a low-volume, high-priced transaction to the aftermarket of the home country, without further adjustment. Thus, dumping was found not because the respondent was selling to similarly situated OEMs at different prices in the two markets, but because the prices being compared were prices to customers that were not, in fact, at the same level of trade with each other (i.e., they were not, functionally, in competition with one another). Although the adjustment for the level of trade substantially mitigates this problem, Commerce has acknowledged that, for CEP sales, there will rarely be an identical level of trade in the home market. As a result, in most CEP cases there will not be an adjustment for the level of trade, but there will be a CEP offset, assuming respondent can provide the necessary documentation and proofs. Because the indirect selling expenses associated with selling to different levels of trade may not, indeed likely will not, fully capture pricing and profit differences between levels of trade, the CEP offset will not remedy the creation of dumping margins from certain cross level of trade matches.

Under domestic price discrimination law, differential pricing to different levels of trade is not actionable, except in certain circumstances not applicable here. Whether expressed in terms of functional discounts, or simply that the less-favored customer does not compete with the favored customer, the result under Robinson-Patman case law is the same: differential pricing to different levels of trade is not actionable price discrimination.

Proposal for reform The Uruguay Round Agreements Act, and the manner in which Commerce has implemented the Act in its antidumping regulations on level of trade, represent substantial reforms over prior practice. Still, large volumes of products subject to antidumping duty orders are sold through affiliated US companies and are thus analyzed as CEP sales. As to those sales, Commerce has determined that it cannot calculate a level of trade adjustment and therefore will, at most, grant only a CEP offset.

Although Commerce has concluded that there is only one level of trade in the United States in CEP sales—the CEP level of trade—the CEP prices remain influenced by the original selling price which, in turn, is a function of the level of trade of the sale in the United States to the unaffiliated customer. Commerce recognizes this in selecting its home-market sales for comparison. It is Commerce's practice to compare a sale to a US unaffiliated OEM to the average normal value for OEM sales in the home market of the same product as a first choice, looking to home-market sales of the same product in the aftermarket as a second choice. In doing so, Commerce recognizes that there are differing price and profit levels associated with sales to different categories of customers in the home market. Commerce should therefore take the next step and calculate a level of trade adjustment applicable for CEP sales based on such differences. This could be accomplished by recognizing different CEP levels of trade, based on the category of the first sale in the United States to an unaffiliated customer, and then applying the level of trade adjustment as it normally would do so in the case of export price sales. This proposal is more in keeping with the Robinson-Patman model advocated here—price discrimination requires some evidence of price differentials that may tend to lessen competition. Where the customers whose prices are being compared do not compete with one another, an appropriate adjustment should be made in all cases, including CEP sales.

Averaging of US Sales

Under US law before 1 January 1995, Commerce examined each individual US sale against a weighted average of sales in the home market in its calculations of antidumping margins. In addition, sales in the United States that were above foreign market value (or, FMV, now normal value [NV]) were treated as having a zero dumping margin rather than a negative dumping margin. As a result, a respondent did not get full credit for having sold some products above fair value and others below fair value. Instead, the sales above fair value were treated as having been sold equal to fair value, with the result that dumping margins were still found even if there were only a handful of sales at less than fair value.

This can best be understood by specific example. Assume that the respondent engaged in five transactions in the United States during the investigation. These transactions were all at the same level of trade and all involved a single product, but they were in different quantities and hence at different unit prices: $4 per unit for 100 units, $3.50 for 200, $3 for 300 or 400, and $2 for 500. Assume further that the exporter engaged in the same five sales transactions in its home market involving the same quantities and the same prices of merchandise, and that these sales produced five FMVs equal to the per-unit US prices listed above. By weight averaging the home-market transactions to produce a single normal value, Commerce will calculate an NV equal to $2.80 for the home market. As a consequence, it would find dumping on one of the five transactions in the United States and calculate a 10.5 percent dumping margin.[32]

Proposal for reform   If the purpose of antidumping law is to address price discrimination between markets, Commerce should calculate the measure of price in each market on the same basis. By failing to do so, the methodology is heavily tilted in favor of finding dumping margins even where price discrimination does not exist, as illustrated in the example above. The dumping margin should therefore be calculated in a manner that gives full credit for sales that are above fair value. This can be accomplished by weight averaging prices on the US side and comparing a single-weighted average export price or constructed export price for a specific period to a single-weighted average NV for a comparable period.

This is, in fact, the approach adopted in the 1994 GATT Antidumping Agreement, Article 2.4.2. US implementing legislation, however, limited such averaging to investigations. Commerce will continue to compare *individual* US sales to average home-market normal values in annual reviews—which is where the actual assessment rates are determined (but see 1994 GATT Antidumping Agreement, Article 18.3, which applies the

---

32. Dumping margins are calculated by the formula

$$\Sigma PUDD/\Sigma USP$$

where $\Sigma PUDD$ (potential uncollected dumping duties) is the sum of all comparisons in which $NV - USP > 0$. Thus, the $PUDD$ in the example equals ($2.80 – $2.00) × 500, or $400. The ΣUSP (the sum of US prices) equals $400 + $700 + $900 + $1,200 + $1,000, or $4,200. By dividing $400 into $4,200, one can calculate a margin of approximately 10.5 percent.

agreement to both investigations and reviews). Alternatively, if Commerce continues to calculate margins on a sale-by-sale basis, as it will apparently do in reviews until reversed in a WTO challenge, it should give full credit for sales that occur above fair value. The calculation of the potential uncollected dumping duty (PUDD) would therefore equal the sum of the pluses and minuses that result from the margin calculation rather than just the sum of the pluses, as now occurs.

Such reform would put the antidumping duty calculation method through a "tightening" process similar to that experienced under the Robinson-Patman Act. Until the early 1980s, a successful plaintiff could collect "automatic" damages, equal to three times the amount of the price difference. However, the US Supreme Court in *J. Truett Payne Co. v. Chrysler Motors Corp.* (451 US 557, 562, 1981), eliminated the rule of automatic damages and firmly established the requirement that there be proof of a direct causal link between an alleged violation of the law and the amount of alleged injury. Further, a plaintiff must prove a direct link between a competitor's lower prices and plaintiff's loss of customers or profits. Mere assertions to that fact have been ruled insufficient for showing actual injury.[33]

Such a strict standard for the awarding of damages under antitrust law would be well applied to relief under antidumping law. Petitioners in dumping cases should be held to a much greater burden of proof to demonstrate that price discrimination by a foreign competitor has caused injury not only to themselves but also to competition. Furthermore, the proposed reform of the duty margin calculation would acknowledge and account for sales both above and below fair value, thereby giving credit for above-fair-value sales in determining the extent to which discrimination has actually occurred. In view of the express language of the GATT Antidumping Agreement and its limited US implementation for investigations only, there would seem to be no principled basis for not extending US price averaging to reviews as well.

Ordinary Course of Trade

Commerce has recognized that it may be inappropriate to include certain types of transactions occurring in the home market in the calculation of the weighted-average NV. Such sales are designated as sales "outside the ordinary course of trade." Typically, these are sales respondents have

---

33. For example, in *Olympia Co. v. Celotex Corp.* (771 F.2d 888, 891-92, 5th Cir. 1985), the plaintiff made assertions regarding profits and sales it "would have made" had it received the same price reduction a competitor had received. That is, the plaintiff claimed that a 5 percent reduction in price (as given to a competitor) would have resulted in increased profits of $38,157.65 over four years, as well as a projected sales increase of 40 percent over a 10-year period. The courts ruled that these projections did not demonstrate injury but were merely unsupported hypotheses.

made at extraordinarily high prices under unusual circumstances—for example, prototype sales, where the product price includes special charges for design and/or tooling. Or, the product in question may be very unusual in the home market and therefore able to command a premium price (e.g., a product scaled in inches in a metric country).[34]

Before Commerce will exclude such sales from the home-market database, however, it requires respondents to produce significant amounts of evidence; mere abnormalities in price/quantity relationships have typically not been sufficient proof. Such a high standard of proof imposed upon respondents is probably defensible, however, given the strong desire of exporters to "cherry pick" the very high-priced home-market sales to eliminate them from the margin calculation. Indeed, we would have no objection with the standard at all if Commerce were to apply comparable standards to transactions in the US market.

In part because of differences in the statutory definitions of normal value and export price, however, Commerce maintains that it must calculate a margin for every sale in the United States during the period of review.[35] Thus, it has only excluded US "sales" where it has found that the transaction in question was in fact not a sale. While the standards for such a finding have varied, Commerce now appears to focus on whether title has passed to the customer, and if so, it deems the event a sale, for which a margin must be calculated.[36]

In determining what constitutes sales in the "ordinary course of trade" for the purpose of price comparisons, Commerce should follow principles analogous to those inherent in section 2(a) of Robinson-Patman, which allow for price differentials and variations resulting from factors that alter the market for, or marketability of, a product. Section 2(a) of Robinson-Patman allows for a "changing conditions defense." That is, in response to conditions such as seasonality or obsolescence of a product, temporary price reductions are not sufficient to sustain a finding of actionable price discrimination (ABA 1992, 426, notes 182, 183). The governing Robinson-Patman language reads:

---

34. The United States has added to this category sales that are below cost within an extended period. This new measure is a significant move away from antitrust principles.

35. But see *Ipsco, Inc. v. United States*, 714 F. Supp. 1211, 1217 (Court of International Trade 1989), reversed on other grounds, 965 F.2d 1056 (Federal Circuit 1992), in which the court ruled that Commerce was not required to include every US sale in calculating margins in investigations.

36. The broad concept of what constitutes a sale conflicts with the narrower scope of generally accepted definitions, such as that found in the Uniform Commercial Code, § 2-106: "A 'sale' consists in the passing of title from the seller to the buyer for a price. . . ." The UCC definition thus excludes transfers in which the transferor receives no valuable consideration from the transferee, while Commerce considers such transfers, in the United States, to be sales.

> . . . nothing herein contained shall prevent price changes from time to time where in response to changing conditions affecting the market for or the marketability of the goods concerned, such as but not limited to actual or imminent deterioration of perishable goods, obsolescence of seasonal goods, distress sales under court process, or sales in good faith in discontinuance of business in the goods concerned. (*US Code* 15, § 13)

The inclusion of such language in the law reflects Congress's intent to allow for price adjustments that reflect changes in the "saleability of goods" (ABA 1992, 426). In its report, the House stated that:

> . . . while it is not believed that the principal prohibitions of Section 2(a) apply in any case to such price changes, nor has such construction ever been suggested or contended for under present Section 2, this specific exemption is included as an added precaution to safeguard the ready disposition of goods characterized by fluid market conditions. (H.R. Rep. No. 2287, 74th Cong., 2d Sess. 11, 1936)

In *Valley Plymouth v. Studebaker-Packard Corp.* and *Peter Satori, Inc. v. Studebaker-Packard Corp.*,[37] lower prices were deemed to be justified by reason of obsolescence and seasonality. In one case, lower-priced cars were found to be obsolete and therefore appropriately reduced in price from earlier sales. In the other case, cars had become less desirable due to the creation of improved models, thus permitting the lower prices. Under Robinson-Patman, the lower-priced sales (in the domestic context) were seen as justified by the market and consequently found to be an inappropriate basis for finding discrimination. In the international context, however, there is no similar acknowledgment of the real-world workings of the marketplace. Commerce continues to view each US transaction as a sale suitable for comparison, regardless of the market conditions or reasons behind the pricing.

Proposal for reform By incorporating Robinson-Patman provisions in its price comparison methods, Commerce would be forced to account for reasonable variations in price differentials rather than being allowed to compare, on a price-to-price basis, US sales which are *not* in the ordinary course of trade but merely priced in response to changing market conditions. Further, applying the same "ordinary course" concepts in both the home and US markets, Commerce ought not to calculate margins on "giveaways," which in commercial terms constitute merely promotional expenses, not sales.

Constructed Value Calculations

Commerce uses constructed value as a basis for NV when there is no foreign like product in the home market, or when identical merchandise

---

37. Found, respectively, in 219 F. Supp. 608 (S.D. Cal. 1963) and 1964 Trade Cas. (CCH) ¶ 71,309 (S.D. Cal. 1964).

is sold in the home market but all such sales are disregarded as being below the cost of production. This use of constructed value has been the target of extensive criticism of US antidumping law. Such criticisms once focused primarily on the fact that the constructed-value calculation before 1 January 1995 included a minimum 10 percent of cost of manufacture to be added for SG&A expenses, plus a minimum profit of 8 percent to be added to the combined cost of manufacture plus SG&A. Thus, dumping was found to have occurred in constructed-value matches whenever the foreign manufacturer elected not to earn on its US sales a profit of at least 8 percent above its fully allocated cost of production.

More recently, the constructed-value statute has been the source of substantial additional mischief. The antidumping law generally considers parties to be "affiliated" if there is a 5 percent or greater stock ownership interest in one party by another. Thus, the statute permits Commerce to reject the transfer prices of inputs manufactured by affiliated parties if it finds that such prices are not at arm's length, and to use "best evidence available" as a substitute for such transfer prices whenever it does reject them. In addition, if the input in question is a "major input," and if Commerce has reason to believe or suspect that the transfer price is below the cost of production, it may substitute the affiliated supplier's cost of production for the transfer price.

The difficulties in responding to Commerce requests for such information, however, are manifold. In many circumstances, the affiliated supplier is the sole source of the particular input, and thus there is no easy way to provide prices of the input purchased from unaffiliated suppliers as a benchmark to test the market values of the affiliated-party transfer price. An even greater problem is that, for suppliers that are only partially owned by the manufacturer, it is often impossible to obtain cost of production information, particularly where the degree of ownership is between 5 and 50 percent. Recently, Commerce applied its "best information available" (now "facts available") rule (which usually means adverse information, often data from the petition or prior reviews) to a respondent that, in its view, had not been able to meet these onerous standards. Moreover, this is an issue of increasing interest to Commerce, fueled in large part by the discovery in the *Minivans* case that certain affiliated suppliers were transferring parts at different prices depending upon the ultimate destination of the minivan.[38]

While we generally do not dispute the need for a cost-based measure of NV, the statutory framework should not be so rigid that it disregards basic commercial realities. The notion that a supplier owned 5 percent by

---

38. "Final Determination of Sales at Less Than Fair Value: New Minivans From Japan," *Federal Register* 57: 21937, 21942 (26 May 1992); James Bovard, "Minivan," *The New Republic*, 22 June 1992, 20.

its customer would offer preferential pricing and/or sell below cost to its minority shareholder lacks any basis in reality. Moreover, the measure of cost that is currently used deviates so far from antitrust norms that it must be rejected in favor of a more modern approach.

Proposal for reform The proposals for reform depend in part on the reason for constructed value being invoked in the first place. When constructed value is used because there is no comparable merchandise sold in the home market, we submit that dumping should not be found unless the US price is less than the variable cost of manufacture of the product in question. Absent unusually compelling circumstances, prices above variable cost of manufacture would not be found to be predatory under US antitrust concepts. Applying the same standard to dumping would help to restore the law to one of its original premises as a predatory price discrimination statute.

Even assuming, however, that a standard based on variable cost of manufacture will be rejected by US domestic interests as unacceptably low, we would suggest that constructed value be simply the manufacturer's total cost of manufacture or, at worst, total cost of production, including its actual SG&A and profit.

The 1994 GATT Antidumping Agreement in fact required the United States to eliminate its minimum additions for SG&A expenses, and for profit. US implementing legislation, however, does not merely require that the profit be that which is actually earned by the exporter on its domestic sales. Rather, the profit that is added for constructed value must be the profit earned on those sales that pass the law's below-cost test. Once below-cost sales are eliminated, an exporter's profit margin may be, indeed is likely to be, much higher than the prior minimum of 8 percent. Here, again, the current US approach takes antidumping law further away from antitrust principles.

If the reason for a constructed-value calculation arises from the existence of sales of comparable merchandise in the home market that have been rejected for being below cost, then our proposal for reform is to revert to price-to-price comparisons. The reason for this is simple: The primary rationale for continuing to have an antidumping law that uses standards different from pure antitrust law is the inability of the US industry to "arbitrage" price differences between the two markets because of private or governmental restrictions on access to the foreign country's market. Profits made through sales in the protected home market, it is argued, can be used to underwrite dumping in the United States because such profits are insulated from arbitrage by US producers. Where, however, the foreign producers are selling below cost in *both* markets, there obviously will not be home-market profits available to subsidize dumping in export markets. Under such circumstances, the proper comparison is price to price, not price to some measure of cost.

Conclusion

The above proposals for reform are not intended to be comprehensive. Rather, they include only the aspects of existing antidumping practice that appear to have diverged the most from existing antitrust practice and represent an attempt to introduce (or in some cases reintroduce) competition-based principles into the antidumping framework. An antidumping regime reformed along the lines suggested here would produce many positive results: Foreign manufacturers would have much greater freedom to compete with US manufacturers on the same terms that other US manufacturers can now compete, and those dumping remedies that are imposed would be limited to a narrower range of products. Moreover, margins would be more likely to reflect the actual degree of discrimination and injury through the use of averaging of US sales.

Some of the proposed reforms were in fact codified in the GATT Antidumping Agreement after the completion of the Uruguay Round. Further, most but not all of the GATT reforms were included in the US implementing legislation for the Uruguay Round agreement. The United States, however, balked at the averaging of prices in reviews and at applying reasonable currency conversion rules in reviews. In other areas, it declined to follow the intent of the GATT changes; for example, in defining the conditions under which injury could be found. Further, the use of only above-cost sales for calculating constructed-value profits, although permitted by the GATT Antidumping Agreement, is not required by it, and undoubtedly will increase margins based on constructed value.

Other reforms could readily be proposed, such as truly automatic sunset provisions on antidumping orders. It is quite clear, however, given the difficulties that plagued antidumping reform in the GATT negotiations, that achievement of even the modest and rational goals suggested here must be considered a long-term project at best. Nonetheless, the first steps of focusing the debate must be taken, and this chapter offers what I hope is a contribution to that process.

References

American Bar Association, Antitrust Section. 1992. *Antitrust Law Developments*, 3d ed. Chicago.

Feltham, I., S. Salen, R. Mathieson, and R. Wonnacott. 1991. *Competition (Antitrust) and Antidumping Laws in the Context of the Canada-US Free Trade Agreement: A Study for the Committee on Canada–United States Relations of the Canadian Chamber of Commerce and the Chamber of Commerce of the United States*. Washington: US Chamber of Commerce.

Hart, M., ed. 1997. *Finding Middle Ground, Reforming the Antidumping Laws in North America*. Centre for Trade Policy and Law, Carleton University.

Lipstein, Robert. 1993. "It's Time to Dump the Dumping Law." *International Economic Insights* (November/December).

US Department of Justice and Federal Trade Commission. 1992. *Horizontal Merger Guidelines* (2 April).

US Government Printing Office. 1992. *1992 Trade Policy Agenda and 1991 Annual Report of the President of the United States on the Trade Agreements Program*. Washington.

US International Trade Commission (ITC). 1991. *High Information Content Flat Panel Displays and Display Glass Therefor from Japan*. Inv. no. 731-TA-469 (Final), USITC Publication 2413 (August). Washington.

US International Trade Commission (ITC). 1993a. *Sulphur Dyes from India*. Final Determination, USITC Publication 2619 (April). Washington.

US International Trade Commission (ITC). 1993b. *Ferrosilicon from Kazakhstan and Ukraine*. Final Determination, USITC Publication 2616 (June). Washington.

US International Trade Commission (ITC). 1993c. *Certain Flat-Rolled Carbon Steel Products from Argentina, Australia, Austria, Belgium, Brazil, Canada, Finland, France, Germany, Italy, Japan, Korea, Mexico, the Netherlands, New Zealand, Poland, Romania, Spain, Sweden, and the United Kingdom*. Final Determination, USITC Publication 2664 (August). Washington.

14

Formal and Informal Measures for Controlling Competition in Japan: Institutional Overview and Theoretical Evaluation

KOTARO SUZUMURA

Enacted in 1947, Japan's original Antimonopoly Law (AML) was a major component of the post–World War II economic democratization policy pursued by the Occupation Forces. Modeled after US antitrust laws, the AML was rigorously procompetitive. Not only was a per se illegal standard for cartels applied, but stringent control over mergers and acquisitions was imposed. However, as time passed, a rigorous competition policy based on the original AML came to be recognized as unrealistic, and several amendments to the AML were introduced with the purpose of relaxing major provisions of the law. As early as 1953, for example, the per se illegality of cartels was modified to a prohibition of cartels only if they restrained competition to the substantial detriment of the "public interest"; recession cartels and rationalization cartels were exempted from the AML under some conditions. Several other laws were introduced that exempted certain anticompetitive agreements among firms from the application of the AML, thereby allowing anticompetitive agreements in such areas as the export-import industry, small enterprises, marine transport, fire and marine insurance, and certain specific areas such as coal and fertilizers.

In addition to these laws and provisions, which explicitly legalized some anticompetitive practices, the Japanese government, in particular the Ministry of International Trade and Industry (MITI), sought administrative guidance as an informal means of achieving industrial policy

Kotaro Suzumura is a professor at the Institute of Economic Research, Hitotsubashi University, Tokyo. An earlier, shorter version of this chapter appeared in Suzumura (1995, appendix A).

objectives. MITI often gave private firms administrative guidance on forming cartels and consolidating private resources and facilities. Such administrative guidance has been applied even when no exempting provision has existed, which occasionally has ignited debates on whether cartels are unlawful even if they are based on MITI's administrative guidance.

Several other measures existed that could be invoked by the government to regulate competition, for example, laws restricting entry, stipulating various qualifications for business start-ups, and controlling prices. These laws, which included public utility regulation, licensing for maintaining health and safety standards, and protection of a specific industry such as agriculture, enabled the government to interfere directly in an industry by entry regulation, price regulation, or both.

In view of these measures for controlling competition in Japan, which not only ranged widely in coverage but were complicated in their stipulations, one naturally is led to wonder why there should be so many channels through which the free working of the competitive market mechanism could be interfered with, despite the deeply rooted consensus among orthodox economists on the welfare-enhancing effects of increased competition. The purpose of this chapter is to present a succinct overview and evaluation of the systems of exemption from the AML and other measures for controlling competition in postwar Japan.

The plan of this chapter is as follows: In section 2, it is shown that the answer to the question as to whether there is room for rationalizable government interference in the free working of the competitive market mechanism hinges on which criterion is selected from among consumers' surplus, producers' surplus, and the social welfare in terms of net market surplus. Addressing this question is helpful in gaining an understanding of the nature and scope of the different stances of MITI, the Fair Trade Commission of Japan (JFTC), the business community at large, and Japan's Supreme Court in the context of whether and to what extent competition should be regulated in the name of promoting the public interest. In section 3, a succinct summary is provided of the system of exemptions from the AML and other exempting laws. In section 4, the problem inherent in entry regulation in terms of administrative guidance is illustrated by a case study of the Large-Scale Retail Store Law and its erosion. Section 5 focuses on the telecommunications industry following the 1985 Telecommunications Reform, whereby competition has been handcuffed by the Ministry of Posts and Telecommunications even subsequent to the industry's liberalization and the Nippon Telegraph and Telephone Public Corporation's privatization by the reform. In section 6, the Antimonopoly Law Guidelines Concerning Joint Research and Development are briefly examined. Conclusions are provided in section 7.

On the Rationale of Interference in Market Competition

Socially Excessive Firm Entry under Private Incentives

To orient subsequent analysis, I begin by examining the welfare effects of firm entry, which capitalizes on Suzumura (1995, part 1).

Consider an industry where n firms are producing a single homogeneous good, where $2 \leq n < +\infty$. The inverse demand function and the cost function of each firm are $p = f(Q)$ and $c(q_i)$, respectively, where p is output price, q_i is output of firm i, and $Q = \sum_{j=1}^{n} q_j$ is industry output. It is assumed that firms are identical, that $f(Q)$ is twice continuously differentiable with $f'(Q) < 0$ for all $Q \geq 0$ such that $f(Q) > 0$, and that $c(q_i)$ is twice continuously differentiable with $c(q_i) > 0$, $c'(q_i) > 0$, and $c''(q_i) > 0$ for all $q \geq 0$.

Consider a game G, which is defined by a set of players $N = \{1, 2, \ldots, n\}$ and a profile of payoff functions $\{\pi^i \mid i \in N\}$, where π^i is defined by $\pi^i(q_i; Q_{-i}) = q_i f(q_i + Q_{-i}) - c(q_i)$, and $Q_{-i} = Q - q_i = \sum_{j \neq i} q_j$. Let $q^N(n) = (q_1^N(n), q_2^N(n), \ldots, q_n^N(n))$ be the Cournot-Nash equilibrium of game G, which is characterized by

$$f(Q^N(n)) + q_i^N(n)f'(Q^N(n)) - C'(q_i^N(n)) = 0, \tag{1}$$

where $Q^N(n) = q_i^N(n) + Q_{-i}^N(n)$. Assuming that firms are identical, we focus on the symmetric Cournot-Nash equilibrium, so that we have $q_i^N(n) = q^N(n)$, say, for all $i \in N$. Throughout this chapter, we assume that the strategic substitutability holds, that is, that $\beta^N(n) < 0$ is satisfied, where $\beta^N(n) = (\partial^2/\partial q_i \partial q_j)\pi^i(q_i^N(n); Q_{-i}^N(n))$ $(i \neq j)$. It is easy to verify that this assumption guarantees $(d/dn)q^N(n) < 0$ and $(d/dn)Q^N(n) > 0$. See Suzumura (1995, chapter 1).

Let $\pi^N(n)$ be the profits earned by each firm at $q^N(n)$; that is,

$$\pi^N(n) = q^N(n)f(Q^N(n)) - C(q^N(n)). \tag{2}$$

Since $\pi^N(n) > $ (or $<$) 0 induces new entry of potential competitors (or exit of incumbent firms), a long-run equilibrium will be attained only if the number of firms reaches the equilibrium value, n_e, which is defined by $\pi^N(n_e) = 0$. Let $CS^N(n)$ and $PS^N(n)$ stand for the consumers' surplus and the producers' surplus, respectively, which are defined by

$$CS^N(n) = \int_0^{Q^N(n)} f(Z)dZ - Q^N(n)f(Q^N(n)) \tag{3}$$

and

$$PS^N(n) = \sum_{i=1}^{n} \{q_i^N(n)f(Q^N(n)) - C(q_i^N(n))\}. \tag{4}$$

By adding up $CS^N(n)$ and $PS^N(n)$, we obtain a social welfare measure in terms of net market surplus, that is, $W^N(n) = CS^N(n) + PS^N(n)$.

To see how these criteria will be affected by an exogenous change in n, we differentiate $CS^N(n)$, $PS^N(n)$, and $W^N(n)$ with respect to n to obtain

$$(d/dn)CS^N(n) = - Q^N(n)f'(Q^N(n))(d/dn)Q^N(n), \tag{5}$$

$$(d/dn)PS^N(n) = \pi^N(n) + Q^N(n)f'(Q^N(n))\{(d/dn)Q^N(n) - (d/dn)q^N(n)\} \tag{6}$$

and

$$(d/dn)W^N(n) = \pi^N(n) - Q^N(n)f'(Q^N(n))(d/dn)q^N(n). \tag{7}$$

It follows from (5) that $(d/dn)CS^N(n) > 0$ holds for all n. Thus, it is always to the benefit of consumers to *increase* the number of firms within the class of models we are envisaging. However, it follows from (6), as well as $(d/dn)q^N(n) < 0$, $(d/dn)Q^N(n) > 0$ and $(d/dn)\pi^N(n) < 0$, which are shown by Suzumura (1995, chapter 1), that $(d/dn)PS^N(n)$ consists of two terms with opposite signs as long as n is less than n_e; however, it becomes unambiguously negative when $n = n_e$, as the first term in (6) will be zero at $n = n_e$. Thus, it is to the benefit of producers to *decrease* the number of firms from $n = n_e$. In fact, the negative effect of $(d/dn)PS^N(n_e)$ is so dominant vis-à-vis the positive effect of $(d/dn)CS^N(n_e)$ that $(d/dn)W^N(n_e)$ will become unambiguously negative. This implies that the social welfare measured in terms of net market surplus is improved by a marginal *decrease* in the number of firms from its equilibrium value. Thus, it is in society's interest for the government to interfere with the free competitive forces so as to keep the number of firms less than its equilibrium value as long as the government is willing to make up for a loss in consumers' surplus with the concomitant gain in producers' surplus.

Socially Excessive Capacity Investment under Private Incentives

Capitalizing on Suzumura (1995, part 2), we now briefly summarize the welfare effects of strategic commitment to cost-reducing research and development in order to confirm the robustness of the above conclusion.

Consider an industry with n firms producing a single homogeneous good, where $2 \leq n < + \infty$. Firms compete in two stages. In the first stage of the game, each firm makes a strategic commitment to R&D investment in full anticipation of the equilibrium in the second stage, where firms compete in terms of quantities.

Let x_i and q_i be the R&D investment and the output of firm i, chosen, respectively, in the first and second stages. The second-stage variable cost function of firm i is $c(x_i)q_i$, where $c(x_i) > 0$ and $c'(x_i) < 0$ for all $x_i > 0$. Given a profile $x = (x_1, x_2, \ldots, x_n)$ of R&D investments, let $G(x)$ be a game defined by a set of players $N = \{1, 2, \ldots, n\}$ and a profile of the second-stage payoff functions $\{\pi^i \mid i \in N\}$, where π^i is defined by $\pi^i (q_i; Q_{-i}; x_i) = \{f(q_i + Q_{-i}) - c(x_i)\}q_i - x_i$, and $Q_{-i} = \Sigma_{j \neq i}^n q_j$.

Let $q^N(x) = (q_1^N(x), q_2^N(x), \ldots, q_n^N(x))$ be the Cournot-Nash equilibrium of the game $G(x)$. Assuming interior optimum, $q^N(x)$ is characterized by

$$q_i^N(x)f(Q^N(x)) + q_i^N(x)f'(Q^N(x)) = c(x_i), \tag{8}$$

where $Q^N(x) = \Sigma_{j=1}^n q_j^N(x)$.

Let G be a game defined by a set of players $N = \{1, 2, \ldots, n\}$ and a profile of the first-stage payoff functions $\{\Pi^i \mid i \in N\}$, where Π^i is defined by $\Pi^i(x) = \pi^i(q_i^N(x); Q_{-i}^N(x); x_i)$. Let x^N be the Nash equilibrium of game G, which may be characterized by

$$\sum_{j=1}^{n} (\partial/\partial q_j)\pi^i(q_i^N(x); Q_{-i}^N(x); x_i^N)(\partial/\partial x_i)q_j^N(x^N) + (\partial/\partial x_i)\pi^i(q_i^N(x); Q_{-i}^N(x); x_i^N) = 0 \tag{9}$$

under the assumption of interior optimum. The equilibrium path $\{x^N, q^N(x^N)\}$ is the subgame-perfect equilibrium of our two-stage game.

Throughout this chapter, we assume that the second-stage Cournot-Nash equilibrium $q^N(x)$ is symmetric for any symmetric R&D profile x, that is, that $q_i^N(x) = q^N(x)$, say, for all $i \in N$ if x is symmetric. We also assume that the first-stage Nash equilibrium x^N is symmetric, i.e., that $x_i^N = x^N$, say, for all $i \in N$.

To see whether there is any room for rationalizable interference in this arena, we introduce the consumers' surplus $CS^N(x)$, the producers' surplus $PS^N(x)$, and the social welfare in terms of the net market surplus $W^N(x)$ by

$$CS^N(x) = \int_0^{Q^N(x)} f(Z)dZ - Q^N(x)f(Q^N(x)), \tag{10}$$

$$PS^N(x) = \sum_{i=1}^{n} [q_i^N(x)\{f(Q^N(x)) - c(x_i)\} - x_i] \tag{11}$$

and $W^N(x) = CS^N(x) + PS^N(x)$.

Differentiating $CS^N(x)$ and $PS^N(x)$ with respect to x_i, we obtain

$$(\partial/\partial x_i)CS^N(x) = - Q^N(x)f'(Q^N(x))(\partial/\partial x_i)Q^N(x) \tag{12}$$

and

$$(\partial/\partial x_i)PS^N(x) = \{f(Q^N(x)) + Q^N(x)f'(Q^N(x))\}(\partial/\partial x_i)Q^N(x)$$
$$- \sum_{j \neq i} c(x_j)(\partial/\partial x_i)q_j^N(x) - c'(x_i)q_i^N(x) - 1. \tag{13}$$

At this stage of our analysis, we assume that the second-order condition for payoff maximization in the game $G(x)$ is satisfied at $q^N(x)$, that is, that $\alpha^N(x) = (\partial^2/\partial q_i^2)\pi^i(q_i^N(x); Q_{-i}^N(x); x_i) < 0$ holds. It is also assumed that the strategic substitutability property holds at $q^N(x)$, i.e., that $\beta^N(x) = (\partial^2/\partial q_i\partial q_j)\pi^i(q_i^N(x); Q_{-i}^N(x); x_i) < 0$ $(i \neq j)$ is satisfied. Under these assumptions, it is verified in Suzumura (1995, chapter 4), that $(\partial/\partial x_i)q_i^N(x) > 0$, $(\partial/\partial x_i)q_j^N(x) < 0$ $(i \neq j)$ and $(\partial/\partial x_i)Q^N(x) > 0$ hold. It follows from (12) that $(\partial/\partial x_i)CS^N(x) > 0$ holds for any x. Thus, the strategic R&D investment is always insufficient from the point of view of consumers; hence, promotion rather than restriction of competition in R&D commitment should be the rational policy prescription from the exclusive viewpoint of consumers' welfare. In contrast, it follows from (13) that the sign of $(\partial/\partial x_i)PS^N(x)$ is ambiguous in general. However, it may be verified by virtue of (8) and (9) that

$$(\partial/\partial x_i)PS^N(x^N) = (n-1)q_i^N(x^N)f'(Q^N(x^N))(\partial/\partial x_i)Q^N(x^N) < 0 \qquad (14)$$

holds at the subgame-perfect equilibrium $\{x^N, q^N(x^N)\}$. It follows that the strategic R&D investment is excessive at the subgame-perfect equilibrium; hence, restriction rather than promotion of strategic R&D competition should be the rational policy prescription from the exclusive point of view of producers' benefit.

Turning to the point of view of social welfare defined by the net market surplus, and putting (12) at x^N and (14) together, we obtain

$$(\partial/\partial x_i)W^N(x^N) = -q_i^N(x^N)f'(Q^N(x^N))\{(\partial/\partial x_i)Q^N(x^N) + (n-1)(\partial/\partial x_i)q_j^N(x^N)\}, \quad (15)$$

which is in general of indeterminate sign. However, it is shown in Suzumura (1995, chapter 4) that $(\partial/\partial x_i)W^N(x^N) < 0$ unambiguously holds if the number of firms n is "large enough," which implies that the strategic R&D investment is marginally excessive at the subgame-perfect equilibrium. Thus, restriction rather than promotion of competition in terms of R&D commitment should be the rational policy prescription from the point of view of social welfare defined by the net market surplus measure.

Empirical Relevance

The above theoretical observations have rather strong empirical relevance in the Japanese context. In postwar Japan, interfirm competition has been consistently kéen and has played a major role in promoting rapid economic growth by embodying new technology through extensive investment in plant and equipment. So keen has this competition been that a dysfunction of the market mechanism has allegedly developed from time to time, and government intervention has been applied in the name of keeping "excessive competition" in investment under control. However, hardly anyone has ever defined the meaning of excessive competition within the standard framework of microeconomics. Indeed, most of the common arguments on excessive competition boil down to the assertion that competition is so keen that some of the incumbent firms are forced to retreat from the competitive arena. If this is all that can be meant by excessive competition, there is no real substance to this esoteric term. If one is to gauge the real relevance of alternative stances taken by the industrial policy authorities represented by MITI, the competition policy authorities represented by JFTC, and the Supreme Court in the context of competition versus regulation, the theoretical meaning, if any, of excessive competition should be explored. Recollect in this context that the "excessive competition in investment . . . tends to develop in industries characterized by heavy overhead capital, homogeneous products, and oligopoly. Examples are iron and steel, petroleum refining, petrochemicals, certain other chemicals, cement, paper and pulp, and sugar refining" (Komiya 1975, 213-14). It is in response to this acute observation that the two models summarized above were developed embodying the three crucial features identified by Komiya.

According to the above analyses, one may clearly identify three situations in which excessive competition in the welfare-theoretic sense does or does not surface:

- There is no such phenomenon as excessive competition if one evaluates the performance of competition exclusively in terms of consumers' surplus.

- If one measures the performance of competition exclusively in terms of producers' surplus, the competitive equilibrium number of firms (or the subgame-perfect equilibrium level of R&D investment) is excessive at the margin in the sense that a marginal decrease in the number of firms from its long-run equilibrium value (or a marginal decrease in the R&D investment from its subgame-perfect equilibrium level) improves the performance of the industry at the margin.

- If one measures the performance of competition exclusively in terms of net market surplus, the competitive equilibrium number of firms (or the subgame-perfect equilibrium level of R&D investment) is excessive at the margin in that a marginal decrease in the number of firms from its long-run equilibrium value (or a marginal decrease in R&D investment from its subgame-perfect equilibrium level) improves the industry performance at the margin.

It is worth emphasizing that the three performance criteria referred to here are of crucial empirical relevance in the Japanese context. According to Article 2-5 (private monopolization) and Article 2-6 (cartels) of the AML, a monopolization or cartel is unlawful if and only if it restrains competition substantially in a particular field of trade "contrary to the public interest." As Matsushita (1990, 16-20) has aptly observed, however, the crucial expression "contrary to the public interest" admits several alternative interpretations, and the choice made among them may dictate the rigor with which one is ready to apply the AML to a private monopolization or cartel. The following three views on the issue of interpretation can be identified, each offering sharply contrasting policy implications:[1]

- **The view taken by JFTC.** According to JFTC, the so-called public interest means nothing more than "free competition." Thus, the expression "contrary to the public interest" simply implies that there is a lack of free competition. This view can be traced back directly to the basic objective of the AML. As stipulated in Article 1, the law is designed to "promote fair and free competition." If one subscribes to this view held by JFTC, there is no room for an independent performance criterion other than free competition itself in judging whether there should be interference in the working of market competition.

- **The view held by the business community.** The business community in general, and the Federation of Economic Organizations in particular, maintains the view that the "public interest" should be construed to mean something far broader than free competition alone, and that its definition should duly acknowledge the importance of balanced development of the national economy, consumer welfare, and cooperation with foreign countries. In other words, rigorous application of the AML should not be construed as an end in itself, and an interference in the working of free competition may be rationalized if it contributes to the enhancement of a suitably defined measure of social welfare, that is, the "public interest."

- **The view of the Supreme Court in the oil cartel decision.** In the context of the 1984 decision in one of the oil cartel cases, the Supreme Court took an intermediate view which struck a balance between the view of JFTC and the view held by the business community. According to the Supreme Court, the "public interest" should in principle mean nothing other than free competition, and, under normal circumstances, an anticompetitive agreement among firms should be deemed contrary to the "public interest." However, inherent in this view is the admission that there are exceptional circumstances under which an anticompetitive agreement may be justified if the disadvantage of interfering in free competition may be offset by the social advantage secured only by an anticompetitive agreement

---

1. The following discussion of the three interpretations of "contrary to the public interest" owes much to Matsushita (1990).

among firms. Inasmuch as the circumscription of the so-called exceptional circumstances is left unclear, the extent to which the Supreme Court's view diverges from the JFTC view is also left opaque. It is worth emphasizing, however, that the real importance of this view lies in the fact that it admits the existence of the areas in which a comparison—in terms of social welfare—between free competition and anticompetitive regulation should be made before a decision is reached on the application of the AML.

This completes this chapter's preliminary analyses of competition, regulation, and welfare. In the following section, I begin a description of the exemption systems laid down by the AML and other anticompetitive policy measures in postwar Japan.

Overview of the AML Exemption Systems

Current Status of the Exemption Systems

The exemption systems of the AML are designed for the exceptional exemption from that law's prohibitive provisions of anticompetitive agreements (cartels) and the like devised by firms and trade associations.

The AML exemption systems are quite extensive. In June 1991 there existed 68 exemption systems under 42 laws, of which 56 exempted cartel systems under 37 laws accounted for the vast majority. Among these, 30 exemption systems under 15 laws were administered with the authorization of JFTC, or by the competent cabinet minister after having obtained the consent of—or having consulted with or notified—JFTC. The number of cartels under these systems has been decreasing, and some of the exempted cartel systems have been dormant for a long time—indeed, some have never been implemented at all since their introduction. There were 1,079 exempted cartels at the end of March 1966, of which 72 percent involved small and medium-size enterprise associations, 21 percent involved foreign trade, and the remainder involved coastal shipping and other associations of various kinds. The number of exempted cartels was reduced to 505 at the end of March 1982, the most dramatic decrease having occurred in the areas of foreign trade (from 225 to 69) and small and medium-size enterprise associations (from 781 to 461). In June 1991, there were 247 active cartels under six laws, of which 170 involved small and medium-size enterprise associations, 34 involved foreign trade, 37 involved hairdressing, and the remaining six involved coastal shipping and fisheries.[2]

---

2. Detailed historical and factual information on the exemption systems in Japan may be found in Fair Trade Commission of Japan (1977; 1991) and Uesugi (1986).

Exempting Laws Currently in Effect

Japan's exemption systems and laws are too numerous to describe here in full detail. In this chapter I refer only to those laws that are both typical and substantially important.

Some exemptions are based on the AML itself, or on components of it such as the Law Concerning Exemption, whereas others are provided for in other laws. AML-based exemptions include natural monopolies (Article 21), intellectual property rights (Article 23), certain activities of cooperatives (Article 24), resale price maintenance (Article 24-2), recession cartels (Article 24-3), and rationalization cartels (Article 24-4).

Table 1 lists the cartels that were exempted from the AML by Article 24-3 (recession cartels) and Article 24-4 (rationalization cartels).

The second category of exemptions includes the following:

- the exemption of legitimate acts performed under laws and regulations, including the Land Traffic Enterprise Coordination Law and the Food Control Law, or orders under such laws and regulations;

- the exemption of organizations and other entities established under specific laws from Article 8 of the AML.

The third category of exemptions is illustrated by the following laws:

- the Marine Transportation Law, which exempts shipping conferences from the AML application;

- the Insurance Business Law, which authorizes rates fixed by fire and marine insurance companies;

- the Road Transportation Law, which exempts trucking, bus, and taxi companies from the AML;

- the Aviation Law, which allows Japanese airline companies to join the international aviation cartels;

- the Export-Import Transactions Law, which authorizes export and import cartels;

- the Small and Medium-Size Business Organizations Law, which allows small enterprises to organize cartels.

Historically Important Exempting Laws

Besides those laws currently in effect, it is worth noting some exempting laws that are of historical importance although they no longer have any influence. The following laws, promulgated on behalf of various manufacturing industries on the basis of their "strategic importance," illustrate the nature of such laws: Law on Temporary Measures for Structural

Table 1 Number of cartels exempted from the Antimonopoly Law, 1954–92

Year	AML Article 24-3	AML Article 24-4
1954	0	0
1955	0	0
1956	0	4
1957	1	6
1958	1	6
1959	5	8
1960	4	9
1961	3	9
1962	0	11
1963	1	11
1964	2	14
1965	2	14
1966	16	14
1967	1	13
1968	0	13
1969	0	12
1970	0	10
1971	0	13
1972	9	10
1973	2	10
1974	0	9
1975	2	0
1976	1	0
1977	1	0
1978	6	1
1979	4	0
1980	1	1
1981	1	1
1982	3	0
1983	2	0
1984	0	0
1985	0	0
1986	0	0
1987	0	0
1988	2	0
1989	2	0
1990	0	0
1991	0	0
1992	0	0

Source: Fair Trade Commission of Japan, Annual Report 1992 (Tokyo: Fair Trade Association, 1993). Attachments, 58–59.

Improvement of Specified Industries (May 1978-June 1988), Law on Special Measures for the Promotion of the Machinery Industry (June 1956-March 1971), Law on Special Measures for the Promotion of Electronics Industry (June 1957-March 1971), Law on Temporary Measures for the Promotion of Specified Electronics Industries and Specified Machinery Industries (April 1971-March 1978), and Law on Temporary Measures for the Promotion of Specified Machinery and Information Industries (July 1978-June 1985).

Table 2 summarizes the historical pattern of cartels that were exempted from the AML by the five laws listed above. Note that all these laws of historical importance had completely ceased to be effective by June 1988 if not earlier.

Evaluations

Most of the modifications of the original and procompetitive AML resulted from tensions between MITI and JFTC, which started soon after the enactment of the AML. The first government-organized cartel was introduced in February 1952, when MITI issued an administrative guidance to 10 large cotton spinners to reduce production by 40 percent. To enforce the quotas assigned by MITI, it was informally suggested that the foreign currency assignments under MITI's control for the following month's supply of raw cotton might be unavailable to those who rejected the quotas. Such cartels, organized as well as enforced by MITI, have proliferated since then, despite the accusation by JFTC that MITI's administrative guidance was illegal. To strengthen MITI's legal position vis-à-vis the AML, MITI soon submitted to the Diet the Law on Special Measures for the Stabilization of Designated Medium Size and Small Enterprises and the Exports Transactions Law, which authorized MITI to create cartels among small businesses without their being constrained by the AML.

This movement toward securing a safeguard against the AML applications was not confined to medium-size and small enterprises. Indeed, in 1953 the Steel Federation, as well as the Federation of Economic Organizations, petitioned the Diet to permit recession cartels and rationalization cartels. MITI also asked for the power to approve not only recession cartels and rationalization cartels but also other cooperative behavior adopted to restrict production and sales. It was against this background that the Diet amended the AML in September 1953 to approve recession and rationalization cartels. Furthermore, beginning with the Law on Special Measures for the Equipment of the Textile Industry (1956), the Law on Special Measures for the Promotion of the Machinery Industry (1956), and the Law on Special Measures for the Promotion of the Electronics Industry (1957), MITI began to implement a series of industry laws which secured exemptions from the AML for the designated industries.

MITI's persistent attempts to secure powerful institutional devices for controlling market competition culminated in its 1958 plan for a "public sales system" for the steel industry, which was, quite surprisingly, approved by JFTC. The widely held perception that JFTC would approve anything that MITI claimed was necessary to the well-being of Japan seems to be deeply rooted in this dark period of competition policy.

Table 2 Number of cartels exempted from the Antimonopoly Law, 1957–88

Year	A	B	C	D	E
1957	–	0	–	–	–
1958	–	0	0	–	–
1959	–	0	0	–	–
1960	–	1	0	–	–
1961	–	1	0	–	–
1962	–	5	0	–	–
1963	–	6	0	–	–
1964	–	14	0	–	–
1965	–	14	1	–	–
1966	–	9	1	–	–
1967	–	6	1	–	–
1968	–	8	0	–	–
1969	–	17	0	–	–
1970	–	16	1	–	–
1971	–	17	2	–	–
1972	–	–	–	0	–
1973	–	–	–	13	–
1974	–	–	–	15	–
1975	–	–	–	17	–
1976	–	–	–	16	–
1977	–	–	–	15	–
1978	–	–	–	9	–
1979	5	–	–	–	1
1980	8	–	–	–	1
1981	8	–	–	–	2
1982	4	–	–	–	1
1983	4	–	–	–	1
1984	5	–	–	–	1
1985	7	–	–	–	1
1986	6	–	–	–	–
1987	5	–	–	–	–
1988	2	–	–	–	–

– = not applicable.
A. Law on Temporary Measures for Structural Improvement of Specified Industries: May 1978–June 1988.
B. Law on Special Measures for the Promotion of the Machinery Industry: June 1956–March 1971.
C. Law on Special Measures for the Promotion of the Electronics Industry: June 1957–March 1971.
D. Law on Temporary Measures for the Promotion of Specified Electronics Industries and Specified Machinery Industries: April 1971–March 1978.
E. Law on Temporary Measures for the Promotion of Specified Machinery and Information Industries: July 1978–June 1985.

Source: Fair Trade Commission of Japan, *Annual Report 1992* (Tokyo: Fair Trade Association, 1993). Attachments, 58–61.

In view of the historical background of the AML exemption systems and other measures for controlling competition, the evaluation of institutional anticompetitive devices becomes almost tantamount to the evaluation of Japanese industrial policy. Leaving this larger task to much more extensive studies such as Itoh et al. (1991), Johnson (1982), Komiya, Okuno, and Suzumura (1988), and Okimoto (1989), I shall make only two brief observations.

First, there is little solid proof, if any, that MITI's protective intervention into the mechanism of free competition through its measures to control competition was indispensable to recovery, rationalization, rapid economic growth, and adjustment to external shocks in the postwar Japanese economy. Indeed, the effectiveness of the government-sanctioned cartels has been seriously questioned. For example, in his analysis of the competitive consequences of Japan's export cartel associations, Dick (1992, 280) concluded that "Japanese export cartels appear to have had no statistically significant effect upon either export prices or quantities," and suggested that "several seemingly anti-competitive provisions of Japanese antitrust law, including the limited antitrust exemption for resale price maintenance and the exemption for private depression cartels, appear in practice to have allowed efficient forms of competition to emerge" (Dick 1992, 291). More recently, Weinstein (1993) concluded in an evaluation of the administrative guidance and cartels in Japan that "MITI's guidance and cartel policies seem to have had rather small impacts on firm behavior," and that "in comparison to the favorable tax treatment, subsidies, protection, and low interest loans that some sectors received, exemptions from the virtually defunct Anti-Monopoly Law seem like relatively mild forms of government intervention."

Second, it can hardly be denied that MITI had often outmaneuvered JFTC, at least until the early 1970s. However, there were two changes in the mid-1970s and thereafter that are worth mentioning. In the first place, there was a sharp and outright confrontation between MITI and JFTC when in February 1974 JFTC charged the Petroleum Association of Japan and 12 petroleum companies with operating an illegal price cartel. The case was turned over to the Tokyo High Public Prosecutor's Office. What was unique about this case was that the petroleum companies pleaded not guilty, saying that whatever they had done collectively had been done in accordance with MITI's administrative guidance. Although MITI was not charged in this context and neither was MITI's administrative guidance openly referred to in the indictment, the very fact that MITI's administrative guidance underlay the first criminal prosecution for a violation of the AML clearly indicated that the day had long passed when MITI could impose its anticompetitive measures on JFTC with impunity. In the second place, the lenient nature of the AML in Japan has become one of the focal issues of the US-Japan Debates on Structural Impediments Initiatives. In response to this external pressure, JFTC has recently reviewed and reevaluated systems of exemption to the AML in Japan. It seems safe to surmise that, whatever effects one may be ready to associate with the current exemption systems and other anticompetitive measures, these systems and measures are in the process of being curtailed, if not actually extinguished.

Case Study I: Entry Regulation in the Japanese Retail Industry

Formal Structure of the Large-Scale Retail Store Law

Since large firms tend to be technically more efficient than small firms, substantial social conflict occurs when a few large firms come to compete with many small firms in a segmented market. From the point of view of technical efficiency, it may be better to have fewer and larger firms rather than more and smaller ones. However, apart from the problem that a larger proportion of overall market power would then be held by these larger firms, there are at least two countervailing considerations. First, more often than not larger firms are newcomers to the segmented ("local") market, in which smaller firms have been engaged in hand-to-mouth business over many years or even generations. Hence, the arrival of larger rivals may be viewed as eradicating fair and rightful business opportunities for those who have been totally committed to the local market. Second, smaller firms, being predominant in number, are capable of exerting strong political pressure on the government, which may result in some governmental measures being taken to regulate, if not blockade, the entry of technically superior and larger firms into a local market. One can best appreciate how these considerations interact, and how they tend to generate a complex and informal system of entry regulation, by examining the local retail markets.

I shall begin by describing the formal system of entry regulation in local retail markets that existed until the recent reform, and will then explain the huge divergence that subsequently developed between this lawful framework and the actual modus operandi of entry regulation.[3] It is my hope that this case study will illustrate the difficulties that must be faced in attempting to design and implement a welfare-enhancing entry regulation, and that it will suggest how great the social cost of less-than-ideal anticompetitive market intervention can be.

The formal structure of the Law Concerning the Adjustment of Retail Activities by Large-Scale Retail Stores (referred to hereafter as the Large-Scale Retail Store Law), which was enacted in 1974 and replaced the foregoing Department Law, is fairly simple and straightforward. According to Article 1 of the law, its purpose is to keep the retail activities of large-scale retail stores under due control, thereby securing fair business opportunities for local small and medium-sized retailers, and to main-

---

3. This section is based essentially on Suzumura (1990c). See also Kusano (1992) and Tsuruta and Yahagi (1991).

tain the well-balanced development of retail industry in the area without sacrificing consumers' benefits.[4]

Whenever a large-scale retailer intends to start a new store whose size exceeds 500 square meters in a local retail market, that retailer must follow the accommodation procedure stipulated by the law.[5] In the first place, those who intend to build the large-scale retail store must notify MITI of their construction plans through the local municipality. This is known as the Article 3 notification. Once this notification is filed, MITI should make it known to those who are likely to be affected by the proposed entry that a formal process of accommodation in accordance with the law is about to start. After this first step is completed, the second notification to MITI, the so-called Article 5 notification, must be filed at least five months before the opening of the store in question through the local municipality by those who are going to engage in retail business activities in the proposed large-scale retail store. This second notification must include such information as opening date, total floor space, and frequency of discount sales. If MITI feels that the opening of the proposed store may adversely affect the business opportunities of small local retailers beyond a reasonable limit, it is within MITI's jurisdiction to recommend that the potential entrant delay the opening of the store or reduce the planned floor space, or both. This recommendation should be made within four months after the Article 5 notification is filed. In doing this, MITI should consult the Large-Scale Retail Store Council, an advisory group under MITI's jurisdiction, for its opinion concerning the necessity and content of a recommendation. The council, being rather distant from local circumstances and opinions, will consult the local Chamber of Commerce for its opinion; the latter in turn will organize a Council to Accommodate Commerce Activities (CACA), whose function is to hold discussions to accommodate local

---

4. This declared purpose of the law seems to contain some possibilities of internal inconsistency. In particular, it is not at all clear how one can protect the "fair" business opportunities of local small retailers by the entry regulation of large-scale stores, which tend to be more efficient and capable of providing a wider product range to local customers, without sacrificing consumers' benefits.

5. According to the original 1974 law, a large-scale retail store is one whose total floor space exceeds 1,500 square meters. This stipulation only induced an increase in the number of retail stores whose total floor space was $1,500 \text{ m}^2 - \varepsilon$, where ε is positive but small. Partly in response to this induced tendency and partly in response to the additional regulations introduced by local municipalities that covered retail stores with total floor space less than 1,500 square meters, the law was modified in 1979 so as to define a large-scale retail store as one whose total floor space exceeds 500 square meters. This definition lasted until January 1992, when the law was again modified in response to the US-Japan Debates on Structural Impediments Initiatives. In order to facilitate new entry of large retailers, the critical total floor space of retail stores was raised to 3,000 square meters. For more factual details on the history and content of the Large-Scale Retail Store Law, see Suzumura (1990b) and Kusano (1992).

interest groups. It is noteworthy that the formal members of CACA consist of local business representatives *excluding* those who are directly affected by the large-scale retail store in question, plus consumer representatives and neutral third parties, including informed academics.[6]

The maximum allowable length of time for this accommodation process is obviously limited by the maximum time allowed between the Article 5 notification and MITI's lawful recommendation. As a matter of fact, MITI's administrative guidance recommended that this period be restricted to two months. Therefore, it should be possible under the law to open a new large-scale retail store within as little as seven months of filing the Article 3 notification, as long as the original entry plan is duly modified in full accordance with any MITI recommendation. If MITI's recommendation is not voluntarily complied with, then it can issue a legal order to enforce its lawful recommendation.

This formal accommodation procedure is briefly summarized in figure 1. It should be clear that the Large-Scale Retail Store Law empowers no one, not even MITI officials and local municipalities, to *reject* new entry into a local retail market, as long as the two notifications are filed in time and MITI's recommendation based on the formal procedure is duly observed.

Actual Working of the System of Entry Accommodation

In reality, actual accommodation procedure has been completely different from what has been described so far. In some cases, the formal accommodation procedure can begin only after quite lengthy and unofficial *ex ante* negotiations with local interest groups have been successfully carried out, which sometimes can take as long as five years. In view of this prolonged and painful process of accommodation, which is obviously costly to those wanting to enter a local retail market, there have been cases in which attempted entry plans were abandoned or shifted to another area. There seem to be at least two reasons why this happens, one involving MITI's administrative guidance and bureaucratic conventions and another involving additional regulations brought in by local municipalities.

The first step in the erosion of the official accommodation procedure is that it soon became a bureaucratic convention that MITI consulted the opinion of the local Chamber of Commerce between the two lawful notifications, the reason presumably being to facilitate better reflection of local opinions in the final settlement. Since the official CACA is formed

---

6. To be precise, there is no explicit stipulation in the law concerning the role of the Council to Accommodate Commerce Activities. It was MITI's administrative guidance that first introduced this council. Its role was made more official in the 1982 revision but was never been formally included in the law itself.

Figure 1 Formal accommodation procedure

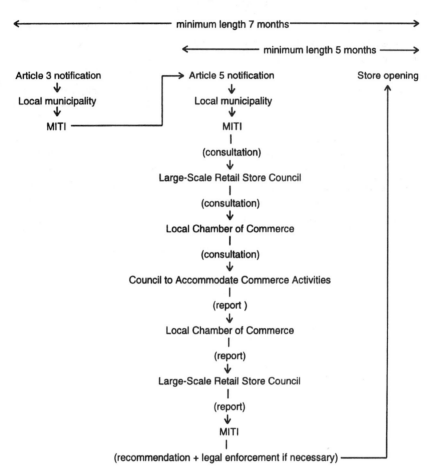

only *after* the Article 5 notification is filed and the Large-Scale Retail Store Council has consulted the local Chamber of Commerce, it was necessary to introduce another informal council, without any lawful status whatsoever, which dealt with the substantial matter of accommodation as it concerned floor space, opening date, holidays, and opening hours. This informal council came to be called the Prior CACA, and it lies completely outside the lawful accommodation procedure, with two regrettable consequences.

First, in contrast to the situation with the official CACA, there was no time limit on the accommodation within the Prior CACA, nor was there any accountable restriction on the Prior CACA's membership. Second, this informal council in effect preempted the formal accommodation procedure as laid down in the Large-Scale Retail Store Law. It was inevitable that much time thereby came to be wasted, but the more serious problem was that the lawful accommodation procedure was deprived of its substance. That the official CACA came to be dubbed the "Confirmation CACA" is symbolic of the extent to which it was undermined by the unofficial Prior CACA.

To rectify the situation, in May 1979 MITI introduced administrative guidance to the effect that the length of time between the Article 3 and Article 5 notifications should not exceed eight months. This, in effect, set an upper limit of eight months on the allowable period of accommodation within the Prior CACA. In response to this administrative guidance, however, a bizarre practice came into being. The Preliminary Explanation by the potential entrant to the local interest groups, which was also introduced by MITI's administrative guidance as a prerequisite to official filing of the Article 3 notification, transformed itself into the Prior-Prior CACA, within which the whole substance of the accommodation procedure was in effect completed. As this Preliminary Explanation had to be completed before filing of the Article 3 notification, there were no legal stipulations on the membership of the Prior-Prior CACA; nor was there any constraint on the content and length of negotiations within it.

Along with this erosion of the entry regulation system administered by the central government, many local municipalities introduced additional entry regulations which made the actual entry accommodation procedure even more opaque and inefficient. On the one hand, some local municipalities required that the agreement concluded within the Prior-Prior CACA be appended to the Article 3 notification. This administrative practice has no legal foundation in the Large-Scale Retail Store Law itself, however.[7] On the other hand, many local municipalities extended the scope of entry regulations based on the Large-Scale Retail Store Law, intending to cover retail stores with floor space far less than the legally stipulated 500 square meters.[8] In extreme cases, local entry regulation was applied to retail stores whose floor space exceeded just one square meter when the store was funded by someone residing outside the municipality in question. Figure 2 summarizes the actual entry regulation system in local retail markets schematically.[9]

Given this labyrinth of informal entry regulations, it is all too common for many large-scale retail stores to be effectively blocked from

---

7. In March 1989, there were 117 local municipalities that had their own entry regulations governing large-scale retail stores, in addition to the regulations based on the Large-Scale Retail Store Law; see Kusano 1992, 28.

8. In March 1989, there were 1,014 local municipalities regulating the entry of retail stores with floor space less than 500 square meters; see Kusano 1992, 28.

9. This scheme persisted until May 1990. It was in response to US criticism of this grotesque arrangement that the first step was taken to make it more efficient and more accountable; see section 4.3 below.

Figure 2 Informal accommodation procedure

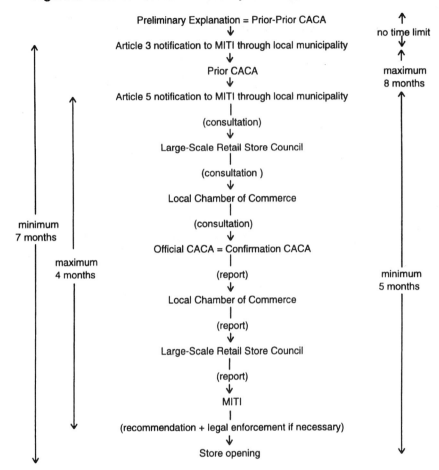

Preliminary Explanation = Prior-Prior CACA
↓
Article 3 notification to MITI through local municipality
↓
Prior CACA
↓
Article 5 notification to MITI through local municipality
|
(consultation)
↓
Large-Scale Retail Store Council
|
(consultation)
↓
Local Chamber of Commerce
|
(consultation)
↓
Official CACA = Confirmation CACA
|
(report)
↓
Local Chamber of Commerce
|
(report)
↓
Large-Scale Retail Store Council
|
(report)
↓
MITI
|
(recommendation + legal enforcement if necessary)
↓
Store opening

no time limit

maximum
8 months

minimum
5 months

minimum
7 months

maximum
4 months

entering local markets, or "voluntarily" to shift away from local markets known for their vigorous entry-preventing activities, to the clear detriment of local consumers. If and when an attempted entry does prove successful, the entry "fee," in the form of forgone imputed rent on the prospective store site, the cost of lengthy negotiations, and pecuniary or nonpecuniary compensations paid out to local retailers, is ultimately passed on to local consumers.

The story told thus far should not be interpreted to suggest that large-scale retailers have been unilaterally sacrificed and exploited by incumbent small and medium-size retailers through the informal mechanism of entry regulations. The reason is as follows: Since most large-scale retailers have repeatedly played this entry regulation game, even when they are compelled to pay compensation for their attempts to enter a local market, the same mechanism effectively protects them from future attempts at entry by their rivals. It follows that the initial entry "fee," which is shifted to customers after entry anyway, is in fact considered money well spent from large-scale retailers' point of view. Thus, not only small and medium-sized retailers, but also the large-scale retailers themselves, are beneficiaries of this informal mechanism of entry regulation. This is one of the crucial reasons why the mechanism has been so robustly preserved, despite its obvious inefficiency, unfairness, and lack of transparency.

Prospects for Regulatory Reform in the Japanese Retail Industry

Entry regulations in the retail industry became the symbolic focus of the US-Japan Debates on Structural Impediments Initiatives. In response to criticisms raised by the US representatives of the supplier-oriented nature of administrative practices in Japan, several important steps have been taken to improve both the formal structure of entry regulations and administrative practices.

The initial step was taken in May 1990, when MITI issued a circular to all municipalities and Chambers of Commerce. In it, the ministry requested that the maximum period of accommodation be shortened to 18 months total, and that the improper use of the Preliminary Explanation as the Prior-Prior CACA be terminated. The law itself was revised in May 1991 and became effective nine months later. The revised law stipulated that the total period of accommodation should be less than one year; it also simplified the accommodation procedure by placing accommodation-related activities exclusively in the hands of the Large-Scale Retail Store Council. It is worth emphasizing that neither the Prior CACA nor the official CACA itself, which symbolized the deformed accommodation procedure, has any role whatsoever in this newly revised procedure.

The immediate response to the revisions was remarkable. Within one month of MITI's May 1990 circular, more than 1,500 large-scale retail stores announced their intention either to open a new store or to upgrade their existing store(s). This figure was three times larger than the total number of Article 3 notifications filed in all of 1989. It spoke eloquently to the severity of the entry regulations and indicated how many potential entries had had to remain latent.

Although implementation of this regulatory reform may not be easy for various reasons, the shift toward more transparent and consumer-oriented entry accommodation mechanisms should be welcomed. Note, however, that the Large-Scale Retail Store Council faces a prodigious task in view of the number of proposed new entries. It is not clear how the council will cope with this responsibility. In addition, it is not clear how the extended use of entry regulations by local municipalities, which was one of the major reasons for the failure of the former accommodation procedure, can be effectively contained without violating the important principle of local autonomy.

With the conclusion of this case study, a general remark seems in order. Even when the formal system of market intervention is straightforward, it may be made complex and internally inconsistent by a sequence of administrative guidances which, by their very nature, lack a basis on any clear and logical procedural restriction. The situation is even worse when the formal system itself contains some internal logical inconsistencies. Indeed, what underlies the quagmire of entry regulations in the Japanese retail industry is a conflict between two very basic requirements of social policy: efficiency of industry performance, on the one hand, and protection of the "right" of those who have been engaged in local business long before the proposed entry of their large rivals, on the other hand.[10] Once it is agreed that the "right" in question is worth social protection, the concomitant loss of social efficiency may be regarded as a cost to be borne collectively. Even in this case, however, one can design a much more efficient and straightforward mechanism for protecting this "right" than leaving the issue to be settled through the complex procedure of endless negotiations and compensations. However, if the general validity of such a "right" is not universally agreed upon, the raison d'être of entangled negotiation procedure will be that much less.

Case Study II: Telecommunications Reform and Handcuffed Competition

Telecommunications Reform of 1985

The telecommunications industry is under the jurisdiction of the Ministry of Posts and Telecommunications (MPT). In 1985, MPT introduced an extensive telecommunications reform which is apparently procompetitive in nature. Before the implementation of this important reform, Nippon Telegraph and Telephone Public Corporation had legally monopolized domestic telecommunications in Japan. My second case study focuses on the nature and aftermath of this reform, with special emphasis on the public decision-making mechanism that led to this reform.[11]

---

10. This basic conflict reflects itself in Article 1 of the law; see footnote 4.

11. For the sake of brevity, the following explanation greatly simplifies matters. See Suzumura (1990a) and Okuno-Fujiwara, Suzumura, and Nambu (1993) for a more detailed account and analysis of the 1985 telecommunications reform.

The origin of the 1985 reform can be traced back to the Third Report of the Second Ad Hoc Commission on Administrative Reform, which was submitted to the prime minister in 1982. To understand the nature of this report and its enforcement, a brief account of the nature of this Ad Hoc Commission is provided here.

Historically speaking, it was the Occupation authorities who encouraged participatory democracy in order to reduce and rectify the arbitrary nature of Japan's prewar administration. With the implementation of the National Administrative Organization Law in 1949, the government ministries began to establish advisory bodies on the level of cabinet ministers, bureau chiefs, and section chiefs. These advisory bodies are classified into "consultative bodies," which deliberate on policies, and "examining bodies," which, by participating in administrative decision making, ensure that the laws are fairly administered. A report submitted by a consultative body is not binding, whereas the resolution of an examining body can serve as a legal constraint on bureaucracy. Thus, it is clear that examining bodies are far stronger administrative committees than consultative bodies in terms of their degree of independent authority; furthermore, examining bodies are grounded in Article 3 of the National Administrative Organization Law.

Although the Second Ad Hoc Commission was a consultative body grounded in Article 8 of the National Administrative Organization Law, its reports were considered virtually legally binding, owing to the fact that the prime minister had publicly promised the chairman of the Second Ad Hoc Commission that his government would faithfully implement its recommendations.

Concerning the telecommunications industry, the Third Report made the following recommendations:

- Nippon Telegraph and Telephone Public Corporation should be privatized.

- This public corporation should be divided into a central corporation, which would manage the long-distance network, and local corporations, which would manage the local networks in their respectively designated areas.

- The telecommunications industry should be liberalized and new entry into the long-distance market should be encouraged.[12]

---

12. The background of these radical recommendations seems to be threefold. First, under the legal monopoly enjoyed by Nippon Telegraph and Telephone Public Corporation, the telecommunications industry in Japan was not responsive enough to rapidly expanding and diversifying customer needs. Second, the extent of the internal inefficiencies of the state monopoly seemed to have far exceeded the limits of public tolerance. Third, owing to innovations in telecommunications technology, the traditional reason for state monopoly, that is, natural monopoly, seemed to have disappeared at least as far as long-distance telecommunications were concerned.

Of these three recommendations, the first two were indeed implemented by the 1985 telecommunications reform. The Nippon Telegraph and Telephone Public Corporation was transformed into a special government-controlled private company called NTT. In addition, in 1987 three new common carriers (NCCs) selectively entered the long-distance market and started telecommunications services in the most profitable market segment. Concerning the third recommendation, however, no firm commitment to its implementation was made in the 1985 reform. It was simply announced that the performance of the new organization of the telecommunications industry in general, and the performance of NTT in particular, would be reviewed after five years with the purpose of deciding what further steps should be taken. At the time of the 1985 reform, therefore, NTT remained a consolidated common carrier and continued to monopolize the local telecommunications market.

The 1984 procompetitive reform notwithstanding, the telecommunications industry has remained highly regulated, and the nascent competition between the privatized NTT and the newly arrived NCCs has been hampered by MPT's incessant interference. Not only NTT, but also the NCCs, have been subject to MPT's price and service regulations, which seem to have been guided by MPT's industrial policy aimed at promoting the NCCs as an effective countervailing power against the bottleneck monopolist, that is, NTT. Indeed, at least up to June 1992, there had always been a 20 percent difference in the NCCs' favor between the rates charged by NTT and the NCCs for long-distance telephone services. This difference sufficed to bring about a rapid shift in the long-distance telephone market from NTT to the NCCs.[13]

Not only the entry of potential firms into this industry, but also the exit of incumbent firms from the industry, is under the strict surveillance of MPT. Since NTT was not divested in the 1985 reform but retained its integrated network, a fundamental asymmetry persists between NTT and the NCCs. Thus, each NCC can complete its long-distance telecommunications service only by being smoothly connected with NTT's local network, whereas NTT can provide a self-contained telecommunications service. Given this structural asymmetry between NTT and the NCCs, it makes sense that there should remain an asymmetric regulation in order to keep NTT's bottleneck monopoly under proper control. However, the current intervention by MPT would seem to go far beyond such rule-oriented and procompetitive regulation and to interfere with the choice of competitive strategies by the market participants. The current method of price regulation, which remains the classical rate-of-

---

13. The NCCs' share of long-distance telephone service between Tokyo and Osaka via Nagoya was already as high as 40 percent in 1990 and came close to 60 percent in 1992. Given that the NCCs started their service only in 1987, this drastic shift in market share is truly remarkable.

return regulation, is not really procompetitive either. Besides, MPT has never allowed NTT to rebalance its rate structure, with the result that the local telephone charge has remained absolutely fixed ever since the 1985 reform, in the face of a sharp decrease in the long-distance telephone charges arising from the introduction of controlled competition in this segment of the market.[14]

In 1988, MPT sought the opinion of the Telecommunications Deliberation Council, the advisory body at MPT level, on further measures to be adopted with the purpose of improving NTT's performance. In March 1990, the council submitted a report to the minister of posts and telecommunications on several possible measures that could be taken, including the vertical divestiture of NTT into two parts: the Long-Distance Network Corporation and the Local Network Corporation. However, this report failed to attract support from other ministries, including MITI and the Ministry of Finance—the ruling Liberal Democratic Party was likewise uninterested—and the implementation of recommendation 2 of the Second Ad Hoc Commission had to be postponed for another five years.

Public Decision-Making Process of the 1985 Reform

In Japan there exists a traditional one-to-one correspondence between an industry and the ministerial bureau, division, or section under whose jurisdiction the industry in question falls. Whenever a new development disrupts or blurs this delicately balanced relationship, inevitably a jurisdictional dispute among ministries breaks out. This was indeed the case in the 1970s and early 1980s, when MPT and MITI had a jurisdictional dispute over data processing. MITI's concern was not to lose its influence in data-processing and information services. In addition, some large corporations under MITI's jurisdiction were complaining that they were being prevented from setting up nationwide value-added networks (VAN) between companies; nor were these companies satisfied by the high cost of long-distance calls and the lack of customized billing. It is true that the Third Report of the Second Ad Hoc Commission on Administrative Reform took a clear initiative in designing NTT's privatization and divestiture, but MITI's strong and explicit concern also played an undeniable role throughout the public debate over the privatization of NTT and the liberalization of the telecommunications industry in general, and over data communications in particular.

---

14. In February 1988, shortly after the NCCs first started providing long-distance telephone services, NTT's charge for the longest-distance telephone service (three minutes, daytime) was ¥360, whereas the corresponding charge by the NCCs was ¥300. These charges were lowered to ¥330 versus ¥280 in February 1989, ¥280 versus ¥240 in March 1990, and ¥240 versus ¥200 in March 1991. During and after this period, NTT's charge for local telephone service (three minutes, day or night) remained absolutely fixed at ¥10.

Although jurisdictional disputes such as the one between MPT and MITI are often viewed cynically, there is a positive side, which is illustrated by looking at the process by which further measures for improving NTT's performance were discussed during 1988–90. NTT being within MPT's jurisdiction, it was the Telecommunications Deliberation Council that came to the fore at this time. As is always the case, the deliberation process within the council was closed to the public, and those who testified in the council's meeting were strongly urged not to disclose any information outside the council. If it were not for other organs, such as the other ministries or business organizations which expressed strong concern and publicized alternative opinions on and scenarios for further telecommunications reform, the general public would not have known what was really at stake. Thus, an imperfect—yet workable—mechanism for checks and balances, that is, the expressed interest of the concerned ministries combined with concomitant jurisdictional disputes, may play some positive role in such a situation by bringing the real policy issues under debate to public awareness.

It goes without saying, however, that it would be much better if there were more dependable and transparent mechanisms through which bureaucratic arbitrariness and unfairness in the form of administrative guidance could be systematically contained. From this point of view, the importance of the Administrative Procedure Law, which was promulgated in November 1993 and stipulates the lawful limits and legitimate procedures of administrative guidance, cannot be overemphasized. For the first time, it is made explicit that compliance with administrative guidance must be strictly voluntary, and there should not be any retaliatory action on the part of the government bureaucracy when the guidance fails to bring about voluntary compliance. It is also significant that the law stipulates that the contents of the administrative guidance, as well as the identity of the person in charge of it, be formally put in writing and provided to those who are subject to the guidance in question. It is hoped that the effective invocation of this law will make administrative procedures in Japan more accountable and transparent in the future.

What's Wrong with Controlled Competition?

In view of the fact that competition has been keen in the long-distance telecommunications market and that customers are gaining from lower long-distance telephone charges without being required to pay higher local telephone charges, a devoted consequentialist may ask: What's wrong with handcuffed competition? However, it seems that such a competition is indeed wrong, for at least two reasons.

First of all, by controlling long-distance telephone charges in such a way that the NCCs can always maintain a substantial competitive edge over NTT, the authority in charge of handcuffed competition is in fact depriving the NCCs of any incentive to compete in terms of strategies other than controlled prices. A regrettable consequence is that customers miss out on the opportunity to choose from a wider range of services that would be competitively provided were it not for artificially maintained differentials in long-distance telephone charges.

Second, by maintaining artificially low local telephone charges, the authority in charge of handcuffed competition is foreclosing on the potential entry of the NCCs into the local telecommunications market where NTT is still maintaining a virtual bottleneck monopoly. If it were not for the prohibition on revisions to local telephone charges, there might be a spontaneous growth of countervailing competitive power in the local telecommunications market.

It cannot be denied that unfettered competition can be downright wasteful, but handcuffed competition can also cause waste by suppressing spontaneous development which only free market competition can nourish. It is not at all clear which is the lesser of the two "evils."

Antimonopoly Law Guidelines Concerning Joint R&D

Positive and Negative Effects of Collaborative R&D

Apart from anticompetitive interference in the form of entry and exit regulations and rationalization and recession cartels under government auspices, there are cases in which government promotes cooperative behavior among competitive firms. The most important example in postwar Japan is public assistance to collaborative R&D activities through pecuniary and nonpecuniary policy measures.[15] A crucial feature of such government-assisted collaborative R&D is that the joint efforts are deliberately focused on "precompetitive" R&D, which is aimed at disseminating knowledge in nonmarketable form in full awareness that the recipient firms commercialize the knowledge or process in the "competitive" stage.[16] There is widespread interest in this institutional arrangement for promoting R&D, and there are proponents who claim that the AML regulations governing this class of collaborative agreements among competing firms should be made more lenient. It is in this context that

---

15. This section is based largely on Suzumura and Goto (1995).

16. The best-known example of government-assisted collaborative R&D is the Very Large-Scale Integrated Circuit Research Association (VLSI, 1976-80), which was designed to develop the advanced semiconductor technology that would enable Japanese computer firms to compete with the fourth-generation IBM computers. See Suzumura and Goto (1995) for an evaluation of the VLSI Research Association.

the AML Guidelines Concerning Joint R&D, which were recently published by JFTC, deserves special attention.

I will start by summarizing the pros and cons of such collaborative R&D agreements in general terms. It is widely believed that collaborative R&D has the following positive effects: First, it is necessary for firms to reveal a portion of information concerning a project if they are to raise funds for R&D individually in imperfect capital markets; this reduces their incentive to embark on such R&D projects. However, collaborative R&D arrangements could overcome this barrier and lead to an increase in aggregate R&D. Second, R&D collaboration may improve R&D efficiency if member firms can bring in complementary expertise.[17] Third, R&D competition with the feature of rank order competition, in which the firm that achieves the R&D goal ahead of others reaps most of the fruits, may motivate firms to scurry simultaneously to accomplish the same R&D objective, with the result being a lower social rate of return on additional private R&D. The device of R&D collaboration may prevent this wasteful duplication of R&D resources.[18] Fourth, an R&D collaboration may cope effectively with the problem of appropriability, thereby increasing the aggregate R&D. Indeed, by internalizing R&D externalities, the member firms of an R&D collaboration can appropriate the benefits of R&D, although outsiders can still free ride on R&D spillovers. The diffusion of technological information among member firms can be easier and more assured under an R&D collaboration than under a regime of competitive R&D.

Against these potential benefits, however, there are certain dangers inherent in the institutional device of collaborative R&D. First, R&D collaborations may lead to an excessively high price for technology by reducing competition in the technology market. Second, R&D collaborations may lead to dynamic inefficiency by reducing R&D efforts collectively. This is a real danger which may be exemplified by the case of the US automobile manufacturers' attempt to slow down R&D in pollution-control technology. Third, collaborative behavior at the R&D level by otherwise competing firms may spill over to the product market, that is, collusion on the R&D stage may pave the way for collusion in the stage of product market competition.

17. For example, a ceramic manufacturer and an automobile manufacturer could develop a ceramic engine more effectively in a collaborative effort than if each of them pursued the same R&D project independently.

18. If various approaches are possible to solve the same research problem, and if each firm pursues a separate approach, then competitive R&D may make more sense. However, this type of parallel R&D through competition is unlikely to materialize. The possibility of duplication is high, because each firm will try to keep its approach secret under the competitive R&D regime. If decision making is centralized through collaborative R&D, it is possible for the firms to diversify their approaches deliberately and pursue parallel development strategy intentionally, thereby making the allocation of R&D resources more efficient.

In order to design an effective collaborative R&D policy, it is clearly necessary to pay due attention to these negative effects along with the previously enumerated positive effects.

JFTC Guidelines

In April 1993, JFTC published the Antimonopoly Law Guidelines Concerning Joint Research and Development (hereafter referred to as the JFTC Guidelines) and clarified its general stance regarding collaborative R&D arrangements. The following salient features of these guidelines are particularly worth noting:

■ The guidelines are universally applicable to all attempts at collaborative R&D as long as they may exert an anticompetitive effect in the Japanese market, irrespective of whether the participants are domestic or foreign firms.

■ Collaborative R&D projects that would encounter problems under the AML would be those undertaken by competitive firms. There is very little likelihood that collaborative R&D projects among noncompetitive firms would pose problems under the AML.

■ In passing judgment on whether or not competition in the market is substantially restrained by a particular joint R&D project, the number of member firms and their share of and position in the market are taken into account. If the combined market share of the members is no more than 20 percent, this will usually present no problem under the AML. Even when the total share exceeds 20 percent, however, this does not automatically pose a problem. Judgment will be made by comprehensively taking matters such as the character of research, need for collaboration, and range of objectives into consideration.

■ Even where the collaborative undertaking of R&D presents no problem of its own under the AML, arrangements accompanying its actual implementation may affect competition in the product market, thereby creating problems under the AML. These problems may occur (a) if an arrangement unjustly restricts the business activities of a participating firm, thereby impeding fair competition, and (b) if competitive business activities relating to the price and quantity of a product are mutually restricted among participating firms. Thus, collaborative R&D presents a problem under the AML if there is a spillover of anticompetitive practices from the precompetitive R&D stage to the stage of product market competition.

■ In principle, under the AML, participants in collaborative R&D can be required (a) to disclose information on technologies necessary for the collaborative R&D project, (b) to report to other participants on the progress of their share of the research work, and (c) to keep secret the information on technologies disclosed to them by other participants in connection with the collaborative R&D.

■ In principle, it does not present any problem under the AML (a) to restrict, within a reasonable period, the marketing of products utilizing a technology that is the fruit of the collaborative R&D project to the participants or a designated firm or firms, if it is deemed necessary to maintain the secrecy of the resulting know-how; or (b) to restrict, within a reasonable time, the source(s) of supply of raw materials or parts for products utilizing the technology resulting from the collaborative R&D project to other participants or to a designated firm or firms to maintain the secrecy of the resulting know-how and ensure the quality of products based on such technology.

■ Other restrictions, even those based on the propriety of one's collaboratively developed technology, such as (a) restrictions on the production or on the territory where the product may be sold, or (b) restrictions on the production or on the volume of sales of the product, may fall into the category of unfair trade practices.

■ To supplement these guidelines, a prior-consultation system has been established whereby any uncertainty about whether a specific collaborative R&D project presents any problems under the AML may be resolved. The party eligible to request prior consultation is the firm or the trade association intending to implement the collaborative R&D, irrespective of whether the firm or the trade association is domestic or foreign.

It is worth noting that the JFTC Guidelines were published for the purpose of facilitating procompetitive collaborative R&D by making the legal constraints on such associations more transparent. Recently, and in a similar spirit, both in the United States and Europe, the antitrust laws and their practical implementation have become clearly more lenient in regard to collaborative R&D with the passage of the National Cooperative Research Act in 1984, and the Block Exemption from Article 85 in the European Community for some categories of R&D agreements in 1985. It is against this background that the following observations on the JFTC Guidelines may be of some relevance.

The first observation is a general one which pertains not only to the JFTC Guidelines on collaborative R&D but to competition policy in general. Although the preliminary analyses laid out earlier in this chapter cast doubts on the universal validity of the common belief in the welfare-improving effects of increased competitiveness, this conventional wisdom seems to persist in the JFTC Guidelines in that collaborative R&D is judged to present no problem under the AML only when it is procompetitive. It seems that the crucial criterion for approving any coordinating device should be whether or not it leads to an improvement in social welfare; to be procompetitive is neither necessary nor sufficient for this crucial criterion to be satisfied.

The second observation pertains to the second guideline. According to this guideline, horizontal R&D collaboration among competing firms and vertical R&D collaboration among noncompeting firms have strongly contrasting implications in that the former, but not the latter, has a nontrivial likelihood of posing problems under the AML. However, it seems that R&D collaboration among vertically related firms—say, a ceramics manufacturer and an automobile manufacturer for the development of a ceramic engine—if successful, may have a serious impact on competitiveness in both the ceramics industry and the automobile industry. In general, the overly sharp demarcation between horizontal and vertical R&D collaborations does not seem to be warranted.

The third observation pertains to the markets whose competitiveness is the focus of the JFTC Guidelines in judging whether or not R&D collaboration presents problems under the AML. One may easily verify that domestic markets are exclusively focused upon in this context, even though the first and last guidelines assert that foreign firms are to be treated on a par with domestic firms. Thus, the effects of the participation of foreign firms in Japanese collaborative R&D on the competitiveness of foreign markets play no role whatsoever in the JFTC judgment on the pro- or anticompetitiveness of R&D collaborations. This insidious feature of the JFTC Guidelines may be in need of further examination from the viewpoint of international harmonization of antimonopoly legislation and its implementation.

Concluding Remarks

This chapter presents a brief overview of formal as well as informal policy measures for controlling competition in Japan, starting with the formal systems of exemption from the Antimonopoly Law and proceeding to informal policy measures—such as administrative guidance—that have been invoked by government ministries in pursuit of industrial policy objectives. In the following paragraphs, I summarize the main points of this chapter.

A rational answer to the crucial question of whether there is any room for justifiable interference in free market competition hinges on the objective function involved. If one measures the performance of market competition in terms of consumers' surplus (or producers' surplus), entry regulation does not improve (or does improve) market performance at the margin for a wide class of economies. If one is prepared to add consumers' surplus and producers' surplus to define net market surplus as a performance criterion, then one is led to conclude that entry regulation improves market performance at the margin. The same conclusions are valid for regulation of R&D investment at the margin as well.

According to the AML, a private monopolization or cartel is unlawful if and only if it restricts competition contrary to the public interest. The crucial term—public interest—admits several alternative interpretations, and the choice made among them dictates the rigor with which the AML is applied to a private monopolization or cartel. I have identified three interpretations, adopted by the JFTC, the Federation of Economic Organizations, and the Supreme Court, respectively, which roughly correspond to the three performance criteria mentioned above, that is, consumers' surplus, producers' surplus, and net market surplus, with their respective welfare implications.

The systems of exemption from the AML are both extensive and complicated, but the number of cartels under these systems has been decreasing, and some of the exempted cartel systems have been dormant for a long time. There are also several exempting laws of historical importance, as typified by the Law on Temporary Measures for Structural Improvement of Specified Industries, the Law on Special Measures for the Promotion of the Machinery Industry, and the Law on Special Measures for the Promotion of the Electronics Industry. However, all these laws of historical importance had ceased to be effective by June 1988, and in some cases much earlier.

Even if the systems of exemption from the AML and other provisions for controlling competition are formally straightforward, the actual implementation of the anticompetition policies may become extremely complicated as well as opaque through informal administrative guidance and bureaucratic conventions. This was illustrated by two case studies: entry regulation in the retail industry and telecommunications reform in 1985. In this context, the newly enacted Administrative Procedure Law, which clarified the lawful limit of and legitimate procedure for administrative guidance, is crucially important.

Collaborative R&D among otherwise competitive firms is often believed to generate welfare-improving effects, and there are proponents who ask for more lenient AML applications to this class of collaborative activities. I have identified positive as well as negative implications of collaborative R&D and critically examined the rationale of the AML Guidelines Concerning Joint Research and Development.

Postscript: June 1997

Japan's AML and competition policy are currently in a state of flux. In June 1997, the original prohibition of pure stock-holding companies was lifted, and in 1999, the exemption of depression and rationalization cartels from the AML is scheduled to end. Despite these substantial changes in competition policy, the main message of our chapter stands without revision.

Japan's telecommunications policy is also radically changing. MPT and NTT came to an historic agreement in December 1996 concerning the plan to split NTT into a long-distance company, two local companies, and a pure stock-holding company that would control these operating companies. This plan was formally implemented by the June 1997 NTT Company Law. Triggered by this radical change in the managerial form of NTT and by concomitant deregulation, the telecommunications business, domestic as well as international, is now subject to a wave of new entries and strategic alliances that are leading toward more competition. Events leading up to the developments summarized in this postscript are described in detail in Suzumura (forthcoming).

References

Dick, A. R. 1992. "The Competitive Consequences of Japan's Export Cartel Association." *Journal of the Japanese and International Economies* 6: 275-98.

Fair Trade Commission of Japan. 1977. *A Thirty-Year History of Japanese Antimonopoly Policy.* Tokyo: Secretariat of the Fair Trade Commission of Japan. In Japanese.

Fair Trade Commission of Japan. 1991. "Report of the Study Group on the Review of the Exemption Systems from the Antimonopoly Act." *FTC/Japan Views* no. 12: 55-73.

Fair Trade Commission of Japan. 1993. *Annual Report 1992.* Tokyo: Fair Trade Association.

Grossman, G., and C. Shapiro. 1986. "Research Joint Ventures: An Antitrust Analysis." *Journal of Law, Economics, and Organization* 2: 315-37.

Hadley, E. M. 1970. *Antitrust in Japan.* Princeton, NJ: Princeton University Press.

Haley, J. O. 1986. "Administrative Guidance versus Formal Regulation: Resolving the Paradox of Industrial Policy." In G. R. Saxonhouse and K. Yamamura, *Law and Trade Issues of the Japanese Economy: American and Japanese Perspectives.* Seattle, WA: University of Washington Press.

Itoh, M., K. Kiyono, M. Okuno-Fujiwara, and K. Suzumura. 1991. *Economic Analysis of Industrial Policy.* New York: Academic Press.

Iyori, H. 1986. "Antitrust and Industrial Policy in Japan: Competition and Cooperation." In G. R. Saxonhouse and K. Yamamura, *Law and Trade Issues of the Japanese Economy: American and Japanese Perspectives.* Seattle, WA: University of Washington Press.

Jacquemin, A. 1988. "Cooperative Agreements in R&D and European Antitrust Policy." *European Economic Review* 32: 551-60.

Jacquemin, A., T. Nambu, and I. Dewez. 1981. "A Dynamic Analysis of Export Cartels: The Japanese Case." *Economic Journal* 91: 685-96.

Johnson, C. 1982. *MITI and the Japanese Miracle: The Growth of Industrial Policy, 1925-1975.* Stanford, CA: Stanford University Press.

Kaneko, H. 1994. *Administrative Procedure Law.* Tokyo: Iwanami Shoten. In Japanese.

Katz, M. L., and J. A. Ordover. 1990. "R&D Cooperation and Competition." *Brookings Papers on Economic Activity, Microeconomics:* 137-203.

Komiya, R. 1975. "Planning in Japan." In M. Bornstein, *Economic Planning: East and West.* Cambridge, MA: Ballinger.

Komiya, R., M. Okuno, and K. Suzumura, eds. 1988. *Industrial Policy of Japan.* New York: Academic Press.

Konishi, H., M. Okuno-Fujiwara, and K. Suzumura. 1990. "Oligopolistic Competition and

Economic Welfare: A General Equilibrium Analysis of Entry Regulation and Tax-Subsidy Schemes." *Journal of Public Economics* 42: 67-88.

Kusano, A. 1992. *Large-Scale Retail Store Law: The Structure of Economic Regulation.* Tokyo: Nihon-Keizai-Shimbun-sha. In Japanese.

Mankiw, N. G., and M. D. Whinston. 1986. "Free Entry and Social Inefficiency." *Rand Journal of Economics* 17: 48-58.

Matsushita, M. 1979. "Export Control and Export Cartels in Japan." *Harvard International Law Journal* 20: 103-25.

Matsushita, M., with J. D. Davis. 1990. *Introduction to Japanese Antimonopoly Law.* Tokyo: Yuhikaku. In English.

Miwa, Y. 1993. "Economic Effects of the Anti-Monopoly and Other Deconcentration Policies in Postwar Japan." In J. Teranishi, J. Kosai, and Y. Kosai, *The Japanese Experience of Economic Reforms.* London: Macmillan.

Nakazawa, T., and L. W. Weiss. 1989. "The Legal Cartels of Japan." *Antitrust Bulletin* (Fall): 641-53.

Okimoto, D. I. 1989. *Between MITI and the Market: Japanese Industrial Policy for High Technology.* Stanford, CA: Stanford University Press.

Okuno-Fujiwara, M., and K. Suzumura. 1993. "Symmetric Cournot Oligopoly and Economic Welfare: A Synthesis." *Economic Theory* 3: 43-59.

Okuno-Fujiwara, M., K. Suzumura, and T. Nambu, eds. 1993. *Telecommunications in Japan: The Economics of Competition and Regulation.* Tokyo: Nihon Keizai Shimbun-sha. In Japanese.

Ordover, J., and W. Baumol. 1988. "Antitrust Policy and High-Technology Industries." *Oxford Review of Economic Policy* 4: 13-34.

Peck, M. 1986. "Joint R&D: The Case of Microelectronics and Computer Technology Corporation." *Research Policy* 15: 219-31.

Peck, M. J., R. C. Levin, and A. Goto. 1987. "Picking Losers: Public Policy toward Declining Industries in Japan." *Journal of Japanese Studies* 13 (Winter): 79-123.

Shindo, M. 1992. *Administrative Guidance.* Tokyo: Iwanami Shoten. In Japanese.

Suzumura, K. 1990a. "Competition and Regulation in the Telecommunications Industry: Present State and Future Tasks of Telecommunications Reform." Discussion Paper 224. Tokyo: Institute of Economic Research, Hitotsubashi University. In Japanese.

Suzumura, K. 1990b. "The Economic Consequences of Entry Regulation in the Japanese Distribution Industry: Or What's Wrong with the Large-Scale Retail Store Law?" Discussion Paper 230. Tokyo: Institute of Economic Research, Hitotsubashi University. In Japanese.

Suzumura, K. 1992. "Cooperative and Non-Cooperative R&D in an Oligopoly with Spillovers." *American Economic Review* 82: 1307-20.

Suzumura, K. 1995. *Competition, Commitment, and Welfare.* Oxford, England: Oxford University Press.

Suzumura K. N.d. "Japan's Industrial Policy for Telecommunications: The 1985 Institutional Reform and its Aftermath." In K. Odaka and J. Teranishi, *Markets and Government: Foes or Friends?* Tokyo: Kinokuniya Publishing Co. Forthcoming.

Suzumura, K., and A. Goto. 1997. "Collaborative R&D and Competition Policy: Economic Analysis in the Light of Japanese Experience." In L. Waverman, W. S. Comanor and A. Goto, *Competition Policy in the Global Economy: Modalities for Cooperation.* London and New York: Routledge, 197-223.

Suzumura, K., and K. Kiyono. 1987. "Entry Barriers and Economic Welfare." *Review of Economic Studies* 54: 157-67.

Tsuruta, T., and Yahagi, T. 1991. "The System of Large-Scale Retail Store Law and Its Hollowing-Out Process." In K. Nishimura and Y. Miwa, *The Distributions in Japanese.* Tokyo: University of Tokyo Press. In Japanese.

Uesugi, A. 1986. "Japan's Cartel System and Its Impact on International Trade." *Harvard International Law Journal* 27 (Special Issue): 389-424.

Vickers, J. S., and G. K. Yarrow. 1988. *Privatization: An Economic Analysis.* Cambridge, MA: MIT Press.

Weinstein, D. E. 1993. "Evaluating Administrative Guidance and Cartels in Japan (1957-1988)." Discussion Paper 1628. Cambridge, MA: Harvard Institute of Economic Research.

Yonezawa, Y. 1993. "National Economic Independence and the Rationalization of Industry." In J. Teranishi and Y. Kosai, *The Japanese Experience of Economic Reforms.* London: Macmillan.

15

VERs, VIEs, and Global Competition

MOTOSHIGE ITOH AND SADAO NAGAOKA

With the rapid industrialization experienced by countries around the world, especially in the economies of East Asia, foreign competition has become a more important factor for industrial firms in developed countries, and even for those in the United States and the European Union that once worried mostly about competing with domestic firms. However, strong import competition has often hurt domestic import-competing industries, leading to the introduction of trade restrictions. One favorite form of such restrictions has been voluntary export restraints (VERs), which have not only nullified the effects of the tariff cuts promoted by successive rounds of the General Agreement on Tariffs and Trade (GATT) but also undermined basic GATT principles (i.e., nondiscrimination and general prohibition of the use of quantitative restrictions). Consequently, it was agreed in December 1993 as part of the Uruguay Round agreement on safeguards that existing VERs be phased out and future use be banned. This chapter will evaluate the safeguards rule and suggest complementary reforms based on our examination of the causes and consequences of VERs.

In addition, a new form of discriminatory, quantity-fixing trade intervention has emerged recently: voluntary import expansions (VIEs). The US government has strongly pressured Japan in bilateral trade talks to commit to setting import targets in sectors in which the US government perceives barriers to market access. The US Japan semiconductor agreements (in 1986 and 1991) were the first consequence. Some US scholars (e.g., Tyson 1992) argue that, whereas VERs restrict trade and

---

Motoshige Itoh and Sadao Nagaoka are economics professors at, respectively, Tokyo University and Hitotsubashi University.

competition, VIEs promote both. This chapter will also assess the validity of this argument.

The Effects of VERs

Who Is Using Them and Who Is Targeted

Among the exporting countries, Japan and South Korea have most frequently restrained their exports through VERs (and not always voluntarily, despite what the name would imply). As table 1 shows, each of these two countries, accounts for slightly more than 10 percent of all VER cases. According to the GATT (1992), 12.5 percent of Japanese exports were subject to VERs in 1989. As table 2 shows, among the importing countries the European Union and the United States have most frequently restrained their imports through VERs. The European Union and the United States account for 50 percent and 26 percent of all the cases, respectively. Clearly, VERs have typically been used to protect the industries of the largest economies from serious competition from the fastest-growing economies.

Textiles, steel, and agricultural products have been most frequently restrained. Many exporting countries have been subject to the restraints in these sectors. On the other hand, in the more technology-intensive sectors such as automobiles, electronics, and machine-tool industries, the restraints have been concentrated in Japan, South Korea, and Taiwan.

Protections for particular sectors, once initiated by VERs, tend to be long-lived. The first VER for the US textile sector was introduced with respect to Japan in 1957, and that sector is still being protected from international competition through the Multi-Fiber Arrangement (or MFA; see table 3 for major VERs restraining Japan). The MFA now covers most importing and exporting countries. The VER for the US steel sector was introduced in 1969. After a series of revisions, the VER agreement expired in March 1993, but the US steel industry filed extensive antidumping and countervailing duty petitions in 1992 before the expiration of the agreement, with the result that steel trade has not yet been fully liberalized.

Why VERs Have Been Used

Voluntary and Involuntary Restraints

VERs have typically been used to avert alternative trade restrictions. They can be characterized as voluntary or involuntary, depending on whether the restrictions to be averted are consistent with GATT rules. When they are used as a substitute for trade restrictions that are con-

Table 1 Number of VERs by industry and exporting country

Industry	EFTA	Canada	EC	Japan	South Korea	China	Taiwan	US	Other	Total
Steel	7	3	6	4	7		2		34	63
Machine tools		1		4			2		1	8
Electronics				8	5		1		3	17
Footwear			1	1	5	1	4		3	15
Textiles					6	6	1		72	85
Agriculture	4	2	3		3	1		4	42	59
Automobiles				16	2					18
Other	3	3		4	6	1			7	24
Total	14	9	10	37	34	9	10	4	162	289

EFTA = European Free Trade Association.

Table 2 Number of VERs by product and importing country

Industry	EFTA	Canada	EC	Japan	Austria	Australia	Switzerland	Former Soviet	US	Total
Steel	1		21			1			40	63
Machine tools			3						5	8
Electronics			14						3	17
Footwear	1	3	10						1	15
Textiles	18	7	21	11	2		7		19	85
Agriculture	4	1	45	4	1		2		2	59
Automobiles		2	13					1	2	18
Other	1		18			1			4	24
Total	25	13	145	15	3	2	9	1	76	289

EFTA = European Free Trade Association.

Source: OECD (1992).

Table 3　Major Japanese VERs

Sector/ importing country	Duration	Affected exports (billions of 1991 dollars)	Cause	Initial tightness of the restriction and reduction from previous year	Development since initial restriction
Automobile					
US	May '81-March '94 (originally 3 years)	21	Section 201 petition failed but imminent threat of quota.	-7.7 (from $1.82 million to $1.68 million)	The level of quota was increased to $2.3 million in 1985 but then reduced to $1.65 million in 1992. Quota unfilled since 1987. Significant local production ($1.2 million in 1992).
EC	July '91-Dec. '99	10	To eliminate five national restrictions.	No export growth is forecasted until 1999.	Binding. Reduction of the restraint from $1.26 million in 1991 to less than $1 million in 1993.
Machine tools					
US	Jan. '87-Dec. '93 (originally 5 years)	0.54	Section 232 investigation conducted.	-20	Withdrawn.
EC	Jan. '81-	0.54	To avoid trade frictions, including dumping disputes.	A floor pricing system for exports and an import monitoring system.	
Color TVs					
US	July '77-June '80	n.a.	Section 201. (Serious injury found.)	-41 (from $2.96 million to $1.75 million)	A large-scale switch to local production, while the US industry shifted overseas.

	Period	Value	Purpose	Type of restraint	Status
Steel					
US	July '69-Mar. '92 (a series of agreements, the most recent from May '85)	3.23	Section 201. (Serious injury found in 1984 and legislative proposal for quota.	Multilateral restraints.	Currently not under the restraint, but antidumping petition filed in August 1992. MSA under negotiation.
EU	1972-74, 1976-90	n.a.	To avoid trade frictions.		Withdrawn.
Textiles					
US	1957- (VER, STA, LTA, VER, and VER)	0.60	To avoid trade frictions.	Multilateral restraints.	End of the bilateral agreements based upon MFA in 1991 for US and in 1977 for EC.
EC	1955- (GATT membership of Japan initially restricted by nonapplication provisions of GATT	0.45	To avoid trade frictions.		
Semiconductors					
US	1986-96 (originally 5 years)	N/A	To prevent dumping of exports.	Collection of price and cost data.	
EU	1990-	N/A	To prevent dumping of exports.	Price surveillance undertaking on DRAMs under EU antidumping procedures.	

n.a. = not applicable.
N/A = not available.

Source: Constructed by the authors. Main information is from *Trade Policy Reviews* (of Japan, the United States, and the European Union), 1992, and General Agreement on Tariffs and Trade (GATT).

sistent with GATT, such as safeguard and antidumping measures, VERs are voluntary for the countries involved. When used to forestall GATT-inconsistent restrictive measures or as a compromise to phase out such measures, such VERs are involuntary for the exporting country. Let us illustrate how these two motivations were involved in three major VER cases involving Japan.

In the case of a 1976 petition by the US industry to restrict color television imports under the safeguards clause, the US International Trade Commission decided that the imports had seriously injured the US industry, and it recommended a substantial tariff increase to provide import relief. The US government, instead of levying a tariff, asked Japan for a VER—specifically, a reduction of Japanese exports to roughly 40 percent of the unrestrained level. Later, South Korea and Taiwan were also included. In this case, the VER was a clear substitute for the safeguard action. Since the safeguard requires the importing country to be nondiscriminatory in its import restriction and since importing countries can be required to render compensation to avoid the exercise of the GATT rights of retaliation by the exporting countries, the VER arrangement has often been found, as in this case, to be more attractive for the importing country. The exporting country also finds VERs preferable because they do not represent a unilateral measure by the importing country, and they leave quota rents to the exporting country.

In the case of a 1980 petition for restricting automobile imports based upon the safeguard clause, the ITC decided that there had been no serious injury. As a result, there was no GATT-consistent measure available under which the US government could restrict the imports. However, faced with increased layoffs in the US automobile industry, the US Congress prepared a bill for restricting the import of the Japanese automobiles through quotas. Once the US government explained the clear risk that the bill might become law, the Japanese government decided to impose the VER for three years, beginning in 1981, in order to forestall protectionist moves by the Congress.

In the case of a 1983 petition to restrict the import of machine tools for national security reasons, the US government conducted the investigation but did not choose to restrict the imports based upon section 232 of the 1962 Trade Expansion Act. Rather, in 1986 the president asked for VERs from the four major exporting countries: Japan, West Germany, Taiwan, and Switzerland. In this case, it was not clear whether the US government could legitimately restrict trade. Although Japan and Taiwan agreed to the restraints, West Germany and Switzerland declined.

Legal Status

Since VERs restrain international trade as well as competition in the import country's market, many have questioned whether VERs could ever be considered consistent with GATT obligations and with the antitrust law of the importing country. In our view, VERs are not consistent with GATT, because GATT Article XI generally prohibits the use of trade-restricting measures other than duties, taxes, and other charges, whether by exporting countries or by importing countries, with exceptions limited only to those explicitly sanctioned by the other GATT articles.[1] GATT Article XIX (on safeguards) does allow countries to adopt import-restricting measures under certain conditions, but such measures have to be administered in a nondiscriminatory manner (GATT Article XIII). VERs do not satisfy these conditions.

However, VERs have not been challenged in the GATT and had remained as gray-area measures until the Uruguay Round agreement on December 1993 explicitly prohibited their future use. There are two reasons for the absence of such challenges. First, VERs are not unilateral measures but are explicitly or implicitly agreed to both by the exporting and importing countries. Second, although VERs do affect third countries, it is not clear whether these countries lose anything from them. In fact, the third country that imports the good affected by the VER should see gains due to lower prices. The import-competing industry in such a country may still complain and demand that its government control the trade diversion. However, when political pressures for restrictions rise, the standard response of the third-country government has been to demand a similar VER from the exporting country rather than to demand the dismantling of the original VER, presumably because import restriction by the importing country through one measure or another is regarded as inevitable. A third country that exports the good affected by the VER gains because the VER expands its export opportunities to the importing country. On the other hand, the third country would clearly lose if a nondiscriminatory import restriction was substituted for the VER.

In many industrialized countries, including the United States, the European Union, and Germany, antitrust law is regarded as applicable to restraints on trade made by foreign exporting firms when such restraints significantly harm domestic competition. However, when a VER is organized at the request—or at least with the consent of—the government of the importing country, that country's competition policy authority has refrained from bringing antitrust suits. If such a suit were brought,

---

1. This applies not only to quantitative restrictions but also to such measures as the minimum import price system and the minimum export price system. This was demonstrated by the ruling of the GATT panel in 1988 that the administrative guidance from Japan's Ministry of International Trade and Industry with respect to the monitoring of the semiconductor export prices was inconsistent with Japan's GATT Article XI obligations, even though such guidance was issued with a view to preventing dumping in third countries, as agreed in the US-Japan semiconductor agreement.

the importing-country government would obviously face a marked contradiction. But sovereign compulsion doctrine, which relieves the exporting firms of the legal responsibility of their joint actions for restraining exports if such actions are forced by the exporting country's government, has been used in the United States in order to avoid such a contradiction.[2]

Anticompetitive Effects

The Static Effects

VERs constrain the competitive behavior of exporting firms, thus reducing and distorting competition in the importing country's markets. The exact manner in which competition and welfare is affected, however, depends upon the strategic nature of competition and market structure, as well as which competitive behaviors VERs constrain. Here, we focus on the case in which VERs restrict quantities (VERs that restrict pricing decisions would have effects similar to antidumping measures).

First, consider the case in which firms compete on price, unconstrained by supply capacities unless VERs constrain export quantities. As demonstrated by Itoh and Ono (1984), Harris (1985), and Krishna (1989) in the context of duopoly competition, VERs enable the domestic and foreign firms to jointly raise prices, even if the export quota is set at the free trade level. This is because, on the one hand, the domestic firm can raise its price without worrying that the affected consumers will buy imports instead of the domestic good. The more concentrated the domestic industry, the stronger this price effect would be. On the other hand, the foreign firm can also profitably raise its price because the VER has ensured that the domestic firm will raise its price, causing excess demand for the products of the foreign firm. Thus, the VER has the effect of constraining price competition, even if it does not directly constrain the pricing behavior of firms. This effect also arises where there is competition between constrained and unconstrained exporters.

The increased prices of both domestic and imported goods imply reduced global welfare. The domestic firm's supply of the good can actually decline after the imposition of a VER due to its increased market power when the VER is not too restrictive. The sharply increased profits of the US automobile industry, unaccompanied by significant output expansion, that occurred just after the imposition of the 1980 VER (Crandall 1987) is consistent with this theoretical prediction. When the VER is not

---

2. Foreign sovereign compulsion requires the government of the exporting country to establish the legal instrument to force the exporting firms to abide by the restraints (US Department of Justice 1988 and 1994).

too restrictive, the exporting firm also gains, thanks to its higher export price; this also happened after the 1980 VER was imposed (Collyns and Dunaway 1987). But in this case, the welfare of the importing country declined more than the foreign firm gained.

This sharply anticompetitive effect depends upon the specific assumption that only price matters in competition. When nonprice dimensions of competition are important, the result has to be modified. Thus we will consider two nonprice dimensions of competition: quality and supply, or output capacity. We will later analyze the effect of VER upon dynamic competition (i.e., competition through cost reduction).

A number of empirical studies suggest that VERs prompt the exporting firm to make significant improvements in quality (Feenstra 1988; Boorstein and Feenstra 1991). When the firm's exports are restricted by a VER, the firm will try to circumvent it by improving the quality of its exports if a higher quality good can simply deliver more services per unit. In this case, the domestic firm will find it difficult to raise its price despite the VER. The quality upgrades may also take place when the VER causes the marginal consumer, who values quality less than the average consumer, to drop out of the market for the export firm's goods (Das and Donnenfeld 1989). In either case, a price increase can be partially accounted for by the quality improvement and should not be fully attributed to the anticompetitive effect of the VER.

Next let us turn to supply capacity. When price competition is constrained by supply capacities, the market can be modeled as a Cournot-Nash equilibrium, in which a firm takes its rival's output as fixed and acts accordingly to supply the rest of the market. In this case, the VER would artificially reduce the foreign firm's supply in the importing country's market and would encourage the domestic firm to build up its capacity. Unlike the case of price competition (a Bertrand-Nash equilibrium in which firms take their rivals' prices as given), the domestic firm always raises its supply capacity in response to the imposition of the VER but not to the extent that it compensates for the reduced import supply. This is because the larger market share of the domestic firm makes it less aggressive. Consequently, the VER is anticompetitive in this context, too, because it reduces the total supply and raises the market price. The foreign firm subject to the restraint always loses. The domestic firm gains, but by less than the combined losses of domestic consumers and the foreign firm (see Smith and Venables 1991 for the empirical analysis of the VER on the Japanese car producers in the European car market).

Moreover, when the VER sets import share rather than import quantity as the ceiling for the imports, its anticompetitive effect is magnified. As is the case in Bertrand-Nash competition, the supply of the domestic firm may also decline when it is monopolistic. This is because the domestic firm can expect that if it can credibly reduce its supply, the exporting firm will be forced to reduce its supply, too, in order to keep its market share within the limit set by the VER. In this case, both the domestic supply and import supply decline due to the VER.

The Tightness of Restraints

All VERs are not created equal: the tightness of the restraint is crucial in determining its effects on competition and welfare. The tighter the restraint, the more restricted is competition in the importing country's market and the less the global welfare.

How do governments determine how tight these restraints should be? From the point of view of bargaining theory, it depends on the outside opportunities of the exporting and importing countries that are negotiating the VERs. Let us assume that the governments (i.e., the trade policy authorities) of both the exporting and importing countries are mainly concerned with securing producers' interests. (For the exporting country, protecting its export industry's interest is equivalent to maximizing national welfare if it does not take into account the effect of possible compensations associated with safeguard measures by the importing country. In the importing country, the government is under strong political pressures for import restriction from the import-competing industry.) We also will assume that firms compete in a Cournot-Nash manner.[3] In this case, when the importing country requests a VER backed up by a credible threat of an alternative restriction that would be more damaging to the exporting firms, the restrictiveness of the VER should be relatively great.

This prediction seems consistent with the tendency of the VER to be more restrictive when the government of the importing country has established a clear legal right to restrict trade. Let us illustrate this point with the three Japanese VERs mentioned earlier. In the case of the color televisions, where the ITC sanctioned the strong safeguard action based upon section 201 of US trade law, the US government initially requested the reduction of exports by as much as 60 percent (that is, a reduction to between 1.2 million and 1.3 million sets per year from the 3.0 million sets exported in 1976) and then settled for 40 percent. In the case of the VER on machine tools, where no clear international standard has yet been established on how extensively trade can be restricted based upon national security reasons, the two governments agreed to reduce exports by 20 percent. In the case of the VER on automobiles, where ITC found no serious injury, the Japanese government settled on a reduction of about 8 percent.

We can also predict that substituting a VER for a safeguard measure based on a tariff will further restrict competition and output. Under a

---

3. Collusion among domestic and foreign firms is assumed to be infeasible, due to antitrust and other constraints.

Cournot-Nash equilibrium, the level of the profit of the export industry declines as the restraint becomes tighter. Moreover, for the same level of export, the VER yields more profit for the export industry than tariff, since the VER leaves quota rent to the export firms. Consequently, the export industry is willing to accept a lower level of export when it is constrained by quota rather than tariff.

The Dynamic Effects

How do VERs affect competition in terms of firms' investments to reduce costs? Let us consider this problem in the framework of a two-stage game, with cost-reducing investment in the first stage and determination of output in the second stage. The incentive for cost-reducing investment rests on the three determinants: size of the market supplied by a firm, its competitor's response to cost reduction, and the policy response to cost reduction.

A VER interferes with all three. It reduces the global supply of the industry, even if it may increase the supply of the domestic firm. Therefore, even if the incentive for cost reduction increases for the domestic firm due to the larger market the VER secures for itself, it tends to decline more for the exporting firm. It also reduces the competitor's negative sales response to cost-reducing investment by each enterprise. In particular, if the VER specifies an import share as a ceiling, the cost-reducing investment by the domestic firm enables the exporting firm to expand its supply because the lower production cost of the domestic firm increases its incentive to expand supply, which in turn allows the foreign firm to export more. Finally, it makes the policy response to cost reduction perverse, unless the VER is credibly temporary. Therefore, the VER is very likely to impede the cost-reducing efforts of the industry as a whole. It is therefore anticompetitive in a dynamic context, too.

VERs as a Safeguard and Adjustment Assistance Mechanism

The preceding discussion has ignored the issue of adjustment difficulties in the import-competing industry. In reality, many VERs have been introduced to reduce unemployment in the industries affected by import surges and to assist the restructuring of these industries.

If a VER can significantly reduce unemployment in the import-competing industry, it may improve welfare. When contraction of output in the import-competing industry leads to more unemployment in that country, the social opportunity cost of production of the import-competing firm can be significantly lower than that of the exporting firm. If this is the case, the VER-induced shift of global demand toward the domestic firm may improve global welfare, with the positive effect of lower unemployment potentially dominating the anticompetitive effect of the VER.

However, there are three major limitations of VERs as a safeguard mechanism. First, a VER may have to be very restrictive to save jobs. As demonstrated earlier, a weak VER may actually reduce the domestic firm's output and the number of domestic jobs because the VER enhances the market power of the domestic firm. Weak substitutability between domestic and imported goods and high production costs of the domestic firm also increase the cost of VERs. A number of empirical studies suggest that consumers' costs per-job-saved is very large (OECD 1985, 1992).

Second, the VER may worsen the labor market distortion, which contributes significantly to unemployment. It is widely recognized that the high wages obtained by strong unions in the US auto and steel industries have exacerbated the unemployment problem in these industries. The VER enhances the monopoly power of such unions and thus allows more aggressive wage demands, since the elasticity of demand for labor declines (Lawrence and Lawrence 1985).

Third, the VER is not the least-cost method for restricting imports, since it is bilateral and discriminatory in nature.

Does a VER aid the adjustment efforts of the import-competing industry? Let us assume that there is significant room for cost reduction by the industry. As pointed out earlier, the incentive for cost reduction by the import-competing industry may or may not increase as a result of the VER. First, output of the domestic industry may decline due to the VER. Second, even if the domestic industry's output expands, the weaker supply response of the foreign competing industry and the perverse policy response of the government to the domestic industry's cost reduction may still reduce the cost-reduction incentive. It is important to note that the net effect on the cost-reduction incentive is more likely to be negative for the more monopolistic domestic industry.

Under certain circumstances, VERs may improve the capacity of the domestic industry for cost reduction. First, if the domestic industry is in a state of financial distress, the VER-induced financial improvement may help the domestic industry to pursue long-term efforts to improve efficiency, although such bailout creates moral-hazard problems. Second, the VER may improve the incentive for technology transfer by the foreign export industry when foreign direct investment by the export industry in green fields is costly. An extensive investment by the Japanese steel industry in the US steel industry may reflect such an incentive.

However, the productivity performance of the industries protected by the VERs has not been encouraging. As Crandall (1987) points out, the productivity performance of the US automobile and steel industry did not improve after the introduction of VERs. A comparison with the performance of other manufacturing sectors of the US economy also suggests that the productivity performance of these two sectors is not particularly high relative to that of other sectors.

Spillover Effects

Competition in the Importing Country's Market

As we discussed in the previous section, VERs have a strong anticompetitive effect. However, this analysis was based on a two-country model, in which third countries are neglected and firms do not have wider options, such as direct investment and local production. Once we introduce these elements, the story becomes more complicated. However, consideration of these complications is necessary because, as we will discuss, spillover to other markets and to other instruments such as direct investment can be observed in various industries.

Foreign Direct Investment

When the amount of exports is regulated by VERs, firms can increase their shares in foreign markets only by producing in those markets. Indeed, many industries have increased foreign direct investment (FDI) after the introduction of VERs.

For example, after VERs were introduced in 1977 for color television exports from Japan to the United States, Japanese companies increased their direct investment to the United States, and local production in the United States by the subsidiaries of the Japanese manufacturers replaced exports from Japan. In 1978, only one year after the start of the VER, the amount of local production exceeded the amount of exports, and in the 1980s, the share of exports in total sales by Japanese firms in the United States was less than one-third.

A similar phenomenon could be observed in automobiles. After a VER was in place, most Japanese manufacturers built subsidiaries in the United States for local production. In 1993, the local production exceeded exports from Japan.[4]

Why do Japanese firms invest abroad when they face VERs? The most important reason seems to be competition among Japanese firms. The export cartelization through VERs does not allow each firm to expand its share of export markets. Thus, each firm must choose whether to stick to the existing voluntary export restraints and obtain a fixed share of cartel profits or to expand its share by making foreign direct investment. In the case of the color television and auto VERs, competition pushed the Japanese firms to choose the latter.

Theoretically, both cases are possible, and the choice between the two depends on various factors. Several factors promote FDI. One is the

---

4. The amount of automobile exports in 1993 was 1.45 million units; the amount of local production was 1.52 million units—three times the volume it was seven years before. In 1986, 2.42 million units were exported, and local production was only about 510,000 units.

number of competing firms, and another is the asymmetry in costs among firms, under which firms with more efficient technology will have a stronger incentive to expand their market shares. Another factor that might be important for understanding the behavior of automobile firms is the perceived growth of profit opportunities. When firms perceive an expanding market, they often engage in aggressive share-taking and growth-maximizing behavior. This is consistent with long-run profit maximization.

The question then arises as to whether the increased direct investment further distorts the allocation of resources beyond that of the simple two-county model, which did not take the FDI option into account. Again, the answer to this question depends on many elements. It is true that the anticompetitive effect of VERs is weakened by expansion of local production. However, even if FDI restores some competitiveness to the market, it is at the cost of substantial outlays of FDI.

Spillover Effects on Third Countries

VERs are usually arranged on a bilateral basis. However, this arrangement may have spillover effects on other countries. When exports to one country are restricted, how is a third country affected?

In an oligopolistic setting, the answer to this question depends on the cost structure of the firm as well as many other factors. When a large portion of production costs are already incurred, and in that sense, sunk, the firms whose exports face the VER restriction in one country will try to recover their production level by expanding exports to third countries. This case can arise when there has been a substantial amount of capital investment before the VERs were instituted and/or when it is difficult to cut the number of workers in the face of the VERs, as is generally the case in Japan because Japanese firms rely less on layoffs and are under stronger pressure to maintain employment levels than are firms in other countries.

Even in a simple static cost function model, if marginal costs are increasing, then restriction of exports to one country will decrease a firm's marginal costs and therefore induce it to take a more aggressive export position with the third country. The opposite would be true under a situation of decreasing marginal costs.

All the cases discussed above are only theoretical possibilities. However, in the real world, when a VER arrangement is made between two countries, it is quite often the case that the third country raises concerns about possible spillover effects of more-aggressive export behavior.

Of course, more-aggressive export behavior directed toward the third country is typically welfare-enhancing for the importing country, since consumers or firms purchasing the products can enjoy lower prices. However, firms in the importing countries that are competing with the imported goods and criticize a VER because of its possible spillover effects have a political impact. Thus, it is possible that a bilateral VER arrangement could spark the forming of another VER arrangement with the third country. For instance, the VERs between Japan and the United States triggered similar arrangements between Japan and European countries in such industries as automobiles.

Competition in Exporting Countries

The effect of VERs on competition in the domestic markets of the exporting countries is similar to the effect on third countries. As with third countries, cost structure is an important indicator of how the behavior of firms in their domestic markets changes under VERs.

When the firms are committed to maintaining their production levels, domestic competition will be intensified. This seems to have actually happened in the Japanese market when the Japanese automobile producers faced VERs in the US market. Furthermore, when the allocation of export quotas among the exporting firms depends on their shares in the domestic market, competition for larger shares in that market may be intensified.

We cannot make any definite general statement about the effects of VERs on competitiveness in the domestic market. However, it appears that only rarely does cartelization through VERs in the firms' export markets actually induce similar cartel behavior in the domestic market.

Voluntary Import Expansions

So-called "voluntary import expansions" (VIEs) have received increased attention since 1986, the year of the semiconductor trade agreement between Japan and the United States. Although there is a dispute between the two governments about what kind of commitment was implied by the agreement—namely, whether achieving import expansion of a certain amount was an obligation of the Japanese government or just an expectation of US industry—we understand that a target was set (in this case, a 20 percent share of the Japanese market) so that imports would exceed this target by the voluntary action of Japanese firms. The success of expanding the share in the Japanese semiconductor market through a VIE encouraged the US industry and the government to use VIEs for other industries such as automobile parts and automobiles, based on the view that the low shares of the US industry in these Japanese markets were due to their import or entry barriers.[5]

---

5. See appendix I for an explanation of how market share comparisons can be misleading in evaluating trade barriers.

The implication of VIEs for competition is similar in some respects to that of VERs: they distort resource allocation. By forcing either buying or selling firms in importing countries to expand the sales of products of exporting countries that are not otherwise competitive, VIEs give rise to the anticompetitive reallocation of resources in the market. This is easy to understand if we imagine a closed economy in which several firms are competing. If the government forces some buying or selling firms to expand the sales of a particular group of suppliers, the resulting market allocation will be distorted considerably. What the US government asked of the Japanese government and industry is similar: to expand the sales of American products in Japan.

VERs and VIEs differ in some respects. While a VER restricts supply, a VIE may not. Thus it is possible, as the US government often claims, that such an arrangement could actually enhance competition in the importing market if there are substantial import barriers and if import goods are highly substitutable for domestic goods. However, even if such barriers exist, the theory of the second best tells us that it is quite possible global welfare would decline under a VIE, although the exporting country can always gain from terms of trade improvements and rent shifting. In order to improve global welfare, it is essential to correct any existing barrier.

It must also be emphasized that a seemingly competition-enhancing VIE that has its effect through forced import expansion may actually have anticompetitive effects just like those of a VER (see appendix II). This is particularly so if the shares of imports are fixed. When the share of US exports to Japan is fixed, and when the Japanese industry and government make commitments to that share, the incentives for US firms to set lower prices will be weakened. They may even raise prices. Facing this less-competitive behavior from exporters that are protected by VIEs and being obliged to help exporters reach the target share, domestic firms will have less incentives to behave competitively or will be constrained from doing so.

More important is the fact that the process of import expansion itself is anticompetitive. Voluntary import expansion is not actually "voluntary." In fact, it is a form of intervention by the government in sales activities. It is also true that firms must coordinate action to successfully expand imports; in other words, there has to be concerted behavior among firms. This does not necessarily imply cartel behavior, but it certainly risks inducing anticompetitive concerted behavior among firms in other activities.

In any case, under normal competitive conditions, it is difficult to effectuate a voluntary import expansion only by the voluntary behavior of firms. Thus, some kind of government intervention, such as allocating import shares among importing firms, is necessary. And this kind of government intervention certainly contradicts the basic idea of free trade.

Directions of Policy Reform

Uruguay Round Agreement on Safeguards

Elimination of VERs

The Uruguay Round Agreement on Safeguards aims at reestablishing multilateral control over safeguards and eliminating measures that escape such control, VERs in particular. The agreed text prohibits and eliminates VERs and sets rules for the application of safeguard measures; these rules are more lenient than would be a stricter interpretation of GATT Article XIX.

Implementation of the agreement will bring about three things, the relative significance of which is hard to judge at this stage. First, in those cases in which imports cause serious injury, the GATT-consistent safeguard measures will be more actively used than they were in the past. Unlike VERs, the measures must follow the explicit rules set out in the agreement and will be monitored by a multilateral committee. But there is a danger that GATT-consistent safeguards replicate the problems of VERs substantially, which we evaluate in a subsequent section.

Second, antidumping and other unilateral measures will be more extensively used because VERs will not be able to forestall activation of such measures. The more active use of these unilateral measures can reduce and distort global competition more than the VERs do, as we will examine later in detail.

Third, free trade may be maintained in the future even in those cases in which GATT-consistent protective measures are unavailable but VERs might have been used in the past. Since the safeguard clause explicitly prohibits both seeking and instituting VERs, free trade may be maintained, even if political pressures mount for protection in importing countries. This, of course, is the most desirable outcome.

Evaluating Agreed Safeguard Rules

The Agreement on Safeguards reflects the three basic principles of the GATT Article XIX: serious injury is a necessary condition for import relief, import restrictions for such relief must be nondiscriminatory, and exporting countries affected by the measure can suspend equivalent concessions for the importing country. However, the agreement reduces the cost to the importing country of using safeguards in three ways:

- An importing country may allocate quotas selectively, departing from the past proportions held by traditional suppliers in the market to deal with disproportionate increases from certain exporting countries.

- An importing country may take a provisional safeguard measure, based upon a preliminary determination of serious injury.

- Affected exporting countries cannot suspend equivalent concessions for the first three years.

The above provisions clearly make safeguards easier to use. In particular, allowing countries to target certain suppliers in quota allocations may induce them to use the safeguards rather than other measures. The European Union had criticized the prohibition against selective import restrictions as well as the necessity of compensation as being rigid. These former constraints on the use of safeguards also prompted the US government to use VERs instead of safeguards in the past. However, the new, selective safeguard measure based upon quotas has exactly the same problems as VERs have: it distorts and reduces global competition by penalizing the most competitive firms, and therefore it is not efficient. Moreover, the restrictions on retaliation will increase the use of trade restrictions as a whole.

However, there is one significant advantage of the Uruguay Round safeguards over VERs. It is rule-based and transparent. The proposed code sets out the following conditions for the safeguard measure:

- The period of a safeguard measure cannot exceed four years. Although extension is feasible upon satisfying certain conditions, the total period cannot exceed eight years.

- The safeguard measure has to be progressively liberalized.

- The quantitative restriction cannot be so restrictive as to reduce imports below the average level of imports in the last three years.

These disciplines, if properly applied, will help correct the past situation, in which VERs dragged on almost indefinitely.

Three major problems with the safeguard code still exist. First, eight years of import protection can significantly retard the adjustment of the domestic industry. Conditions for the extension of the safeguard measure can be further tightened so that the measure can be applied in a disciplined manner. Second, the use of quotas as a safeguard measure, besides being more likely to be discriminatory, has a strong anticompetitive effect, especially when the market structure of the importing country is concentrated. As pointed out earlier, quotas also tend to constrict imports more than tariffs do, although the proposed agreement sets the floor for the level of the quota restraint. The most important constraint for switching quotas to tariffs would be compensation for the exporting country. One solution might be to restrict the use of quotas as a safeguard measure in exchange for tight disciplines on the level and period of the tariff protection. Third, the elimination of existing VERs is allowed to take place slowly, over a period ending in 1999.

Tighter Disciplines on Antidumping and Other Unilateral Measures

There is a serious danger that prohibition of VERs will lead simply to more active use of antidumping and other unilateral protectionist measures. Antidumping can be worse than VERs in reducing and distorting global competition. In particular, antidumping measures often result in a complete ban of exports, since they force exporters to price their exports above both artificially calculated production costs and home-market sales prices. In contrast, VERs secure at least some level of exports for the exporters. Moreover, antidumping measures, once set, can last a long time, especially in the United States. It is reported that more than one-third of the current antidumping measures on Japanese exports in the United States have lasted for more than 10 years; for example, those on color televisions have lasted more than 22 years (MITI 1993). Despite these problems, the Uruguay Round has made only small progress in tightening the discipline on antidumping.

A similar danger of increased abuse exists for countervailing duty measures and import restrictions based upon national security reasons. In addition to the abuse of these GATT-consistent unilateral measures, GATT-inconsistent unilateral measures, such as the one proposed in the import quota bill for Japanese automobile exports in 1981, may be used to restrict imports. Consequently, it is important to make further multilateral efforts to significantly tighten the discipline on antidumping and other unilateral measures as complements to the prohibition of VERs.

Can Competition Policy Substitute for Trade Restrictions?

Can competition policy intervention properly substitute for trade restrictions in providing safeguard and adjustment assistance? Such intervention may include policy changes favoring more lenient attitudes toward mergers and cartels among domestic firms. If successful, this could help the domestic industry restructure more quickly under the pressure of unrestricted international competition.

However, there is a major limitation on the use of competition policy as a safeguard measure. It is very unlikely that relaxation of competition policy, unlike trade restrictions, will reduce unemployment. It is more likely to have a perverse effect, since the increased market power of the domestic firms results in the contraction of its output and, therefore, in demand for workers. Thus, relaxation of competition policy only provides financial relief for industry, unlike trade restrictions, which protect jobs as well as industries.

Flexible competition policy responses toward restructuring, based upon an adequate assessment of the strength of import competition, could promote industrial adjustment. Mergers and increased specialization through acquisitions and sales of some divisions of firms could help domestic industry enhance its productivity and efficiency, as long as overall competitive pressures remain strong. Such restructuring would help achieve economies of scale and scope and increase the appropriability of cost-reducing investment.

The challenge for competition policy is that the standard market-share criteria, such as those based upon the Herfindahl-Hirschman index of industry concentration, can be biased against such restructuring when the competitive position of the domestic industry is declining rapidly. This is because, while market shares are calculated based upon historical data, such shares can change dramatically over a short period when import competition becomes strong. Therefore, the results of standard market-share analysis should be applied cautiously in the case of the industries subject to intensifying import competition, provided that international trade remains unrestricted so that industrial restructuring to improve efficiency can take place smoothly.

On the other hand, production and sales cartels do not strengthen incentives for cost reduction. On the contrary, they reduce competitive discipline and do not increase the appropriability of cost-reducing investment. Cartels may further lead to the creation of import barriers when domestic firms taken together have a large degree of market power, even if imports remain unrestricted by trade policy. Therefore, it is not clear whether competition-policy changes to provide financial relief to industry is less costly in terms of competition and long-run effects than is relief based on trade policy. This is especially the case when trade relief is provided by nondiscriminatory and credibly temporary tariffs. On the other hand, cooperation in research and development, as well as in other efforts to improve technology and efficiency, can play a positive role, as long as competitive discipline from imports remains strong.

In sum, it is unlikely that competition policy can substitute for trade policy in providing safeguards. However, competition policy can correct potential biases against industrial restructuring and against cooperative efforts to improve technology when the competitive position of domestic industry is eroding.

Conclusion

VERs are typically introduced to contain large economies' threats of alternative trade restrictions, some of which are GATT-consistent and some of which are not. The stronger such a threat is, the more restrictive the VER becomes. VERs are anticompetitive in both static and dynamic contexts. They tend to reduce global output, as well as global efforts for higher efficiency. Anticompetitive effects are stronger the more monopolistic the import-competing industry is.

VERs have spillover effects both in the importing country's market as well as in the exporting country's market. Both FDI and the growth of third-country exports in the importing country's market tend to undo the anticompetitive effects of VERs, but only imperfectly and with substantial costs. VERs may actually enhance domestic competition in the exporting country's market, since capacity constraints become less restrictive and punishment against deviation from implicit cartels becomes less effective. Nevertheless, a possible negative, anticompetitive spillover has to be prevented through vigorous antitrust policy.

VIEs are also anticompetitive. When the target is defined in terms of market share and the exporting industry is monopolistic, the VIE reduces global output as well as global efforts for higher efficiency, just as VERs do.

Elimination of VERs, as agreed in the Uruguay Round, is a critical step for enhancing global competition. However, if such a step is to truly enhance competition and improve welfare, multilateral disciplines over unilateral trade restrictions, including antidumping measures, have to be tightened. Moreover, the agreed safeguard rule has to be employed in a disciplined manner. GATT-consistent safeguards could replicate the problems of VERs substantially, since the major constraints on the safeguard actions (i.e., nondiscrimination and retaliation) seem to have been relaxed by the new rules and protection is allowed to persist for eight years. Competition policy is not likely to substitute for trade policy in providing safeguards, but it can correct potential biases against industrial restructuring and against cooperative efforts to improve technology in order to promote adjustment.

Global competition policy objectives provide hardly any justification for VIEs. International dialogue and negotiations over the improvement of market access should focus upon import and entry barriers in a truly economic sense but not upon the results of commercial transactions. Thus, VIEs should also be banned multilaterally.

Appendix I: Do Low Market Shares in a Foreign Market Signify Closedness?

The fact that an industry in country A has a lower market share in country B than in the rest of the world has sometimes been used as proof of the closedness of country B's market. For example, Bergsten and Noland (1993, 134-35) argue that "the 20 percent market share [the target set by the Semiconductor Trade Agreement] appears to have been a lower-bound estimate of what the foreign producer market share would have been if the Japanese market were like markets elsewhere in the world"; as evidence they cite that "in 1986, US firms had a 40 percent share of the European market and a 66 percent share of the world market excluding Japan." They then take a permissive view of the VIE approach as the "second-best" solution.

However, such an argument, based upon a simple market-share comparison, is not well-grounded and can be highly misleading, since it ignores a number of critical factors influencing international differences of market shares of a particular industry. In the case of the semiconductor market, the neglect of the following factors makes the comparison a dubious one.

- **International differences in demand structure.** The semiconductor market covers a number of highly heterogeneous products, the structure of demand for which varies significantly across countries. For example, final use of semiconductors for consumer products accounted for 40 percent of the Japanese market but only 5 percent of the US market and 16 percent of the West European market in 1992. Moreover, the industry of a particular country has comparative advantages in those products for which its home market is important (i.e., there is home-market bias in comparative advantage, presumably because the home-market influences the product development efforts of a firm more than the foreign market does). Thus, the Japanese industry has more market shares in the Japanese market, as does the US industry in the US market.

- **Trade barriers in comparator countries.** The issue could be that the market shares of US industry in the US market are too high rather than that the shares of the US industry in the Japanese market are too low. In the US and EU markets, antidumping regulations have been powerful deterrents to the rapid expansion of exports by foreign firms. While the practice of "forward pricing" is regarded as a normal business practice if exercised by domestic firms, it is regarded as dumping if exercised by foreign firms and can be subject to high duties. The antidumping duties determined by the US Commerce Department for 256K DRAM exports by Japanese firms in 1985 amounted to 109 percent. Tariff rates for semiconductors are higher in the European Union and the United States (generally 14 percent and 4.2 percent, respectively) than in Japan (0 percent).

- **Foreign direct investment.** Trade barriers in the EU market have favored the US industry more than the Japanese industry, since the US industry made direct investments in the EU market much earlier and much more significantly than did the Japanese industry.

Figure 1 Effects of a voluntary import expansion

Capacity of the foreign firm

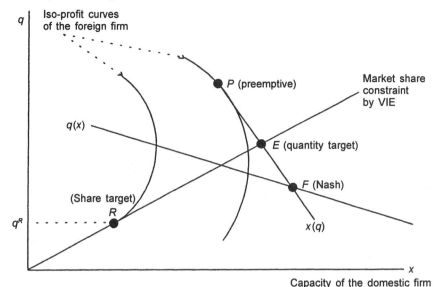

Capacity of the domestic firm

- **Transportation and communication costs.** Local firms have competitive advantages over foreign firms in supplying local markets, due to transportation and communication costs.

Appendix II: A Simple Economic Analysis of VIEs[6]

Let us analyze the effect of VIEs in the framework of duopoly competition. The foreign and domestic firms are assumed to compete in supply capacities (i.e., Cournot-Nash competition). If unconstrained, neither firm has the first-mover advantage, so that the equilibrium is a Nash equilibrium (point F in figure 1). However, if a VIE is imposed on the domestic firm, the foreign firm gains the first-mover advantage, since the domestic firm now cannot unilaterally decide its capacity.

First, let us assume that the target of the VIE is given in terms of market share. It is clear that the foreign firm now has the strategic incentive to reduce its export supply, because if it reduces its supply, the domestic firm is also forced to reduce its supply. In figure 1, the equilibrium is now at point R instead of the point F; q^R, which is located on the iso-profit line just tangent to the VIE constraint forced on the

---

6. This section had been written before Irwin (1994) was available. He analyzed the VIE in the case of market share target and reached a similar conclusion.

domestic firm, becomes the choice for the foreign firm if it produces more profit for the foreign firm than the strategy of preemptive capacity expansion (point P).

When point R is realized as the equilibrium, it is clear that while the foreign firm's market share increases, its supply, as well as the total supply in the domestic market, declines. Thus, a VIE can reduce trade and competition just as a VER can, contrary to the analysis by Tyson (1992).

The foreign firm gains on the following two accounts. First, it can gain more market share for each level of the total supply—that is, the rent-shifting effect. Second, it can reduce the total supply and increase the price level—this is the market-power effect. The domestic firm may or may not gain, depending on the dominance of the market-power effect over the rent-shifting effect. The welfare of the foreign country always increases, while the welfare of the importing country always declines since the loss of the domestic firm dominates any existing consumer gains. Thus, a VIE is a beggar-your-neighbor policy.

Next let us consider the case where the VIE target is in terms of import quantity. In this case the equilibrium is now given by point E in figure 1. The domestic firm's supply declines compared with the Nash equilibrium F, but the total supply increases, since the smaller market share of the domestic firm makes it more willing to accept the lower profit margin due to its supply expansion. Thus, a VIE expands output and trade in this case.

However, efficiency (the sum of the producers' surplus and the consumers' surplus) can still decline, since the VIE shifts production from the low-cost firm to the high-cost firm, assuming that the foreign firm seeking the VIE has a higher supply cost in the domestic market than does the domestic firm. The foreign firm and the foreign country always gain from a VIE; the domestic country necessarily loses when efficiency declines (the loss of the domestic firm surpasses the consumer welfare gain).

References

Bergsten, C. F., and M. Noland. 1993. *Reconcilable Differences? United States-Japan Economic Conflict.* Washington: Institute for International Economics.

Boorstein, R., and R. C. Feenstra. 1991. "Quality Upgrading and Its Welfare Cost in US Steel Imports 1964-74." In E. Helpman and A. Razin, *International Trade and Trade Policy.* Cambridge, MA: MIT Press.

Crandall, R. W. 1987. "The Effects of US Trade Protection for Autos and Steel." *Brookings Papers on Economic Activity* 1: 271-88.

Collyns, C., and S. Dunaway. 1987. *The Cost of Trade Restraints: The Case of Japanese Automobile Exports to the United States.* International Monetary Fund Staff Papers No. 1 Washington: International Monetary Fund (March).

Das, S., and S. Donnenfeld. 1989. "Oligopolistic Competition and International Trade-Quantity and Quality Restrictions." *Journal of International Economics* 27: 299-318.

Feenstra, R. C. 1988. "Quality Change under Trade Restraints in Japanese Autos." *Quarterly Journal of Economics* 103, no. 1 (February): 131-46.

General Agreement on Tariffs and Trade (GATT). 1992. *Trade Policy Review: Japan.* Geneva: GATT.

Harris, R. 1985. "Why Voluntary Export Restraints are Voluntary." *Canadian Journal of Economics* 18: 799-809.

Irwin, D. A. 1994. *Managed Trade: The Case against Import Targets.* Washington: American Enterprise Institute.

Itoh, M., and Y. Ono. 1984. "Tariffs vs. Quotas under Duopoly of Heterogeneous Goods." *Journal of International Economics* 16: 359-73.

Krishna, K. 1989. "Trade Restrictions as Facilitating Practices." *Journal of International Economics* 26: 257-70.

Lawrence, C., and R. Z. Lawrence. 1985. "Manufacturing Wage Dispersion: An End Game Interpretation." *Brookings Papers on Economic Activity* 1: 47-106.

Ministry of International Trade and Industry, Japan (MITI). 1993. *Report on Unfair Trade Practices.* Tokyo: MITI.

Organization for Economic Cooperation and Development (OECD). 1985. *The Costs and Benefits of Protection.* Paris: OECD.

Organization for Economic Cooperation and Development (OECD). 1992. *Barriers to Trade and Competition.* Paris: OECD.

Smith, A., and A. J. Venables. 1991. "Counting the Cost of Voluntary Export Restraints in the European Car Market." In E. Helpman and A. Razin, *International Trade and Trade Policy.* Cambridge, MA: MIT Press.

Tyson, L. 1992. *Who's Bashing Whom: Trade Conflict in High-Technology Industries.* Washington: Institute for International Economics.

US Department of Justice. 1988. *Antitrust Enforcement Guidelines for International Operation.* Washington.

US Department of Justice. 1994. Antitrust Enforcement Guidelines for International Operation. Draft. Washington.

16

Keiretsu, Competition, and Market Access

PAUL SHEARD

Japan's distinctive forms of interfirm business organization, known as *keiretsu,* have become a contentious issue in policy and academic debates concerning the nature of competition in Japan, the openness of the Japanese market, and Japan's place in the international trading system. *Keiretsu,* in Japanese, is an informal term used to refer to various forms of interfirm relationships and sets of related firms. Three forms of *keiretsu* are usually distinguished: financial *keiretsu* or enterprise groups such as the Sumitomo group or the Mitsubishi group; vertical *keiretsu* or supplier networks centering on assembly firms such as Toyota or Matsushita; and distribution *keiretsu* or the networks of affiliated wholesalers and retailers that manufacturers of consumer goods use to distribute their products.

Two contrasting views about *keiretsu* can be found, roughly corresponding to the US and the Japanese policy positions. One is that *keiretsu* are collusive, anticompetitive, and exclusionary and that they allow

Paul Sheard is strategist with Baring Asset Management (Japan). This paper was written while the author was International Cooperation (Osaka Gas) Associate Professor in the Faculty of Economics at Osaka University. It draws on earlier work carried out when the author was a visiting scholar at the Institute of Social and Economic Research, Osaka University, and the Foundation for Advanced Information Research, Japan. Support from the International Cooperation (Osaka Gas) research fund at Osaka University is gratefully acknowledged. Useful comments were received from the editors and participants in the project and from participants in seminars at the Australia-Japan Research Centre, Columbia University, Foundation for Advanced Information and Research, Japan (FAIR), Keio University, the Kisei to Kyoso Kenkyu Forum, Kyoto University, Macquarie University, Osaka University, Osaka University of Economics, and Stanford University.

Japanese firms to gain an unfair advantage in domestic and international competition and to close off the Japanese market to foreign entrants. This view has become predominant in US policy thinking, spurred in large part by the so-called revisionist literature on Japan (Johnson 1987, 1990a, and 1990b). Japanese observers frequently counter that *keiretsu* are misunderstood in the West and that they represent efficient forms of economic organization, conditioned by historical circumstance and well adapted to Japan's unique business and market environment (Komiya 1990, 186; Yoshitomi 1990). Advocates on both sides of the debate can point to studies that support their position and marshal confirming anecdotal and survey evidence. (For recent surveys of these arguments see Goto and Suzumura 1994; Lawrence 1991b and 1993; Saxonhouse 1993; Sheard 1991 and 1992).

Keiretsu have become a contentious issue in the context of US-Japan trade frictions. There is a deep-rooted feeling in US policy and business circles that the Japanese market is closed to imports, particularly of manufactures, that the closedness of the market is a primary cause of the large and persistent US current account deficit with Japan, and that *keiretsu* are an important factor contributing to this closedness. (For academic views see Bergsten and Noland 1993; Dornbusch 1990; Johnson 1990a; Krugman 1991; Lawrence 1991b and 1993; Noland 1992; Yamamura 1990.) In this view, *keiretsu* are a "problem" and a legitimate target of policy action, such as the application of antitrust policy or trade pressure. Descriptions of *keiretsu* as cartels or as collusive or exclusionary reinforce this perception. An influential study by Lawrence (1991a) on the effects of *keiretsu* on Japanese imports and exports and a much-cited survey by Kreinen (1988) on the purchasing preferences of Japanese firms seem to provide the hard evidence.

Other observers see *keiretsu* as being more about how Japanese firms have organized their input and ownership structures to compete successfully in domestic and international markets (Aoki 1994). Supplier systems that capture the benefits of both hierarchical coordination and market incentives have been identified as a key factor in the success of Japan's machinery industries in achieving cost and quality competitiveness and leading world market shares (Dyer 1993; Fruin 1992; Nishiguchi 1994; Sako 1992; Smitka 1991). The financial *keiretsu* have attracted attention for their role in corporate governance, providing a stable but disciplined environment for corporate management. Stable shareholding arrangements, centering on key financiers and trading partners, and relations with the group's so-called main bank create an insider-based system of contingent corporate governance, which balances the benefits of managerial autonomy against the need for the capital market to monitor and intervene. (For detailed arguments see Abegglen and Stalk 1985, chapter 7; Aoki et al. 1994; Gilson and Roe 1993; Hoshi 1994; Sheard 1994a, 1994d, and 1994e. For important empirical evidence see Kang and Shivdasani

1994; Kaplan 1994; Kaplan and Minton 1994; Morck and Nakamura 1992; Sheard 1994c).

In terms of outcomes, the two views about *keiretsu* yield similar predictions. In both, *keiretsu* structures are associated with Japanese firms capturing or holding on to market share. The two hypotheses are difficult to distinguish by simply observing economic or market outcomes. The mechanisms involved and the implications for policymakers and business persons, however, are quite different. If the advantage to *keiretsu* organization rests on unfair and anticompetitive practices, a strong policy response is called for, and the burden of action should fall on the Japanese side. If, on the other hand, *keiretsu* structures reflect legitimate competitive strategies on the part of Japanese firms, it may be less a public policy than a corporate strategy response that is called for, with the burden of action resting on the side of US and other foreign business.

Quantitative studies can shed light on this dispute. Indeed, a large literature examining the economic effects of *keiretsu* organization has developed, part of it concerned with the market access issue.[1] Useful as it is, however, the empirical literature on *keiretsu* has been inconclusive. *Keiretsu* relationships are complex, multidimensional, and variable across firms, yet empirical studies, partly because of data limitations and the demands of tractability, have taken a crude, black-box approach to their measurement and modeling. Much insight into the issues raised in the *keiretsu* debate can be gained, however, by carefully considering the economic logic of the arguments in the light of what is known about Japanese industrial organization. That is the approach taken in this chapter.

The term *keiretsu* in Japanese is both vague and ambiguous, and the phenomena it refers to are both diverse and inherently imprecise, so much so that *keiretsu* is almost a synonym for "Japanese industrial organization." Partly because of this, and partly because so much is at stake in the US-Japan economic relationship, confusions and misunderstandings have abounded. Some of these are at a factual level, and some relate to conceptual issues. One aim of this chapter is to contribute to the policy debate by presenting some key facts and conceptual insights about *keiretsu*.

Two kinds of policy issue arise in the *keiretsu* debate, namely, antitrust and market access. In the debate to date, there has been a tendency to lump antitrust issues and market access issues together in an indiscriminate manner. The issues do overlap, but it is necessary to maintain a clear distinction between them. Anticompetitive practices in a domes-

---

1. On the trade issue, see in particular Fung (1991), Lawrence (1991a, 1991b), Noland (1992), Petri (1991), and Weinstein and Yafeh (1993), and on economic effects more generally the line of studies following Nakatani (1984) by Beason (1994), Ferris and Sarin (1993), Hoshi et al. (1990a, 1990b, and 1991), Kato (1994), Kato and Schallheim (1993), and Prowse (1992).

tic market can be a cause of market access being limited. But market access can be limited for reasons other than anticompetitive behavior.

One set of claims is that *keiretsu* are anticompetitive, that is, that they facilitate collusive practices and cartels, that they create entry barriers to markets, that they allow firms to behave in a predatory fashion both domestically and in international markets, and that they involve exclusionary practices, particularly in the distribution of intermediate and final products.[2] If *keiretsu* serve to cartelize markets and exclude imports, as some suggest, this would constitute a market access issue.

On the other hand, there are market access issues raised by *keiretsu* that go beyond traditional antitrust concerns of cartelization and market foreclosure. It is argued that the nature of interfirm ties in Japan implies that markets are not as open there as elsewhere.[3] In this view, it is not that there is anything particularly "wrong" with Japanese corporate organization; it is just that it is different, and that this difference creates problems for Japan's trading partners. Private preferences create barriers to trade (Noland 1992). As Dore (1986, 248) puts it, "Imports penetrate into markets, and where there *are* no markets, only a network of established 'customer relationships,' it is hard for them to make headway."

It is important to be clear about the policy issue involved. If antitrust concerns about *keiretsu* prove valid, the onus for a policy response lies on the Japanese side, and stronger antitrust oversight and enforcement to eliminate anticompetitive and undesirable effects are called for. If, however, the difficulties of market access reflect the lack of competitiveness of foreign firms in the Japanese market or systems of business that do not mesh, the appropriate policy response is less clear. Constructive efforts by governments to facilitate entry, as opposed to attempts at managed trade and market sharing, may help. It may be more a case, however, of foreign business needing to devise entry strategies that are suited to the Japanese market.

The *keiretsu* debate reflects deeper conceptual and policy issues relating to the problems that cross-country differences in economic organization and business practices pose for international trade, competition, and

---

2. This image of *keiretsu* has been projected particularly by so-called revisionist writers such as Johnson (1990a, 1990b) and by business people frustrated in their dealings with Japanese firms or attempts to sell into Japanese markets. Lawrence (1991a) calls this the "trust-busting" position. Lincoln (1990, 5) claimed that the US policy position was essentially an antitrust position.

3. The Office of the US Trade Representative (1989, 112) has argued that "Japan's *keiretsu* system involves close intercompany linkages which impede the importation of many U.S. products into the Japanese market." As Tyson and Zysman (1989a, xix) put it, "even when the government reduces policy barriers to market access in Japan, foreign firms continue to confront barriers that stem from the long-term contractual relationships among Japanese firms" and this results in the market being "[sealed off] at very low levels of import penetration" (1989b, 126).

market access. Trade policy is traditionally concerned with access to markets; its aim is to remove artificial barriers to markets. Competition policy is concerned with firm behavior in markets; it sets the rules under which firms compete with one another in markets. A key insight of the new industrial organization literature (on transaction cost economics and contractual theories of the firm) concerns the endogenous nature of markets, especially in intermediate products: which markets are open and how they operate depends on where firms locate their own boundaries and how they choose to contract across those boundaries. Firms do not just operate *in* markets; their contractual choices help to shape the design of markets. Economic organization varies across countries. Neither "firms" nor "markets," particularly intermediate product markets, are necessarily the same in each country.

Intermediate product markets do not exist independently of the way in which firms have organized themselves and their interfirm transactions. Prying opening markets that have been closed because of direct or indirect government restrictions on trade is a relatively straightforward matter (to contemplate, but not necessarily to implement). Opening markets that are closed because firms have internalized them or turned them into markets for long-term contracts presents a qualitatively different set of issues. The issues raised by *keiretsu* are in the latter category. The debate has been confused, however, because there has been an understandable tendency to use the vocabulary of traditional trade and competition policy—to speak of "closed markets," "collusive behavior," and "exclusionary practices"—to come at these issues. In this paper, I hope to provide some insights into the policy issues raised by the fact that firms in different national economies draw and manage their boundaries in different ways.

The paper is organized as follows. The next section provides some background information on the structure of *keiretsu*. The following two sections examine the antitrust arguments about *keiretsu*, namely, that they are collusive and that they foreclose markets through vertical relationships among member firms. The paper concludes with a discussion of the market access concerns that arise from the vertical organization of firms and markets in Japan.

The Structure of *Keiretsu*

Because the term *keiretsu* has entered the vocabulary of trade negotiators, academics, businesspeople, and even the general public interested in Japan, it is important that all who use the term have a clear understanding of what *keiretsu* means in Japanese and what aspects of Japanese industrial organization it refers to. The word *keiretsu* is written in Japanese with two Chinese characters *kei*, meaning "lineage" or "system," and *retsu,* meaning "row" or "line" (Nelson 1974). In general use, the word means "ordered sequence" or "series." As an economic term, as we have seen, *keiretsu* is widely used to refer to various forms of corporate affiliation or the groups of firms formed by such affiliations. The first character is frequently used by itself as a suffix indicating affiliation, as in *Nissan-kei no kaisha,* "a firm affiliated with Nissan." In Japanese at least, the term *keiretsu,* in and of itself, is vague and nonspecific. The affiliation to which it refers can fall within a range of forms, from parent-subsidiary relations to close trading ties between independent firms. It is not surprising, then, that Japanese have often appeared perplexed, defensive, or even dismissive when confronted with broad claims by Westerners about the effects of *keiretsu.*

As already noted, it is common to distinguish three kinds of *keiretsu.* One of these, financial *keiretsu,* involves a collection of leading firms from a diverse range of industrial sectors. Six major financial *keiretsu* are commonly identified in Japan, all of them based around major city banks and related financial institutions. Four of these groups (Mitsui, Mitsubishi, Sumitomo, and Fuyo) evolved from the prewar *zaibatsu,* which were broken up after World War II, and the other two (Sanwa and Daiichi Kangyo) formed around major banks in the high-growth era of the 1950s and 1960s. Firms in these groupings are linked by interlocking shareholdings, close relations with a common main bank and a general trading company (GTC), and supply relationships, and the core firms participate in executive gatherings known as presidents' clubs (*shachokai*). In 1991, 8 percent of firms listed on Japanese stock exchanges belonged to one or more presidents' clubs (Toyo Keizai Shinposha 1991, 50, 100). Classifying firms on the basis of financial and other ties, Keizai Chosa Kyokai (1992, 1) identified 59 percent of nonfinancial firms listed in the first section of the Tokyo exchange as being affiliated with one of the six groups.

Table 1 provides some data on interfirm ties among these group-affiliated firms. Whether the groups are defined narrowly or broadly, the average level of intragroup shareholding is about the same, at around 18 percent, as is the average level of intragroup bank and insurance company financing, also about 18 percent. On average, 9 percent of input purchases are from other member firms (almost two-thirds of these from the GTC), and 8 percent of sales are made to other member firms (three-quarters of these to the GTC).

A second form of *keiretsu* comprises a large parent firm and its network of subsidiaries and affiliated suppliers. Typical examples are the Toyota and Nissan groups in the automobile industry; the Matsushita, Hitachi, and Toshiba groups in the electrical goods industry; and the Nippon Steel group in that basic materials industry. A leading Japanese corporate directory lists 40 main "pyramid-style" groups of this kind, each having on average 192 subsidiaries or associated companies (Toyo

Table 1 Measures of intragroup ties in the six enterprise groupings, 1990[a] (percentages except in first row)

Measure	Mitsui	Mitsubishi	Sumitomo	Fuyo	Sanwa	DKB	Average
Number of firms in group	24	29	20	29	44	47	32
	106	130	107	117	60	88	101
Intragroup borrowing[b]	19.6	19.4	21.5	17.4	18.2	12.5	18.1
	15.6	20.2	14.1	18.9	18.4	15.8	17.2
Intragroup shareholding[c]	16.5	26.9	24.1	15.4	16.4	12.1	18.6
	(19.5)	35.5	27.5	16.4	16.5	14.6	21.7)
	17.4	25.2	23.7	17.1	10.6	13.6	17.9
Intragroup directors[d]	2.2	12.9	8.7	2.4	5.0	6.9	6.4
Intragroup purchases[e]	7.7	16.1	12.8	7.1	4.2	3.3	8.9
Of which GTC purchases[f]	4.5	10.8	9.5	5.4	2.4	2.3	5.8
Intragroup sales[g]	6.5	14.3	12.2	6.4	3.6	4.8	8.0
Of which sales to GTC[h]	4.0	9.3	9.0	7.5	4.8	2.1	6.1
Purchases from GTC[i]	10.1	9.9	13.2	2.0	2.6	3.0	6.8
Sales to GTC[j]	13.6	20.3	33.6	10.2	4.2	5.9	14.6

GTC = general trading company.

a. Upper- or single-row figures are for the groups as defined by membership in a presidents's club (*shachokai*); lower row figures, where they appear, are for the same groups as more extensively defined by the *Nenpo keiretsu no kenkyu* annual directory. For the row in brackets, see note c.

b. Percentage of member firms' total borrowings supplied by the group financial institutions (city bank, trust bank, life and casualty insurance companies).

c. Percentage of member firms' shares held within the group. The first row is calculated only for the top 20 (in a small number of cases, the top 10) shareholdings. The second (bracketed) row, from Kosei Torihiki Iinkai (1992), is also for presidents's club members (for 1989) and appears to include non-top 20 shareholdings.

d. Percentage of total directors of member firms who moved to the firm from another member firm (or are serving concurrently as part-time directors).

e. Percentage of total input purchases of nonfinancial member firm supplied by member firms (including general trading companies).

f. Percentage of total input purchases of nonfinancial member firms (including GTC) supplied by group GTC.

g. Percentage of total output sales of nonfinancial member firms going to member firms (including GTCs).

h. Percentage of total output sales of nonfinancial member firms (including GTC) going to group GTC.

i. Percentage of total input purchases of nonfinancial member firms (excluding GTC) made from group GTC.

j. Percentage of total output sales of nonfinancial member firms (excluding GTC) sales made to group GTC.

Sources: Keizai Chosa Kyokai, 1992, 3 and 5; Kosei Torihiki Iinkai, 1992, 124; Toyo Keizai Shinposha, 1991, 40-49.

Keizai Shinposha 1991, 54). Most attention has focused on the vertical *keiretsu* of the automakers, which comprise hierarchically structured supplier networks. For instance, data for 1977 show Toyota having 168 first-tier suppliers, which in turn had 5,437 suppliers (indirect or second-tier suppliers to Toyota), which in turn had 41,703 lower-level suppliers (Fruin 1992, 271).[4]

Table 2 provides some data on four of the best-known supplier groups, two from the automobile industry and two from the electrical goods and machinery industry. Toyota's 41 most important first-tier direct suppliers and subcontractors, shown in table 2, accounted for 75 percent of its total purchases of inputs in the 1991 financial year. These suppliers are not totally independent of Toyota. There is partial vertical integration in an ownership sense, with Toyota having an average shareholding of 25 percent in these firms. On average, these firms supplied 43 percent of their output to Toyota. The situation with Nissan is similar. The 30 suppliers shown accounted for 70 percent of Nissan's input purchases in the 1991 financial year and supplied on average 55 percent of their output to Nissan, with the automaker owning 30 percent of their shares on average. Matsushita's 15 principal subsidiaries and suppliers accounted for 49 percent of its purchases of final products and material inputs and supplied on average 51 percent of their output to the parent company, which had an average ownership share in them of 54 percent. Hitachi's 16 principal subsidiaries and suppliers accounted for 39 percent of its purchases, and on average they supplied 30 percent of their output to Hitachi, which owned on average 50 percent of their shares.

The third form of *keiretsu* consists of a parent firm and the set of firms that comprise its distribution system or network. Conceptually, these "distribution *keiretsu*" are analogous to supplier *keiretsu*: they involve vertical ties, which, however, are downstream rather than upstream (Flath 1989). Less attention has been paid to this aspect of corporate organization, particularly in a comparative context, although vertical ties loom large in discussions of anticompetitive behavior.

The notion of a "distribution *keiretsu*" is very broad, as every large firm in Japan has some kind of distribution system, and the nature of these varies greatly by industry and even across leading firms in a given industry (Ariga et al. 1991, Itoh 1992, Miwa and Nishimura 1992). Producers of final consumer goods distribute these goods through affiliated dealer and chain store networks. These networks tend to be vertically integrated in a product market sense—outlets specialize in the brand names of the maker—but only partially integrated in an ownership sense.

---

4. Strictly speaking, however, this type should be distinguished from cases where subsidiaries produce related final (or intermediate) products rather than supply intermediate inputs to the parent firm. So-called vertical *keiretsu* comprise a mixture of the two types.

Table 2 Shareholding and output links in four leading vertical subsidiary/supplier groups, 1992

Toyota group

Name of subsidiary or supplier	Product/ operations	Toyota's shareholding[a] (percent)	Sales to Toyota[b] (millions of yen)	Share of output sold to Toyota
Nippon Denso	Electrical parts	23.5	742,738	na
Toyota Body	Vehicle assembly	43.1	495,000 (223,151)	98
Toyota Auto Loom	Vehicle assembly	23	416,180 (186,339)	71.3
Kanto Motors	Vehicle assemby	49.4	382,582 (222,568)	99.9
Aishin Seiki	Transmissions	21.9	373,661 (46,032)	67.5
Toyoda Trading	Trading company	21.8	349,026 (197,065)	16.4
Hino Motors	Deisel trucks	11.2	251,106	39.4
Daihatsu Ind.	Light vehicles	15.4	210,960	26.1
Aishin A.W.	Automatic transmissions	41.1	209,226	na
Toyoda Gosei	Synthetic resins, rubber	41.1	145,154 (8,728)	59.1
Tokai Rika Elec.	Switches, locks, seat belts	30.8	125,738 (9,657)	62.3
Toyoda Koki	Machining tools, components	21.4	118,352 (17,573)	67.8
Kojima Press	Press, resins	3.7	101,340	na
Takashimaya Hatsujo Ind.	Interior parts	24.2	94,144 (47,605)	na
Central Motors	Bodies	47	92,279 (57,585)	na
Fujitsu Ten	Audio equipment	35	91,138	na
Futaba Ind.	Mufflers	13.2	77,406	54.6
Koito Manuf.	Lamps	19	72,610	46.4
Aisan Ind.	Electronic fuel injection equipment	31.8	61,346	73.8
Aishin Takaoka	Brake drums	37.3	56,175	na
Koyo Seiko	Bearings	21.9	55,542	19
Horie Metal Ind.	Fuel tanks	50	50,996	na
Shiroki Ind.	Door frames	14.1	45,730	51.2
Toyo Rubber	Tires	4.5	37,014	16.6
Topi Ind.	Press, wheels	na	28,319	17
Chuo Hatsujo	Springs, cable	23.6	28,000 (891)	42.8

(Continued on next page)

Table 2 Shareholding and output links in four leading vertical subsidiary/supplier groups, 1992 (continued)

Toyota group

Name of subsidiary or supplier	Product/ operations	Toyota's shareholding[a] (percent)	Sales to Toyota[b] (millions of yen)	Share of output sold to Toyota
Taiheiyo Ind.	Tire valves	45.8	21,858	45.8
Nihon Hatsujo	Springs, seats	1.1	18,879	11.7
Ichiko Ind.	Lamps	6.1	18,304	16
Toyoda Spinning	Filters, interior	9.3	11,588	24.8
Jeko	Auto clocks	34.3	10,476	38.3
Chuo Katan Ind.	Forging, casting	5.1	9,186	44.3
Toyo Radiators	Radiators	4.9	7,560	13.9
Trinity Ind.	Painting equipment	30.2	7,422	64.1
Teikoku Piston Rings	Piston rings	6.8	5,630	18.8
Nihon Gaskette	Gaskets	0.3	4,427	70.5
Araki Works	Lifting equipment	na	3,689	na
Ohari Seiki	Screws, forged products	5.2	3,326	23.5
Tokyo Shoketsu	Products, pumps	25.3	2,070	17.2
Kyoto Machinery	Tools	na	1,805	13.3
Kyowa Leather	Interior leather	33.5	220	na
Average/total		24.7	4,838,202	42.9

Nissan group

Name of subsidiary or supplier	Product/ operations	Nissan's shareholding[a] (percent)	Sales to Nissan[b] (millions of yen)	Share of output sold to Nissan
Nissan Body	Vehicle assembly	43.4	568,048 (260,267)	99.8
Aichi Machinery	Vehicle assembly	33.5	281,047 (135,634)	99.0
Karusonikku	Radiators	33.8	169,034 (7,209)	76.1
Atsugi Yunishia	Parts	34.0	139,131 (7,423)	77.6
Nissan Deisel	Truck assembly	40.2	101,877 (33,119)	26.2
Ikeda Bussan	Seats	58.0	89,324 (3,802)	62.2
Kansei	Meters	32.1	84,402 (134)	68.8
Yamakawa Ind.	Pressed components	30.3	60,261 (18,865)	72.0

Table 2 Shareholding and output links in four leading vertical subsidiary/supplier groups, 1992 (continued)

Nissan group

Name of subsidiary or supplier	Product/ operations	Nissan's shareholding[a] (percent)	Sales to Nissan[b] (millions of yen)	Share of output sold to Nissan
Ichiko Ind.	Lamps	20.9	52,621	46.0
Fuji Heavy Ind.	Vehicle assembly	4.3	51,153 (44,935)	na
Clarion	Audio equipment	11.5	50,626	33.1
Kawanishi Ind.	Doors	23.1	47,178 (637)	64.7
Yorozu	Locks	28.5	44,100 (15,748)	64.9
Kinugawa Rubber	Rubber components	29.1	42,544 (279)	56.2
Sekuseru	Fuel injection pumps	11.2	39,403	15.3
Hashimoto Forming	Exterior components	25.2	37,899 (2,325)	55.3
Fuji Yunibansu	Transmissions	34.4	37,794 (7,209)	68.0
Fuji Kiko	Belts, seats	24.1	32,637 (4,977)	54.5
Daiwa Ind.	Pressed components	34.0	32,547 (659)	na
Daii Works	Suspensions	29.0	29,969 (4,423)	63.3
Tsuchiya Works	Air filters	57.2	28,965 (1,341)	54.1
Tachiesu	Seats	20.5	27,596 (3,354)	26.0
Nihon Plastics	Resin products	27.3	23,224 (621)	43.2
Jidosha Electric	Control parts	25.0	23,101	40.0
Nairusu Parts	Electrical components	40.0	22,168 (1)	na
Akebono Brake	Brakes	15.6	18,267	16.9
Tochigi Fuji Ind.	Axles	21.0	18,069	43.6
Kisei Machinery	Brake drums	50.6	16,621 (1,415)	58.8
Nihon Kikaki	Converters	24.2	13,452	43.9
Tosoku	Parts	28.5	9,186 (275)	44.9
Average/total		29.7	2,192,244	54.6

(Continued on next page)

Table 2 Shareholding and output links in four leading vertical subsidiary/supplier groups, 1992 (continued)

Matsushita group

Name of subsidiary or supplier	Product/ operations	Matsushita's shareholding[a] (percent)	Sales to Matsushita[b] (millions of yen)	Share of output sold to Mitsushita
Matsushita Communications	Communications, auto equipment	57.0	442,199 (11,305)	96.6
Kyushu Matsushita Electric	Electrical equipment, parts	52.0	329,255 (7,498)	94.9
Matsushita Electronic Parts	Electronics materials, parts	98.7	322,683 (17,269)	84.5
Matsushita Reiki	Refrigerators, vending machines, air conditioners	51.8	200,607 (9,521)	98.8
Matsushita Battery Ind.	Batteries	97.6	178,389 (3,710)	89.2
Matsushita Judenshi Ind.	Visual, audio, heating equipment	57.7	171,561 (22,387)	62.9
Matsushita Seiko	Air conditioning, fans	59.0	91,241 (3,048)	96.1
Matsushita Denso	Fax machines	60.0	58,084 (10,937)	70.4
Matsushita Denko	Lighting, electrical, information equipment	32.0	29,480 (38,331)	2.9
Matsushita Butsuryu	Warehousing, transportation	30.0	27,479	na
Miyata Ind.	Bicycles, fire extinguishers	44.4	1,596	5.0
Nihon Victor	Visual, audio equipment	52.4	1,488 (41,194)	0.2
Wakayama Precision Ind.	Compressors	54.0	533 (726)	13.0
National Housing Ind.	Housing, housing materials	26.3	336 (2,851)	0.2
National Securities	Securities	29.1	17	0.1
Matsushita Electronics Ind.	Semiconductors, light bulbs, TV screens	65.0	na (na)	na
Average/total		54.2	1,854,948	51.1

(*continued on next page*)

Table 2   Shareholding and output links in four leading vertical subsidiary/supplier groups, 1992 (continued)

Hitachi group

Name of subsidiary or supplier	Product/ operations	Hitachi's shareholding[a] (percent)	Sales to Hitachi[b] (millions of yen)	Share of output sold to Hitachi
Hitachi Plant Construction	Plant construction	56.0	159,816 (1,519)	65.5
Hitachi Butsuryu	Transportation, warehousing	62.0	85,823 (3,984)	41.3
Nissei Ind.	Electronic equipment sales	58.1	84,529 (225,712)	14.4
Hitachi Software Engineering	Software	64.2	57,549 (16,872)	62.9
Kokusai Electric	Communications equipment, electronics components	21.9	56,446	45.6
Hitachi Electric Wire	Electric wire, copper wire	52.3	36,128 (999)	10.8
Hitachi Koki	Electrical tools	31.6	32,215	24.9
Hitachi Information Systems	Software	64.1	30,281 (15,201)	27.6
Hitachi Kasei Ind.	Electronics components, housing equipment	57.2	26,088 (907)	8.4
Faicomu High-Tech	Calculator sales, software	50.0	25,808	na
Hitachi Electronics	Broadcasting, video, information equipment	64.4	21,885 (1,199)	35.8
Tokiko	Hydraulic equipment	38.7	14,014 (1,380)	12.9
Nakayo Communications Equip.	Telephones, switchboards	21.5	11,509 (1,149)	43.4
Hitachi Kiden Ind.	Cranes, water treatment equipment	65.8	11,197 (536)	48.3
Hitachi Metal	Special steel, magnetic materials	54.5	7,913 (9,083)	2.4
Shinmeiwa Ind.	Special vehicles, industrial machinery	29.4	6,849	5.2
Average/total		49.5	668,050	30.0

na = not available.
a. Including some indirect holdings.
b. Figures in parentheses are amount of purchases from the parent company.
Source: Toyo Keizai Shinposha, 1992, 18-25.

For example, Japan's nine automakers in 1992 had 3,759 affiliated dealers, with a total of 17,423 dedicated outlets (Kosei Torihiki Iinkai 1993a). In almost all cases, the dealers sold only the affiliated parent's vehicles. In only 16 percent of cases did the automakers own shares in the dealerships. However, for the largest dealers (the 14 percent with ¥100 million—about $1 million—or more in capital) the picture was different: close to half (45 percent) were wholly owned by the automakers; on the other hand, in nearly a third of cases the automakers had no shareholding. Shareholding levels vary widely even for the same maker. Toyota's three Tokyo dealers are all consolidated subsidiaries, but Toyota does not even figure as a top-20 shareholder in its main dealer in its home prefecture of Aichi, Aichi Toyota Motor, even though this firm alone accounts for about 4 percent of Toyota's domestic passenger vehicle sales (as calculated from Nihon Keizai Shinbunsha 1994).

Firms producing intermediate products frequently distribute their outputs to user firms through wholesalers and sales outlets, which carry out informational, order processing, transportation, inventory, financing, and in some cases finishing, processing, and assembly operations. For example, the three leading makers of sheet glass distribute their outputs through 381 wholesale agencies, which in turn deal with a further 15,000 sales outlets (Kosei Torihiki Iinkai 1993b). Almost all of the agencies handle only their affiliated maker's products. The glassmakers hold shares in the wholesalers in about one-quarter of cases, and in 80 percent they hold a majority of shares.

The Small and Medium Enterprise Agency's periodic survey of wholesale and retail industry defines "being in a *keiretsu*" as "having entered into a special agency (*tokuyakuten*) contract or agency (*dairiten*) contract or being in receipt of managerial or other assistance from a transaction partner, and in return selling the transaction partner's products on a preferential basis." Although not rigorous or conceptually founded, this definition is a practical one understandable to business people. On this basis, the 1992 Basic Survey found that 30.7 percent of wholesale firms and 28.9 percent of retail firms (most having fewer than 50 employees) said that they belonged to a *keiretsu*, with 67.4 percent and 68.7 percent, respectively, replying that they did not. *Keiretsu* affiliation was most prevalent in household equipment and utensils retailing (74.4 percent), fuel retailing (71.1 percent), and pharmaceuticals and cosmetics wholesaling (50.8 percent), and least prevalent in knitwear and clothing retailing (17.0 percent), furniture and fixtures retailing (17.3 percent), recycled materials wholesaling (18.1 percent), and textiles wholesaling (19.7 percent; Chusho Kigyocho 1994, 62-65).

A key point is that, from an industrial organization viewpoint, the relations observed in all three forms of *keiretsu* are not horizontal. Firms associated with supplier or distribution *keiretsu* are firms that are linked in vertical input-output supply relations. Firms associated with financial *keiretsu* are either linked in vertical relations (including factor inputs in the case of bank-firm ties) or operate in different intermediate or final product markets. Firms in a given *keiretsu*, generally speaking, are not direct competitors in a given market. For instance, Central Glass and Nissan are in a vertical relationship because the former supplies material inputs to Nissan, and both are in vertical relationships with the distribution outlets through which Central Glass supplies its output to Nissan. Nissan and Tokyo Nissan Auto Sales are in a vertical relationship because Nissan supplies the latter's inputs. Fuji Bank supplies capital to Nissan in the form of loans and equity, and thus can also be viewed as an upstream supplier of inputs.

Although analytically the relations involved are vertical, there are important differences between the various forms of *keiretsu*. One is that financial *keiretsu* are highly diversified across sectors at a groupwide level (although particular firm pairs within them may have direct vertical relations), whereas supplier and distribution *keiretsu* involve firms producing a single product or related set of products. A second difference is that, although both types of grouping involve financial and input-output ties, these differ between the three types. In financial *keiretsu*, financial ties are based mainly on extensive, diffuse interlocking shareholdings and main bank financing relations. In supplier networks (and subsidiary networks more generally) shareholdings are centered on parent firms: the parent firm holds shares in subsidiaries (and not the other way around to any large extent), and the shareholdings are often majority or large minority holdings. As regards transactional ties, these are strong within and lie at the heart of supplier networks, but apart from particular pairs of firms they are fairly minor in the financial *keiretsu*. Many firms identified as belonging to a particular financial *keiretsu* have minimal or no direct contact or ties with each other. However, they do share the same group banks and trading company for financing and handling of inputs and outputs (table 1). At the risk of oversimplification, it can be said that production links are the driving force in supplier networks, and financial (financing and interlocking shareholding) ties the main aspect of multimarket groups.

The different kinds of *keiretsu* are not mutually exclusive. Leading industrial firms in financial *keiretsu* typically are parent firms in their own supplier networks, distribution networks, or subsidiary groups. Although financial and supplier *keiretsu* are presented as separate categories in empirical work such as Lawrence (1991a), there is considerable overlap in their membership, with firms in assembly-supplier systems such as Toyota or Matsushita or parent-subsidiary firm groups such as Nippon Steel being associated with a financial *keiretsu* as well, either as a member of a presidents' club, as in the case of Hitachi (member of the Fuyo, Sanwa, and DKB presidents' clubs), Toyota (Mitsui), Nissan (Fuyo), and Toshiba (Mitsui), or through a main bank relationship as with Matsushita (Sumitomo Bank) and Nippon Steel (Industrial Bank of Japan).[5]

Relations in a given *keiretsu* are multifaceted, involving such aspects as ownership, financing, transfers of intermediate products, movement of personnel, sharing of information, and joint research and product development, even between a given pair of firms. Not only is membership better conceived in terms of a continuum rather than a zero-one condition, but it is also better viewed as connoting a vector of attributes rather than a single one. Indeed, it is the bundling together of various attributes that makes these business structures so interesting from the viewpoint of industrial organization theory (Aoki 1994; Flath 1992) and that magnifies the concerns about them with respect to competition policy and market access.

Keiretsu and Collusion

Terms such as "cartel-like," "collusive," and "exclusionary" are often used to suggest that *keiretsu* have anticompetitive aspects.[6] In general, however, these concerns are not warranted—the language of antitrust has been applied in far too cavalier a fashion to these relationships.

Any antitrust issues raised by *keiretsu* must relate to their vertical organization. To characterize *keiretsu* as "cartels" or "collusive" is therefore misleading. Cartels and collusion involve firms selling the same products fixing prices or tacitly coordinating on a monopoly price (Jacquemin and Slade 1989; Tirole 1989, chapter 6).[7] Firms in a *keiretsu* cannot form cartels or collude because they do not operate in the same market. It is spurious to associate *keiretsu* affiliation with cartels or collusion.

The potential confusion is exacerbated by a widespread misuse of terminology in the literature. Following the tradition in the Japanese literature, financial *keiretsu* are sometimes referred to as "horizontal" or "horizontally connected" groupings. But this terminology reflects an

---

5. Lawrence does not make clear how he handled this overlap issue in his empirical estimation.

6. For instance, Taira (1993) defined *keiretsu* as "cartel-like alliances of firms," and Pickens (1992) defined them as "government-sponsored cartels." Lawrence (1991a, 324) referred to the possibility of "collusive behavior by *keiretsu* firms."

7. *The MIT Dictionary of Modern Economics* defines a cartel as a "formal agreement between firms in an oligopolistic market to co-operate with regard to agreed procedures on such variables as price and output," collusion as "agreement between firms to cooperate in order to avoid mutually damaging rivalry," horizontal as "at the same stage of production," and vertical as "belonging different stages of the same production process" (Pearce 1992). It follows from both formal and economic logic that vertically related firms cannot collude or form cartels.

implicit theory of power relations rather than any industrial organization concept. Financial *keiretsu* comprise leading firms in distinct industries, some of which are vertically linked. They are loosely conglomerate, but the product-market transactions between these firms are vertical. "Horizontal" in this context captures the notion of equality in status or lack of hierarchy, in the sense that no firm stands at the pinnacle of the group in an ownership or decision-making sense.

"Horizontal" in industrial organization and antitrust, on the other hand, refers to behavior in a market. For example, a "horizontal merger" is a merger between two firms in a market (Jacquemin and Slade 1989), and "horizontal shareholding" is shareholding among competing firms (Flath 1994). If *keiretsu* were horizontal in an antitrust sense, issues of collusion or cartel formation would warrant consideration. But they are not. To use terms such as "horizontal groups" and "collusion" or "cartel-like" in the same context is to invite the misconception that *keiretsu* links exist between firms in a given market. Although there are instances of this, it is not common.

This kind of confusion is evident in Lawrence's (1991a, 329) influential paper. He summarized his results as follows:

> While antitrust violations should be punished, there are cases where keiretsu relationships improve efficiency. As might be expected, these efficiencies tend to be associated with vertical rather than horizontal linkages. Given the complexity and pervasiveness of the vertical keiretsu, it is difficult to support extreme approaches that would either entirely ban these linkages or unreservedly tolerate them. Instead, vigilance and a "rule of reason" approach, which pays particular attention to horizontal linkages, seems most appropriate.

Lawrence is correct to point to the need for vigilance regarding "horizontal linkages," but the analysis of "horizontal *keiretsu*" in his paper has nothing to do with that issue, because what he terms "horizontal *keiretsu*" in fact involve vertical linkages or conglomeratelike (multimarket) linkages, not within-market horizontal linkages.

The confusion of important substantive issues by misleading terminology is clearly in evidence in the general discussion following Lawrence's paper in the Brookings Papers, as the following passage shows:

> Steven Salop [noted] that more recently antitrust economists and lawyers have become increasingly concerned with vertical restraints on trade, especially where they are accompanied by horizontal restraints. As vertical and horizontal keiretsu often coexist, there was probable cause for antitrust concerns. Lawrence observed that if antitrust policy was concerned with efficiency, it should look closely at horizontal keiretsu which, according to his findings, might lead to discrimination against foreign goods while not increasing efficiency. (Lawrence 1991a, 337)

The term "horizontal" is being used in two different senses here, the first corresponding to the normal antitrust usage, the second borrowing the usage peculiar to Japanese, which has nothing to do with "horizontal" in the antitrust sense. Exactly the same confusion is evident in the continuation of the above passage:

> The panelists discussed some ambiguities in the empirical results. Nordhaus noted that horizontal concentration increased imports while horizontal *keiretsu* reduced them. (Lawrence 1991a, 337)

There is only an ambiguity if the first "horizontal" is being used in the same sense as the second, which readers of this passage would assume to be the case, but which the above discussion makes clear is not the case.

It is a small step from here to another fallacy, namely, to conclude that, because particular markets appear to be dominated by firms with *keiretsu* ties and *keiretsu* are believed to be characterized by cozy insider relations, the market somehow is prone to be collusive. The firms in question belong to different *keiretsu* and compete with one another; firms in the same *keiretsu* may have cozy relations but these are relations *across* two vertically linked markets, not between firms in the same market.

Collusion and cartel formation do occur in Japanese markets, but they involve firms belonging to different *keiretsu* that operate in the same market. Any collusion that occurs must be across *keiretsu* lines. Cartels in Japan, like those elsewhere, are typically organized, sanctioned, or facilitated by some kind of government action. Financial and insurance markets, in which the government regulates prices and restricts entry (McKenzie 1992); *dango,* or public-procurement bidding cartels, which involve the government as buyer (McMillan 1991); and government-sanctioned recession, structural depression, and export cartels readily come to mind (Dick 1992). But these have little or nothing to do with *keiretsu.*

There are two possible ways in which *keiretsu,* given their structure, could conceivably lead to cartelization or collusion. The first is a multimarket collusion story that focuses on the loosely conglomerate nature of the diversified financial *keiretsu*. Because these groups comprise firms from diverse markets, as described above, they may facilitate multimarket collusion as studied in the industrial organization literature (Tirole 1989). Lawrence (1993) makes reference to this possibility. Although interesting at a theoretical level, this argument is totally lacking in plausibility as it applies to actual Japanese circumstances.

First of all, multimarket oligopoly models are developed for oligopolists operating in multiple markets that are *single* decision-making units. Financial *keiretsu* are loose collections of *independent* firms. It is implausible to suggest that these loose collections can coordinate their actions sufficiently well to implement the credible multimarket retaliation strategies necessary for the multimarket effect to appear. The assumptions of the model are stringent enough for a single decision-making multimarket unit, let alone an organization with multiple decentralized decision units.

Equilibrium in the model would involve firms in all *keiretsu* tacitly colluding on a monopoly price in each market. The model would require, for example, that if Nissan, a Fuyo group firm, undercut Mitsubishi Motors, a Mitsubishi group firm, not only would Mitsubishi Motors retaliate against Nissan with reversion to competitive (technically Bertrand or Cournot) behavior in all future periods, but all other Mitsubishi firms (and firms in all other groups) would retaliate against all other Fuyo group firms in their markets, even though no defection took place there. One theoretical possibility is that the main bank in each group provides the coordinating function. Main banks do play an important role in investment and corporate governance (Aoki et al. 1994), but it stretches credulity to its limits to suggest that they can control product market decisions such as prices and outputs.

Second, multimarket oligopoly models have in mind a set of unrelated final product markets. The argument does not make sense for firms linked in vertical input-output relations, because this would lead to successive monopolies and double (or multiple) marginalization effects, raising costs through the input-output production chain and leading to final-product market prices above their monopoly price levels (Tirole 1989, 174-75). The argument only makes sense in relation to final product markets, in which the groups tend to be less represented anyway.

These considerations raise a serious doubt about the way in which Lawrence (1991a) interpreted his results. Lawrence found that the prevalence of horizontal *keiretsu* was associated with a reduction in imports but no increase in exports, whereas vertical *keiretsu* were associated with both a reduction in imports and an increase in exports. Lawrence interpreted the latter result to mean that there may be some efficiency gains from vertical *keiretsu*, but he took the absence of an export-promoting effect for horizontal *keiretsu* as evidence for his trust-busting hypothesis "that *keiretsu* create entry barriers for newcomers and engage in anticompetitive practices" (1991a, 314). As argued above, however, it is difficult to identify anything anticompetitive in the structure of financial *keiretsu*.[8] The diversified composition of the groups does not, of itself, raise any anticompetitive concerns, and the vertical input-output supply linkages, which have been weakening over time, are generally less tight than those found in the supplier *keiretsu*. It is hard to see any logical reason why one set of supplier ties would be anticompetitive and another efficient.

There is a more innocuous explanation for Lawrence's results, which is consistent with the historical development of these business forms. It is well documented in the literature that in the high-growth period of the 1950s and 1960s the financial *keiretsu* exhibited a form of herd investment behavior, in which each of the six groups strove to establish a group

---

8. See also the comment on Lawrence's paper by Saxonhouse (1991a) and Saxonhouse's (1991b) comment on Lawrence (1991b).

presence in each major industry. This is the "one set" phenomenon documented by Miyazaki (1967). As a result, each of the six groups, as defined by presidents' club membership, today has a presence in the commercial banking, life insurance, wholesale trading, construction, chemicals, cement, steel, engineering and shipbuilding, and electrical machinery industries; five have a presence in the trust banking, casualty insurance, fiber and textiles, nonferrous metals, automobile, and shipping industries; and four have a presence in the real estate, oil refining, paper, and warehousing industries (Gerlach 1992, 83-84).

There seem to be two main factors at work. First, in an economy that was growing rapidly but was relatively closed (particularly the financial sector), the banks found it useful to forge close ties (main bank relations) with the leading firms in key sectors, and so carry out their role as financial intermediaries and promote their own growth. Second, given that the banks were going to hold diversified portfolios of major corporate investments, it made sense to link these investments in a coherent input-output way. If a bank is going to finance a major capital investment, it wants to make sure that the firm making the investment has a stable supply of high-quality inputs and a market for its output. Investing as a main bank in both upstream and downstream firms linked to the firm in question is a way of helping to ensure this. There was also a legacy of concerns about stability of supply and production bottlenecks from the earlier wartime planned economy and postwar recovery (Okazaki 1994). By organizing their investments into affiliated groups of vertically linked firms, banks could reduce uncertainties associated with input supplies and output demands and internalize spillover effects (Goto 1982). There is nothing anticompetitive about any of this, although the coordination mechanism is surely different from a pure market mechanism (for more discussion, see Sheard 1994b). It is more a description of how investment and production coordination was achieved and competitive forces played out in an economy that was growing rapidly but had a highly regulated financial system.

This historical perspective suggests that it is the investment behavior more than the trading behavior of groups that lies at the root of foreign concerns about multimarket keiretsu. A common complaint has been that there is preferential intragroup trading among affiliated firms and that this reduces market access for imports. There is some truth in this, but it is important to consider the mechanisms through which this comes about and understand the policy implications. In the real world, particularly in industries requiring large capital investments, investment decisions and decisions about how inputs will be procured and outputs disposed of in the future are made simultaneously. The fact that two firms transact on a continuous basis, making it difficult for new firms to break in, is likely to reflect the fact that the firms made prior capital investments with a view to having a supply relationship, rather than exclusionary behavior or inherent group preferences. At the macroeconomic level, if *keiretsu* impede imports, it is mainly because investment decisions have been made to source inputs from particular domestic sources rather than from elsewhere. These may have been good or bad investment decisions, but it is not necessary to resort to the language of antitrust to describe their ramifications.

Another possibility regarding *keiretsu* and collusion that needs to be considered is that firms use vertical ties to maintain higher prices, that is, that they tacitly collude with other firms (in other *keiretsu*) at their stage of production. This is an argument that has been debated at length in the US antitrust literature and largely rejected (Demsetz 1992). The argument rests on the assumption that firms at a given stage, rather than directly colluding among themselves, can better enforce collusion indirectly through relations with downstream firms, in particular distributors or retailers. Firms that are vertically linked cannot collude to set a monopoly price. Such collusion has to be between competing firms. But their joint action may enhance the ability of competing upstream firms to collude on a monopoly price. For instance, long-term contracts with downstream firms, by creating captive customers, may be a better way of committing not to undercut rivals' prices than tacit collusion in an environment of arm's-length relations with downstream customers (conceptually, it is analogous to creating a form of product differentiation, in that lock-in effects reduce substitutability with rivals' outputs).

The problem with this argument is that the upstream and downstream firms' interests are diametrically opposed, since upstream monopoly prices translate into higher costs for downstream firms. The argument requires that downstream firms willingly agree to a course of action that is detrimental to their interests. Although one can generate hypothetical examples where this kind of prisoners' dilemma behavior is induced, it is hardly a robust theory of corporate behavior in Japan or elsewhere (Rasmusen et al. 1991).

Vertical Foreclosure and Market Access

Observers who characterize *keiretsu* as cartel-like or collusive seem to have in mind a market foreclosure argument of the antitrust kind, namely, that *keiretsu* firms use upstream-downstream links to exclude competing firms from entering either the upstream or downstream market. However, the foreclosure argument does not apply automatically to the market access issues raised in the *keiretsu* debate. It is necessary to examine the arguments carefully to ascertain when it does.

Vertical (or market) foreclosure occurs when a firm at one stage of production "closes off" a vertically adjacent stage of production to its rivals. Vertical foreclosure involves contracts or agreements between upstream and downstream firms aimed at other firms at either stage (but not both stages, because that would lead to "double marginalization"). Vertical foreclosure can take either of two forms, depending on whether the foreclosing firm is upstream or downstream. *Downstream foreclosure* occurs when an upstream firm enters into contracts with downstream firms with the aim of shutting out other upstream firms from its output market (the downstream input market). *Upstream foreclosure* occurs when a downstream firm enters into contracts with upstream firms with the aim of putting other downstream firms in its output market at a disadvantage by raising the costs of supply of inputs. For instance, a traditional concern in the antitrust literature involves the case of a downstream monopolist foreclosing entry to its market by denying the potential entrant access to an essential input that it controls.

Two market access issues are raised in relation to *keiretsu*. One concerns the alleged closedness of parts-supply systems and intermediate product markets. The second concerns the distribution system. Arguments about the distribution system have been raised at two levels: the final distribution system and the distribution system between firms in intermediate product markets. It is useful to examine these market access issues from the perspective of vertical foreclosure.

The argument that *keiretsu* are exclusionary and limit market access for imported parts and products concerns the allocation of Japanese downstream firm input demand. Foreign exporters complain that Japanese firms allocate their input demands to affiliated suppliers or group-related firms under preferential purchasing arrangements. For instance, in the case of supplier systems (so-called vertical *keiretsu*), much policy pressure has been directed at the downstream assembly firms (e.g., the automakers) to open up their input purchases to foreign parts suppliers. In the case of the presidents' club enterprise groups (financial *keiretsu*), concerns have been expressed about high levels of intragroup trading based on group purchasing preferences. For example, Nissan, a downstream firm, purchases a large part of its glass inputs from Central Glass, and both are members of the Fuyo group presidents' club. In the case of distribution *keiretsu,* much concern is expressed about exclusive trading relationships between manufacturers and downstream affiliated distributors who take all or a large fraction of their inputs from a related upstream manufacturer.

The Japan Fair Trade Commission conducts regular surveys on the extent of within-group trading by the big six enterprise groups. According to the most recent survey, in the 1989 financial year (on average for each grouping), 7.3 percent of the total sales of nonfinancial presidents' club member firms were to other member firms; 8.1 percent of member firm input purchases were from other member firms (table 1). The averages for the Mitsui, Mitsubishi, and Sumitomo groups (the core former *zaibatsu* groups), 11.1 percent of sales and 12.2 percent of input purchases, respectively, were considerably higher than for the Fuyo, Sanwa, and DKB groups, at 4.9 percent and 5.4 percent, respectively.

It is important to note that arguments relating to how Japanese firms allocate their input demands are not issues of foreclosure. A basic principle of a free enterprise market economy is that firms are free to decide how to allocate their input purchases as they see fit, including to their own plants. Indeed, decisions about such issues are key decisions in the firm's competitive arsenal, analogous to decisions about product mix, R&D strategy, human resource management, advertising, and design of decision-making structures. It can be assumed that the firm will seek to allocate these input demands in a cost-minimizing way (adjusted for quality and dynamic considerations). If a given firm exhibits a "preference" for dealing with a particular upstream supplier, presumably it is because that supplier suits its needs well and the firm perceives benefits from the ongoing relationship. Outside observers sometimes term these relationships as "cozy," but management scholars would probably term them "value-adding partnerships" (Johnston and Wallace 1988).

To see more clearly that the market access concerns raised in connection with parts-supply systems and intermediate product markets are not issues of foreclosure, consider the case of the automobile industry. Downstream foreclosure would correspond to the case where suppliers of parts or of material inputs such as glass and steel tried to exercise market power in their output markets by tying up the downstream automakers' input markets and foreclosing them to other suppliers, including foreign ones. In this case it is not the automakers but the upstream suppliers that are keeping foreign supplies out. As noted earlier, it is not in the interest of the automakers to allow upstream firms to monopolize their output markets, as it only serves to raise their costs.

The second possibility is upstream vertical foreclosure by the Japanese automakers. This corresponds to the case where Japanese automakers put their foreign rivals at a disadvantage by not allowing them access to their supply networks. This has not been raised as a serious issue. US automakers are not complaining that Toyota, Nissan, and other Japanese automakers are limiting their ability to compete by discouraging their affiliated suppliers from supplying them. Rather, US parts suppliers are complaining that the Japanese automakers will not buy from them (in sufficient amounts, at least). The US automakers are not complaining that the Japanese glassmakers will not supply them; rather the US glassmakers are complaining that the customers of the Japanese glassmakers will not buy from them. Ironically enough, were Japanese assembly firms to open up their input markets to foreign suppliers by bringing them into their *keiretsu* structures, they would be acting in a way that more closely resembled classic vertical foreclosure behavior.[9]

The arguments about the distribution system, however, correspond more closely to a foreclosure argument and need to be considered more seriously. Distribution refers to various activities associated with the sup-ply of output to customers: either other firms in the case of intermediate product market transactions, or individual consumers in the case of sales of final products. Distribution occurs after production and so can be thought of as being downstream from the seller and upstream from the buyer. Conceptually, however, it more useful to think of distribution as being another kind of input that the seller uses in producing its output.

Viewed in this light, the market access arguments about distribution can be given an interpretation in terms of upstream foreclosure. Upstream foreclosure in this setting would involve Japanese manufacturers using their control of distribution channels to put foreign suppliers at a disadvantage by denying them access to a needed input. Vertical foreclosure concerns about distribution are more acute than those about other inputs such as raw materials or parts, because distribution has in large measure the characteristics of a nontraded good. If Japanese glassmakers or auto parts suppliers refused to supply US automakers, this would not prevent the latter from producing automobiles and attempting to market them in Japan. However, "distribution of outputs in Japan" is not a service that can be acquired in the exporter's home market or in the world market; at least some component must be procured in Japan.

It is unlikely, however, that foreign firms with competitive products could be shut out of the Japanese market through refusal of competing Japanese firms to supply the distribution inputs that they control. The conditions under which vertical foreclosure can occur are strict in theory (Hart and Tirole 1990). Attempts at foreclosure are made difficult by two things. Firms that attempt to foreclose can do so only by denying competitors access to the upstream or downstream units that they control. A firm faced with foreclosure always has the option of mobilizing resources itself, for example, by vertically integrating or by securing its own suppliers or distribution outlets. This means that, except in exceptional circumstances, vertical foreclosure is unlikely to be sustainable in the long run. It is unlikely that a firm with a competitive product (that is, lower

---

9. As should be clear from the earlier discussion, this is not to imply that they could achieve foreclosure or would even be trying to do so. It is only to say that the behavior involved, namely, extending supply relations to rivals' upstream suppliers, would more clearly resemble a foreclosure argument than if downstream firms dedicated their input demand to a particular set of established upstream suppliers.

prices, and therefore lower input costs for customers) will be prevented from entering the market in the long run.

The second factor making it difficult to implement foreclosure strategies is that, as in the earlier example, the interests of upstream and downstream firms are opposed. In downstream foreclosure, the upstream firm enters into contracts with downstream firms to lock out other upstream suppliers. But downstream firms will have incentives to enter into such contracts only if it lowers their costs, which contradicts the assumption that the upstream firm is exercising market power. In the case of upstream foreclosure, the downstream firm may be able to transfer some of the rents it captures in its output market to the monopsonized upstream suppliers. However, the point remains that, if successful, vertical foreclosure strategies must be raising costs at some point in the vertical chain. Downstream firms have no incentives to participate in arrangements that raise their costs, and if they are unwilling victims of such attempts upstream, they have every incentive to switch their input demands to lower cost supplies. Foreclosure, like cartelization, contains the seeds of its own destruction, because if it is successful, monopoly profits must be being earned at some horizontal stage, and these will provide incentives for entry to occur.

Firms enter long-term contracts because they make themselves better off by doing so. There are two ways they can do this, namely, by generating value through lowering joint costs or raising demand (e.g., by increasing quality), or by capturing monopoly rents. It is obvious that firms linked in vertical transactions have incentives to lower costs and raise demand for their outputs. How efficiently the firm acquires its inputs influences the price and quality of its outputs. To a large extent, final producers of assembly goods establish their competitiveness and compete with one another through the design of their production systems, including how they procure inputs. It is misleading to describe this process in antitrust or market closure terms.

While vertically related firms have clear incentives to jointly minimize costs, which leads to an expansion in output, they do not have incentives to exercise joint monopoly power, which must involve a restriction of output. For a firm in a vertical production chain to capture monopoly profits, it has to charge monopoly prices to the purchasers of its outputs or behave as a monopsonist with respect to its input purchasers. Such monopoly gains ultimately can only come from outside the vertical chain; otherwise one party is gaining at the expense of the other, and the arrangement is inherently unstable. But monopolizing vertical chains also tend to be unstable because the extraction of monopoly profits from suppliers or customers itself creates profitable opportunities for new entry. Incentives to engage in cost saving are endemic, but incentives to exercise monopoly power among vertically related firms, unlike among competitors at the same stage of production, are not automatic.

Vertical Organization and Market Access

Although the language of foreclosure is used, the market access concerns raised by *keiretsu* do not appear to be of the traditional market foreclosure kind. Rather they appear to relate to the vertical contractual organization of Japanese firms and not directly related to antitrust issues as such.

At an analytical level, issues relating to *keiretsu* can be thought of as organizational and contracting issues relating to the vertical structure of the firm. Vertical issues in industrial organization have to do with where firms locate their boundaries and how firms organize transactions across those boundaries. A key insight from the industrial organization literature is that the vertical organization of the firm is endogenous in an economic sense. Consider two units in adjacent vertical stages of production or distribution, for example steel production and steel fabrication, or parts production and assembly, or final production and distribution. The two stages could be linked in various ways. At one extreme is vertical integration—the two plants belong to the same firm; at the other extreme are arm's-length contracting or pure-market transactions. In between is a continuum of possible intermediate forms of organization, including the patterns described as *keiretsu*.

The vertical organization of firms and markets in Japan (as elsewhere) reflects the choices that firms have made about where to locate their boundaries and how to structure their transactions there (Katz 1989; Perry 1989; Williamson 1985). Market access concerns can arise purely from differences in the vertical organization of firms and markets. It is important to keep the distinction in mind, because it is blurred by the language that is used. All firms are vertically integrated to a certain extent, and some more than others, but it is only in rare cases that vertical integration has anything to do with vertical market foreclosure (Perry 1989). The same can be said for *keiretsu*. *Keiretsu* have a lot to do with vertical organization but probably little to do with vertical foreclosure. That does not mean that *keiretsu* pose no problems for business managers and trade negotiators who want to see their firm or country have a larger market share in Japan. Rather the market access problem is of a different dimension from either traditional antitrust or traditional trade policy. The market access problems concerning *keiretsu* are better seen as systemic ones stemming from the contracting and organizational choices of firms rather than reflecting strategies at the individual firm level aimed at creating market power. There is just too much competition among existing firms in the market for foreclosure of the antitrust kind to be a plausible argument.

The argument that *keiretsu* ties are exclusionary or based on preferential trading biases, reinforced by interlocking shareholdings, needs to be examined with care. Analytically, *keiretsu* relations are just various forms of long-term contracting or, in some cases, degrees of vertical integration between vertically related firms. A number of points can be noted.

First of all, a distinction needs to be made between the use of the term "exclusionary" in the long-term contracting sense and its use in an antitrust context. By definition, all long-term contracts are exclusionary ex post, when the contract is carried out, because the parties have committed themselves to a certain course of action. For instance, if a parts supplier signs a contract with a parent firm to supply it with goods in the next period, when the next period comes the parent firm cannot unilaterally turn to the spot market without breaching the contract. Spot market suppliers in that period will find themselves excluded from supplying that part of the firm's input demand.

In a world of long-term contracts or transaction arrangements, a clear distinction needs to be made between ex post and ex ante exclusion. Whereas ex post exclusion merely reflects the implementation of long-term contracts, ex ante exclusion means that potential suppliers are prevented from bidding for contracts at the initial stage (or, in the real world, at the recontracting stage). Needless to say, ex ante exclusion is a stronger concept than ex post exclusion and has more serious trade consequences, because it says that new suppliers can never enter. It is an unlikely situation, however, because a downstream firm in a vertical production process has no interest in permanently excluding potential suppliers from competing with its current sources of supply. The downstream firm's interest is in obtaining supply on advantageous terms, which, besides price, include a vector of quality attributes such as low defect rates, reliability, stability of supply, follow-up service, and ability to respond to contingencies. Permanently shielding one's suppliers from potential competition neither makes sense economically nor corresponds to what is known about the way markets operate in Japan. It is true that, when it comes to recontracting—at the time of a model change or retooling, for example—incumbent suppliers will enjoy incumbency advantages due to learning effects, accumulation of goodwill capital, and switching costs. However, this is a general argument about industrial production and does not apply only, or even particularly, to Japan.

The cost-minimizing calculus will not be a static, unidimensional one but rather a dynamic, multidimensional one. A customer firm will not switch to a new supplier in a given period just because a lower price is offered; it will also consider switching costs (sunk investments and learning costs), a vector of quality attributes, and its expectation of the likely future path of costs. A spot market supplier might have to charge a high price next period, making the discounted expected cost over two periods higher than the expected cost if the established supplier is used.

The logic can be illustrated with a simple example. Let e_j and i_j denote the costs of the outside supplier (a new entrant) and the incumbent supplier, respectively, in time period j, where $j = 1, 2$. Suppose that $e_1 < i_1$. In a single time period setting, the parent firm should switch to the new supplier, but it will not necessarily do so in a dynamic, multiperiod setting, which needless to say better captures business reality. It may be that the expected price in the spot market next period, $E(e_2)$, is higher than the expected price of the existing supplier, $E(i_2)$. Allowing for a discount factor δ, a rational parent firm will not switch if $i_1 + \delta E(i_2) < e_1 + \delta E(e_2)$. In this situation it is true algebraically that $e_1 + \delta E(i_2) < i_1 + \delta E(i_2)$; that is, the parent firm would be better off if it could choose the spot market supplier when it offered a lower cost and switch back to the established supplier when it offered a lower cost. This is not likely to be a feasible strategy, however. It can be assumed that the ability of the established supplier to offer a lower price next period is predicated on it being able to transact with the parent company in the current period, reflecting the existence of specific investment effects, learning effects, contract-economizing effects, or incentive or other effects that have been identified in the literature as providing benefits to repeated transactions. The parent firm cannot have its cake and eat it, too.

An important feature of the vertical structure of *keiretsu* and industrial organization in Japan more generally is that firms that have long-term trading ties also tend to hold each other's shares. Firms that expect to have a long-term trading relationship commonly take up minor equity positions (typically less than 1 percent) in each other. But when the small equity positions of a large number of transaction partners are combined with the larger holdings of financial institutions, the result is that the typical Japanese firm is 60 percent owned by firms with which it does business.

Table 3 presents evidence on interlocking shareholdings between Japanese automakers and their suppliers for four important upstream input markets. Three pieces of information are presented: the percentage shareholding that each firm has in the other, the market value of this shareholding, and the market value expressed as a percentage of the value of the automaker's total input purchases or the supplier's sales. The third item has no intrinsic meaning but is presented to provide a measure of relative size from the shareholding firm's perspective. In 70 (55 percent) of the 128 potential relationships, there was evidence of a shareholding relationship, and in more than half of these cases (54 percent) shareholding was in both directions.[10] In 108 (42 percent) of the 256 potential cases,

---

10. Reliable information on supply relationships was available only for the sheet glass industry. In that case, there was clear evidence that cross-shareholdings and transactional ties were correlated. In 9 out of the 10 cases in which there was evidence of a major transactional relationship (the automaker appeared on the firm's list of principal sources of accounts receivable), shareholding relations were in evidence. In only 3 of the 13 cases in which there was no evidence of a major transactional relationship were shareholding relations observed.

Table 3 Interlocking shareholdings between Japanese automakers and their transaction partners[a]

| | Steel makers | | | | | | | | | |
| | Nippon Steel (25.6) | | Nippon Kokan (11.1) | | Kawasaki Steel (10.2) | | Sumitomo Metal (10.2) | | Kobe Steel (5.7) | |
Automaker	Automaker's share in supplier	Supplier's share in automaker	Automaker's share in supplier	Supplier's share in automaker	Automaker's share in supplier	Supplier's share in automaker	Automaker's share in supplier	Supplier's share in automaker	Automaker's share in supplier	Supplier's share in automaker
Toyota (36.4)										
Percent shares	0.29	0.76	0.21	0.28	–	0.13	–	0.40	–	0.22
Market value (in millions of dollars)	69.0	618.6	18.5	227.7	–	102.1	–	322.4	–	182.1
As share of material purchases or sales	0.11	2.87	0.03	1.89	–	1.02	–	3.09	–	1.70
Nissan (19.2)										
Percent shares	0.32	0.99	0.21	0.22	0.40	0.95	–	0.44	0.30	0.26
Market value (in millions of dollars)	75.2	217.5	19.0	48.3	46.2	209.6	–	97.4	23.8	56.2
As share of material purchases or sales	0.29	1.01	0.07	0.40	0.18	2.08	–	0.93	0.09	0.53
Honda (12.4)										
Percent shares	0.10	1.15	–	–	0.04	0.59	–	0.12	–	–
Market value (in millions of dollars)	22.6	193.2	–	–	4.4	99.3	–	20.7	–	–
As share of material purchases or sales	0.15	0.89	–	–	0.03	0.99	–	0.20	–	–
Mitsubishi (10.3)										
Percent shares	–	–	–	–	–	–	–	–	–	–
Market value (in millions of dollars)	–	–	–	–	–	–	–	–	–	–
As share of material purchases or sales	–	–	–	–	–	–	–	–	–	–

(continued on next page)

Table 3 Interlocking shareholdings between Japanese automakers and their transaction partners[a] (continued)

	Steel makers									
	Nippon Steel (25.6)		Nippon Kokan (11.1)		Kawasaki Steel (10.2)		Sumitomo Metal (10.2)		Kobe Steel (5.7)	
Automaker	Automaker's share in supplier	Supplier's share in automaker	Automaker's share in supplier	Supplier's share in automaker	Automaker's share in supplier	Supplier's share in automaker	Automaker's share in supplier	Supplier's share in automaker	Automaker's share in supplier	Supplier's share in automaker
Mazda (8.3)										
Percent share	0.05	0.54	—	—	—	0.46	0.03	0.53	0.04	0.19
Market value (in millions of dollars)	11.2	28.9	—	—	—	24.8	2.8	28.7	2.8	10.3
As share of material purchases or sales	0.08	0.13	—	—	—	0.25	0.02	0.28	0.02	0.10
Suzuki (5.0)										
Percent shares	—	—	—	—	—	—	—	0.51	—	—
Market value (in millions of dollars)	—	—	—	—	—	—	—	30.1	—	—
As share of material purchases or sales	—	—	—	—	—	—	—	0.29	—	—
Fuji H.I. (4.3)										
Percent shares	0.04	0.53	0.06	0.70	—	—	—	—	—	—
Market value (in millions of dollars)	10.5	12.2	4.9	16.1	—	—	—	—	—	—
As share of material purchases or sales	0.20	0.06	0.09	0.13	—	—	—	—	—	—
Daihatsu (4.1)										
Percent shares	—	—	—	—	—	—	—	—	—	—
Market value (in millions of dollars)	—	—	—	—	—	—	—	—	—	—
As share of material purchases or sales	—	—	—	—	—	—	—	—	—	—

Sheet glass suppliers

Automaker	Asahi Glass (48.0)		Nippon Sheet Glass (32.0)		Central Glass (20.0)	
	Automaker's share in supplier	Supplier's share in automaker	Automaker's share in supplier	Supplier's share in automaker	Automaker's share in supplier	Supplier's share in automaker
Toyota						
Percent shares	0.85	0.48	2.19	0.22	—	—
Market value (in millions of dollars)	108.0	391.7	52.7	175.8	—	—
As share of material purchases or sales	0.17	4.06	0.08	8.19	—	—
Nissan						
Percent shares	0.32	0.41	1.17	0.26	7.80	0.43
Market value (in millions of dollars)	41.0	91.0	28.2	56.5	69.3	94.2
As share of material purchases or sales	0.16	0.94	0.11	2.63	0.26	6.34
Honda						
Percent shares	0.07	0.51	—	—	—	—
Market value (in millions of dollars)	9.3	85.3	—	—	—	—
As share of material purchases or sales	0.06	0.88	—	—	—	—
Mitsubishi						
Percent shares	0.15	0.82	—	—	—	—
Market value (in millions of dollars)	19.0	61.6	—	—	—	—
As share of material purchases or sales	0.12	0.64	—	—	—	—

(continued on next page)

Table 3 Interlocking shareholdings between Japanese automakers and their transaction partners[a] (continued)

Automaker	Sheet glass suppliers					
	Asahi Glass (48.0)		Nippon Sheet Glass (32.0)		Central Glass (20.0)	
	Automaker's share in supplier	Supplier's share in automaker	Automaker's share in supplier	Supplier's share in automaker	Automaker's share in supplier	Supplier's share in automaker
Mazda						
Percent shares	—	—	0.78	0.54	—	—
Market value (in millions of dollars)	—	—	18.9	28.9	—	—
As share of material purchases or sales	—	—	0.14	1.35	—	—
Suzuki						
Percent shares	—	—	—	—	0.26	0.47
Market value (in millions of dollars)	—	—	—	—	2.0	27.7
As share of material purchases or sales	—	—	—	—	0.03	1.86
Fuji H.I.						
Percent shares	—	—	0.15	0.21	0.63	0.25
Market value (in millions of dollars)	—	—	3.7	4.9	5.6	5.8
As share of material purchases or sales	—	—	0.07	0.23	0.11	0.39
Daihatsu						
Percent shares	0.03	—	—	—	—	—
Market value (in millions of dollars)	3.4	—	—	—	—	—
As share of material purchases or sales	0.08	—	—	—	—	—

Tire suppliers

Automaker	Bridgestone (46.4)		Yokohama Rubber (20.0)		Sumitomo Rubber (13.8)		Toyo Rubber (12.0)	
	Automaker's share in supplier	Supplier's share in automaker	Automaker's share in supplier	Supplier's share in automaker	Automaker's share in supplier	Supplier's share in automaker	Automaker's share in supplier	Supplier's share in automaker
Toyota								
Percent shares	0.52	0.04	0.98	0.13	—	0.04	4.56	0.12
Market value (in millions of dollars)	49.9	31.5	15.2	106.4	—	33.5	39.3	98.7
As share of material purchases or sales	0.08	0.50	0.02	4.12	—	1.41	0.06	5.27
Nissan								
Percent shares	—	0.14	0.20	—	—	0.03	2.50	0.21
Market value (in millions of dollars)	—	31.9	—	44.8	—	5.9	21.5	47.0
As share of material purchases or sales	—	—	—	1.73	—	0.25	0.08	2.51
Honda								
Percent shares	0.03	0.30	0.33	0.16	0.73	0.17	—	—
Market value (in millions of dollars)	2.5	49.6	5.1	27.0	11.4	27.7	—	—
As share of material purchases or sales	0.02	0.79	0.3	1.05	0.08	1.17	—	—
Mitsubishi								
Percent shares	—	0.06	0.28	0.15	—	—	—	0.02
Market value (in millions of dollars)	—	4.4	4.3	11.4	—	—	—	0.9
As share of material purchases or sales	—	0.07	0.03	0.44	—	—	—	0.05

(continued on next page)

Table 3 Interlocking shareholdings between Japanese automakers and their transaction partners[a] (continued)

	Tire suppliers							
	Bridgestone (46.4)		Yokohama Rubber (20.0)		Sumitomo Rubber (13.8)		Toyo Rubber (12.0)	
Automaker	Automaker's share in supplier	Supplier's share in automaker	Automaker's share in supplier	Supplier's share in automaker	Automaker's share in supplier	Supplier's share in automaker	Automaker's share in supplier	Supplier's share in automaker
Mazda								
Percent shares	–	0.43	0.14	0.09	–	0.01	–	–
Market value (in millions of dollars)	–	23.1	2.1	5.0	–	0.6	–	–
As share of material purchases or sales	–	0.37	0.02	0.19	–	0.02	–	–
Suzuki								
Percent shares	–	0.28	0.11	0.18	–	0.04	–	–
Market value (in millions of dollars)	–	16.4	1.8	10.8	–	2.1	–	–
As share of material purchases or sales	–	0.26	0.02	0.42	–	0.09	–	–
Fuji H.I.								
Percent shares	–	0.67	–	0.06	–	–	–	–
Market value (in millions of dollars)	–	15.3	–	1.3	–	–	–	–
As share of material purchases or sales	–	0.24	–	0.05	–	–	–	–
Daihatsu								
Percent shares	–	0.47	–	–	–	–	–	0.07
Market value (in millions of dollars)	–	10.3	–	–	–	–	–	1.5
As share of material purchases or sales	–	0.16	–	–	–	–	–	0.08

Paint suppliers

Automaker	Kansai Paint (21.3)		Nippon Paint (20.3)		Dainippon Paint (8.2)		Shinto Paint (4.5)	
	Automaker's share in supplier	Supplier's share in automaker	Automaker's share in supplier	Supplier's share in automaker	Automaker's share in supplier	Supplier's share in automaker	Automaker's share in supplier	Supplier's share in automaker
Toyota								
Percent shares	2.99	0.03	1.93	0.05	–	–	–	0.003
Market value (in millions of dollars)	40.3	23.2	31.0	44.2	–	–	–	2.8
As share of material purchases or sales	0.06	1.49	0.05	2.96	–	–	–	0.73
Nissan								
Percent shares	–	–	0.93	0.06	–	–	–	0.002
Market value (in millions of dollars)	–	–	15.0	12.8	–	–	–	0.5
As share of material purchases or sales	–	–	0.06	0.86	–	–	–	0.13
Honda								
Percent shares	–	–	–	0.06	–	0.04	–	0.001
Market value (in millions of dollars)	–	–	–	10.4	–	7.0	–	0.2
As share of material purchases or sales	–	–	–	0.70	–	11.2	–	0.45
Mitsubishi								
Percent shares	–	–	–	–	–	0.003	–	–
Market value (in millions of dollars)	–	–	–	–	–	0.3	–	–
As share of material purchases or sales	–	–	–	–	–	0.44	–	–

(continued on next page)

Table 3 Interlocking shareholdings between Japanese automakers and their transaction partners^a (continued)

	Paint suppliers							
	Kansai Paint (21.3)		Nippon Paint (20.3)		Dainippon Paint (8.2)		Shinto Paint (4.5)	
Automaker	Automaker's share in supplier	Supplier's share in automaker	Automaker's share in supplier	Supplier's share in automaker	Automaker's share in supplier	Supplier's share in automaker	Automaker's share in supplier	Supplier's share in automaker
Mazda								
Percent shares	–	–	0.38	0.21	–	–	–	–
Market value (in millions of dollars)	–	–	6.1	11.6	–	–	–	–
As share of material purchases or sales	–	–	0.04	0.77	–	–	–	–
Suzuki								
Percent shares	–	–	–	0.05	–	–	–	–
Market value (in millions of dollars)	–	–	–	3.1	–	–	–	–
As share of material purchases or sales	–	–	–	0.21	–	–	–	–
Fuji H.I.								
Percent shares	–	–	–	0.03	–	–	–	0.001
Market value (in millions of dollars)	–	–	–	0.8	–	–	–	0.03
As share of material purchases or sales	–	–	–	0.05	–	–	–	0.07

Daihatsu							
Percent shares	0.21	—	—	—	—	—	—
Market value (in millions of dollars)	2.9	—	—	—	—	—	—
As share of material purchases or sales	0.07	—	—	—	—	—	—

— = the other firm does not appear in that firm's list of principal shareholdings.

a. Market values are calculated using an average of the high and low share price of firm in the last month of fiscal 1993 using an exchange rate of US$1=¥100. The market value of shareholdings are shown as percentages of total material purchases for automaker's shareholdings and of total sales for other firms. Numbers in parentheses are market shares.

Sources: Yuka shoken hokokusho soran, No. 16-21 (Toyota Jidosha Kabushiki Kaisha), No. 16-19 (Nissan Jidosha Kabushiki Kaisha), No. 16-35 (Honda Giken Kogyo Kabushiki Kaisha), No. 16-30 (Matsuda Kabushiki Kaisha), No. 16-92 (Mitsubishi Jidosha Kogyo Kabushiki Kaisha), No. 16-37 (Fuji Juko Kogyo Kabushiki Kaisha), No. 16-36 (Suzuki Kabushiki Kaisha), No. 16-31 (Daihatsu Kogyo Kabushiki Kaisha), No. 10-1 (Asahi Garasu Kabushiki Kaisha), No. 10-2 (Nippon Ita Garasu Kabushiki Kaisha), No. 7-22 (Sentoraru Garasu Kabushiki Kaisha), No. 9-8 (Kabushiki Kaisha Burijisuton), No. 9-1 (Yokohama Gomu Kabushiki Kaisha), No. 9-16 (Sumitomo Gomu Kogyo Kabushiki Kaisha), No. 7-72 (Kansai Peinto Kabushiki Kaisha), No. 7-71 (Nippon Peinto Kabushiki Kaisha), No. 7-70 (Dainippon Toryo Kabushiki Kaisha), No. 7-123 (Shinto Toryo Kabushiki Kaisha), Okurasho Insatsukyoku, Tokyo, 1994 (fiscal 1993 corporate financial reports of companies); Nihon Keizai Shinbunsha, 1993: *Shijo senyuritsu '94* (Market shares '94), Tokyo, Nihon Keizai Shinbunsha; Nihon Keizai Shinbunsha, 1994: *Nikkei kaisha joho '94-IV shugo* (Nikkei company information, 1994 4th quarter autumn edition), Nihon Keizai Shinbun, Tokyo.

there was evidence of shareholding. The shareholdings were typically minor in percentage terms: less than 1 percent in 100 out of 108 cases (93 percent) and less than half a percent in 81 cases (75 percent).

Interlocking shareholding among trading partners is closely related to the Japanese system of corporate governance (Berglof and Perotti 1994 and Sheard 1994a). In effect, the system of interlocking shareholdings and main bank relations creates a situation where the stakeholders in a large Japanese firm constitute a latent corporate governance coalition, able collectively to block hostile takeover bids by external parties but also able to exercise corporate control rights if circumstances require.

Whether interlocking shareholdings have an effect on purchasing behavior is a subtle issue. Japanese businessmen claim that share interlocks help to cement business relations and support long-term transactions: in a recent survey, 27.0 percent of listed firms surveyed cited "long-term stabilization of business transactions" as the most important merit of interlocking shareholdings, and an additional 69.4 percent viewed it as an important merit (Fuji Research Institute Corporation 1993, 106). Interlocking shareholdings may result in trading biases, although the magnitudes involved seem too small to have other than fairly marginal effects (Flath 1992).

Even if there is a trading bias, however, this does not mean that such practices are anticompetitive or unfair to other firms (Flath 1994). Following the earlier logic, the aim of interlocking shareholdings must be to lower the costs of doing business; otherwise firms would not have a positive incentive to engage in them. To the extent that share interlocks create lock-in effects, it is the logic of long-term contracting and commitment that applies rather than antitrust. Any lock-in effects of vertical interlocking shareholdings must be anticipated and factored into the intertemporal calculus of the costs and benefits of doing business.

There exists an important distinction, not sufficiently stressed in the literature on economic organization, between final and intermediate product markets, that is relevant to the issues raised in the market access debate. For all intents and purposes, we can take the set of final goods markets as given (by technology and consumer preferences). Whether these markets are open or closed is an important trade policy issue. For advocates of free trade, the existence of a closed market is cause for concern, and arguments justifying closure (such as those marshalled to justify protection of the Japanese rice market) are viewed with a healthy dose of skepticism, if not antipathy.

The situation for intermediate product markets is quite different. Issues of access to intermediate as opposed to final goods, markets are complicated, because whether and in what form an intermediate market exists depends on where and how the entities we call firms have located their boundaries, *and* on what goes on at that boundary in the contracting between firms. An intermediate market may fail to exist, or to be visible as an "open market," because upstream firms have internalized (vertically integrated across) that stage of the vertical production chain, or it may exist but depart from the arm's-length interactions that characterize relations between buyers and sellers in final goods markets. That a market may be "closed" may be more a statement about the extent and nature of vertical integration than about barriers to trade of the kind that traditionally concern advocates of free trade.

A stylized example, abstracting from the particular structures of *keiretsu*, highlights the key point that intermediate markets reflect the vertical organization of firms. Consider a production process comprising three stages—parts production, subassembly, and final assembly—and compare the structure of the industry in two countries. Suppose that in country A final producers purchase parts and carry out subassembly and final assembly in-house, whereas in country J final producers specialize in final assembly and purchase subassemblies from suppliers that are integrated over subassembly and parts production. In this case the degree of vertical integration is the same in both countries, but the intermediate product markets differ. In country A the intermediate product market is for parts, whereas in country J it is for subassemblies. The degree of vertical integration and the location of firms' boundaries influence whether a given intermediate good is transferred to the downstream stage internally or between firms as a market transaction.

The implications of differences in vertical organization for international trade and market access are immediately apparent. Suppose that parts suppliers in country A want to export their output to country J; they would find that the intermediate product market was internalized or "closed," and similar circumstances exist for producers of subassemblies in country J, should they attempt to export to country A. To say that an intermediate product market is closed in this way is quite different from saying that a final product market is closed. Market access concerns about *keiretsu* seem to be mainly issues of this kind, relating to differences in vertical contractual organization, that is, differences in the mechanisms used to coordinate the production process, rather than vertical foreclosure in the antitrust sense.

Actual comparisons of the openness or closedness of intermediate product markets in national economies are more complicated. To say which system is more open or closed requires a reckoning not only of how transactions are structured at the boundary of the firm—say, between arm's-length and long-term contracting—but of how extensive the internal organization of the firm is as well. For example, it is well known that US automakers are more vertically integrated than Japanese automakers and that interfirm relations for the former are more arm's-length and for the latter more long-term oriented. Dyer (1993) presents some interesting data on this: he finds that 48 percent of total component cost is internal for US automakers, versus 27 percent for Japan, but that for

Japanese makers 38 percent of cost is accounted for by partner suppliers as against 18 percent for the United States; Japanese automakers utilize arm's-length suppliers for 35 percent and US makers for 42 percent. On this reckoning, the level of openness (crudely measured) of the two systems is roughly comparable. Absent comparable data for the whole range of industrial sectors, it may be premature to conclude that the level of closedness of the Japanese economy—measured in terms of tightness of vertical links—is more or less than that of other economies.

Failure to distinguish between arguments at the level of the firm and at the level of the industry or the overall economy is a source of confusion in the market access debate. Arguments about *keiretsu* are arguments at the firm level, that is, about the way individual firms have structured their input, output, and financial contracts. Arguments about market access, however, are pitched at the aggregate level of the market or the economy as a whole. Arguments about *keiretsu* and market closure confuse the two. To say that, by preferentially allocating its purchases to a given set of *keiretsu* suppliers, a firm "closes the market" to outside suppliers is misleading, because a single firm, in allocating its demand for inputs, can "control" only that part of the market that relates to its own purchases. It is meaningless to say that an individual firm "closes the market" when it allocates its input demand to certain suppliers; it does not control "the market," but only its own purchases. At this level of analysis, "closing the market" and "procuring its inputs" are just two ways of describing the same thing, as are, from the viewpoint of a supplier, "failing to win the deal" and "being denied access."

Market access concerns at the firm level appear misguided. When an individual firm allocates its input demand (including its demand for distribution inputs), it is not closing the market; rather it is organizing its production and distribution system, and presumably doing so in a cost-minimizing way. It might allocate that demand by deciding to produce the input itself, it might rely on arm's-length transactions, or it might attempt to secure a long-term supply under a long-term contract or under a regime conducive to continuous transactions.

Aggregating up to the industry level, however, presents a somewhat different picture, and this is the level at which trade negotiators operate. It is easy to understand foreign frustration with the degree of openness of access to Japanese intermediate product markets when potential sellers observe the entire population of potential buyers tied up in long-term contracts or enjoying established incumbency advantages. This defines a challenge for business, however, more than an agenda for politicians and trade negotiators.

A final point to note, relating to the distinction between intermediate and final product markets, is that even if, because of decisions about procurement and organizational design, intermediate product markets are closed to foreign suppliers, it does not mean that suppliers are excluded from the market. As long as the final market is open they are able, in principle, to access the final market through supply relations with other firms. The demand for parts or intermediate products is a derived demand; that is, demand for the input derives from the demand that exists for the final product. Even if foreign parts makers are excluded from supplying Japanese automakers because of the structure of Japanese parts supply systems, they are not necessarily excluded from the final market. They can supply the final market as long as they can supply other downstream firms selling into the final market. It is the relative loss of market share by the firms that they traditionally supplied, rather than the exclusionary behavior of Japanese automakers, that lies at the root of foreign parts suppliers' calls to open the Japanese market. These in effect are demands for their competitors in the Japanese parts supply market to give up part of their market share through trade deals rather than competition. Japanese automakers are not competing with US parts suppliers; Japanese parts suppliers are. That is not to deny that there is room for policy measures to improve market access for foreign suppliers. It is merely to say that government interference in how firms structure their procurement systems and interfirm ties does not qualify as one of them.

Conclusion

This chapter has attempted to clarify the arguments surrounding *keiretsu*, competition, and access to the Japanese market. The key argument is that *keiretsu* rest on vertical and financial ties that reflect the organization of firms and markets in Japan. Despite the frequent use of terms such as "cartel-like" and "collusive" to describe them, *keiretsu* are not anticompetitive and have nothing to do with price-fixing. Market access concerns about *keiretsu* reflect the vertical organization of firms and intermediate product markets and the way in which firms have structured their input transactions. Vertical foreclosure due to *keiretsu* does not appear to be a serious concern, even in distribution markets, where the vertical foreclosure argument carries most force. It is more fruitful to regard *keiretsu* as reflecting the way that firms have structured their boundaries and organized their interfirm transactions to achieve competitive advantage, involving relationships with financiers, with input suppliers, trading companies, and distributors, and with customer firms, all of which participate in corporate governance through cross-holdings of equity. It may be convenient to apply the language of trade policy and negotiation to *keiretsu*, but it is not correct. The markets that are closed to new entrants because of *keiretsu* ties are markets that, in the main, need to be pried open by the excluded firms themselves, not by government officials. Japanese firms have no sensible interest in shielding their suppliers from foreign competition. They do not need Japanese or US government officials to guide them to make cost-minimizing input purchase decisions. There may be good reasons to increase foreign access to the Japanese market. The justification for these actions, however, must lie elsewhere than in the anticompetitive and market foreclosure rhetoric in which they are clothed.

References

Abegglen, James C., and George Stalk Jr. 1985. *Kaisha, The Japanese Corporation*. Tokyo: Charles E. Tuttle.

Aoki, Masahiko. 1994. "The Japanese Firm as a System of Attributes: A Survey and Research Agenda." In Masahiko Aoki and Ronald Dore, *The Japanese Firm: The Sources of Competitive Strength*. Oxford, UK: Oxford University Press.

Aoki, Masahiko, Hugh Patrick, and Paul Sheard. 1994. "The Japanese Main Bank System: An Introductory Overview." In Masahiko Aoki and Hugh Patrick, *The Japanese Main Bank System: Its Relevancy for Developing and Transforming Economies*. Oxford, UK: Oxford University Press.

Ariga, Kenn, Yasushi Ohkusa, and Hisashi Namikawa. 1991. "The Japanese Distribution System." *Ricerche Economiche* 45, nos. 2-3: 185-230.

Beason, Richard. 1994. "Keiretsu Affiliation and Share Price Volatility in Japan." Bank of Japan, Tokyo. Photocopy.

Berglof, Erik, and Enrico Perotti. 1994. "The Governance Structure of the Japanese Financial Keiretsu." *Journal of Financial Economics* 36: 259-84.

Bergsten, C. Fred, and Marcus Noland. 1993. *Reconcilable Differences? United States–Japan Economic Conflict*. Washington: Institute for International Economics.

Chusho Kigyocho (Small and Medium Enterprise Agency). 1994. *Dai 6kai shogyo jittai kihon chosa hokokusho-heisei 4nen 10gatsu 1nichi genzaishirabe-sokuho* (Report on the 6th Basic Survey of Commercial Structure and Activity, as of October 1, 1992, Preliminary Report). Tokyo: Chusho Kigyocho.

Demsetz, Harold. 1992. "How Many Cheers for Antitrust's 100 Years?" *Economic Inquiry* 30: 207-17.

Dick, Andrew R. 1992. "The Competitive Consequences of Japan's Export Cartel Associations." *Journal of the Japanese and International Economies* 6, no. 3: 275-98.

Dore, Ronald. 1986. *Flexible Rigidities: Industrial Policy and Structural Adjustment in the Japanese Economy 1971–80*. Stanford, CA: Stanford University Press.

Dornbusch, Rudiger W. 1990. "Policy Options for Freer Trade: The Case for Bilateralism." In Robert Z. Lawrence and Charles L. Schultze, *An American Trade Strategy: Options for the 1990s*. Washington: Brookings Institution.

Dyer, Jeffrey H. 1993. "The Japanese Vertical *Keiretsu* as a Source of Competitive Advantage." University of Pennsylvania, Philadelphia. Photocopy.

Ferris, Stephen P., and Atulya Sarin. 1993. "The Role of Corporate Groupings in Controlling Agency Conflicts: The Case of *Keiretsu*." University of Missouri, Columbia. Photocopy.

Flath, David. 1989. "Vertical Restraints in Japan." *Japan and the World Economy* 1: 187-203.

Flath, David. 1992. "The *Keiretsu* Puzzle." North Carolina State University, Raleigh. Photocopy.

Flath, David. 1994. "*Keiretsu* Shareholding Ties: Antitrust Issues." *Contemporary Economic Policy* 12, no. 1: 24-36.

Fruin, W. Mark. 1992. *The Japanese Enterprise System: Cooperative Structures and Competitive Strategies*. Oxford, UK: Clarendon Press.

Fuji Research Institute Corporation. 1993. *Meinbanku shisutemu oyobi kabushiki mochiai' ni tsuite no chosa hokokusho* (Investigative Report on the Main Bank System and Interlocking Shareholdings). Tokyo.

Fung, K. C. 1991. "Characteristics of Japanese Industrial Groups and Their Potential Impact on U.S.-Japan Trade." In Robert Baldwin, *Empirical Studies of Commercial Policy.* Chicago: University of Chicago Press.

Gerlach, Michael L. 1992. *Alliance Capitalism: The Social Organization of Japanese Business.* Berkeley: University of California Press.

Gilson, Ronald J., and Mark J. Roe. 1993. "Understanding the Japanese Keiretsu: Overlaps Between Corporate Governance and Industrial Organization." *Yale Law Journal* 102: 871-906.

Goto, Akira. 1982. "Business Groups in a Market Economy." *European Economic Review* 19: 53-70.

Goto, Akira, and Kotaro Suzumura. 1994. "Keiretsu Inter-firm Relationship in Japan." Hitotsubashi University. Photocopy.

Hart, Oliver, and Jean Tirole. 1990. "Vertical Integration and Market Foreclosure." *Brookings Papers: Microeconomics 1990.* Washington: Brookings Institution.

Hoshi, Takeo. 1994. "The Economic Role of Corporate Groupings and the Main Bank System." In Masahiko Aoki and Ronald Dore, *The Japanese Firm: The Sources of Competitive Strength.* Oxford, UK: Oxford University Press.

Hoshi, Takeo, Anil Kashyap, and David Scharfstein. 1990a. "Bank Monitoring and Investment: Evidence from the Changing Structure of Japanese Corporate Banking Relationships." In R. Glenn Hubbard, *Asymmetric Information, Corporate Finance and Investment.* Chicago: University of Chicago Press.

Hoshi, Takeo, Anil Kashyap, and David Scharfstein. 1990b. "The Role of Banks in Reducing the Costs of Financial Distress in Japan." *Journal of Financial Economics* 27, no. 1: 67-88.

Hoshi, Takeo, Anil Kashyap, and David Scharfstein. 1991. "Corporate Structure, Liquidity and Investment: Evidence from Japanese Panel Data." *Quarterly Journal of Economics* 106: 33-60.

Itoh, Motoshige. 1992. "Organizational Transactions and Access to the Japanese Import Market." In Paul Sheard, *International Adjustment and the Japanese Firm.* St. Leonards, Australia: Allen & Unwin.

Jacquemin, Alexis, and Margaret E. Slade. 1989. "Cartels, Collusion, and Horizontal Merger." In Richard Schmalensee and Robert D. Willig, *Handbook of Industrial Organization,* vol. 1. Amsterdam: North-Holland.

Johnson, Chalmers. 1987. "How to Think About Economic Competition from Japan." In Kenneth B. Pyle, *The Trade Crisis: How Will Japan Respond?* Seattle: Society for Japanese Studies.

Johnson, Chalmers. 1990a. "Trade, Revisionism, and the Future of Japanese-American Relations." In Kozo Yamamura, *Japan's Economic Structure: Should It Change?* Seattle: Society for Japanese Studies.

Johnson, Chalmers. 1990b. "*Keiretsu*: An Outsider's View." *International Economic Insights* 1, no. 2: 15-17.

Johnston, K., and P. Wallace. 1988. "Beyond Vertical Integration: The Rise of the Value-Adding Partnership." *Harvard Business Review* (July-August): 94-101.

Kang, Jun-Koo, and Anil Shivdasani. 1994. "Firm Performance, Corporate Governance, and Top Executive Turnover in Japan." Draft. Michigan State University, East Lansing.

Kaplan, Steven N. 1994. "Top Executive Rewards and Firm Performance: A Comparison of Japan and the United States." *Journal of Political Economy* 102, no. 3: 510-46.

Kaplan, Steven N., and Bernadette Alcamo Minton. 1994. "Appointments of Outsiders to Japanese Corporate Boards: Determinants and Implications for Managers." *Journal of Financial Economics* 36, no. 2: 225-58.

Kato, Takao. 1994. "Chief Executive Compensation and Corporate Groups in Japan: New Evidence from Micro Data." Colgate University, Hamilton, NY. Photocopy.

Kato, Kiyoshi, and James S. Schallheim. 1993. "Private Equity Financings in Japan and Corporate Grouping (Keiretsu)." *Pacific-Basin Finance Journal* 1: 287-307.

Katz, Michael L. 1989. "Vertical Contractual Relations." In Richard Schmalensee and Robert Willig, *Handbook of Industrial Organization*, vol. 1. Amsterdam: North-Holland.

Keizai Chosa Kyokai. 1992. *Nenpo "Keiretsu no kenkyu" dai32shu (1992): daiichibu jojo kigyohen* [Corporate Affiliation Research Annual, no. 32 (1992): First-Section Listed Firm Edition]. Tokyo.

Komiya, Ryutaro. 1990. *The Japanese Economy: Trade, Industry, and Government.* Tokyo: University of Tokyo Press.

Kosei Torihiki Iinkai (Fair Trade Commission). 1992. *Heisei 4 nenban Kosei Torihiki Iinkai nenji hokoku (dokusen kinshi hakusho)* (1992 Fair Trade Commission Annual Report: The Antimonopoly White Paper). Tokyo: Okurasho Insatsukyoku.

Kosei Torihiki Iinkai (Fair Trade Commission). 1993a. *"Joyosha no ryutsu jittai chosa"* (Report on the State of Passenger Vehicle Distribution). Tokyo.

Kosei Torihiki Iinkai (Fair Trade Commission). 1993b. "Ita garasu no ryutsu ni kansuru kigyokan torihiki no jittai chosa" (Report on the State of Interfirm Transactions Relating to Sheet Glass Distribution). Tokyo.

Kreinen, Mordechai E. 1988. "How Closed Is Japan's Market? Additional Evidence." *World Economy* 11: 529-42.

Krugman, Paul, ed. 1991. *Trade with Japan: Has the Door Opened Wider?* Chicago: University of Chicago Press.

Lawrence, Robert Z. 1991a. "Efficient or Exclusionist? The Import Behavior of Japanese Corporate Groups." *Brookings Papers on Economic Activity* 1: 311-41.

Lawrence, Robert Z. 1991b. "How Open Is Japan?" In Paul Krugman, *Trade with Japan: Has the Door Opened Wider?* Chicago: University of Chicago Press.

Lawrence, Robert Z. 1993. "Japan's Different Trade Regime: An Analysis with Particular Reference to *Keiretsu*." *Journal of Economic Perspectives* 7, no. 3: 3-19.

Lincoln, Edward J. 1990. *Japan's Unequal Trade.* Washington: Brookings Institution.

McKenzie, Colin. 1992. "Stable Shareholdings and the Role of Japanese Life Insurance Companies." In Paul Sheard, *International Adjustment and the Japanese Firm.* St. Leonards, Australia: Allen & Unwin.

McMillan, John. 1991. "*Dango*: Japan's Price-Fixing Conspiracies." *Economics and Philosophy* 3: 201-18.

Miwa, Yoshiro, and Kiyohiko Nishimura, eds. 1992. *Nihon no ryutsu* (Japanese Distribution). Tokyo: University of Tokyo Press.

Miyazaki, Yoshikazu. 1967. "Rapid Economic Growth in Post-War Japan: With Special Reference to 'Excessive Competition' and the Formation of '*Keiretsu*.' " *The Developing Economies* 5, no. 2: 329-50.

Morck, Randall, and Masao Nakamura. 1992. "Banks and Corporate Control in Japan." Photocopy. University of Alberta, Edmonton.

Nakatani, Iwao. 1984. "The Economic Role of Financial Corporate Grouping." In Masahiko Aoki, *The Economic Analysis of the Japanese Firm.* Amsterdam: North-Holland.

Nelson, Andrew N. 1974. *The Modern Reader's Japanese-English Character Dictionary.* Rutland, VT, and Tokyo: Charles E. Tuttle.

Nihon Keizai Shinbunsha. 1994. *Nikkei kaisha joho '94-IV shugo* (Nikkei Company Information, 1994 4th Quarter Autumn Edition). Tokyo.

Nishiguchi, Toshihiro. 1994. *Strategic Industrial Sourcing.* New York: Oxford University Press.

Noland, Marcus. 1992. "Public Policy, Private Preferences, and the Japanese Trade Pattern." Washington: Institute for International Economics.

Office of the United States Trade Representative. 1989. *1989 National Trade Estimate Report on Foreign Trade Barriers.* Washington: Government Printing Office.

Okazaki, Tetsuji. 1994. "Relationship Between Government and Firm in the Post WWII Economic Recovery: Policy of Industrial Rationalization and Firm." University of Tokyo.

Pearce, David W. 1992. *The MIT Dictionary of Modern Economics*, 4th ed. Cambridge, MA: MIT Press.

Perry, Martin K. 1989. "Vertical Integration: Determinants and Effects." In Richard Schmalensee and Robert Willig, *Handbook of Industrial Organization*, vol. 1. Amsterdam: North-Holland.

Petri, Peter. 1991. "Market Structure, Comparative Advantage, and Japanese Trade Under the Strong Yen." In Paul Krugman, *Trade with Japan: Has the Door Opened Wider?* Chicago: University of Chicago Press.

Pickens, Boone. 1992. "How to Compete with the Japanese—And Win." *Business Week* (17 February): 5.

Prowse, Stephen D. 1992. "The Structure of Corporate Ownership in Japan." *Journal of Financial Economics* 47, no. 3: 1121-40.

Rasmusen, Eric B., J. Mark Ramseyer, and John S. Wiley Jr. 1991. "Naked Exclusion." *American Economic Review* 81, no. 5: 1137-45.

Sako, Mari. 1992. *Prices, Quality and Trust: Inter-firm Relations in Britain and Japan.* Cambridge, UK: Cambridge University Press.

Saxonhouse, Gary R. 1991a. "Comments and Discussion." *Brookings Papers on Economic Activity* 1331-36.

Saxonhouse, Gary R. 1991b. "Comment." In Paul Krugman, *Trade with Japan: Has the Door Opened Wider?* Chicago: University of Chicago Press.

Saxonhouse, Gary R. 1993. "What Does Japanese Trade Structure Tell Us About Japanese Trade Policy?" *Journal of Economic Perspectives* 7, no. 3: 21-43.

Sheard, Paul. 1991. "The Economics of Japanese Corporate Organization and the 'Structural Impediments' Debate: A Critical Review." *Japanese Economic Studies* 19, no. 4: 30-78.

Sheard, Paul. 1992. *Keiretsu and Closedness of the Japanese Market: An Economic Appraisal.* Institute of Social and Economic Research Discussion Papers 273. Osaka University.

Sheard, Paul. 1994a. "Interlocking Shareholding and Corporate Governance." In Masahiko Aoki and Ronald Dore, *The Japanese Firm: The Sources of Competitive Strength.* Oxford, UK: Oxford University Press.

Sheard, Paul. 1994b. "The Role of Government in Different Market Economy Systems: Observations from the Japanese Case." In *Papers and Proceedings of the Eleventh ERI International Symposium, International Comparison of the Systems of Market Economy.* Tokyo: Economic Research Institute, Economic Planning Agency, Government of Japan.

Sheard, Paul. 1994c. "Bank Executives on Japanese Corporate Boards." *Bank of Japan Monetary and Economic Studies* 12, no. 2.

Sheard, Paul. 1994d. "Main Banks and the Governance of Financial Distress." In Masahiko Aoki and Hugh Patrick, *The Japanese Main Bank System: Its Relevancy for Developing and Transforming Economies.* New York: Oxford University Press.

Sheard, Paul. 1994e. "Long-termism and the Japanese Firm." In Mitsuaki Okabe, *The Japanese Economy in Transition.* New York: Macmillan.

Smitka, Michael J. 1991. *Competitive Ties: Subcontracting in the Japanese Automobile Industry.* New York: Columbia University Press.

Taira, Koji. 1993. Review of Koji Matsumoto, *The Rise of the Japanese Corporate System: The Inside View of a MITI Official. Journal of Economic Literature* 31, no. 2: 918-20.

Tirole, Jean. 1989. *The Theory of Industrial Organization.* Cambridge, MA: MIT Press.

Toyo Keizai Shinposha. 1991. *Kigyo keiretsu soran 1992nenban* (Corporate affiliation directory, 1992 edition). Tokyo.

Toyo Keizai Shinposha. 1992. *Kigyo keiretsu soran 1993nenban* (Corporate Affiliation Directory, 1993 edition). Tokyo.

Tyson, Laura D'Andrea, and John Zysman. 1989a. "Preface: The Argument Outlined." In

Chalmers Johnson, Laura D'Andrea Tyson, and John Zysman, *Politics and Productivity: The Real Story of Why Japan Works*. Cambridge, MA: Ballinger.

Tyson, Laura D'Andrea, and John Zysman. 1989b. "Developmental Strategy and Production Innovation in Japan." In Chalmers Johnson, Laura D'Andrea Tyson, and John Zysman, *Politics and Productivity: The Real Story of Why Japan Works*. Cambridge, MA: Ballinger.

Weinstein, David, and Yishay Yafeh. 1993. "Japan's Corporate Groups: Collusive or Competitive? An Empirical Investigation of Keiretsu Behavior." Harvard Institute of Economic Research Discussion Papers 1623. Harvard University, Cambridge, MA.

Williamson, Oliver E. 1985. *The Economic Institutions of Capitalism*. New York: Free Press.

Yamamura, Kozo, ed. 1990. *Japan's Economic Structure: Should It Change?* Seattle: Society for Japanese Studies.

Yoshitomi, Masaru. 1990. "Keiretsu: An Insider's Guide to Japan's Conglomerates." *International Economic Insights* 1, no. 2: 10-14.

IV

CONCLUSIONS

17

Conclusions and Recommendations

EDWARD M. GRAHAM AND J. DAVID RICHARDSON

Introduction

Because many trade disputes of the past 10 years have involved issues of competition policy, the World Trade Organization's (WTO) multilateral trading rules should recognize their importance. That is the main premise of this volume (see chapter 1). The existing rules are ill suited to deal with these disputes, so new approaches are urgently needed. There are, however, significant problems in creating competition-policy rules to fit the WTO framework. These include substantive problems: among domestic competition agencies in the major trading nations, there is no consensus on the appropriate standards for competition policy,[1] nor do scholars who specialize in the study of the underlying economics agree on the normatively best competition policies.[2] In addition, there is no agreement on the most appropriate enforcement mechanisms.

In spite of these problems, there are many approaches to the internationalization of competition policy, not all of which center around the WTO nor even involve it. Indeed, some do not require consensus among nations on appropriate substantive and enforcement standards. Rather, nations would agree to define and enforce their own standards above some threshold and recognize the outcomes of other nations' competition

---

1. Fox compares US and EU competition policy in chapter 10, and Rosenthal and Matsushita compare US and Japanese competition standards in chapter 9.

2. See chapter 1.

policies. It would be a major step forward if every nation had a competition law and enforcement mechanism.[3]

Even so, the WTO might help to ensure that where competition issues are at the heart of trade disputes, the interests of all disputing nations are heard. To whatever extent possible, it could also ensure that those disputes are resolved under rules and procedures subscribed to by all member nations.[4] Later in this chapter, we spell out some specific WTO initiatives.

Meanwhile, what is competition policy's role in the multilateral trading system? That depends on how effectively competition policy can eliminate or reduce market access barriers that remain after the traditional barriers to trade tariffs, quotas, and other nontariff barriers are dismantled. We address this question next.

Competition Policy and International Market Access

Many trade disputes in recent years have centered on market access—that is, on barriers to foreign entry that are not the result of traditional trade policy instruments. Instead, these barriers result from private business practices that might be facilitated by domestic regulation or policies. Most competition-policy issues, including disputes over these international barriers, are specific to a sector and/or to a region or nation (e.g., the US-Japan auto parts dispute outlined in chapter 1). Thus, the right answer to a specific issue (or even the right approach to addressing this issue) might not be applicable in a different sector and/or a different region or nation. For example, the horizontal merger of two competing firms that each have 20 percent of a given market might not be deemed anticompetitive, whereas a merger in some other market between two firms that each have less than 20 percent market share might be. Thus, other factors might explain the apparent contradiction (e.g., conditions affecting entry of new sellers and the availability of close substitutes for the products or services). That different circumstances lead to different normative conclusions is one reason why so many areas of competition policy, even at the level of basic economic analysis, remain murky (see chapter 1). It is also why many cases are subject to rule-of-reason—specific

---

3. All new member nations of the European Union are required to have a competition law and enforcement mechanism.

4. To some extent, the WTO can already play this role, because under the 1960 General Agreement on Tariffs and Trade (GATT) decision on restrictive business practices (see chapter 1), where such practices lead to alleged impairment of trade, consultations can be held under the auspices of the WTO. However, this role is limited and has rarely been invoked.

business practices are often neither per se legal or illegal. Instead, the legality depends on how the practices are employed.

Thus, whether competition policy reduces market access barriers depends on the characteristics of a given market. For example, in some markets competition policy cannot effectively reach structural barriers that reduce opportunities for competition (and hence market access). Also, some markets are characterized by natural monopoly, wherein only one supplier of a good or service (or few suppliers) can operate efficiently. Natural monopoly is characterized by large and unrecoverable front-end expenditures (sunk costs) that cannot be amortized if entry and increased competition drive prices too low. Thus, the sunk cost acts as a structural barrier to entry.

Competition policy only partially answers the question of how to increase competition when the conditions for natural monopoly exist. For example, firms seeking to supply a good or service to a market characterized by natural monopoly might be periodically required to bid for the franchise to serve as this supplier. If the bidding is competitive, the bid for the franchise will equal the present value of expected future rents. Thus, the public will recover the supplier's rents. However, even this approach might not be feasible in some cases: the sunk costs associated with switching suppliers may be so great as to preclude such switching.

However, competition policy can help to ensure that unnatural monopoly (where a single supplier attempts to masquerade as a natural monopolist) does not persist. Although the provision of a service that requires a huge sunk cost might be a natural monopoly, all aspects of the sale of services need not be monopolized. For example, the fixed costs of creating a basic telecommunications network might preclude the existence of two parallel networks in any given place. However, even in the provision of basic telecommunications services, many, if not most, value-added services can be sold competitively, if all relevant service suppliers have equal access to the common good (e.g., Petrazzini 1996).

Whether competition policy can reduce market access barriers also depends on the substantive standards enforced by competition agencies. Part II of this book showed that the substantive standards of competition policies vary significantly from nation to nation (where we count the European Union as a nation). For example, under EU law and policy, the authorities tend to see certain vertical restraints as competition reducing. Where such restraints can be identified, they can be addressed by competition policy. In contrast, similar restraints in the United States might be seen as efficiency enhancing and, hence, not subject to competition policy. Consequently, EU law is generally less forgiving of vertical restraints that act as market access barriers than is US law.[5] Some argue

---

5. However, some sectors in Europe are subject to block exemptions, under which otherwise illegal vertical practices are specifically made legal.

that if the issues in the US-Japan auto parts dispute had been adjudicated under competition policy, the US trade representative's case would have likely done better under EU law than US law.

But what are the correct substantive standards? As has been emphasized throughout this book, there is only modest consensus on this question, even with respect to what is normatively best from an economics point of view (see chapter 1). This lack of full consensus is usually not a matter of ideology. Rather, whether a specific practice is deemed bad or good from an economics perspective often depends on the underlying economic conditions. For example, should resale price maintenance (RPM) be per se illegal?[6] If the objective of RPM regulation is to maximize overall welfare, whether this objective is attained can be conditional on the elasticity of demand of inframarginal buyers. Under some conditions, RPM might enhance overall welfare and should be legal in those cases. But under other conditions, RPM would unequivocally harm welfare and should be illegal. Thus, the correct policy may not easily flow from the underlying economics. The difficulty is not that analytic tools are lacking. Rather, the difficulty lies in correctly assessing the circumstances under which the tools must be applied.

Lack of consensus on substantive standards constitutes a major dilemma of competition policy. The murkiness of much of the underlying economics exacerbates a second, related dilemma. Not only are substantive standards different across nations, they have also been significantly revised over time within some nations. For example, in the United States under the Reagan administration (under the influence of the so-called Chicago School) competition policy became considerably less interventionist than it was during the 1960s and 1970s (see chapters 10, 7, and 11 by Fox, Fox and Pitofsky, and Rosenthal and Nicolaides, respectively).

Some scholars therefore question whether international consensus on the substantive standards for competition policy would be desirable. These scholars argue that such a consensus could lock the world into standards that seem right now but, at some time, might become discredited. They point to US efforts during the 1970s to encourage other nations to adopt US standards and argue that had this occurred and had the standards not been revised, global competition policy would now be based on standards that the United States itself no longer accepts. Because the underlying economics of competition policy are murky, such scholars argue that it is better to allow for policy competition, under which different ideas would compete in different regions, because policy would evolve parallel to what is best practice.

A third dilemma of competition policy as a means of increasing international market access is that there is often no consensus on who has standing to bring a case. In the United States, for example, there is

---

6. For a discussion of RPM, see Scherer and Ross (1990, 541-58).

relatively easy private right of action. US officials vigorously defend this, maintaining that without easy private right of action, many violations of competition law would go unchallenged. By contrast, EU officials argue that too easy a private right of action leads to far too many court cases, imposing costs on society.[7] In many East Asian nations, it is argued that moral persuasion can work better than overt legal action to enforce competition standards (see Liu 1996). Few competition experts in Western nations would agree, however.

The issue of resources is tied to that of private right of action. In the United States, the professional staff of the Antitrust Division of the Department of Justice numbers 500. There are 275 more employed at the Federal Trade Commission. The DGIV of the European Commission, which enforces competition policy in a market somewhat larger than that of the United States, employs a total professional staff of 450. The EU commission does not make public the exact breakdown of its staff. However, the 450 includes junior-grade staff that would probably not be classed as professional staff in other countries and includes staff whose primary mission is to investigate state aids to industry and regions. Because there are fewer resources devoted to enforcement in the European Union, it can be argued that a higher percentage of suspected violations of competition law are never investigated or prosecuted in Europe than in the United States. In particular, some legal experts allege that there are many cartels in existence that would, if prosecuted, be found in violation of Article 85 of the Treaty of Rome (see Fox's arguments in chapter 10 on US-EU competition law). In other nations, resources for enforcement are even more meager. The professional staff of the Japanese Fair Trade Commission (JFTC) numbers 250, for example. China, although it has an unfair business-practices law and is contemplating an antimonopolies law, has no enforcement agency at all (see Ma 1995).

The priority that nations place on competition is also related to the issue of resources. Many nations do not have competition laws. However, many of these nations are now contemplating them. Also, the competition laws of many nations are incomplete. Meanwhile, Mexico, Venezuela, Taiwan, and other nations have broad but largely untried competition laws.

It is alleged that competition policies often go unenforced in nations that have had such a policy for a decade or more. Thus, practices that create market access barriers and are, in principle, in violation of the law are tolerated nonetheless. Such allegations, for example, have been voiced against Japan and South Korea.

---

7. On this matter, however, there are advocates within Directorate General IV (DGIV) of the European Commission who argue that private right of action should be made less restrictive, on the grounds that the resources of the official agency in Brussels are too limited to handle all cases that are brought to its attention. See Fox's arguments in chapter 10 on US-EU competition law.

This issue should be distinguished from the point made above that competition-policy enforcement varies from nation to nation. The issue is whether in some nations enforcement is so slack or selective, perhaps purposefully so, that the net effect nullifies the law and policy. In these nations, however, enforcement appears to be improving (e.g., in Taiwan, where a competition law and enforcement agency has been in place since the late 1980s, but where enforcement, until quite recently, has been quite lax).

Even in those countries where competition law has historically been taken seriously, competition goals are not always paramount. In chapter 11, Rosenthal and Nicolaides argue that

> Competition law and policy in the United States, Japan, and Canada is relatively weak vis-à-vis five sets of national laws and economic policies that most directly restrict national and global competition: (1) protectionist trade measures, (2) measures intended to attract or exclude categories of foreign investors, (3) nonborder regulations that confer a competitive advantage on local products or firms, (4) industrial policies intended to promote national champions and save jobs, (5) overly broad protection of intellectual property rights in some nations, which has had the effect of discouraging innovation and competition not involving industrial pirates. . . . Because competition policy is weak nationally, it is necessarily weak in multilateral forums.

In particular, certain laws and policies pertaining to imports offset the goals of competition policy. For example, antidumping policies, as implemented by many nations, could reinforce anticompetitive practices and, hence, work against the goals of competition policy. The threat of antidumping action against an importer could give an incentive to that importer to set prices at levels sought by a domestic cartel, even if the cartel were violating competition laws. We further address the issue of antidumping later in this chapter.

Thus, competition policies seem to stop at the border. In addition to antidumping, national laws permitting domestic exporters to set up export cartels would seem to work against the goals of competition policy. Another example of trade laws that might have anticompetitive effects are those that prohibit parallel imports of branded products. Under these laws, such products bought legitimately in one national market may not be imported into another market. Such a prohibition allows the producer of the product to price discriminate in different national markets.

Other exceptions to competition policy also present problems. In some nations, certain sectors are off-limits to competition policy. For example, a sector is often set aside for a state-run monopoly. And entry into other sectors is often closely regulated, and in some cases new entry is effectively barred. Sectors falling into these categories include some of the most dynamic and important ones (e.g., natural resource extraction, telecommunications, banking, and civil aviation). In the European Union, industries can be granted block exemptions, under which otherwise illegal practices are allowed (i.e., exclusive dealing relationships in the automotive industry). Suzumura, in chapter 14, looks specifically at exceptions in Japan and argues that sometimes such exceptions are economically justified. In contrast, we argue that most exceptions are unwarranted on economic grounds and that the exceptions foster economic inefficiency, reduce buyer choice, and impede market access by firms wishing to do business across national borders.

The issue of exceptions to competition policy impinges on such WTO issues as sectoral liberalization (e.g., the recently completed telecommunications agreement and the ongoing negotiations within the WTO to liberalize financial services as part of the effort to supplement the liberalization commitments under the General Agreement on Trade in Services (GATS). This issue also impinges on whether government regulation acts as an undesirable market access barrier and to what extent deregulation is appropriate. As is often the case with competition-policy issues, the answer to the problems caused by exceptions are likely to be nation and sector specific.

Some aspects of competition may be so international in scope that they cannot be handled by national law. Certain so-called strategic alliances, for example, might have anticompetitive aspects to them, but if the alliance involves firms of multiple nationalities, it might not fall under the purview of any nation in which it operates. Arguably, there are some sectors where natural monopoly might exist on a global scale. For example, the sunk costs of creating the next generation of wide-body passenger aircraft might prove to be so great that it becomes a global natural monopoly.

Transborder mergers are a recognized area for cooperation between national officials, but more must be addressed in this area. Certain cartel-like arrangements (e.g., ocean-shipping conferences) largely escape the scrutiny of competition-policy authorities, often because these arrangements are exempt from competition policy. Other possible problems associated with international oligopoly might also escape the scrutiny of national authorities. These might include tacit collusion among firms supplying an international market, enabling the firms to act as a de facto cartel.

A Taxonomy of Trade and Investment-Related Competition Issues

Drawing from chapter 1 and the various studies in this volume, we have identified the priority trade and investment issues in international competition policies and grouped them in tables 1 and 2 (table 1 provides full details and table 2, a summary). The tables show our appraisal of whether there is enough intellectual and policy consensus on any of these issues to warrant an international agreement.

Table 1 Criteria for a global competition-policy agenda: detail

		State of convergence		Feasibility of further convergence[b]	Gains from further convergence[b]	
	Economic clarity	Toward best practice	Toward each other		Efficiency gains	Conflict reduction
Issues pertaining to market structure						
Cartelization	Clear	Low	High	Moderate	High	Moderate/high
Unwarranted horizontal restraints	Clear	Moderate	Moderate	Moderate	High	Low/moderate
Vertical arrangements						
Resale price arrangements	Murky	Controversial[a]	Low	Moderate	Low	Low
Foreclosure	Murky	Controversial[a]	Low	Low	Moderate	High
Strategic alliances	Murky	Controversial[a]	Low	Indeterminate	Moderate	Indeterminate
Mergers and acquisitions regulation	Clear minus	Moderate	Moderate	Moderate/high	Moderate	Moderate
Issues pertaining to firm conduct						
Predation	Clear minus	Controversial[a]	Moderate	Low	High	High[b]
Price fixing	Clear	High	High	High	High	Low
Price discrimination	Clear minus	Controversial[a]	Moderate	Low/moderate	Low	High
Abuse of market power	Murky	Controversial[a]	Low	Low	Indeterminate	Low
Exemptions						
Functional (e.g., for research and development)	Murky	Controversial[a]	Moderate	Moderate	Low/moderate	High
Sectorial (e.g., telecommunications)	Murky	Controversial[a]	Moderate	Low but improving	Moderate	High
Temporal (e.g., for recession cartels)	Murky	Controversial[a]	Low	Moderate	Moderate	Moderate
Efficiency defense	Murky	Controversial[a]	Low	Low	Indeterminate	Moderate

Trade policy measures raising competition concerns						
VERs, OMAs, etc.	Clear	Low	Low	High[b]	High	Moderate
VIEs	Clear minus	Moderate	Low	Indeterminate	High	High
Antidumping	Clear	Low	Low but increasing	Low	High	High
National treatment issues						
For imports	Clear	High	High	In place	Low	Low
For foreign direct investors	Clear	Moderate	Moderate but decreasing	Moderate	Moderate/high	Moderate but increasing
Other related issues						
Intellectual property protection	Murky	Controversial	Moderate but becoming higher	Moderate/high[c]	Moderate	High
State aids to industry/subsidies						
Research and development	Murky	Controversial	Low	Moderate[c]	Moderate	Moderate/high
Production	Clear minus	Moderate	Low	Moderate[c]	Moderate	Moderate/high

a. Best practice is not clearly delineated or is controversial.
b. Toward each other or toward best practice.
c. Based on successes and failures in GATT negotiations during the Uruguay Round.

Table 2 Criteria for a global competition-policy agenda: summary

		State of convergence			Gains from further convergence[b]	
	Economic clarity	Toward best practice	Toward each other	Feasibility of further convergence[b]	Efficiency gains	Conflict reduction
Issues pertaining to market structure	Clear minus	Moderate	Moderate	Moderate	Moderate	Moderate
Issues pertaining to firm conduct	Clear minus	Controversial[a]	Moderate	Low	Moderate	Moderate
Exemptions	Murky	Controversial[a]	Low	Moderate	Moderate	High
Trade policy measures raising competition concerns	Clear	Low	Moderate	Moderate	High	High
Other related issues	Murky	Controversial[a]	Moderate	Moderate	Moderate	High

a. Best practice is not clearly delineated or is controversial.
b. Toward each other or toward best practice.

The first column in each table classifies the issue under market structure, exemptions, firm conduct, trade policy, or other. These issue areas are not always mutually exclusive. Nonetheless, we put substantively similar issues in separate categories if the typical regulatory process treats them separately.

The second column in each table categorizes these issues according to the criterion of economic clarity presented in chapter 1 of this volume— (i.e., whether there is strong consensus among economists on what is substantively best practice). If there is such a consensus, we label the issue clear: if there is no such consensus, we label the issue murky. On issues where there is a majority consensus but some dissention, we place the label clear minus.

If there is to be any sort of international convergence on the issues listed, the best practice with respect to the issue should be clear or, minimally, clear minus.[8] If there is no intellectual consensus on the best

---

8. In what follows, convergence pertains both to convergence among the laws and policies of nations (necessary if any sort of international accord is to be reached) and convergence between trade policy and competition policy positions on issues that overlap (e.g., predation and antidumping). Presumably, convergence (in both contexts) toward best practice is desired and not convergence for its own sake.

practice, international convergence would be useless or, worse yet, counterproductive (i.e., what is the point of converging on a bad practice?).

The remaining columns describe aspects of convergence with respect to each practice. The columns labeled state of convergence describe the status quo; the columns labeled feasibility of further convergence and gains from further convergence describe the feasibility and desirability of changing the status quo. Desirability is assessed with respect to reducing both inefficiency and international conflict. The second and third columns record our assessment of the state of convergence, first toward best practice (when a consensus exists) and, second, across national practices.

The fourth column indicates the feasibility of further convergence. Feasibility in this context means political feasibility (i.e., is there any consensus among policy officials and legislatures on what would be normatively better practice?). We classify issues as low feasibility if either (1) there are substantial differences among officials of different nations on desirable practice, or (2) there is a substantial difference between branches of a single government as to desirable practice.[9] If an issue is not characterized by a high or at least moderate level of feasibility in this sense, there is probably little hope at this time for reasonable convergence.

The fifth column represents an effort to judge what might be gained, in terms of economic efficiency, from moving from the present policy regime to a convergence on best practice. In areas where we judged the substantively best practice to be murky, we attempted to judge the efficiency implications of continuing practices that economists agree lead to inefficiencies. One way of looking at this judgment is to ask: If we could agree on a substantive best practice, and this agreement had economic merit, what would we gain? The final column indicates issues for which we judge that success in reaching any sort of convergence will lead to conflict resolution. Several issues are labeled at least moderate for three of the following: clarity, feasibility, efficiency, and conflict reduction. The common thread through most of them is market access, and virtually all involve barriers to the contestability of markets. Those issues are

■ cartelization;

■ other horizontal restraints;

■ mergers and acquisitions;

■ price fixing;

■ voluntary export restraints (VERs), orderly marketing arrangements (OMAs), and other similar practices; and

■ national treatment for foreign direct investors and services.

---

9. For example, trade policy officials may defend existing antidumping statutes, but competition policy officials may see these as irrational when evaluated by standards for predation or price discrimination.

Many issues do not make this list, but have high efficiency and conflict-reduction implications. These include predation or antidumping and voluntary import expansions (VIEs) (for which likely efficiency gains would be substantial if there were the political will to implement significant reform of the existing system);[10] vertical practices (for which the underlying economics remains murky);[11] intellectual property and related issues (for which the debate over the welfare tradeoff between strong intellectual property protection, and greater rivalry among innovators will likely never be fully resolved); and state aids to industry (Is there such thing as a good subsidy?). Of these issues, the last three do not make the list because the underlying economics of the issue remains murky and, hence, what is normatively best practice is difficult to determine.

This distillation provides a useful means for categorizing alternative policy recommendations. It provides the substance of a desirable agreement on Trade-Related Antitrust Measures (TRAMs), akin to the current Trade-Related Intellectual Property (TRIPs) measures and Trade-Related Investment Measures (TRIMs), and also provides an agenda for reform of some of the least efficient and least equitable aspects of current trade and investment rules.

How Might Competition Policy Be Internationalized?

In principle, there are many ways to extend competition policy beyond national borders. They include

- Creation of an international body of law and an enforcement agency to enforce competition policy on a global basis. (e.g., Scherer 1994).

- Harmonization of competition law and policy among nations, because differences in substance and enforcement among the laws and policies of different nations are among the most prominent obstacles to internationalization.

- Adoption of a WTO agreement on TRAMs and integration of competition issues into the dispute-settlement procedures of the WTO.

- Cooperative arrangements among the enforcement agencies of major nations (and the European Union).

- Aggressive unilateralism, whereby the competition laws and policies of one nation (or the European Union) are extended extraterritorially so that jurisdictions not under the sovereign control of the relevant

---

10. See chapter 15 by Itoh and Nagaoka and chapter 13 by Lipstein.

11. For example, there is room for reasoned debate as to whether vertical *keiretsu* in Japan are efficiency enhancing or otherwise. Sheard argues in chapter 16 that efficiency-enhancing effects dominate on balance.

government are forced to comply with the competition laws and policies of that government.

Because some border measures nullify the objectives of competition policy, a sixth alternative should be listed. This alternative could be implemented as a complement to any of the first five:

■ World trade laws should be reformed so that they do not thwart the objectives of competition policy. Such laws include antidumping statutes and those permitting export cartels. Reform of these laws could be undertaken in the context of the TRAMs code or as a stand-alone exercise.

The following sections develop these alternatives in more detail.

A WTO DGIV

The most straightforward way to integrate competition policy into the world trading system would be to create an international body of law enforced by an international enforcement agency as part of the WTO. A WTO enforcement agency might be similar to the existing DGIV of the European Union, which has broad powers to deal with competition-policy issues. Just as the powers of the DGIV impinge on the sovereignty of the European member states (see chapter 8 by Nicolaïdis and Vernon), so would a WTO enforcement agency impinge on the sovereignty of WTO member nations. In Europe, the DGIV's powers have been sustained by European Court of Justice decisions and by the willingness of the member nations of the European Union to abide by these decisions, even when the effect has been to erode sovereignty. There is no worldwide equivalent to the European Court of Justice and no evident willingness of nations to allow a supranational agency to hold powers equivalent to those of DGIV. An international body of law enforced by an international agency under the aegis of the WTO would be feasible only if there were a strong and enduring consensus on the substantive principles of competition policy. These considerations suggest that a WTO version of the DGIV is not yet practical.

The lack of substantive consensus does not necessarily rule out the desirability of an international law and agency. Lack of consensus, however, would make it difficult to negotiate a workable agreement. Nonetheless, if the political will to create such a law and agency were present, the difficulties would be overcome.

But political will is also wanting. More specifically, there is no worldwide political consensus to build the institutional framework for an international law and enforcement agency. Without this framework, such a law and agency would not be able to function.

To establish an effective framework, considerable sovereign power would be sacrificed. For example, chapter 7 on the United States by Fox and Pitofsky emphasizes that US antitrust policy is ultimately determined by the courts and often by the US Supreme Court.[12] Meanwhile, if an international agency is to be effective, its decisions must be heard by an appellate body whose decision would be final. This appellate body would necessarily be international in scope, because no nation would be willing to accept the national courts of another nation as the ultimate arbiter. This would imply that, in the domain of antitrust, the appellate body's decisions could override those of US courts, including the Supreme Court. It is unlikely that the United States would allow a multilateral agency to exercise this power.

Nevertheless, we have already noted many substantive arguments in favor of such an approach. Because many important industries now compete on a global scale (see Graham 1996), it is easily argued that competition policy should also be enforced on a global scale. Also, for a variety of reasons, a national government might be reluctant to take action against a local firm. An international agency would presumably be empowered to deal with such cases that have an international dimension. Thus, although a supranational agency with powers to enforce an internationally agreed upon body of law is not feasible at this time, the possibility of such an agency in the future should not be discounted completely. In particular, if globalization continues and national borders cease to define markets, a global approach might be the only pragmatic way to implement competition policy.

Harmonization of Competition Laws and Policies

Harmonization in this context means that nations adopt nearly uniform substantive and enforcement standards by means of negotiation and agreement. Full harmonization of competition laws and policies appears impractical for the same reason that negotiation of global standards is not feasible. There is a lack of both political and intellectual consensus on what standards should be adopted, either substantively or in terms of enforcement. And, a number of key nations that currently appear unwilling to negotiate global standards also appear unwilling to change current national standards to achieve such a consensus.[13]

Nonetheless, some subsets of competition laws and policies might be harmonized. Most nations, for example, have laws prohibiting price-

---

12. Meanwhile, enforcement retain a major role in the determination of policy.

13. Neither the United States nor the European Union are prepared to adopt the other's substantive standards where there are substantial differences. And, without a consensus between them, there is no chance for a larger international consensus.

fixing and other cartel arrangements. The substantive provisions of these laws are not widely divergent. Thus, there could be harmonization of substantive laws on the control of cartels (see Fox 1997).

In other domains, rather than deliberate harmonization of competition law, there might occur a process of convergence, that is, uniformity achieved through cross-fertilization of ideas among experts and officials. Convergence, however, also seems unlikely to move quickly on a global scale, given the lack of consensus on normative standards.

Nonetheless, there might be some process of convergence among certain subsets of nations. In particular, members of the European Union and nonmembers seem to be achieving convergence. This is largely because members typically seek national law and policy that does not conflict with EU law and policy (see chapters 6, 3, and 4 by Hay, Jenny, and Kühn, respectively); nonmembers seeking to join the European Union must have a competition law that is compatible with EU law and policy.

It is possible to envisage that these incentives might create some sort of critical mass around the EU approach to competition policy. That is, nations neither currently members of the European Union nor contemplating becoming members might nonetheless seek to adopt EU standards so that its law and policy does not conflict with that held by so many leading nations. Thus, for example, some nations in the Asia Pacific area have looked to EU law and policy as a possible model. EU standards might very well become world standards, because a large number of nations will harmonize their own laws and policies around them.

However, it is doubtful that EU standards will become accepted on a truly global basis, because certain major nations, such as the United States and Japan, are unlikely to adopt them (see chapter 10 by Fox). Indeed, in canvassing the opinions of the US business community regarding competition policy in preparation for the 1996 WTO ministerial meeting, the Office of the US Trade Representative learned that major US firms opposed any movement in the WTO toward global recognition of certain European standards, especially those associated with Article 85 of the Treaty of Rome (abuse of a dominant market position by a firm). Thus, while much of the world might converge on EU standards, those nations not converging will be of such importance to the world economy that no claim could be made that worldwide convergence had occurred.

Integration of Competition Policy into the WTO Dispute Settlement Procedures

Many proposals that would inject elements of competition policy into the WTO have been made (e.g., Fox 1997; Graham 1995). Possibly the best thinking on this matter is that of Fox (1997), who explores a *de minimis* framework for putting competition issues into the WTO that is compatible with its dispute settlement procedures. Indeed, our main recommendation is that a variant of this proposal be adopted. However, before exploring this option, a short digression into the workings of the WTO and its dispute resolution procedures will prove useful.

The WTO's authority is embodied in a series of agreements (e.g., the General Agreement on Trade and Tariffs (GATT), the GATS, the plurilateral Agreement on Civil Aviation)[14] Each of these is a set of rules (or obligations) to which nations voluntarily agree to be bound, subject to a series of stated exceptions. Each WTO member nation is obliged to bring its national law and policy into compliance with these rules.

If a WTO member nation believes that its trading interests are adversely affected because some other member nation is not complying with an obligation, the aggrieved nation can lodge a complaint with the WTO. The dispute can then be taken to WTO dispute settlement procedures. Under these procedures, the disputants must first try to settle via good-faith consultation. Failing a resolution of the conflict by this means, the dispute is brought before a panel of experts, who hear the complaint and make recommendations with respect to (1) whether the obligation has been broached as alleged and, if so, (2) a remedy to correct the failed obligation. These recommendations are accepted by the WTO unless the decision is appealed to the WTO Appellate Body, or there is a unanimous consensus among the WTO member governments to block the recommendations.[15] If a decision is appealed, the Appellate Body must review the decision within 60 days on "issues of law covered in the panel report and legal interpretations developed by the panel" (Schott and Buurman 1994). The decision of the Appellate Body is accepted unless there is a unanimous decision among the WTO member governments not to accept it. If the panel's recommendations for a remedy are not promptly complied with by the offending nation, sanctions against that nation can be taken by the complaining nation. However, sanctions are not allowed if the complaint involves a nonviolation, (i.e., nullification and impairment under GATT Article XXIII), a point to which we shall return.

The language of GATT Article XXIII on nullification or impairment has led us to believe that the WTO dispute settlement procedure could

---

14. A plurilateral agreement is one to which a subset of WTO members agree to be bound. There currently are agreements on government procurement, civil aviation, dairy products, and bovine meat products.

15. These are new procedures created by the Uruguay Round agreements. Prior to 1995, a panel decision had to be accepted unanimously by the contracting parties (the member nations of the precedent GATT agreement), implying that one nation could veto the decision (this nation could have been the one against whom the original complaint was lodged). Also, prior to 1995, there was no Appellate Body.

be used to resolve some competition-policy issues (Graham 1995; Richardson 1995). Paragraph I of that article states:

> If any (member nation) should consider that any benefit accruing to it directly or indirectly under this Agreement is being nullified or impaired or that the attainment of any objective of the Agreement is being impeded as the result of (a) the failure of another (member nation) to carry out its obligations under this Agreement, or (b) the application by another (member nation) of any measure, whether or not it conflicts with the provisions of this Agreement, or (c) the existence of any other situation, the (aggrieved member nation) may, with a view to the satisfactory adjustment of the matter, make written representations or proposals to the other (member nation or nations) which it considers to be concerned. Any (member nation) thus approached shall give sympathetic consideration to the representations or proposals made to it.

Paragraph 2 of the article indicates that if the dispute is not satisfactorily resolved by the nations involved, the issue can be brought before the WTO and resolved through the dispute settlement process.

Thus, it would appear that a private business action that blocks market access and that might be remedied by competition policy is, in the language of Article XXIII, paragraph 1, a nullification or impairment of a benefit brought on by "(c) the existence of any other situation . . ." (Graham 1995; Richardson 1995). In this case, the benefit would be increased exports, enabled by the reduced border measures brought about by GATT. Under the article, "written representations or proposals" could be made by the aggrieved nation (that which suffers reduced exports) to the putatively offending nation (that which harbors the market-access barrier). Such good-faith consultation, part of the traditional WTO dispute resolution process, would be in the spirit of so-called positive comity, a loose doctrine whereby, when administering domestic law and policy, the officials of one nation listen sympathetically to the concerns of other national governments and act accordingly.

If the aggrieved nation felt that the putatively offending nation had not acted with positive comity, a dispute could be lodged with the WTO (Graham 1995; Richardson 1995). Just as occurs in traditional trade disputes not solved by good-faith consultation, a panel of experts would be formed. In this case, the panel would be empowered to determine whether the complaint was valid and whether the government of the putatively offending nation had properly enforced its competition law to address this market-access problem. In our view, the panel would stop there. It would issue a report only indicating whether there was a problem of market access and whether competition law in the defendant nation could be (and had been) used to address this problem. The panel would not be empowered to recommend a remedy to the problem, as it does for other trade disputes.

Our earlier proposal is consistent with the Uruguay Round clarification of Article XXIII, paragraph 1(c).[16] Under that clarification, it would appear that a panel can hear any dispute involving GATT-enabled export opportunities that are nullified or impaired by "any other situation" (in this case, nonenforcement of competition law). However, the nation under scrutiny does not appear to be obligated to adopt any recommendation of the panel.

However, this approach to implementing competition policy in the context of GATT Article XXIII is open to legal questioning. In particular, a GATT working group in 1960 recommended that this article not be invoked by nations seeking to redress market-access barriers created by private business practices. The group argued that GATT contains no language on such practices and that substantive provisions that had not been explicitly agreed on by the contracting parties should not be introduced through Article XXIII. This recommendation does not have the force of law, but it does establish a precedent against use of Article XXIII for the purpose of raising and resolving competition-policy issues within the WTO.

Also, international legal experts have pointed out a further legal flaw with our approach. WTO panels do not pass judgment on the failure of member governments to enforce their national laws and policies if these laws and policies are not germane to specific WTO obligations.[17] For a panel to do so in the case of competition policy would set a precedent that member governments would undoubtedly not accept. The problems

---

16. The clarification states:

> Where the provisions of paragraph 1(c) of Article XXIII of GATT 1994 are applicable to a covered agreement, a panel may only make rulings and recommendations where a party considers that any benefit accruing to it directly or indirectly under the relevant covered agreement is being nullified or impaired or the attainment of any objective of that Agreement is being impeded as a result of the existence of any situation other than those to which the provisions of paragraphs 1(a) and 1(b) of Article XXIII of GATT 1994 are applicable. Where and to the extent that such party considers and a panel determines that the matter is covered by this paragraph, the procedures of this Understanding shall apply only up to and including the point in the proceedings where the panel report has been circulated to the Members. The dispute settlement rules and procedures contained in the Decision of 12 April 1989 (BISD 36S/61-67) shall apply to consideration for adoption, and surveillance and implementation of recommendations and rulings. The following shall also apply: (a) the complaining party shall present a detailed justification in support of any argument made with respect to issues covered under this paragraph; (b) in cases involving matters covered by this paragraph, if a panel finds that cases also involve dispute settlement matters other than those covered by this paragraph, the panel shall circulate a report to the DSB addressing any such matters an a separate report on matters falling under this paragraph.

17. A WTO panel would consider a government's failure to enforce its own law where this law reflected a WTO obligation.

would be greatest in those nations that enforce competition law largely through judicial proceedings (e.g., the United States). WTO review of how national law is enforced would be seen as an unacceptable impingement on national sovereignty and, in particular, on the powers of the judiciary.

The WTO is much more comfortable with disputes involving putative violation (i.e., failure of a member nation to adhere to an obligation under a WTO agreement) than those involving nonviolation (i.e., nullification and impairment under Article XXIII, paragraphs 1(b) or 1(c)).

Cognizant of this and of the 1960 working group recommendation, Fox (1997) suggests that a new agreement be negotiated within the WTO, which she would label TRAMs, in the spirit of the existing agreements on TRIMs and, especially, TRIPs. Rather than negotiate a comprehensive agreement on all aspects of com-petition policy, she proposes that a new agreement focus only on those subdomains that are most relevant to issues of market access. In her judgment, these include

- cartels with boycotts;

- vertical arrangements that tend to foreclose outside vendors or block established channels of distribution to new entrants; and

- monopolistic discriminations and exclusions.

In principle, we agree with her approach. However, we disagree with the specifics. Fox acknowledges that, while agreement on the first subdomain could be relatively straightforward, the second and third are problematic. Vertical arrangements have been ubiquitous to many recent trade disputes. However, these arrangements can also be efficiency enhancing. Efficiency defenses have been used to defend the existence of so-called production *keiretsu* in Japan, which have been at the heart of many recent disputes (see chapter 16 by Sheard). It is largely for this reason that the economic consensus on vertical arrangements is, according to our taxonomy of competition issues, murky. Substantial differences also exist between US and EU doctrine toward vertical arrangements, with the United States generally accepting efficiency defenses for arrangements that might be prohibited in the European Union. Similar differences exist in US and EU policies on horizontal market power. For example, US policy, except under specific circumstances, allows monopolistic firms to refuse to deal with a customer, whereas EU policy holds that dominant firms have a duty not to discriminate among customers or refuse to deal.

These differences are sufficiently great among the three largest WTO members as to preclude them from being able to agree on a common set of standards. Also, we have discussed the unwillingness of most WTO members, including these three, to relinquish sovereign powers to rule on competition-policy issues to an international body. This is true of the European Union, even though individual member nations of the European Union relinquish such powers to an international body, the European Commission.

We suggest that Fox's general TRAMs agreement focus on contestability. Our analysis of feasibility (see tables 1 and 2) suggests a focus on five areas:

- national treatment for local affiliates of foreign firms,

- international control of cartels and cartel-like behavior,

- enlargement of WTO consultative procedures,

- mergers and acquisitions notification, and,

- more speculatively, what we call TRAMs plus.

TRAMS plus is an approach to dealing with industries in decline that demand trade protection and might qualify for escape-clause (GATT Article XIX) relief. Our proposals in each of these areas provide a positive role for the WTO but do not obligate WTO members to relinquish sovereign powers. We will examine each of these issues.

National Treatment for Local Affiliates of Foreign Firms

Firms' concern with market access often has to do with the right to establish a presence in a local market by creating (or acquiring) a local subsidiary. Such market presence is virtually a prerequisite for international trade in the fast-growing services sector. This point has been well recognized in the Uruguay Round's still unfinished GATS. Although not an absolute prerequisite in most manufacturing activities, local market presence is nonetheless desirable. These considerations suggest that a vital component of market access is that governments not discriminate against the establishment or operation of a local affiliate of a foreign firm. In other words, these affiliates should be granted full-national treatment (see Graham 1996).

National treatment for foreign-controlled enterprises is most often thought of as an international investment issue, because lack of national treatment is a major impediment to foreign direct investment (FDI). However, any impediment to FDI is also an impediment to market entry and, hence, to increased market contestability. And, given that increased market contestability is one of the major goals of competition policy, national treatment is also a competition-policy issue. Indeed, it might be the issue with the highest priority. Many trade-policy issues that concern market access would simply fade away if governments were obligated to grant national treatment to foreign-controlled firms.

Our views on how national treatment for foreign-controlled enterprises should be implemented have been published in detail elsewhere (see Graham 1996). Here, we summarize a few points. First, no government is ever likely to endorse full, unqualified national treatment for foreign-controlled enterprises. Hence, there is a practical requirement for lists of exceptions. For reasons of transparency, a list of exceptions is preferable to the so-called positive list approach of the GATS, whereby governments commit themselves to granting national treatment for foreign-controlled enterprises for only those sectors that are explicitly listed. Second, national treatment is not an isolated investment issue that can be dealt with successfully in an agreement that exists independent of the WTO agreements. Rather, it is an issue that cuts across trade and investment policy and is also highly relevant to competition policy. Hence, the Multilateral Agreement on Investment (MAI) being negotiated within the Organization for Economic Cooperation and Development (OECD) is not the correct way to place this concept into multilateral trade law, although the OECD work might yield a constructive precursor to a future WTO agreement. Implementation of a WTO agreement on national treatment for foreign-controlled enterprises will likely require some modification of WTO dispute settlement procedures. In particular some provision for enterprise-to-state dispute settlement will need to be established. On this, the North American Free Trade Agreement might provide a useful model (see Graham and Wilkie 1994).

International Control of Cartels and Cartel-Like Behavior

Virtually all competition-policy specialists agree that under most circumstances, cartels are bad. Thus, nearly all competition laws in place include anticartel provisions. Furthermore, convergence already exists. Thus, it would be relatively easy to achieve international consensus on a worldwide agreement to ban most cartels.

If many nations already have such a ban in place, why strike an international agreement? First, not all WTO member nations have competition policies, and, hence, in many nations there are no prohibitions on cartels. Under a WTO agreement, all nations would be required to bring national law into conformity. Second, even in nations with competition laws, enforcement of anticartel provisions has often been lax. A WTO agreement would step up enforcement of these laws, especially where the existence of a cartel in one nation creates tension in another nation. Third, some cartels exist purely in international markets. Many of these are legal because of various exemptions or loopholes in national laws.

In particular, many nations permit export cartels on the theory that their exporters need to have some sort of countervailing power to compete effectively with foreign rivals.[18] However, if every nation allows exporters to form cartels, any national benefit would be offset by the actions of other nations' export cartels. In the end, the cartels limit output and raise price, to the detriment of buyers of the cartelized product or service and to the benefit of no one. Therefore, a WTO agreement on cartels should include a ban on most export cartels. There are some exceptions, to be discussed below.

A WTO agreement on cartels would require some minor changes in existing dispute settlement procedures. If a panel, responding to a complaint by a member country, found cause to believe that a cartel existed in violation of the agreement, it would recommend that competition authorities in the nation where the alleged violation took place investigate the situation and, where appropriate, take remedial action. If the authorities failed to act, sanctions could be applied by the aggrieved nation (or nations) following standard WTO procedures.

What if the relevant authorities in the violating nation agreed to pursue the case, but found in favor of the defendant firm or firms? For example, if the problem were the putative existence of a producers' cartel that boycotted any distributor that handled imported products,[19] the relevant authorities might conclude that no such cartel existed, or that, if it did, its existence did not constitute a violation of national law (in principle, national law would be in conformity with the agreement). In this case, a detailed report would be transmitted to the panel indicating why the authorities reached the conclusion that they did. The panel could be empowered to review the report and accept or reject it. If it were accepted, the case would be terminated.

If it were not accepted, withdrawal of WTO concessions (sanctions in the sense used by WTO) might be authorized.[20] Grounds for nonacceptance could be procedural (e.g., the factual investigation had been impaired somehow, or due process was not followed) or substantive (the panel might determine that the relevant national standards did not conform with the WTO agreement).

However, if it were rejected, bolder alternatives than sanctions might be envisaged. For example, the panel (or some other agent) might have standing to pursue the case in the national courts (or, in the case of the European Union, the supranational courts) of the violating WTO member.

---

18. If national exporters can collectively exercise market power in foreign markets, they can appropriate rents from foreigners to the benefit of domestic residents.

19. Such a cartel has been alleged, for example, in the case of the flat glass industry in Japan.

20. Fox (1997) argues for fines rather than sanctions. The WTO presently cannot impose fines and would have to be given that power.

Enlargement of WTO Consultative Procedures

On trade-related issues other than cartels, there is little likelihood of international agreement on substantive rules to which the above procedures could be applied. However, there is room for new procedural rules. Particularly, existing WTO consultation procedures could be enlarged. As we have already seen, the 1960 GATT decision called for consultation between or among nations if private business practices had alleged effects of foreclosing exports. Similarly, WTO member nations could commit to enter into consultations over export or investment foreclosure. A comprehensive list of private practices, which could be the basis for member countries to request consultations, could be compiled. If the list included a private practice, that would not constitute a prescription against the practice but would indicate that consultations could be initiated. Such a list should include vertical restraints that might foreclose exports (e.g., exclusive-dealing contracts) and monopolistic discriminations as identified by Fox (1997). We would enlarge this list and make it more detailed.

Consultations could be bilateral or multilateral, as circumstances dictate. There would be no requirement to resolve the problem via consultations. And the consultations would not preclude formal dispute settlement procedures, if those procedures were applicable to a particular case. Indeed, relevant parties are required under these procedures to attempt to solve a dispute via consultation and negotiation before the dispute comes before a panel. Nonetheless, we believe that many disputes involving private practices could be resolved via consultation, especially if nations were to proceed in the spirit of positive comity.

Mergers and Acquisitions Notification

We advocate mandatory notification for mergers and acquisitions likely to have significant international effects (e.g., a merger of two firms having sales outside the home country or countries that exceed certain threshold levels). We envisage that most cross-border mergers or acquisitions would be subject to this requirement. The notification might consist of the following:

- an announcement that a certain merger or acquisition is pending,

- publication of basic information regarding the parties to the transaction (e.g., the basic income statement and balance sheet), and

- indication of whether national authorities of the home nation or nations of the parties to the transaction intend to review the merger.

Other countries with substantial interest in the transaction (i.e., the transaction, if completed, would have material effects in the domestic market of the relevant country) could request consultation with the home country's competition authorities, as per the mandatory consultation provision outlined above. The home country's competition officials would determine whether such effects were present. Such a determination would be sufficient to show that such effects were present.

Are such procedures for mandatory consultations really necessary? After all, many cases that might have been covered by this procedure (including the Boeing-McDonnell Douglas merger and the US-Japan dispute over auto parts but not including the US-Japan dispute over photographic film and paper) have in practice been resolved, apparently to everyone's satisfaction, via bilateral procedures. Nonetheless, the WTO procedures would be there when and if nations sought to use them. WTO procedures might be utilized by smaller nations more than by larger ones, especially if a bilateral resolution were to come at the expense of smaller nations. But WTO procedures might also be used to resolve disputes over merger approval among larger nations, especially if more than two nations were party to the dispute.

TRAMs Plus: A Competition-Policy Safeguard Mechanism

As globalization encompasses more regions and more issues (e.g., services), downsizing and rationalization pressures will grow as fast as opportunities for firms to expand and prosper in other sectors. Ad hoc safeguard mechanisms, such as enhanced antidumping procedures (which are new in many smaller WTO members) and creative subsidization, are already burgeoning to cope with downsizing and rationalization. But these often have high efficiency costs (see chapter 1) and are administered in ways that are at best cumbersome and at worst capricious, creating rancor and inequity.

Competition policies in Japan and parts of Europe have historically handled rationalization and downsizing better than elsewhere, though they have hardly handled them perfectly (see various chapters on Japan and Europe). They do so sometimes through functional exceptions such as rationalization cartels and sometimes through sectoral exceptions such as in European basic metals. Mergers between strong firms and weak ones are both efficient and fair, if the only other real alternative is extinction of the weak. The most important key to free entry is often rational exit (see chapter 1). In that spirit of contestability and market access, there is great potential in a competition-policy-oriented safeguard agreement that could eventually become part of the TRAMs and that would presumably use the same dispute settlement procedures.[21]

---

21. Messerlin (1996) sees little merit in a TRAMs agreement except to discipline ad hoc safeguard mechanisms.

We think a TRAMS agreement is even more feasible than tables 1 and 2 make it appear. First, cooperative unilateralism and multilateralism along the lines sketched above, will, if successful, build the networks, trust, and precedents for a more ambitious TRAMs agenda. Second, the inefficiencies and inequities of current ad hoc safeguard mechanisms will soon become untenable, as firms and countries that have historically gained from them become their new victims at the hands of powerful emerging rivals.

Cooperative Arrangements among Nations

WTO initiatives will work best if supported by less-formal bilateral and regional cooperation on these issues. Cooperative arrangements already exist among the competition authorities of various nations, and more such arrangements are easily visualized (see chapter 10 by Fox on US-EU arrangements, chapter 2 by Goldman, Bodrug, and Warner on Canada, and chapter 12 by Thomson on Australia-New Zealand). These could run the spectrum from informal consultation to joint legal action.

For example, the United States and the European Union already have a cooperative agreement that provides for consultation between relevant authorities in Washington and Brussels whenever a merger or acquisition comes under the scrutiny of both. In most cases, the authorities will agree on who has the most pressing interest in the case. The authorities with lesser interest will agree not to contest the findings of the authority with greater interest. Because the substantive standards for merger and acquisition differ, a merger that might not be allowed to stand on one side of the Atlantic, if allowed to stand on the other side, will not be contested. Alternatively, a merger that might be allowed to stand on one side of the Atlantic might be blocked on the other side, without objection by the authorities who would have allowed it.

The US-EU agreement does not, however, allow for detailed information sharing, because enforcement standards differ greatly. In the United States, those who violate certain antitrust laws can receive criminal penalties, whereas only civil penalties are invoked in the European Union. Thus, EU authorities have been unwilling to consider information-sharing cooperative agreements because information disclosed by DGIV to the Antitrust Division of the US Department of Justice could lead to criminal charges against European nationals for violations that would not be considered criminal in Europe. Similarly, the possibility that criminal charges might be pressed in the United States for violations that elsewhere would not be considered criminal has deterred cooperative arrangements between the United States and other nations, including Japan.

The United States also has limited joint enforcement agreements with Canada. Under these agreements, there is cooperation in fact-finding if both nations suspect a criminal violation (see chapter 2 by Goldman, Bodrug, and Warner).

There have been proposals for even bolder cooperative arrangements, including one for joint US-Japan enforcement of antitrust laws (see Bergsten and Noland 1993). The rationale for such cooperation is that, by investigating and, where appropriate, prosecuting violations jointly, the joint interests of the cooperating nations will be carried out. However, because of substantial differences in penalties and other provisions of law enforcement, there is considerable reluctance on the part of a nation to grant any discovery powers (powers to investigate in order to accumulate evidence of possible violation) to foreign authorities. In the preceding paragraph, we noted that this includes a reluctance to share information. But joint enforcement would necessarily require discovery powers that go well beyond simple information sharing. The issue of standing poses problems (i.e., would enforcement authorities of one nation be granted standing in the courts of another?).

Unilateral Enforcement of National Antitrust Laws Internationally

Competition-policy issues will not dissolve in the absence of multilateral, regional, or bilateral action. But we do not recommend the unilateralism that currently exists. As already noted, the European Union and the United States have unilaterally enforced antitrust laws extraterritorially (i.e., outside the sovereign territory of the relevant authority). The European Union has exercised its authority only in cases involving mergers of firms with significant European presence (in fact, all such cases have involved at least one firm headquartered in Europe). The United States has exercised a broader reach. US law and policy encompasses the effects doctrine, which asserts that US law can reach any foreign conduct having direct, substantial, and foreseeable effects on the US economy.[22] (In cases involving cartels, it must also be established that the intent of the cartel was to raise prices in US markets directly, substantially, and foreseeably.) US courts have admitted such cases under US law.

Practices that have alleged effects on producers (such as alleged foreclosure of US exports from foreign markets) would not, however, normally raise domestic prices or restrict output. In the short run, it seems that US domestic supply for the relevant good or service would be greater if an export restriction existed.[23] Thus, such cases do not fall under the effects doctrine.

---

22. The effects doctrine was established in US law in 1911 in the case *United States versus American Tobacco*, 221 US 106.

23. But this might not be the case if the export foreclosure prevented domestic producers from achieving static or dynamic economies of scale.

US courts have held, nonetheless, that in some instances export fore-closure can be subject to US antitrust law. Specifically, the courts have identified opportunities for US exports that are hindered by practices in foreign countries that would be illegal in the United States. However, during the Reagan administration it was announced that the US Department of Justice would not pursue any extraterritorial action unless there were a demonstrated a loss to US consumer welfare because of raised prices or reduced quantities (US Department of Justice 1988, note 159). However, just four years later, Bush administration Assistant Attorney General for Antitrust, James Rill, indicated that the Antitrust Division would consider suits against foreign import cartels that limit US exports, if those cartels are illegal under the law of the country of import, and that country fails to enforce its law.

This policy shift was apparently made to give impetus to the Structural Impediments Initiative (SII), a then ongoing effort by the United States and Japan to break down structural barriers to trade between each other.[24] During the Clinton administration's early years, then-Assistant Attorney General for Antitrust, Anne Bingaman, indicated that she would pursue practices that foreclose US exports or limit the ability of US firms to invest directly in a foreign market. However, no court case based on this new doctrine was ever actually pursued, and the idea seems to have been dropped during the second Clinton administration. Thus, it is impossible to know with certainty how the courts would currently treat export foreclosure cases. However, courts have in the past ruled that such cases can fall under US jurisdiction.

The contrast between the Clinton administration's enthusiasm to prose-cute cases involving export foreclosure, and its failure to bring to frui-tion a successful case after a three-and-a-half year effort illustrates one of the flaws in the unilateral approach. To prosecute a case under US law, evidentiary standards are very high (the case must be proven by means of hard evidence). Staff at the Antitrust Division have indicated that lack of hard evidence has impeded efforts to develop a case.

US authorities have no power of discovery outside the United States—that is, they cannot compel firms that do not have a US presence to submit company records that might (or might not) substantiate the alle-gations.[25] And, where cases are pursued unilaterally, foreign authorities are generally reluctant to use their powers of discovery to assist US efforts. Indeed, other nations (including Canada and the United King-dom) have passed blocking statutes that would forbid firms operating within their jurisdictions to comply with US requests for information.

---

24. We say "shift in policy" to emphasize that there was no shift in US case law.

25. However, many foreign firms now have US subsidiaries, and discovery could be compelled through these subsidiaries.

Blocking statutes illustrate the major flaw with unilateral extraterritorial enforcement of competition laws: other nations typically resent such actions, even if the relevant authorities in the affected nations might have sympathy with the case on substantive grounds. Other nations have viewed the US extraterritorial application of antitrust laws as a violation of their sovereignty.

We do not see much future in unilateral enforcement of antitrust laws, especially in light of the Clinton administration's record. However, the Department of Justice did seek and identify cases where it felt that the practices involved had particularly egregious effects. But, as a practical matter, it found that it could not build successful cases because it lacked powers of discovery outside the United States. Without discovery powers, evidence of wrongdoing under US law could not be accumulated. And, had such a case been successfully undertaken, the outrage of foreign nations would likely have been great even if the substantive merits of the case had been strong.

Reform of Anticompetitive World Trade Laws

Most reform of anticompetitive world trade laws could be internalized within a TRAMS agreement. For example, such an agreement would, as noted above, deal with cartels that use boycotts to foreclose entry. Export cartels could be banned. Thus, antidumping reform could be included in the negotiation of a TRAMS agreement.

However, antidumping reform would likely be one of the most contentious issues in the negotiation of a TRAMs agreement. Many trade specialists see antidumping as a necessary safeguard in international trade law, because it protects domestic producers from imports priced below cost. However, antidumping provisions are detested by most economists, because they raise prices and reduce consumer welfare on the basis of specious price or cost tests that bear no relation to below-cost pricing. However, most economists agree that predation exists (see chapter 1). Competition law in most countries that have such a law directly or implicitly deals with predation. Thus, antidumping could be eliminated entirely, and nations could apply competition law instead.[26] This alternative is consistent with concepts of national treatment: under competition law, low-priced imports would be dealt with no differently than low-priced equivalent domestic goods or services. In the application of competition law, imports are not discriminated against, whereas antidumping law is directed solely at imports (and hence, because dumping

---

26. This is of course what is done inside the European Union (see chapter 8 by Nicolaïdis and Vernon) as well as between Australia and New Zealand (see chapter 12 by Thomson).

is easier to prove than is predation, imports are effectively discriminated against).[27]

There are two objections to this alternative. First, in many countries (e.g., the United States) it is difficult and costly to prove predation. Second, in those countries that apply antidumping law, the intent of the lawmakers is that it be easier to apply measures against low-priced imports than against low-priced equivalent domestic goods or services. In other words, the intent of antidumping is to create an easier standard to act as a safeguard against low-priced imports. Thus, antidumping is an internationally agreed on exception to the principle of national treatment. As Lipstein points out in chapter 13, there have been rationales for this exception (e.g., the inability of domestic producers to arbitrage international price discrimination), but these rationales lose their validity over time. Meanwhile, the divergence between predation standards and antidumping standards has widened.

Antidumping policies exist mostly because there is often a significant political constituency in favor of their continuance. Offsetting this is a growing number of internationally oriented firms that are alarmed by the widespread use of antidumping policies in recent years. Indeed, as recently as 10 years ago nations could be divided into two groups: those nations that were primarily users of antidumping (e.g., Australia, Canada, the European Union, New Zealand, and the United States) and those nations that were primarily victims of this use (the newly industrializing nations, including, at one time, Japan). Today, given the proliferation of antidumping (mostly by nations that were once victims), more of the world's trading nations are simultaneously both users and victims of antidumping.

The true victims of this proliferation of antidumping are the world's international firms. These firms have not, to date, formed an effective constituency against antidumping, but their numbers are growing (see

---

27. See chapter 13 by Lipstein. To recapitulate, to demonstrate that dumping occurs, it is necessary under US law to show that imports are sold at prices below those in the country of origin. To establish this, the US Department of Commerce, which makes antidumping determinations administratively, uses procedures that many analysts believe are stacked against the importer (e.g., dumping can be found even if average price in the United States is exactly equal to average price in the country of origin, because the procedures allow for certain observed values of the price to be discarded). Alternatively, the Department of Commerce can use, in place of prices in the country of origin, either prices in a third country or a "constructed cost" measure. Both are subject to similar biases. To invoke antidumping remedies (extra duties), material injury to US producers must also be shown. Lipstein notes that such harm, defined as "harm which is not inconsequential, immaterial, or important," is almost trivial to establish. It can be established if sales, profits, or employment by US producers is reduced as a result of the dumping.

Graham 1996). Thus, the call for significant reform or abolition of anti-dumping will grow louder in the years to come.[28]

The existing antidumping law could be reformed instead of eliminated. Lipstein argues in chapter 13 that certain provisions of the US Robinson-Patman Act would, if incorporated into antidumping law, defend exporters against charges of dumping and, on balance, tip the scales slightly in their favor. We support Lipstein's proposals, which in summary form are:[29]

■ To apply antitrust principles to a definition of domestic-like products and injury determination. In particular, Lipstein advocates the use of narrower product categories (to eliminate present absurdities, such as an importer being found guilty of dumping product into the United States if no similar domestic product is even produced) and elimination of cumulation (adding together the imports of several firms or from several countries) in injury determination tests.

■ To establish a "meeting the competition" defense, whereby an exporter of products to the United States would not be found guilty of dumping if it lowered prices to meet those being charged by domestic competitors. The burden of proof, however, would be on the exporter.

■ To narrow the criteria for the standing of antidumping petitioners (to ensure that the petitioner represents all domestic producers of the product in question).

■ To require the Department of Commerce to examine products of similar grade and quality (an antitrust concept) when determining whether dumping occurs and by what margins. The Department of Commerce under present standards can, in effect, compare apples to oranges. The Commerce Department would also be required to make its comparisons at the same level of trade (i.e., it could not compare prices charged by exporters to large scale wholesalers in the United States with those charged to small scale distributors in the home country).

Lipstein notes that elements of these proposals were incorporated in the Uruguay Round Antidumping Code (and in the US enabling legislation) and that both the existing code and the counterpart US laws are still tipped in favor of the plaintiff.

---

28. The Uruguay Round antidumping reforms, however, tended to make it easier for plaintiffs in antidumping cases. See Schott and Buurman (1994).

29. In chapter 13, Lipstein presents these as reforms of US law. However, it is easy to envisage equivalent reforms of international law as embodied in the GATT.

Lipstein begs the question: Should some sort of predation standard be incorporated into antidumping law? As noted, predation is notoriously difficult to define in measurable terms (how does one measure intent to monopolize?), and, under US law and policy, it is difficult to prove in a court of law.

Although antidumping might, in principle, bear some resemblance to competition law regarding predation, in practice, antidumping is often used to grant relief to sectors in which domestic producers are facing intensified international competition (i.e., sectors in which a particular nation is losing comparative advantage). Such sectors are often termed industries in decline. Given this, it has been proposed that antidumping might be replaced by policies designed to protect industries in decline for a period long enough for adjustment to occur. In this case, adjustment means that the domestic industry shrinks as a result of disinvestment and worker relocation. Such policies might resemble antidumping, in the sense that tariff rates above those bound in GATT Article II would be permitted during an adjustment period. However, these tariffs would be determined not on the basis of artificial concepts such as dumping margins. And whether an industry would be eligible for relief would not be determined by injury tests. Rather, an optimal (or at least reasonable) rate of industry contraction would be determined, and levels and duration of tariffs would be set to permit such a contraction to occur at minimal cost.

Conclusions and Recommendations

Recent cases demonstrate that competition policy, in some form, belongs in the multilateral rules for world trade. The WTO recognizes this and now has a working group in place whose mission is to explore how trade and competition policy might interact.

We recommend that an activist approach be followed. In line with the discussion in this chapter, the approach entails two elements:

- All WTO member nations should be required to have in place a law on competition and the institutional means to enforce it, and

- This requirement should be negotiated as part of a WTO agreement on TRAMs.

Our version of the TRAMs proposal is not necessarily the ultimate framework for how competition policy might be implemented at the international level. Rather, it would be a first step in the right direction. As national economies become more and more integrated with one another and business organizations become increasingly global, national governments will likely rethink whether it is in their best interests to retain full sovereignty over competition policy. At present, many policymakers realize that increasing world economic integration poses new challenges for competition policy. Nonetheless, they are unwilling to cede any national sovereignty in this domain. Thus, our TRAMs proposal is meant to be a first, modest, and experimental step toward a more international approach to competition policy. The proposal makes maximum use of existing WTO rules and procedures—substantive new rules would be needed in only two areas, but these are high priority areas where there is already some consensus of views: national treatment for foreign-owned firms and regulation of cartels. Otherwise, what we propose is that national authorities extend a practice in which they are already engaged, and consultation with one another over specific cases where the interests of more than one national authority are at stake. In addition, certain mergers and acquisitions would be formally notified to the WTO (so that basic information pertaining to these cases is available to all national authorities), and consultation among national authorities would be mandatory if at least one national authority in a specific case requests it. We believe that implementation of these proposals would neither diminish sovereignty nor transfer it to the WTO.

In short, our proposals are a modest first step in the right direction. Once this step is taken, and after some experience with the new procedures has been accumulated, nations can decide on the next step.

References

Bergsten, C. Fred, and Marcus Noland. 1993. *Reconcilable Differences? United States-Japan Economic Conflict*. Washington: Institute for International Economics.

Fox, Eleanor M. 1997. Toward World Antitrust and Market Access. *The American Journal of International Law 91*, no. 1 (January).

Graham, Edward M. 1995. Competition Policy and the New Trade Agenda. In *New Dimensions of Market Access in a Globalizing Economy*. OECD Documents. Paris: Organization for Economic Cooperation and Development.

Graham, Edward M. 1996. *Global Corporations and National Governments*. Washington: Institute for International Economics.

Graham, Edward M., and Christopher Wilkie. 1994. Multinationals and the Investment Provisions of the NAFTA. *The International Trade Journal 8*, no. 3 (Spring).

Liu, Lawrence S. 1996. In Search of Fair and Free Trade: The Experience of the Republic of China on Taiwan as an Asian Model of Implementing Competition Policy and Law. In *Competition Regulation in the Pacific Rim*, ed. by Carl Green and Douglas Rosenthal. Dobbs Ferry, New York: Oceana Press.

Ma, Jun. 1995. Defining the Limits of Local Government Power in China: The Relevance of International Experience. *Journal of Contemporary China 10*.

Messerlin, Patrick A. 1996. Competition Policy and Antidumping Reform: An Exercise in Transition. In *The World Trading System: Challenges Ahead*, ed. by Jeffrey J. Schott. Washington: Institute for International Economics.

Petrazzini, Ben A. 1996. *Global Telecom Talks: A Trillion Dollar Deal*. POLICY ANALYSES IN INTERNATIONAL ECONOMICS 44. Washington: Institute for International Economics.

Richardson, J. David. 1995. Comment on Can Dispute Settlement Contribute to and International Agreement (Institutional Order) on Locational Competition? (by J. Michael Finger) In *Locational Competition in the World Economy: Symposium 1994*, ed. by Horst Siebert. Tubingen, Germany: J. C. B. Mohr (Paul Siebeck).

Scherer, F. M. 1994. *Competition Policies for an Integrated World Economy.* Washington: Brookings Institution.

Scherer, F. M., and David Ross. 1990. *Industrial Market Structure and Economic Performance,* 3d. ed. Boston: Houghton Mifflin.

Schott, Jeffrey J., and Johanna W. Buurman. 1994. *The Uruguay Round: An Assessment.* Washington: Institute for International Economics

US Department of Justice, Antitrust Division. 1988. *Enforcement Guidelines for International Operations,* revised. Washington: US Department of Justice, Antitrust Division.

Warner, Mark A. A. 1994. Efficiencies and Merger Review in Canada, the European Community, and the United States: Implications for Convergence and Harmonization. *Vanderbilt Journal of Transnational Law* 26: 1059.

Index

Australian competition policy (*Cont.*)
  reforms in 1990s, 387-89
  replacement of trade law with, 369, 391-92, 398-402
  third-line forcing, 387
  tolerance of anticompetitive behavior, 385-86, 392-93
Australia/New Zealand Closer Economic Relations Trade Agreement (CER), 392, 394, 395, 398-402
Austria, 380-81
automobile industry
  Canadian, 72-73
  Japanese, 191-92, 319, 331, 508, 514, 523-24, 528
  joint ventures, 253
  in United Kingdom, 221-22
  in United States, 317, 426, 539-40
  voluntary export restraints, 480, 482-83, 484, 487
autoparts, US-Japan dispute, 549-50

banks. *See* financial institutions; financial *keiretsu*
Barr, William, 265
barriers to market entry
  distribution arrangements, 6b, 184-85, 200, 524
  in Japanese retailing, 453-60
  keiretsu seen as, 502, 522
  market shares as measurement of, 495-97
  predatory behavior, 200
  set-up and withdrawal costs, 20
  standards, 215-16
  strategic, 18
  trade disputes over, 6b
  See also voluntary import expansions
Baxter, Bill, 378
Benedict, Ruth, 313-14
Bergsten, C. F., 495-96, 502, 578
bid rigging. *See* price-fixing agreements
Bingaman, Anne, 324, 325, 573
Boeing, 11, 12, 23, 25, 27, 303, 368
Boston Consulting Group (BCG), 322
Britain. *See* United Kingdom
British Telecom (BT), 216, 220
Brittan, Sir Leon, 268, 362
Bush, George, 262

Canada
  economic policies, 48-49
  foreign investment from, 49
  foreign investment in, 48, 67-70
  mutual legal assistance treaty (MLAT), 62-64
  trade policy, 48, 49, 71-80
  trade with United States, 48
  See also North American Free Trade Agreement (NAFTA)

Canada-US Free Trade Agreement, 49, 75-76, 77-78, 369, 409
Canadian competition law
  abuse of dominance, 56-58, 78-80
  collusion, 54-56
  Competition Act, 50-69, 72, 78-82
  enforcement, 50-51, 52, 58
  enforcement agreement with United States, 63-64, 267
  export cartels, 80
  extraterritoriality, 62-67
  history, 50
  mergers, 53-54, 58-62, 323
  predatory pricing, 78-80
  research joint ventures, 80-82
Canadian International Trade Tribunal (CITT), 71, 72-75
cartels
  benefits, 32
  crisis, 123, 342, 361
  efficiency defense, 121-23, 124
  EU law, 223, 285-87, 342-43, 361
  French law, 92, 93
  German law, 120-25
  history in Europe, 116-17, 273-74
  import, 123, 125, 153, 176
  international control, 567-68
  Japanese policy, 151, 152, 154, 157, 170-76
  legal in Japan, 176-77, 317, 439, 447, 449t, 450, 451t
  restructuring, 121-22, 223, 450
  US law, 245-47, 252-53, 341-42
  See also export cartels
Celler-Kefauver Merger Act, 236, 241
CER. *See* Australia/New Zealand Closer Economic Relations Trade Agreement (CER)
Chapman, William, 314
China, 262, 410
CITT. *See* Canadian International Trade Tribunal
Clayton Act, 236, 240, 249, 259, 260
Clinton, Bill, 317
collusion, 23, 26
  Canadian law on, 54-56
  French law, 88-89
  suspected in *keiretsu*, 191-92, 516-21
  See also cartels; cooperation; price-fixing
competition
  attribute, 17-18
  best-practice, 18-19
  excessive, 445
  goals, 317-18
  in Japanese culture, 313-14, 316, 319-21, 328
  perfect, 29
  preferences of individual companies, 11
  rationale for interference in, 441-47, 469-70
  Schumpeterian, 28-29
  welfare effects, 441-42
Competition Act (Canada), 50-69, 72, 78-82

Competition Act (United Kingdom), 202, 204, 206
Competition Bureau (Canada), 52
Competition Council (France), 87-88, 89-90, 91-93
   approach, 95-96, 97-98, 104-6
   cases referred to, 91-92, 92*t*
   merger reviews, 112
   price discrimination cases, 106-7
competition policy
   compromises in, 318-19
   cooperative arrangements, 571-72
   dealing with import competition, 493-94
   enforcement, 549, 573-74
   exclusion of sectors from, 552
   exemptions, 554*t*
   firm behavior, 13-23
   harmonization of. *See* harmonization
   history, 358-60
   interaction with trade policy, 4-5, 6*b*, 199-202, 272-73, 335, 357, 377-83
   internationalization of, 547
   lifetime behavior, 27-33
   and market access, 548-53
   in market systems, 5-6
   objectives, 7-13
   political opposition to, 375-77
   relational behavior, 23-27
   sectoral differences, 34
   social objectives, 33-35, 375, 379
   unilateral enforcement, 572-74
   See also specific countries and issues
Competition Tribunal (Canada), 50, 53, 57, 60
computers. *See* information technology
conglomerates, 36, 37, 39
   mergers, 135-36, 182, 349
Conseil de la concurrence. *See* Competition Council (France)
conspiracies. *See* collusion; price-fixing
constructed export price (CEP), 412, 434-36
consumer protection issues, 154, 236-37, 327-28
contestability, 19-20
cooperation among firms
   efficiency increased by, 10, 24
   horizontal, 24-25, 26-27, 100-103, 219-20
   vertical, 24, 25-27
copyright. *See* intellectual property protection
cultural issues, 34, 68, 70

Daimler Benz, 134-35, 144
de Gaulle, Charles, 278
de Havilland, 61-62, 302, 350, 368
Deming, W. Edwards, 321
deregulation
   in Australia, 394
   in European Union, 303
   in Germany, 146
   in Japan, 175, 315, 317, 329, 334, 460-65, 471
   telecommunications industries, 378-79, 460-65, 471
   in United States, 378-79

DGFT. *See* Director General of Fair Trading
DGIV. *See* Directorate-General IV
Directorate-General IV (DGIV), European Commission, 207, 208, 360, 368-69, 377, 551
Director General of Fair Trading (DGFT; United Kingdom), 203
distribution
   barriers to foreign firms, 200, 524
   contracting arrangements, 527-28
   French system, 105-6, 110
   Japanese system, 6*b*, 184-85, 522-23
   See also resale price maintenance; vertical restraints
distribution *keiretsu*, 191, 508, 514, 515
dominance. *See* abuse of dominance
dominant firms. *See* monopolies
dumping. *See* antidumping measures

EC. *See* European Community
ECSC. *See* European Coal and Steel Community
EEAA. *See* European Economic Area Agreement
efficiency
   allocative, 237
   best-practice competition, 18-19
   defense, 554*t*
   dynamic, 8, 10-11, 28
   economywide, 35-39
   lack of in state-owned enterprises, 37
   as objective of competition policy, 7-13
   over long term, 27-28
   static, 8, 10
   tradeoffs with fairness, 9-12
enforcement of competition laws
   in European Union, 341, 342-43, 353
   international coordination agreements, 63-64, 266-69, 303, 355-56, 374, 397-98
   See also extraterritoriality; *and specific countries*
ESPRIT (European Strategic Program for Research and Development in Information Technology), 301
ET. *See* extraterritoriality
EU. *See* European Union
European Coal and Steel Community (ECSC), 275-76, 285, 364
European Commission, 277-78, 302
   Directorate-General IV (DGIV), 207, 208, 360, 368-69, 377
European Community (EC)
   antitrust cooperation agreement with United States, 268, 269, 303, 355-56
   competition policy. *See* European Union (EU) competition policy
   formation, 273, 276-77
   Single European Act, 277, 290, 294-97, 361
   trade among members, 280-81, 297
   trade policies, 280-85, 305
   transborder mergers and acquisitions, 297

European Court of Justice, 109, 207, 278-79, 296
European Economic Area Agreement (EEAA), 356
European Union (EU)
  antidumping measures, 283-84, 363, 378
  competition with United States and Japan, 295-96
  industrial policy, 361-62
  intellectual property protection, 363
  international negotiations, 279, 283
  investment policy, 362
  mutual recognition of national standards, 215-16, 296, 297, 298-99, 300-301, 364
  regulatory powers, 364-65
  technological cooperation, 301-2
  trade policies, 361-62, 363-64, 380-81
  voluntary export restraints imposed by, 476, 478-79t
European Union (EU) competition policy
  abuse of dominance, 206-7, 212-13, 222, 227, 290-92, 303, 343-44
  administration of, 277-79, 288-90, 302, 342-43
  administrative fines, 161, 162
  cartels, 285-87, 342-43
  comparison to US law, 339-54
  cooperation with United States, 571-72
  criticisms, 208, 209
  enforcement, 89, 99-100, 341, 342-43, 353
  exempted cartels, 223, 285-86, 287, 342, 361
  export cartels, 228
  extraterritoriality, 287, 303, 373
  goals, 206, 207, 305, 340-41
  history, 273-77
  interaction with trade policy, 304-5
  joint ventures, 229, 350
  merger reviews, 27, 93, 208, 211, 227, 292, 302-3, 348, 350-51, 353
  monopolies, 227, 290, 303-5, 364-65
  potential conflicts with national policy, 144-48, 209-13, 231-32
  predatory pricing, 351, 352
  price discrimination, 16, 219
  public procurement, 215
  as replacement for members' trade laws, 369
  research and development joint ventures, 228-29, 289-90
  restrictive agreements, 206, 211-12
  role of national competition authorities, 89, 144-45
  specialization agreements, 229, 342
  state aids, 230, 277, 292-94, 362, 380-81
  supremacy over national law, 279
  vertical restraints, 220, 221, 287-89, 346-47
  See also Treaty of Rome
exclusive-dealing arrangements, 219-20, 221-22
  Australian law, 386
  of Boeing and airlines, 12, 25
  EU law, 220

German law, 138-39
Japanese law, 187, 188-89
UK law, 220, 221-22
US law, 236, 240, 259
export cartels, 26, 552
  Canadian law, 80
  efficiency gains, 11
  in European Union, 228
  German law, 123, 125
  in Japan, 153, 176, 452
  in United Kingdom, 228
  in United States, 224, 260-61, 264
exports. *See* voluntary export restraints (VERS)
extraterritoriality
  in Canadian competition law, 62-67
  in EU competition law, 214, 287, 303, 373
  in intellectual property protection, 373
  opposition to, 397
  in trade law, 373
  in UK competition law, 213-14
  in US competition law, 64-66, 80, 263-66, 330, 370-75

fairness
  economywide, 39-40
  international differences in meaning, 8-9
  as objective of competition policy, 7-13
  over long term, 28
  tradeoffs with efficiency, 9-12
Fair Trade Act (FTA; United Kingdom), 202, 203-4, 206
Fair Trade Commission of Japan (FTCJ), 155-56, 158-59, 171, 326-27, 333
  creation, 152
  definition of public interest, 446
  Designation of Unfair Business Practices, 193, 194
  distribution guidelines, 184, 188-90
  enforcement, 160-70, 452, 551
  guidelines on joint research and development, 467-69
  merger reviews, 182-83, 322-23
  powers, 178
  procedures, 158-60
  studies of *keiretsu*, 522-23
Federal Cartel Office (Germany), 119, 142
Federal Trade Commission (FTC; United States), 242, 265, 341, 352, 367, 420, 551
Federation of Economic Organizations. *See* Keidanren
financial institutions
  Canadian, 57
  Japanese, 193, 317
  mergers, in United Kingdom, 216-17
  supervision in European Union, 300
financial *keiretsu*, 502, 506, 507t, 515, 516-18, 519-20, 522-23
firms
  competitive behavior, 13-23
  lifetime behavior, 27-33

International Antitrust Enforcement Assistance
    Act (IAEAA), 268, 355, 398
investment. *See* foreign direct investment
Investment Canada Act (ICA), 67-70
ITC. *See* US International Trade Commission

Japan
    central planning, 316-17
    competition in culture, 313-14, 316, 319-21,
        328
    corporate accountability, 333-34
    deregulation, 175, 315, 317, 329, 334
    distribution system, 6b, 184-85, 522-23
    economic trends, 314-15, 336
    financial markets, 173-74
    foreign firms' access to market, 6b, 332-33,
        335-36, 523-24, 540
    industrial policy, 173
    innovation in, 320
    jurisdictional disputes among ministries,
        463-64
    Ministry of Finance, 173-74, 317
    relations with United States, 152, 316, 330-
        34
    sectoral exceptions to competition policy,
        552-53
    semiconductor trade agreements, 332, 475,
        489, 495-96
    Structural Impediments Initiative (SII), 155-
        56, 161, 164, 184, 188, 239, 265, 452,
        459
    as target of voluntary export restraints, 476,
        478-79t
    trade with Asia, 330
    trade associations, 170, 171, 173, 324
    trade policy, 315-16, 327
    trade with United States, 6b, 8, 239, 475
    See also Ministry of International Trade and
        Industry (MITI); Ministry of Posts
        and Telecommunications (MPT)
Japanese competition policy
    abuse of dependency, 152
    abuse of dominance, 156-57, 192-95
    administrative guidance, 173-76, 450, 452
    administrative surcharges, 159, 161-63, 163t,
        165
    cartels, 151, 152, 154, 157, 170-76, 450, 452
    consumer protection issues, 154, 327-28
    enforcement, 153, 154, 155, 158-70, 191, 196,
        323-26, 551
    exempted cartels, 176-77, 317, 439, 447, 449t,
        450, 451t
    exemptions, 153, 171, 447-52
    history, 151-56, 314, 439-40, 461
    link to trade disputes, 190-91, 194-95
    mergers, 156, 178, 181-83, 322-23
    monopolies, 156, 178-81
    price-fixing agreements, 154, 323-24
    price-reporting system, 154-55
    private damage actions, 160, 166-69, 325, 334

protection of specific industries, 448-49, 450
public interest consideration, 446-47
recent changes, 470-71
reforms recommended, 326-27, 335
resale price maintenance, 151, 152, 168-69,
    179, 185-86, 189, 323, 326
research and development collaboration,
    465-69
retail entry regulations, 453-60
unfair business practices, 157-58
vertical restraints, 167-68, 184-92
Western ideas in, 322-27
See also Antimonopoly Law (AML)
Japan Fair Trade Commission (JFTC). *See* Fair
    Trade Commission of Japan (FTCJ)
joint ventures, 554t
    definition, 23n
    EU law, 229, 350
    multinational, 553
    UK law, 229
    US law, 238-39, 240, 243-45, 252-55, 263, 349-
        50
    See also research and development joint
        ventures

Kao Cosmetics, 169, 326
Keidanren (Federation of Economic Organiza-
    tions), 172, 328, 329, 446, 450
keiretsu
    antitrust issues, 503-4
    contracting arrangements, 526-28, 538-41
    distribution, 191, 508, 514, 515
    effects, 501-3
    financial, 502, 506, 507t, 515, 516-18, 519-20,
        522-23
    formation, 519-20
    forms, 501, 506, 508, 514-16
    interlocking shareholdings, 509-13t, 528,
        529-37t, 538
    market access issues, 190-91, 504, 522, 526-
        28, 538-41
    meaning of term, 184-85, 505-6
    opposing views of, 501-3
    organizational boundaries, 538-41
    potential anticompetitive effects, 518-21
    unwarranted suspicion of collusion, 191-92,
        516-21
    vertical, 506, 508, 509-13t, 515, 519, 522
    within-group trading, 522-23

labor unions, 36, 260
Large-Scale Retail Store Law (Japan), 453-55
    accommodation procedure, 454-60, 456f,
        458f
less than fair value (LTFV), 411, 412
like products, 412, 417-19, 420-23, 427-28

MAI. *See under* OECD
market foreclosure, 220-21, 521-25, 554t
    See also barriers to market entry

oil
- cartels in Japan, 154, 161, 163-64, 166-67, 172-73, 174-75, 446-47, 452
- price agreements in France, 102-3
- price caps in Germany, 128-29

oligopoly, 15

OMA, *see* orderly marketing arrangements

orderly marketing arrangements (OMA), 555t

Organization for Economic Cooperation and Development. *See* OECD

Ozawa, Ichiro, 327

patents. *See* intellectual property protection

positive comity, 563

predatory behavior, 19, 554t
- as barrier to entry of foreign firms, 200
- product changes, 255
- types, 218-19

predatory pricing, 218, 219, 220, 554t
- Canadian law, 78-80
- dumping compared to, 376, 407-10
- EU law, 351, 352
- French law, 109
- German law, 129-30
- US law, 255-56, 351-52
- *See also* price discrimination

Presidents' clubs. *See* financial *keiretsu*

price controls, 89-90, 128-29, 390

price discrimination, 15-17, 25-26, 218, 554t
- Canadian law, 79-80
- difficulty of proving, 405-6
- divergent responses to domestic products and imports, 407-20, 424
- EU law, 16, 219
- French law, 91, 106-7, 110
- German law, 139-40
- US law, 80, 236, 240, 241, 256-57, 406-9, 419-20
- *See also* antidumping measures

Price fixing, 554t

price-fixing agreements
- Australian law, 386
- Canadian law, 55
- French law, 101-2
- Japanese law, 154, 323-24
- US law, 245-47, 257, 342

prices, predatory. *See* predatory pricing

price setting power, 14-15, 25-26
- *See also* resale price maintenance

Private right of action, 551

privatization
- in European Union, 304
- in Japan, 462, 471
- of state monopolies, 34-35, 216, 304, 462, 471
- in United Kingdom, 216

public interest, 203-4, 226, 446-47

quotas, 492-93

reciprocal-dealing arrangements, 189, 259

regulations. *See* deregulation; standards

resale price maintenance (RPM), 25-26, 550, 554t
- Australian law, 386, 388
- French cases, 105-6
- German law, 118, 137-38
- Japanese law, 151, 152, 168-69, 179, 185-86, 189, 323, 326
- UK law, 205
- US law, 257-58, 345

Resale Prices Act (RPA; United Kingdom), 202, 206

research and development, 555t
- Australian policies, 395
- effect of market structure, 29-33
- EU programs, 301-2
- German policies, 141-42, 147
- UK policies, 228
- welfare effects, 442-44

research and development joint ventures
- Canadian law, 80-82
- EU law, 228-29, 289-90
- German law, 141-43
- Japanese law, 465-69
- US law, 238-39, 263, 365

restraint of trade, horizontal, 554t. *See also* collusion

restrictions on entry of foreign firms. *See* barriers to market entry

Restrictive Trade Practices Act (RTPA; United Kingdom), 202, 203, 205, 206, 213, 220

retailing
- abuse of dominance, in Japan, 194
- entry regulations in Japan, 453-60
- predatory pricing, in Germany, 129-30
- *See also* distribution *keiretsu*; resale price maintenance

Rill, James, 239, 265, 573

Robinson-Patman Anti-Price Discrimination Act, 80, 236, 241, 256-57, 419-20, 576

RPM. *See* resale price maintenance

safeguards
- compared to voluntary export restraints, 492
- competition policy as, 493-94
- GATT agreement, 475, 481, 491-93
- voluntary export restraints as, 485-86

semiconductor trade agreements, 332, 475, 489, 495-96

services
- state monopolies, 303-5
- trade in, 297-301
- *See also* financial institutions; telecommunications

Sherman Antitrust Act, 64, 235-36, 240, 241-42, 263, 266

Shiseido, 168-69

SII. *See* Structural Impediments Initiative

SIMA. *See* Special Import Measures Act
Single European Act, 277, 290, 294-97, 361
small business
    promotion of, 34, 122-23, 208, 342
    protection of, 192, 236-37, 453-60
South Korea, 36, 37, 476, 480, 551
sovereignty, 560
Special Import Measures Act (SIMA; Canada),
    71-75
specialization agreements, 229, 342
standards
    agreements among firms, 123
    as barrier to foreign firms, 215-16
    harmonization, 295, 297-301, 306
    mutual recognition, 215-16, 296, 297, 298-99,
        300-301, 364
state aids, 555t
    EU law, 230, 277, 292-94, 362, 380-81
    prohibited in free trade agreements, 380-81,
        399
    UK law, 230
    from US states, 375
state-owned enterprises
    application of competition law to, 93-95,
        125
    Australian, 388, 394
    foreign investment by, 262
    privatization, 34-35, 216, 304, 462, 471
    x-inefficiency, 37
    See also monopolies, state
strategic alliances, 554t. *See also* joint ventures
Structural Impediments Initiative (SII), 155-56,
    161, 164, 184, 188, 239, 265, 452, 459
subsidies. *See* state aids
suppliers
    contracts, 527-28
    See also distribution; vertical *keiretsu*

Taiwan, 480, 551
takeovers. *See* mergers
Tebbit, Norman, 226
telecommunications
    in Canada, 58
    deregulation, 378-79, 460-65, 471
    international competition, 226-27
    in Japan, 460-65, 471
    monopolies, 21, 216, 249, 303-5, 460-65
    in United States, 378-79
    vertical integration, 220
televisions, voluntary export restraints, 480,
    484, 487
territorial restrictions
    EU law, 347
    Japanese law, 186-87, 189-90
    US law, 258-59, 346
tie-in arrangements
    German law, 140-41
    Japanese cases, 167-68, 187-88
    UK law, 204
    US law, 236, 240, 259-60, 346

Toshiba Elevator, 167-68, 325
trade disputes
    differences over competition policy, 4-5, 6b,
        199-202
    Japanese competition policy and, 190-91,
        194-95
    settlement mechanisms, 75-78
    See also antidumping measures
trademarks. *See* intellectual property
    protection
trade policy
    after World War II, 358-59
    Australian, 393-94
    Canadian, 48, 49, 71-80
    effect of organizational differences, 504-5
    of European Union, 280-85, 305
    extraterritoriality, 373
    German, 147-48
    import restrictions, 223
    interaction with competition policy, 4-5, 6b,
        199-202, 335, 357, 377-83
    measuring closedness of foreign markets,
        495-97
    New Zealand, 393-94
    substituting competition policy for, 272-73,
        369, 391-92, 398-402
    United States, 239-40, 256, 261, 372
    voluntary import expansions (VIEs), 475-76,
        489-90, 495, 497-98
    See also antidumping measures; voluntary
        export restraints (VERS)
Trade-Related Antitrust Measures (TRAMs),
    558-59, 565, 570-71
TRAMS. *See* Trade-Related Antitrust Measures
Treaty of Rome, 271-72, 273, 276-77, 360
    Article 85, 104, 206, 285-87, 289-90, 561
    Article 86, 206-7, 208, 227, 290-92, 343-44
    Article 90, 290
    Article 92, 230, 277, 293
    Article 94, 293
    extraterritorial application, 214

UNCTAD (United Nations Committee on
    Trade and Development), 369-70
United Kingdom
    foreign direct investment, 214-17
    privatizations, 216
United Kingdom competition policy
    abuse of dominance, 212-13
    administration of, 202, 203-4
    anti-competitive practices, 204-5
    criticism, 205-6
    export cartels, 228
    extraterritoriality, 213-14
    foreign access to domestic market, 214-17
    joint ventures, 229
    laws, 202-6
    mergers, 204, 211, 216-17, 226-27
    monopolies, 203-4, 206, 225-26

United Kingdom competition policy (*Cont.*)
potential conflicts with EU policy, 209-13, 231-32
public procurement, 215
research and development agreements, 228
specialization agreements, 229
state aids, 230
vertical restraints, 204, 205, 220, 221-22
United Nations Committee on Trade and Development (UNCTAD), 369-70
United States
antidumping law, 256, 405-6, 409, 410-19
Canada-US Free Trade Agreement, 49, 75-76, 77-78, 369, 409
export cartels, 224, 260-61, 264
foreign direct investment in, 49
industrial policy, 238-39, 317, 340
investment policy, 365-66
mutual legal assistance treaty (MLAT), 62-64
National Economic Council (NEC), 261
relations with Japan, 152, 316, 330-34
semiconductor trade agreements, 332, 475, 489, 495-96
short-term focus of business, 320
Structural Impediments Initiative (SII), 155-56, 161, 164, 184, 188, 239, 265, 452, 459
technological innovation, 328-29
telecommunications deregulation, 378-79
trade with Canada, 48
trade with Japan, 6*b*, 8, 239, 475
trade policy, 239-40, 256, 261, 372
voluntary export restraints imposed by, 476, 478-79*t*, 480, 482-83, 484, 487
See also North American Free Trade Agreement (NAFTA)
US Commerce Department, 411, 414-15, 417-18, 421, 425-36, 576
United States competition policy
abuse of dominance, 343
cartels, 245-47, 252-53, 341-42
comparison to EU law, 339-54
coordination agreements with other countries, 63-64, 266-69, 303, 355-56, 374, 397-98, 571-72
efficiency exemption, 251
enforcement, 237, 241-43, 341, 342, 352-53, 360, 366-67, 378
exemptions, 260-61
extraterritoriality, 64-66, 80, 263-66, 330, 370-75
federal statutes, 235-36, 240-41
goals, 235-38, 340
history, 235-37, 239
influence of trade policy, 239-40, 261
joint ventures, 238-39, 240, 243-45, 252-55, 263, 349-50
mergers, 11, 236, 239, 240, 243-45, 249-52, 347-49

monopolies, 240, 241, 247-49
national security considerations, 261-62
predatory behavior, 255-56, 351-52
price discrimination, 80, 236, 240, 241, 256-57, 406-9, 419-20
price-fixing agreements, 245-47, 257, 342
research and development joint ventures, 238-39, 263, 365
state statutes, 241, 243
vertical restraints, 236, 240, 257-60, 345-46
unilateral enforcement, 572-74
US Congress, 372, 381
US Department of Justice, Antitrust Division, 241-42, 264-65, 268-69, 325, 341, 342, 352, 367, 551
US International Trade Commission (ITC), 411, 415-19, 420-23, 480
US Supreme Court, 236, 266, 371, 375-77, 379
uranium industries, 65, 372, 374, 397
Uruguay Round. *See* GATT
utilities
deregulation, 146
privatizations, 216, 304
state monopolies, 216, 303, 304

Van Miert, Karel, 362
Venezuela, 551
Vernon, Raymond, 382
VERs. *See* voluntary export restraints
Vertical arrangements, 565
vertical foreclosure, 25, 220-21, 521-25
vertical integration, 220-21, 526, 539-40
vertical *keiretsu*, 506, 508, 509-13*t*, 515, 519, 522
vertical restraints, 25-27, 554*t*
Canadian law, 62
EU law, 220, 221, 287-89, 346-47
French law, 103-6
German law, 136-41
Japanese law, 184-92
refusal to supply, 138-39
territorial, 186-87, 189-90, 258-59, 346, 347
UK law, 221-22
US law, 240, 257-60, 345-46
See also exclusive-dealing arrangements; price-fixing; resale price maintenance; tie-in arrangements
VIEs. *See* voluntary import expansions
voluntary export restraints (VERs), 223-24, 475, 555*t*
adjustment assistance, 485-86
anticompetitive effects, 482-86
duration, 476
industries applied to, 476, 477*t*, 480
Japanese, 478-79*t*
legal status, 224, 480-82, 491
spillover effects, 487-89
tightness of restraints, 484-85
use of, 224, 476, 480

voluntary import expansions (VIEs), 475-76, 489-90, 495, 555*t*, 558
    effects, 490, 497-98, 497*f*

World Trade Organization (WTO), 5*b*, 33, 547-79
    Appellate Body, 562-66

competition policy enforcement agency, 559-60
consultative procedures and competition policy, 569
dispute settlement and competition policy, 561-66
    See also GATT
WTO. *See* World Trade Organization

Other Publications from the
Institute for International Economics

Economic Sanctions Reconsidered: History and Current Policy
Gary Clyde Hufbauer, Jeffrey J. Schott, and Kimberly Ann Elliott/*December 1990*
ISBN cloth 0-88132-136-2 288 pp.
ISBN paper 0-88132-140-0 288 pp.

Pacific Basin Developing Countries: Prospects for the Future
Marcus Noland/*January 1991* ISBN cloth 0-88132-141-9 250 pp.
(out of print) ISBN paper 0-88132-081-1 250 pp.

Currency Convertibility in Eastern Europe
John Williamson, editor/*October 1991*
ISBN paper 0-88132-128-1 396 pp.

International Adjustment and Financing: The Lessons of 1985-1991
C. Fred Bergsten, editor/*January 1992*
ISBN paper 0-88132-112-5 336 pp.

North American Free Trade: Issues and Recommendations
Gary Clyde Hufbauer and Jeffrey J. Schott/*April 1992*
ISBN paper 0-88132-120-6 392 pp.

Narrowing the U.S. Current Account Deficit
Allen J. Lenz/*June 1992*
(out of print) ISBN paper 0-88132-103-6 640 pp.

The Economics of Global Warming
William R. Cline/*June 1992* ISBN paper 0-88132-132-X 416 pp.

U.S. Taxation of International Income: Blueprint for Reform
Gary Clyde Hufbauer, assisted by Joanna M. van Rooij/*October 1992*
ISBN cloth 0-88132-178-8 304 pp.
ISBN paper 0-88132-134-6 304 pp.

Who's Bashing Whom? Trade Conflict in High-Technology Industries
Laura D'Andrea Tyson/*November 1992*
ISBN paper 0-88132-106-0 352 pp.

Korea in the World Economy
Il SaKong/*January 1993* ISBN paper 0-88132-106-0 328 pp.

Pacific Dynamism and the International Economic System
C. Fred Bergsten and Marcus Noland, editors/*May 1993*
ISBN paper 0-88132-196-6 424 pp.

Economic Consequences of Soviet Disintegration
John Williamson, editor/*May 1993*
ISBN paper 0-88132-190-7 664 pp.

Reconcilable Differences? United States-Japan Economic Conflict
C. Fred Bergsten and Marcus Noland/*June 1993*
ISBN paper 0-88132-129-X 296 pp.

Does Foreign Exchange Intervention Work?
Kathryn M. Dominguez and Jeffrey A. Frankel/*September 1993*
ISBN paper 0-88132-104-4 192 pp.

Sizing Up U.S. Export Disincentives
J. David Richardson/*September 1993*
ISBN paper 0-88132-107-9 192 pp.

NAFTA: An Assessment
Gary Clyde Hufbauer and Jeffrey J. Schott/*rev. ed. October 1993*
ISBN paper 0-88132-199-0 216 pp.

Adjusting to Volatile Energy Prices
Philip K. Verleger, Jr./*November 1993*
ISBN paper 0-88132-069-2 288 pp.

The Political Economy of Policy Reform
John Williamson, editor/*January 1994*
ISBN paper 0-88132-195-8 624 pp.

Measuring the Costs of Protection in the United States
Gary Clyde Hufbauer and Kimberly Ann Elliott/*January 1994*
ISBN paper 0-88132-108-7 144 pp.

The Dynamics of Korean Economic Development
Cho Soon/*March 1994*
ISBN paper 0-88132-162-1 272 pp.

The Trading System After the Uruguay Round
John Whalley and Colleen Hamilton/*July 1996*
ISBN paper 0-88132-131-1   224 pp.

Private Capital Flows to Emerging Markets After the Mexican Crisis
Guillermo A. Calvo, Morris Goldstein, and Eduard Hochreiter/*September 1996*
ISBN paper 0-88132-232-6   352 pp.

The Crawling Band as an Exchange Rate Regime:
Lessons from Chile, Colombia, and Israel
John Williamson/*September 1996*
ISBN paper 0-88132-231-8   192 pp.

Flying High: Civil Aviation in the Asia Pacific
Gary Clyde Hufbauer and Christopher Findlay/*November 1996*
ISBN paper 0-88132-231-8   232 pp.

Measuring the Costs of Visible Protection in Korea
Namdoo Kim/*November 1996*
ISBN paper 0-88132-236-9   112 pp.

The World Trading System: Challenges Ahead
Jeffrey J. Schott/*December 1996*
ISBN paper 0-88132-235-0   350 pp.

Has Globalization Gone Too Far?
Dani Rodrik/*March 1997*   ISBN cloth 0-88132-243-1   128 pp.

Korea-United States Economic Relationship
C. Fred Bergsten and Il SaKong, editors/*March 1997*
ISBN paper 0-88132-240-7   152 pp.

Summitry in the Americas: A Progress Report
Richard E. Feinberg/*April 1997*
ISBN paper 0-88132-242-3   272 pp.

Corruption and the Global Economy
Kimberly Ann Elliott/*June 1997*
ISBN paper 0-88132-233-4   256 pp.

Regional Trading Blocs in the World Economic System
Jeffrey A. Frankel/*October 1997*
ISBN paper 0-88132-202-4   346 pp.

Sustaining the Asia Pacific Miracle: Environmental Protection and
Economic Integration
André Dua and Daniel C. Esty/*October 1997*
ISBN paper 0-88132-250-4   232 pp.

Trade and Income Distribution
William R. Cline/*November1997*
ISBN paper 0-88132-216-4   296 pp.

Global Competition Policy
Edward M. Graham and J. David Richardson/*December 1997*
ISBN paper 0-88132-166-4   616 pp.

SPECIAL REPORTS

1   Promoting World Recovery: A Statement on Global Economic Strategy
    by Twenty-six Economists from Fourteen Countries/*December 1982*
    (out of print)   ISBN paper 0-88132-013-7   45 pp.
2   Prospects for Adjustment in Argentina, Brazil, and Mexico:
    Responding to the Debt Crisis   (out of print)
    John Williamson, editor/*June 1983*
                                ISBN paper 0-88132-016-1   71 pp.
3   Inflation and Indexation: Argentina, Brazil, and Israel
    John Williamson, editor/*March 1985*
                                ISBN paper 0-88132-037-4   191 pp.
4   Global Economic Imbalances
    C. Fred Bergsten, editor/*March 1986*
                                ISBN cloth 0-88132-038-2   126 pp.

WORKS IN PROGRESS

Visit our website at: http://www.iie.com   **E-mail address:** orders@iie.com